DATE DUE

MR 6			
NO 18 '97			
MY 10 04			
MY 24 05			

DEMCO 38-296

CIVIL RIGHTS TITLES
FROM WILEY LAW PUBLICATIONS

AIDS AND THE LAW
THIRD EDITION

SUBSCRIPTION NOTICE

This Wiley product is updated on a periodic basis with supplements to reflect important changes in the subject matter. If you purchased this product directly from John Wiley & Sons, Inc., we have already recorded your subscription for this update service.

If, however, you purchased this product from a bookstore and wish to receive (1) the current update at no additional charge, and (2) future updates and revised or related volumes billed separately with a 30-day examination review, please send your name, company name (if applicable), address and the title of the product to:

Supplement Department
John Wiley & Sons, Inc.
One Wiley Drive
Somerset, NJ 08875
1-800-225-5945

For customers outside the United States, please contact the Wiley office nearest you.

Professional and Reference Division
John Wiley & Sons Canada, Ltd.
22 Worcester Road
Rexdale, Ontario M9W 1L1
CANADA
(416) 675-3580
1-800-567-4797
FAX (416) 675-6599

John Wiley & Sons, Ltd.
Baffins Lane
Chichester
West Sussex, PO19 1UD
UNITED KINGDOM
(44) (243) 779777

Jacaranda Wiley Ltd.
PRT Division
P.O. Box 174
North Ryde, NSW 2113
AUSTRALIA
(02) 805-1100
FAX (02) 805-1597

John Wiley & Sons (SEA)
  Pte. Ltd.
2 Clementi Loop
#02-01 Jin Xing Distripark
SINGAPORE 0512
4632400
FAX 4634604

AIDS AND THE LAW
THIRD EDITION

DAVID W. WEBBER, EDITOR

Philadelphia, Pennsylvania

Wiley Law Publications

JOHN WILEY & SONS, INC.

New York • Chichester • Weinheim • Brisbane • Singapore • Toronto

Library of Congress Cataloging-in-Publication Data

ISBN 0-471-13542-9

Printed in the United States of America

10 9 8 7 6 5 4 3 2 1

To advocates worldwide, seeking to make the law an instrument of justice and compassion for those affected by the HIV epidemic.

FOREWORD

This third edition of *AIDS and the Law* is an excellent treatise providing comprehensive coverage of the legal aspects of the HIV epidemic. This is not just a book for the legal community, but will be a valuable book for health care and social service professionals, community-based organizations, schools, businesses, and the public in general. It addresses issues that should be of concern to all of us in the context of HIV, such as housing, education, business, immigration, and rights of privacy, among others. That is, the basic rights of an individual who happens to be living with HIV. It is written in a very sincere, clear, and concise form, and, hopefully, will keep alive interest in the myriad laws and policy issues that continue to confront us as a result of this epidemic. This book also serves as a reminder that the law and its institutions need to respond humanely and in a fair, positive, and affirmative way to the needs of individuals with HIV who are now among those most marginalized by our society, namely, minorities, women, and children.

We have learned a lot in the 10 years since the first edition of this book was published, but we still do not have a cure or a vaccine. We have learned that this disease does not discriminate on the basis of religion, race, education, sexual preference, or income. More than 29 million people worldwide have been infected with HIV, and 3.1 million new cases were added in 1996.

After years of being treated as a political football based on fears and "isms," HIV/AIDS has finally gained acceptance as a medical infectious disease. Research has revealed a great deal of valuable medical, scientific, and public health information about HIV/AIDS. Unfortunately, not all of this information has been used to serve those afflicted with this disease or, for that matter, the rest of the world. *AIDS and the Law* helps to bring us the information we need to make good decisions. When we are reluctant to examine our own assumptions and prejudices, our vision is clouded. The results are often fatal. We must not let people perish for lack of this knowledge.

Researchers have isolated the HIV virus, determined its genetic sequence, and discovered its replication mechanisms and how it causes disease. The virus initially binds to CD4 receptors and co-receptors on the surface of T cells, enters the cells, and then attacks the body's own disease-fighting immune system. Cellular RNA is converted into double-stranded DNA by a viral enzyme called reverse transcriptase. Next, another viral enzyme, integrase, incorporates the virus's genetic material within the T cells' DNA. The viral DNA thus uses the cells' own manufacturing processes to produce viral RNA and proteins. Protease enzymes cut the viral proteins into shorter pieces so they can be incorporated into newly produced viruses. Once complete, the newly replicated viruses bud off to attack other T cells. HIV does not lie dormant for 10 years as previously thought.

Knowledge of the mechanisms of binding, replication, incorporation, and release of viral particles has been used to develop drug therapies to attack this virus. Therapeutic cocktails, which combine protease inhibitors with other antiviral drugs, appear to be changing AIDS from a fatal disease to a chronic disease. Investigators are finding that we can decrease viral load, increase CD4 counts, and improve the clinical status of patients with HIV illness. Most importantly, we can change our *outlook* on HIV. To take advantage of this new scientific information, we must educate our people, continue the research, and make care accessible to all.

AIDS is now the leading cause of death among African-American men and women between the ages of 25 to 44. Over half of these deaths are related to injection drugs. Yet, the United States refuses to approve funding for clean needles or syringes. *AIDS and the Law* addresses some of the public health interventions and laws that we could change to substantially reduce the spread of HIV among injection drug users. We have got to be about *preventing* disease. We must permit both the possession of sterile needles and the nonprescription sale of sterile needles by pharmacies, as well as the funding of needle exchange programs and provision of treatment for drug users who need it. The federal government must support needle exchange programs, and the criminalization of harm-reduction activists must stop. Why can't we reduce the harm of spreading HIV disease by providing clean needles when all our research says that needle exchange programs *do not increase* drug use but *do decrease* the spread of HIV?

We have disregarded most of what we know about public health in addressing HIV/AIDS. We must now begin to deal with the problems related to prevention and access to care. We must make sure that all people are allowed the opportunity to receive benefits from the drugs that have been developed and not be denied therapy simply on the basis of cost. We still do not have a cure, but HIV disease has become a chronic disease that we may be able to control. We must now develop a system for people to live with HIV disease, rather than simply to die with AIDS.

Politics should not determine public health policies. Public health policies should be based on strong scientific evidence and principles. Education is still the most powerful weapon we have against this disease. Haven't we already learned from this disease that ignorance is *not* bliss?

Little Rock, Arkansas   JOYCELYN ELDERS, M.D.
                                    United States Surgeon General, 1993–1994

PREFACE

This third edition of *AIDS and the Law* covers a broad range of legal subjects, as well as the underlying medical, scientific, and social issues, that are of most significance to individuals with HIV in our society. Although the chapters cover diverse legal fields, ranging, for example, from employment to immigration law, we frequently return to an underlying theme: the risk of HIV transmission in these varying contexts, and how the legal system assesses that risk and what conclusions are drawn from that assessment. In that sense, much of this book charts the interaction between law and science in the context of the HIV epidemic.

Although *AIDS and the Law* is intended primarily as a resource for legal professionals, it should have value far beyond that readership. Health care and social service professionals are frequently called upon to act as advocates for their patients and clients. They also need to understand how the law defines their own professional duties and responsibilities. Public health professionals and policy makers in other areas, such as those responsible for formulating and implementing employment policy, should also find that *AIDS and the Law* addresses crucial issues in their fields. These professionals frequently shape and influence law and policy, affecting the lives of individuals with HIV perhaps more frequently and more profoundly than do lawyers and judges.

Our society's response to the epidemic certainly appears to have shifted in the 10 years since the first edition of this book. That shift, however, in which fear has been replaced with indifference, combined with the increasing impact of the epidemic on the least well-resourced individuals in our society, indicates that the need for advocacy in this area is as great now as at any point in the past.

Chapter 1 is a comprehensive introduction to the medical aspects of HIV disease. For anyone truly wishing to understand the legal issues of the epidemic, this chapter is the necessary starting point. The core of the chapter covers in detail what is frequently the primary factual issue underlying HIV-related disputes: the means of transmission and the associated risks. This chapter also provides an overview of tests for HIV. Although HIV testing is obviously an important health service, it is frequently considered for purposes other than the medical benefit of the individual being tested. Testing methods and the meaning and significance of the test results need to be fully understood. Finally, this chapter deepens our understanding of the disease process, by examining the concept of "HIV disease" itself in light of recent developments in diagnosis and treatment.

Chapter 2 surveys public health law and policy responses to the epidemic. Two fundamental but conflicting responses to the epidemic have sought to effect changes in behavior that will reduce or eliminate HIV transmission. Coercive or punitive measures, on the one hand, and measures that encourage voluntary cooperation, on the other, are outlined. The coercive measures include mandatory testing for HIV and the disclosure of results, restrictions on sexually oriented commercial activities, criminalization of syringe exchange activities or possession of sterile needles and syringes, and limitations, such as quarantine, imposed to restrict the liberty of individuals with HIV. Voluntary efforts are encouraged through the availability of HIV testing and counseling, HIV education (including availability of condoms in schools), and access to health care and related services (such as those provided under the Ryan White CARE Act). Censorship and other limits on dissemination of HIV/AIDS educational information are covered, as well as state and local efforts to make sterile syringes and related services available to reduce HIV transmission among injecting drug users.

The next four chapters (**Chapters 3** through **6**) form what is essentially a "quadrilogy" in terms of legal prohibitions against HIV-related discrimination. Each chapter focuses on nondiscrimination standards in a different context, beginning with employment (**Chapter 3**), moving next to public accommodations and services (**Chapter 4**), then to schools and other educational settings (**Chapter 5**), and concluding with nondiscrimination in housing (**Chapter 6**). To some degree, these chapters overlap and cross-reference each other, reflecting the continuing history of congressional efforts to address HIV discrimination in a series of enactments and amendments to existing legislation, including the Fair Housing Act, the Rehabilitation Act, and, perhaps most significantly, the Americans with Disabilities Act. These chapters are not, however, limited exclusively to discrimination issues. **Chapter 3** covers HIV in the workplace more broadly, including topics such as workplace safety standards and the Family and Medical Leave Act as it applies in the context of HIV. **Chapter 5** covers the Individuals with Disabilities in Education Act in detail, but also addresses confidentiality and school HIV policy issues. **Chapter 6** considers the problem of housing for individuals with HIV not just as a direct result of discriminatory treatment, but also as a result of poverty; federal housing assistance, provided by the Housing for Persons with AIDS program, is also covered.

The next two chapters examine, in turn, criminal and civil liability for transmission of HIV. **Chapter 7** covers HIV and the criminal law, including a review of the substantive criminal law prohibitions on HIV transmission. It answers, in essence, the question of when and under what circumstances persons with HIV can be criminally prosecuted for transmission or risking transmission to others. Equally important, though, but often overlooked, the chapter also considers *whether* such prosecutions can be justified from a public health point of view. Also, privacy rights in the context of criminal law are examined from both statutory and constitutional standpoints. Next, **Chapter 8** covers tort law issues pertaining to the HIV epidemic. In reality, and unlike the criminal prosecutions

considered in **Chapter 7,** wrongful transmission of HIV has not been widely litigated against individuals with HIV. The risk of such litigation, however, particularly against third parties, is a frequent concern in the formulation of policies
that attempt, for example, to balance the value of protecting confidentiality against
the risk of a lawsuit for failing to disclose HIV information. The more numerous
cases involving claims based on fear of exposure to HIV, but without actual
transmission, are collected and critically analyzed.

Chapter 9 covers public benefits programs for individuals with HIV, a subject that is routinely of importance to virtually every HIV-infected individual.
Benefits advocates in many professions and settings should find this chapter to
be key to understanding the arcane workings of the benefits bureaucracy. For the
convenience of practitioners, this chapter also reprints the Social Security Administration's standards for determining disability based on HIV disease.

Chapter 10 provides a global perspective by examining international legal
efforts in response to the HIV epidemic. Although the other chapters of this book
are concerned almost exclusively with U.S. law, it is a grave error to think that
the epidemic is limited or entirely unique to the United States or that efforts in
response to the epidemic can be successful if limited to one country, without
taking the international response into account. In fact, the impact of HIV is far
more serious in other parts of the world, which have far fewer resources to
respond than does the United States.

Chapter 11 covers U.S. immigration law in regard to HIV. The history and
scope of the exclusion applicable to immigrants with HIV are reviewed, and
guidance is provided regarding the availability of waivers for that exclusion.
Immigration law imposes one of the few mandatory HIV testing requirements
under U.S. law, and this chapter provides a concise review of that requirement
and its potential impact on immigrants. The chapter also outlines the impact that
recent changes in U.S. law will have on the availability of government benefits
for noncitizens with HIV.

The appendixes include several items for the convenience of practitioners.
Appendix A summarizes HIV-related statutes on HIV testing, confidentiality,
and related issues, thus providing a quick introduction to these state laws for
practitioners not otherwise familiar with them. These issues have typically been
addressed under state, not federal, laws, and thus this starting point for state-by-
state research and analysis is important. **Appendix B** reprints the Occupational
Safety and Health Administration's bloodborne pathogens standard, which regulates workplace safety in regard to HIV under the Occupational Safety and
Health Act, covered in **Chapter 3. Appendix C** reprints the Centers for Disease
Control and Prevention's recommendations for preventing transmission of HIV
to patients during exposure-prone invasive procedures, also covered in **Chapter 3.**

Philadelphia, Pennsylvania   DAVID W. WEBBER
February 1997

ACKNOWLEDGMENTS

I consider myself fortunate to have worked with the staff at John Wiley & Sons, Inc., who consistently have been as gracious, kind, and patient as they are professionally skilled. It would be an injustice indeed if their names did not appear somewhere in this book. From the beginning, Teri Peisner has guided this project with a tirelessness and enthusiasm that even I find remarkable; Lynn Castillo produced from a series of diskettes what was beginning to appear to be an intractable and unmanageable manuscript; Martha Freeman and Karen Hoefer efficiently managed the copy editing process, while Belinda Conter and Tom Waters found numerous ways to improve a manuscript that I somehow had come to believe was already perfect; Sharon Langworthy and Karen Ferguson have handled the actual production of the book, a process that, happily, I don't even need to understand, given their excellent efforts.

Much of my research for this book was completed at the Jenkins Memorial Law Library, Philadelphia, Pennsylvania. I've probably received assistance at least once from every staff member, but the reference librarians in particular deserve my thanks for the depth of their knowledge and the unfailing courtesies they've shown me. Roughly 10 years ago, when I handled the initial nonprofit incorporation of a nascent AIDS library here in Philadelphia, I had no idea that it would grow into a nationally significant collection of AIDS materials, the AIDS Information Network. That resource has been indispensable in the researching of this book, the staff a delight to work with.

In preparing a work of such a wide scope, I frequently asked colleagues and friends to review portions of the manuscript. It has benefited in countless ways from their generosity. I thank Paula Berg, Michael Braffman, Fernando Chang-Muy, Rondee Goldfein, John T. McFeely, Leonard Rieser, and David Rudovsky. Edwin J. Greenlee has contributed significantly to this publication, both by preparing the state statutory summary in **Appendix A** and by ably fielding miscellaneous legal research questions that I've sent his way. I owe special thanks to Henry H. Perritt, Jr., who is perhaps more responsible for this book than he knows, having first involved me years ago with John Wiley & Sons, Inc., and to whose own publications I look as the standard in terms of scholarship for the practitioner. I thank also Lawrence O. Gostin, whose encouragement from the very start has meant a great deal to me. Ed Hermance, proprietor of Giovanni's Room, which is surely among the finest bookstores in the world, has tracked down numerous titles at my request and called my attention to others.

I also acknowledge Morris Goldman, and our many mutual friends and associates, who routinely throughout this project reminded me of the benefit of living in a society governed by the rule of law.

Finally, I thank Felicia Sarner. Without her support, it's fair to say, this book would never have been completed.

D.W.W.

ABOUT THE EDITOR

David W. Webber, J.D., is a Philadelphia lawyer who specializes in AIDS/HIV and other infectious disease legal issues. In 1988, he founded the AIDS Law Project of Pennsylvania, a nonprofit public interest law firm. He has served both as the Law Project's executive director and director of education and policy. In addition to his extensive experience in counseling and representing clients with HIV, as well as others affected by the epidemic, Mr. Webber conducts numerous lectures and seminars on AIDS legal issues in many forums. Mr. Webber received a B.A. degree from the University of Pennsylvania and a J.D. degree from Temple University.

ABOUT THE CONTRIBUTORS

Ignatius Bau, J.D., is both the HIV program coordinator and the policy director at the Asian and Pacific Islander American Health Forum, a national health advocacy organization in San Francisco. He was formerly a staff attorney at the Lawyers' Committee for Civil Rights of the San Francisco Bay Area, working on civil rights, immigration, public benefits, and employment issues. He received his law and undergraduate degrees from the University of California, Berkeley.

Karen L. Black, J.D., is a staff attorney with the Public Interest Law Center of Philadelphia, a private nonprofit law firm dedicated to realizing social justice, freedom from abuse and discrimination, and equal participation in the law for children, minorities, individuals with disabilities, and victims of violence and discrimination. In 1992, she founded the Law Center's Fair Housing Project, which seeks to eliminate discriminatory housing practices through litigation and empower housing consumers through legal representation, counseling, and education. In addition to her extensive experience in counseling and representing victims of housing discrimination, Ms. Black also serves as a legal consultant for private law firms and fair housing groups in the Delaware Valley area. A graduate of Williams College and University of California at Los Angeles Law School, Ms. Black is an accomplished lecturer in the area of civil rights and has written numerous articles about housing discrimination.

Linda D. Headley, J.D., is the senior managing attorney of New Jersey Protection and Advocacy, Inc., a private nonprofit public interest law firm dedicated to protecting the civil, legal, and human rights of people with disabilities. Ms. Headley is a graduate of the National Law Center of the George Washington University, and the University of Delaware. Her practice has focused on disability rights issues since 1983, through individual client representation, public policy initiatives, public education, and regulatory and legislative advocacy.

Elizabeth T. Hey, J.D., is a trial attorney with the Defender Association of Philadelphia, Federal Court Division. She received her undergraduate degree from Vassar College, her law degree from Villanova University School of Law, and a Ph.D. in clinical psychology from Hahnemann University.

J. Michael Howe, M.S.L.S., is the manager and librarian of the Department of Veterans Affairs AIDS Information Center located at the San Francisco VA Medical

Center. He is responsible for managing information services to support the National VA HIV/AIDS Education Program and to provide timely information to staff throughout the VA system. He is the editor and publisher of one of the most widely distributed electronic HIV/AIDS newsletters in the country. He has prepared documents for educational programs, represented the VA as a presenter at conferences, and published extensive reviews of HIV/AIDS resources. He is an acknowledged leader in the field of information services and has been recognized by VA Headquarters and other organizations for facilitating authoritative information access and exchange about HIV disease on a national and international level.

Peter C. Jensen, M.D., is acting chief of infectious diseases at the San Francisco VA Medical Center. He received his training in infectious diseases at the University of California, San Francisco (UCSF), where he is now clinical professor of medicine. In 1985, Dr. Jensen established the San Francisco VA Medical Center HIV/AIDS program including the clinic where more than 2,000 patients have received care. He is active in the clinical research of HIV disease and its associated opportunistic infections. He has served as faculty in various HIV educational programs and has been active in the National VA HIV/AIDS Education Program since its inception in 1989. With his colleagues at UCSF, Dr. Jensen established one of the first programs in the country for health care workers who experience high risk occupational exposures to blood borne pathogens.

Irwin E. Keller, J.D., is the executive director of the AIDS Legal Referral Panel of the San Francisco Bay Area. The AIDS Legal Referral Panel (ALRP) provides legal counseling and representation to over 3,000 HIV-positive Bay Area residents each year through the active volunteerism of over 600 private attorneys. For over three years Mr. Keller was ALRP's benefits program director, specializing in insurance, government benefits, and bankruptcy law. He has published articles and manuals on social security and HIV, insurance coverage for experimental HIV treatments, and needle exchange legal defense. He was also principal author of the Chicago Human Rights ordinance, which was passed into law in December 1988. Mr. Keller received a B.A. degree from the University of Illinois and a J.D. degree from the University of Chicago Law School.

David L. McColgin, J.D., is a staff attorney with the Defender Association of Philadelphia, Federal Court Division. Mr. McColgin focuses on federal criminal appeals. He received a B.A. degree from Lawrence University and a J.D. degree from New York University Law School. He has written and lectured on a variety of criminal law topics.

Julie Shapiro, J.D., is an associate professor of law at Seattle University School of Law, where she teaches civil procedure, constitutional litigation, and family law. Before entering teaching, her legal practice experience included trial and appellate litigation of civil and constitutional rights, police misconduct, and civil RICO claims. As a volunteer attorney with the AIDS Law Project of Pennsylvania, she litigated employment and access to health care discrimination cases, as well as challenges to nonconsensual HIV testing. Ms. Shapiro received a J.D. degree from the University of Pennsylvania.

Jean R. Sternlight, J.D., is an assistant professor of law at Florida State University College of Law. She received a B.A. degree from Swarthmore College and a J.D. degree from Harvard University. She has written and lectured regarding HIV in various settings and also teaches a seminar entitled "AIDS and the Law."

Mark E. Wojcik, J.D., LL.M, is an assistant professor of law at John Marshall Law School in Chicago. He received his undergraduate degree in international studies from Bradley University and law degrees from John Marshall Law School and New York University School of Law. He has written several articles on AIDS, and he coauthored the first law school casebook on AIDS. Mr. Wojcik has spoken on human rights and AIDS at conferences in Canada, Germany, India, Italy, Japan, Palau, and across the United States.

SUMMARY CONTENTS

DETAILED CONTENTS

SHORT REFERENCE LIST

Short Reference	Full Reference
ADA	Americans with Disabilities Act of 1990
AFDC	Aid to Families with Dependent Children
AIDS	acquired immune deficiency syndrome
ALJ	administrative law judge
AZT	azidothymidine
CARE Act	Ryan White Comprehensive AIDS Resources Emergency (CARE) Act of 1990
CDC	Centers for Disease Control and Prevention
COBRA	Consolidated Omnibus Budget Reconciliation Act of 1985
DOD	Department of Defense
DOL	Department of Labor
EEOC	Equal Employment Opportunity Commission
ELISA	enzyme-linked immunosorbent assay
FDA	Food and Drug Administration
FHA	Fair Housing Act
FMLA	Family and Medical Leave Act of 1993
HIV	human immunodeficiency virus
HOPWA	Housing Opportunities for Persons with AIDS program
HUD	Department of Housing and Urban Development
IDEA	Individuals with Disabilities Education Act

Short Reference	Full Reference
INS	Immigration and Naturalization Service
IRCA	Immigration Reform and Control Act of 1986
JAMA	Journal of the American Medical Association
MMWR	Morbidity and Mortality Weekly Report
OSHA	Occupational Safety and Health Administration
PHS	Public Health Service
SSA	Social Security Administration
SSDI	Social Security Disability Income
SSI	Supplemental Security Income
UNAIDS	U.N. Program on AIDS
VA	Department of Veterans Affairs
WHO	World Health Organization
ZOV	zidovudine

CHAPTER 1

AN INTRODUCTION TO THE MEDICAL ASPECTS OF HIV DISEASE

J. Michael Howe

Peter C. Jensen*

---

* The viewpoints presented in this chapter are those of the authors and do not necessarily reflect the policy of the U.S. Department of Veterans Affairs.

§ 1.1   Introduction

HIV disease[1] has had a significant impact on society and perhaps more than any other illness has profoundly affected the way in which medical, legal, public health, and information services are provided. Fortunately, the epidemic arrived at a time of unprecedented strides in biotechnology and information access. Had the first cases of AIDS been reported in the decade of the 1950s rather than the 1980s, for example, individuals involved in the clinical treatment of HIV disease or the provision of information services would have been in a more difficult position. The biotechnology that made possible the laboratory diagnostics, the design of drugs, and the unraveling of the immune system provided significant insight into a complex and complicated biology and generated new knowledge at an incredible pace. In addition, the availability of this medical information through computer technologies facilitated access to an extensive body of literature.

This introductory chapter provides an overview of the basic aspects of HIV disease based on the medical literature. No single chapter can adequately address all medical issues related to HIV; therefore, this chapter provides extensive references, including recommendations and guidelines published by the Centers for Disease Control and Prevention (CDC),[2] for those who require more detailed information.

---

[1] *HIV disease* refers to the continuum of HIV infection: from the moment the virus first enters the body until the time, usually years later, when the full consequences of its effects have rendered the individual ill. Like most other infectious diseases, HIV has a clinically "silent" period that proceeds the appearance of symptoms. During this time, antibodies to HIV appear in the bloodstream (seroconversion), rendering an HIV antibody test positive. Unlike most other encounters between infectious agents and susceptible hosts, however, these antibodies are simply markers of infection; they do not fight it and, thus, the disease progresses until predictable clinical events occur. Before objective laboratory measures of immune suppression (CD4 cell counts) or viral activity (viral load), patients and their physicians used clinical events to mark the progression of infection. Thus, *AIDS* was defined as a syndrome characterized by certain sentinel events such as pneumocystis carinii pneumonia or Kaposi's sarcoma. Less severe conditions, such as oral candida infections (thrush), were called AIDS-Related Complex (ARC). With the ability to measure key laboratory markers of immune suppression, the terms AIDS and ARC became much less clinically relevant than the CD4 count or the viral load. The term AIDS, however, remains useful for classifying individuals for public health registries and other administrative purposes.

[2] The CDC is an agency within the Public Health Service, U.S. Department of Health and Human Services, charged with protecting the public health of the nation by providing leadership and direction in the prevention and control of diseases and other preventable conditions and responding to public health emergencies. For more information about the role of the CDC in this area, see Verla S. Neslund et al., *The Role of CDC in the Development of AIDS Recommendations and Guidelines,* 15 Law Med. & Health Care 73 (1987). The CDC issues the *Morbidity and Mortality Weekly Report* [hereinafter MMWR], a primary source of CDC recommendations and guidelines. In addition to the print copy, the MMWR is available on the CDC's Internet home page, http://www.cdc.gov.

Section 1.2 provides an historical overview of the first reported cases of immunodeficiency that eventually became known as acquired immunodeficiency syndrome (AIDS). **Section 1.3** briefly describes human retroviruses to provide a perspective on HIV in relation to other viruses belonging to the lentivirus family. Epidemiologic data is provided in §§ **1.4** through **1.6,** including CDC surveillance for HIV infection and diagnosed AIDS cases. Infection begins with the transmission of HIV, and this is discussed in detail in §§ **1.7** through **1.13.** HIV tests, among a wide variety available, are then described in §§ **1.14** through **1.17.** The chapter concludes with an overview of the clinical progression of HIV disease in §§ **1.18** through **1.21.**

§ 1.2 Historical Background

The CDC reported in June 1981 that five young, gay men were treated for pneumocystis carinii pneumonia (PCP) at three different hospitals in Los Angeles, California, between October 1980 and May 1981.[3] Pneumocystis pneumonia in the United States was almost exclusively limited to severely immunosuppressed patients.[4] The occurrence of this illness in these five individuals without a clinically apparent underlying immunodeficiency was unusual, but the fact that these patients were all gay men suggested either an association between the illness and some aspect of the patients' lifestyle or a disease acquired through sexual contact.

In July 1981, the CDC reported 10 more cases of PCP and 26 diagnoses of Kaposi's sarcoma (KS), an uncommonly reported malignancy in the United States, in gay men.[5] The range in age of these patients was 26 to 51 (mean 39 years); eight of these patients died within 24 months after KS was diagnosed. The following month, an additional 70 cases of PCP and KS in predominantly white, gay men were reported.[6] These cases of both PCP and KS again implied a common underlying factor, with both diseases being linked to immunosuppression.[7] Similar cases of immunosuppression were subsequently identified in, but not exclusively limited to, other populations, including injecting drug users,[8]

---

[3] CDC, *Pneumocystis Pneumonia—Los Angeles,* 30 MMWR 250 (1981).

[4] Peter D. Walzer et al., *Pneumocystis Carinii Pneumonia in the United States: Epidemiologic, Diagnostic, and Clinical Features,* 80 Annals Internal Med. 83 (1974).

[5] CDC, *Kaposi's Sarcoma and Pneumocystis Pneumonia Among Homosexual Men—New York City and California,* 30 MMWR 305 (1981).

[6] CDC, *Follow-up on Kaposi's Sarcoma and Pneumocystis Pneumonia,* 30 MMWR 409 (1981).

[7] R.W. Gange & E.W. Jones, *Kaposi's Sarcoma and Immunosuppressive Therapy: An Appraisal,* 3 Clinical Experimental Dermatology 135 (1978); Israel Penn, *Kaposi's Sarcoma in Organ Transplant Recipients: Report of 20 Cases,* 27 Transplantation 8 (1979).

[8] CDC, *Update on Acquired Immune Deficiency Syndrome (AIDS)—United States,* 31 MMWR 507 (1982).

people with hemophilia,[9] blood transfusion recipients,[10] infants,[11] and immigrants from certain countries.[12]

These first r   ~ts of unexplained opportunistic infections,[13] such as PCP and KS as well as cases of persistent lymphadenopathy,[14] alerted physicians and public health officials to unusual conditions of immunosuppression. It soon became evident that these patients had a common immunologic deficit, an impairment in cell-mediated immunity.[15] This cellular immunodeficiency would eventually be labeled the *acquired immunodeficiency syndrome* (AIDS) and the cause would be identified as a virus called the *human immunodeficiency virus* (HIV).[16]

§ 1.3 Human Retroviruses

Four types of human retroviruses,[17] also known as human T-lymphotropic viruses (HTLV), have been identified to date. These include: HTLV-I; HTLV-II; HTLV-III,

---

[9] CDC, *Pneumocystis Carinii Pneumonia Among Persons with Hemophilia A*, 31 MMWR 365 (1982).

[10] CDC, *Possible Transfusion-Associated Acquired Immune Deficiency Syndrome (AIDS)*, 31 MMWR 652 (1982).

[11] CDC, *Unexplained Immunodeficiency and Opportunistic Infection in Infants—New York, New Jersey, California*, 31 MMWR 665 (1982).

[12] CDC, *Opportunistic Infections and Kaposi's Sarcoma Among Haitians in the United States*, 31 MMWR 353 (1982). In 1981, when the first cases of AIDS were reported in the United States, similar cases were reported among Haitian immigrants to the United States. Michele Barry et al., *Haiti and the AIDS Connection*, 37 J. Chronic Diseases 593 (1984). Haiti was identified as a potential index location for HIV. Gary W. Shannon et al., The Geography of AIDS: Origins and Course of an Epidemic 40 (1990). This early focus, however, was later abandoned. *See* Paul Farmer, AIDS and Accusation: Haiti and the Geography of Blame 210 (1992).

[13] An *opportunistic infection* is an illness caused by an organism that usually does not cause disease in a person with a normal immune system. People with advanced HIV infection suffer opportunistic infections of the lungs, brain, eyes, and other organs. Opportunistic infections common in AIDS patients other than PCP and KS include mycobacterium avium complex, toxoplasmosis, cryptosporidiosis, candidiasis, and other parasitic, viral, and fungal infections, and some types of cancers.

[14] CDC, *Persistent, Generalized Lymphadenopathy Among Homosexual Males*, 31 MMWR 249 (1982).

[15] Michael S. Gottlieb et al., *Pneumocystis Carinii Pneumonia and Mucosal Candidiasis in Previously Healthy Homosexual Men: Evidence of a New Acquired Cellular Immunodeficiency*, 305 New Eng. J. Med. 1425 (1981); Henry Masur et al., *An Outbreak of Community-Acquired Pneumocystis Carinii Pneumonia: Initial Manifestation of Cellular Immune Dysfunction*, 305 New Eng. J. Med. 1431 (1981).

[16] For a brief overview of this new infectious disease, see Myron Essex, *Origin of AIDS, in* AIDS: Etiology, Diagnosis, Treatment, and Prevention 3 (Vincent T. DeVita, Jr. et al. eds., 4th ed. 1997).

[17] A *retrovirus* is a virus that, when not infecting a cell, stores its genetic information on a single-stranded RNA molecule instead of the more usual double-stranded DNA. After a retrovirus penetrates a cell, it constructs a DNA version of its genes using a special enzyme,

now termed HIV-1; and HTLV-IV, also known as HIV-2. Retroviruses belong to the lentivirus family and generally cause chronic infections characterized by a long clinical latency period, nervous system involvement, and high levels of virus in the blood. Other lentiviruses infect nonhuman species. For example, the feline immunodeficiency virus (FIV) infects cats and the simian immunodeficiency virus (SIV) infects monkeys and other nonhuman primates. These and other viruses as well as their animal hosts are used by researchers as models of HIV disease.

HIV-1. HIV-1 was initially assigned different names, including lymphadenopathy-associated virus (LAV),[18] human T-lymphotropic virus III (HTLV-III),[19] and AIDS-associated retrovirus (ARV).[20] In 1986, *human immunodeficiency virus* became the accepted term for this retrovirus.[21] Although some authors have argued that HIV is not the cause of AIDS,[22] the overwhelming evidence for HIV's primary role in the pathogenesis of this disease has been well established.[23]

HIV-1 Subtypes. The genetic variation of HIV is extremely high, and several subtypes, also termed *clades* or *genotypes* and designated as group M strains, of HIV-1 isolates have been classified.[24] The distribution of these subtypes is dispersed and intermixed geographically.[25] Subtype B, for example, is predominant in North America and Europe; subtypes A, C, and D are common in Africa; and subtype E is prevalent in Thailand.

The spread of subtypes does occur, however, as confirmed by two *Lancet* reports. In the first, the authors documented multiple introductions of subtype

---

reverse transcriptase. Reverse transcriptase is a viral enzyme that constructs DNA from an RNA template, which is an essential step in the life-cycle of a retrovirus such as HIV. For more information about human retroviruses, see Robert Gallo, Virus Hunting: AIDS, Cancer, and the Human Retrovirus (1991).

[18] Francoise Barre-Sinoussi et al., *Isolation of a T-Lymphotropic Retrovirus from a Patient at Risk for Acquired Immune Deficiency Syndrome (AIDS),* 220 Science 868 (1983).

[19] Robert C. Gallo et al., *Frequent Detection and Isolation of Cytopathic Retroviruses (HTLV-III) from Patients with AIDS and at Risk for AIDS,* 224 Science 500 (1984).

[20] Jay A. Levy et al., *Isolation of Lymphocytopathic Retroviruses from San Francisco Patients with AIDS,* 225 Science 840 (1984).

[21] John Coffin et al., *Human Immunodeficiency Virus,* 232 Science 697 (1986).

[22] *See, e.g.,* Peter Duesberg, Inventing the AIDS Virus (1996); Robert S. Root-Bernstein, Rethinking AIDS: The Tragic Cost of Premature Consensus (1993).

[23] *See* National Inst. of Allergy & Infectious Disease, The Relationship Between the Human Immunodeficiency Virus and the Acquired Immunodeficiency Syndrome (1995). This document is available via the Internet. The NIAID gopher address is gopher.niaid.nih.gov. The World Wide Web address is http://www.niaid.nih.gov.

[24] David J. Hu et al., *The Emerging Genetic Diversity of HIV: The Importance of Global Surveillance for Diagnostics, Research, and Prevention,* 275 JAMA 210 (1996).

[25] Los Alamos Nat'l Lab., *Human Retroviruses and AIDS 1994: A Compilation and Analysis of Nucleic Acid and Amino Acid Sequences* (G. Myers et al. eds., 1995). Entries are regularly updated and available via the Internet at http://hiv-web.lanl.gov.

E into the western hemisphere and suggested that all regions of the world may eventually harbor multiple subtypes.[26] In the second report, the authors described the first documented cases of native U.S. residents (five U.S. servicemen who were infected with subtypes A, D, and E during overseas deployments) acquiring infection with subtypes other than B and the first reported introduction of subtypes A and E into the United States.[27] This provided evidence of the presence of subtypes of HIV other than the well-characterized B subtype prevalent in the United States and suggested that strains other than B are being introduced in this country. This genetic diversity of the global HIV pandemic will need to be considered when developing strategies for epidemic control.

The existence of significant biological or immunological differences among HIV-1 subtypes has important implications for the development of vaccines as well.[28] Because of the predominance of subtype B viruses in Europe and the United States, most resources for vaccine development have been focused on this group. Vaccines based on this subtype, however, may not provide immunity to protect against other subtypes prevalent in other parts of the world; therefore, a vaccine for all subtypes may be required in order to be effective worldwide. Similarly, the development and evaluation of the currently used diagnostic tests have been based primarily on subtype B. Thus, whether these tests can be used in detecting divergent strains other than subtype B needs to be further evaluated.[29]

Another group of HIV subtypes that are characterized by extensive genetic divergence from group M was identified recently and classified as group O viruses. Group O viruses or evidence of group O infection have been reported in individuals primarily from West and Central Africa.[30] In July 1996, however, the first recognized case of HIV-1 group O infection in the United States was documented.[31] This infection was not detected consistently by standard HIV laboratory detection methods, which has important implications for medical diagnosis and blood safety. The recognition of this case (and the potential for emergence of other highly divergent strains) also underscores the importance of maintaining active surveillance for HIV variants.[32]

---

[26] Andrew W. Artenstein et al., *Multiple Introductions of HIV-1 Subtype E into the Western Hemisphere,* 346 Lancet 1197 (1995).

[27] S.K. Brodine et al., *Detection of Diverse HIV-Genetic Subtypes in the USA,* 346 Lancet 1199 (1995).

[28] Paul M. Rowe, *HIV Subtypes Raise Vaccine Anxieties,* 347 Lancet 603 (1996).

[29] David J. Hu et al., *The Emerging Genetic Diversity of HIV: The Importance of Global Surveillance for Diagnostics, Research, and Prevention,* 275 JAMA 210, 212 (1996).

[30] *Id.* at 210.

[31] CDC, *Identification of HIV-1 Group O Infection—Los Angeles County, California, 1996,* 45 MMWR (1996).

[32] *See, e.g.,* C.P. Pau et al., *Surveillance for Human Immunodeficiency Virus Type 1 Group O Infections in the United States,* 36 Transfusion 398 (1996).

HIV-2.   HIV-2 was isolated in 1986 from patients in West Africa, where it may have been present decades earlier.[33] Although HIV-1 and HIV-2 are similar in their viral structure, modes of transmission, and resulting opportunistic infections, they have differed in their geographic patterns of infection. The first case of HIV-2 infection in the United States was diagnosed in 1987,[34] but relatively few cases have been reported.[35] HIV-2 is spread through contaminated blood and sexual contact but, unlike HIV-1, perinatal (that is, between mother and newborn) transmission is limited. HIV-2 is genetically related to SIV much more closely than to HIV-1; biological and demographic data suggest that HIV-2 may have originally been transmitted from monkeys to humans.[36] Although HIV-2 causes AIDS, the asymptomatic incubation period after infection with HIV-2 appears to be substantially longer than that following HIV-1 infection.[37]

HTLV-I/HTLV-II.   HTLV-I, the first known human retrovirus and a cause of adult T-cell leukemia/lymphoma, was initially isolated in 1979 from patients in both the United States and Japan.[38] HTLV-II, which was isolated from a patient with hairy cell leukemia, shares a close relationship with HTLV-I and was isolated in 1982.[39]

§ 1.4   Epidemiology

The epidemic's impact was highlighted during 1995, when the cumulative number of reported AIDS cases in the United States surpassed one-half million.[40] As

---

[33] Francois Clavel et al., *Isolation of a New Retrovirus from West African Patients with AIDS,* 233 Science 343 (1986). For an overview of HIV-2 in the decade since this virus was first described, see Richard Marlink, *Lessons from the Second AIDS Virus, HIV-2,* 10 AIDS 689 (1996).

[34] CDC, *Update: HIV-2 Infection—United States,* 38 MMWR 572 (1989).

[35] Kevin M. DeCock et al., *Epidemiology and Transmission of HIV-2—Why There Is No Pandemic,* 270 JAMA 2083 (1993); Thomas R. O'Brien, *Human Immunodeficiency Virus Type 2 Infection in the United States: Epidemiology, Diagnosis, and Public Health Implications,* 267 JAMA 2775 (1992).

[36] Russell F. Doolittle, *The Simian-Human Connection,* 339 Nature 338 (1989).

[37] David M. Markovitz, *Infection with the Human Immunodeficiency Virus Type 2,* 118 Annals Internal Med. 211 (1993); *see also* Phyllis J. Kanki, *Biologic Features of HIV-2: An Update,* in AIDS Clinical Review 1991 at 17 (Paul Volberding & Mark A. Jacobson eds., 1991).

[38] Yorio Hinuma et al., *Adult T-Cell Leukemia: Antigen in an ATL Cell Line and Detection of Antibodies to the Antigen in Human Sera,* 78 Proc. Nat'l Acad. Sci. 6476 (1981); Bernard J. Poiesz et al., *Detection and Isolation of Type-C Retrovirus Particles From Fresh and Cultured Lymphocytes of a Patient with Cutaneous T-Cell Lymphoma,* 77 Proc. Nat'l Acad. Sci. 7415 (1980).

[39] V.S. Kalyanaraman et al., *A New Subtype of Human T-Cell Leukemia Virus (HTLV-II) Associated with a T-Cell Variant of Hairy Cell Leukemia,* 218 Science 571 (1982).

[40] CDC, *First 500,000 AIDS Cases—United States, 1995,* 44 MMWR 849 (1995).

of December 1995, a total of 513,486 individuals had been diagnosed with AIDS and reported to the CDC by state and territorial health departments; over 62 percent (319,849) had died.[41] The demographic characteristics, behavioral risks, and geographic distribution of persons with AIDS reported during 1995 reflect shifts in the populations at risk, most notably the changing racial/ethnic shift from whites to minorities, especially blacks and Hispanics, who are disproportionately affected. In 1995, for the first time, the proportion of persons reported with AIDS who are black was equal to the proportion who are white (40 percent). In previous years, the incidence of AIDS had been higher among black and Hispanic men than among white men,[42] but in 1995, blacks and Hispanics represented the majority of cases among men (54 percent) as well as women (76 percent). The reported AIDS incidence rate per 100,000 among blacks (92.6) was 6 times higher than that among whites (15.4) and 2 times higher than among Hispanics (46.2). Factors contributing to the increased risk among racial/ethnic minorities include decreased access to HIV-prevention services, higher rates of sexually transmitted diseases,[43] and culturally inappropriate HIV prevention activities.[44]

Men who have sex with men account for the largest proportion of AIDS cases.[45] In 1994, there were 34,974 cases of AIDS among men whose only reported HIV exposure was sexual contact with other men.[46] Although previous reports indicated progressively smaller annual increases in AIDS cases for men who have sex with men,[47] male-to-male sexual contact again accounted for the largest proportion of AIDS cases (51 percent) in 1995. Among young men (ages 20 to 24 years), male-to-male sexual contact and/or injecting drug use accounted for 76 percent of AIDS cases and 63 percent of HIV infection cases reported in 1995.

---

[41] CDC, *HIV/AIDS Surveillance Report* 20 (year-end ed., Dec. 1995).

[42] CDC, *AIDS Among Racial/Ethnic Minorities—United States, 1993,* 43 MMWR 644 (1994).

[43] National Comm'n on Acquired Immune Deficiency Syndrome, The Challenge of HIV/AIDS in Communities of Color (1992). The risk of contracting HIV infection is higher among persons with previous or concomitant sexually transmitted disease. *See, e.g.,* Francis A. Plummer et al., *Cofactors in Male-Female Sexual Transmission of Human Immunodeficiency Virus Type 1,* 163 J. Infectious Diseases 233 (1991); Anne M. Rompalo et al., *Syphilis as a Cofactor in the Natural History of Human Immunodeficiency Virus Infection, in* Cofactors in HIV-1 Infection and AIDS 113 (Ronald Ross Watson ed., 1990); Walter E. Stamm et al., *The Association Between Genital Ulcer Disease and Acquisition of HIV Infection in Homosexual Men,* 260 JAMA 1429 (1988).

[44] U.S. Conference of Mayors, Assessing the HIV-Prevention Needs of Gay and Bisexual Men of Color (1993).

[45] CDC, *Update: Trends in AIDS Among Men Who Have Sex with Men—United States, 1989–1994,* 44 MMWR 401 (1995).

[46] *Id.* at 401.

[47] John M. Karon et al., *The Geographic and Ethnic Diversity of AIDS Incidence in Homosexual/Bisexual Men in the United States,* 4 J. Acquired Immune Deficiency Syndrome 1179 (1991).

The majority of reported AIDS cases in 1994 among women were based on criteria added in the 1993 CDC expanded AIDS surveillance case definition.[48] In 1995, women accounted for 19 percent of adult/adolescent AIDS cases, the highest proportion yet reported among women. HIV infection among women has been related primarily to two modes of HIV transmission: injecting drug use and heterosexual contact with an at-risk partner,[49] and this remained true in 1995 as most women acquired HIV infection through injecting drug use (38 percent) or sexual contact with a man with or at risk for HIV infection (38 percent).

The epidemic in women is reflected in the epidemic in children, nearly all of whom acquired HIV infection perinatally. In 1995, 84 percent of children reported with AIDS were black or Hispanic, and AIDS rates per 100,000 population among black and Hispanic children were 16 and 6 times higher (6.4 and 2.3, respectively) than among white children (0.4).[50] The number of children reported with AIDS in 1995 (800) was lower than that reported in 1994 (1,034). Changes in surveillance practices, the number of infected women giving birth, and the clinical management of women and children may each have contributed to this decline.

Although men who have sex with men continued to account for the largest proportion of cases, injecting drug use is the second most frequently reported risk behavior for HIV infection.[51] Syringe sharing and related behaviors involved in injection of illegal drugs is the risk behavior that most frequently results in heterosexual and mother-to-infant transmission in the United States. HIV transmission among injection drug users (IDUs) and their sex and syringe-sharing partners, as well as transmission to their newborn infants, is a major factor in the continuing spread of HIV, especially among racial/ethnic minority populations.

Of the total reported AIDS cases through December 1995, 184,359 (36 percent) were directly or indirectly associated with injecting drug use; 25,860 (35 percent) of the cases were reported in 1995. When analyzed by gender, 66 percent of AIDS cases reported among women and 85 percent among heterosexual men with an identified exposure category were related to injecting drug use. Although annual increases in the number of cases associated with IDUs continue to occur, these increases have been progressively smaller whereas AIDS incidence among heterosexual partners of IDUs and minorities has continued to increase steadily.[52]

Provisional mortality data for 1993 and 1994, the most recent available, indicate a continuing increase in HIV infection as a leading cause of death in the United States.[53] HIV infection became the eighth leading cause of death overall

---

[48] CDC, *Update: AIDS Among Women—United States, 1994,* 44 MMWR 82 (1995).

[49] *Id.* at 82.

[50] CDC, *HIV/AIDS Surveillance Report* 13 (year-end ed., Dec. 1995).

[51] CDC, *AIDS Associated with Injecting-Drug Use—United States, 1995,* 45 MMWR 392 (1996).

[52] *Id.* at 392, 395.

[53] CDC, *Update: Mortality Attributable to HIV Infection Among Persons Aged 25–44 Years— United States, 1994,* 45 MMWR 121 (1996).

in 1994, accounting for 2 percent of all deaths. HIV infection also became a leading cause of premature mortality and is the fourth leading cause of years of potential life lost before age 65.

An estimated 41,930 U.S. residents died from HIV infection in 1994; of these, 3 percent were aged less than 25 years; 72 percent were 25 to 44 years; and 25 percent were 45 years or older. HIV infection is the leading cause of death in men who are 25 to 44 years old. The death rate among this age group was almost four times as high for black men as for white men and nine times as high for black women as for white women, again reflecting changes in the demographic patterns of the HIV epidemic. Racial differences in death rates probably reflect social, economic, behavioral, and other factors related to HIV transmission risks.[54]

HIV infection is the third leading cause of death for women among persons 25 to 44 years old. The increasing death rate for women is particularly noteworthy because it affects the care of their children: the estimated 80,000 HIV infected women of childbearing age who were alive in 1992 will leave approximately 125,000 to 150,000 children when they die.[55]

§ 1.5   U.S. Surveillance of HIV Infection

For surveillance reporting, individuals older than 18 months of age are considered HIV infected if they have at least one positive Western Blot (or other positive confirmatory test) or had a diagnosis of HIV infection documented by a physician.[56] In 1987, CDC published a classification system for children infected with HIV.[57] New knowledge about the progression of HIV disease in children warranted revision of the 1987 classification system to better reflect the disease process; therefore, the laboratory and diagnostic criteria for the 1987 pediatric case definition were updated in 1994.[58] Before October 1994, children less than 15 months of age were considered HIV infected if they met the definition stated in the 1987 pediatric classification system for HIV infection. Beginning in October 1994, however, children less than 18 months of age are considered HIV infected if they meet the definition stated in the 1994 pediatric classification system for HIV infection. Also included are children who were diagnosed as HIV infected by a physician. Although many states monitor reports

---

[54] *Id.* at 123.

[55] M. Blake Caldwell et al., *Estimated Number of AIDS Orphans in the United States,* 90 Pediatrics 482 (1992).

[56] CDC, *HIV/AIDS Surveillance Report* 31 (mid-year ed., June 1996).

[57] CDC, *Classification System for Human Immunodeficiency Virus (HIV) Infection in Children Under 13 Years of Age,* 36 MMWR 225 (1987).

[58] CDC, *1994 Revised Classification System for Human Immunodeficiency Virus Infection in Children Less Than 13 Years of Age,* 43 MMWR 1 (RR-12, 1994).

of children born to infected mothers, only those with a documented diagnosis of HIV infection are included in CDC surveillance reports.

HIV positive test results, unlike all diagnosed AIDS cases, are not reportable in all states. Through June 1996, 26 states had laws or regulations requiring confidential reporting by name of all persons with confirmed HIV infection, in addition to reporting of persons with AIDS.[59] Two other states, Connecticut and Texas, require reporting of HIV infection by name only for children less than 13 years of age.

HIV infection data should be interpreted with caution for several reasons. First, HIV surveillance reports are not representative of all persons with HIV infection. Because many HIV reporting states also offer anonymous HIV testing, confidential HIV infection reports are not representative of all persons who are being tested in these areas.[60] Furthermore, many factors may influence testing patterns, including the extent that testing is targeted or routinely offered to specific groups and the availability and access to medical care and testing services. CDC data thus provide a minimum estimate of the number of persons with HIV infection. Persons reported with HIV (not AIDS), however, are younger, more likely to be women and black or Hispanic minorities, and more recently infected than persons reported with AIDS.[61]

Second, because states initiated reporting on different dates, the length of time reporting has been in place influences the number of HIV infection cases reported. For example, data presented for a given annual period may include cases reported during only a portion of the year. Prior to statewide HIV reporting, some states collected reports of HIV infection in selected populations. Therefore, these states have reports prior to initiation of statewide confidential reporting.

Finally, before 1991, surveillance of HIV infection was not standardized and reporting was based primarily on a voluntary basis. Consequently, many reported cases do not have complete information. Since 1991, CDC has assisted states in conducting active surveillance of HIV infection using standardized report forms and software. However, collection of demographic and risk information still varies greatly among states.

---

[59] CDC, *HIV/AIDS Surveillance Report* 30 (mid-year ed., June 1996).

[60] Anonymous testing does not require any identification, and names for contact tracing and partner notification are not provided. Confidential testing does require a name, although individuals have the option of using a pseudonym at confidential test sites. Supporters of confidential testing and named HIV reporting claim that this strategy may enhance the notification of partners of individuals who test positive and potentially reduce the spread of HIV. *See* CDC, *Partner Notification for Preventing Human Immunodeficiency Virus Infection— Colorado, Idaho, South Carolina, Virginia,* 37 MMWR 393 (1988); John J. Potterat et al., *Partner Notification in the Control of Human Immunodeficiency Virus Infection,* 79 Am. J. Pub. Health 874 (1989). Colorado was one of the first states to adopt a voluntary, confidential HIV testing program and require laboratories to report individuals' names who test positive; the debate about this method of disease control remains a subject of controversy. *See, e.g.,* Tamara Hoxworth et al., *Anonymous HIV Testing: Does It Attract Clients Who Would Not Seek Confidential Testing,* 9 AIDS & Pub. Pol'y J. 182 (1994).

[61] CDC, *HIV/AIDS Surveillance Report* 24–28 (mid-year ed., June 1996).

§ 1.6   U.S. Surveillance of AIDS Cases

AIDS was initially defined as "Kaposi's sarcoma and opportunistic infections in previously healthy persons."[62] Later, several staging systems were proposed for classification and staging.[63] One of the first, the Walter Reed Staging Classification for HTLV-LAV Infection, was adopted by the U.S. Army but never achieved widespread use.[64] In 1990, the World Health Organization (WHO) published an interim proposal for a staging system.[65] Case definitions in countries outside of the United States have also been developed.[66]

The term *AIDS* was first used by the CDC in 1982 to describe "a disease, at least moderately predictive of a defect in cell-mediated immunity, occurring with no known cause for diminished resistance to that disease."[67] The initial CDC list of AIDS-defining conditions included KS, PCP, and Mycobacterium avium complex (MAC), among others. This first AIDS surveillance case definition was developed in response to the need for public health agencies to monitor a disease resulting from HIV infection in the United States. The definition was modified in 1985,[68] 1987,[69] and 1992.[70] The last revision became effective in January 1993.

The most recent definition encompasses CD4 cell[71] counts and is an improvement over the previous staging system (which placed no emphasis on CD4 counts)

---

[62] CDC, *Update on Kaposi's Sarcoma and Opportunistic Infections in Previously Healthy Persons—United States,* 31 MMWR 294 (1982).

[63] *See, e.g.,* CDC, *Classification System for Human T-Lymphotropic Virus Type III/Lymphadenopathy-Associated Virus Infections,* 35 MMWR 334 (1986); Harry W. Haverkos et al., *Classification of HTLV-III/LAV-Related Diseases,* 152 J. Infectious Diseases 1095 (1985); Amy C. Justice et al., *A New Prognostic Staging System for the Acquired Immunodeficiency Syndrome,* 320 New Eng. J. Med. 1388 (1989); R.A. Royce et al., *The Natural History of HIV-1 Infection: Staging Classification of Disease,* 5 AIDS 355 (1991).

[64] Robert R. Redfield, *The Walter Reed Staging Classification for HTLV-LAV Infection,* 314 New Eng. J. Med. 131 (1986).

[65] World Health Org. (WHO), *Interim Proposal for a WHO Staging System for HIV Infection and Diseases,* 65 Wkly. Epidemiological Rec. 221 (1990).

[66] *See, e.g.,* R.A. Ancelle-Park, *European AIDS Definition,* 339 Lancet 671 (1992); L. Belec et al., *Surveillance of Acquired Immunodeficiency Syndrome in Africa: An Analysis of Evaluations of the World Health Organization and Other Clinical Definitions,* 16 Epidemiological Rev. 3 (1994); Robert Colebunders et al., *Evaluation of a Clinical Case Definition of Acquired Immunodeficiency Syndrome in Africa,* 1 Lancet 492 (1987); Kevin M. DeCock et al., *AIDS Surveillance in Africa: A Re-Appraisal of Case Definitions,* 303 Brit. Med. J. 1185 (1991).

[67] CDC, *Update on Acquired Immune Deficiency Syndrome (AIDS)—United States,* 31 MMWR 507 (1982).

[68] CDC, *Revision of the Case Definition of Acquired Immunodeficiency Syndrome for National Reporting—United States,* 34 MMWR 373 (1985).

[69] CDC, *Revision of the CDC Surveillance Case Definition for Acquired Immunodeficiency Syndrome,* 36 MMWR 1 (Supp. 1, 1987).

[70] CDC, *1993 Revised Classification System for HIV Infection and Expanded Surveillance Case Definition for AIDS Among Adolescents and Adults,* 41 MMWR 1-19 (RR-17, 1992).

[71] *CD4+ T-lymphocytes* (CD4s) are white blood cells that are produced in the lymphoid organs. They are the primary target for HIV infection. *See, e.g.,* J.S. McDougal et al., *Binding of the*

because this parameter consistently correlates with HIV-related immune dysfunction and disease progression.[72] They are also used to guide clinical and therapeutic management of HIV infected persons.[73] In addition to the 23 clinical conditions in the 1987 definition, the 1993 case definition for adults and adolescents includes: (1) HIV infected persons with CD4 counts of less than 200 cells per milliliter or a CD4 percentage of less than 14, and (2) the addition of three clinical conditions—pulmonary tuberculosis, recurrent pneumonia, and invasive cervical cancer. All conditions added to the 1993 definition require laboratory confirmation of HIV infection.

All 50 states, the District of Columbia, U.S. dependencies and possessions, and independent nations in association with the United States[74] report diagnosed AIDS cases to the CDC using this uniform surveillance case definition.[75] Although completeness of AIDS case reporting to state and local health departments varies by geographic region and patient population, studies conducted by state and

---

HTLV-III/LAV to T4+ T-Cells by a Complex of the 110K Molecule and the T4 Molecule, 231 Science 382 (1985). These cells have a docking molecule on their surface called *cluster designation 4* (CD4). Cells with this molecule are known as *CD4 positive* (CD4+) cells. A healthy, uninfected person usually has 800 to 1200 CD4+ cells per cubic milliliter of blood. CD4s coordinate a number of important immunologic functions, and a loss of these functions results in progressive impairment of the immune response. For an overview of the immune system, including the function of lymphocytes, see National Cancer Institute & National Institute of Allergy & Infectious Diseases, Understanding the Immune System, NIH Pub. No. 92-529 (Oct. 1991). This document is available on NIAID's World Wide Web home page at http://www.niaid.nih.gov.

[72] *See, e.g.,* John L. Fahey et al., *The Prognostic Value of Cellular and Serologic Markers in Infection with Human Immunodeficiency Virus Type 1,* 322 New Eng. J. Med. 166 (1990); Eduardo Fernandez-Cruz et al., *Immunological and Serological Markers Predictive of Progression to AIDS in a Cohort of HIV-Infected Drug users,* 4 AIDS 987 (1990); James J. Goedert et al., *Effect of T4 Count and Cofactors on the Incidence of AIDS in Homosexual Men Infected with Human Immunodeficiency Virus,* 257 JAMA 331 (1987); William Lang et al., *Patterns of T Lymphocyte Changes with Human Immunodeficiency Virus Infection: From Seroconversion to the Development of AIDS,* 2 J. Acquired Immune Deficiency Syndrome 63 (1989); Joep M.A. Lange et al., *Markers for Progression of HIV Infection,* 3 AIDS 153 (Supp. 1, 1989); Henry Masur et al., *CD4 Counts as Predictors of Opportunistic Pneumonias in Human Immunodeficiency Virus (HIV) Infection,* 111 Annals Internal Med. 223 (1989); Janet K.A. Nicholson, *Serial Determination of HIV-1 Titers in HIV-Infected Homosexual Men: Association of Rising Titers with CD4 T Cell Depletion and Progression to AIDS,* 5 AIDS Res. & Human Retroviruses 205 (1989); Jeremy M.G. Taylor et al., *CD4 Percentage, CD4 Numbers, and CD4:CD8 Ration in HIV Infection: Which to Choose and How to Use,* 2 J. Acquired Immune Deficiency Syndrome 114 (1989).

[73] National Insts. of Health (NIH), *State-of-the-Art Conference on Azidothymidine Therapy for Early HIV Infection,* 89 Am. J. Med. 335 (1990); U.S. Pub. Health Serv. & Infectious Diseases Soc'y of Am., *USPHS/IDSA Guidelines for the Prevention of Opportunistic Infections in Persons Infected with Human Immunodeficiency Virus,* 21 Annals Internal Med. 1 (Supp. 1, 1996).

[74] Included among the dependencies, possessions, and independent nations are Puerto Rico, the U.S. Virgin Islands, Guam, American Samoa, the Republic of Palau, the Republic of the Marshall Islands, the Commonwealth of the Northern Mariana Islands, and the Federated States of Micronesia. The latter five comprise the category of Pacific Islands, U.S.

[75] CDC, *HIV/AIDS Surveillance Report* 30 (mid-year ed., June 1996).

local health departments indicate that reporting in most areas of the United States is more than 85 percent complete.[76]

Following the initial report in 1982 of diagnosed AIDS in children,[77] it became evident that the clinical characteristics of AIDS in children were different from those in adults. The laboratory and diagnostic criteria for the 1987 pediatric case definition[78] were updated in 1994.[79] For children of any age with an AIDS-defining condition that requires evidence of HIV infection, a single positive HIV detection test is sufficient for a reportable AIDS diagnosis if the diagnosis is confirmed by a clinician. The revised 1994 pediatric definition for HIV encephalopathy and HIV wasting syndrome reflects increased knowledge of these conditions in children and replaces the 1987 definition. The definition of HIV encephalopathy follows the recommendations of the American Academy of Neurology AIDS Task Force.[80]

§ 1.7 HIV Transmission

HIV is a blood borne pathogen that is transmitted *primarily:* (1) between sex partners through contact of blood with anal or genital mucosa; (2) by direct inoculation of infected blood or blood-containing tissues through transfusion of blood or blood products, transplantation of organs or certain tissues, reuse of contaminated needles or other injection equipment, or penetrating injuries with needles or other sharp objects contaminated with blood; and (3) from a mother with HIV infection to her newborn during pregnancy, delivery, or breast feeding.[81] In the health care setting, relatively few workers have been infected. Those cases have occurred as a result of being stuck with needles containing HIV infected blood or, less frequently, after infected blood gets into the worker's bloodstream through an open cut or splashes into a mucous membrane, for example, the eyes or inside of the nose.

---

[76] James W. Buehler et al., *The Completeness of AIDS Surveillance,* 5 J. Acquired Immune Deficiency Syndrome 257 (1992); Lisa Rosenblum et al., *The Completeness of AIDS Case Reporting, 1988: A Multisite Collaborative Surveillance Project,* 82 Am. J. Pub. Health 1495 (1992).

[77] CDC, *Unexplained Immunodeficiency and Opportunistic Infection in Infants—New York, New Jersey, California,* 31 MMWR 665 (1982).

[78] CDC, *Classification System for Human Immunodeficiency Virus (HIV) Infection in Children Under 13 Years of Age,* 36 MMWR 225 (1987).

[79] CDC, *1994 Revised Classification System for Human Immunodeficiency Virus Infection in Children Less Than 13 Years of Age,* 43 MMWR 1 (RR-12, 1994).

[80] Working Group of the Am. Acad. of Neurology AIDS Task Force, *Nomenclature and Research Case Definitions for Neurologic Manifestations of Human Immunodeficiency Virus-Type 1 (HIV-1) Infection,* 41 Neurology 778 (1991).

[81] James W. Curran et al., *Epidemiology of HIV Infection and AIDS in the United States,* 239 Science 610 (1988).

HIV has also been found in semen[82] and pre-ejaculatory fluid,[83] vaginal and cervical secretions,[84] amniotic fluid,[85] breast milk,[86] alveolar fluid,[87] saliva,[88] tears,[89] throat swabs,[90] and cerebrospinal fluid.[91] HIV nucleic acid sequences, but not the virus, have been detected in urine.[92] HIV has not been found in feces or vomitus; however, these fluids theoretically may contain HIV if they are contaminated with blood. These fluids contain relatively low levels of HIV; thus transmission by these fluids is lower when compared to blood because transmission is greatly influenced by the amount of infectious virus in a body fluid and the extent of contact with that body fluid. **Section 1.13** examines in more detail some of these fluids as factors in HIV transmission.[93]

---

[82] Pietro L. Vernazza et al., *Detection and Biologic Characterization of Infectious HIV-1 in Semen of Seropositive Men,* 8 AIDS 1325 (1994); Omar Bagasra et al., *Detection of HIV-1 Proviral DNA in Sperm from HIV-1 Infected Men,* 8 AIDS 1669 (1994); John N. Krieger et al., *Intermittent Shedding of Human Immunodeficiency Virus in Semen: Implications for Sexual Transmission,* 154 J. Urology 1035 (1995).

[83] Jeffrey Pudney et al., *Pre-Ejaculatory Fluid as Potential Vector for Sexual Transmission of HIV-1,* 340 Lancet 1470 (1992); Gerard Ilaria et al., *Detection of HIV-1 DNA Sequences in Pre-Ejaculatory Fluid,* 340 Lancet 1469 (1992).

[84] Roger J. Pomerantz et al., *Human Immunodeficiency Virus Infection of the Uterine Cervix,* 108 Annals Internal Med. 321 (1988); Marcus W. Vogt et al., *Isolation of HTLV III/LAV from Cervical Secretions of Women at Risk for AIDS,* 1 Lancet 525 (1986); Catherine Wofsy et al., *Isolation of AIDS-Associated Retrovirus from Genital Secretions of Women with Antibodies to the Virus,* 1 Lancet 527 (1986).

[85] David C. Mundy et al., *Human Immunodeficiency Virus Isolated from Amniotic Fluid,* 2 Lancet 459 (1987).

[86] L. Thiry et al., *Isolation of AIDS Virus from Cell-Free Breast Milk of Three Healthy Carriers,* 2 Lancet 891 (1985).

[87] J. Ziza et al., *Lymphadenopathy-Associated Virus Isolated From Bronchoalveolar Lavage Fluid in AIDS-Related Complex With Lymphoid Interstitial Pneumonitis,* 313 New Eng. J. Med. 183 (1985).

[88] Jerome E. Groopman et al., *HTLV-III in Saliva of People with AIDS-Related Complex and Healthy Homosexual Men,* 226 Science 447 (1984); David D. Ho et al., *Infrequency of Isolation of HTLV-III Virus from Saliva in AIDS,* 313 New Eng. J. Med. 1606 (1985); Jay A. Levy & Deborah Greenspan, *HIV in Saliva,* 2 Lancet 1248 (1988).

[89] Leslie S. Fujikawa et al., *Isolation of Human T-Lymphotropic Virus Type III from the Tears of a Patient with the Acquired Immunodeficiency Syndrome,* 2 Lancet 529 (1985).

[90] Hisashi Kawashima et al., *Excretion of Human Immunodeficiency Virus Type 1 in the Throat but Not in Urine of Infected Children,* 118 J. Pediatrics 80 (1991).

[91] David D. Ho et al., *Isolation of HTLV-III from Cerebrospinal Fluid and Neural Tissues of Patients with Neurologic Syndromes Related to the Acquired Immunodeficiency Syndrome,* 313 New Eng. J. Med. 1493 (1985).

[92] Jay A. Levy, *Pathogenesis of Human Immunodeficiency Virus Infection,* 57 Microbiological Revs. 183, 191 (1993).

[93] *See id.* at 189–91.

§ 1.8 —Sexual Contact

Male-to-male sexual contact is the most frequently reported mode of HIV transmission in the United States. HIV infection among gay and bisexual men results
primarily from receptive anal intercourse.[94] Although receptive anal intercourse
is more efficient than other sexual activities and is associated with the greatest
risk, other reports have suggested transmission by insertive anal intercourse.[95]

A similarly high risk may pertain to women who engage in receptive anal intercourse with infected male partners.[96] The prevalence of heterosexual anal intercourse is poorly documented, although efforts to study its frequency have suggested
that it is more widespread and frequent than commonly believed. Insertive heterosexual anal intercourse and vaginal intercourse appear to carry lower levels of
risk.[97]

As noted in § 1.7, HIV has been identified in semen and pre-ejaculatory fluid
as well as cervical and vaginal secretions. Vaginal-penile intercourse, therefore,
can transmit HIV to either the male or the female. A number of studies, however,
show that male-to-female transmission is more common than female-to-male transmission in the United States,[98] although female-to-male transmission is prevalent in other countries.[99] Although some studies failed to find a link between risk

---

[94] William W. Darrow et al., *Risk Factors for Human Immunodeficiency Virus (HIV) Infections in Homosexual Men,* 77 Am. J. Pub. Health 479 (1987); Harold M. Ginzburg et al., *Selected Public Health Observations Derived from the Multicenter AIDS Cohort Study,* 1 J. Acquired Immune Deficiency Syndrome 2 (1988); Lawrence A. Kingsley et al., *Risk Factors for Seroconversion to Human Immunodeficiency Virus Among Male Homosexuals: Results from the Multicenter AIDS Cohort Study,* 1 Lancet 345 (1987); Andrew R. Moss et al., *Risk Factors for AIDS and HIV Seropositivity in Homosexual Men,* 125 Am. J. Epidemiology 1035 (1987); Warren Winkelstein Jr. et al., *Sexual Practices and Risk of Infection by the Human Immunodeficiency Virus: The San Francisco Men's Health Study,* 257 JAMA 321 (1987).

[95] Alan R. Lifson et al., *Recent HIV Seroconverters in a San Francisco Cohort of Homo-sexual/Bisexual Men: Risk Factors for New Infection,* Fifth Int'l Conf. on AIDS 127 (Montreal, Canada, Abstract No. WAP46, 1989, AIDSLINE S.I. No. ICA5/00044189).

[96] European Study Group, *Risk Factors for Male to Female Transmission of HIV,* 198 Brit. Med. J. 411 (1989); Mads Melbye et al., *Anal Intercourse as a Possible Factor in Hetero-sexual Transmission of HTLV-III to Spouses of Hemophiliacs,* 312 New Eng. J. Med. 857 (1985).

[97] June E. Osborn, *Public Health, HIV, and AIDS, in* Textbook of AIDS Medicine 135 (Samuel Broder et al. eds., 1994).

[98] *See, e.g.,* Nancy Padian et al., *Male-to-Female Transmission of Human Immunodeficiency Virus,* 258 JAMA 788 (1987); Thomas A. Peterman et al., *Risk of Human Immunodeficiency Virus Transmission from Heterosexual Adults with Transfusion-Associated Infections,* 259 JAMA 55 (1988).

[99] For a discussion of the factors that may be relevant in explaining prevalent female-to-male transmission in other countries, see Nancy S. Padian et al., *Female-to-Male Transmission of Human Immunodeficiency Virus,* 266 JAMA 1666 (1991).

of infection and number of sexual contacts with an HIV positive partner,[100] the risk of infection from a single sexual contact is estimated to be low.[101] Epidemiology studies suggest that some individuals are resistant to HIV infection,[102] while other individuals remain uninfected despite multiple high-risk sexual exposures.[103] Female partners of HIV infected hemophiliacs, for example, who have had frequent unprotected sexual contact over a period of years but remain uninfected, suggest that HIV is not always transmitted from an HIV positive male to a female.[104] In another study, the authors investigated the relationship between the number of unprotected heterosexual contacts with an HIV infected person and the probability of HIV transmission.[105] The percentage of female partners infected ranged from 10 percent, among those with less than 10 unprotected contacts with an infected male, to 23 percent after 2,000 unprotected contacts. These results suggest that the association between the number of unprotected sexual contacts and the probability of infection is relatively low.

In contrast some individuals appear to have been infected after only one or two sexual exposures.[106] One study showed that the number of contacts with an infected individual increases the risk of transmission.[107] This variation in transmissibility could be caused by varying susceptibility to infection among the partners; by changing degrees of infectiousness in the HIV infected individual over time; by differences in strains of HIV, which in turn might vary in an individual carrier over time; by varying distributions of cofactors that might

---

[100] Thomas A. Peterman et al., *Risk of Human Immunodeficiency Virus Transmission from Heterosexual Adults with Transfusion-Associated Infections,* 259 JAMA 55 (1988); Margaret A. Fischl et al., *Evaluation of Heterosexual Partners, Children, and Household Contacts of Adults with AIDS,* 257 JAMA 640 (1987).

[101] Victor DeGruttola et al., *Infectiousness of HIV Between Male Homosexual Partners,* 42 J. Clinical Epidemiology 849 (1989); D. Rebecca Prevots et al., *The Epidemiology of Heterosexually Acquired HIV Infection and AIDS in Western Industrialized Countries,* 8 AIDS 109 (Supp. 1, 1994).

[102] Roger Detels et al., *Resistance to HIV-1 Infection,* 7 J. Acquired Immune Deficiency Syndrome 1263 (1994); R. Taylor, *Quiet Clues to HIV-1 Immunity: Do Some People Resist Infection?,* 6 J. Nat'l Inst. Health Res. 29 (1994).

[103] William A. Paxton et al., *Relative Resistance to HIV-1 Infection of CD4 Lymphocytes from Persons Who Remain Uninfected Despite Multiple High-Risk Sexual Exposures,* 2 Nature Med. 412 (1996).

[104] Peter Jones et al., *AIDS and Hemophilia: Morbidity and Mortality in a Well-Defined Population,* 291 Brit. Med. J. 695 (1985).

[105] Angela M. Downs & Isabelle De Vincenzi, *Probability of Heterosexual Transmission of HIV: Relationship to the Number of Unprotected Sexual Contacts,* 11 J. Acquired Immune Deficiency Syndrome 388 (1996).

[106] Thomas A. Peterman et al., *Risk of Human Immunodeficiency Virus Transmission from Heterosexual Adults with Transfusion-Associated Infections,* 259 JAMA 55 (1988).

[107] Nancy S. Padian, *The Effect of Number of Exposures on the Risk of Heterosexual HIV Transmission,* 161 J. Infectious Diseases 883 (1990).

enhance or limit transmission probabilities;[108] or by some combination of all of these possibilities.[109] The difficulty in identifying frequency of sexual contact as enhancing risk in many transmission studies demonstrates that although the number of contacts does increase risk, the variability of infectiousness over time may be a more significant determinant of transmission risk.[110]

The role of oral sex has been difficult to determine in regard to HIV transmission because it usually is not the only reported sexual activity. In addition, risk factors facilitating transmission through such exposures have not been conclusively identified. In one study, however, researchers found that six of seven monkeys became infected with SIV when the virus was placed on the backs of their tongues.[111] The minimal virus dose needed to achieve infection after oral exposure was 6000 times lower than the dose required to achieve infection after rectal exposure. Unprotected receptive oral intercourse, therefore, should not be considered risk-free. The authors point out, however, that the amount of SIV required for infection was relatively high, and it is unlikely that anyone could become infected from casual contact, such as kissing or sharing a fork.

Exposure through receptive oral sex can occur either with or without ejaculation. In one report, two gay men became HIV infected although both men reported no insertive or receptive anal intercourse for at least five years before the estimated seroconversion date, but they did report multiple episodes of receptive oral intercourse with ejaculation.[112] Little is known about the risk of receptive oral intercourse without ejaculation, but HIV is present in pre-ejaculatory fluids; therefore, the possibility for HIV transmission exists.[113]

Information about oral-vaginal transmission is limited, but one report described HIV infection in a man who had both fellatio and cunnilingus with an HIV infected woman, although HIV transmission could not be conclusively proven.[114] Two reports of possible female to female transmission have appeared in the literature. In a letter published in the *Annals of Internal Medicine,* the authors documented an apparent female to female sexual transmission as a result of digital,

---

[108] For a list of cofactors, see Dennis H. Osmond & Nancy Padian, *Sexual Transmission of HIV, in* The AIDS Knowledge Base 1.9-1, 1.9-9 (P.T. Cohen et al. eds., 2d ed. 1994) (Table 3 sets forth factors associated with heterosexual transmission of HIV).

[109] *Id.* at 1.9-2.

[110] *Id.* at 1.9-7.

[111] Timothy W. Baba et al., *Infection and AIDS in Adult Macaques After Nontraumatic Oral Exposure to Cell-Free SIV,* 272 Science 1486 (1996).

[112] Alan R. Lifson et al., *HIV Seroconversion in Two Homosexual Men After Receptive Oral Intercourse With Ejaculation: Implications for Counseling Concerning Safe Sexual Practices,* 80 Am. J. Pub. Health 1509 (1990).

[113] Gerard Ilaria et al., *Detection of HIV-1 DNA Sequences in Pre-Ejaculatory Fluid,* 340 Lancet 1469 (1992); Jeffrey Pudney et al., *Pre-Ejaculatory Fluid as Potential Vector for Sexual Transmission of HIV-1,* 340 Lancet 1470 (1992).

[114] Peter G. Spitzer & Neil J. Weiner, *Transmission of HIV Infection from a Woman to a Man by Oral Sex,* 320 New Eng. J. Med. 251 (1989).

oral-genital, and oral-anal contact which allowed exposure to vaginal blood.[115] In another report,[116] the authors described a 24-year-old woman infected with HIV whose sole reported risk behavior was prior oral-genital contact with an HIV infected woman. These cases provide some evidence that lesbian activity can be a risk behavior for HIV transmission, although such behavior may be an inefficient means of transmission. The assertion that the low level of risk from female to female sex does not place individuals at risk, however, is unwarranted.[117]

Regardless of risk levels of sexual activities, studies of sexually active persons have shown that correct and consistent use of latex condoms is highly effective in preventing HIV infection.[118] The effectiveness of consistent condom use is evident from epidemiologic studies of serodiscordant heterosexual couples (that is, one partner is HIV infected and the other is not).[119] Despite the widespread understanding that HIV infection is transmitted sexually, however, most sexually active Americans have intercourse without using condoms. In one study, for example, only 6 percent of heterosexual males with multiple sex partners reported always using condoms; a much higher proportion (48 percent) of gay and bisexual men reported always using condoms.[120] In another study, only about 20 percent of sexually active American women reported that their male partners used condoms, but even among these couples, condom use was inconsistent; only one in five who reported condom use said they were used during the last sexual intercourse activity.[121]

§ 1.9 —Injecting Drug Use

HIV (as well as hepatitis B and C virus) is transmitted through the reuse and sharing of contaminated injecting drug equipment which allows the exchange of

---

[115] Michael Marmor et al., *Possible Female-to-Female Transmission of Human Immunodeficiency Virus,* 105 Annals Internal Med. 969 (1986).

[116] Ofelia T. Monzon et al., *Female-to-Female Transmission of HIV,* 2 Lancet 40 (1987).

[117] Barbara G. Dicker, *Risk of AIDS Among Lesbians,* 70 Am. J. Pub. Health 1569 (1989).

[118] W. Cates & K.M. Stone, *Family Planning, Sexually Transmitted Diseases and Contraceptive Choice: A Literature Update: Part I,* 24 Fam. Plan. Persp. 75 (1992).

[119] Y. Laurian et al., *HIV Infection in Sexual Partners of HIV Seropositive Patients with Hemophilia,* 320 New Eng. J. Med. 183 (1989); European Study Group on Heterosexual Transmission of HIV, *Comparison of Female to Male and Male to Female Transmission of HIV in 563 Stable Couples,* 304 Brit. Med. J. 809 (1992); Isabelle de Vincenzi, *A Longitudinal Study of Human Immunodeficiency Virus Transmission by Heterosexual Partners,* 331 New Eng. J. Med. 341 (1994).

[120] Joseph A. Catania et al., *Condom Use in Multi-Ethnic Neighborhoods of San Francisco: The Population-Based AMEN (AIDS in Multi-Ethnic Neighborhoods) Study,* 82 Am. J. Pub. Health 284 (1992).

[121] K. Kost & J.D. Forrest, *American Women's Sexual Behavior and Exposure to Risk of Sexually Transmitted Diseases,* 24 Fam. Plan. Persp. 244 (1992).

blood.[122] HIV can be transmitted through injection drug use when the blood of an HIV infected drug user is transferred to a drug user who is not yet HIV infected. Needles and syringes are the primary drug injection equipment involved in transferring HIV infected blood between drug injectors. This transfer of HIV infected blood occurs almost exclusively through multiperson use, or sharing, of drug injection equipment. There are two primary drug injection activities that involve introducing blood into the needle and syringe. The first activity is to draw blood into the syringe to verify that the needle is inside a vein so the drug can be injected intravenously. The second, following drug injection, is to refill the syringe several times with blood from the vein to "wash out" any heroin, cocaine, or other drug left in the syringe after the initial injection. If a small amount of HIV infected blood is left in the syringe, HIV can be transmitted to the next user.

Some sexually active, HIV infected IDUs also continue to practice sexual activities that place them and their partners at risk, including those who trade sex for noninjected drugs, particularly "crack" cocaine.[123] Trading sex for drugs often is associated with unprotected sex and having multiple sex partners. In a CDC study that analyzed data about sexual risk behavior among HIV positive IDUs, for example, the results showed that men who reported not using condoms were more likely to trade sex for money or drugs than did men who reported using condoms.[124] Further, the use of noninjected drugs or alcohol can place a person at risk in part because these substances lessen inhibitions and reduce reluctance to engage in unsafe sex.

Abstaining from the sharing of injection drug equipment eliminates the risk of HIV transmission; disinfection of needles and syringes with household bleach can reduce this risk.[125] Since the mid-1980s, HIV-prevention programs for IDUs in the United States have recommended using bleach for disinfection of drug-injection equipment previously used by another person to reduce the possibility of HIV transmission. More recent studies, however, suggested that the

---

[122] Ellie E. Schoenbaum et al., *Risk Factors for Human Immunodeficiency Virus Infection in Intravenous Drug Users*, 321 New Eng. J. Med. 874 (1989); *see also* Richard S. Garfein et al., *Viral Infections in Short-Term Injection Drug Users: The Prevalence of the Hepatitis C, Hepatitis B, Human Immunodeficiency, and Human T-Lymphotropic Virus*, 86 Am. J. Pub. Health 655 (1996).

[123] B.K. Singh et al., *Sexual Risk Behavior Among Injection Drug-Using Human Immunodeficiency Virus-Positive Clients*, 28 Int'l J. Addictions 735 (1993).

[124] CDC, *Continued Sexual Risk Behavior Among HIV-Seropositive Drug-Using Men—Atlanta; Washington, D.C.; and San Juan, Puerto Rico, 1993*, 45 MMWR 151 (1996).

[125] Linda S. Martin, *Disinfection and Inactivation of the Human T Lymphotropic Virus Type III/Lymphadenopathy-Associated Virus*, 152 J. Infectious Diseases 400 (1985); Lionel Resnick et al., *Stability and Inactivation of HTLV-III/LAV Under Clinical and Laboratory Environments*, 255 JAMA 1887 (1986); B. Spire et al., *Inactivation of Lymphadenopathy Associated Virus by Chemical Disinfectants*, 2 Lancet 899 (1984).

effectiveness of bleach disinfection may be limited.[126] As a result, two national bulletins were issued in early 1993 that described disinfection procedures that would increase the likelihood of disinfection.[127] They included provisional recommendations for the use of bleach to disinfect needles and syringes, including the recommendation for the use of full-strength household bleach.

To determine whether these new recommendations had been disseminated effectively to IDUs, the CDC published data about knowledge of bleach use for disinfection among persons who reported injecting drugs.[128] Although the findings were subject to at least three limitations, the results indicated that only one-fifth of the active IDUs reported sharing injection equipment. However, of those who did share, only one-fourth used bleach consistently, and of all the active IDUs, only one-third knew both recommendations for correct bleach use, regardless of whether they shared injection equipment or used bleach. Because of inconsistent use and incomplete knowledge, active IDUs who reuse syringes that have been used by other IDUs are at high risk for HIV infection.

One report concluded that IDUs who continue to share syringes should not be urged to clean used equipment but should be ensured a routine and reliable source of sterile equipment.[129] In July 1991, the National Commission on AIDS recommended that legal barriers to the purchase and possession of needles and syringes be removed as part of a strategy for reducing the spread of HIV among IDUs unable or unwilling to enter drug treatment.[130] Given the importance of IDU access to sterile needles and syringes, the CDC and others have recommended that public health officials review local laws and regulations that affect needle/syringe availability and possession.[131] Other measures suggested for reducing transmission include preventing the initiation of injecting drug use, increasing the number of IDUs in drug treatment, encouraging safer injecting practices

---

[126] See, e.g., Paul Shapshak et al., *Inactivation of Human Immunodeficiency Virus-1 at Short Time Intervals Using Undiluted Bleach,* 6 J. Acquired Immune Deficiency Syndrome 218 (1993).

[127] CDC Ctr. for Substance Abuse Treatment & Nat'l Inst. on Drug Abuse, *HIV AIDS Prevention Bulletin* (Apr. 19, 1993); National Inst. on Drug Abuse, *Community Alert Bulletin* (Mar. 25, 1993).

[128] CDC, *Knowledge and Practices Among Injecting-Drug Users of Bleach Use for Equipment Disinfection—New York City, 1993,* 43 MMWR 439 (1994).

[129] Martin C. Donoghoe & Robert Power, *Household Bleach as Disinfectant for Use by Injecting Drug Users,* 341 Lancet 1658 (1993).

[130] National Comm'n on Acquired Immune Deficiency Syndrome, Report: The Twin Epidemics of Substance Use and HIV 10 (1991).

[131] CDC, *Impact of New Legislation on Needle and Syringe Purchase and Possession—Connecticut, 1992,* 42 MMWR 145 (1993); *see also* Kaiser Forums, Henry J. Kaiser Family Foundation, Dimensions of HIV Prevention: Needle Exchange (Jeff Stryker & Mark Smith eds., 1993). Legal issues posed by syringe exchange programs are discussed in **Ch. 2.**

among IUDs, and promoting safer sexual behaviors among IDUs and their sex partners.[132]

§ 1.10 —Blood Transfusions and Products

HIV transmission by blood transfusions was recognized in the early 1980s.[133] Transmission has been reported by transfusion of whole or cellular blood components.[134] The frequency of HIV infected blood donations was estimated as high as 1 in 100 donations in some areas of the United States in 1982,[135] with the risks varying in large measure on the geographic region where the donated blood was collected.[136]

Steps were taken between 1983 and 1985 to control HIV transmission. Since March 1983, the U.S. Public Health Service (PHS) has recommended that individuals at increased risk for HIV infection refrain from donating plasma and/or blood.[137] The risk of transmission associated with the administration of blood or blood products at that time accounted for about 2 percent of all reported AIDS cases in the United States.[138] Anonymous test sites were established to discourage people from donating blood solely to be tested, but some individuals with known risk factors continued to donate blood.[139]

---

[132] Don C. Des Jarlais et al., *Continuity and Change Within an HIV Epidemic: Injecting Drug Users in New York City, 1984 Through 1992,* 271 JAMA 121 (1994); Laugher Roehrich et al., *Behavioral Interventions for In-Treatment Injecting Drug Users, in* Preventing AIDS: Theories and Methods of Behavioral Interventions 189 (R.J. DiClemente & J.L. Peterson eds., 1994).

[133] CDC, *Possible Transfusion-Associated Acquired Immune Deficiency Syndrome (AIDS)— California,* 31 MMWR 652 (1982).

[134] CDC, *Changing Patterns of Acquired Immunodeficiency Syndrome in Hemophilia Patients— United States,* 34 MMWR 241 (1985).

[135] M.P. Busch et al., *Risk of Human Immunodeficiency Virus (HIV) Transmission by Blood Transfusions Before the Implementation of HIV-1 Antibody Screening,* 31 Transfusion 4 (1991).

[136] R.M. Selik et al., *Trends in Transfusion-Associated Acquired Immune Deficiency Syndrome in the United States, 1982 Through 1991,* 33 Transfusion 890 (1993).

[137] CDC, *Prevention of Acquired Immune Deficiency Syndrome (AIDS): A Report of Inter Agency Recommendations,* 32 MMWR 101 (1983).

[138] CDC, *Provisional Public Health Service Inter-Agency Recommendations for Screening Donated Blood and Plasma for Antibody to the Virus Causing Acquired Immunodeficiency Syndrome,* 34 MMWR 1 (1985).

[139] *See, e.g.,* L.S. Doll et al., *Human Immunodeficiency Virus Type 1-Infected Blood Donors: Behavioral Characteristics and Reasons for Donation,* 31 Transfusion 704 (1991); L.R. Petersen et al., *Human Immunodeficiency Virus Type 1-Infected Blood Donors: Epidemiologic, Laboratory and Donation Characteristics,* 31 Transfusion 698 (1991).

In January 1985, CDC recommended that *all* blood used for transfusion or for the manufacture of blood products be screened for HIV.[140] Blood screening involves both donor screening and blood testing.[141] Donor screening begins when blood donors complete questionnaires designed to promote self-exclusion by those who have engaged in high-risk behaviors.[142] An interview process eliminates additional donors who fail to meet criteria for protecting the blood supply, and potential donors are examined for evidence of fever or illicit drug use. Donors are generally provided a third opportunity for confidential self-exclusion. HIV infected individuals are permanently excluded from donating and all blood donation centers have access to a computerized list of disqualified donors. In March 1985, blood and plasma collection centers in the United States introduced HIV screening, and the risk of transmission was reduced to 1 in 40,000 or less.[143]

An individual could be HIV infected, however, yet still have a negative antibody test result. According to a recent CDC study that analyzed data obtained from regions served by the American Red Cross, transmission of HIV by blood transfusion occurs almost exclusively in the United States when recently infected donors are infectious but have not yet developed detectable levels of HIV antibody, the *window period*.[144] The CDC study estimated that from 1 in 450,000 to 1 in 660,000 blood donations in the United States were infectious for HIV but not detected.[145] A more recent report estimated that the risk of giving blood during an infectious window period was 1 in 493,000.[146]

---

[140] CDC, *Provisional Public Health Service Inter-Agency Recommendations for Screening Donated Blood and Plasma for Antibody to the Virus Causing Acquired Immunodeficiency Syndrome*, 34 MMWR 2 (1985).

[141] For a discussion of this two-phase process, see Elaine M. Sloand et al., *Safety of the Blood Supply*, 274 JAMA 1368 (1995).

[142] Elaine M. Sloand et al., *HIV Testing: State of the Art*, 266 JAMA 2864 (1991).

[143] M.P. Busch et al., *Risk of Human Immunodeficiency Virus (HIV) Transmission by Blood Transfusions Before Implementation of HIV-1 Antibody Screening*, 31 Transfusion 9 (1991).

[144] When the first tests were used to screen blood donations from 1985 through 1990, the average length of the window period was 45 days. *See, e.g.,* L.R. Petersen et al., *Duration of Time from Onset of Human Immunodeficiency Virus Type 1 Infectiousness to Development of Detectable Antibody*, 33 Transfusion 890 (1993). The average window period for the most sensitive current assays for HIV-1 and HIV-2 antibodies is 25 days. M.P. Busch et al., *Time Course of Detection of Viral and Serologic Markers Preceding Human Immunodeficiency Virus Type 1 Seroconversion: Implications for Screening of Blood and Tissue Donors*, 35 Transfusion 91 (1995).

[145] Eve M. Lackritz et al., *Estimated Risk of Transmission of the Human Immunodeficiency Virus by Screened Blood in the United States*, 333 New Eng. J. Med. 1721 (1995).

[146] George B. Schreiber et al., *The Risk of Transfusion-Transmitted Viral Infections*, 334 New Eng. J. Med. 1685 (1996).

Although epidemiologic data indicate that the prevalence of HIV-2 infections in persons in the United States is extremely low, the Food and Drug Administration (FDA) recommended that all donated blood be screened for antibodies to HIV-2 beginning no later than June 1, 1992. In accordance with those recommendations, blood centers began testing all donated whole blood, blood components, and source plasma for antibodies to HIV-2.[147] This can be accomplished by either using a single combination test for HIV-1/HIV-2 or by using two independent tests, one for HIV-1 and one for HIV-2.[148]

Screening donated blood and plasma for HIV-2 infection raises issues concerning appropriate strategies for testing for both viruses, HIV-2 testing in other settings, and notification of HIV-1 and HIV-2 test results. Although the CDC does not recommend *routine* testing for HIV-2 in settings other than blood centers, recommendations for the diagnosis of HIV-1 and HIV-2 infections in persons being tested in settings other than blood centers have been published as well as CDC/FDA guidelines for serologic testing when combination HIV-1/HIV-2 screening tests are used.[149]

§ 1.11 —Mother-to-Infant

HIV is transmitted from mother to infant during pregnancy, labor and delivery, or through breast feeding. Almost all children infected with HIV acquire the

---

[147] FDA, Revised Recommendations for the Prevention of Human Immunodeficiency Virus (HIV) Transmission by Blood and Blood Products (1992).

[148] On April 25, 1990, the FDA licensed an enzyme immunoassay (EIA) test kit for detection of antibodies to HIV-2 in human serum or plasma; on September 25, 1991, it licensed the first HIV-1/HIV-2 EIA; and on February 14, 1992, it licensed the HIVAB HIV-1/HIV-2 (rDNA) EIA. These tests permit simultaneous testing for both HIV-1 and HIV-2 in human serum or plasma. They are used for donor screening without increasing the number of screening tests performed by blood banks and as an aid in the diagnosis of potential infection with HIV-1 and/or HIV-2.

[149] When HIV testing is indicated, however, tests for antibodies to both HIV-1 and HIV-2 should be obtained if epidemiologic risk factors for HIV-2 infection are present, if clinical evidence exists for HIV disease in the absence of a positive test for antibodies to HIV-2, or if HIV-1 Western Blot results exhibit an unusual indeterminate pattern. *See* CDC, *Testing for Antibodies to Human Immunodeficiency Virus Type 2 in the United States,* 41 MMWR 1 (RR-12, 1992). Testing for HIV-2 antibody is recommended for persons with risk factors for HIV-2 infection, for example, West Africans who have engaged in high risk behaviors, sex partners of West Africans, persons who have received blood transfusions in West Africa, and children born of HIV-2 infected mothers. HIV-2 testing is also indicated in persons with an illness that suggests HIV infection (such as an HIV associated opportunistic infection) in whom HIV-1 testing is not positive. Testing of persons infected with HIV-2 shows a similar antibody development to persons infected with HIV-1 and antibody seems to become generally detectable within three months of infection, *see* CDC, *Update: HIV-2 Infection Among Blood and Plasma Donors—United States, June 1992–June 1995,* 44 MMWR 603 (1995).

virus from their mothers before or during birth,[150] a process called *perinatal transmission.* In the United States, approximately 25 percent of pregnant HIV infected women have passed on the virus to their babies, although reported rates vary from 12 to 35 percent.[151] The factors influencing transfer of virus from the mother to the newborn are not completely known, but several possibilities have been described.[152] According to one study, risk of perinatal transmission varies with maternal immunologic, virologic, and placental factors.[153]

Breast feeding plays a potential role in mother-to-child transmission because HIV has been isolated from breast milk. Nine cases that strongly suggest transmission of HIV by breast feeding have been described.[154] The transmission risk attributable to breast feeding and the factors that enhance or inhibit transmission are presently unknown, although one mechanism by which breast milk might inhibit HIV transmission is the presence of specific antibodies directed against HIV in breast milk of seropositive mothers.[155] Results have also shown that duration of breast feeding significantly increased the risk of transmission.[156]

The PHS has recommended that HIV infected women avoid breast feeding because safe alternatives to breast milk are available in the United States.[157]

---

[150] CDC, *Recommendations for Assisting in the Prevention of Perinatal Transmission of Human T-Lymphotropic Virus Type III/Lymphadenopathy-Associated Virus and Acquired Immunodeficiency Syndrome,* 34 MMWR 721 (1985).

[151] *See, e.g.,* Susan F. Davis, *Prevalence and Incidence of Vertically Acquired HIV Infection in the United States,* 274 JAMA 952 (1995); James J. Goedert et al., *Mother-to-Infant Transmission of Human Immunodeficiency Virus Type 1: Association with Prematurity or Low Anti-GP 120,* 2 Lancet 1351 (1989); *see also* European Collaborative Study, *Children Born to Women With HIV-1 Infection: Natural History and Risk of Transmission,* 337 Lancet 253 (1991).

[152] Jay A. Levy, *Features of HIV Transmission and Acute Infection, in* HIV and the Pathogenesis of AIDS 22 (Jay A. Levy ed., 1994).

[153] Sheldon H. Landesman et al., *Obstetrical Factors and the Transmission of Human Immunodeficiency Virus Type 1 from Mother to Child,* 334 New Eng. J. Med. 1617 (1996); Michael E. St. Louis et al., *Risk for Perinatal HIV-1 Transmission According to Maternal Immunologic, Virologic, and Placental Factors,* 269 JAMA 2851 (1993).

[154] For a review of the virological and epidemiological data available on HIV transmission by breast feeding, see Philippe Van de Perre, *Mother-to-Infant Transmission of Human Immunodeficiency Virus by Breast Milk: Presumed Innocent or Presumed Guilty?,* 15 Clinical Infectious Diseases 502 (1992).

[155] C. Duprat, *Human Immunodeficiency Virus Type 1 IgA Antibody in Breast Milk and Serum,* 13 Pediatric Infectious Disease J. 603 (1994).

[156] Italian Reg. for HIV Infection in Children, *Human Immunodeficiency Virus Type 1 Infection and Breast Milk,* 400 Acta Paediatrica Supp. 51 (1994); Maurizio de Martino, *HIV-1 Transmission Through Breast-Milk: Appraisal of Risk According to Duration of Feeding,* 6 AIDS 991 (1992).

[157] CDC, *Recommendations for Assisting in the Prevention of Perinatal Transmission of Human T-Lymphotropic Virus Type III/Lymphadenopathy-Associated Virus and Acquired Immunodeficiency Syndrome,* 34 MMWR 725 (1985).

Nutritional concerns and other health-promoting benefits, however, may outweigh the risk of transmission, especially in developing countries,[158] and the World Health Organization has recommended breast feeding in those areas where safe alternatives do not exist.[159]

Early strategies for reducing perinatally acquired HIV infection in the United States included preventing HIV infection among women and, for HIV infected women, avoiding pregnancy or refraining from breast feeding their infants.[160] In 1994, the preliminary results of a clinical trial indicated the effectiveness of zidovudine (ZDV, formerly known as azidothymidine or AZT) for the prevention of perinatal transmission, although the findings are subject to limitations.[161] The PHS, however, has recommended the use of ZDV to reduce perinatal transmission because the results from these clinical trials demonstrated that ZDV can reduce the risk of perinatal HIV infection by approximately two-thirds.[162] The PHS has also published guidelines for HIV counseling and voluntary testing for pregnant women.[163]

§ 1.12 —Health Care Environment

Only one demonstrated case has been reported of a patient's being infected by a health care worker; this involved transmission from an infected dentist to six patients.[164] CDC investigations of more than 22,000 patients of 63 HIV infected

---

[158] Angus Nicoll et al., *HIV and Infant Feeding Practices: Epidemiological Implications for Sub-Saharan African Countries,* 4 AIDS 661 (1990).

[159] Special Programme on AIDS, WHO, Statement from the Consultation on Breast-Feeding/ Breast Milk and Human Immunodeficiency Virus (HIV) 23 (1987).

[160] CDC, *Recommendations for Assisting in the Prevention of Perinatal Transmission of Human T-Lymphotropic Virus Type III/Lymphadenopathy-Associated Virus and Acquired Immunodeficiency Syndrome,* 34 MMWR 725 (1985).

[161] CDC, *Zidovudine for the Prevention of HIV Transmission from Mother to Infant,* 43 MMWR 285 (1994).

[162] CDC, *Recommendations of the U.S. Public Health Service Task Force on the Use of Zidovudine to Reduce Perinatal Transmission of Human Immunodeficiency Virus,* 43 MMWR 1 (RR-11, 1994).

[163] CDC, *U.S. Public Health Service Recommendations for Human Immunodeficiency Virus Counseling and Voluntary Testing for Pregnant Women,* 44 MMWR 1 (RR-7, 1995).

[164] CDC, *Update: Transmission of HIV Infection During Invasive Dental Procedures—Florida,* 40 MMWR 377 (1991). This case remains the subject of controversy and debate. As recently as 1994, a magazine article, a newspaper article, and a segment of the television newsmagazine *60 Minutes* presented the information that casts doubt on the CDC's conclusion that the dentist had infected his patients. Although unanswered questions about the case remain, the evidence continues to overwhelmingly support the CDC's theory. The criticism of the CDC investigation consists largely of assertions that contrary evidence theoretically might exist. *See* Stephen Barr, *The 1990 Florida Dental Investigation: Is the Case Really Closed,* 124 Annals Internal Med. 250 (1996); David Brown, *The 1990 Florida Dental Investigation: Theory and Fact, id.* at 255.

doctors and dentists showed that no other cases of this type of transmission have been identified.[165] The dental case, however, prompted the CDC in 1991 to revise the guidelines for preventing HIV and hepatitis B transmission during exposure-prone invasive procedures.[166] One published report, however, states that the current CDC recommendations could be considered overly conservative and the recommendations to protect patients undergoing invasive procedures are not warranted.[167] States, however, are required to implement these guidelines or their equivalent as a condition for continued funding under the U.S. Public Health Service Act.

Based on assessments of health care workers exposed to HIV infected blood, the risk for HIV transmission has been estimated to be less than 0.1 percent for a single mucous-membrane exposure[168] and 0.3 percent after a percutaneous exposure (that is, a needlestick or cut with a sharp object) to HIV infected blood.[169] The risk is probably lower for intact skin exposures to HIV infected blood and even lower, if present at all, for skin exposures to body secretions and excretions without visible blood.[170] Recommendations for the prevention of HIV transmission in health care settings were published in 1987[171] and updated in 1988.[172]

Through June 1996, 51 documented cases were reported as a result of occupational transmission, and 102 documented cases were reported as a result of possible occupational transmission.[173] Many health care workers, however, say that the true number of occupational HIV infections is greatly underreported; the CDC acknowledges that seroconversions are underreported because reporting is voluntary and often hindered by litigation and fear of confidentiality breaches.[174]

---

[165] Laugher M. Robert et al., *Investigations of Patients of Health Care Workers Infected With HIV: The Centers for Disease Control and Prevention Database,* 122 Annals Internal Med. 653 (1995).

[166] CDC, *Recommendations for Preventing Transmission of Human Immunodeficiency Virus and Hepatitis B Virus to Patients During Exposure-Prone Invasive Procedures,* 40 MMWR 1 (1991).

[167] Julie Louise Gerberding, *The Infected Health Care Provider,* 334 New Eng. J. Med. 94 (1996).

[168] Giuseppe Ippolito et al., *The Risk of Occupational Human Immunodeficiency Virus Infection in Health Care Workers: Italian Multicenter Study,* 153 Archive Internal Med. 1451 (1993).

[169] David K. Henderson, *HIV-1 in the Health Care Setting, in* Principles and Practice of Infectious Diseases 2637 (G.L. Mandel et al. eds., 4th ed. 1995).

[170] *Id.* at 2633; *see also* David K. Henderson et al., *Risk for Occupational Transmission of Human Immunodeficiency Virus Type 1 (HIV-1) Associated With Clinical Exposures: A Prospective Evaluation,* 113 Annals Internal Med. 740 (1990).

[171] CDC, *Recommendations for Prevention of HIV Transmission in Health-Care Settings,* 36 MMWR 1 (Supp. 2, 1987).

[172] CDC, *Update: Universal Precautions for Prevention of Transmission of Human Immunodeficiency Virus, Hepatitis B Virus, and Other Bloodborne Pathogens in Health-Care Settings,* 37 MMWR 377 (1988).

[173] CDC, *HIV/AIDS Surveillance Report* 15 (mid-year ed., June 1996).

[174] *"Gross Underestimation" of Occupational HIV Infection,* 11 AIDS Alert 5 (1996).

The CDC recently published the first case-control study of health care workers that assessed the effectiveness of prophylactic antiretroviral therapy using zidovudine (ZDV) after exposure to HIV.[175] After controlling for other factors associated with HIV transmission risk, the report indicated that the risk of HIV infection among health care workers who used ZDV was reduced by approximately 79 percent, although the limitations of the study design should be considered when interpreting these results. Failures of postexposure ZDV to prevent HIV infection in health care workers have been documented,[176] and studies involving animals have yielded inconclusive results.[177] In addition, ZDV is not approved by the FDA for use after occupational exposure.

The PHS concluded in 1990 that a recommendation could not be made for or against the use of ZDV after exposure because of limited knowledge regarding its efficacy and toxicity.[178] This statement was updated in June 1996 to include six recommendations for postexposure management.[179] These recommendations are provisional, however, because they are based on the limited data from the CDC case-control study regarding efficacy and toxicity of postexposure prophylaxis and risk for HIV infection after different types of occupational exposure.

§ 1.13 —Other Transmission Factors

Saliva.   Contact with saliva has never been shown to result in transmission of HIV. HIV is present at low levels in saliva; one study estimated that 1 milliliter of saliva contains less than one infectious HIV particle.[180] In another study, the findings raised the possibility that, in most cases, salivary inhibitors render the

---

[175] CDC, *Case-Control Study of HIV Seroconversion in Health-Care Workers After Percutaneous Exposure to HIV-Infected Blood—France, United Kingdom, and United States, January 1988—August 1994*, 44 MMWR 929 (1995).

[176] *HIV Seroconversion After Occupational Exposure Despite Early Prophylactic Zidovudine Therapy*, 341 Lancet 1077 (1993); Jerome I. Tokars et al., *Surveillance of HIV Infection and Zidovudine Use Among Health Care Workers After Occupational Exposure to HIV-Infected Blood*, 118 Annals Internal Med. 913 (1993).

[177] Douglas N. Fish, *Prophylaxis of HIV Infection Following Occupational Exposure*, 27 Annals Pharmacotherapy 1246 (1993).

[178] CDC, *Public Health Service Statement on Management of Occupational Exposure to Human Immunodeficiency Virus, Including Considerations Regarding Zidovudine Postexposure Use*, 39 MMWR 1 (RR-1, 1990) (recommends that health care workers who may be at risk for occupational exposure to HIV infection be informed of the considerations pertaining to the use of ZDV for postexposure prophylaxis, including the risk for HIV transmission after the exposure, factors that may increase or decrease this risk, and the limited knowledge regarding the potential efficacy and toxicity of zidovudine postexposure prophylaxis; if a decision is made to use postexposure prophylaxis, it should be initiated promptly).

[179] CDC, *Update: Provisional Public Health Service Recommendations for Chemoprophylaxis after Occupational Exposure to HIV*, 45 MMWR 468 (1996).

[180] Jay A. Levy & Deborah Greenspan, *HIV in Saliva*, 2 Lancet 1248 (1988).

virus noninfectious.[181] However, HIV infected blood in saliva does pose a potential risk of transmission.[182] Because of the theoretical potential for contact with blood during kissing,[183] CDC recommends against engaging in this activity with an infected person. However, no case reported to CDC can be attributed to transmission through kissing.

Biting. Although biting is not a common way of transmitting HIV,[184] several published reports have suggested that HIV was transmitted by a bite. In a *Lancet* report, two adult sisters had a violent fight during which several of the HIV positive sister's teeth were broken and knocked out when she was punched in the mouth.[185] She then bit her HIV negative sister, who was an injecting drug user, and tore the skin, which resulted in blood-to-blood contact. The sister subsequently tested HIV positive. In another *Lancet* report, a bite was suggested as the mode of HIV transmission between two brothers in Germany, although the source and other possible modes of transmission were not thoroughly investigated.[186] In contrast, four studies of a total of 22 persons who were bitten by HIV infected individuals found that none of the bitten persons became infected.[187]

In 1995, however, an investigation was conducted of an incident that suggested blood-to-blood transmission by a human bite.[188] An HIV positive prostitute with bleeding gums bit a 91-year-old man, inflicting extensive tissue damage that caused bleeding. Other possible routes of HIV transmission (for example, syringe sharing or sexual contact) were thoroughly investigated. The evidence that supported the bite as the route of transmission is that the man was exposed to the blood of an HIV infected person. He subsequently seroconverted, and

---

[181] Barbara E. Moore, *HIV Recovery From Saliva Before and After Dental Treatment: Inhibitors May Have Critical Role in Viral Inactivation,* 124 J. Am. Dental Ass'n 67 (1993).

[182] Marcello Piazza et al., *Blood in Saliva of Patients with Acquired Immunodeficiency Syndrome: Possible Implication in Sexual Transmission of the Disease,* 42 J. Med. Virology 38 (1994).

[183] Marcello Piazza et al., *Passionate Kissing and Microlesions of the Oral Mucosa: Possible Role in AIDS Transmission,* 261 JAMA 244 (1989).

[184] Katherine M. Rickman & Leland S. Rickman, *The Potential for Transmission of Human Immunodeficiency Virus Through Human Bites,* 6 J. Acquired Immune Deficiency Syndrome 402 (1993).

[185] *Transmission of HIV by Human Bite,* 2 Lancet 522 (1987).

[186] Volker Wahn et al., *Horizontal Transmission of HIV Infection Between Two Siblings,* 2 Lancet 694 (1986).

[187] John A. Drummond, *Seronegative 18 Months After Being Bitten by a Patient with AIDS,* 256 JAMA 2342 (1986); Martha F. Rogers et al., *Lack of Transmission of Human Immunodeficiency Virus from Infected Children to Their Household Contacts,* 85 Pediatrics 210 (1990); L.R. Shirley & S.A. Ross, *Risk of Transmission of Human Immunodeficiency Virus by Bite of an Infected Toddler,* 114 J. Pediatrics 425 (1989); Chris M. Tsoukas et al., *Lack of Transmission of HIV Through Human Bites and Scratches,* 1 J. Acquired Immune Deficiency Syndrome 505 (1988).

[188] CDC, *National AIDS Hotline Training Bulletin,* No. 163 (1995).

testing showed that the virus from the woman and the virus from the man were closely related, suggesting person-to-person transmission.

Because transmission was attributed to a bite, this case raised concerns about the possibility of HIV transmission in settings in which biting often occurs, such as day care centers. The nature of the bite in this instance, however, is unlike most bites that occur among children, whose bites rarely involve blood or breaking the skin. Current recommendations, therefore, are not being altered.[189]

Tears.   HIV has been isolated from tears and from contact lenses worn for 14 to 16 hours by seropositive volunteers.[190] Although no cases of transmission have been reported, the CDC has developed guidelines for health care workers to reduce the possibility of HIV transmission during ophthalmologic examinations.[191]

Insects.   From the onset of the HIV epidemic, there has been concern about HIV transmission by blood-sucking insects such as mosquitoes, bedbugs, fleas, biting flies, and lice. However, current laboratory and epidemiologic data continue to provide no support for insect transmission of HIV.[192]

Theoretically, there are two mechanisms through which biting insects might transmit HIV. First, when bloodsucking insects feed on an HIV infected person, the virus might be ingested with blood, reproduce and multiply in the insect, migrate to the insect's salivary glands, and be injected into uninfected persons on whom the insect subsequently fed. This is known as *biological transmission* and is the mode through which diseases such as malaria are transmitted. The second possible mechanism through which bloodsucking insects might transmit HIV is known as *mechanical transmission.* The insect might begin to feed on an HIV infected person and be interrupted for one reason or another. Instead of returning to its original host, the insect might move on to another, uninfected person to complete its meal. The insect might transfer part of the flesh blood remaining on its mouthparts from its previous feeding attempt to the uninfected person and might also regurgitate some of its previous meal of blood.

With respect to biologic transmission, in one study HIV replication was not detected in bedbugs or mosquitoes after inoculation.[193] Other studies have shown

[189] *Infectious Bite Treated as Bloodborne Transmission,* 10 AIDS Alert 155 (1995).

[190] Timo Tervo et al., *Recovery of HTLV-III from Contact Lenses,* 1 Lancet 379 (1986).

[191] CDC, *Recommendations for Preventing Possible Transmission of Human T-Lymphotropic Virus Type III/Lymphadenopathy-Associated Virus from Tears,* 34 MMWR 533 (1985).

[192] Alan R. Lifson, *Transmission of the Human Immunodeficiency Virus, in* AIDS: Etiology, Diagnosis, Treatment, and Prevention 116 (Vincent T. DeVita, Jr., et al. eds., 1992); *see also* Alan R. Lifson, *Do Alternate Modes for Transmission of Human Immunodeficiency Virus Exist?: A Review,* 259 JAMA 1355 (1988).

[193] Patricia A. Webb et al., *Potential for Insect Transmission of HIV: Experimental Exposure of Cimex Hemipterous and Toxorhynchites Amboinensis to Human Immunodeficiency Virus,* 160 J. Infectious Diseases 970 (1989).

that HIV does not replicate in cell lines derived from insects.[194] With respect to mechanical transmission, although HIV was cultured in one study from bedbugs but not mosquitoes up to four hours after engorging on blood containing high concentrations of HIV, bedbugs were unable to transmit HIV from infected to uninfected blood during interrupted feeding experiments.[195] In part this may be a result of the extremely small amount of blood on the mouthparts.[196]

Household Settings.   HIV transmission has been reported in households in which health care has been provided to HIV infected individuals and between children residing in the same household, but transmission of HIV is rare in this setting.[197] The two most recent cases of transmission in households were reported in 1994; they apparently occurred following contact with blood or other body secretions or excretions in individuals who received care from, or provided care to, HIV infected family members residing in the same household. In both instances, exposures occurred after the HIV positive members had developed AIDS; consequently, relatively high HIV titers may have been present in their blood. The CDC has published recommended precautions to reduce exposures to blood and other bloody fluids.[198]

Service Workers.   There is no known risk of HIV transmission to co-workers, clients, or consumers from contact in industries such as food service establishments. Food service workers known to be infected with HIV need not be restricted

---

[194] Lawrence Miike, Office Tech. Assessment, U.S. Congress, Staff Paper No. 1, *Do Insects Transmit AIDS?* (1987); *see also* Arie J. Zuckerman, *HIV Transmission and Insects, in* Cofactors in HIV-1 Infection and AIDS 121 (Ronald Ross Watson ed., 1990).

[195] Peter G. Jupp & Susan F. Lyons, *Experimental Assessment of Bedbugs (Cimex Lectularius and Cimex Hemipterous) and Mosquitoes (Aedes Aegypti Formosus) as Vectors of Human Immunodeficiency Virus,* 1 AIDS 171 (1987).

[196] Lawrence Miike, Office Tech. Assessment, U.S. Congress, Staff Paper No. 1, *Do Insects Transmit AIDS?* (1987).

[197] CDC, *Apparent Transmission of Human T-Lymphotropic Virus Type III/Lymphadenopathy-Associated Virus from a Child to a Mother Providing Health Care,* 35 MMWR 76 (1986); CDC, *HIV Infection in Two Brothers Receiving Intravenous Therapy for Hemophilia,* 41 MMWR 228 (1992); CDC, *HIV Transmission Between Two Adolescent Brothers with Hemophilia,* 42 MMWR 948 (1993); Joseph E. Fitzgibbon et al., *Transmission from One Child to Another of Human Immunodeficiency Virus Type 1 with a Zidovudine-Resistance Mutation,* 329 New Eng. J. Med. 1835 (1993); P. Grint & M. McEvoy, *Two Associated Cases of the Acquired Immunodeficiency Syndrome (AIDS),* 42 Communicable Disease Rep. 4 (1985); R. Ellen Koenig, *Unusual Intrafamilial Transmission of Human Immunodeficiency Virus,* 2 Lancet 627 (1986); Volker Wahn et al., *Horizontal Transmission of HIV Infection Between Two Siblings,* 2 Lancet 694 (1986).

[198] CDC, *Update: Universal Precautions for Prevention of Transmission of Human Immunodeficiency Virus, Hepatitis B Virus, and Other Bloodborne Pathogens in Health-Care Settings,* 27 MMWR 377 (1988).

from work unless they have other infections or illnesses (such as diarrhea or hepatitis A) for which any food service worker, regardless of HIV infection status, should be restricted.

In 1985, CDC issued routine precautions that all personal service workers (for example, hairdressers, barbers, cosmetologists, massage therapists) should follow.[199] Those recommendations state that instruments used to penetrate the skin (for instance, tattooing and acupuncture needles, ear piercing devices) should be used once and disposed of, or thoroughly cleaned and sterilized, after each use, and instruments not intended to penetrate the skin but which may become contaminated with blood (for example, razors) should be used for only one client and disposed of, or thoroughly cleaned and disinfected, after each use. Personal service workers can use the same cleaning procedures that are recommended for health care institutions.

§ 1.14 HIV Detection: Laboratory Methods

The development of sensitive and specific[200] tests for antibody to HIV progressed rapidly after this retrovirus was identified as the cause of AIDS in 1983. These blood serum tests have been used for various purposes, including clinical diagnosis of HIV infection (for symptomatic and asymptomatic patients in counseling and testing programs), seroprevalence surveys, and blood donor screening. All blood tests are designed to detect, either directly or indirectly, the presence of underlying HIV infection.[201] Thus, the practice of referring to these tests as "AIDS tests" is medically incorrect because AIDS is a syndrome characterized by a wide spectrum of opportunistic infections associated with the impairment of cellular immunity.

---

[199] CDC, *Recommendations for Preventing Transmission of Infection with Human T-Lymphotropic Virus Type III/Lymphadenopathy-Associated Virus in the Workplace,* 34 MMWR 693 (1985).

[200] *Sensitivity* refers to the test's ability to correctly identify all specimens with HIV antibody; therefore, if the test is 99 percent sensitive, 99 of 100 specimens with antibody would be identified as having antibody, although one negative specimen would also be identified as being positive. *Specificity* refers to the test's ability to identify all specimens that do not have HIV antibodies; therefore, a test that is 99 percent specific would correctly identify 99 of 100 specimens as not containing antibody but incorrectly identify one as positive. The test incorrectly identified is considered a *false positive.* Test accuracy has been discussed in a number of publications. *See, e.g.,* Ron Brookmeyer & Mitchell H. Gail, *Screening and Accuracy of Tests for HIV, in* AIDS Epidemiology: A Quantitative Approach 169 (Ron Brookmeyer & Mitchell H. Gail eds., 1994); *see also* Niel T. Constantine et al., *Indicators of the Value of Diagnostic Tests, in* Retroviral Testing: Essentials for Quality Control and Laboratory Diagnosis 113 (1992).

[201] Michael Saag, *AIDS Testing Now and in the Future, in* The Medical Management of AIDS 65 (Paul A. Volberding & Mark A. Sande eds., 1995).

The CDC published recommendations for HIV counseling and testing services in March 1985 when serologic tests first became available to detect HIV antibodies.[202] In August 1987, CDC guidelines were published for counseling and antibody testing to prevent HIV infection,[203] and these guidelines remain in effect.[204] Counseling guidelines have also been developed by the American Medical Association[205] and the Canadian Medical Association.[206]

§ 1.15 —Antibody Detection

HIV antibody testing was first licensed by the FDA in 1985. Most of the current testing procedures, called *enzyme immunoassays* (EIAs), rely on detecting HIV-1 antibodies. The most widely used test is the enzyme-linked immunosorbent assay (ELISA) used in conjunction with a confirmatory test, the Western Blot, when the ELISA test result is positive.[207]

ELISAs were chosen because these types of tests had been used successfully to detect a variety of other infectious agents. The ELISA is considered the best available screening procedure because of its standardization, high reliability, and relatively quick turn-around.[208] ELISA kits have reported greater than 99 percent sensitivity and specificity, although the figure varies with the population being tested.[209] False positive screening results may result from biological variations in the manner in which a blood sample responds to a test, human laboratory errors, or health conditions such as hemophilia, autoimmune disorders, and alcohol-related hepatitis.[210]

---

[202] CDC, *Recommendation for Assisting in the Prevention of Perinatal Transmission of Human T-Lymphotropic Virus Type III/Lymphadenopathy-Associated Virus and Acquired Immunodeficiency Syndrome,* 34 MMWR 721 (1985); *see also* CDC, *Additional Recommendations to Reduce Sexual and Drug Abuse-Related Transmission of Human T-Lymphotropic Virus Type III/Lymphadenopathy-Associated Virus,* 35 MMWR 152 (1986).

[203] CDC, *Public Health Service Guidelines for Counseling and Antibody Testing to Prevent HIV Infection and AIDS,* 36 MMWR 509 (1987).

[204] CDC, *Technical Guidance on HIV Counseling,* 42 MMWR 11 (RR-2, 1993).

[205] Division of Health Sciences, Am. Med. Ass'n, HIV Blood Test Counseling: AMA Physician Guidelines (2d ed. 1993). The guidelines are available from the AMA Internet home page at http://www.ama-assn.org.

[206] Canadian Med. Ass'n, *Counselling Guidelines for HIV Testing* (1995). The guidelines are available from the CMA Internet home page at http://www.cma.ca.

[207] Elaine Sloand et al., *HIV Testing: State of the Art,* 266 JAMA 2861 (1991).

[208] J. Sanford Schwartz et al., *Strategies for Screening Human Immunodeficiency Virus Antibody,* 259 JAMA 2574 (1988).

[209] CDC, *Update: Serological Testing for HIV-1 Antibody,* 39 MMWR 380 (1990); F. Michaelski, *The Diagnosis of Human Immunodeficiency Virus Infection,* 62 Yale J. Biology & Med. 93 (1989).

[210] D.J. Bylund, *Review of Testing for Human Immunodeficiency Virus,* 12 Clinics Laboratory Med. 305 (1992).

Although ELISA tests detect HIV antibodies very effectively in HIV positive populations, their use in nondiseased populations has presented a challenge.[211] The occurrence of even a small number of false positives by these tests can have profound implications when testing a population at low risk for infection. This is especially true when testing blood donors, since false positive results waste resources in discarded blood units and require verification of reactive results using more expensive tests. In addition, a false negative result, indicating that an infected individual is not infected, can have serious consequences for the blood recipient. Therefore, attempts to improve tests have been a continuous challenge.

The CDC has published recommended procedures for HIV antibody testing. These include using an ELISA test to detect HIV antibodies and a confirmatory test with a more specific assay (for example, Western Blot). All tests should be performed and conducted according to manufacturers' instructions and applicable state and federal laboratory guidelines. Laboratories performing these tests should be certified as competent by the College of American Pathologists to ensure compliance with good laboratory practices, including quality control procedures and performance testing.[212]

Serum samples that are repeatedly reactive in the EIA for HIV antibody are retested with a supplemental and more specific test, the most common being the Western Blot.[213] Although the overall sensitivity and specificity of the Western Blot for detection of antibodies are high, there has been substantial debate regarding the interpretive criteria.[214] The licensed DuPont Western Blot test

---

[211] Klemens B. Meyer et al., *Screening for HIV: Can We Afford the False-Positive Rate?,* 317 New Eng. J. Med. 238 (1987).

[212] Regulation of all decentralized testing falls under the Clinical Laboratory Improvement Amendments of 1988, 42 U.S.C. § 263a (1994). Two organizations, the Joint Commission on Accreditation of Health Care Organizations and the College of American Pathologists, have received deemed status for their voluntary standards from the Health Care Financing Administration. *Deemed status* means that the organizations' voluntary standards meet or exceed the federal requirements. The decentralized testing sites can exercise several options in determining which organization, and hence which set of standards, will be used to regulate their testing processes. *See* Ronald H. Laessig et al., AACC Workshop 201: Complying with Regulations (CLIA, JCAHO, CAP, COLA) and Passing Inspections (1995) (outlining regulatory requirements, providing insights into the interrelationship of each, and offering a framework for decentralized testing sites to meet the requirements).

[213] CDC, *Provisional Public Health Service Inter-Agency Recommendations for Screening Donated Blood and Plasma for Antibody to the Virus Causing Acquired Immunodeficiency Syndrome,* 34 MMWR 1 (1985); CDC, *Update: Serologic Testing for Antibody to Human Immunodeficiency Virus,* 36 MMWR 833–40 (1988).

[214] CDC, *Interpretation and Use of the Western Blot Assay for Serodiagnosis of Human Immunodeficiency Virus Type 1 Infections,* 38 MMWR 1 (Supp. 7, 1989); CDC, *Interpretive Criteria Used to Report Western Blot Results for HIV-1 Antibody Testing—United States,* 40 MMWR 692 (1991); Roger Y. Dodd & Chyang T. Fang, *The Western Immunoblot Procedure for HIV Antibodies and Its Interpretation,* 114 Archives Pathology & Laboratory Med. 240 (1990).

interpretation scheme maximizes the specificity of the assay and is, therefore, useful in all clinical settings, including blood donation centers.[215] Alternative criteria have been proposed by various groups, including the Association of State and Territorial Public Health Laboratory Directors (ASTPHLD),[216] the Consortium for Retrovirus Serology Standardization (CRSS),[217] and the American Red Cross.[218] The CDC has concurred with the ASTPHLD criteria and recommended their use in public health and clinical practice.[219]

The recommendations state that laboratories should identify test results as positive, indeterminate, or negative. No positive test results should be given to clients/patients until a screening test has been repeatedly reactive (that is, greater than or equal to two tests) on the same specimen and a supplemental, more specific test such as the Western Blot has been used to validate those results.[220] Because of the variability of unlicensed reagents, laboratories using non-FDA-licensed Western Blots should compare, on a routine basis, their tests with the FDA-licensed Western Blot kit using well-characterized serum specimens.

A person whose Western Blot test results continue to be consistently indeterminate for at least six months—in the absence of any known risk factors, clinical symptoms, or other findings—may be considered to be negative for antibodies to HIV-1. These persons should be reassured that they are almost certainly not infected with HIV-1. However, no large-scale studies have been done to provide virologic data to confirm independently the serologic findings from the studies of clients whose Western Blot test results are consistently indeterminate. In contrast, an asymptomatic person who has an indeterminate Western Blot test result and a history of possible exposure to or symptoms compatible with HIV infection requires additional diagnostic follow-up. This should include conducting serial Western Blot testing, assessing the function of the individual's immune system, and eliciting, if appropriate, the cooperation of the person's sexual and syringe-sharing partners to determine whether they are infected. Individuals with a pattern of indeterminate Western Blot test results should not donate blood or plasma for either transfusion or use in manufactured blood products.

---

[215] DuPont Diagnostics, Human Immunodeficiency Virus (HIV): Biotech/DuPont HIV Western Blot Kit for Detection of Antibodies to HIV (1987).

[216] W.J. Hausler, Jr. & Jane P. Getchell, *Report of the Fourth Consensus Conference on HIV Testing Sponsored by the Association of State and Territorial Public Health Laboratory Directors (ASTPHLD),* 10 Infection Control Hosp. Epidemiology 354 (1989).

[217] Consortium for Retrovirus Serology Standardization, *Serological Diagnosis of Human Immunodeficiency Virus Infection by Western Blot Testing,* 260 JAMA 674 (1988).

[218] S.G. Sandler et al., *Diagnostic Tests for HIV Infection, in* AIDS: Etiology, Treatment, and Prevention 1211 (Vincent T. DeVita, Jr., et al. eds., 2d ed. 1988).

[219] CDC, *Interpretation and Use of the Western Blot Assay for Serodiagnosis of Human Immunodeficiency Virus Type 1 Infections,* 38 MMWR 1 (Supp. 7, 1989).

[220] CDC, *Update: Serologic Testing for Antibody to Human Immunodeficiency Virus,* 36 MMWR 833 (1988).

§ 1.16 —Viral Detection

P24 antigen, the core structural protein of HIV, is detectable two to three weeks after HIV infection. During this time, the blood of infected individuals is highly infectious, and tests for p24 antigen are usually positive.[221] On average, p24 antigen is detected an estimated six days before HIV antibody tests become positive.[222] When antibodies to HIV become detectable, however, p24 antigen is often no longer detectable.

In August 1995, the FDA recommended that all blood and plasma donations be screened for p24 antigen effective within three months of licensure of a test. This recommendation was made as an additional safety measure because recent studies indicated that p24 screening reduces the infectious window period, implementation of p24 antigen testing had become possible for mass screening, and such testing would reduce the risk for HIV infection for individuals who receive donated blood or blood products.[223] FDA, however, regarded donor screening for p24 antigen as an interim measure pending the availability of technology that would further reduce the risk for HIV transmission from blood donated during the infectious window period.

The first antigen test kit performed on serum or plasma was approved in March 1996. P24 antigen screening is expected to detect four to six infectious donations that would not be identified by other screening tests for the 12 million annual blood donations in the United States. In the same month, the PHS issued guidelines for testing and counseling blood/plasma donors for HIV antigen.[224] This report provided guidelines for interpreting p24 antigen assay results, counseling and follow-up of blood and plasma donors who have positive or indeterminate antigen test results, and using p24 antigen testing in settings other than blood blanks. Initiation of routine p24 antigen testing in publicly funded HIV counseling and testing sites, physicians' offices, or other non-blood bank settings is not recommended, however.

In addition to p24 antigen testing, three viral detection methods are used to directly measure HIV: branched DNA (bDNA), Nucleic Acid Sequence-Based Amplification (NASBA), and polymerase chain reaction (PCR). These tests are often called *DNA fingerprinting* because they are based on the production of multiple copies of a DNA sequence.[225] In June 1996, the FDA approved the first test to accurately measure quantities of virus in the blood using PCR technology.

---

[221] D.R. Henrard et al., *Detection of Human Immunodeficiency Virus Type 1 p24 Antigen and Plasma RNA: Relevance to Indeterminate Serologic Tests,* 34 Transfusion 376 (1994).

[222] J.L. Galarda et al., *Early Detection of Antibody to Human Immunodeficiency Virus Type 1 by Using an Antigen Conjugate Immunoassay Correlates with the Presence of Immunoglobulin M Antibody,* 30 J. Clinical Epidemiology 2379 (1992).

[223] Center for Biologics Evaluation & Res., FDA, Recommendations for Donor Screening with a Licensed Test for HIV-1 Antigen (1995).

[224] CDC, *U.S. Public Health Service Guidelines for Testing and Counseling Blood and Plasma Donors for Human Immunodeficiency Virus Type 1 Antigen,* 45 MMWR 1 (RR-2, 1996).

[225] Bill Barrick & Susan Vogel, *Application of Laboratory Diagnostics in HIV Nursing,* 31 Nursing Clinics N. Am. 41 (1996).

PCR has proven valuable for detecting infection in seronegative individuals, measuring the amount of virus in the blood, typing HIV infections, early diagnosis of perinatal transmission of HIV, and resolving indeterminate Western blots.[226] The PCR assay, however, is not sufficiently accurate to be used for the diagnosis of HIV infection without confirmation in adults, and it should be limited to situations in which antibody tests are known to be insufficient.[227] Although the PCR is among the best tests for HIV diagnosis in infants, it is not definitive[228] and the clinical utility of the assay as a predictor of perinatal transmission remains undefined.[229] The major problem, as well as the greatest strength, with a PCR assay is its sensitivity. Inadvertent contamination can lead to false positive results even in laboratories with the most experienced staff.[230] This can be avoided, however, by applying strict laboratory routines.[231]

§ 1.17   —Other Tests

Murex Single Use Diagnostic System (SUDS) HIV-1 Test.   Although the ELISA and the Western Blot are the tests most commonly used for antibody tests, other techniques have been developed. In 1992, the FDA licensed a 10-minute diagnostic test kit which can be used to quickly and reliably detect HIV antibodies in human serum or plasma.[232] This test can be used in health care settings where traditional diagnostic test kits are impractical or unavailable.

Saliva Tests.   In December 1994, the FDA approved the first oral fluid HIV antibody test system in the United States for use in individuals 13 years of age or older.[233] The new test system is less sensitive and less specific than tests using blood. Individuals who test positive must have follow-up testing using a blood specimen. This collection device is available by prescription only. The test

---

[226] Gerald Schochetman & John J. Sninsky, *Direct Detection of Human Immunodeficiency Virus Infection Using the Polymerase Chain Reaction, in* AIDS Testing: Methodology and Management Issues 105 (Gerald Schochetman & J. Richard George eds., 1992).

[227] Douglas K. Owens et al., *Polymerase Chain Reaction for the Diagnosis of HIV Infection in Adults: A Meta-Analysis With Recommendations for Clinical Practice and Study Design,* 124 Annals Internal Med. 803 (1996).

[228] Douglas K. Owens et al., *A Meta-Analytic Evaluation of the Polymerase Chain Reaction for the Diagnosis of HIV Infection in Infants,* 275 JAMA 1342 (1996).

[229] Sheldon H. Landesman & David Burns, *Quantifying HIV,* 275 JAMA 640 (1996).

[230] Alan R. Lifson et al., *Detection of Human Immunodeficiency Virus DNA Using the Polymerase Chain Reaction in a Well-Characterized Group of Homosexual and Bisexual Men,* 161 J. Infectious Diseases 436 (1990).

[231] Shirley Kwok & Russell Higuchi, *Avoiding False Positives with PCR,* 339 Nature 237 (1989).

[232] FDA, *Talk Paper* (May 27, 1992). This information is available via the Internet at the FDA World Wide Web page at http://www.fda.gov.

[233] Stuart L. Nightingale, *Oral Fluid Specimen Test System for HIV-1 Approved,* 273 JAMA 613 (1995).

system is marketed under significant restrictions: it must be administered only by trained "collectors;" individuals must be given an information pamphlet that explains the test system's limitations; and it must not be given to individuals for home use or used to screen blood donors. Physicians are required to sign a letter assuming certain responsibilities related to proper use of the system, including training of the specimen collectors, who may be nonmedical personnel. Materials for training the collectors are supplied to the physician by the company. Training and proficiency control materials also are provided to laboratories that want to become qualified to process and test the oral fluid specimens. In June 1996, the FDA granted approval for a Western Blot kit to confirm HIV infections in samples taken orally.

Urine Tests.   Urine specimens have also been proposed as an alternative to blood for HIV antibody testing. Several companies have developed new tests to screen for HIV in urine that would make the procedure easier and simpler (especially for developing countries with scarce medical facilities) because the need for trained medical personnel to draw blood is eliminated. In August 1996, the FDA approved the first test to detect HIV antibodies in urine samples, but positive results must be confirmed by a blood test. The urine test was not approved for screening blood donations because the test is not as accurate as serum tests.

Home Tests.   In May 1996, the FDA approved the first HIV test system that includes collection of blood samples at home.[234] Clinical studies showed that the test identified negative samples 99.95 percent of the time and correctly identified 100 percent of 150 known positive samples. The new testing system is comprised of three integrated components: an over-the-counter home blood collection kit, HIV antibody testing at a certified lab, and a test result center that anonymously provides test results, counseling, and referral. Technological advances in the accuracy of testing, the availability of treatments for people who are infected but do not yet have symptoms, and the public health benefits that would accrue from more people's being aware of their HIV status all contributed to the agency's decision to approve the kit.

§ 1.18   Clinical Progression of HIV Disease

HIV disease is now viewed as a continuous, progressive process, beginning with primary HIV infection, continuing with a chronic phase that is usually asymptomatic, leading to progressively severe symptoms and, ultimately, profound immunodeficiency which in turn results in opportunistic infections,[235] commonly

---

[234] FDA, *FDA Approves First HIV Home Test System* (May 14, 1996) (press release).

[235] Anthony S. Fauci, *Multifactorial Nature of Human Immunodeficiency Virus Disease: Implications for Therapy,* 262 Science 1011 (1993).

designated as AIDS. Previously, persons with HIV were classified as having either AIDS, AIDS-related complex (ARC), or asymptomatic disease, but these terms are now outdated. The term *AIDS* has very little clinical utility; its use is confined to an epidemiological role in tracking the number of cases in a consistent manner. Clinically, AIDS represents only the advanced stage of HIV disease. Some researchers prefer to speak of HIV disease and its early, middle, and advanced stages to emphasize the fact that asymptomatic, recently infected individuals have the same chronic, progressive, ultimately fatal disease as persons with severe immunosuppression who meet the criteria for CDC-defined AIDS.[236]

§ 1.19 —CD4 Cell Counts and Viral Markers

Stages of HIV disease progression, as well as initiation of therapy,[237] are monitored by using clinical, also known as surrogate, markers.[238] The CD4 cell count is most frequently used because these cells are the major cellular receptors for HIV.[239] HIV infection causes the depletion of CD4 cells, and this depletion is a measure of immunodeficiency which results in increased clinical complications. As the number of CD4s decreases, the immune system can no longer protect the body from bacteria, viruses, and other organisms that can cause infections. In clinical practice, measurements of immune function, notably levels of CD4 cells, are used to guide the clinical and therapeutic treatment of HIV infected individuals,[240] because they are useful for predicting the onset of

---

[236] P.T. Cohen & Paul A. Volberding, *Clinical Spectrum of HIV Disease, in* The AIDS Knowledge Base 4.1-4 (P.T. Cohen et al. eds., 2d ed. 1994).

[237] For an overview of antiretroviral therapy, see Victoria A. Johnson, *New Developments in Antiretroviral Drug Therapy for HIV-1 Infections, in* AIDS Clinical Review 1995/1996 at 305 (Paul Volberding & Mark A. Jacobson eds., 1996).

[238] For an overview of laboratory and clinical markers, see Nancy A. Hessol & Susan P. Buchbinder, *Predictors of HIV Disease Progression in the Era of Prophylactic Therapies, in* AIDS Clinical Review 1992 at 25 (Paul Volberding & Mark A. Jacobson eds., 1992).

[239] A.G. Dalgleish et al., *The CD4 (T4) Antigen is an Essential Component of the Receptor for the AIDS Retrovirus,* 312 Nature 763 (1984); D. Klatzmann et al., *T-Lymphocyte T4 Molecule Behaves as Receptor for Human Retrovirus LAV,* 312 Nature 767 (1984).

[240] Several authoritative texts have been published that provide detailed information about the management of HIV disease. *See, e.g.,* The AIDS Knowledge Base: A Textbook on HIV Disease from the University of California, San Francisco, and the San Francisco General Hospital (P.T. Cohen et al. eds., 2d ed. 1994); HIV Infection: A Primary Care Manual (Howard Libman & Robert A. Witzburg eds., 3d ed. 1996); The Johns Hopkins Hospital Guide to Medical Care of Patients With HIV Infection (John G. Bartlett ed., 5th ed. 1995); The Medical Management of AIDS (Merle A. Sande & Paul A. Volberding eds., 4th ed. 1995); Textbook of AIDS Medicine (Samuel Broder et al. eds., 1994); *see also* Jonathan E. Kaplan et al., *USPHS/IDSA Guidelines for the Prevention of Opportunistic Infections in Persons Infected with Human Immunodeficiency Virus,* 21 Clinical Infectious Diseases 1 (Supp. 1, 1995). But standards change rapidly and updates are available, among other Internet sources, at http://www.ama-assn.org.

diseases generally termed opportunistic because they take advantage of the opportunity provided by the hosts' immunodeficient, weakened state as CD4 cells decline.[241] In HIV infected adults and adolescents, serious opportunistic infections generally do not develop until the CD4 count falls below 200, but an individual is diagnosed with AIDS when the count decreases to 200 whether or not the individual has developed an AIDS-defining opportunistic infection.

CD4 counts can be variable, and some caution should be exercised in the interpretation of results.[242] The white blood cell count, for example, can vary substantially from day to day and may account for shifts of as much as 50 to 150 in normal adults, although the degree of this change is less in individuals with lower CD4 counts. Also, substantial variability exists from laboratory to laboratory; those that do not perform cell count procedures frequently or do not have quality assurance programs may produce inaccurate test results.[243] Compounding this problem, an extended delay of more than 48 hours between the time of sampling and actual specimen processing will result in inaccurate values. Therefore, if a laboratory does not perform the test on a daily basis, or if, for example, blood is drawn on Friday and processed on Monday, the test results may be inaccurate. Another common source of inaccuracy is refrigeration of the blood sample.

In view of the variability in CD4 cell count values, some clinicians follow the absolute CD4 count or a combination of absolute count and CD4 percentage values.[244] Although the debate continues, the authors agree with those who advocate the use of CD4 percentage as a more stable marker than the use of absolute CD4 count.

More recently, research has shown the usefulness of viral load measurements in determining the prognosis of infected individuals. One study showed that a single measurement of plasma viral load can predict the subsequent risk of AIDS or death independent of CD4 cell counts.[245] The results of another study showed that changes in plasma viral load explain the effect of treatment on clinical

---

[241] *See, e.g.,* Henry Masur et al., *CD4 Counts as Predictors of Opportunistic Pneumonias in Human Immunodeficiency Virus (HIV) Infection,* 111 Annals Internal Med. 223 (1989).

[242] Barbara J. Turner et al., *CD4+ T-Lymphocyte Measures in the Treatment of Individuals Infected With Human Immunodeficiency Virus Type 1,* 154 Archives Internal Med. 1562 (1994).

[243] CDC published guidelines in 1992 for laboratories performing assays to enumerate CD4+ T-cell levels. *See* CDC, *Guidelines for the Performance of CD4+ T-Cell Determinations in Persons with Human Immunodeficiency Virus Infection,* 41 MMWR 1 (RR-8, 1992). These guidelines addressed issues about hematology measures as well as flow cytometric measures, which are combined for enumerating CD4+ T-cells. The guidelines were revised in 1994 to reflect more current technology and to guide laboratories in proper quality assurance and quality control. *See* CDC, *1994 Revised Guidelines for the Performance of CD4+ T-Cell Determinations in Persons with Human Immunodeficiency Virus (HIV) Infection,* 43 MMWR 1 (RR-3, 1994).

[244] *See, e.g.,* J. Burcham et al., *CD4+ Is the Best Predictor of Development of AIDS in a Cohort of HIV-Infected Homosexual Men,* 5 AIDS 365 (1991).

[245] John W. Mellors et al., *Prognosis in HIV-1 Infection Predicted by the Quantity of Virus in Plasma,* 272 Science 1167 (1996).

outcome the most reliably whereas changes in the CD4 count provide additional information.[246] These and other findings indicate that viral load determinations are an important prognostic marker of disease progression and provide a valuable tool for the management of individual patients.[247] Despite increasing evidence demonstrating the value of viral load determinations, many practitioners are uncertain about the optimal use of these tests; therefore, recommendations by the International AIDS Society-USA for the use of viral load markers in clinical practice were published in June 1996.[248] The Society has also published recommendations for new approaches to antiretroviral therapy which reflect agreement on the importance of plasma measurements for predicting risk of clinical progression, as well as the recent demonstration from clinical trials of combination therapies that reductions in levels are associated with increased survival and decreased progression to AIDS.[249] Although viral load levels provide unique information regarding the stage of HIV disease, the role of using viral load data in clinical management of patients with HIV infection remains an evolving science. The rate of progression through stages of HIV disease, the clinical response of patients to treatment for HIV infection, and decisions regarding the prevention of opportunistic infections and for the classification of the stages of HIV disease remain dependent in large measure on the CD4 lymphocyte count.

§ 1.20   —Time Periods for HIV Disease Progression

The median time period between infection with HIV and the onset of clinically apparent disease is approximately 10 years in western countries, according to prospective studies of gay men in which dates of seroconversion are known.[250]

---

[246] Els Hogervorst et al., *Predictor for Non- and Slow Progression in Human Immunodeficiency Virus (HIV) Type 1 Infection,* 171 J. Infectious Diseases 811 (1995); John W. Mellors et al., *Quantitation of HIV-1 RNA in Plasma Predicts Outcome After Seroconversion,* 122 Annals Internal Med. 573 (1995).

[247] William A. O'Brien et al., *Changes in Plasma HIV-1 RNA and CD4+ Lymphocyte Counts and the Risk of Progression to AIDS,* 334 New Eng. J. Med. 426 (1996).

[248] David D. Ho, *Viral Counts Count in HIV Infection,* 272 Science 1124 (1996).

[249] Charles C.J. Carpenter et al., *Antiretroviral Therapy for HIV Infection in 1996: Recommendations of an International Panel,* 276 JAMA 146 (1996). Information about the nine FDA-approved drugs for antiretroviral therapy (ZDV, ddI (didanosine), ddC (deoxycytidine), d4T (stavudine), 3TC (lamivudine), nevirapine (Viramune), saquinavir (Invirase), retonavir (Novir), and indinavir (Crixivan)) and combination therapy is included in abstracts from the XIth International Conference on AIDS, held July 7–12, 1996, in Vancouver, Canada. These are located on the World Wide Web at http://sis.nlm.nih.gov/aidsabs.htm.

[250] Nancy A. Hessol et al., *Progression of Human Immunodeficiency Virus Type 1 (HIV-1) Infection Among Homosexual Men in Hepatitis B Vaccine Trial Cohorts in Amsterdam, New York City and San Francisco, 1978–1991,* 139 Am. J. Epidemiology 1077 (1994); George F. Lemp et al., *Projections of AIDS Morbidity and Mortality in San Francisco,* 263 JAMA 1497 (1990).

Similar estimates of asymptomatic periods have been made for HIV infected blood transfusion recipients, injecting drug users, and adult hemophiliacs.[251] One study, for example, analyzed the progression of HIV infection from seroconversion to AIDS and death in 403 homosexual/bisexual men with documented dates of seroconversion.[252] After merging data from four cohort studies on three continents, the researchers reported a median time from HIV seroconversion to AIDS of 8.3 years and from seroconversion to death of 8.9 years. Another report analyzed 362 documented seroconverters from three hepatitis B vaccine trial cohorts on two continents.[253] The authors reported a median time from seroconversion to AIDS of 10.2 years and from seroconversion to death of 12.3 years.

HIV disease, however, is not uniformly expressed in all individuals. A small proportion of HIV infected individuals progress rapidly and die within months following initial infection, whereas approximately 5 percent of HIV infected individuals exhibit no signs of disease progression after 12 years.[254] In some cases no clinical evidence of HIV disease is apparent after more than 10 years[255] or even 15 years.[256] Some researchers have estimated that between 32 and 40 percent of gay/bisexual men will be free from clinical AIDS 12 years from seroconversion, and approximately 13 percent may remain so for more than 20 years.[257]

A number of variables, termed *clinical illness promotion factors* or *cofactors,* may influence the onset of clinical disease.[258] These include host immune factors such as age or genetic differences among individuals, the level of virulence of the individual strain of virus, as well as influences such as co-infection with

[251] P. Alcabes et al., *Incubation Period of Human Immunodeficiency Virus,* 15 Epidemiology Rev. 303 (1993).

[252] P.J. Veugelers et al., *Determinants of HIV Disease Progression Among Homosexual Men Registered in the Tricontinental Seroconverter Study,* 140 Am. J. Epidemiology 747 (1994).

[253] N.A. Hessol et al., *Determinants of Human Immunodeficiency Virus Type 1 (HIV-1) Infection Among Homosexual Men in Hepatitis B Vaccine Trial Cohorts in Amsterdam, New York City, and San Francisco, 1978–1991,* 139 Am. J. Epidemiology 1077 (1994).

[254] Yunzhen Cao et al., *Virologic and Immunologic Characterization of Long-Term Survivors of Human Immunodeficiency Virus Type 1 Infection,* 332 New Eng. J. Med. 201 (1995); Giuseppe Pantaleo et al., *Studies in Subjects With Long-Term Nonprogressive Human Immunodeficiency Virus Infection,* 332 New Eng. J. Med. 209 (1995).

[255] Haynes W. Sheppart & William Lang, *Factors Influencing Long-Term Nonprogression of HIV Disease,* 4 AIDS Reader 199 (1994).

[256] Susan P. Buchbinder et al., *Long-Term HIV-1 Infection Without Immunologic Progression,* 8 AIDS 1123 (1994).

[257] Alvaro Munoz et al., *Long-Term Survivors with HIV-1 Infection: Incubation Period and Longitudinal Patterns of CD4+ Lymphocytes,* 8 J. Acquired Immune Deficiency Syndrome 499 (1995).

[258] A.S. Evans, *The Clinical Illness Promotion Factor: A Third Ingredient,* 55 Yale J. Biological Med. 193 (1982).

other microbes.[259] According to a recent study,[260] however, neither disease progression nor survival was related to sex, race, injecting drug use, or socio-economic status. Rather, HIV disease progression appears to be best predicted by CD4 cell count, receipt of antiretroviral therapy, and age. The study showed that HIV infected persons were twice as likely to progress to AIDS or die from their infection if they had a low CD4 cell count (201 to 350 cells) and were symptomatic at study enrollment. They had nearly twice the risk (1.7 twice the normal) if they received antiretroviral therapy prior to study enrollment. Older age was associated linearly with a greater risk of death (relative risk per year of age, 1.02 percentage points). These results provide strong evidence that the more rapid disease progression and shorter survival observed among women and blacks, for example, are likely the result of inadequate medical care rather than biologic differences among groups in the natural history of HIV infections. In one study, researchers found that blacks are much less likely than whites to receive therapy for HIV-related illnesses.[261]

Estimates of survival after an AIDS diagnosis have increased six to twelve months over the past decade.[262] One study found that an overall increase in survival was a result of an increase in survival among those with PCP, but not among those with other diagnoses.[263] Other studies have shown that therapy with ZDV improves survival,[264] although the effect of ZDV on improving survival is

---

[259] Sarah C. Darby et al., *Importance of Age at Infection with HIV-1 for Survival and Development of AIDS in UK Haemophilia Population,* 347 Lancet 1573 (1996); Anthony S. Fauci, *Multifactorial Nature of Human Immunodeficiency Virus Disease: Implications for Therapy,* 262 Science 1011 (1993); R.A. Kaslow et al., *Influence of Combinations of Human Major Histocompatibility Complex Genes on the Course of HIV-1 Infection,* 2 Nature Med. 405 (1996); Giuseppe Pantaleo et al., *The Immunopathogenesis of Human Immunodeficiency Virus Infection,* 328 New Eng. J. Med. 327 (1993).

[260] Richard E. Chaisson et al., *Race, Sex, Drug Use, and Progression of Human Immunodeficiency Virus Disease,* 333 New Eng. J. Med. 751 (1995).

[261] Richard D. Moore, *Racial Differences in the Use of Drug Therapy for HIV Disease in an Urban Community,* 330 New Eng. J. Med. 763 (1994); *see also* Stephen Crystal, *The Diffusion of Innovation in AIDS Treatment: Zidovudine Use in Two New Jersey Cohorts,* 30 Health Servs. Res. 593 (1995).

[262] L.P. Jacobson et al., *Changes in Survival After Acquired Immunodeficiency Syndrome (AIDS): 1984–1991,* 138 Am. J. Epidemiology 952 (1993); George F. Lemp et al., *Survival Trends for Patients with AIDS,* 263 JAMA 402 (1990); Dennis Osmond et al., *Changes in AIDS Survival Time in Two San Francisco Cohorts of Homosexual Men, 1983–1993,* 271 JAMA 1083 (1994).

[263] Richard Rothenberg et al., *Survival with the Acquired Immunodeficiency Syndrome: Experience with 5833 Cases in New York City,* 317 New Eng. J. Med. 1297 (1987).

[264] *See, e.g.,* Elisabeth Buira et al., *Influence of Treatment with Zidovudine (ZDV) on the Long-Term Survival of AIDS Patients,* 5 J. Acquired Immune Deficiency Syndrome 737 (1992); Neil M.H. Graham et al., *The Effects on Survival of Early Treatment of Human Immunodeficiency Virus Infection,* 326 New Eng. J. Med. 1037 (1992); Alfred J. Saah et al.,

transient.[265] Improvements in diagnosis of AIDS-defining conditions and modifications in the CDC case definition of AIDS leading to earlier AIDS diagnoses may also partially explain this increase in survival.[266] Although survival has improved and new treatment strategies hold some promise, the impact on survival is, as yet, uncertain.[267]

Other reports in the literature provide additional insights into the variability in HIV disease progression. Researchers from the National Cancer Institute, including Dr. Robert Gallo, the co-discoverer of HIV, isolated three potential suppressor substances secreted by white blood cells that inhibit HIV.[268] Other researchers have stated that nonprogressors show an immune response to HIV that is quantitatively and qualitatively better than the immune response in rapid progressors.[269] Yet others, however, argue that the powerful immune response enabling many patients to remain healthy for years is finally undermined by continuous mutation of HIV that exceeds the immune system's ability to regulate the virus.[270] This hypothesis was contradicted, however, in a recently published study in which the researchers reported that greater viral diversity is not related to the rate of disease progression.[271]

§ 1.21   —Stages of HIV Disease

After infection with HIV, seroconversion can occur within days, but generally antibodies to HIV appear in one to four weeks. In some studies, however,

---

Factors Influencing Survival After AIDS: Report from the Multicenter AIDS Cohort Study (MACS), 7 J. Acquired Immune Deficiency Syndrome 287 (1994).

[265] Concorde Coordinating Comm., *Concorde: MRC/ANRS Randomised Double-Blind Controlled Trial of Immediate and Deferred Zidovudine in Symptom-Free HIV Infection,* 343 Lancet 871 (1994); John D. Hamilton et al., *A Controlled Trial of Early Versus Late Treatment with Zidovudine in Symptomatic Human Immunodeficiency Virus Infection: Results of the Veterans Affairs Cooperative Study,* 326 New Eng. J. Med. 437 (1992); Jens D. Lundgren et al., *Comparison of Long-Term Prognosis of Patients with AIDS Treated and Not Treated with Zidovudine,* 271 JAMA 1088 (1994); Paul A. Volberding et al., *The Duration of Zidovudine Benefit in Persons with Asymptomatic HIV Infection: Prolonged Evaluation of Protocol 019 of the AIDS Clinical Trials Group,* 272 JAMA 437 (1994).

[266] Cheryl Enger et al., *Survival from Early, Intermediate, and Late Stages of HIV Infection,* 275 JAMA 1329 (1996).

[267] *Id.* at 1333.

[268] Michael Balter, *Elusive HIV-Suppressor Factors Found,* 270 Science 1560 (1995).

[269] Giuseppe Pantaleo et al., *Toward an Understanding of the Correlates of Protective Immunity to HIV Infection,* 271 Science 326 (1996).

[270] Martin A. Nowak & Andrew J. McMichael, *How HIV Defeats the Immune System,* 273 Sci. Am. 58 (1995).

[271] Steven M. Wolinsky et al., *Adaptive Evolution of Human Immunodeficiency Virus-Type 1 During the Natural Course of Infection,* 272 Science 537 (1996).

antibodies were first detected as early as six days after infection in some subjects.[272]

Early Stage (Acute or Primary Infection).   HIV infected individuals initially enter the acute or primary infection phase, which usually lasts a few weeks and is characterized by very high viral levels[273] and an abrupt decline in CD4 cell counts.[274] Two to four weeks after transmission, up to 70 percent of HIV infected individuals suffer flu-like symptoms related to the acute infection, which usually lasts one to three weeks. In a review of 139 cases, researchers found that the most common physical signs and symptoms were fever (97 percent), swollen lymph glands (77 percent), sore throat (73 percent), rash (70 percent), and muscle aches and joint pains (58 percent).[275] During this acute phase, HIV is also present in the cerebrospinal fluid[276] and semen,[277] the latter indicating the potential for

---

[272] David A. Cooper et al., *Acute AIDS Retrovirus Infection: Definition of a Clinical Illness Associated with Seroconversion*, 1 Lancet 537 (1985); Hans Gaines et al., *Detection of Immunoglobulin M Antibody in Primary Human Immunodeficiency Virus Infection*, 2 AIDS 11 (1988).

[273] High viral levels, occurring in very early and very late stages of infection, are directly related to transmissibility. Susan A. Fiscus, *Transient High Titers of HIV-1 in Plasma and Progression of Disease*, 9 J. Acquired Immune Deficiency Syndrome 51 (1995). One study showed that levels of infectious virus are increased in individuals with AIDS, and infection from such individuals with advanced disease may therefore contain a larger viral load. David D. Ho et al., *Quantification of Human Immunodeficiency Virus Type 1 in the Blood of Infected Persons*, 313 New Eng. J. Med. 1621 (1989). There is also limited evidence that persons who acquire HIV infection from an individual with late-stage disease may have a higher incidence of symptomatic primary infection and an accelerated development of severe disease than those who acquire infection from an asymptomatic individual. *See, e.g.*, I.P. Keet et al., *Predictors of Rapid Progression to AIDS in HIV-1 Seroconverters*, 7 AIDS 51 (1993); *see also* G.J. Griensven et al., *Risk Factors for Progression of Human Immunodeficiency Virus (HIV) Infection Among Seroconverted and Seropositive Homosexual Men*, 132 Am. J. Epidemiology 203 (1990). Other researchers have hypothesized that the infectivity in the initial infection might be as much as 100- to 1,000-fold higher than in the following long asymptomatic period. *See* John A. Jacquez, *Role of the Primary Infection in Epidemics of HIV Infection in Gay Cohorts*, 7 J. Acquired Immune Deficiency Syndrome 1169 (1994). According to this view, the rate of HIV transmission in a given population is higher when individuals are newly infected and thus in a more highly infectious stage of the illness, but as these individuals move into a less infectious, asymptomatic stage, the rate of transmission rapidly declines.

[274] Eric S. Daar et al., *Transient High Levels of Viremia in Patients with Primary Human Immunodeficiency Virus Type 1 Infection*, 324 New Eng. J. Med. 961 (1991).

[275] S.J. Clark et al., *High Titers of Cytopathic Virus in Plasma of Patients with Symptomatic Primary HIV-1 Infection*, 324 New Eng. J. Med. 954 (1991).

[276] David D. Ho et al., *Isolation of HTLV-III from Cerebrospinal Fluid and Neural Tissues of Patients with Neurologic Syndromes Related to the Acquired Immunodeficiency Syndrome*, 313 New Eng. J. Med. 1493 (1985).

[277] B. Tindall et al., *Identification of HIV-1 in Seminal Fluid Following Primary HIV-1 Infection*, 6 AIDS 949 (1991).

HIV transmission through sexual contact. Three to four months after the primary virus infection, CD4 cells usually rise to nearly normal levels and then generally decrease steadily.[278]

Middle Stage (Asymptomatic Infection).   Individuals usually have few symptoms during this period, which may last from many months to years. The development of severe HIV-related disease within the first two years after infection is rare, although some cases have been reported.[279] In general, HIV infected individuals with CD4 cell counts greater than 500 are asymptomatic and have nearly normal immune defenses. Patients with counts of 200 to 500 are often asymptomatic but may have occasional complications that usually are due to relatively virulent pathogens. There is usually a gradual decline in the CD4 cell count averaging 30 to 60 per year according to sequential assays in large cohorts of patients followed for prolonged periods.[280]

A characteristic of HIV disease is the typically long delay in the onset of symptomatic illness after initial infection, the so-called *latent period.* Although infected individuals usually exhibit a period of clinical latency with few symptoms of disease, the virus is never truly latent. The term *latent* was initially useful not only because it described a time period of limited clinical signs, but also because in early stages of HIV disease the quantity of HIV in peripheral blood is relatively small, misleadingly suggesting a period of minimal HIV replication.[281] In 1993, however, researchers reported that virus is disseminated to the lymphoid tissue at very early stages and that viral replication in these tissues is continuous throughout the asymptomatic phase of HIV infection.[282] This replication results in the rapid establishment of a high total body viral burden and subsequent extensive infection of CD4 cells as well as macrophages in the lymph and spleen and continues over the course of infection.[283] As a result of these events, immunosuppression develops, marked by a decline in CD4 cell count and eventual clinical manifestations. Thus the lack of symptoms, or clinical latency, in middle stage HIV disease does not indicate true latency of the HIV disease process.

---

[278] W. Lang et al., *Patterns of T Lymphocyte Changes with Human Immunodeficiency Virus Infection: From Seroconversion to the Development of AIDS,* 2 J. Acquired Immune Deficiency Syndrome 63 (1989).

[279] B. Isaksson et al., *AIDS Two Months After Primary Human Immunodeficiency Virus Infection,* 158 J. Infectious Diseases 866 (1988).

[280] Daniel S. Stein, *CD4+ Lymphocyte Cell Enumeration for Prediction of Clinical Course of Human Immunodeficiency Virus Disease: A Review,* 165 J. Infectious Diseases 352 (1992).

[281] P.T. Cohen & Paul A. Volberding, *Clinical Spectrum of HIV Disease, in* The AIDS Knowledge Base 4.1-3 (P.T. Cohen et al. eds., 2d ed. 1994).

[282] Janet Embretson et al., *Massive Covert Infection of Helper T Lymphocytes and Macrophages by HIV During the Incubation Period of AIDS,* 362 Nature 359 (1993); Giuseppe Panteleo et al., *HIV Infection is Active and Progressive in Lymphoid Tissue During the Clinically Latent Stage of Disease,* 362 Nature 355 (1993).

[283] A.T. Haase, *New Molecular Technology in HIV Research,* Xth Int'l Conf. on AIDS (Yokohama, Japan, Abstract No. PS16, 1994, AIDSLINE S.I. No. ICA10/94370803).

Advanced Stage (Symptomatic HIV Infection). Typically, individuals with advanced disease have less than 200 CD4 cell counts, and the levels of HIV in the blood and lymph nodes tend to increase sometimes to levels as high as those in primary infection. In some cases, the number of CD4 cells can drop precipitously over just a few months, most likely reflecting a return to high-level virus production.[284] The risk of developing AIDS-defining conditions, particularly OIs, rises substantially when CD4 counts drop below 200.[285] In fact, prophylactic therapy to prevent pneumocystis carinii pneumonia, the most common opportunistic infection, is recommended when CD4 counts fall to this level.[286] Individuals with CD4 cell counts of less than 50 have limited life expectancy (median survival 12 to 18 months) and most who die with AIDS-related complications are in this CD4 strata.[287]

In conclusion, HIV disease is a chronic progressive process that begins with HIV infection and replication and leads to the destruction of the immune system. The spectrum of HIV disease is marked by high viral replication in early and late stages of the process. Although the time period from HIV infection to clinical AIDS is variable, the median time appears to be 10 years for adults. The appearance of clinical symptoms, however, is predicted by the extent of immune deficiency. Severe immunosuppression results in advanced HIV disease, referred to as AIDS as defined by the CDC. HIV disease progression, as measured by the CD4 cell count, is emphasized in this section because staging provides prognostic information useful for treatment decisions and the clinical management of the disease. An understanding of the stages of HIV disease also provides useful information for individuals who must meet eligibility requirements for needed social services.

---

[284] Jay A. Levy, *The Mysteries of HIV: Challenges for Therapy and Prevention*, 333 Nature 519 (1988); P.T. Schellekens et al., *Biphasic Rate of CD4+ Cell Count Decline During Progression to AIDS Correlates with HIV-1 Phenotype*, 6 AIDS 665 (1992).

[285] K.B. MacDonell et al., *Predicting Progression to AIDS: Combined Usefulness of CD4 Lymphocyte Counts and p24 Antigenemia*, 89 Am. J. Med. 706 (1990).

[286] CDC, *Recommendations for Prophylaxis Against Pneumocystis Carinii Pneumonia for Adults and Adolescents Infected with Human Immunodeficiency Virus*, 41 MMWR 1 (RR-4, 1992).

[287] Philippa J. Easterbrook et al., *Progress CD4 Cell Depletion and Death in Zidovudine-Treated Patients*, 6 J. Acquired Immune Deficiency Syndrome 927 (1993); Andrew N. Philips et al., *Immunodeficiency and the Risk of Death in HIV Infection*, 268 JAMA 2662 (1992).

CHAPTER 2

HIV AND PUBLIC HEALTH LAW

David W. Webber

§ 2.1   Introduction

In context of the HIV epidemic, public health law can be generally understood as the set of legal rules concerned with infection control. In its most elementary formulation, this body of law sets limits on governmental authority to separate or distance in some manner the infected from the uninfected. The idea of separation in this context can take a variety of forms and be achieved by a variety of policies, some more effective than others. For example, barrier protections between patient and health care professional can prevent HIV transmission, AIDS education can enable individuals to avoid infection by limiting sexual activities or using safer sex techniques, and, perhaps the most drastic and rare example, some individuals who are known to persist in exposing others to HIV may have their liberty restricted by civil detention.

This chapter addresses some of the most persistent and ongoing issues involving public health law and HIV.[1] Two frequently conflicting strategies are considered. One involves the cooperation of individuals at risk for HIV infection and offers voluntary testing, assurances of confidentiality, and protection from discrimination. The other involves imposing coercive measures, such as mandatory testing and contact tracing with its risk of disclosure and lack of confidentiality, which in turn risks further loss of confidentiality and discrimination.[2] The first approach seeks to encourage cooperation and voluntary actions by assuring certain benefits, such as the protection of privacy. The other strategy, however, attempts to change behavior by coercion, typically by imposing or threatening to impose some penalty, such as disclosure of HIV status, which, in turn, results in discrimination. Obviously, the strategy of separating the infected from the uninfected by coercive measures has a significant cultural history and is profoundly rooted in the beliefs and fears that have emerged in response to the HIV epidemic, despite that fact that this response is counterproductive.[3]

These conflicting strategies are brought into sharp relief in *New York State Society of Surgeons v. Axelrod*.[4] The case resulted from a lawsuit brought by four physicians' organizations, which contested the New York state health commissioner's failure to place HIV on the official list of communicable or sexually transmitted diseases that are dangerous to the public health. Although there was no dispute that HIV was sexually transmitted and posed a public health danger, placing it on the list had significant public health implications: listed diseases are subject to state statutory provisions requiring isolation and quarantine, case reporting, mandatory testing, and contact tracing.[5] The physicians' challenge, it

---

[1] For further coverage of public health issues in the context of the HIV epidemic, see Judith Areen et al., Law, Science and Medicine 484–686 (2d ed. 1996); Arthur S. Leonard et al., *Traditional Public Health Law Approaches, in* AIDS Law and Policy 69–144 (1995); Larry Gostin, *Traditional Public Health Strategies, in* AIDS Law Today: A New Guide for the Public 59–81 (Scott Burris et al. eds., 1993).

[2] For a fuller discussion of these issues, see Ronald Bayer, *AIDS, Public Health, and Civil Liberties: Consensus and Conflict in Policy, in* AIDS & Ethics 26–49 (Frederic G. Reamer ed., 1991).

[3] *See generally* William A. Rushing, The AIDS Epidemic: Social Dimensions of an Infectious Disease (1995); Joni N. Gray et al., *AIDS, Fear, and Science, in* Ethical and Legal Issues in AIDS Research 163–72 (1995); Allan M. Brandt, *AIDS in Historical Perspective: Four Lessons from the History of Sexually Transmitted Diseases,* 78 Am. J. Pub. Health 367 (1988), *reprinted in* The AIDS Reader: Social, Political, and Ethical Issues 313 (Nancy F. McKenzie ed., 1991).

[4] 555 N.Y.S.2d 911 (App. Div. 1990).

[5] *See* N.Y. Pub. Health Law §§ 2300–2301 (1987) (providing for compulsory testing and isolation of individuals for STDs by public health officer upon "reasonable ground" to believe individual is infected).

should be noted, was far from altruistic; they were motivated as much by fear of infection from patients with HIV as they were by a desire to advance broader public health goals.[6] Although the court did not directly address the physicians' fears, the CDC's recommended use of universal precautions is one means of addressing that concern without imposing coercive measures against individuals with HIV, as discussed in **Chapter 3.** The Appellate Division of the New York Supreme Court, in a 3-2 decision, rejected the physicians' challenge. The majority concluded that the health commissioner's duty to place diseases on the list was discretionary, and his exercise of discretion in not listing HIV was rationally based. The rationality of his decision rested on view that "the voluntary cooperation of high-risk individuals will be acquired by existing programs and by the elimination of the fear that coercive measures will be taken."[7] The existing programs included the voluntary testing (including anonymous testing), contact tracing limitations, and statutory HIV confidentiality requirements of New York law.[8] However, two dissenting justices, although conceding that the voluntary cooperation of individuals with HIV might be lost as a result of the more coercive measures, were persuaded that the "current, dangerously critical level [of] the epidemic" required such coercive measures and that the health commissioner's voluntary cooperation strategy "sidesteps . . . the physician's right and responsibility to know if their [sic] patients are infected and to proceed accordingly."[9] On appeal, that argument was not persuasive, and the New York Court of Appeals affirmed.[10]

This chapter begins by reviewing some of the more coercive measures, such as that of mandatory testing and disclosure (**§ 2.2**), restricting business activities that are believed to contribute to the spread of HIV (**§ 2.3**), and imposing restrictions directly on the liberty of infected individuals, as is the case with civil detention statutes (**§ 2.4**).

In contrast to the coercive strategies, education and access to information has been widely favored. The appeal of this approach is based on the notion that individuals will act rationally in reducing their risk of HIV infection if they are given appropriate information and education. A corollary to this approach makes HIV counseling and voluntary testing available, and adds confidentiality[11] and nondiscrimination protections.[12] For example, the availability of home HIV testing is one recent development that provides testing in a setting that maximizes

---

[6] New York State Soc'y of Surgeons v. Axelrod, 555 N.Y.S.2d at 915 (Kane, J.P., dissenting).

[7] *Id.* at 914.

[8] *See* N.Y. Pub. Health Law §§ 2780–2790 (providing for voluntary, consensual HIV testing, confidentiality, and exceptions).

[9] New York State Soc'y of Surgeons v. Axelrod, 555 N.Y.S.2d at 914.

[10] 572 N.E.2d 605 (N.Y. 1991).

[11] *See generally* **App. A;** Lawrence O. Gostin, Legislative Survey of State Confidentiality Laws, with Specific Emphasis on HIV and Immunization (1996) (available from the CDC AIDS Information Clearinghouse; 1-800-458-5231); *id., Health Information Privacy,* 80 Cornell L. Rev. 101 (1995).

[12] Nondiscrimination protections are covered generally in **Chs. 3** through **6.**

privacy, thus extending the appeal of testing to individuals who might not otherwise be tested, although it does so at the potential expense of the educational
benefits that can result from pre- and post-test counseling, which are frequently
required by law.[13]

Although individuals may not have any constitutional right to AIDS education, § 2.5 considers government attempts to restrict or manipulate the message,
and the legal limitations on that. AIDS education and prevention programs are
addressed in two specific contexts. **Section 2.6** addresses the problem of Internet censorship in relation to the epidemic, and § 2.7 addresses the issues posed
by providing AIDS education in the schools and, in particular, the controversies
that have surrounded condom distribution programs.

In addition to access to information and education, the epidemic poses many
problems in regard to access to health care and related services. **Section 2.8** is
an overview of the most important of the congressional enactments, the Ryan
White Comprehensive AIDS Resources Emergency (CARE) Act. Two aspects
of that legislation are then covered separately: the controversial provisions concerning testing of pregnant women and newborns (§ 2.9) and the CARE Act's
funding restrictions, which are largely politically motivated. The controversy
concerning access to medical marijuana, just one of many issues involved in research and treatment for HIV disease,[14] is covered in § 2.11, and the perhaps even
more controversial issues concerning syringe exchange programs are discussed
in §§ 2.12 to 2.15.

LEGAL RESTRICTIONS TO PREVENT TRANSMISSION

§ 2.2 Mandatory Testing and Disclosure

In the United States, mandatory HIV testing or screening has been imposed only
in specific, limited areas and frequently has been subject to challenge and controversy. Under federal law, testing requirements apply to the armed forces (see
Chapter 3), immigrants (see **Chapter 11**), the foreign service,[15] and certain other

---

[13] William O. Fabbri, *Home HIV Testing and Conflicts with State HIV Testing Regulations,* 11
Am. J. L. & Med. 419 (1995).

[14] For further discussion of issues in this area, see Joni N. Gray et al., Ethical and Legal Issues
in AIDS Research (1995); Carol Levine, *AIDS and the Ethics of Human Subjects Research, in*
AIDS & Ethics 77–104 (Frederic G. Reamer ed., 1991).

[15] *See* Local 1812, Am. Fed'n of Gov't Employees v. U.S. Dep't of State, 662 F. Supp. 50
(D.D.C. 1987) (upholding State Dep't policy of HIV testing for foreign service employees).

federal programs.[16] Under state laws, mandatory testing has been imposed primarily within the criminal justice system. See **Chapter 7.** Mandatory counseling of pregnant women has been required in some states.[17] In the private sector, mandatory HIV testing policies have rarely been adopted, with the exception of HIV screening for applicants for life or disability insurance policies.

Once a reliable means of determining HIV antibody status became available in 1985, it was inevitable that the test would be proposed for widespread identification of those infected, or at least imposed on a mandatory basis for individuals within certain settings, such as hospital patients. Many proponents of mandatory testing for HIV appear to have been motivated merely by a desire to inflict harm or punishment on those infected. According to former Surgeon General C. Everett Koop, for example, one proponent of mandatory HIV testing, Congressman William Dannemeyer, expressed an attitude that has been widely held, but not as widely voiced, stating that if all persons with HIV infection in the United States could be identified, that information could be used to "[w]ipe them off the face of the earth!"[18] Societal response in the form of scapegoating those infected should not be surprising, however, and has been a feature of other societies' experience with epidemics.[19]

Over the years, however, mandatory testing has proven to be the exception, not the norm, largely for several practical as well as ethical and legal reasons[20]

---

[16] The federal Peace Corps and Job Corps have required HIV testing, although abandonment of that policy, at least in regard to the Job Corps, is apparently under consideration. *See* Presidential Advisory Council on HIV/AIDS, Progress Report: Implementation of Advisory Council Recommendations 49 (July 8, 1996); Dorsey v. U.S. Dep't of Labor, 41 F.3d 1551 (D.D.C. 1994) (challenge to Job Corps HIV policy).

[17] *See* Fla. Stat. Ann. § 384.31 (West Supp. 1997) (requiring health care provider counseling of pregnant women regarding HIV testing); N.J. Stat. Ann. § 26:5C-16 (West 1996) (same); N.Y. Pub. Health Law § 2500-f (McKinney Supp. 1997) (requiring comprehensive program for testing newborns). This issue was also addressed in the 1996 amendments to the Ryan White CARE Act. See § **2.9.**

[18] C. Everett Koop, Koop: The Memoirs of America's Family Doctor 208 (1991).

[19] *See generally* William A. Rushing, The AIDS Epidemic: Social Dimensions of an Infectious Disease (1995) (examining the social response to AIDS in light of other infectious diseases historically).

[20] *See generally* Institute of Medicine, Nat'l Academy of Sciences, Confronting AIDS: Update 1988, 75–80 (1988) (endorsing mandatory testing policies in only limited circumstances); Ronald Bayer et al., *HIV Antibody Screening: An Ethical Framework for Evaluating Proposed Programs,* 256 JAMA 1768 (1986), *reprinted in* The AIDS Reader: Social, Political, Ethical Issues 327–46 (Nancy F. McKenzie ed., 1991) (examining screening programs from an ethical perspective, concluding that universal mandatory screening cannot be justified); *see also* Allan M. Brandt et al., *Routine Hospital Testing for HIV: Health Policy Considerations, in* AIDS and the Health Care System 125–39 (Lawrence O. Gostin ed., 1990) (concluding that compulsory routine testing in programs in hospitals is "fundamentally flawed").

that can be summarized briefly. First, the setting in which the testing is required may simply be avoided by many individuals, whether or not they are at risk for HIV, thus rendering the screening ineffective if it is meant to have any broad public health value. Additionally, many individuals may forego a valuable benefit in order to avoid testing. For example, requiring all hospital patients to be tested may have the negative effect of deterring potential patients from seeking hospital care. Similarly, any rule that requires the disclosure of test results provides an incentive for individuals to avoid being tested. Along those lines, a proposal in Congress to require physicians to disclose their HIV infection to patients before performing invasive procedures was rejected on the basis that it would discourage voluntary testing.[21] Instead, a less coercive measure was adopted.[22] From a cost-benefit perspective, widespread testing of populations with relatively low prevalence of HIV requires a significant expenditure of funds in relation to the few individuals with HIV who are identified. Finally, even generally reliable tests can result in erroneous results, raising the issue of how positive tests will be verified or confirmed. In light of these considerations, alternatives to mandatory testing, such as AIDS education programs and the availability of voluntary, confidential HIV testing, appear particularly attractive.

Attempts to regulate marriage by imposing HIV testing illustrate these problems. Imposing HIV testing as a prerequisite to marriage, or by forbidding marriage between persons with HIV, have been proposed in many states but not widely adopted. These legal measures should now be viewed as futile. Illinois and Louisiana previously imposed HIV testing as part of their required premarital exam, but both those standards have been repealed.[23] These statutes did not prohibit marriage for those testing positive but did require the HIV positive person to disclose that to the other partner before marriage. As is the case with mandatory screening programs imposed on populations that are not, overall, at high risk for HIV, the Illinois program resulted in very few HIV positive test results. Many people apparently avoided the HIV test by applying for marriage licenses in neighboring states, where HIV testing was not required.[24]

---

[21] *See* 137 Cong. Rec. S10,331–63 (daily ed. July 18, 1991) (debate on Helms amendment to 1992 Treasury Appropriations bill).

[22] The so-called Dole amendment is discussed in § **3.12.**

[23] Ill. Rev. Stat. ch. 40, ¶ 204 (1987) (repealed); La. Rev. Stat. Ann. § 9:229 (West 1991) (repealed); *cf.* 20 Ill. Comp. Stat. Ann. § 2310/55.55 (free brochures on HIV for marriage license applicants).

[24] *See* Bernard J. Turnock & Chester J. Kelly, *Mandatory Pre-Marital Testing for Human Immunodeficiency Virus: The Illinois Experience,* 261 JAMA 3415 (1989) (noting that after six months of experience with mandatory HIV testing, seroprevalence rate was .011 percent, with a resulting cost of $312,000 per individual identified as HIV-infected; at the same time, rate of marriage license issuance in Illinois declined 22.5 percent); Stephen C. Joseph, *Premarital AIDS Testing: Public Policy Abandoned at the Altar,* 261 JAMA 3456 (1989) (editorial by New York's commissioner of health).

Alternatives to mandatory testing certainly seem attractive. Some states require that HIV counseling be provided to prospective marriage partners. Since 1987, for example, California has required that applicants for marriage certify that they have received an offer of HIV testing from the physician who conducted the premarital examination.[25] West Virginia requires that the marriage license issuer provide the applicants with information on HIV testing. The provision of the education materials must then be documented with the marriage license forms.[26]

§ 2.3 Restricting Sexually Oriented Commercial Activities

The AIDS epidemic has provided government officials with a new rationale for attacking sexually oriented commercial activities, by utilizing not the criminal law but coercive civil legal authority instead. The risk of HIV transmission has been proffered in support of regulation or closure of businesses that foster or promote sexual activities on their premises. Although the sexual activities themselves are frequently not commercial in nature,[27] they occur in settings that are commercial (for example, bookstores, movie theaters, and bathhouses).

Video Booths.   Cases involving state or local laws prohibiting commercial operation of private video booths, so-called open door ordinances, are legion. The intent behind this legislation, frequently adopted in response to the AIDS epidemic, is to prevent patrons from using the private video booths for sexual activities. The defendants in these cases do not appear to have argued that their establishments were committed to HIV education activities or to ensuring that sexual activities that occurred posed no risk of transmission. Generally, the courts have applied the analysis set forth in *City of Renton v. Playtime Theatres, Inc.,*[28] which provides that the legislation meet three criteria. First, the regulation must be content neutral, that is, the intent must not be to suppress the constitutionally protected expressive activity. Second, the regulation must be narrowly tailored to serve a substantial governmental interest. Finally, there must

---

[25] Cal. Fam. Code Ann. § 358 (West 1994).

[26] W. Va. Code Ann. § 16-3C-2(g) (1995).

[27] Criminal law prohibitions on commercial sexual activities such as prostitution are covered in **Ch. 7.** Although some courts have concluded that prostitution offenses occur on the premises of commercial businesses and thus justify their closure, that does not appear to be the primary commercial purpose of the businesses.

[28] 475 U.S. 41, 47 (1986). Some courts have applied the similar time, place, and manner analysis of United States v. O'Brien, 391 U.S. 367 (1968). *See* Mitchell v. Commission on Adult Entertainment Establishments, 10 F.3d 123, 130–31 n.7 (3d Cir. 1993), *cited approvingly in* City of Colo. Springs v. 2354 Inc., 896 P.2d 272, 297 n.19 (Colo. 1995).

be alternative channels of communication not closed by the regulation. Rulings in at least seven circuit courts of appeal have all upheld such regulation[29] and several state courts have ruled similarly.[30]

In identifying the substantial governmental interest underlying these enactments, it appears to be accepted, almost as a matter of law, that requiring booths to be open to view "promote[s] the public health and general welfare," as the U.S. District Court for Connecticut concluded in *Grunberg v. Town of East Hartford*,[31] without even mentioning the public health threat of HIV transmission. Nevertheless, at least some of the decisions do not specifically identify the precise nature of the public health threat, perhaps indicating that those seeking to regulate the business are motivated in part by moral disdain for the activities in question. In some cases, however, the courts' conclusion that the operation of the closed booths posed a threat to the public health were based on evidence that criminal activities, such as prostitution, or unprotected sexual contact that poses a risk of HIV transmission occur in these settings. In *Broadway Books, Inc. v. Roberts*,[32] for example, the court relied on testimony of a local public health official that blood and semen in booths, as well as unspecified sexual activities, could transmit "the HTLV-III virus that carries AIDS."[33] Similarly, *Matney v. County of Kenosha*[34] upheld against constitutional challenge an open

---

[29] Mitchell v. Commission on Adult Entertainment Establishments, 10 F.3d 123 (3d Cir. 1993), *aff'g* 802 F. Supp. 1112 (D. Del. 1992); Bamon Corp. v. City of Dayton, 923 F.2d 470 (6th Cir. 1991); Postscript Enters. v. City of Bridgeton, 905 F.2d 223, 227 (8th Cir. 1990) (upholding open booth ordinance but without reference to public health issues), *aff'g* 699 F. Supp. 1393 (E.D. Mo. 1988); Doe v. City of Minneapolis, 898 F.2d 612 (8th Cir. 1990), *aff'g* 693 F. Supp. 774 (D. Minn. 1988); Berg v. Health & Hosp. Corp., 865 F.2d 797, 803–04 (7th Cir. 1989) (occurrence of anonymous, high-risk sexual activities in closed booths), *aff'g* 667 F. Supp. 639 (S.D. Ind. 1987); FW/PBS, Inc. v. City of Dallas, 873 F.2d 1298, 1304 (5th Cir. 1988) (concluding that closed booths encourage illegal and unsanitary sexual activity in adult theaters), *vacated in part on other grounds,* 493 U.S. 215 (1990); Wall Distribs., Inc. v. City of Newport News, 782 F.2d 1165, 1169 (4th Cir. 1986) (noting public health interests, but without identifying HIV specifically, upheld open door legislation); Ellwest Stereo Theaters, Inc. v. Wenner, 681 F.2d 1243, 1247–48 (9th Cir. 1982) (upholding open booth ordinance, but without reference to public health justification; no constitutional right to engage in private sexual activity in closed booth).

[30] Marsoner v. Pima County, 803 P.2d 897 (Ariz. 1991) (upholding AIDS-specific regulation requiring that adult amusement establishments not just remove their booth doors, but allow public health inspections and other measures intended to end sexual transmission of HIV); City of Colo. Springs v. 2354 Inc., 896 P.2d 272, 297–98 (Colo. 1995) (upholding design and one-person occupancy requirements for video booths); City of Lincoln v. ABC Books, Inc., 470 N.W.2d 760, 766 (Neb. 1991).

[31] 736 F. Supp. 430, 432–33 (D. Conn. 1989).

[32] 642 F. Supp. 486 (E.D. Tenn. 1986); *see also* DLS, Inc. v. City of Chattanooga, 894 F. Supp. 1140, 1145 (E.D. Tenn. 1995) (citing *Broadway Books* approvingly); City of Lincoln v. ABC Books, Inc., 470 N.W.2d 760, 766 (Neb. 1991) (noting that closed booths were shown to have promoted masturbation, fondling, and indecent exposure).

[33] Broadway Books, Inc. v. Roberts, 642 F. Supp. at 491.

[34] 887 F. Supp. 1235, 1239 (E.D. Wis. 1995).

door ordinance on the basis that the ordinance was intended to prevent sexually transmitted disease and, more generally, unsanitary conditions. The precise connection between the unsanitary conditions and disease prevention was not explained. But in *Suburban Video, Inc. v. City of Delafield,*[35] the court expressed a far more scientifically sound view: neither masturbation nor presence of semen on walls or floors poses a risk of HIV transmission. The court nevertheless upheld the local ordinance on the basis that other sexual activities did pose a threat of HIV transmission. In one case, *Ellwest Stereo Theater, Inc. v. Boner,*[36] the court referenced testimony that health department records indicated that the local incidence of AIDS was traceable to adult-oriented establishments, although the precise nature of this evidence was unexplained. In *Movie & Video World, Inc. v. Board of County Commissioners,*[37] the court concluded that even the possibility of HIV transmission on the premises was an adequate basis for regulation.

In *Commonwealth ex rel. Preate v. Danny's New Adam & Eve Bookstore,*[38] the attorney general for Pennsylvania used a real estate nuisance statute as the basis for petitioning for an injunction against operation of video viewing booths and a "California Couch Dancing area" in adult bookstores. Referencing the common law definition of nuisance,[39] the Pennsylvania Commonwealth Court upheld the lower court's grant of injunctive relief. The lower court had concluded that sexual conduct occurred on the premises that "could lead to the spread of HIV which may result in AIDS." According to the court, this view was supported by expert testimony, not explained in the opinion, and testimony of one patron, who testified that he was infected with HIV and engaged in sexual intercourse in the bookstore.[40] On appeal, the majority did not identify the specific risk of transmission, but it implied that sexual intercourse occurred without the use of a condom and without disclosing the patron's HIV status to an individual who was not aware of the patron's HIV infection. However, the dissent argued that sexual conduct within the booths was not illegal and thus could not be a basis for an injunction; on the other hand, the risk of HIV transmission needed to be shown to be "practically certain, not merely probable," and, because the sexual activities were masturbation or oral intercourse, the evidence of record showed little risk of HIV transmission from such activities. The risk of transmission was "theoretical, at best." The dissent noted, however, that if evidence showed that prostitution occurred on the premises, there would be a clear basis for granting the commonwealth's requested injunction.

---

[35] 694 F. Supp. 585, 589–90 (E.D. Wis. 1988).

[36] 718 F. Supp. 1553, 1563 (M.D. Tenn. 1989).

[37] 723 F. Supp. 695 (S.D. Fla. 1989).

[38] 625 A.2d 119 (Pa. Commw. Ct. 1993).

[39] *See* Restatement (Second) of Torts § 821B (1985) (an "unreasonable interference with a right common to the general public").

[40] One wonders whether the patron was offered a grant of immunity for his testimony regarding his own sexual activities, because that testimony would appear to be an admission of the commission of criminal offenses, as discussed in **Ch. 7.**

Movie Theaters. The New York City Health Department obtained an injunction against the operation of a movie theater in *City of New York v. Dana.*[41] The city and its health department relied on the prohibited facilities regulation[42] in a case based on evidence that high-risk sexual activities occurred in the theater. Health inspectors observed numerous acts of high-risk sex (anal intercourse and fellatio) on the premises during the weeks preceding the commencement of the injunction action. The theater's management was then given written notice in advance of the commencement of the action, but it failed to end the sexual activities on the premises. In granting the injunction, the court distinguished *People ex rel. Arcara v. Cloud Books, Inc.,*[43] which rejected a prosecutor's attempt to obtain a court order closing a bookstore on the basis that closure was an overly broad remedy, given the importance of the First Amendment interest. In *Dana,* the health department had warned the proprietor to limit sexual activities on the premises, to no avail. As a result, closure was deemed justified as the only effective way to abate the nuisance. Additionally, unlike *Arcara,* the threat of HIV transmission was involved at the theater, a health risk not referred to in *Arcara.*

Bathhouses. Since the beginning of the epidemic, the regulation of bathhouses or sex clubs has been a controversial aspect of the public health response.[44] Unlike the commercial establishments discussed above, in the context of bathhouses and sex clubs, there has been less dispute about whether sexual activities that pose a risk of HIV transmission take place. Also unlike the bookstore video booth cases, First Amendment free expression protections are not implicated, because the regulation is generally of sexual conduct itself, not in a setting implicating First Amendment protections. Instead, the question is what is the appropriate public health response. Some public health advocates have argued that closing bathhouses and like businesses simply forces the patrons to engage in the same activities in settings in which they cannot be reached with safe sex messages.[45] Nevertheless, closure of such businesses has been upheld. In *City*

---

[41] 627 N.Y.S.2d 273 (Sup. Ct. N.Y. County 1995).

[42] N.Y. Comp. Codes R. & Regs. tit. 10, § 24-2.1–.3 (1994).

[43] 503 N.E.2d 492 (N.Y. 1986) (applying state constitutional standards); *cf.* Arcara v. Cloud Books, Inc., 478 U.S. 697, 705 (1986) (because unlawful public sexual activities are not protected under federal constitution, there is no constitutional bar to bookstore closure on basis that such activities occur on the premises).

[44] *See* Ronald Bayer, *Sex and the Bathhouses: The Politics of Privacy, in* Private Acts, Social Consequences: AIDS and the Politics of Public Health 20–71 (1989); Dennis Altman, AIDS in the Mind of America 147–55 (1987); Randy Shilts, And the Band Played On: Politics, People, and the AIDS Epidemic 19–20 (1987); *see also* Stephen C. Joseph, Dragon Within the Gates: The Once and Future AIDS Epidemic 103–08 (1992) (account by former New York City Health Commissioner).

[45] *See, e.g.,* Ronald Bayer, *Sex and the Bathhouses: The Politics of Privacy, in* Private Acts, Social Consequences: AIDS and the Politics of Public Health 53–54 (1989) (quoting New York City Health Commissioner David Sencer as stating that "changing the habitat is [not] necessarily going to change behavior").

of New York v. New Saint Mark's Baths,[46] for example, based on evidence of high-risk sexual activities' taking place on the premises, the court upheld the closing of a bathhouse. The court noted that the parties opposed to the closure challenged the scientific judgments regarding the risk of HIV transmission and whether closure would in fact limit transmission, given the facility's efforts to educate its patrons regarding the risk of HIV transmission. On that point, however, the court simply deferred to the views of the city health department. In regard to the First Amendment issues implicated by the closure, the court questioned whether sexual activities taking place in a commercial establishment are constitutionally protected and concluded that the "tangential impact upon association or expression is insufficient to obstruct the exercise of the State's police power to protect the public health and safety."[47]

Recent attempts to forge a public health-private business partnership are one approach, involving continued operation of such businesses, but with the requirement that safer sex standards be enforced and educational services or programs be provided to support changes in high-risk sexual behaviors.[48] In the New York City area, for example, public health officials have noted the proliferation of approximately 50 sex clubs, two-thirds of which are gay, and one-third cater to heterosexuals. Health officials are reported to have attempted to work in a conciliatory manner with the owners in order to provide patrons with information regarding risk reduction measures, as opposed to seeking to close the clubs.[49]

§ 2.4 Quarantine and Other Restrictions

Among the most traditional of public health approaches to infectious disease is quarantine. *Quarantine* is generally defined as limiting the movement of individuals who have been exposed to a communicable disease for a period of time equal to the longest usual incubation period, so that they do not expose others.[50] Federal authority to control diseases through limitations on individual liberty is set forth in several constitutional provisions[51] and addressed both by statute and

---

[46] 497 N.Y.S.2d 979 (Sup. Ct. N.Y. County 1986).

[47] *Id.* at 983.

[48] *See* V. Kegebein et al., *Keeping San Francisco Sex Clubs Open and Safe: Community/Public Health Partnerships,* S.F. Dep't of Pub. Health, AIDS Office, *abstracted in* AIDSWeekly, Aug. 3, 1992. A similar approach was approved by the court in California v. Pi-Acqua, Inc., No. BC004578 (Stipulation of Entry of Final Judgment) (Cal. Super. Ct. L.A. County, July 29, 1992).

[49] Mireya Navarro, *In the Age of AIDS, Sex Clubs Proliferate Again,* N.Y. Times, Mar. 3, 1993, at B1.

[50] *See* Frank P. Grad, Public Health Law Manual 74–78 (2d ed. 1990); Sherston Baker, The Laws Relating to Quarantine 2–3 (1879). For a history of quarantine provisions, see Wendy E. Parmet, *AIDS and Quarantine: The Revival of an Archaic Doctrine,* 14 Hofstra L. Rev. 53, 55–71 (1985).

[51] U.S. Const. art. I, § 8, cls. 1 (general welfare) and 3 (regulation of interstate and foreign commerce).

regulations governing entry into and interstate travel within the United States.[52] Because these laws address diseases that are communicated far more readily than HIV, such as by airborne transmission, HIV has never been included among diseases listed for quarantine.[53] The laws of many states include similar restrictive provisions.[54]

The surgeon general in his 1987 AIDS report took only one sentence to dismiss the idea of quarantine: "Quarantine has no role in the management of AIDS because AIDS is not spread by casual contact."[55] In considering the issue in 1985, one legal scholar commented that "courts must recognize that quarantine cannot be constitutionally justified today unless the state can show that the particular method chosen is carefully tailored to meet its goal—public health protection."[56] The notion of imposing quarantine on persons in the United States has thus never been considered a realistic approach to the AIDS epidemic.

Part of the problem with imposing quarantine is the practical one of identifying persons appropriate for quarantine. In terms of the AIDS epidemic, prior to antibody tests availability in 1985, only those persons with symptomatic disease could have been identified. Once the test was available, the process of testing all residents of the United States posed huge logistical and financial burdens. Presumably, all residents testing negative would then be tested repeatedly, because at least some would not have developed antibodies at the time of the previous testing and might have infected others during the interim. Given the extent of HIV infection in the population by the time HIV antibody testing became available, the problem of separately housing or confining the large number of persons subject to quarantine was immense. Additionally, not all persons who test positive for the virus necessarily pose a risk of transmission to others because, unlike the diseases traditionally subject to quarantine, transmission of HIV generally occurs as a result of specific, generally voluntary behaviors. Identifying on a widespread basis individuals who might engage in such behavior in the future is a difficult if not impossible task. In an island country like Cuba, mandatory testing and quarantine might at least be an option. Cuba has made the isolation of persons with HIV the cornerstone of its HIV policy, with

---

[52] 42 U.S.C. §§ 264–266 (1994) (apprehension and detention of individuals for purpose of preventing disease); 42 C.F.R. pt. 71 (1995) (prevention of introduction of communicable diseases from foreign countries); 21 C.F.R. pt. 1240 (1996) (restrictions on travel between states); Exec. Order No. 12,452, 48 Fed. Reg. 56,927 (1983), *set forth as note to* 42 U.S.C. § 264. As explained in **Ch. 11,** HIV infection is relevant to immigration into the United States, but that policy is no longer justified on the basis of infection control.

[53] *See* 42 C.F.R. § 71.32 (1995), 21 C.F.R. § 1240.54 (1996) (listing of specific diseases subject to quarantine).

[54] *See, e.g.,* Cal. Gov't Code § 202; Cal. Health & Safety Code §§ 3110–3125; Fla. Stat. Ann. §§ 384.28, .281 (West 1993 & Supp. 1997) (quarantine limitation).

[55] C. Everett Koop, Surgeon General's Report on Acquired Immune Deficiency Syndrome 34 (1987).

[56] Wendy E. Parmet, *AIDS and Quarantine: The Revival of an Archaic Doctrine,* 14 Hofstra L. Rev. 53, 90 (1985).

apparent success in limiting the spread of HIV within Cuban society, although at a significant cost in terms of the rights of the individuals who are subject to that policy.[57]

The courts have traditionally upheld broad public health powers, although the rationale offered in older cases is hardly persuasive in terms of current constitutional standards. The Supreme Court's 1905 decision, *Jacobson v. Massachusetts*,[58] is a frequently cited precedent in this area. In that case, a Massachusetts smallpox vaccination law was challenged as unconstitutional. Without subjecting the vaccination law to any real scrutiny, the court upheld it, noting that there are "manifold restraints to which every person is necessarily subject for the common good."[59] Other cases have upheld wartime confinement or limitations on liberty of Japanese-Americans during World War II,[60] but those cases now may serve as nothing more than examples of the Supreme Court's fallibility.[61]

More recently, however, the Supreme Court has considered the issue of detention in contexts other than the public health. These cases provide the outlines for constitutional analysis of detention statutes in the field of public health. In *United States v. Salerno*,[62] the Supreme Court upheld a federal pretrial criminal detention statute, which allows pretrial detention of persons accused of federal felonies. The statute was viewed as not having been enacted as a punitive measure. But unlike public health detention for an individual with HIV, which could be indefinite in length, the period of detention under consideration in *Salerno* was limited by federal law that requires that the accused's trial must occur within a relatively short period of time. The detention, then, could not extend beyond the trial, unless the accused was convicted, the conviction then being the basis for confinement. Similarly, venereal disease "detain and treat" statutes provide a model for restricting the personal liberties of individuals with an

---

[57] *See* Marvin Leiner, *AIDS: Cuba's Effort to Contain, in* Sexual Politics in Cuba: Machismo, Homosexuality, and AIDS 117–57 (1994); Sarah Santana et al., *Human Immunodeficiency Virus in Cuba: The Public Health Response of a Third World Country,* 21 Int'l J. Health Servs. 511 (1991), *reprinted in* AIDS: The Politics of Survival 167 (Nancy Krieger & Glen Margo eds., 1994); Nancy Scheper-Hughes, *AIDS, Public Health, and Human Rights in Cuba,* 342 Lancet 965 (1993), *reprinted in* AIDS Reference Guide ¶ 223 (1993) (noting success of Cuban policy in limiting AIDS to 927 cases (111 deaths) as of May 31, 1993, as compared, for example, to Puerto Rico, which has one-third the population of Cuba but over 8,000 cases of AIDS); Ronald Bayer & Cheryl Heaton, *Controlling AIDS in Cuba: The Logic of Quarantine,* 320 New Eng. J. Med. 1022 (1989); Ronald Bayer, *Cuba's HIV Quarantine Takes Toll in Liberty,* N.Y. Times, July 30, 1993, at A26 (letter); Robert Bazell, *Happy Campers: Cuba's Sanitarium for AIDS Patients,* New Republic, Mar. 9, 1992, at 12.

[58] 197 U.S. 11 (1905).

[59] *Id.* at 26.

[60] *See* Korematsu v. United States, 323 U.S. 214 (1944).

[61] *See, e.g.,* Laurence H. Tribe, American Constitutional Law § 16-6 (2d ed. 1988) (*Korematsu* "represents the nefarious impact that war and racism can have on institutional integrity and cultural health").

[62] 481 U.S. 739 (1987). *See also* United States v. Estreda, 488 U.S. 361 (1989).

infectious disease in which casual contact is not involved but, again, detention is for the limited period of time it takes to test for or treat the infection.[63]

In another line of cases, courts have upheld the detention of individuals found to be both dangerous and mentally unstable[64] or of criminal defendants who are both incompetent to stand trial and dangerous.[65] Although it seems too obvious to mention, the Supreme Court has explicitly stated that public intolerance or animosity cannot be a basis for confinement.[66]

The relatively rare use of civil detention against individuals with HIV is demonstrated by one survey of public health authorities' actions in that regard, which concluded that from 1981 to 1990, 24 state health departments either had no means of taking action or took no action upon receiving reports about persons whose behavior posed a risk of HIV transmission. In states that did respond to such situations, cease and desist orders were used most frequently; 10 instances of quarantine were reported, typically for relatively brief periods. The survey authors concluded that the central focus of HIV prevention efforts must remain "education, counselling, voluntary testing and partner notification, drug abuse treatment, and needle exchange programs."[67]

One reported case that considers the issues involved in confining an individual who appears to put others at risk of HIV infection is *In re Stilinovich*.[68] The trial court had concluded that Robert Stilinovich, who was infected with HIV, had engaged in violent and aggressive conduct, including spitting, scratching, fighting, and making terroristic threats regarding his intentions to transmit HIV to others. The trial court also concluded that he had expressed his intention

---

[63] *See* Reynolds v. McNichols, 488 F.2d 1378 (10th Cir. 1973). Individuals with Hansen's disease were subjected to indefinite confinement despite evidence that the illness was not easily transmitted to others, although the policy of confinement was apparently not challenged. *See* Rick Bragg, *Lives Stolen by Treatment, Not by Disease,* N.Y. Times, June 19, 1995, at A1 (describing closure of National Hansen's Disease Center); Douglas Shenson, *When Fear Conquers: A Doctor Learns About AIDS from Leprosy,* N.Y. Times, Feb. 28, 1988, at 35 (magazine).

[64] Foucha v. Louisiana, 504 U.S. 71 (1992); Addington v. Texas, 441 U.S. 418 (1979). *See also* Young v. Weston, 898 F. Supp. 744 (W.D. Wash. 1995); *In re* Hendricks, 914 P.2d 129 (Kan.), *cert. granted sub nom.* Kansas v. Hendricks, 116 S. Ct. 2522 (1996) (challenge to confinement pursuant to violent sexual predator statute, which requires finding of dangerousness and mental abnormality); *In re* Young, 857 P.2d 989 (Wash. 1993). For a discussion of mental health issues in regard to patients posing a risk of HIV transmission, see Gregory A. Carlson, *Management of HIV-Positive Psychiatric Patients Who Fail to Reduce High-Risk Behaviors,* 40 Hosp. & Community Psychiatry 511 (1989).

[65] Jackson v. Indiana, 406 U.S. 715 (1972); Greenwood v. United States, 350 U.S. 366 (1956). *See also* Vitek v. Jones, 445 U.S. 480 (1980) (right to counsel in commitment case); Greene v. Edwards, 263 S.E.2d 661 (W. Va. 1980), (per curiam) (right to counsel in involuntary confinement for active tuberculosis).

[66] O'Connor v. Donaldson, 422 U.S. 563, 575 (1975).

[67] Ronald Bayer & Amy Fairchild-Carrino, *AIDS and the Limits of Control: Public Health Orders, Quarantine, and Recalcitrant Behavior,* 83 Am. J. Pub. Health 1471 (1993).

[68] 479 N.W.2d 731 (Minn. Ct. App. 1992).

to have sexual intercourse with others without disclosing his status, and that he would use intimidation and even force in order to engage in such relations. Stilinovich's problems apparently stemmed from his pattern of pathological drug abuse, which resulted in brief episodes of psychosis. Concluding that the criminal justice system was not adequate to address this problem, the trial court ordered Stilinovich committed for an indeterminate period as a "psychopathic personality." On appeal, the court upheld the factual findings as to the threat that Stilinovich posed, but it concluded that because the reason for his commitment was the fact that his HIV status posed a danger to others, commitment should have been pursuant to Minnesota's Health Threat Procedures Act,[69] which provides a means for adjudicating cases in which an individual is alleged to pose a health threat to others by means of HIV transmission. The court reversed the trial court's commitment order, noting, however, that because the court's reversal order would not be effective for 30 days, Stilinovich would remain in custody during that time period, thus giving the commissioner of health an opportunity to petition for his confinement under the Health Threat Procedures Act.

INFORMATION ACCESS, CENSORSHIP, AND EDUCATION

§ 2.5 Access to Information and Censorship

Education and prevention efforts in response to the AIDS epidemic have been subject to control, censorship, and manipulation, largely as a result of conflicting political or ideological agendas. Educational efforts have necessarily introduced topics of a traditionally sensitive or private nature into public discourse, including issues concerning human sexuality (specifically, homosexuality and bisexuality, as well as adolescent sexuality) and illicit drug use. What is acceptable and relevant information to one recipient may be offensive and pointless to another. However, despite attempts to control or direct public discourse in this area, it is fair to say that the epidemic has forced a significant change in what is acceptable in public discussion.

In AIDS education, the potentially controversial contents of the message on religious, moral, or political grounds is compounded by the fact that underlying scientific issues may be disputed. Thus, for example, recommending use of condoms as a means of preventing HIV transmission may be unacceptable on either a moral basis or as being scientifically unsound.[70] Despite the need for

---

[69] Minn. Stat. Ann. §§ 144.4171–.4186 (West 1989 & Supp. 1997).

[70] *See, e.g.,* Steven Epstein, Impure Science: AIDS, Activism, and the Politics of Knowledge 96–97 (1996) (noting support of scientific theory of viral transmission for "sex positive" message emphasizing condom use as opposed to message stressing monogamous sexual relationships); William L. Roper et al., Commentary: *Condoms and HIV/STD Prevention: Clarifying the*

scientific research on issues relevant to AIDS education and prevention, limitations have been imposed there as well. Government research restrictions, frequently imposed because the subject matter was viewed as too controversial for scientific inquiry and discussion,[71] have been criticized by the National Commission on AIDS[72] and the subject of congressional inquiry.[73]

Attempts to ideologically influence and restrict public AIDS education and dissemination of AIDS information have taken many forms and have occurred repeatedly; examples abound.[74] The Recommendations of the Domestic Policy Council, approved by President Reagan in 1987, failed to mention risk reduction through the use of condoms and appear to limit AIDS education only to heterosexuals by emphasizing that "[a]ny health information developed by the Federal Government that will be used for education should encourage responsible sexual behavior—based on fidelity, commitment, and maturity, placing sexuality within the context of marriage."[75] Despite his reputation for outspokenness on AIDS issues in the late 1980s, C. Everett Koop abided by Reagan administration directives to remain silent on AIDS issues during the first half of his tenure as United States Surgeon General.[76] Lack of reticence about speaking publicly about AIDS and sexuality caused President Clinton to fire his surgeon general, Joycelyn Elders, who, in responding to a question posed at the United Nations during a World AIDS Day program, stated that teaching about masturbation should be included in comprehensive sex education programs.[77] Ironically, the question posed to Dr. Elders included reference to the fact that "the campaign against AIDS has already destroyed many taboos about discussion of sex in

---

Message, 83 Am. J. Pub. Health 498 (1993) (emphasizing evidence of condoms' reliability in preventing HIV transmission); Lauran Neergaard, *CDC: Condoms Can Block AIDS,* Phila. Inquirer, Aug. 6, 1993, at A19 (describing CDC's efforts to end controversy regarding condom reliability by referencing studies of sero-discordant couples).

[71] For a general discussion of the constitutional protections afforded scientific discourse, see Steven Goldberg, Culture Clash: Law and Science in America 28–31 (1994) (observing that suppression of scientific information, like suppression of political speech, is inconsistent with the democratic political process).

[72] National Comm'n on AIDS, Behavioral and Social Sciences and the HIV/AIDS Epidemic 36–39 (1993).

[73] *See* The Politics of AIDS Prevention at the Centers for Disease Control: Hearings Before the Human Resources and Intergovernmental Relations Subcomm. of the House Comm. on Government Operations, 102d Cong., 2d Sess. (July 2, 1992).

[74] For further discussion of the issues in this area, see Scott Burris, *Education to Reduce the Spread of HIV, in* AIDS Law Today: A New Guide for the Public 82–114 (1993).

[75] President's Domestic Policy Council's Principles of AIDS Education (1987), *set forth as app. I to* CDC, *Guidelines for Effective School Health Education to Prevent the Spread of AIDS,* 37 MMWR 1, 10 (Supp. 2 1988).

[76] C. Everett Koop, Koop: The Memoirs of America's Family Doctor 195–96, 202–03 (1991).

[77] Douglas Jehl, *Surgeon General Forced to Resign by White House,* N.Y. Times, Dec. 10, 1994, at A1. For Dr. Elders' account of her firing, see Joycelyn Elders & David Chanoff, Joycelyn Elders, M.D.: From Sharecropper's Daughter to Surgeon General of the United States of America 331–35 (1996).

public."[78] The AIDS prevention program of the American Red Cross, funded in 1995 by a $5 million federal grant, was "toned down" in response to the wishes of the organization's president, Elizabeth Hanford Dole, wife of then-presidential candidate Bob Dole. The materials were deemed too explicit in terms of sexual matters. The action resulted in the criticism from AIDS education advocates that the Red Cross was substituting Mrs. Dole's husband's political aspirations for a sound approach to AIDS prevention and education.[79]

Federal AIDS education efforts have been subject to congressional or administrative restrictions that may not be consistent with effective education.[80] Although there may be no legally recognized right to receive information or education on health issues, such as HIV transmission, from the government, in reality governmental public health agencies are frequently the primary, if not exclusive, source of information. If those agencies do not directly undertake education efforts, they are frequently undertaken by nongovernmental agencies with government funds and the conditions attached to receipt of such funds. In that regard, Congress has specified that programs of education and information on AIDS "shall include information about the harmful effects of promiscuous sexual activity and intravenous substance abuse, and the benefits of abstaining from such activities."[81] But federal funds may not be used to provide education and information "designed to promote or encourage, directly, homosexual or heterosexual sexual activity or intravenous substance abuse."[82] However, this limitation is not to be read to restrict the ability of an education program that includes information on abstinence from those activities to provide "accurate information about various means to reduce an individual's risk of exposure" to HIV.

In any event, informational materials may not be obscene.[83] Whether AIDS education materials could be found to be obscene seems unlikely. They would very likely be found either to lack prurient value or to have scientific value.[84]

---

[78] *See President Clinton Forces Surgeon General to Quit—Comments After Speech at the U.N.,* Wash. Post, Dec. 10, 1994, at A12.

[79] *See* Richard L. Berke, *Red Cross Tones Down AIDS Materials,* N.Y. Times, Sept. 13, 1995, at A20.

[80] Congressional directives in this area have their origin in the Departments of Labor, Health and Human Services, and Education, and Related Agencies Appropriations Act of 1988, Pub. L. No. 100-202, Title V, § 514, 1987 U.S.C.C.A.N. (101 Stat.) 1329-256, 1329-289, and Health Omnibus Programs Extension Act of 1988, Pub. L. No. 100-607, Title II, § 221, 1988 U.S.C.C.A.N. (102 Stat.) 3048, 3093 (codified at 42 U.S.C. § 300ee). For a more specific discussion of congressional reaction to AIDS education activities, see Mark Barnes, *Toward Ghastly Death: The Censorship of AIDS Education,* 89 Colum. L. Rev. 698, 712–18 (1989) (book review).

[81] 42 U.S.C. § 300ee(b).

[82] *Id.* § 300ee(c).

[83] *Id.* § 300ee(d).

[84] *See* Miller v. California, 413 U.S. 15, 22 (1973); *Cf.* Rees v. Texas, 909 S.W.2d 264 (Tex. Ct. App. 1995), *cert. denied,* 117 S. Ct. 169 (1996) (affirming obscenity conviction for cable television broadcast of purported safer sex educational video).

Attempts by the CDC to administratively prohibit "offensive" terms or displays in federally funded AIDS education materials, however, were rejected as unconstitutionally vague and beyond the CDC's statutory authority in *Gay Men's Health Crisis v. Sullivan.*[85] The CDC's standards were intended to screen out AIDS materials that might be offensive to a majority of the intended audience or to a majority of the adults outside the intended audience, unless the "potential offensiveness of such materials is outweighed by the potential effectiveness in communicating an important HIV prevention message."[86]

Governmental limitations on AIDS education activities of individuals and private organizations have been successfully challenged under the First Amendment. Significant efforts in AIDS education have come not from the government but from private organizations. In *AIDS Action Committee, Inc. v. Massachusetts Bay Transportation Authority,*[87] a local AIDS advocacy organization challenged the transportation authority's rejection of seven public service advertisements for display on subway and trolley cars. The advertisements were intended to promote the use of latex condoms and used sexual innuendo and double entendre in a humorous manner to convey the safer sex message most effectively. Without reaching the issue of whether the transportation system's advertising areas constituted a public forum, the court held that the nonobscene advertisements had been rejected on the basis of their content and that the rejection gave rise to the unrebutted appearance of viewpoint discrimination. The record indicated that after previous advertisements for condoms were run, the transportation authority received 36 letters complaining about them, one-third of which, the court noted, contained explicit homophobic statements, even though the advertisements did not refer even indirectly to homosexuality. The court's opinion is accompanied by reprints of the advertisements in question, including those for the movie "Basic Instinct," which the transportation authority did accept, although there was no dispute that those advertisements were as sexually explicit as those proposed by the AIDS Action Committee.[88]

§ 2.6 —Internet Information Control

Legislation enacted by Congress in 1996 attempts to prohibit the availability of "indecent" and "sexually explicit" information or materials on the Internet to

---

[85] 792 F. Supp. 278 (S.D.N.Y. 1992), *prior opinion,* 733 F. Supp. 619 (S.D.N.Y. 1989).

[86] *Id.* at 281, *quoting* 55 Fed. Reg. 23,4143 (1990). The CDC's previous standard was significantly more restrictive. *See* 792 F. Supp. at 281 n.3, *quoting* 54 Fed. Reg. 10,049 (1989).

[87] 42 F.3d 1 (1st Cir. 1994), *aff'g on other grounds* 849 F. Supp. 79 (D. Mass. 1993). For a discussion of a similar, unreported case, Kupona Network v. Chicago Transit Auth., No. 89C 6908 (N.D. Ill. Sept. 13, 1989), see Scott Burris, *Education to Reduce the Spread of HIV, in* AIDS Law Today: A New Guide for the Public 100–02 (1993).

[88] AIDS Action Comm., Inc. v. Massachusetts Bay Transp. Auth., 42 F.3d at 14–25.

persons under the age of 18. The Communications Decency Act of 1996 (CDA), included as a provision in the Telecommunications Act of 1996,[89] is intended to prevent minors from being exposed to pornography. Although this enactment threatens the availability of many types of information on the Internet, its application in the context of HIV/AIDS information services could have a potentially profound impact. In addition to regulating the availability of information to minors, the CDA also includes, among others, provisions on sexually explicit cable service transmissions[90] and enhanced parental control of violent television programming.[91]

The Internet, or what the CDA defines as the "international computer network of both Federal and non-federal interoperable packet switched data networks,"[92] has been described as playing a significant role in current and future AIDS education efforts. Information can be provided or obtained in privacy, and, if they so choose, the recipients may even remain anonymous. To the extent that Internet services are available from commercial service providers, educational institutions, or governmental organizations, political and geographical boundaries are not a barrier to dissemination of information, even on a world-wide basis. Information can be made available in areas where it would not otherwise be available locally. For many users, both those who distribute information and those who receive it, the direct cost is insignificant, particularly in comparison to publication or retrieval of information in other media. New information can be made available far more quickly than by more traditional means. Furthermore, advocates for Internet AIDS education activities point out that the interactive nature of the medium enhances the value of the Internet for AIDS education, providing opportunities for debate about issues not available in other media, particularly in terms that would not be acceptable in many other forums. Because the CDA has the potential to limit these activities, it was criticized on this basis during its consideration by Congress.[93]

The CDA controls information provided by two different facilities: interactive computer services and telecommunications devices. First, section 502(2) of the CDA directly affects Internet service providers by making it a crime either to knowingly use "an interactive computer service to send to" or "to display in a manner available to" a person under 18 years of age "any comment, request, suggestion, proposal, image, or other communication that, in context, depicts or describes, in terms patently offensive as measured by contemporary community

---

[89] Pub. L. No. 104-104, Title V, §§ 501–509, 1996 U.S.C.C.A.N. (110 Stat.) 56, 133 (to be codified at 47 U.S.C. § 223(a)–(h)).

[90] Pub. L. No. 104-104, § 505, 1996 U.S.C.C.A.N. (110 Stat.) 136.

[91] *Id.* § 551, 1996 U.S.C.C.A.N. (110 Stat.) 139–42.

[92] *Id.* § 509, 1996 U.S.C.C.A.N. (110 Stat.) 139.

[93] *See* Bruce Mirken, *Exon Amendment: Threat to AIDS Prevention and Activism?*, AIDS Treatment News, July 21, 1995, at 5; *id., Internet Censorship: Congress Moves Toward Final Decision,* AIDS Treatment News, Dec. 1, 1995, at 8.

standards, sexual or excretory activities or organs, regardless of whether the user of such service placed the call or initiated the communication."[94] Additionally, the CDA makes it a crime for anyone who "knowingly permits any telecommunications facility under such person's control" to be used for any such prohibited activity with the intent that it be used for such activity.[95] An *interactive computer service* is defined as "any information service, system, or access software provider that provides or enables computer access by multiple users to a computer server, including specifically a service or system that provides access to the Internet and such systems operated or services offered by libraries or educational institutions."[96]

Section 502(1) of the CDA provides that whoever by means of a telecommunications device knowingly "makes, creates, or solicits, and . . . initiates the transmission of, any comment, request, suggestion, proposal, image, or other communication which is obscene or indecent, knowing that the recipient of the communication is under 18 years of age, regardless of whether the maker of such communication placed the call or initiated the communication" is subject to fines and imprisonment of not more than two years, or both.[97] Additionally, anyone who "knowingly permits any telecommunications facility under his control" to be used for any such prohibited activity "with the intent that it be used for such activity" is also subject to criminal penalties.[98] The definition of *telecommunications device* does not, however, include interactive computer service,[99] and therefore the limitations on "indecent" communications via telecommunication devices do not appear to extend to the interactive computer service provisions. However, because of the use of modems, which can be viewed as telecommunications devices under the CDA, with computers, the two provisions relating to telecommunication devices and interactive computer services may be coextensive in terms of the indecency prohibition. Under this interpretation of the CDA, the CDA's indecency standard also applies to communications undertaken by modem-linked computers. In sum, the CDA criminalizes both the "sending" of "patently offensive" sexual or excretory information or material to minors as well as the "displaying" of such information so that it is available to minors under the age of 18 years.

The CDA provides that it is a defense that the person "has taken, in good faith, reasonable, effective, and appropriate actions under the circumstances to restrict or prevent access by minors to a [prohibited] communication, which may involve any appropriate measures to restrict minors from such communications, including any method which is feasible under available technology."[100] Because

---

[94] 47 U.S.C.A. § 223(d)(1).

[95] *Id.* § 223(d)(2).

[96] U.S.C.A. § 230(e)(2), *referenced in* 47 U.S.C.A. § 223(h).

[97] 47 U.S.C.A. § 223(a)(1)(B).

[98] *Id.* § 223(a)(2).

[99] *Id.* § 223(h)(1)(B).

[100] 42 U.S.C.A. § 223(e)(5)(A).

of the controversial nature of the CDA, it provides for expedited review by the Supreme Court. Any civil challenge to the CDA is heard by a district court of three judges. If any provision in the CDA is ruled unconstitutional by the three-judge court, the CDA then provides an appeal by right directly to the Supreme Court.[101]

In regard to its regulation of interactive computer services, the CDA thus sets as its goal the regulation of sexually explicit information that is available to minors, while providers of such information have to determine whether the information offends community standards in the place in which the information is received. There is little question that prosecution of dissemination of obscene materials, as opposed to indecent materials, by means of the Internet can be undertaken under current federal obscenity statutes.[102]

Despite the sexually explicit nature of the information or materials that address HIV prevention issues, they presumably would not be obscene under *Miller v. California*,[103] given their political or scientific value. The discussion of AIDS prevention issues, particularly on the Internet, opens scientific discourse to a broad public, ranging from the professional scientific researchers and scholars, to AIDS activists, to persons whose interest is only casual. Like the sexual content in safe sex messages or other materials made available in other contexts ranging from school curricula to mass transit bus advertisements, the basis of the information is fairly characterized as scientific, for example, identification of sexual behaviors that are believed by medical experts to transmit or prevent transmission of HIV, although in order to be understood and accepted, that essentially scientific message is expressed in language that some persons may find to be patently offensive. The CDA's attempt to regulate indecent and patently offensive materials, however, poses special problems for Internet service providers. An Internet provider of materials that discuss HIV prevention issues is faced with the daunting task of keeping such materials from persons under age 18 while not restricting access of adults. In particular, it is impossible to prevent access to information by minors without significantly altering the way that the Internet functions. As a result, full compliance with the CDA can be achieved only by limiting information available to all users, including adults.

Several service providers have established World Wide Web pages that provide information of a sexually explicit nature, including information pertaining to AIDS. These sites typically advise the user in advance of using the site

---

[101] 1996 U.S.C.C.A.N. (110 Stat.) 142–43.

[102] *See, e.g.,* United States v. Thomas, 74 F.3d 701 (6th Cir. 1996) (affirming convictions under the federal obscenity law, 18 U.S.C. §§ 1462, 1465, for computer bulletin board system operators for making obscene materials available to subscribers in graphic interchange (GIF) format); United States v. Maxwell, 42 M.J. 568 (A.F. Ct. Crim. App. 1995) (affirming conviction under federal obscenity statute for transmission of obscene images using commercial computer service). For a general overview of regulation of obscene or indecent material in the context of the Internet, see Henry H. Perritt, Jr., Law and the Information Superhighway § 6.7 (1996).

[103] 413 U.S. 15 (1973).

materials of the sexually explicit nature of the information offered. Some commercial online services attempt to limit subscribers' access and distribution of sexually explicit information, although it is unclear to what extent those provisions are enforced by the services, particularly in regard to sexually explicit material pertaining to HIV. Critics of the CDA argue that controlling availability of information to minors by regulating Internet service providers is misguided and ineffective, and that the only effective way to regulate minors' access to such material is at the point of receipt of materials. This can be accomplished by limiting access to specific discussion lists or World Wide Web sites, or preventing the user from receiving information containing specified terms or vocabulary, features available from some online service providers or through the use of software products installed on the recipient's computer. Such approaches allow parents to control their children's access to certain materials but does not otherwise affect their availability on the Internet.

Signed into law by President Clinton on February 8, 1996, the CDA was promptly challenged in two civil actions filed by two groups of 47 plaintiffs, including the American Civil Liberties Union, Internet service providers, news organizations, software manufacturers, public interest groups, and individual users, including AIDS information providers.[104]

In a ruling that frequently referenced the significance of HIV/AIDS information on the Internet, the three-judge court unanimously concluded that the CDA is unconstitutional on its face and granted the plaintiffs' request for a preliminary injunction. The opinion of Chief Judge Sloviter of the Court of Appeals for the Third Circuit concluded that because of the CDA's regulation of constitutionally protected speech, it was subject to strict scrutiny, and that the government's burden in defending the CDA was to show both a compelling governmental interest and that the means chosen was the least restrictive. The court concluded that the CDA failed on both points. The court pointed out that the government had failed to show any compelling interest in preventing minors' access to certain indecent materials, while the CDA nevertheless threatened those who make such materials available:

> [P]laintiffs presented testimony that material that could be considered indecent, such as that offered by . . . Critical Path AIDS project, may be critically important for certain older minors. For example, there was testimony that one quarter of all new HIV infections in the United States is estimated to occur in young people between the ages of 13 and 20, an estimate the government made no effort to rebut. The witnesses believed that graphic material that their organizations post on the Internet could help save lives, but were concerned about the CDA's effect on their right to do so.[105]

A concurring opinion by District Judge Buckwalter agreed with Chief Judge Sloviter's conclusion that the CDA is unconstitutional on its face, but he further

---

[104] American Civil Liberties Union v. Reno, 929 F. Supp. 824 (E.D. Pa. 1996).

[105] *Id.* at 853. *See also id.* at 871 (Dalzell J., concurring).

concluded that the CDA's terms "indecent" and "patently offensive" are unconstitutionally vague.[106] A concurring opinion by District Judge Dalzell, however, concluded that although the terms of the CDA are not unconstitutionally vague, it nonetheless could not pass constitutional scrutiny. Indeed, in a strong endorsement of free, unregulated speech on the Internet, Judge Dalzell concluded "that the disruptive effect of the CDA on Internet communication, as well as the CDA's broad reach into protected speech, not only render the Act unconstitutional but also would render unconstitutional any regulation of protected speech on this new medium."[107]

The Supreme Court noted probable jurisdiction for the government's appeal in the case.[108]

§ 2.7   —School Curriculum Issues

AIDS school education programs have been particularly controversial in some areas.[109] Frequently, conflicts have arisen regarding the content of such programs in specific regard to whether sexual abstinence should be stressed or whether teens' responsibility to undertake sexual activities, if at all, with the risk of HIV reduced, through the use of condoms, should at least be acknowledged, if not emphasized. Going even further, some sexual health programs include making condoms available to students.

School policies and programs are traditionally left to the states and local school boards. The federal role in assisting development of AIDS education in the schools was initially very restrained. The President's Domestic Policy Council recommendations, approved by President Reagan in 1987, took a particularly restricted view of the federal government's role, which, although limited, was not without an ideological tilt, stating only that "[a]ny health information provided by the Federal Government that might be used in schools should teach that children should not engage in sex."[110] The CDC issued guidelines in 1988 that emphasized that school programs should provide education that enables and encourages young people to abstain from sex "until they are ready to establish a mutually monogamous relationship within the context of marriage."[111] However,

---

[106] *Id.* at 858.

[107] *Id.* at 867.

[108] 117 S. Ct. 554 (1996).

[109] For more information about these programs, contact the National School Boards Association, which maintains an HIV and AIDS Resource Database, 1680 Duke Street, Alexandria, VA 22314; (703) 838-NSBA.

[110] The President's Domestic Policy Council's Principles of AIDS Education (1987), *set forth as appendix to* CDC, *Guidelines for Effective School Health Education to Prevent the Spread of AIDS,* 37 MMWR 1, 10 (Supp. 2 1988) (app. I).

[111] CDC, *Guidelines for Effective School Health Education to Prevent the Spread of AIDS,* 37 MMWR 1, 4 (Supp. 2 1988).

the CDC also recommended that school systems, in consultation with parents and health officials, should provide AIDS education programs that address preventive types of behavior, including use of latex condoms, although the CDC stopped short of suggesting that condoms be made available to students. The National Commission on AIDS has recommended that "[c]omprehensive HIV prevention should include information, exploration of values and attitudes, skill building, and access to health care and social services, including condom availability."[112] Additionally, the commission noted that both abstinence messages and skills building about other means of reducing risk of HIV transmission, such as use of condoms, should be included.[113]

States like California have adopted legislation mandating AIDS education for junior and senior high schools but do not include distribution of condoms as part of the program.[114] Similar requirements apply to education of children who are wards of the state.[115] Other states, such as Arkansas, require parental consent;[116] others prohibit distribution only under certain circumstances[117] or prohibit condom distribution altogether.[118] These programs have been designed to allow only voluntary participation.[119] In some cases, the condom distribution activities take place outside of the classroom, but in others the parents can elect to remove their children from the program or from having condoms available for their children.

Although condom distribution programs in the schools are highly controversial in many areas, the reality of teenage sexual activity and the risk of HIV transmission has begun to set in in some areas, and programs that include distribution of condoms have been increasing.[120] Condom distribution programs, already in place in New York City, have been advocated for suburban high schools in the area.[121] New Haven, which has the highest level of AIDS cases in Connecticut, has initiated a condom distribution program beginning with fifth graders in its public school system.[122] Condoms have been shown to be effective, and

---

[112] National Comm'n on AIDS, Preventing HIV/AIDS in Adolescents 19 (1993).

[113] Id.

[114] Cal. Ed. Code § 51201.5 (West Supp. 1996).

[115] Cal. Welf. & Inst. Code § 1123 (West Supp. 1997).

[116] Ark. Code Ann. § 6-18-703 (1993).

[117] Md. Ann. Code art. 27, § 41A (prohibiting sale by vending machine).

[118] La. Rev. Stat. Ann. tit. 17, § 281; id. tit. 40, § 31.3; Mich. Comp. Laws Ann. § 380.1507 [6] (prohibiting distribution); S.C. Code Ann. § 59-1-405 (same).

[119] U.S. Conference of Mayors AIDS/HIV Program, *Condom Availability in High School: A Local Response,* AIDS Information Exchange (Dec. 1992).

[120] CDC, *HIV Instruction and Selected HIV-Risk Behaviors Among High School Students— United States, 1989–1991,* 41 MMWR 866 (1992) (documenting HIV instruction in school grades 9–12 as increasing significantly, from 54 to 83 percent, during 1989 to 1991). For an overview of such programs, see generally The Kaiser Forums, Condoms in the Schools (Sarah E. Samuels & Mark D. Smith eds., 1993) (app. IV listing of condom programs as of Jan. 26, 1993).

[121] Joseph Berger, *Distribution of Condoms Is Advocated,* N.Y. Times, Apr. 13, 1993, at B4.

[122] Clifford J. Levy, *Fifth Graders Get Condoms in New Haven,* N.Y. Times, July 28, 1992, at B1.

advocacy concerning their availability has been shown not to increase sexual activity among adolescents.[123]

AIDS education programs in high schools, for example, may still face serious barriers insofar as they are opposed by school boards or administrators, as illustrated in *Planned Parenthood v. Clark County School District*,[124] which upheld a school district's right to exclude an outside organization's health-related advertisements in school newspapers, yearbooks, and athletic programs. In places where AIDS education programs have official sanction, however, parents' groups have challenged the inclusion of their children in such programs, as in *Ware v. Valley Stream High School District*.[125] In that case, members of a religious organization, the Plymouth Brethren, challenged an AIDS-related health education program mandated by the New York State Education Department. Although Brethren children were granted exemptions from the health and hygiene curriculum relating to human sexuality, their request for exemption from the AIDS curriculum was denied by the commissioner of education on the basis that their claim was outweighed by the state's interest in providing universal AIDS education. Although it did not reach the merits of the constitutional issue, the New York Court of Appeals reversed the lower court's summary judgment ruling in favor of the defendant school district. The Court of Appeals concluded that the constitutional claim of the Brethren presented material questions as to both the Brethren's claim that their sincerely held religious belief was burdened by the AIDS education requirement and that granting the exemption would not substantially impede a compelling governmental purpose. But in *Brown v. Hot, Sexy & Safer Productions, Inc.*,[126] the court rejected a series of statutory and constitutional challenges to a mandatory AIDS awareness program presented during high school assembly.

In contrast, *Alfonso v. Fernandez*,[127] upheld a condom distribution program against parents' challenges that it violated health services law requiring parental consent and constitutional rights. Since participation in the condom distribution program was entirely voluntary, unlike the compulsory AIDS education program in *Ware*, the court ruled that there was no violation of the First Amendment free exercise of religion clause. But on appeal, however, that ruling was reversed.[128] The New York Supreme Court, Appellate Division, in a 3-2 vote, determined that because the condom program, although entirely voluntary, did not include a parental opt-out provision, it violated the parents' constitutional rights. Under New York law, adolescents (18 years old or younger) are deemed incapable of

---

[123] *See* William L. Roper et al., *Commentary: Condoms and HIV/STD Prevention: Clarifying the Message,* 83 Am. J. Pub. Health 498 (1993).

[124] 941 F.2d 817 (9th Cir. 1991) (en banc).

[125] 550 N.E.2d 420 (N.Y. 1989) (parents' First Amendment freedom of religion challenge AIDS education for their children).

[126] 68 F.3d 525 (1st Cir. 1995), *cert. denied,* 116 S. Ct. 1044 (1996).

[127] 584 N.Y.S.2d 406 (Sup. Ct. Richmond County 1992).

[128] 606 N.Y.S.2d 259 (App. Div. 1993), *motion for leave to appeal dismissed,* 637 N.E.2d 279 (N.Y. 1994).

providing a valid consent for health services, except as specifically provided by statute. There is no statutory provision allowing for minors' consent to receive condoms. The ruling was based on the court's conclusion that condom distribution is a health service, as opposed to health education, as had been argued by the school board. In that regard, the court distinguished health education activities, such as providing instruction to students on the proper method of condom use and the risks and benefits resulting from the use of condoms. Thus, student consent for the receipt of condoms was invalid. Additionally, the court concluded that the program violated the constitutional rights of the parents, under both the federal and New York constitutions. Specifically, the court determined that the parents' due process right to rear their children as they see fit was violated. On the other hand, the court also noted that the parents' claim that the program violated their First Amendment freedom of religion right was without merit. A dissenting opinion disagreed with the majority's view that condom distribution is a health service. The dissent also noted that if the majority is correct that the program is a health service, then parental consent for participation is required, not just an opt-out provision for parents who do not wish to have their children participate. Despite urging from the New York Civil Liberties Project,[129] the school board decided not to appeal the court's ruling. Instead, the school board responded to the court's ruling by amending its policy to provide for a parental opt-out provision.[130] To assure compliance with the parental opt-out direction, any student requesting condoms has to identify him or herself so that the school can verify that the student's parents have not opted out of the program. The opt-out provision has been criticized in that regard because it limits confidentiality in the provision of condoms, potentially discouraging some students from requesting them. A survey of parents and their children concluded that only 2 percent of the parents chose to opt out of the program.[131]

In another public school condom distribution case, *Curtis v. School Committee*,[132] the Supreme Judicial Court of Massachusetts upheld the program of the senior and junior high schools in Falmouth, Massachusetts, against a federal constitutional challenge. The challenge was focussed on the program's lack of both an opt-out provision and a system of parental notification of a child's request for a condom. In the junior high school, condoms were available without charge upon request to the school nurse, who would also provide counseling concerning sexually transmitted diseases. In the senior high school, free condoms were

---

[129] *See* Donna Lieberman, *Why Condoms Decision Needs to Be Appealed,* N.Y. Times, Jan. 21, 1994, at A26 (letter).

[130] Sam Dillon, *Controversial Yet Convenient,* N.Y. Times, Jan. 11, 1994, at A26; Josh Barbenel, *Board of Education Appears Ready to Let Parents Make the Call on Condoms,* N.Y. Times, Jan. 6, 1994, at B3.

[131] *Parents, Students Support School Condom Programs,* AIDS Alert, Nov. 1995, at 141.

[132] 652 N.E.2d 580 (Mass. 1995). For background information on the Falmouth program, see Beverly Wright & Kevin Cranston, *Condom Availability in a Small Town: Lessons from Falmouth, Massachusetts,* SIECUS Rep., Oct.–Nov. 1992, at 13–17.

available from the school nurse, who again would provide counseling, or they could be purchased from vending machines. Counseling from trained faculty was available upon request. The program was designed to emphasize abstinence as the only certain method of avoiding sexually transmitted diseases. Noting that the program is in all respects voluntary, the court held that it does not violate constitutionally protected rights, either by interfering with parental rights to control the upbringing of their children or with the families' free exercise of their religion. The court concluded that "[p]arents have no right to tailor public school programs to meet their individual religious or moral preferences."[133] The court also rejected the reasoning of the *Alfonso* decision on the issue of whether providing condoms is a medical service.

In another case, *Parents United for Better Schools v. School District,*[134] Philadelphia's condom distribution program was upheld against challenge. That program does allow for parental opt-out; as a result, the court ruled that parents lacked standing to challenge it. On appeal, however, that ruling was reversed and the case remanded.[135] The court held that although the parents could and, in fact, did elect to prevent their teenage children from participating in the condom distribution program, they nevertheless had standing to challenge the program's reliance on the participation of teenagers on the basis of their parent's tacit as proposed to express consent. Without defining the scope of the parental right to provide an express consent in advance of a minor child's receiving medical treatment, or the precise application of that right to this case, the court concluded that Pennsylvania law recognizes such a right. Because the parents challenging the condom distribution policy were asserting that right, the court found that they did indeed have standing to challenge it. A dissenting opinion argued that because the parents challenging the policy had already obtained the only relief to which there were entitled (preventing their children from receiving condoms by failing to expressly consent), the only remedy available to them would be to limit the access of other parents' teenagers to the condoms, a form of relief to which they were not, in the dissent's view, entitled.

ACCESS TO HEALTH CARE AND OTHER SERVICES

§ 2.8 Ryan White Comprehensive AIDS Resources Emergency Act

Federal legislative attention to the AIDS epidemic has found its most focussed and positive response in one piece of legislation: the Ryan White Comprehensive

---

[133] 652 N.E.2d at 589.

[134] 25 Phila. 27 (P.A. Common Pleas Ct. 1993).

[135] 646 A.2d 689 (Pa. Commw. Ct. 1994).

AIDS Resources Emergency (CARE) Act of 1990.[136] The CARE Act is dedicated to the memory of the 70,000 persons who had lost their lives to AIDS as of the date of the law's enactment in 1990 and to the memory of Ryan White, who died on April 8, 1990, after living with AIDS for six years, from the age of 13.[137] The CARE Act was initially authorized for five years and was amended and extended for another five years in 1996.[138]

The CARE Act establishes an HIV Health Care Services Program "to provide emergency assistance to localities that are disproportionately affected" by the epidemic and to fund states and other public or private nonprofit entities "to provide for the development, organization, coordination and operation of more effective and cost efficient systems for the delivery of essential services to individuals and families with HIV disease."[139]

Funding Structure.   As originally enacted in 1990, the CARE Act was divided into four titles. Title I (the Emergency Relief grants program) provided emergency relief for areas with substantial need: eligible metropolitan areas (EMAs) with 2,000 or more cases of AIDS or per capita incidence of cumulative cases of not less than 0.00025.[140] Initially, the funding formula relied on cases reported by June 30, 1990, for fiscal year 1991, then as of March 31 of the most recent fiscal year for which data is available for a grant in any subsequent fiscal year.

This funding structure was criticized and was modified by the 1996 amendments. In 1995, for example, the General Accounting Office (GAO) undertook a review of the CARE Act Title I and II funding structure and concluded that the formulas resulted in funding inequity insofar as they resulted in significant per-case variations in funding that were not attributable to differences in cost of care.[141] The GAO attributed this finding primarily to the fact that EMA's AIDS cases are double counted, once under Title I for medical services and again under Title II for state medical and other services. A state that did not have an EMA, for example, received disproportionately less funding than a state that had an EMA. Additionally, Title I funding took into account the EMA's cumulative number of reported AIDS cases, even though as many as 60 percent of those individuals had died. The formula thus favored EMAs that were earliest affected

---

[136] Pub. L. No. 101-381, 1990 U.S.C.C.A.N. (104 Stat.) 576, principally adding to the Public Health Service Act a new Title XXVI (codified at 42 U.S.C. §§ 300ff, 300ff-1, 300ff-11–18, 300ff-21–29, 300ff-41–55, 300ff-61–67 (1994)).

[137] Rep. No. 273, 101st Cong., 2d Sess. 1–2, *reprinted in* 1990 U.S.C.C.A.N. 862, 862–63.

[138] Ryan White CARE Act Amendments of 1996, Pub. L. No. 104-146, 1996 U.S.C.C.A.N. (110 Stat.) 1346. Generally, the amendments were effective October 1, 1996, although some provisions, such as those pertaining to perinatal transmission of HIV, were effective upon enactment. *Id.* § 13, 1996 U.S.C.C.A.N. (110 Stat.) 1346, 1374.

[139] 42 U.S.C. § 300ff (1994).

[140] *Id.* § 300ff-11.

[141] General Accounting Office, Ryan White CARE Act of 1990: Opportunities to Enhance Funding Equity 2 (GAO/HEHS-96-26, 1995).

by AIDS, but other areas that may have had more recent increases in cases received less funding.

In 1996, these concerns were addressed when Title I was amended to eliminate the per capita incidence and total cumulative case count requirement for EMAs.[142] Instead, a five-year cumulative total is used, combined with the original requirement that the EMA have at least 2,000 reported AIDS cases. New grants are available only to cities with a population of 500,000 or more, although cities receiving funds under the original formula are grandfathered. Grantees funded under the original formula will lose no more than 5 percent of their funding over the five years following the 1996 amendment. The formula for determining grant amounts was also modified in 1996 to use a distribution factor based on the estimated number of individuals living with AIDS; the estimate is based on a 10-year weighted case count intended to reflect the rate of mortality.[143]

CARE Act Title I funding is directed to the "chief elected official of the city or urban county that administers the public health agency that provides outpatient and ambulatory services to the greatest number of individuals with AIDS."[144] Agreements reached with political subdivisions must have not less than 10 percent of the number of such cases reported for the EMA.

Health Service Planning Councils. Title I establishes HIV health services planning councils,[145] which include representatives of health care providers, community-based and AIDS service organizations, social service providers, mental health care providers, local public health agencies, hospital planning agencies or health care planning agencies, affected communities (including individuals with HIV disease), nonelected community leaders, state government, public and nonprofit private entities that provide early intervention services,[146] and the lead agency of any health resources and services administration adult and pediatric HIV-related care demonstration project operating in the EMA. The planning council establishes priorities for the allocation of funds within the EMA, develops a comprehensive plan for health services,[147] and assesses the "efficiency of the administrative mechanism in rapidly allocating funds to the areas of greatest need within the eligible area, and at the discretion of the planning council . . . the effectiveness . . . of the services offered in meeting the identified

---

[142] Pub. L. No. 104-146, § 3, 1996 U.S.C.C.A.N. (110 Stat.) 1346, 1346–47, *amending* 42 U.S.C. § 300ff-11.

[143] Pub. L. No. 104-146, § 4, 1996 U.S.C.C.A.N. (110 Stat.) 1346, 1364–65, *amending* 42 U.S.C. § 300ff-13(a)(3).

[144] 42 U.S.C. § 300ff-12(a)(1).

[145] *Id.* § 300ff-12(b), *amended by* Pub. L. No. 104-146, § 3, 1996 U.S.C.C.A.N. (110 Stat.) 1346, 1347–48.

[146] 42 U.S.C. § 300ff-51, referencing entities described in § 300ff-52.

[147] *Id.* § 300ff-12(b)(4)(B), *amended by* Pub. L. No. 104-146, § 3(b)(1)(D), 1996 U.S.C.C.A.N. (110 Stat.) 1346, 1348, *referencing* 42 U.S.C. § 300ff-14.

needs."[148] The planning council's priorities must be followed in the allocation of funds by the political subdivision.[149] Thus, the original design of the HIV planning councils institutionalized a conflict of interest insofar as grantees were represented on the body charged with identifying funding priorities. This issue was addressed in the renewal of the CARE Act in 1996. The HIV planning council provisions were amended to add specified representatives and require that the composition of the councils reflect the demographics of the area, to clarify the factors to be used in establishing funding priorities, to avoid conflicts of interest and establish a grievance procedure (model procedures are to be developed by the secretary of Health and Human Services), and to require participation in a statewide coordinated statement of need.[150]

Distribution of Title I Grants.   One-half of Title I grants are distributed by a formula, one-half on a competitive application basis.[151] The grant formula uses both the EMA's cumulative reported number of AIDS cases and the cumulative AIDS incidence rate. Grants are intended for the primary purposes of both outpatient and inpatient care and support services, including case management services. The 1996 amendments specifically include substance abuse treatment and mental health treatment, as well as "treatment education and prophylactic treatment for opportunistic infections" among the treatment services.[152]

Distribution of Title II Grants.   Title II (the CARE Grant program) grants are made to states upon application.[153] Title II grants, like those under Title I, are distributed according to a formula. As originally enacted, the Title II formula used the number of AIDS cases reported in the two most recent fiscal years and the per capita income for the state. The Title II distribution formula was amended in 1996. As a result, distribution of Title II grants is based on a 10-year weighted case count, used to calculate two distribution factors, one for the state (weighted at 80 percent) and one for the state's non-EMA case count (weighted at 20 percent).[154] Because the new formula resulted in a transfer of funds among states, the resulting funding losses are capped so as not to exceed

---

[148] *Id.* § 300ff-12(b)(4)(C), *amended by* Pub. L. No. 104-146, § 3(b)(1)(C), 1996 U.S.C.C.A.N. (110 Stat.) 1346, 1347.

[149] *Id.* § 300ff-14(a); Pub. L. No. 104-146, § 3(b)(3)(C), 1996 U.S.C.C.A.N. (110 Stat.) 1346, 1351 (codified at 42 U.S.C. § 300ff-13(c)) (requiring compliance with planning council priorities for preceding year as condition for continued funding).

[150] Pub. L. No. 104-146, § 3(b), 1996 U.S.C.C.A.N. (110 Stat.) 1346, 1347–50, *amending* 42 U.S.C. § 300ff-12(b).

[151] 42 U.S.C. § 300ff-13(a)(3).

[152] Pub. L. No. 104-146, § 3(b)(4), 1996 U.S.C.C.A.N. (110 Stat.) 1346, 1347–50, *amending* 42 U.S.C. § 300ff-14(b).

[153] 42 U.S.C. § 300ff-27.

[154] Pub. L. No. 104-146, § 5, 1996 U.S.C.C.A.N. (110 Stat.) 1346, 1365–66, *amending* 42 U.S.C. § 300ff-28(b).

5 percent, and the 5 percent is to be phased in over five years. As originally enacted, Title II funded Special Projects of National Significance, up to 10 percent of the Title II funds subject to formula distribution;[155] those grants are now made under Title V.[156]

The degree of access to CARE Act services by traditionally underserved populations has been a significant concern[157] and was addressed by several of the 1996 amendments. For example, the amendments require that Title I and II grantees set aside a portion of their funding for health and support services for women, children, and infants equivalent to the ratio of such persons with AIDS to the general population of persons with AIDS within the state.[158] This funding set-aside includes among its purposes the prevention of perinatal transmission of HIV.

Funding of Title III Grants.   Title IIIa of the CARE Act, which provides early intervention grants to states, has never been funded. Title IIIb provides categorical grants for early intervention services to be provided by migrant health centers, community health centers, health care providers for the homeless, family planning clinics, comprehensive hemophilia diagnostic and treatment centers, federally qualified health centers under the Social Security Act,[159] and nonprofit private entities that provide comprehensive primary care services to populations at risk for HIV disease.[160] Equitable allocation of funds among urban and rural areas is required. Early intervention services include HIV counseling and testing (counseling requirements are included in the CARE Act[161]), including diagnosis of the extent of the deficiency in the immune system to determine therapeutic interventions, referrals to other CARE Act-funded agencies, experimental treatment facilities, community based organizations, or grantees providing services for pediatric patients funded pursuant to 42 U.S.C. § 300ff-71.

---

[155] 42 U.S.C. § 300ff-28(a).

[156] Pub. L. No. 104-146, § 3(g), 1996 U.S.C.C.A.N. (110 Stat.) 1346, 1362–64 (codified at 42 U.S.C. § 300ff-101).

[157] *See* General Accounting Office, Ryan White CARE Act: Access to Services by Minorities, Women, and Substance Abusers (GAO/HEHS-95-49, 1995). A series of HRSA-sponsored work group reports also address this issue: HIV/AIDS Work Group on Health Care Access Issues for Women (DHHS Pub. No. HRSA-RD-SP-93-7); HIV/AIDS Work Group on Health Care Access Issues for African Americans (DHHS Pub. No. HRSA-94-023); HIV/AIDS Work Group on Health Care Access Issues for Hispanic Americans (DHHS Pub. No. HRSA-RD-SP-93-8); HIV/AIDS Work Group on Health Care Access Issues for American Indians/ Alaska Natives (DHHS Pub. No. HRSA-RD-SP-93-7).

[158] Pub. L. No. 104-146, § 3(b)(4)(C), 1996 U.S.C.C.A.N. (110 Stat.) 1346, 1351 (codified at 42 U.S.C. § 300ff-14(b)(3) (Title I amendment)); Pub. L. No. 104-146, § 3(c)(1), 1996 U.S.C.C.A.N. (110 Stat.) 1346, 1353 (codified at 42 U.S.C. § 300ff-21(b) (Title II amendment)).

[159] 42 U.S.C. § 1396d(1)(2)(B).

[160] *Id.* § 300ff-51.

[161] *Id.* § 300ff-62.

Titles IV and V Grants.   The 1996 amendments modified Title IV and added a new Title V. Title IV provides grants to primary health care providers to enhance opportunities for women, infants, children, and youth to voluntarily participate as subjects in research of potential clinical benefit. For the third or subsequent fiscal year for which an applicant seeks funding under Title IV, the applicant must assure that a significant number of these individuals who are patients of the applicant are participating in research projects. If the applicant is temporarily unable to comply with this requirement, a waiver is available from the secretary of Health and Human Services under limited circumstances.

Title V provides for grants for Special Projects of National Significance (SPNS), which previously had been included in Title II. SPNS fund special programs for the care and treatment of individuals with HIV disease in specifically defined areas. These include delivery of HIV health care and support services to underserved populations, such as persons in rural communities, adolescents, Native Americans, homeless individuals and families, hemophiliacs, and incarcerated individuals. The 1996 amendments also included the AIDS Education and Training Center program and AIDS Dental Reimbursement Program, which are funded as separate programs under Title V.[162]

§ 2.9 —Testing of Pregnant Women and Newborns

Perhaps the most controversial aspect of the CARE Act renewal process in 1996 was the proposal to include mandatory HIV testing for pregnant women and newborn children. As noted in **Chapter 1,** providing antiretroviral therapy during pregnancy has been shown in some studies to reduce perinatal transmission of HIV and thus has been recommended for pregnant women with HIV. HIV testing is seen as a prerequisite to making this treatment option available. Previously, a bill addressing this issue, the Newborn Infant HIV Notification Act,[163] was introduced in Congress but not passed. Instead, the enactment of the CARE Act amendments emphasizes pre-test counseling and voluntary, as opposed to mandatory, HIV testing of pregnant women, consistent with the CDC's recommendations.[164] The statement of congressional findings concludes that "routine HIV counseling and voluntary testing of pregnant women should become the standard of care."[165] In effect, however, the threatened loss of federal CARE grant funding may frequently result in testing under circumstances that are not fully voluntary or testing on a mandatory basis.

---

[162] Pub. L. No. 104-146, § 3(h), 1996 U.S.C.C.A.N. (110 Stat.) 1346, 1363 (to be codified at 42 U.S.C. § 300ff-111(e) (AIDS Education and Training Centers)).

[163] H.R. 1289, 104th Cong., 1st Sess. (1995).

[164] CDC, *U.S. Public Health Service Recommendations for Human Immunodeficiency Virus Counseling and Voluntary Testing for Pregnant Women,* 44 MMWR 1 (RR-7, 1995).

[165] Pub. L. No. 104-146, § 7(a)(7)(A), 1996 U.S.C.C.A.N. (110 Stat.) 1346, 1368.

The CARE Act amendments required that in order to receive CARE Act funding for HIV counseling and testing, states must have certified to the secretary of Health and Human Services by September 1996 that they adopted the CDC recommendations for HIV counseling and voluntary testing for pregnant women.[166] Additionally, Congress authorized $10 million per year from 1996 to 2000 to assist states in implementing the guidelines, providing outreach efforts to pregnant women at high risk for HIV, and making voluntary HIV testing available. States that have the "greatest proportion of HIV seroprevalence among child bearing women" are given priority in the awarding of grants.[167]

Congress then mandated that the CDC, in consultation with the states, develop a reporting system by September 1996 to determine the rate of new cases of perinatal transmission and the possible causes, such as inadequacy of the counseling available to women during pregnancy. The Department of Health and Human Services is then required to consult with the Institute of Medicine, evaluate the problem of perinatal transmission, and report to Congress by May 1998. By September 1998, the secretary of Health and Human Services must determine whether mandatory testing of infants born to women who have not undergone prenatal testing has become a routine practice. If the secretary determines that mandatory infant testing has become routine, then states have 18 months (until March 2000) to demonstrate: (1) a 50 percent reduction in rate of perinatal transmission compared to 1993 rates; (2) at least 95 percent of women who have received at least two prenatal visits with a health care provider have been tested for HIV; or (3) a program of mandatory testing of all newborns whose mothers have not undergone prenatal HIV testing. If a state cannot meet one of these three conditions, the state loses its CARE grant (Title II) funding.[168] States that have mandatory newborn testing requirements must also require that health insurers not discontinue insurance solely as a result of the insured's HIV status.[169]

§ 2.10 —Funding Restrictions and
Miscellaneous Provisions

The CARE Act, as amended, includes several funding restrictions, as well as several miscellaneous provisions that are not directly related to the purpose of the Act. First, as originally enacted, CARE Act funds may not be used for syringe exchange programs.[170] Additionally, the 1996 amendments require that

---

[166] Pub. L. No. 104-146, § 7, 1996 U.S.C.C.A.N. (110 Stat.) 1346, 1369 (codified at 42 U.S.C. § 300ff-____).

[167] *Id.,* 1996 U.S.C.C.A.N. (110 Stat.) 1346, 1369 (codified at 42 U.S.C. § 300ff-33(c)(3)).

[168] *Id.,* 1996 U.S.C.C.A.N. (110 Stat.) 1346, 1370 (codified at 42 U.S.C. § 300ff-34(e)(2)).

[169] *Id.,* § 7, 1996 U.S.C.C.A.N. (110 Stat.) 1346, 1372 (codified at 42 U.S.C. § 300ff-37).

[170] *Id.* § 300ff-1 (prohibiting use of funds to provide individuals with "hypodermic needles or syringes so that such individuals may use illegal drugs"). Limitations on funding for syringe exchange programs are discussed in **§ 2.12.**

CARE Act funds may not be used to fund programs or materials "designed to promote or encourage, directly or indirectly, intravenous drug use or sexual activity, whether heterosexual or homosexual."[171]

Although not directly related to its purpose, the CARE Act, as originally enacted, required the secretary of Health and Human Services to develop a list of potentially life-threatening infectious diseases to which emergency response employees (EREs) may be exposed in responding to emergencies.[172] The 1996 amendments added funeral-service practitioners to the definition of ERE.[173] HIV is included on the secretary's list. The CARE Act then sets forth a process by which EREs at risk for exposure may seek to obtain information about the infectious status of the emergency victim. That provision of the CARE Act is covered in more detail in **Chapter 3.**

The 1996 amendments include several additional miscellaneous provisions. In order to be eligible for CARE grant funding, states must "take administrative or legislative action to require a good faith effort to notify the spouse of a known HIV-infected patient that such spouse may have been exposed to [HIV] and should seek testing."[174] The scope of this provision is potentially far-reaching, given that the definition of *spouse* includes not just the current marriage partner but also any person who was the infected individuals's marriage partner at any time within 10 years prior to the diagnosis of HIV infection. Although acceptable means of compliance with this provision are not set forth, the Conference Committee's joint explanatory statement emphasizes that it is not to be construed to require states to adopt HIV name reporting.[175] Modification of this provision in conference also indicates that it is not intended to require disclosure of the identity of the infected patient, although, obviously, in many cases the spouse will be able to infer the identity of the individual who has placed him or her at risk for infection.

Next, federal employees are guaranteed the right to refuse to participate in AIDS education programs in the workplace, unless the educational program is necessary to protect their health and safety.[176]

Finally, total federal AIDS and HIV activity funding cannot exceed the total amounts expended for activities related to cancer in any fiscal year.[177]

---

[171] Pub. L. No. 104-146, § 10, 1996 U.S.C.C.A.N. (110 Stat.) 1346, 1373 (codified at 42 U.S.C. § 300ff-78).

[172] *Id.* §§ 300ff-81 to -90.

[173] Pub. L. No. 104-146, § 12(a), 1996 U.S.C.C.A.N. (110 Stat.) 1346, 1373, *amending* 42 U.S.C. § 300ff-76(4).

[174] Pub. L. No. 104-146, § 8, 1996 U.S.C.C.A.N. (110 Stat.) 1346, 1372 (codified at 42 U.S.C. § 300ff-37).

[175] Conf. Rep. No. 545, 104th Cong., 2d Sess. 46–47, *reprinted in* 1996 U.S.C.C.A.N. 1021, 1034–35.

[176] Pub. L. No. 104-146, § 9, 1996 U.S.C.C.A.N. (110 Stat.) 1346, 1373.

[177] Pub. L. No. 104-146, § 11, 1996 U.S.C.C.A.N. (110 Stat.) 1346, 1373.

§ 2.11   Regulation of Medicinal Marijuana

AIDS treatments, like zidovudine (ZDV), frequently produce severe nausea as side effects. Some interest has been expressed in making marijuana available on a medically approved basis to counteract these side effects. Federal government opposition to marijuana's availability has caused some researchers to label marijuana the "forbidden medicine."[178] Ironically, opposition to its medicinal use is frequently based on the lack of scientific evidence regarding its safety and efficacy. But attempts to undertake research on whether marijuana has medicinal properties have also been opposed on the basis that there is no evidence of marijuana's effectiveness as a medicine. Whether medicinal use of marijuana should even be studied in clinical trials has thus engendered debate.[179]

Since 1970, marijuana has been listed on Schedule I of the Controlled Substances Act.[180] Drugs on Schedule I, the most restrictive classification, are available only on approval by the Food and Drug Administration (FDA) for restricted research protocols. Reclassification to Schedule II would permit physicians to prescribe marijuana more generally for medical purposes. Attempts to obtain a reclassification of marijuana have been unsuccessful.[181] In the latest chapter of this more than 20-year effort, *Alliance for Cannabis Therapeutics v. Drug Enforcement Administration,*[182] the Court of Appeals for the District of Columbia Circuit rejected arguments that the decision of the Drug Enforcement Administration (DEA) to deny reclassification was biased and ignored the record evidence of marijuana's medicinal value. Instead, the court concluded that the denial was based on substantial evidence of record. Previously, the Public Health Service's single-patient investigational new drug program, which was created in 1976 to provide patient access to marijuana, was closed to new applicants in 1991. The number of applicants had significantly increased as AIDS patients sought access.[183] In response, cannabis buyers clubs have sprung up to make marijuana available to patients, similar to drug buyers' clubs, which make available medications not approved by the FDA.

---

[178] The medical uses for marijuana, including treatment of certain aspects of HIV illness, are discussed at length in Lester Grinspoon & James B. Bakalar, Marihuana: The Forbidden Medicine 85–92 (1993).

[179] Richard Doblin & Mark Kleiman, *The Medical Use of Marijuana: The Case for Clinical Trials, and* Richard H. Schwartz & Eric A. Voth, *Marijuana as Medicine: Making a Silk Purse out of a Sow's Ear,* 14 J. Addictive Diseases 5, 15 (1995); Lester Grinspoon & James B. Bakalar, *Marijuana as Medicine: A Plea for Reconsideration,* 273 JAMA 1875 (1995).

[180] 21 U.S.C. § 812 (1994). For a more detailed discussion of the legal status of marijuana, see generally Richard Glan Boire, Marijuana Law (2d ed. 1996).

[181] *See* 57 Fed. Reg. 10,499 (1992) (final order of Drug Enforcement Administrator denying reclassification).

[182] 15 F.3d 1131, 1133 (D.C. Cir. 1994).

[183] *See* Paul Cotton, *Government Extinguishes Marijuana Access, Advocates Smell Politics,* 267 JAMA 2573 (1992).

A synthetic version of cannabis' active agent (tetrahydrocannabinol), which does not provide a psychoactive high and is administered orally, has been approved by the FDA for marketing under the clinical name "dronabinol" and is sold under the trade name "Marinol." In 1986, the DEA rescheduled this synthetic to Schedule II. Some studies have shown that dronabinol is effective in treating weight loss caused by HIV illness.[184]

Beginning in 1992, Donald Abrams, a researcher at the University of California, San Francisco, attempted for several years to undertake a pilot clinical study of the efficacy of marijuana as an appetite stimulant for AIDS patients with HIV-related anorexia and weight loss. The proposed study would have compared the effects of smoked marijuana with those of dronabinol. Although the study protocol was accepted by the FDA and the sponsoring institution's review board, the National Institute on Drug Abuse, which has marijuana available for research purposes, refused to provide the marijuana or approve the use of marijuana from other sources.[185]

Criminal prosecution of persons with HIV disease for possession of marijuana or others for distributing marijuana to individuals with serious illnesses are occasionally reported.[186] In several cases, defendants have successfully offered medical necessity defenses. For example, when Kenneth and Barbara Jenks were prosecuted for backyard marijuana growing, they argued, with their physician's support, that there was no effective treatment for their nausea, which was so severe that it threatened their lives if left untreated.[187] They started using marijuana after a member of their AIDS support group recommended it. They grew their own because they did not want to have to purchase it on the street. The Florida District Court of Appeals, clearly sympathetic to their plight, recognized a common law medical necessity defense and set aside their convictions.

In another medical necessity case, a Maryland trial court granted the defendant's motion for allowance to present a medical necessity defense to the jury.[188]

---

[184] See J.E. Beal et al., *Dronabinol as a Treatment for Anorexia Associated with Weight Loss in Patients with AIDS,* 10 J. Pain & Symptom Management 89 (1995); T.F. Plasse et al., *Recent Clinical Experience with Dronabinol,* 40 Pharmacology, Biochem. & Behav. 695 (1991).

[185] Eric Bailey, *Politics Curbs Studies of Pot as Medicine, Scientists Say,* L.A. Times, Oct. 30, 1996, at A1; Peter Gwynne, *Trials of Marijuana's Medical Potential Languish as Government Just Says No,* Scientist, Nov. 27, 1995, at 1; Rick Doblin, *AIDS Wasting Syndrome Protocol Update,* Bull. Multidisciplinary Ass'n for Psychedelic Stud., Spring 1996, at 67; id., *Medical Marijuana—AIDS Wasting Syndrome Research: The Latest Obstacle,* Bull. Multidisciplinary Ass'n for Psychedelic Stud., Autumn 1995, at 43.

[186] See Tim Golden, *Agents Crack Down on Marijuana Buying Club,* N.Y. Times, Aug. 8, 1996, at A8 (describing raid of Cannabis Buyers' Club of San Francisco by California state attorney general after federal and local law enforcement officials declined prosecution); *Prohibition of Marijuana Prescriptions Will Be Tested in Ohio,* N.Y. Times, Sept. 17, 1995, at 29 (describing arrest of cancer patient with 30 pounds of marijuana intended for use by other patients).

[187] Jenks v. State, 582 So. 2d 676 (Fla. Dist. Ct. App.), *review denied,* 589 So. 2d 292 (Fla. 1991).

[188] State v. Mensch, Crim. No. 94-07 (Md. Cir. Ct. Charles County Feb. 7, 1995) (opinion and order).

The defendant had been charged with manufacture and possession of marijuana. In its opinion granting the motion, the court noted that the defendant testified that he had AIDS and suffered from wasting syndrome resulting from antiviral treatments, but that using marijuana improved his health and enabled him to remain employed. His physician testified that he believed that Marinol was less effective than marijuana and had side effects not caused by marijuana.

In a New York case, a misdemeanor charge for distributing marijuana for medical purposes was conditionally dismissed by the prosecutor, the court noting that the dismissal indicated that the defendant "should not be held criminally liable" since he intended to distribute the marijuana for medical purposes and not for his personal profit.[189] In another case involving a defendant with HIV, a medical necessity defense resulted in a California jury's acquitting a defendant of two felony charges arising from his cultivation of his own marijuana for medical purposes.[190]

In 1996, voters in California and Arizona approved referendum provisions that make marijuana available for medical purposes by physician prescription. In California, Proposition 215 amended the state's crimes code provisions on possession and cultivation of marijuana[191] to exempt from prosecution any "patient, or . . . patient's primary caregiver, who possesses or cultivates marijuana for the personal medical purposes of the patient upon the written or oral recommendation or approval of a physician."[192] Proposition 215 specifically referenced availability of marijuana to treat AIDS, among other illnesses, as the purpose for its enactment. In Arizona, Proposition 200 provided that "any medical doctor licensed to practice in Arizona may prescribe a controlled substance included in schedule I [of the Arizona Controlled Substance Act] to treat a disease, or to relieve the pain and suffering of a seriously ill patient or a terminally ill patient."[193] Before prescribing marijuana, or any other controlled substance, the physician must document that scientific research exists that supports its use in treatment, obtain a written opinion from another physician that the prescription is appropriate, and obtain the patient's written consent. Receiving, possessing, or using a controlled substance prescribed by a physician is exempted from the Arizona criminal code, although the defendant bears the burden of proving that defense.[194]

In response to these voter initiatives, the federal government has threatened to exclude physicians who prescribe marijuana from participation in the Medicare

---

[189] State v. Moore, No. 96N066699 (Crim. Ct. N.Y. County Apr. 3, 1996, tr. at 3) (transcript on file with author).

[190] *Marijuana User Is Out of Prison,* N.Y. Times, Mar. 6, 1994, at 32 (AP rep.).

[191] Cal. Health & Safety Code §§ 11357, 11358.

[192] Cal. Prop. 215, Compassionate Use Act of 1996, § 1 (codified at Cal. Health & Safety Code § 11365.5(d)).

[193] Ariz. Prop. 200, Drug Medicalization, Prevention, and Control Act of 1996, § 7 (codified at Ariz. Rev. Stat. Ann. § 13-3412.01).

[194] *Id.* § 6 (codified at Ariz. Rev. Stat. Ann. § 13-3412.1.9).

and Medicaid programs and from the DEA registry that allows them to prescribe drugs, and in some cases to commence criminal prosecutions of physicians.[195]

§ 2.12   Syringe Exchange Programs

One of the best examples of how the AIDS epidemic has caused a reexamination of what previously seemed to be unchallengeable expectations about criminal law and public health policy is the development of syringe exchange programs in the United States. The sharing of what the National Commission on AIDS has referred to as "injection drug equipment" (paraphernalia that carry the potential for contamination and transmission through shared use: syringes, needles, "cookers," cotton and rinse water) has been recognized since the beginning of the epidemic as a means of HIV transmission. Syringe exchange programs have been characterized as one means of harm reduction, in which the programs seek to reduce the harm that can result from the risky behavior but do not attempt to impose a complete prohibition against the behavior as a means of eliminating the harm altogether.[196]

The problem of HIV infection through syringe sharing has grown to serious proportions. The National Commission on AIDS, citing CDC statistics, reported in 1991 that 32 percent of all adult and adolescent AIDS cases are related to injection drug use; 70 percent of all pediatric AIDS cases related to a mother at risk for HIV infection are directly related to the mother's exposure to HIV through injection drug use or sex with an injecting drug user; 71 percent of all female AIDS cases are linked directly or indirectly to injection drug use; 19 percent of male AIDS cases are directly linked to injection drug use; and an additional 7 percent of male AIDS cases are linked to both homosexual/bisexual contact and injection drug use. The National Commission on AIDS has also reported that in New York City alone, there are an estimated 200,000 injection drug users, half of whom are HIV-infected, but there are only 38,000 publicly funded treatment slots.[197] Minority communities are particularly hard-hit by drug use and HIV: African-Americans make up 28 percent and Hispanics 16 percent of all AIDS cases, but in cases attributed to injection drug use, African-Americans account for 45 percent and Hispanics 26 percent of the cases.

---

[195] *Doctors Given Federal Threat on Marijuana,* N.Y. Times, Dec. 31, 1996, at 1 (AP rep.); Eric Bailey, *Drug Czar Warns Doctors That U.S. Would Prosecute,* L.A. Times, Oct. 30, 1996, at A12; *see also* Christopher S. Wren, *Doctors Criticize Move Against State Measures,* N.Y. Times, Dec. 31, 1996, at D18.

[196] *See* Don C. Des Jarlais, *Editorial: Harm Reduction—A Framework for Incorporating Science into Drug Policy,* 85 Am. J. Pub. Health 10 (1995).

[197] National Comm'n on AIDS, Report: The Twin Epidemics of Substance Use and HIV 4–5 (1991).

Epidemiological data for 1994 showed a dramatic change in the direction of the epidemic in regard to drug users. Although half of the persons diagnosed with AIDS in 1993 (individuals infected in the early or mid-1980s) were gay males, little more than a quarter were intravenous drug users; fewer than 10 percent were heterosexuals. In 1994, however, nearly three-quarters of the 40,000 new infections with HIV in 1994 were among addicts, half of which were among drug users who share needles. This trend has continued. By the end of 1995, injecting-drug use was the second most frequently reported risk behavior for HIV infection, and 36 percent of AIDS cases reported to the CDC were directly or indirectly attributed to injecting drug use.[198]

In addition to recommending the removal of legal barriers to the "purchase and possession of injection equipment," the Commission has recommended expansion of drug treatment programs, focused federal leadership in addressing the issues of drug use and HIV, increased funding of research and epidemiologic studies of drug use and HIV transmission, and led "a serious and sustained attack" by all levels of government and the private sector "on the social problems that promote licit and illicit drug use in American society."[199]

Programs that advocate for and provide sterile needles or syringes (both activities are referred to here as *syringe exchange*) have resulted. Typically, these programs require the user to return a used syringe or needle in order to obtain a sterile one. Advocates for syringe exchange programs have identified several reasons to support them, including the need to save lives through timely intervention, the fact that the exchange programs are far less costly than the cost of treating a person once he or she becomes infected, and the fact that the programs frequently provide one of the few effective means of public health outreach to injecting drug users and can serve as a means of getting addicted drug users into treatment programs.[200]

It is not clear that alternative prevention strategies are more effective. The effort to end drug use through treatment or for users to use only sterile syringes was strengthened, for example, by findings that the use of bleach to clean syringes is not as effective as once thought. In one study, no difference was found between injecting drug users who used disinfectants and those who did

---

[198] CDC, *AIDS Associated with Injecting-Drug Use—United States, 1995,* 45 MMWR 392 (1996).

[199] National Comm'n on AIDS, Report: The Twin Epidemics of Substance Use and HIV (1991).

[200] *See, e.g.,* Tracey Hooker, State Legislative Representative of the Nat'l Conference of State Legislators, Getting to the Point: HIV, Drug Abuse and Syringe Exchange in the United States (1992); Gostin, *The Needle-Borne HIV Epidemic: Causes and Public Health Responses,* 9 Behav. Sci. & L. 287 (1991); Gostin, *The Interconnected Epidemics of Drug Dependency and HIV,* 26 Harv. C.R.-C.L. L. Rev. 113 (1991). Syringe exchange programs have also been reviewed from a variety of perspectives in The Kaiser Forums, Dimensions of HIV Prevention: Needle Exchange (Jeff Stryker & Mark Smith eds., 1993).

not. Public health authorities now recommend that full-strength bleach be used by injecting drug users who have no other option but to reuse or share a needle and syringe.[201] Another recent study concludes that injecting drug users do not consistently use bleach to clean shared drug injection equipment.[202]

Syringe exchange programs have been criticized on several grounds.[203] First, insofar as they are viewed as receiving the government's endorsement, they appear to officially condone illicit drug use, and may even encourage an increase in illicit drug use, contrary to the government's commitment against such activities. Syringe exchange programs are also viewed as being ineffective in changing syringe-sharing behavior. Given limitations on resources, syringe exchange funding is questioned, because that funding could go directly to rehabilitation programs or other services. Finally, syringe exchange programs are viewed as bringing criminal law standards into contempt, insofar as federal or state laws are viewed as criminalizing the activities of such programs.

In April 1995, a national survey undertaken by the North American Syringe Exchange Network found that 60 needle exchange programs operated in 21 states, an 82 percent increase over the 33 programs identified and surveyed in a federally supported 1993 study. The legal status of these programs was categorized as either *legal* (operating in a state that had no law requiring a prescription to purchase a hypodermic syringe or had an exemption to the state prescription law allowing operation of the program), *illegal-but-tolerated* (operating in a state that has a prescription law, but having received a vote of approval from a local elected body), or *illegal/underground* (operating in a state that has a prescription law and without support from local elected officials). Fifty-five percent of those surveyed reported that the program was legal; 32 percent were illegal-but-tolerated; 13 percent were illegal/underground. The programs reported distributing more than 8 million syringes during 1994. Additionally, 45 programs provided condoms, 23 provided HIV counseling and testing, 12 provided tuberculin skin testing, and 10 provided primary health care and directly observed tuberculosis therapy.[204]

---

[201] *See Use of Bleach for Disinfection of Drug Injection Equipment,* 42 MMWR 418 (1993) (summarizing bulletin issued in Apr. 1993 by National Institute of Drug Abuse).

[202] CDC, *Knowledge and Practices Among Injecting-Drug Users of Bleach Use for Equipment Disinfection—New York City, 1993,* 43 MMWR 439 (1994).

[203] *See generally* Nat'l Research Council & Inst. of Medicine, *Community Views, in* Preventing HIV Transmission: The Role of Sterile Needles and Bleach 103–42 (Jacques Normand et al. eds., 1995) (table 4.3 sets forth summary of community concerns); Sana Loue et al., *Ethical Issues Raised by Needle Exchange Programs,* 23 J. L. Med. & Ethics 382 (1995); Daniel Fernando, *Fundamental Limitations of Needle Exchange Programs as a Strategy for HIV Prevention Among IVDUs in the United States,* 6 AIDS & Pub. Pol'y J. 116 (1991); Maura O'Brien, *Needle Exchange Programs: Ethical and Policy Issues,* 4 AIDS & Pub. Pol'y J. 75 (1989); Harlon L. Dalton, *AIDS in Blackface,* 118 Daedalus 205, 209–10 (1989).

[204] CDC, *Syringe Exchange Programs—United States, 1994–1995,* 44 MMWR 684 (1995). For surveys, see Lawrence O. Gostin et al., *Prevention of HIV/AIDS and Other Blood-Borne Diseases Among Injection Drug Users: A National Survey on the Regulation of Syringes and Needles,* 277 JAMA 53 (1997); Scott Burris et al., *The Legal Strategies Used in Operating Syringe Exchange Programs in the United States,* 86 Am. J. Pub. Health 1163 (1996).

§ 2.13 —Federal Policies and Funding Restrictions

The federal government has withheld support for syringe exchange programs, principally by prohibiting the use of federal funds for such activities. The Ryan White Comprehensive AIDS Resources Emergency (CARE) Act of 1990 includes a prohibition against the use of funds appropriated under that Act to "provide individuals with hypodermic needles or syringes so that such individuals may use illegal drugs."[205] Amendments to the 1988 Health Omnibus Programs Extension Act prohibit the use of federal funds appropriated under it to "provide individuals with hypodermic needles or syringes so that such individuals may use illegal drugs," unless the surgeon general "determines that a demonstration needle exchange program would be effective in reducing drug abuse and the risk that the public will become infected" with HIV.[206] Similar restrictions have been contained in appropriations legislation. A prohibition against the use of funds for syringe exchanges unless the president certified that syringe exchange programs are effective in stopping the spread of HIV and do not encourage the use of illegal drugs was included in the Department of Labor, Health and Human Services, and Education and Related Agencies Appropriations Acts for 1990 and 1991,[207] although no such provision was included in the Appropriation Act for 1992. The Appropriations Act for 1993, however, included a provision that prohibits sterile needle distribution unless the surgeon general determines that such programs are effective in preventing the spread of HIV and do not promote illegal drug use,[208] except that such funds "may be used for such purposes in furtherance of demonstrations or studies authorized in the ADAMHA [Alcohol, Drug Abuse, and Mental Health Administration] Reorganization Act (P.L. 102-321)."[209] The requirement of certification by the surgeon general was then included in the Appropriations Acts for 1994 and 1995.[210] The Alcohol, Drug Abuse, and Mental Health Administration (ADAMHA) Reorganization Act, in turn, provides that grants may be made "to conduct outreach activities to [drug abusers] regarding the prevention of exposure to and the transmission of [HIV], and to encourage the individuals to seek treatment for such abuse."[211] In a 1993 report, the General Accounting Office concluded that this provision of the ADAMHA Reorganization Act would allow the Department of Health and

---

[205] 42 U.S.C. § 300ff-1 (1994).

[206] *Id.* § 300ee-5.

[207] *See* Pub. L. No. 101-166, § 520, 1989 U.S.C.C.A.N. (103 Stat.) 1159, 1192; Pub. L. No. 101-517, § 513, 1990 U.S.C.C.A.N. (104 Stat.) 2190, 2222.

[208] In its 1995 report, the National Research Council specifically called for the surgeon general to make the determination necessary to rescind the prohibition against the use of federal funds under this statute. Nat'l Research Council & Inst. of Medicine, Preventing HIV Transmission: The Role of Sterile Needles and Bleach 7 (Jacques Normand et al. eds., 1995).

[209] Pub. L. No. 102-394, § 514, 1992 U.S.C.C.A.N. (106 Stat.) 1792, 1827.

[210] Pub. L. No. 103-112, § 506, 1993 U.S.C.C.A.N. (107 Stat.) 1082, 1113; Pub. L. No. 103-333, § 506, 1994 U.S.C.C.A.N. (108 Stat.) 2539, 2572.

[211] 42 U.S.C. § 290bb-3(b)(6) (1994).

Human Services "to conduct demonstration and research projects that could involve the provision of needles."[212]

Studies of syringe exchanges, including those funded by the federal government, have reached favorable conclusions regarding syringe exchange programs. In a federally supported report issued in October 1993, a panel of researchers concluded that syringe exchange programs are effective.[213] A 1993 report of the General Accounting Office also reviewed the results reported from syringe exchange programs, concluding that evidence supports the conclusion that syringe exchange programs are effective in several respects without increasing the use of injection drug equipment.[214] In New York City, an expanded syringe exchange program was termed a success even in early months of operation, given the large of number of addicts who participated in the program (5,000), positive changes in behavior (reduced sharing of needles, no increase in drug use), and referrals of participants to other service programs, such as HIV test sites and drug treatment programs.[215] More recently, the evaluation of a program in New York City resulted in preliminary findings of effectiveness after two of three years of study funded by the American Foundation for AIDS Research (AmFAR).[216]

Perhaps the most significant study of syringe exchange programs was that of the National Research Council, which released its book-length report in September 1995. The report's authors concluded that needle exchange programs would be an effective component of a comprehensive strategy to prevent transmission of HIV and other infectious diseases.[217] The report, mandated by congress in 1992,[218] specifically recommends that the surgeon general certify that federal funds be made available to support syringe exchange programs.[219]

---

[212] General Accounting Office, Needle Exchange Programs: Research Suggests Promise as an AIDS Prevention Strategy 4 (1993) (HRD-93-60).

[213] Peter Lurie et al., The Public Health Impact of Needle Exchange Programs in the United States and Abroad (1993) (study prepared for the Centers for Disease Control and Prevention). Copies of the panel's report are available from the CDC National AIDS Clearinghouse, 1-800-458-5231 (voice) or 1-800-243-7012 (TTD).

[214] General Accounting Office, Needle Exchange Programs: Research Suggests Promise as an AIDS Prevention Strategy (1993) (HRD-93-60).

[215] Mireya Navarro, *New York Needle Exchanges Called Surprisingly Effective,* N.Y. Times, Feb. 18, 1993, at A1.

[216] Felicia R. Lee, *Data Show Needle Exchange Curbs HIV Among Addicts,* N.Y. Times, Nov. 26, 1994, at A1 (noting other AmFAR-funded evaluation programs in Los Angeles, Chicago, and Austin, TX); *see also Clean Needles Slow AIDS,* N.Y. Times, Dec. 6, 1994, at A22 (editorial).

[217] Nat'l Research Council & Inst. of Medicine, Preventing HIV Transmission: The Role of Sterile Needles and Bleach (Jacques Normand et al. eds., 1995).

[218] Alcohol, Drug Abuse, and Mental Health Administration Reorganization Act, Pub. L. No. 102-321, § 706, 1992 U.S.C.C.A.N. (106 Stat.) 323, 439, *reprinted as note to* 42 U.S.C. § 285o-3 (1994).

[219] Nat'l Research Council & Inst. of Medicine, Preventing HIV Transmission: The Role of Sterile Needles and Bleach 7 (Jacques Normand et al. eds., 1995).

Despite the growing body of scientific evidence that needle exchange programs are effective and do not increase the use of illegal drugs, no action has been taken by federal officials to make federal funds available for syringe exchange programs other than on the experimental basis noted above.[220] On that point, President Clinton was criticized by his own Advisory Council on HIV/AIDS, which noted that "[f]ederal policy regarding needle-exchange programs is not consistent with current knowledge and understanding regarding the impact of such programs on HIV prevention efforts."[221] Researchers estimate that failure to adopt and publicly fund syringe exchange programs will result in 11,000 new cases of HIV infection by the end of the decade, an estimate that some researchers in this field regard as conservative.[222]

§ 2.14   —Federal and State Criminal Laws

Sale of sterile needles or syringes is criminalized under federal law,[223] and nine states and the District of Columbia criminalize the sale or transfer of needles without a prescription.[224] Numerous other states prohibit the possession of drug paraphernalia, including needles and syringes.[225]

The existence of state law prohibitions on syringe exchange activities has posed a major obstacle for needle exchange programs. Individuals, frequently volunteers, who staff the programs face prosecution for their activities; individuals who receive the needles face potential arrest going to or from needle exchange sites; and state or local government and foundation sources that might wish to support syringe exchange programs cannot, because their action would be directly or indirectly supporting criminal activities.

---

[220] In response to this governmental inaction, in March 1995 the Drug Policy Foundation, Washington, D.C., released copies of internal CDC reports not previously released to the public, which conclude that the benefits of needle exchange programs exceed the theoretical risks. Copies of the reports are available from the Drug Policy Foundation; 202-537-5005. *See also* John Schwartz, *Reports Back Needle Exchange Programs,* Wash. Post, Feb. 16, 1995, at A6.

[221] Presidential Advisory Council on HIV/AIDS, Progress Report: Implementation of Advisory Counsel Recommendations 36 (July 8, 1996).

[222] Amanda Bennett, *Needle-Swap Programs Spark Life-and-Death Debates,* Wall St. J., July 10, 1996 at B1; *see also* Wayne Hearn, *AIDS Researchers Hit U.S. Refusal on Needle Exchanges,* Am. Med. News, Feb. 2, 1996, at 8.

[223] 21 U.S.C. § 863 (1994).

[224] *See, e.g.,* Cal. Bus. & Prof. Code § 4143 (West 1990); Fla. Stat. § 893.147 (West 1994); Ga. Code Ann. § 16-13-32–32.2 (1996); N.Y. Pub. Health Law § 3381–3381a (McKinney 1993); 10 N.Y. Admin. Codes R. & Regs, ch. II, § 80.131–.133; 35 Pa. Cons. Stat. Ann. §§ 780-101 to -144 (1993); Pa. Code, ch. 49, § 27.18(s)(2); *cf.* Mass. Gen. Laws ch. 94C § 27(f) (West Supp. 1996) (exception for pilot syringe exchange program); R.I. Gen. Laws § 21-28-4.04(1)(c) (Michie Supp. 1996) (same).

[225] *E.g.,* Fla. Stat. § 893.147.

Individuals facing prosecution for their activities in regard to syringe exchange programs have been successful in obtaining acquittals in several cases by arguing a necessity defense, based on the theory that their actions in distributing needles avoids the greater harm of HIV transmission.[226] In *People v. Bordowitz*,[227] for example, prosecution of syringe exchange volunteers for possession of hypodermic syringes resulted in a judgment of acquittal. Similarly, in People v. *Cezar*,[228] possession charges were dismissed against an activist who displayed syringes at a demonstration held to call public attention to the problem posed by contaminated syringes.

The necessity defense was not available to the defendants in *Commonwealth v. Leno*[229] and their resulting convictions were affirmed. The Supreme Judicial Court of Massachusetts reasoned that the harm (transmission of HIV) the defendants sought to prevent was not sufficiently imminent to allow the defense. A concurring opinion agreed that the harm at issue was not imminent but expressed hope that the "overwhelming and uncontroverted expert evidence presented at trial describing the effectiveness of needle exchange programs in curbing the spread of AIDS will . . . indicate to the Legislature the importance of joining the vast majority of jurisdictions that have decriminalized possession and distribution of hypodermic syringes."[230]

Although staff of needle exchange programs have sometimes faced prosecution, an additional concern has been that addicts going to or coming from a needle exchange site would be harassed by arrest and prosecution, and the justification defense might not be successful for them as individual users of the prohibited paraphernalia. No such prosecutions have been reported. One case involving prosecution of a needle exchange participant in New York City, who was not in the vicinity of a needle exchange site resulted from the defendant's arrest for attempting to sell heroin to an undercover police officer.[231] When the heroin turned out to be fake, the transfer of heroin charge was dropped. Instead, the defendant was prosecuted for possessing the nine new hypodermic syringes, in their original packaging, that he had on his person at the time of his arrest. Although he was carrying a card indicating that he was a participant in the New York needle exchange program, the defendant's syringes were not those distributed by the needle exchange program, because they were not marked as such. The court refused to dismiss the indictment, noting that the New York regulation establishing the program did not extend to possession of syringes not distributed from the program. To dismiss the indictment, the court reasoned, would undermine public confidence in the needle exchange program itself, particularly

---

[226] *See* Scott Burris et al., *The Legal Strategies Used in Operating Syringe Exchange Programs in the United States,* 86 Am. J. Pub. Health 1161, 1162 (1996) (survey of reported and unreported prosecutions of syringe exchange workers showing nine cases of resulting in acquittal and two cases resulting in conviction).

[227] 588 N.Y.S.2d 507 (Crim Ct. N.Y. County 1991).

[228] 573 N.Y.S.2d 352 (N.Y. County Crim. Ct. 1991).

[229] 616 N.E.2d 453 (Mass. 1993).

[230] *Id.* at 457.

[231] People v. Monroe, 593 N.Y.S.2d 742 (Crim. Ct. New York County 1992).

because the activity that resulted in the defendant's arrest was not protected by the needle exchange regulation.

In *State v. Sorge,*[232] however, the New Jersey Superior Court denied the defendants' motion to dismiss charges on the basis that their conduct in distributing clean hypodermic needles was too trivial to warrant prosecution or that the legislature, in criminalizing the possession or distribution of needles, did not intend the statute to apply to such situations.

In June 1995, the California attorney general issued an opinion in response to the request of a California state assembly member on three questions pertaining to needle exchange programs under California law.[233] The opinion is significant in that it directly discusses several legal aspects of needle exchange programs. Although grounded on California law, the same conclusions may be reached under the laws of other states. First, the attorney general concluded that the operation of a needle exchange program by a local county would violate California criminal law standards, specifically the misdemeanor statute.[234] Although that statute provides an exception for distribution "except as authorized by law," that exception would not apply in terms of county law, because the state law would continue in effect. Next, the attorney general concluded that needle exchange programs would not be lawful even under a county's declaration of a public health emergency. The emergency declaration would not render the state law ineffective. Finally, the attorney general concluded that the necessity defense, even if it were a cognizable defense, would be inapposite, given the narrow definition of the defense under California law. The opinion advises that in addition to the needle exchange prohibition itself, any public official responsible for public moneys who appropriated funds for such programs could be prosecuted for the misuse of those funds. The opinion also notes that the California legislature twice adopted needle exchange pilot program laws, but they were vetoed by the governor. The opinion does not discuss the issue of law enforcement officials' and agencies' foregoing prosecution, an option potentially available under prosecutorial guidelines.

§ 2.15 —State and Local Public Health Responses

State legislatures and public health officials have responded to the issue of needle exchange in a number of different ways. Despite the general view that syringe exchange programs violate drug laws, however, it may be possible for many programs to function legally, based on interpretations of state or local public health laws.[235] In several states, programs have been started, with legislative

---

[232] 591 A.2d 1382 (N.J. Super. Ct. 1991).

[233] No. 94-1104, 95 C.D.O.S. 4555, 78 Ops. Cal. Atty. Gen. 171 (June 7, 1995).

[234] Cal. Health & Safety Code Ann. § 11364.7 (a) (West Supp. 1997).

[235] Scott Burris et al., *The Legal Strategies Used in Operating Syringe Exchange Programs in the United States,* 86 Am. J. Pub. Health 1161, 1164 (1996) (identifying 11 local governments that conduct syringe exchange programs under state and local law).

approval that obviates the risk of criminal prosecution.[236] Rhode Island, for example, provides a priority listing for drug treatment for persons with HIV infection.[237]

Connecticut has enacted a law allowing the purchase of up to 10 needles and syringes without a prescription; possession of up to 10 needles and syringes is also permitted.[238] Sixty percent of Connecticut's AIDS cases reported in 1992 are the result of injection drug use. A study undertaken in Hartford, Connecticut, after the law went into effect showed that needle and syringe sales in pharmacies increased significantly during the months following the change in the law. A survey of injection drug users after the law went into effect indicated that although there was fairly widespread knowledge regarding the availability of syringe and needle purchases without prescriptions in pharmacies, purchasing of syringes and needles occurred more frequently (59 percent) on the street than in pharmacies (41 percent). Reports of needle sharing activity remained unchanged for the period before and the period after the change in the law. Thirty-six percent of the survey participants reported at least one incident of needle sharing. A review of law enforcement personnel injury reports did not show any increase in the number of reported needle-stick injuries after the change in the law.[239] More recent studies have also confirmed that sales of syringes from pharmacies have increased,[240] and shared use of injection equipment has decreased.[241]

In New Jersey, the Governor's Advisory Council on AIDS recommended the state should develop syringe exchange programs regulated by the health department and amend its prescription law. New Jersey Governor Whitman, however, rejected the recommendation, stating that "[s]cientific theories regarding 'needle exchange' programs do not outweigh the longstanding legal, public policy and philosophical determinations embodied in [New Jersey's drug paraphernalia] Act."[242] In making its recommendation, the Governor's Advisory Council on AIDS noted that at year-end 1994, New Jersey ranked first among the states in its proportion of AIDS cases related to injection drug use.

---

[236] *See, e.g.,* Conn. Gen. Stat. §§ 19a-124 (West Supp. 1996) (authorizing syringe exchange program); Haw. Rev. Stat. tit. 19, §§ 325-111 to -117 (1993) (same); Mass. Gen. Laws ch. 111, § 215 (West 1996) (authorizing pilot program); R.I. Gen. Laws § 23-11-19 (same).

[237] R.I. Gen. Laws § 21-28-4.20(d) (Michie Supp. 1996).

[238] Conn. Gen. Stat. § 21a-65 (West 1994 & Supp. 1996).

[239] CDC, *Impact of New Legislation on Needle and Syringe Purchase and Possession—Connecticut, 1992,* 42 MMWR 145 (1993).

[240] Linda A. Valleroy et al., *Impact of Increased Legal Access to Needles and Syringes on Community Pharmacies' Needle and Syringe Sales—Connecticut, 1992–1993,* 10 J. Acquired Immune Deficiency Syndrome 73 (1995).

[241] Samuel L. Groseclose et al., *Impact of Increased Legal Access to Needles and Syringes on Practices of Injecting Drug Users and Police Officers—Connecticut, 1992–1993,* 10 J. Acquired Immune Deficiency Syndrome 82 (1995).

[242] *AIDS Council Recommendations on Needle Programs Opposed by Whitman,* 5 Health L. Rep. (BNA) 542 (1996).

In Washington, public health officials have been successful in starting a needle exchange program under existing public health statutes[243] that exempt public health officials from the criminal law provisions that would otherwise apply to such activities.

In a declaratory judgment action, the Washington Supreme Court upheld Spokane County's needle exchange program, which included one-for-one syringe exchange, provided condoms, bleach, and information on risk reduction for injecting drug users, and offered referrals for HIV testing and counselling as well as drug treatment programs.[244] Similar programs already in place in Tacoma and Seattle prompted the Washington attorney general to issue an opinion to the effect that drug paraphernalia distribution was illegal under Washington's criminal law. Washington criminalized both transfer and possession with intent to transfer hypodermic needles and syringes used for the purpose of injecting illicit drugs.[245] The court ruled that Washington's constitution, which reserves to local health authorities the authority to adopt health measures, combined with the Washington legislature's adoption of AIDS legislation that endorsed "intervention strategies . . . possibly including needle sterilization,"[246] established a bar to enforcement of the criminal laws.

In other states, legislation that would repeal prohibitions against exchange of needles has been introduced, although such reforms have not yet been enacted. In Los Angeles, a mayoral declaration of a state of emergency was intended to allow needle exchange programs to proceed without law enforcement interference, but local neighborhood groups placed needle distributors under citizens' arrest, and police said they had no choice but to arrest the distributors. The neighborhood groups were reportedly concerned that the exchange program attracted "derelicts."[247] Despite the general view that syringe exchange programs violate drug laws, however, it may be possible for many programs to function legally, based on interpretations of state or local public health laws.[248]

---

[243] Wash. Rev. Code Ann. § 69.50.506(c) (1985), § 70.24.400(3) (1992).

[244] Spokane County Health Dist. v. Brockett, 839 P.2d 324 (Wash. 1992).

[245] Wash. Rev. Code Ann. §§ 69.50.412(2), 69.50.102(a)(11) (1985).

[246] *Id.* § 70.24.400(3)(b)(v) (1992).

[247] *Citizen Arrests Challenge Needle Exchanges,* N.Y. Times, Sept. 18, 1994, at 38.

[248] Scott Burris et al., *The Legal Strategies Used in Operating Syringe Exchange Programs in the United States,* 86 Am. J. Pub. Health 1161, 1164 (1996) (identifying 11 local governments that conduct syringe exchange programs under state and local law).

CHAPTER 3

HIV/AIDS IN THE WORKPLACE

David W. Webber

§ 3.1   Introduction

The AIDS epidemic has had a profound and widespread effect on workplace policies and legal standards pertaining to employment throughout the United States. With U.S. Public Health Service estimates of the extent of the epidemic indicating significant rates of HIV infection among working-age individuals in this country,[1] few if any workplaces will remain untouched by this epidemic. As treatment of HIV illness becomes more widespread and effective, the number of persons with HIV infection in the work force will increase even more.

Review of the legal standards applicable to HIV in the workplace involves in many cases potentially overlapping and not necessarily consistent federal, state, and local legislation, regulations, and court decisions explicating nondiscrimination in employment standards. These standards range from general prohibitions against disability discrimination to HIV-specific nondiscrimination standards. Discrimination protection includes not just those diagnosed with AIDS, but frequently extends to a far broader class of individuals, including, in some cases, employees who associate with persons suspected of being HIV infected.

At the same time that employers are prohibited from acts of unlawful discrimination in employment decisionmaking, workplace policies must also comply with legal standards governing workplace safety issues resulting from the risk of occupational transmission of HIV. Employment of persons with HIV infection in certain occupations, such as that of a surgeon or dentist performing certain

---

[1] National Comm'n on AIDS, HIV/AIDS: A Challenge for the Workplace (1993); CDC, *HIV Prevalence, Projected AIDS Case Estimates,* 39 MMWR 110 (1990).

invasive procedures, has been controversial and presents special problems in formulating employment policies.

HIV information pertaining to employees is highly volatile. Employers may face claims for disclosing such information, particularly when specific HIV confidentiality provisions apply. Finally, common law wrongful discharge and related tort claims such as invasion of privacy may arise in the workplace affected by the epidemic.

Employers should formulate a workplace policy on HIV/AIDS, including an educational component to raise awareness of HIV transmission issues among employees. This would help to avoid workplace disruption resulting from co-workers' negative reactions to an employee with HIV infection, as well as avoid the potential liability that can result from uninformed decisionmaking.

§ 3.2   Public Health Policy and AIDS Employment Law

The development of AIDS nondiscrimination in employment standards has frequently relied on a rationale derived primarily from AIDS public health policy. Compliance with AIDS nondiscrimination legislation can be viewed as requiring employer participation in, and even enforcement of, an AIDS public health strategy. Thus, the public health strategy towards the epidemic is important background for understanding the development of AIDS employment law principles.

Formulation of appropriate policy in response to the AIDS epidemic has occasioned considerable public debate and controversy. Quite remarkably, however, a consensus has emerged among medical and public health authorities regarding an approach to fighting the epidemic.[2] First, to further the goal of stopping transmission of HIV, persons who are infected or at risk for infection need to obtain information about preventing HIV transmission. As a result of such education, persons with HIV infection know how to avoid transmission of the infection to others, and those not infected will know how they can avoid infection in the future. Linked with the public education strategy as a means of prevention is the utilization of HIV antibody testing, which, if undertaken with thorough pre- and post-test counselling, has a significant educational effect itself[3] and makes possible early treatment of the illness. Workplace policy should conform to and advance these objectives.

Because persons most at risk for infection should access testing and education services, two strategies ensure that they will select such programs: first, an

---

[2] For more detailed discussion of public health policy in relation to the AIDS epidemic and its politics, see **Ch. 2.**

[3] At least 35 states have adopted legislation requiring informed consent for HIV antibody testing, often requiring that testing include pre- and post-test counselling. See **App. A.**

assurance of confidentiality of the HIV information pertaining to them, and, second, in those instances when HIV status is disclosed to others, an assurance that the disclosure will not result in discrimination.[4] Obviously, those who think they may be HIV-infected have a strong disincentive to seek counselling, testing, or treatment if they are concerned that the information concerning their infection will be disclosed without their permission and with resulting loss of employment or other important benefits. Although alternative approaches to this public health problem have been advanced, in general they have not been persuasive or widely adopted.[5]

This infection control strategy is set forth in the conclusions of the *Report of the Presidential Commission on the Human Immunodeficiency Virus Epidemic,*[6] which gave significant impetus to the enactment of AIDS discrimination provisions in federal law. The President's HIV Commission report concludes:

> As long as discrimination occurs, and no strong national policy with rapid and effective remedies against discrimination is established, individuals who are infected with HIV will be reluctant to come forward for testing, counseling, and care. This fear of potential discrimination . . . will undermine our efforts to contain the HIV epidemic and will leave HIV-infected individuals isolated and alone.[7]

---

[4] Numerous states have also adopted AIDS confidentiality protections as well as nondiscrimination provisions in public accommodations and housing. See **App. A.** *See also* Lawrence O. Gostin, Legislative Survey of State Confidentiality Laws, with Specific Emphasis on HIV and Immunization (1996) (available from AIDS Information Clearinghouse). Discrimination in public services and accommodations is covered in **Ch. 4;** housing discrimination is discussed in **Ch. 6.**

[5] Opponents of extending nondiscrimination standards for persons with HIV infection have argued that such persons have (1) become infected as a result of their own (morally blameworthy) behavior and/or (2) pose a risk of infection to others that cannot be eliminated, and thus are not deserving of special legal protection. These arguments were made by congressional opponents to the Americans with Disabilities Act in regard to extending employment discrimination protection to homosexuals based on their HIV status and in regard to protection for food service workers with HIV infection. As discussed in § **3.6,** Congress rejected these arguments.

[6] The Commission was established by Executive Order 12,601, 52 Fed. Reg. 24,129 (1987), to undertake a comprehensive study of the AIDS epidemic and to make recommendations to end further spread of HIV, to assist in finding a cure for HIV disease, and to provide care for persons already infected.

[7] Report of the Presidential Commission on the Human Immunodeficiency Virus Epidemic 119 (1988). This excerpt from the Presidential Commission Report was quoted approvingly by congressional committees endorsing passage of the Americans with Disabilities Act. H.R. Rep. 485, pt. 2, 101st Cong., 2d Sess. 31, *reprinted in* 1990 U.S.C.C.A.N. 303, 313, 330 (also quoting Presidential Commission report to effect that both symptomatic and asymptomatic individuals with HIV are protected); S. Rep. No. 116, 101st Cong., 1st Sess. 8 (1989). *See also* H.R. Rep. No. 485, pt. 4, 101st Cong., 2d Sess. 25, *reprinted in* 1990 U.S.C.C.A.N. 512, 514 (noting recommendation of the Presidential HIV Commission for "legislation of this type").

These points were also made by Louis W. Sullivan, MD, Secretary of Health and Human Services, in his speech at the Sixth International Conference on AIDS, in which the enactment of nondiscrimination standards was urged because the discrimination "is not medically or morally justified."[8]

State and local policymaking bodies also have supported the adoption of such standards, sometimes on a voluntary basis for employers, sometimes through recommending new legislation.[9] For example, in 1988, the Citizens Commission on AIDS for New York City and Northern New Jersey recommended 10 principles that received the endorsement of employers with a total of 3.5 million employees in the greater New York City area.[10] The first local nondiscrimination ordinance was adopted in Los Angeles in 1985,[11] and claims of discrimination have arisen frequently under state or local nondiscrimination laws.[12] Enforcement of nondiscrimination standards has taken place under both pre-AIDS disability or handicap statutory provisions, but the epidemic has resulted in numerous local enactments, aimed specifically at protecting the employment rights of those with HIV.[13]

An employer's role in the AIDS epidemic need not be limited merely to passive compliance with nondiscrimination standards. Workplace education programs have been an affirmative response, whether required by law or undertaken by the employer's own initiative, as discussed in § 3.3. In Philadelphia, for example, local law requires all employers with three or more employees to undertake a mandatory AIDS education program for their employees, consisting of an "oral discourse" by a senior management official, regarding the ways HIV can and cannot be transmitted, as well as the rights of affected employees.[14] Standards for health care providers promulgated by the Occupational Safety and

---

[8] *Reprinted in* 136 Cong. Rec. S8667 (daily ed. June 25, 1990).

[9] *See generally* Paul Barron et al., *State Statutes Dealing with HIV and AIDS: A Comprehensive State-by-State Summary,* 5 L. & Sexuality 1 (1995); Charles Konigsberg, Jr. & Martha F. Barerra, *Local Public Health Perspectives on the Acquired Immune Deficiency Syndrome (AIDS) Epidemic,* 12 Nova L. Rev. 1141 (1988); U.S. Conference of Mayors, Local AIDS Policies (1988); Intergovernmental Health Policy Project, George Washington Univ., AIDS—A Public Health Challenge: State Issues, Policies and Programs (1987).

[10] *Principles on AIDS in the Workplace Have Gained Support, Commission Says,* 35 Daily Lab. Rep. (BNA) A-5 (Feb. 21, 1991). The Citizens Commission recommendations are reprinted in AIDS in the Workplace: Resource Material (BNA) § F-1 (3d ed. 1989).

[11] Ordinance 160,289 (Aug. 16, 1985), *reprinted in* 3 Emp. Prac. Guide (CCH) ¶ 20950A (1985), and AIDS in the Workplace: Resource Material (BNA) § C-88 (3d ed. 1989).

[12] For a survey of AIDS litigation matters, see Lawrence O. Gostin, The AIDS Litigation Project III: A Look at HIV/AIDS in the Courts of the 1990s (Pub. No. 1164, 1996) (single copies available from the Kaiser Family Foundation, 1-800-656-4533).

[13] State and local discrimination issues are discussed in §§ **3.26–3.28.**

[14] Philadelphia, Pa., Code ch. 9-1700 (bill no. 369) (1990). Whether such an "educational" program is effective is open to debate, however, as discussed in § 3.3.

Health Administration mandate HIV education training programs, which necessarily involve basic AIDS education.[15] In Los Angeles, city policy requires AIDS education for city employees and establishes confidentiality and nondiscrimination standards.[16]

Employment policy, whether embodied in legislation, agency rule or regulation, or judicial decision, should be evaluated to determine if it is consonant with this public health strategy. Thus, for example, a court decision upholding a hospital's requirement that a nurse disclose the results of his HIV test can be read as providing a disincentive for health care workers or others to seek testing.[17] This result could only be justified by a showing that disclosure of the nurse's test result was the only means to protect against transmission of HIV to others. On the other hand, prohibiting an employer from inquiring into an employee's HIV status prevents discrimination that might result from the disclosure of HIV status.[18] These prohibitions also contribute to the "climate of increased emphasis on health promotion and disease prevention" urged by the Secretary of Health and Human Services,[19] by encouraging persons to seek testing and counselling without fear of employer inquiries regarding their test.

§ 3.3   Workplace HIV/AIDS Education Programs

Education is widely viewed as a primary weapon in response to the AIDS epidemic. In the workplace, educational programs may have several objectives. First, increased employee knowledge and reduced fear about HIV transmission reduces the potential for workplace disputes and disruption and any liability that can potentially result. In turn, education programs can achieve the related purpose of ensuring compliance with nondiscrimination standards (including internal employer policies, if they are already in place, on disability nondiscrimination) regarding HIV in the workplace, thus limiting liability for discrimination against employees, customers, or patients who may experience discrimination by employees.[20] Even if an HIV-related employment dispute arises, the adoption of

---

[15] OSHA workplace safety standards are discussed in § 3.29.

[16] David L. Schulman, *AIDS Discrimination: Its Nature, Meaning and Function,* 12 Nova L. Rev. 1113, 1133–34 (1988), *reprinted in* The Aids Reader: Social, Political, and Ethical Issues 463–90 (Nancy F. McKenzie ed., 1991) (describing Los Angeles education program); *Los Angeles Adopts AIDS Policy for City Government Employees,* 201 Daily Lab. Rep. (BNA) A-16 (Oct. 17, 1990).

[17] *See, e.g.,* Leckelt v. Board of Comm'rs, 909 F.2d 820 (5th Cir. 1990), discussed more fully in **§ 3.12.**

[18] Limitations on employer inquiries in pre-employment and employment examinations under the Americans with Disabilities Act are discussed in **§ 3.9.**

[19] 136 Cong. Rec. S8667 (daily ed. June 25, 1990).

[20] Many reported cases of HIV discrimination have as their starting point the decisionmaking about HIV in the workplace that is uninformed and fearful. For example, one of the leading AIDS discrimination cases, Cain v. Hyatt, 734 F. Supp. 671 (E.D. Pa. 1990), involved an employment dispute that originated in a supervisor's fear of contact with a co-worker with AIDS.

employment policy and provision of training may be relevant to a claim for punitive damages based on allegations of the employer's failure to provide a good
faith accommodation of the employee's disability under the Americans with
Disabilities Act.[21] Finally, education may be required to provide a reasonably
safe workplace as mandated by the Occupational Safety and Health Administration or equivalent state agencies.[22]

In June 1993, the National Commission on AIDS issued its report, *HIV/AIDS:
A Challenge for the Workplace,* pointing out that AIDS is affecting an age
group very likely to be employed in the United States during the next few years.
At the same time, however, only about one-fourth of the largest private-sector
employers have policies and programs to guide their response to HIV disease.
The National Commission's report contains a number of recommendations, the
including the initiation of an ongoing federal workplace AIDS program, enhanced
emphasis by the Attorney General on the need for enforcing the Americans with
Disabilities Act, enhanced compliance with OSHA workplace safety standards,
and the expansion of Centers for Disease Control and Prevention's (CDC) educational program.

Although the idea of HIV education in the workplace is fairly commonplace,
it may be controversial in some workplaces or among some employees. HIV
cannot be discussed fully without including topics such as homosexuality and
drug abuse that are not frequently aired in workplace education programs. Views
on these topics are divergent, strongly held, and often laden with emotion. Employers attempting to address these issues face a challenge to make the program
appropriately accurate and informative without offending at least some employees, whose underlying attitudes will remain unaffected. The federal government's AIDS education program, for example, proved sufficiently offensive to
at least some employees that in 1996 Congress prohibited federal agencies from
requiring their employees to attend AIDS or HIV training programs if the employee refuses to consent to attend or participate, unless the training is necessary
to protect the health and safety of the employee and the individuals served by
the employee.[23] On the other hand, a training program that is not adequately
forthright in addressing these issues may lack credibility for other employees or
signal management's lack of commitment to the training objectives and underlying workplace policies. Educational programs that are highly superficial seem,
at best, questionably useful and potentially counterproductive. As one commentator

---

[21] *See* 42 U.S.C. §§ 12117, 1981a.

[22] Workplace safety issues are discussed more fully in **§ 3.30.** The OSHA blood-borne pathogens standard explicitly requires annual employee training on infection control. Employee
training must include a general explanation of the epidemiology and symptoms of HIV disease
and an explanation of the modes of transmission of HIV. 29 C.F.R. § 1910.1030(g)(2)
(1996).

[23] Pub. L. No. 104-146, § 9, 1996 U.S.C.C.A.N. (110 Stat.) 1346, 1373, to be added as note to
5 U.S.C. § 4103. The provision was originally included in the Senate version of the bill, S.
641. The House bill did not include such a provision. In conference committee, the house
receded with an amendment that exempts federal training programs necessary to protect
health and safety. Ryan White CARE Act Amendments of 1996, H.R. Conf. Rep. No. 545,
104th Cong., 2d Sess. 47 (1996), *reprinted in* 1996 U.S.C.C.A.N. 1021, 1035 para. 26.

has concluded, some AIDS workplace education programs have little or no impact on changing workers' attitudes, and legal nondiscrimination standards, such as those embodied in the Americans with Disabilities Act, will be effective educational tools regarding the epidemic only if they receive significant support from the government and political leadership.[24]

There are resources available to assist in this area. The National AIDS Clearinghouse, a service of the CDC located in Rockville, Maryland, has a Business Responds to AIDS Program that maintains a database of AIDS educational materials and publications dealing with AIDS in the workplace.[25] This program makes available several listings of database materials on standard workplace issues.[26] Additionally, several publications from the National Leadership Coalition on AIDS are available. For example, *Sample Policies* provides reprints of model employer policies, either in the form of policies addressing life-threatening illnesses (including Bank of America, Northwestern Mutual Life Insurance Company, and Syntex (U.S.A.), Inc.) or HIV-specific policies (including RJR Nabisco, Inc., the San Francisco AIDS Foundation, and Wells Fargo Bank). Also available is a survey of employer AIDS programs in response to the epidemic.[27] The National Leadership Coalition on AIDS has also published a survey of 10 case studies of employer efforts to help their HIV-infected employees continue working as long as possible, within the context of the Americans with Disabilities Act.[28] Finally, the National AIDS Clearinghouse also has available a Manager's Kit, a self-help collection of materials to assist managers and union leaders through the process of developing an AIDS in the workplace program. The kit contains brochures, resource guides, and publication catalogs, as well as materials that can be used in workplace education programs for employees.

§ 3.4 Alternative Dispute Resolution Considerations

Although unquestionably the AIDS epidemic has resulted in a huge number of disputes resulting in litigation, many of which have arisen in the empl y-ment context, attorneys and other advocates should be aware of alternatives to

---

[24] Deborah Weinstein, *Employment Discrimination: AIDS Education and Compliance with the Law,* 1 Temple Pol. & C.R. L. Rev. 85 (1992).

[25] Employers seeking information and assistance can contact the National AIDS Clearinghouse at 1-800-458-5231 (voice) or 1-800-243-7012 (deaf access/TTD).

[26] *E.g.,* HIV/AIDS Workplace Policy Development (Dec. 1995); HIV/AIDS and Workplace Safety (Dec. 1995); HIV/AIDS and Managers/Supervisors (Jan. 1996); HIV/AIDS and Employees (Jan. 1996).

[27] Alan Emery, The Workplace Profiles Project: Common Features & Profiles of HIV/AIDS in the Workplace Programs (1994) (a project of the National Leadership Coalition on AIDS).

[28] Accommodating Employees with HIV Infection and AIDS: Case Studies of Employer Assistance (1994); Managing Tuberculosis and HIV Infection in Today's General Workplace (brochure). For more information, contact National Leadership Coalition on AIDS, 1400 I Street, NW, Suite 1220, Washington, DC 20005; 202/408-4848.

litigation.[29] *Alternative dispute resolution* (ADR) refers generally to a wide range of approaches, from so-called open door policies, intended to encourage communication and negotiation, to binding arbitration, involving an adversarial proceeding that is less formal than a judicial proceeding but is heard by a neutral third party. ADR methods, particularly mediation,[30] may prove valuable in many cases. This section provides an introduction to ADR considerations that may be relevant in workplace disputes, although many of the considerations noted here are relevant to dispute resolution regarding HIV issues in a broad range of settings, from managed care plans to governance of local AIDS service organizations.[31]

The Americans with Disabilities Act (ADA), the primary legislation setting nondiscrimination standards in the context of HIV,[32] specifically endorses the use of ADR: "Where appropriate and to the extent authorized by law, the use of alternative means of dispute resolution, including settlement negotiations, conciliation, facilitation, mediation, factfinding, minitrials, and arbitration is encouraged to resolve disputes arising under this Act."[33] Also, the ADA's Title I employment nondiscrimination provisions require the exhaustion of administrative remedies, which potentially provide an alternative means of resolving disputes before commencing judicial proceedings. ADA employment claims are first filed with the Equal Employment Opportunity Commission (EEOC). The EEOC then investigates the charge to determine if there is reasonable cause to believe that the charge is true. If the EEOC makes that determination, it is

---

[29] The literature on ADR is vast. Advocates unfamiliar with practice in this area may wish to consult John W. Cooley, Mediation Advocacy (National Inst. for Trial Advocacy (NITA) 1996); John W. Cooley & Steven Lubet, Arbitration Advocacy (NITA 1996); Stephen B. Goldberg et al., Dispute Resolution: Negotiation, Mediation, and Other Processes (2d ed. 1992); Leonard L. Riskin & James E. Westbrook, Dispute Resolution and Lawyers (1987); Christopher W. Moore, The Mediation Process (1986); Jay Folberg & Alison Taylor, Mediation (1984). For an excellent ongoing resource in this area, consult *The Alternate Newsletter: A Resource Newsletter on Dispute Resolution* (James B. Boskey, ed.) (available from Seton Hall Law School, 1 Newark Center, Newark, NJ 07102-5210; telephone: (201) 642-8811).

[30] *Mediation* is defined as a process in which a disinterested third party (the neutral) assists the parties in reaching a voluntary settlement that defines their future behavior. The parties themselves, with the assistance of the neutral, make the resolution decision. In contrast, *arbitration* is a process in which, after hearing evidence and argument from the parties, one or more neutrals render a decision resolving the dispute. The decision may be either binding or nonbinding, as prearranged by the parties. *See* John W. Cooley, Mediation Advocacy 2 (1996).

[31] Under amendments to the Ryan White CARE Act, planning councils funded under the CARE Act are required to adopt procedures to address grievances resulting from funding decisions, including procedures for binding arbitrary for grievances not otherwise resolved. Pub. L. No. 104-146, § 3(b)(1), 1996 U.S.C.C.A.N. (110 Stat.) 1346, 1349 (amending 42 U.S.C. § 300ff-12(b)).

[32] The ADA's employment provisions are covered more generally in **§§ 3.5–3.13,** and its access to services and public accommodation provision is discussed in **Ch. 4.**

[33] 42 U.S.C. § 12212. This Title V provision applies not just to the Title I employment provisions, but also to the other nondiscrimination provisions of the ADA.

required to "endeavor to eliminate any such unlawful employment practice by informal methods of conference, conciliation, and persuasion."[34] In reality, however, given the EEOC's significant backlog of cases, it is questionable whether the EEOC is able to fulfill its statutory obligation to assist in the resolution of cases in any meaningful way. As a result, ADR has been viewed as a particularly effective means to address the EEOC caseload problem.[35]

Whether or not ADR is appropriate in HIV cases is necessarily a case-specific determination. Several factors weigh in favor in ADR, particularly mediation, to resolve HIV disputes. These factors are likely to be attractive to both parties. First, ADR processes can be expeditious, an important factor for an employee who wishes to return to work promptly and may be facing an uncertain future in terms of the ability to continue to work. Generally, the litigation process involves significant delays, despite the availability of case-expediting mechanisms in the courts. Employers, too, may wish to resolve a dispute involving HIV promptly, given the potential for highly emotional controversy, workplace disruption, and adverse publicity that can result if the dispute is not ended. Insofar as the parties are involved in an ongoing employee-employer relationship, the conciliatory and nonadversarial features of mediation may be particularly valuable in defining the parties' relationship in the future. In many HIV disputes, as is true of disability-based disputes generally, a central issue is resolution of conflict about what accommodation of the employee's disability is reasonable. Mediation is particularly well suited to working out these accommodations by involving the employer and employee in a highly fact-specific dialogue. Many employees with HIV may wish to educate their employers about HIV, and receive assurance that the employer has accurate and reliable information about HIV and that the employer will treat information about the employee confidentially. Again, ADR may provide an opportunity to reach an understanding regarding these issues or at least identify a neutral source of information or guidance. Some HIV claims may involve profound emotional issues for both the employer and employee, touching deeply held fears about HIV and the consequences of working with an employee with HIV, but may not involve large, easily determined monetary claims. These conflicts may best be addressed through ADR means, such as workplace education programs, as well as if not better than through the courts. Accordingly, advocates should assess cases for their ADR potential at the very outset and then act on that assessment before filing any discrimination charge or complaint. Also, depending on the parties' agreement before pursuing ADR, they need not give up their right to litigate the case later, should they fail to resolve the dispute. Finally, because ADR can take place privately, involving just the parties, their attorneys (if they are represented by counsel), and, depending on the method used, a mediator or other neutral, confidentiality

---

[34] *Id.* § 2000e-5.

[35] *See* Ann C. Hodges, *Mediation and the Americans with Disabilities Act,* 30 Georgia L. Rev. 431, 442–51 (1996) (reviewing EEOC's caseload problem and discussing ADR as means of addressing it).

regarding the fact that HIV is an issue in the dispute, an interest that the parties are likely to share in many cases, can be better maintained than in the courts or administrative agencies.[36]

Several factors, however, may weigh against the use of ADR. Perhaps the most significant is the interest of individuals with HIV in establishing legal precedents of widespread application regarding the rights of such individuals. For this reason, a dispute that involves novel or unprecedented claims that are viewed as potentially successful for litigation may not be attractive for ADR. A potential plaintiff may wish to pursue the case in court with the risk that it may not be successful but with the expectation that it may result in a precedent, instead of resolving the dispute more informally and privately. As the legal principles regarding HIV in the workplace become more clearly established, the perceived need to establish these precedents may wane. Along the same lines, a potential plaintiff may wish to expose the potential defendant to the public attention that can result from filing a claim that alleges unlawful HIV employment practices as a means of informing the public more generally about the law in this area.

As ADR becomes increasingly popular, particularly for employment disputes,[37] an issue not fully resolved is the legal effect of contractually required ADR, particularly in the context of unionized workplaces. Frequently, employers or service providers require arbitration or some other binding means of dispute resolution. Although a full discussion of this complex issue is beyond the scope of this section, practitioners should note that in regard to the ADA, the provision encouraging the use of ADR was included originally in the House version of the bill, and then adopted by the conference committee to emphasize the understanding that ADR should be fully voluntary and not implemented to limit statutory rights. In their report, the conferees stated, "Under no condition would an arbitration clause in a collective bargaining agreement or employment contract prevent an individual from pursuing . . . rights under the ADA."[38] The conferees adopted the view of the House Judiciary Committee that the ADR provision was to "supplement, not supplant, the remedies provided by the

---

[36] Although many plaintiffs have brought claims under a pseudonym such as "John Doe," and the courts have been generally receptive to such practices to protect their identity, there are reports of problems in maintaining confidentiality in judicial and administrative proceedings. *See, e.g.,* Doe v. City of New York, 15 F.3d 264 (2d Cir. 1994) (claimant's privacy rights violated by disclosure of information by city nondiscrimination agency); Lee v. Calhoun, 948 F.2d 1162 (10th Cir. 1991) (physicians' disclosure of patient's HIV infection privileged given patient's public figure status resulting from litigation); Flynn v. Doe, 553 N.Y.S.2d 288 (App. Div. 1990) (denying request for pseudonym to protect identity of individual who had died of AIDS).

[37] U.S. Gen. Accounting Office, Employment Discrimination: Most Private-Sector Employers Use Alternative Dispute Resolution (1995) (noting that high percentage of employers with more than 100 employees use at least one means of ADR).

[38] H.R. Conf. Rep. No. 596, 101st Cong., 2d Sess., para. 81, at 89, *reprinted in* 1990 U.S.C.C.A.N. 565, 598.

[ADA]."[39] Not all courts have ruled in favor of fully voluntary ADR, however, but have instead upheld mandatory ADR requirements regarding statutory discrimination claims in some cases.[40]

FEDERAL EMPLOYMENT STANDARDS

§ 3.5   Americans with Disabilities Act of 1990

The Americans with Disabilities Act of 1990 (ADA)[41] is perhaps the most significant civil rights legislation since the enactment of the Civil Rights Act of 1964,[42] and certainly the most important disability statute since the passage of the Rehabilitation Act of 1973.[43] Although AIDS or HIV is not mentioned in the text of the ADA, there is no question that the ADA provides broad protection against AIDS or HIV discrimination.

Like the Rehabilitation Act, Title I of the ADA prohibits disability discrimination in employment. Unlike the Rehabilitation Act, however, its coverage is not limited to federal contractors, employers receiving federal funding, or federal agencies. Instead, it extends nondiscrimination coverage to many public and private workplaces, including states and their political subdivisions.[44]

---

[39] H.R. Rep. No. 485, pt. 3, 101st Cong., 2d Sess. at 76–77, *reprinted in* 1990 U.S.C.C.A.N. 445, 499–500 (citing Alexander v. Gardner-Denver Co., 415 U.S. 36 (1974), approvingly).

[40] *E.g.,* Austin v. Owens-Brockway Glass Container, Inc., 844 F. Supp. 1103, 1106–07 (W.D. Va. 1994) (ADA claim estoppel based on mandatory arbitration provision in collective bargaining agreement); *cf.* Block v. Art Iron, Inc., 866 F. Supp. 380 (N.D. Ind. 1994) (ADA claim not subject to mandatory arbitration clause). *See also* Gilmer v. Interstate/Johnson Lane Corp., 500 U.S. 20 (1990) (upholding mandatory arbitration of age discrimination claim); Toney v. U.S. Healthcare, 838 F. Supp. 201, 204–05 (E.D. Pa. 1993) (Rehabilitation Act discrimination claims dismissed because of plaintiff's failure to pursue internal, nonbinding grievance procedure that had been approved by state oversight agency).

[41] Pub. L. No. 101-336, 1990 U.S.C.C.A.N. (104 Stat.) 327 (codified at 29 U.S.C. § 706, 42 U.S.C. §§ 12101–12102, 12111–12117, 12131–12134, 12141–12150, 12161–12165, 12181–12189, 12201–12213 (1994)). Title I of the ADA contains the nondiscrimination in employment provisions. Title V includes miscellaneous provisions relevant to the employment title, including provisions on insurance, attorney's fees, waiver of state immunity, and the ADA's relationship to other state and federal laws. For a general discussion of the ADA, see Henry H. Perritt, Jr., Americans with Disabilities Act Handbook (John Wiley & Sons, Inc. 2d ed. 1991 & Supp. 1996).

[42] Pub. L. No. 88-352, 78 Stat. 214, 1964 U.S.C.C.A.N. 287 (codified at 42 U.S.C. §§ 2000a–2000h-6 (1994)).

[43] HIV issues under the Rehabilitation Act are covered in §§ **3.14–3.17.**

[44] 42 U.S.C. § 12202. Congress intended to waive 11th Amendment state immunity in conformity with Atascadero State Hospital v. Scanlon, 473 U.S. 234 (1985).

The ADA's nondiscrimination standards apply to job application procedures, hiring, advancement, and discharge of employees.[45] Discrimination in compensation, job training, "and other terms, conditions, and privileges of employment" are covered.[46] *Discrimination* as defined by the ADA also includes limiting, segregating, or classifying a job applicant or employee in a way that adversely affects the opportunities or status of the applicant or employee because of the disability.[47] All aspects of an employer's relationship with an employee thus appear to be covered by the ADA. Employers[48] of 15 or more employees are covered by the ADA.[49] In 1991, Congress amended the ADA's extraterritorial coverage by modifying the definition of *employee* to include U.S. citizens employed in foreign countries, subject to certain limitations.[50]

The Equal Employment Opportunity Commission (EEOC) has, pursuant to its ADA rulemaking authority,[51] issued regulations interpreting the ADA's Title I employment discrimination provisions.[52]

§ 3.6 —Legislative History in Regard to HIV

Before the consideration and passage of the ADA by the 101st Congress in 1990, several other legislative proposals in Congress addressed the issue of AIDS discrimination. The passage of the ADA in 1990, three years after federal AIDS nondiscrimination standards were first proposed, should be understood against this background.[53]

---

[45] For a disparate treatment case involving proof of HIV discrimination, see Runnebaum v. NationsBank of Md., No. 94-2200, 65 U.S.L.W. 2272 (4th Cir. Sept. 19, 1996).

[46] 42 U.S.C. § 12112(a).

[47] *Id.* § 12112(b).

[48] The ADA's definition of *covered entity* includes "employer, employment agency, labor organization, or joint labor-management committee." 42 U.S.C. § 12111(2). However, the ADA exempts from coverage the United States, any corporation wholly owned by the United States or an Indian tribe, and bona fide private membership clubs. *Id.* § 12111(5)(B).

[49] 42 U.S.C. § 12111(5)(A) and Pub. L. No. 101-336, Title I, § 108, 1990 U.S.C.C.A.N. (104 Stat.) 327, 337, *reprinted in note to* 42 U.S.C. § 12111 (establishing effective date for employment provisions of the ADA).

[50] Civil Rights Act of 1991, Pub. L. No. 102-166, § 109, 1991 U.S.C.C.A.N. (105 Stat.) 1071, 1077 (amending 42 U.S.C. §§ 12111–12112).

[51] 42 U.S.C. § 12116.

[52] 29 C.F.R. pt. 1630 (1996); *see also* 29 C.F.R. pt. 1640 (1996) (procedures for processing complaints of discrimination under ADA and Rehabilitation Act section 504). The EEOC regulations have also been published by the EEOC and U.S. Department of Justice with an accompanying interpretive analysis in Americans with Disabilities Act Handbook (1991).

[53] Proposals to add general disability or handicap discrimination protections to federal law predate the AIDS epidemic. *See, e.g.,* S. 466/H.R. 5510, 96st Cong., 1st Sess. (1979) (amending Title VII of the Civil Rights Act of 1964 to prohibit handicap discrimination).

First, legislation introduced in 1987 would have amended the Public Health Service Act to add protection from discrimination in employment, housing, public accommodations, and governmental services.[54] This nondiscrimination protection was specific to individuals infected or regarded as infected with "the etiologic agent for acquired immune deficiency syndrome."[55] This proposal made no distinction between symptomatic and asymptomatic infection, and because it specifically identified infection with HIV as the protected disability, no further attempt to define that concept was necessary. This approach was unlike that of the ADA, which is not specific to any disability and thus attempts to define the concept of disability with reference to a generic notion of "impairment" that must meet generally defined severity or durational requirements.

This legislation also addressed the issue of risk of HIV transmission in the workplace. The Senate bill, S. 1575, provided that an individual with HIV is not otherwise qualified for employment if, under guidelines issued by the Secretary of Health and Human Services, "a bona fide medical determination is made that the individual will, under the specific circumstances involved, expose other individuals to a material risk of being infected."[56] The House bill, H.R. 3071, similarly provided that an individual is not otherwise qualified if under the secretary's guidelines, "a public health officer makes a bona fide determination that the individual will, under the circumstances involved, expose other individuals to a significant possibility of being infected."[57]

Both the Senate and House bills authorized enforcement by the secretary, providing civil penalties and injunctive relief as well as creating a private cause of action for actual and punitive damages. Attorneys' fees for prevailing parties were also authorized. Hearings were held on this legislation in both the House[58] and Senate[59] in 1987, but no further action was taken.

Next, legislation introduced in 1988 was also intended to address the issue of AIDS discrimination.[60] Unlike the HIV-specific legislation proposed during the

[54] AIDS Federal Policy Act of 1987, S. 1575/H.R. 3071, 100th Cong., 1st Sess. (1987), 133 Cong. Rec. 21,903 (1987) (text of Senate bill as introduced).

[55] S. 1575/H.R. 3071, § 2341.

[56] S. 1575, § 2341(b)(1), 133 Cong. Rec. at 21,906.

[57] H.R. 3071, § 2341(b)(1).

[58] *Bills and Resolution to Improve AIDS Counseling and Education, and to Encourage Better Testing and Reporting Practices to Help Protect the General Public Against AIDS Infection: Hearings on H.R. 338, H.R. 339, H.R. 344, H.R. 345, H.R. 2272, H.R. 2273, H.R. 3071, and H. Con. Res. 8 Before the Subcomm. on Health and the Environment of the House Comm. on Energy and Commerce,* 100th Cong., 1st Sess. (1988).

[59] *To Amend the Public Health Service Act to Establish a Grant Program to Provide for Counseling and Testing Services Relating to Acquired Immune Deficiency Syndrome and to Establish Certain Prohibitions for the Purpose of Protecting Individuals with Acquired Immune Deficiency Syndrome or Related Conditions: Hearings on S. 1575 Before the Senate Comm. on Labor and Human Resources,* 100th Cong., 1st Sess. (1988).

[60] S. 2345/H.R. 4498, 100th Cong., 2d Sess. (1988). *See* 134 Cong. Rec. S7211 (daily ed. June 6, 1988) (statement of Sen. Weicker in support of S. 2345, citing Presidential Commission Report recommendation for HIV discrimination legislation).

previous year, this proposal was a specific precursor to the ADA, including a generalized definition of disability, without being disability-specific. A joint House and Senate hearing was held,[61] but again no further action was taken.

In the next Congress, a revised ADA was introduced.[62] Throughout the consideration of this legislation during the 101st Congress, protection from discrimination for persons with HIV infection was a stated objective. Additionally, congressional resolution of the disputed issue of coverage of individuals with HIV infection employed in food preparation or handling activities illustrated congressional intent to base the ADA on sound medical and scientific findings regarding disease transmission issues, thus further supporting protection for persons with HIV infection.

The Senate version of the ADA, S. 933, was referred to the Committee on Labor and Human Resources, which considered the issue of HIV infection as a disability.[63] The House version, H.R. 2273, was introduced in four committees, two of which considered the issue of HIV infection as a disability under the ADA: the Committee on Labor and Education[64] and the Committee on the Judiciary.[65] All legislative reports that consider the issue conclude that HIV infection is an impairment under the ADA and apparently assume that the impairment caused by HIV is substantial, although congressional consideration of that issue was not explicitly articulated but instead apparently was assumed. Given the ADA's definition of disability, which includes individuals merely "perceived as" having a disability, as well as those who actually have a disability (see § 3.7), it is not surprising that congressional discussion of that issue is not more detailed, because consideration of the ADA took place against a background of widespread public perception that HIV infection resulted in a significant physical impairment and individuals with HIV infection were thus routinely assumed to have a disability, without regard to the actual severity of the impairment caused by HIV. In short, Congress did not consider the possibility that an individual with HIV might not be impaired or, if impaired, that the impairment would

---

[61] *Americans with Disabilities Act of 1988: Joint Hearing of the Subcomm. on the Handicapped of the Senate Comm. on Labor and Human Resources and the Subcomm. on Select Education of the House Comm. on Education and Labor,* 100th Cong., 2d Sess. (1988).

[62] S. Res. 933, 101st Cong., 1st Sess. (1989); H.R. Res. 2273, 101st Cong., 1st Sess. (1989). For a detailed discussion of the overall legislative history of the ADA in the 101st Congress, see Henry H. Perritt, Jr., Americans with Disabilities Act Handbook §§ 2.1–2.6 (John Wiley & Sons, Inc. 2d ed. 1991).

[63] Senate Comm. on Labor and Human Resources, Americans with Disabilities Act of 1989, S. Rep. 116, 101st Cong., 2d Sess. 8 (1989); *see also* statements upon Senate approval, 135 Cong. Rec. S10,789 (Sen. Kennedy); 135 Cong. Rec. S10,794 (Sen. Moynihan); 135 Cong. Rec. S10,800 (daily ed. Sept. 7, 1989) (Sen. Simon).

[64] H.R. Rep. No. 485, pt. 2, 101st Cong., 2d Sess. 51 [hereinafter House Labor Report], *reprinted in* 1990 U.S.C.C.A.N. 303, 333.

[65] H.R. Rep. No. 485, pt. 3, 101st Cong., 2d Sess. 28 n.18, *reprinted in* 1990 U.S.C.C.A.N 445, 451 n.18 [hereinafter House Judiciary Report] (citing approvingly 1988 Department of Justice memorandum for conclusion that individuals with HIV infection have an impairment that substantially limits a major life activity and thus are disabled).

not be substantial. Indeed, it is debatable whether HIV infection is ever not an actual disability under the ADA.

Furthermore, most of the congressional consideration of HIV focused on the issue of whether HIV, as an infectious disease, should be treated differently from other disabilities under the ADA. Attempts by critics of the ADA to exclude persons with infectious or communicable diseases from coverage under the ADA were unsuccessful, which again emphasizes congressional intent in extending protections.[66]

Perhaps even more significantly, the ADA's definition of disability is adopted from the Rehabilitation Act, which at the time of congressional consideration of the ADA was widely viewed as including individuals with HIV infection within its protection, as discussed in § **3.15.** Congress indicated that the ADA is to be read in light of existing standards under the Rehabilitation Act.[67]

The House version of the ADA was amended in the Judiciary Committee to include clarification of the direct threat defense for employers.[68] That provision was expanded from individuals with contagious diseases to individuals with any disability.[69]

The ADA was approved first in the Senate on September 7, 1989, by a vote of 76 to 8.[70]

The Food Handling Controversy

Congress's resolution of the issue of coverage for persons with HIV infection employed as food service workers illustrates the ADA's reliance on medical and scientific fact in defining extent of coverage. The extent of congressional debate

---

[66] 136 Cong. Rec. H4613 (daily ed. July 12, 1990) (statement of Rep. Dannemeyer in opposition to coverage of persons with communicable diseases); *House Judiciary Committee Begins Markup of Bill to Prohibit Bias Against Disabled,* 85 Daily Lab. Rep. (BNA) A-10 (May 2, 1990) (House Judiciary Committee's rejection of amendment offered by Rep. Dannemeyer to exclude homosexuals infected with HIV from coverage under the ADA). Debate on H.R. 2273 was limited in the House under H. Res. 394, 136 Cong. Rec. 10,839 (1990), and thus the general question of whether individuals with infectious diseases should be covered by nondiscrimination standards was not be debated. *See* 136 Cong. Rec. 10,851–52 (1990) (statement of Rep. Dannemeyer in opposition to including individuals with communicable diseases within the definition of disability).

[67] House Labor Report at 52, *reprinted in* 1990 U.S.C.C.A.N. 303, 334 (citing approvingly U.S. Department of Justice's 1988 opinion that HIV infection is a disability under the Rehabilitation Act because of substantial limitation on procreation and intimate sexual relationships); House Judiciary Report at 28–29, *reprinted in* 1990 U.S.C.C.A.N. 445, 451 (same).

[68] H.R. 2273, § § 101(3) and 103(b) (subsequently enacted, 42 U.S.C. §§ 12111(3), 12113(b)).

[69] H.R. Conf. Rep. No. 596, 101st Cong., 2d Sess. 60, *reprinted in* 1990 U.S.C.C.A.N. 565, 569 [hereinafter Conference Report]. The conference committee adopted the explanation of *direct threat* contained in Senate Comm. on Labor & Human Resources, Americans with Disabilities Act of 1989, S. Rep. No. 116, 101st Cong., 1st Sess. (1989).

[70] 135 Cong. Rec. S10803 (daily ed. Sept. 7, 1989).

on this issue demonstrates the level of fear concerning HIV transmission, particularly by food or beverages, even in the face of overwhelming evidence that HIV was not transmitted in that way.

Before final approval of the bill in the House, Representative Chapman offered the following amendment to section 103, relating to employer defenses:

> (d) FOOD HANDLING JOB. —It shall not be a violation of this Act for an employer to refuse to assign or continue to assign any employee with an infectious or communicable disease of public health significance to a job involving food handling, provided that the employer shall make reasonable accommodation that would offer an alternative employment opportunity for which the employee is qualified and for which the employee would sustain no economic damage.[71]

Although the amendment was not without significant ambiguities, as was pointed out by its congressional critics,[72] and was potentially applicable to illnesses other than HIV, its proponents intended to guarantee the right of restaurateurs or other food service employers to remove an HIV-infected employee from food handling activities. Under the direct threat provisions contained in the version of the ADA under consideration at the time the Chapman amendment was proposed[73] and as subsequently enacted,[74] an employee with a communicable disease employed in food handling activities who poses a risk of infection to others is not protected if the risk of transmission cannot be eliminated by reasonable accommodation. The Chapman amendment was thus necessary to address the situation in which the employee with a communicable does not pose such a threat. As explained by Representative Chapman:

> Today I offer an amendment which would allow employers to move an employee with a communicable or infectious disease of public health significance out of a food handling position while at the same time making a reasonable accommodation of an offer of reassignment to another position for which the individual is qualified and for which the employee would sustain no economic damage.

---

[71] 136 Cong. Rec. 10,911 (1990). *See also id.* at 11,478 (Chapman amendment in House version of ADA, prior to Conference Committee revision); *id.* at 13,037 (Chapman amendment in House version of ADA, as presented to Senate); *cf.* 136 Cong. Rec. 10,884 (1990) (H.R. 2273 prior to Chapman amendment, as considered in House).

[72] *See* 136 Cong. Rec. 10,912 (1990) (statement of Rep. Rowland); *id.* at 10,913–14 (statement of Rep. Byron); 136 Cong. Rec. H2480-81 (daily ed. May 17, 1990) (statement of Rep. Hoyer). The Chapman amendment did not define "communicable disease," "of public health significance," or "food handler"—the most critical terms in the amendment.

[73] H.R. 2273, §§ 101(3), 103(b), 136 Cong. Rec. 10,883–84 (1990). *See also* House Judiciary Report at 93–94, *reprinted in* 1990 U.S.C.C.A.N 445, 511 (dissenting views of Rep. Douglas, noting that without amendment the ADA would prohibit a food service operator from transferring an HIV infected employee, because the CDC guidelines consistently state that HIV is not transmitted by food or beverages).

[74] 42 U.S.C. §§ 12111(3), 12113(b).

. . . the bill as currently drafted will not provide an employer the flexibility to move an employee out of food-handling position if that employee were diagnosed as having an infectious or contagious disease such as AIDS.[75]

The Chapman amendment was not based on the view that HIV is actually transmitted in serving or preparing food, but only that the public perceived it to be transmitted that way. In short, as one congressional supporter of the amendment explained, citing the support of the National Restaurant Association, the amendment was necessary "because perception is reality."[76] As explained by Representative Chapman:

> The reality is that many Americans would refuse to patronize any food establishment if an employee were known to have a communicable disease. Damage to the business can be severe and not only cause the owner the loss of his business but could cause the loss of all the jobs of the employees that work there and result in the loss of their livelihood.[77]

Representative Chapman did not, however, suggest that HIV was known to be transmitted by food preparation activities:

> Let me hasten to add that I am not here to say that there is any evidence that AIDS can be transferred in the process of handling food. To the contrary, the Center [sic] for Disease Control seems to say or does say that there is not a case that they can determine or document found in over 130,000 cases through April 1990 of the disease of AIDS being transmitted in this way. At the same time, however, the Center for Disease Control said as of yesterday that there are 4,428 cases of AIDS where the cause is undetermined or unknown.[78]

Arguing against the amendment, congressional critics pointed out that the amendment would effectively codify the prejudices of the uninformed, analogous to allowing a business to practice racial discrimination because the business's customers shared that prejudice.[79] Nevertheless, the House approved the Chapman

---

[75] 136 Cong. Rec. 10,911 (1990). As discussed in **§ 3.9,** Rep. Chapman's view that reassignment to another position is appropriate as an accommodation is not a correct reading of the reasonable accommodation requirement under the ADA. *Reasonable accommodation* is modification of the job held or desired by the individual with a disability, such that with the modification the individual is able to perform the essential job function.

[76] *Id.* at 10,914 (statement of Rep. Douglas); *see also* 136 Cong. Rec. 13,050–51, 13,062 (1990) (statement of Sen. Helms in support of Chapman amendment).

[77] 136 Cong. Rec. 10,911 (1990).

[78] *Id.* at 10,911–12. Correspondence from the National Restaurant Association in support of the amendment, conceding no actual risk of transmission but noting public fears, was included the Senate debate on the amendment. *See* 136 Cong. Rec. S7437 (daily ed. June 6, 1990).

[79] 136 Cong. Rec. 10,915 (1990) (statement of Rep. Miller); *id.* at 10,914 (statement of Rep. Lewis); *id.* at 10,915–16 (statement of Rep. Hoyer). Similar arguments were made in opposition in the Senate. *See* 136 Cong. Rec. 13,051 (1990) (statement of Sen. Harkin); *id.* at 13,057 (statement of Sen. Kennedy); *id.* at 13,059 (statement of Sen. Cranston); *id.* at 13,060 (statement of Sen. Durenberger); *id.* at 13,061 (statement of Sen. Akaka).

amendment on May 17, 1990, by a vote of 199 to 187.[80] On May 22, 1990, the House passed H.R. 2273, as modified by the Chapman amendment.[81]

Hatch Amendment

Because the House did not approve the version of the ADA passed approximately eight months earlier by the Senate, the differences were to be resolved in the House-Senate Conference Committee. In the Senate, a nonbinding motion by Senator Helms to instruct the Senate conferees to agree to the Chapman amendment was approved on June 6, 1990, by a vote of 53 to 40.[82] Subsequently, the amendment was then deleted in conference, at the request of the Senate conferees.[83]

At that point, the congressional impasse on the issue of employment of HIV-infected food service workers threatened to delay, possibly indefinitely, the passage of the ADA. Senator Hatch, however, offered a compromise proposal on the Senate floor, substituting for the Chapman amendment to § 103(d) an amendment that would require the secretary of Health and Human Services to publish by "wide dissemination" to the general public a list of "infectious and communicable diseases which are transmitted through the handling of the food supply."[84] The methods of transmission of those diseases were also to be published. The compromise amendment further gave employers the right to reassign employees who presented a disease transmission risk if the risk could not be eliminated by reasonable accommodation. The amendment also provided for limitations on its preemptive effect on state law. The secretary's communicable disease list was to be reviewed and revised annually.[85]

In the face of the compromise proposal, Senator Helms's motion to recommit the bill to the conference committee with instructions to include the Chapman amendment was defeated by a vote of 39 to 61.[86] Instead, the Hatch amendment, in slightly modified form,[87] was then approved for inclusion in the Conference

---

[80] 136 Cong. Rec. 10,917 (1990).

[81] *Id.* 11,466–67.

[82] 136 Cong. Rec. 13,062–63 (1990).

[83] H.R. Conf. Rep. No. 558, 101st Cong., 2d Sess., *reprinted in* 136 Cong. Rec. H4169 (daily ed. June 26, 1990); *Conferees Clear Disability Rights Bill after Deleting House-Passed AIDS Amendment,* 123 Daily Lab. Rep. (BNA) A-11 (June 26, 1990) (House conferees agree to delete food handler provision at insistence of Senate conferees).

[84] 136 Cong. Rec. S9593 (daily ed. July 11, 1990).

[85] 136 Cong. Rec. S9543 (daily ed. July 1, 1990).

[86] 136 Cong. Rec. S9555, S9593 (daily ed. July 11, 1990).

[87] The Hatch amendment was modified prior to final approval in conference. Instead of requiring the secretary to review all diseases that "are" transmitted through the handling of the food supply, the final version requires the secretary's review to include all diseases that "may be" so transmitted. The secretary's published list then is to include only those diseases that "are" so transmitted. *See* 136 Cong. Rec. S9556 (daily ed. July 1, 1990) (comments of Sen. Hatch regarding agreement to make final amendments in conference). These changes were apparently suggested to satisfy opponents to the amendment by making the secretary's review process more thorough.

Report, by a vote of 99 to 1 on July 11, 1990, with Senator Helms casting the sole dissenting vote.[88] The amendment to § 103(d) was approved in conference as follows:

(d) LIST OF INFECTIOUS AND COMMUNICABLE DISEASES.—

(1) IN GENERAL.—The Secretary of Health and Human Services, not later than 6 months after enactment of this Act, shall—

(A) review all infectious and communicable diseases which may be transmitted through handling the food supply;

(B) publish a list of infectious and communicable diseases which are transmitted through handling the food supply;

(C) publish the methods by which such diseases are transmitted; and

(D) widely disseminate such information regarding the list of diseases and their modes of transmissibility to the general public. Such list shall be updated annually.

(2) APPLICATIONS.—In any case in which an individual has an infectious or communicable disease that is transmitted to others through the handling of food that is included on the list developed by the Secretary of Health and Human Services under paragraph (A) and which cannot be eliminated by reasonable accommodation, a covered entity may refuse to assign or continue to assign such individual to a job involving food handling.

(3) CONSTRUCTION.—Nothing in this Act shall be construed to preempt, modify, or amend any state, county, or local law, ordinance, or regulation applicable to food handling which is designed to protect the public health from individuals who pose a significant risk to the health or safety of others, which cannot be eliminated by reasonable accommodation, pursuant to the list of infectious or communicable diseases and the modes of transmissibility published by the Secretary of Health and Human Services.[89]

On the floor of the House, a motion to recommit the bill to conference with instructions to include the Chapman amendment was rejected, and the bill, including the Hatch compromise amendment, then received final House approval by a vote of 377 to 28 on July 12, 1990.[90] The Senate then voted final approval, 91 to 6, on July 13, 1990.[91] On July 26, 1990, President Bush signed the ADA into law.[92]

Because the secretary of Health and Human Services opposed the Chapman amendment (as did all other public health officials involved in the legislative process) on the basis that HIV is "not transmitted during the preparation or serving

[88] 136 Cong. Rec. S9555–56 (daily ed. July 11, 1990).

[89] Conference Report at 61–63, *reprinted in* 1990 U.S.C.C.A.N. 565, 570–72 (enacted, 42 U.S.C. § 12113(d)).

[90] 136 Cong. Rec. H4629 (daily ed. July 12, 1990).

[91] 136 Cong. Rec. S9695 (daily ed. July 13, 1990).

[92] 26 Weekly Comp. Pres. Docs. 1165 (1990), *reprinted in* 1990 U.S.C.C.A.N. 601.

of food or beverages,"[93] and the U.S. Public Health Service was already officially on record that HIV is not transmitted through food preparation activities,[94] approval of the Hatch amendment meant that food workers with HIV infection would be protected by the ADA. Moreover, in approving the Hatch compromise amendment, Congress disapproved the notion that negative reaction from customers or others could be a legitimate factor in defense of an employer's decision to discriminate against persons with HIV infection. Instead, Congress placed the authority to decide scientific and medical risk of transmission issues with the federal government agency traditionally charged with policy formulation in that area.[95]

In § 103(d)(3) of the ADA, Congress stated the relationship between the Hatch amendment and existing state or local laws pertaining to food safety standards:

> Nothing in this Act shall be construed to preempt, modify, or amend any State, county, or local law, ordinance, or regulation applicable to food handling which is designed to protect the public health from individuals who pose a significant risk to the health or safety of others, which cannot be eliminated by reasonable accommodation, pursuant to the list of infectious or communicable diseases and the modes of transmissibility published by the Secretary of Health and Human Services.[96]

As explained in the Conference Committee Report, this provision means simply that the ADA does not preempt state and local disease control or public health law requirements applicable to certain job categories, such as required hygienic procedures that do not discriminate against persons with disabilities, including HIV. Nor would the ADA preempt state or local regulation of employment of persons with infectious or communicable diseases (such as limitations on the employment of persons with infectious tuberculosis) that do pose a direct threat to the health or safety of others.[97] Many broadly worded state and local laws on infection control, however, particularly those applicable to food service businesses, must be given a more restrictive reading in order to avoid the preemptive effect of the ADA.

---

[93] Letter of Louis W. Sullivan, MD, Secretary of Health and Human Services, *reprinted in* 136 Cong. Rec. S9545 (daily ed. July 11, 1990).

[94] HIV transmission standards for food service workers were stated in CDC, *Summary: Recommendations for Preventing Transmission of Infection with Human T-Lymphotropic Virus Type III/Lymphadenopathy-Associated Virus in the Workplace,* 34 MMWR 681, 693–94 (1985), *reprinted in* 136 Cong. Rec. S9546 (daily ed. July 11, 1990) (Senate debate concerning Chapman amendment).

[95] Obviously, HIV is not included on the secretary's list. *See* Diseases Transmitted Through the Food Supply, 56 Fed. Reg. 40,897 (1991), 57 Fed. Reg. 40,917 (1992), 59 Fed. Reg. 1949 (1994).

[96] 42 U.S.C. § 12113(d)(3).

[97] Conference Report at 63, 84, *reprinted in* 1990 U.S.C.C.A.N. 565, 572, 593 (explaining relationship to state law).

§ 3.7 —HIV Infection as Disability

The ADA's definition of disability is a general one and does not identify any one or more specific conditions that might constitute a disability. This is in keeping with the view that any listing of disabilities may be inadequate and need to be supplemented or revised in the future.

The ADA has three definitions of *disability:*

1. Having a physical or mental impairment that substantially limits one or more major life activities;
2. Having a record of such an impairment; or
3. Being regarded as having such an impairment.[98]

Although the ADA does not specifically refer to HIV disease as a disability, as discussed in **§ 3.6,** the legislative history of the ADA leaves no question that in general Congress intended HIV disease to be included within that definition.

The three definitions of disability are broadly protective of persons with or thought to be infected with HIV. Because the ADA definition of disability is the same as that in other federal disability nondiscrimination statutes, reference to rulings under those statutes is also relevant to the ADA definition.[99]

Limitation of Major Life Activity

In determining coverage under this standard, an individual must have an impairment[100] that causes a substantial limitation on a major life activity. The EEOC defines *substantial limitation* as being "unable to perform a major life-activity that the average person in the general population can perform" or "[s]ignificantly restricted as to the condition, manner or duration under which an individual can perform a particular major life activity as compared to the condition, manner or duration under which the average person in the general population can perform that same major life activity."[101] *Major life activities* include caring for oneself, performing manual tasks, walking, seeing, hearing, speaking, breathing, learning, working, participating in community activities,[102] and also sexual

---

[98] 42 U.S.C. § 12102(2).

[99] Specifically, the Rehabilitation Act, covered in **§ 3.15,** and the Fair Housing Act, covered in **Ch. 6.**

[100] EEOC interpretative guidance for § 1630.2(i) specifically refers to HIV infection as an impairment. 29 C.F.R. pt. 1630, app. at 339 (1996) (HIV is "inherently substantially limiting"). As noted in **§ 3.6,** the ADA's legislative history also refers specifically to HIV infection as an impairment. House Labor Report at 51; House Judiciary Report at 28. As discussed in **Ch. 1,** HIV affects immune function very rapidly after infection, and as a result there has been little question that HIV infection is an impairment.

[101] 29 C.F.R. § 1630.2(j)(1)(i), (ii).

[102] *See* House Labor Report at 52, 1990 U.S.C.C.A.N. at 334. The EEOC includes these items, with the exception of "participating in community activities" in its definition. 29 C.F.R. § 1630.2(i) (1996).

functioning and reproduction.[103] In many cases, because of the extent of illness, the question of whether an individual diagnosed with AIDS has a disability was not disputed by defendants or was assumed by the courts with little if any discussion.[104] Also, because many plaintiffs have prevailed on their claim that they were "perceived as" having a disability, there has been little need to consider whether they in fact have a disability.[105]

Whether asymptomatic HIV disease or HIV disease with mild symptoms is a disability requires further analysis. Several views of HIV infection support the conclusion that it is a disability under the ADA, without regard to the severity of any symptoms of the illness. First, in regulations of the EEOC, HIV infection has been considered "inherently" substantially limiting.[106] Next, HIV infection has been viewed as an impairment of the hemic or lymphatic systems, which, depending on the individual's symptoms, may or may not be viewed as imposing substantial limitations. More specifically, HIV is considered to be an impairment substantially limiting a major life activity because of the limitations HIV places on procreative and sexual functioning.[107]

---

[103] It should be noted that an individual need not prove that he or she would actually engage in sexual activities or childbearing in order to be protected by the ADA; the substantial limitation exists whether or not the individual chooses to engage in that activity.

[104] *See, e.g.,* Howe v. Hull, 873 F. Supp. 72 (N.D. Ohio 1994) (individual with AIDS covered under ADA); Mauro v. Borgess Medical Ctr., 886 F. Supp. 1349 (W.D. Mich. 1995) (HIV infection as disability not discussed, given disposition on other grounds). In some court opinions, the lack of precise terminology makes it difficult to determine whether the court viewed the plaintiff as having symptoms of HIV illness or being infected with HIV but asymptomatic. *See* Severino v. North Fort Myers Fire Control Dist., 935 F.2d 1179 (11th Cir. 1991) (references to plaintiff as being "AIDS infected"); Doe v. Garrett, 903 F.2d 1455, 1459 (11th Cir. 1990) ("it is well established that infection with AIDS constitutes a handicap"). Note treatment of this issue in Rehabilitation Act cases in § **3.15** and Fair Housing Act cases in **Ch. 6.**

[105] *See* Gates v. Rowland, 39 F.3d 1439, 1446 (9th Cir. 1994) (holding that HIV infection is a disability under ADA based on perceived risk of transmission).

[106] 56 Fed. Reg. 53,741 (1991). *See also* House Labor Report at 48, *reprinted in* 1990 U.S.C.C.A.N. 303, 330 (citing approvingly *Report of the Presidential Commission on the Human Immunodeficiency Virus Epidemic* recommendation regarding coverage of "all persons with symptomatic or asymptomatic HIV infection"). This view may be the result of the conclusion that discrimination against individuals in our society is both widespread and inherently unfair, and thus there is no logical reason for distinguishing between symptomatic and asymptomatic infection. Substantial limitations thus result from widespread discrimination. For example, inclusion of individuals with HIV infection was also endorsed by President Bush in his speech to the National Leadership Coalition on AIDS prior to the ADA's passage. *Bush Endorses Protections for HIV-Positive Contained in Americans with Disabilities Act,* 62 Daily Lab. Rep. A-4 (BNA) (Mar. 30, 1990) (urging passage of ADA "that prohibits discrimination against those with HIV and AIDS").

[107] That was the view of Congress in enacting the ADA. House Labor Report at 52, *reprinted in* 1990 U.S.C.C.A.N. 303, 334 (citing approvingly U.S. Department of Justice's 1988 opinion that HIV infection is a disability under the Rehabilitation Act because of substantial limitation on procreation and intimate sexual relationships); House Judiciary Report at 28–29, *reprinted in* 1990 U.S.C.C.A.N. 445, 451 (same). Not all courts, however, accept the conclusion that child-bearing is a major life activity. *Compare* Krauel v. Iowa Methodist Medical Ctr., No. 95-3768, 65 U.S.L.W. 2186, 8 Nat'l Disab. L. Rep. (LRP) 1 (8th Cir. 1996, Sept. 11,

One of the first cases to analyze the issue of HIV infection under the ADA was *Doe v. Kohn Nast & Graf, P.C.,*[108] which is illustrative of the scope of the ADA's definition of disability in the context of HIV disease in which the symptoms are not severe enough to interfere with work activities. In *Kohn Nast,* the defendant law firm argued that the plaintiff attorney's HIV infection was not a disability under the ADA because it did not result in any limitation on his job-related activities. In doing so, the employer advanced a novel theory of disability discrimination in which the employee must show that his or her impairment is somehow related to employment in order to be deemed a disability. As the court correctly ruled, the ADA imposes no such requirement.[109] The court then concluded, for several reasons, including the fact that HIV infection creates a physiological disorder of the hemic and lymphatic systems and that plaintiff had some symptoms of HIV disease, that the plaintiff suffered from a physical impairment. Then, the court went on to conclude that HIV infection is a substantial limitation on the major life activity of procreation, despite the fact that the "factual record in this case is thin, indeed, as to whether HIV status is a disorder or condition that affects the 'reproductive' system."[110]

The Fourth Circuit Court of Appeals noted this issue in *Ennis v. National Ass'n of Business and Educational Radio, Inc.,*[111] an unusual case in which the plaintiff's ADA employment discrimination claim was based not on the plaintiff's HIV status but on that of her adopted son, whose age is not stated in the court's opinion. The plaintiff claimed that she was discharged from employment because of the employer's fear that medical treatment for her son would be too costly; the employer claimed that the plaintiff was discharged for poor work

---

1996) (procreation and caring for others not major life activities), Cortes v. McDonald's Corp., No. 5-95-CV-827-H1, AIDS Pol'y & L. (LRP), Dec. 27, 1996, at 1 (E.D.N.C. Oct. 3, 1996), *and* Zatarain v. WDSU-Television, Inc., 881 F. Supp. 240, 243–44 (E.D. La. 1995) (same, without discussing legislative history), *aff'd without opinion,* 79 F.3d 1143 (5th Cir. 1996), *with* Pacourek v. Inland Steel Co., 858 F. Supp. 1393, 1404–05 (N.D. Ill. 1994) (reproduction deemed major life activity); *see also* Burgess v. Your House of Raleigh, Inc., 388 S.E.2d 134, 138–39 (N.C. 1990) (applying "more restrictive" N.C. law, procreation not major life activity).

[108] 862 F. Supp. 1310 (E.D. Pa. 1994). The court also noted several symptoms of HIV infection suffered by the plaintiff, which the court considered to be physical impairments, although they were not severe enough to impose a significant limitation on the plaintiff's major life activities. *Id.* at 1319–20.

[109] *Id.* at 1320. *See* 42 U.S.C. § 12102(2)(A); 29 C.F.R. § 1630.2(j).

[110] 862 F. Supp. at 1320. In reaching that conclusion, the court referred to the ADA's legislative history on the question of asymptomatic HIV infection and the regulations of the Justice Department under Title II. The court also concluded that the plaintiff was perceived by the defendants to have a disability. *Id.* at 1322–23.

[111] 53 F.3d 55 (4th Cir. 1995). The case is unusual in that it involved an employment discrimination claim based not on the employee's HIV status, but on the employee's association with an individual with HIV. As a result, the employee did not have the option of arguing that she was perceived to have a disability; the ADA only protects an employee who has a known association with an individual with a known disability. 42 U.S.C. § 12112(b)(4).

performance. Considering the claim that the plaintiff was discriminated against because of her relationship with an individual with a disability, the court noted that determining whether an individual has a disability is a case-by-case inquiry, and that there should be no per se rule that persons with HIV infection are deemed to be disabled under the ADA. Although the fact of the son's HIV infection was undisputed, the court concluded that "there is no evidence in the record before us that [the plaintiff's son] is impaired, to any degree, or that he currently endures any limitation, much less a substantial limitation, on any major life activity."[112] Nevertheless, given the less than fully developed record on this issue, the court assumed that the son had a disability, but it ruled against the plaintiff on other grounds.

Record of Disability

This provision is intended to protect individuals who may have recovered from their disability but whose records reflect the disability in their background.[113] In many cases, an individual with a record of impairment would also be perceived as being impaired. The intent behind this provision is to protect individuals whose medical records include information, possibly erroneous, that is known to an employer. The individual may in fact not have a disability, either because the information is erroneous or because he or she has fully recovered from the disability. In either case, the individual would be unable to claim that he or she is a individual with a disability, and, depending on the employer's view of the condition, the individual may or may not be perceived as having a disability. Nevertheless, discrimination against that individual would be as unfair as discrimination against a person who has a current disability. In such cases it should make no difference if there is a single reference to the disability or a series of references reflecting a history of disability.

The court in *Doe v. Kohn Nast & Graf, P.C.*,[114] however, rejected the plaintiff's argument that he had a record of impairment known to his employer, even though he had alleged that his employer was aware of the contents of a letter from his physician, which could be interpreted as indicating that the plaintiff either had HIV infection or AIDS. The court concluded that because the plaintiff's diagnosis with HIV occurred only a few months before the events that gave rise to the lawsuit, he did not have an adequate history of impairment, despite having an apparent record of impairment. The court's view on this point is open to criticism. The ADA refers to a "record" of impairment and does not use the

---

[112] 53 F.3d at 60. The court limited its review of the record to whether there was evidence that the son actually had a disability.

[113] The fact that the effects of an impairment are controlled by medication is not a basis for concluding that the individual does not have a disability. House Labor Report at 52, *reprinted in* 1990 U.S.C.C.A.N. 303, 334.

[114] 862 F. Supp. 1310, 1322 (E.D. Pa. 1994).

term "history of impairment." Although "history of impairment" was used almost interchangeably in the legislative history with "record of impairment,"[115] the legislative history does not suggest that Congress intended any durational requirement be read into this provision of the ADA.

Perceived as Disabled

Individuals who are perceived to have a disability are protected, whether or not they are actually impaired or have an actual disability. Thus, individuals who are suspected of being HIV-infected are protected insofar as HIV infection itself is a disability or perceived as such.[116]

This protection extends to individuals identified as being "at risk" for HIV infection regardless of the fact that they are not infected or are not even members of the group thought to be at risk. For example, an employee terminated from employment because he is suspected of being HIV infected because the employer believes that he is gay would be protected even though he is not HIV infected and is not gay. Whether he is HIV infected is irrelevant, because it is the employer's perception that is the critical element of the employee's claim, not the employee's actual HIV status. Whether he is homosexual is also irrelevant under the ADA. In that regard, the House Judiciary Committee rejected an amendment that would have provided that homosexuals viewed as HIV infected would not be protected by the ADA. As the Judiciary Report states:

> [h]omosexuality and bisexuality are not impairments and as such are not disabilities under the ADA. Sexual preference is not considered a disability under the ADA, and has not been considered a handicap under the Rehabilitation Act. Individuals who are homosexual or bisexual, and are discriminated against because they have a disability, such as infection with the Human Immunodeficiency Virus, are protected under the ADA.[117]

The ADA extends nondiscrimination standards even further by protecting persons who have a "relationship or association" with someone with HIV.[118] Thus,

---

[115] See House Labor Report at 52–53, *reprinted in* U.S.C.C.A.N. 303, 334–35; *see also* 29 C.F.R. § 1630.2(k) (1996).

[116] See Gates v. Rowland, 39 F.3d 1439, 1446 (9th Cir. 1994) (holding that HIV infection is a disability under ADA-based perceived possibility of transmission); Doe v. Kohn Nast & Graf, P.C., 862 F. Supp. 1310 (E.D. Pa. 1994) (denying summary judgment for defendant based on plaintiff's claim that he was perceived to be HIV infected). Frequently, it is assumed that HIV infection is itself an actual disability under these circumstances. That issue, however, may be irrelevant insofar as the individual in question has experienced a substantial limitation on a major life activity as a result of the perception (for example, the individual has been terminated from employment).

[117] House Judiciary Report at 75, *reprinted in* 1990 U.S.C.C.A.N. 445, 498; *compare* H.R. Rep. No. 485, pt. 4, 101st Cong., 2d Sess. 82–83, *reprinted in* 1990 U.S.C.C.A.N. 512, 564–65 (dissenting statement of Reps. Dannemeyer, Burton, and Ritter to effect that the ADA is a "homosexual rights bill in disguise").

[118] 42 U.S.C. § 12112(b)(4). *See* Ennis v. National Ass'n of Business & Educ. Radio, 53 F.3d 55 (4th Cir. 1995).

the House Judiciary Report states that "it would be discriminatory for an employer to discriminate against a qualified employee who did volunteer work for people with AIDS, if the employer knew of the employee's relationship or association with the people with AIDS, and if the employer was motivated by that relationship or association."[119] The report also states that the relationship or association could be with a family member or friend,[120] and thus an employee whose same-sex lover is known by the employer to have HIV infection and whose employer discriminates against him on that basis is protected. The ADA also extends protection to individuals retaliated against because of their opposition to unlawful acts or practices under the ADA.[121]

§ 3.8   —ADA's Definition of Qualified Individual

To come within the protection of the ADA, the employee or applicant for employment must be deemed *qualified,* that is, be an individual "who, with or without reasonable accommodation, can perform the essential functions of the employment position that such individual holds or desires."[122] Individuals with entirely asymptomatic HIV infection would thus not experience any limitation in regard to most employment situations as a result of their disability. Rarely indeed would HIV-negative status per se be a qualification for employment. On the other hand, however, individuals with advanced HIV disease may experience such significant impairment that, even with reasonable accommodation, they could not perform the essential job function. In regard to this point, it should be noted that in several cases, the courts have ruled that plaintiffs are estopped from claiming protection under the ADA if they had previously applied for disability benefits claiming that they were unable to work.[123]

The ADA further provides that "consideration shall be given to the employer's judgment as to what functions of a job are essential, and if an employer has prepared a written description before advertising or interviewing applicants for the job, this description shall be considered evidence of the essential functions

---

[119] House Judiciary Report at 39, *reprinted in* 1990 U.S.C.C.A.N. 445, 461.

[120] *Id.*

[121] 42 U.S.C. § 12203. Enforcement of these protective provisions is the same as that provided for the underlying unlawful act or practice, as defined in ADA Titles I, II, or III, respectively. Accordingly, an employee terminated for opposing a public entity's (Title II) violation of the ADA would seek redress under that title, not the employment title (Title I). *See* Finley v. Giacobbe, 827 F. Supp. 215 (S.D.N.Y. 1993) (former medical director of a county hospital claimed ADA violation when her employment was terminated because of her advocacy for access to services for persons with AIDS at the hospital).

[122] 42 U.S.C. § 12111(8).

[123] *See, e.g.,* McNemar v. Disney Stores, Inc., 91 F.3d 610 (3d Cir. 1996) (plaintiff with HIV disease estopped from asserting ADA claim based on application for social security disability benefits); Reigel v. Kaiser Found. Health Plan, 859 F. Supp. 963 (E.D.N.C. 1994); *cf.* Smith v. Dovenmuehle Mortgage, Inc., 859 F. Supp. 1138 (N.D. Ill. 1994); Mohamed v. Marriott Int'l, Inc., No. 94 Civ. 2336, 65 U.S.L.W. 2343 (S.D.N.Y. Oct. 31, 1996); Kupperschmidt v. Runyon, 827 F. Supp. 570 (E.D. Wis. 1993).

of the job."[124] Although the employer's definition of *essential function* is a factor to be considered, and if it is reduced to writing it is perhaps evidence of essential job function, the employee or applicant can still challenge the employer's determination.

Because the job function must be an essential one, criteria relating to factors not relevant to job function are not allowed. For example, a specific attendance schedule, not in any way necessary for the successful performance of the employee's duties, could be viewed as nonessential. In that case, the employee's inability to comply with the attendance schedule would not mean that he or she was not qualified for the position. On the other hand, however, if the employee is supervised directly on the job or if the employee must be present at specific times to meet with other staff, that would make the ability to comply with the schedule an essential function of the job.[125] The employer, however, bears the burden of establishing that its criteria are "job-related and based on business necessity."[126]

Finally, the assessment of the employee's or applicant's qualifications for employment should be of present ability to perform the job, not future ability.[127] Thus, under the ADA, an employer could not discriminate against the currently qualified individual with AIDS because of the concern that future illness may render the individual unqualified.

§ 3.9   —Requirement of Reasonable Accommodation

As discussed in **§ 3.8,** the ADA defines a qualified individual with a disability as someone who, "with or without reasonable accommodation, can perform the essential functions of the employment position."[128] The ADA defines *discrimination* to include an employer's failure to make "reasonable accommodations to the known physical or mental limitations of an otherwise qualified individual with a disability, who is an applicant or employee, unless such covered entity can demonstrate that the accommodation would impose an undue hardship on

---

[124] 42 U.S.C. § 12111(8).

[125] *See* Vande Zande v. State of Wis. Dep't of Admin., 44 F.3d 538 (7th Cir. 1995).

[126] House Labor Report at 56, *reprinted in* 1990 U.S.C.C.A.N. 303, 338.

[127] *See* House Judiciary Committee at 34, *reprinted in* 1990 U.S.C.C.A.N. 445, 456 (whether an individual is qualified should "not be based on the possibility that the employee or applicant will become incapacitated and unqualified in the future"); House Labor Committee at 55, *reprinted in* 1990 U.S.C.C.A.N. 303, 337 (question is "whether the individual is qualified at the time of the job action in question; the possibility of future incapacity does not by itself render the person not qualified"). *Compare* Local 1812, Am. Fed'n of Gov't Employees v. U.S. Dep't of State, 662 F. Supp. 50 (D.D.C. 1987) (upholding mandatory employee testing policy on basis that HIV-infected foreign service employee may develop illness in the future during overseas assignment).

[128] 42 U.S.C. § 12111(8).

the operation of the business of such covered entity."[129] Discriminating against a qualified applicant or employee because of the employer's need to provide a reasonable accommodation is also prohibited.[130] Thus, in the case of an applicant or employee with HIV infection, the employer must undertake steps to accommodate that individual's disability. As the Seventh Circuit Court of Appeals has noted, "an intermittent impairment that is a characteristic manifestation of an admitted disability is . . . a part of the underlying disability and hence a condition that the employer must reasonably accommodate."[131] The accommodation must be requested by the employee, however, in order to trigger the employer's duty to accommodate. One problem for employees with HIV illness is when to disclose their illness to the employer. Some employees may believe that their potential claim of discrimination would be strengthened because the employer, having been told that the employee has a disability, cannot deny knowledge of the employee's HIV status when defending a subsequent discrimination claim.[132] At the same time, however, the employee may fear that disclosure of HIV illness will provoke, at some point, discriminatory treatment, if the employer is sufficiently devious to develop a successful pretextual reason for its treatment of the employee. At the point that accommodation of the employee's illness is required, however, disclosure of the disability is necessary.

The employer's duty to accommodate is not unlimited; that duty ends at the point the accommodation imposes "significant difficulty or expense" when considered in light of a listing of four factors:

(i) the nature and cost of the accommodation needed;

(ii) the overall financial resources of the facility or facilities involved in the provision of the reasonable accommodation; the number of persons employed at such facility; the effect on expenses and resources, or the impact otherwise of such accommodation upon the operation of the facility;

(iii) the overall financial resources of the covered entity; the overall size of the business of a covered entity with respect to the number of its employees; the number, type, and location of its facilities; and

(iv) the type of operation or operations of the covered entity, including the composition, structure, and functions of the workforce of such entity; the geographic separateness, administrative, or fiscal relationship of the facility or facilities in question to the covered entity.[133]

---

[129] *Id.* § 12112(b)(5)(A).

[130] *Id.* § 12112(b)(5)(B).

[131] Vande Zande v. State of Wis. Dep't of Admin., 44 F.3d 538, 544 (7th Cir. 1995).

[132] *See* Phelps v. Field Real Estate Co., 991 F.2d 645 (10th Cir. 1993) (successful defense of HIV discrimination claim based on lack of proof of defendant employer's knowledge of employee's status), *aff'g* 793 F. Supp. 1535 (D. Colo. 1991); Brown v. Sprint, 891 F. Supp. 396 (E.D. Mich. 1995) (same); Dutson v. Farmers Ins. Exch., 815 F. Supp. 349 (D. Or. 1993) (same).

[133] 42 U.S.C. § 12111(10).

The ADA contemplates a case-by-case assessment of these factors. The employer has the burden of showing that the accommodation imposes an undue hardship. Each case must be analyzed on its facts, however, and attempts in Congress to amend the ADA to provide a precise limit to the employer's expense were not successful.[134]

The ADA is clear, however, that the accommodation pertains to the employment position held or desired by the employee or applicant.[135] Therefore, reassignment of the qualified employee to another position can never be a way of meeting the reasonable accommodation requirement. In considering employment of food service workers with HIV infection, discussed in § 3.6, Congress rejected the notion that reassignment, even when it does not result in economic damage to the employee, is an alternative to accommodation in the employment position sought or held by the applicant or employee. In that regard, proponents of the Chapman amendment cited cases of food service businesses' failing as a result of rumors concerning an employee with HIV infection.[136] Nevertheless, the ADA provides that the expense of accommodation is an expense resulting from modifying the employment position or providing assistance or aid to the employee so that the employee can perform the essential job function. The employer's argument that it will lose business as a result of employing the person with HIV infection is not a defense allowed under the reasonable accommodation provision of the ADA. The lost revenue is not a cost of enabling the employee with the disability to do his job. Congress rejected any approach that would have allowed customer or co-worker preference, not founded on medical fact, to dictate a definition of coverage. To have allowed such a defense under the ADA would have permitted evidence of future losses caused by employment of an HIV-infected employee, which would be necessarily speculative. Furthermore, such a defense would provide the employer with an incentive to disclose the employee's HIV status, because the fact that the employee's HIV status was widely known would support such a defense by the employer. The ADA's rejection of this defense instead serves as an incentive for employers to support greater public education concerning the transmission issue.

The employer's duty to accommodate an employee with HIV illness is illustrated in *Buckingham v. United States*.[137] Melvin Buckingham, a postal worker with HIV illness, requested that the United States Postal Service provide him with reassignment from Columbus, Mississippi, to Los Angeles so that he could obtain better medical care. The Postal Service denied his request on the basis that it would violate the rights of other employees under a collective bargaining agreement. The court rejected that interpretation of the collective agreement as

---

[134] *See* 136 Cong. Rec. H2471–75 (daily ed. May 17, 1990) (debate and rejection of amendment requiring a 10 percent cap, based on annualized salary or hourly rate of employee position in question, on employer expense to meet reasonable accommodation requirement).

[135] 42 U.S.C. § 12101(8).

[136] *See, e.g.,* 136 Cong. Rec. S9543–44 (daily ed. July 11, 1990) (statement of Sen. Helms).

[137] 998 F.2d 735 (9th Cir. 1993).

groundless.[138] Turning to the reasonable accommodation issue, the court held that an employer is required to accommodate (in this case by transfer) the employee's disability, even if the accommodation is not directly related to enabling the employee to perform the essential job function but instead will enable the employee to pursue therapy or treatment for the disability. The court thus rejected the Postal Service's argument that transfer for medical treatment is precluded as a matter of law from being a reasonable accommodation. The court further indicated that, on remand, there were two ways Buckingham could meet his burden regarding the reasonableness of the accommodation he was seeking. First, he could show that the requested accommodation would, more probably than not, result in his being able to perform the essential job functions. The court imposed the probability as opposed to certainty standard, because Buckingham had not had the opportunity to show that in fact he was qualified for the job as a result of the accommodation. Alternatively, if Buckingham's position was that he was already qualified for the job, he must then show that there was a causal connection between his disability and his need for the requested accommodation, and, additionally, that it was more likely than not that the accommodation would confer the claimed benefit.

§ 3.10   —Employer Inquiries and Tests for HIV

The ADA's limitations on an employer's inquiries and use of medical examinations, both for applicants and employees, eliminates an employer's ability to screen out applicants or employees unfairly when HIV status does not bear any relationship to job qualifications. Pre-employment inquiries are limited to whether the applicant can perform job-related functions; inquiries concerning the existence of a disability, such as HIV infection, are prohibited.[139] Although the ADA does allow the use of an employment entrance examination *after* an offer of employment has been made to the applicant,[140] it imposes significant limitations on the examination process and use of the results. Post-employment examinations must conform to two limitations: (1) they must be required of all entering employees, regardless of disability; and (2) the information obtained regarding the "medical condition or history of the applicant" must be maintained in confidential medical files segregated from other employment records. Information in the medical files may be disclosed only to: (1) the employee's supervisors in regard to restrictions on the work or duties of the employee resulting from the disability; (2) first aid personnel, in the case of a disability that might require emergency treatment; and (3) government officials investigating compliance with the ADA.[141] As a result of these restrictions on using HIV-related information in

---

[138] *Id.* at 742.

[139] 42 U.S.C. § 12112(c).

[140] *Id.* § 12113(d)(3).

[141] *See* 29 C.F.R. § 1630.14 (1996).

post-employment examinations, at least one commentator has written that few employers may wish to do pre-employment HIV testing because the results cannot be used to withdraw conditional job offers and inadvertent violation of the ADA's confidentiality provisions may subject the employer to liability.[142] Additionally, such testing may violate state law informed consent requirements, and in jurisdictions that require pre- and post-test counselling or related services, the testing process may prove to be expensive.[143]

Although the ADA allows the employer to use an employment entrance examination, post-hire inquiry or examination regarding an employee's HIV status are prohibited unless the inquiry or examination "is shown to be job-related and consistent with business necessity."[144] The employer can only inquire into the employee's ability to perform job-related functions. Rarely, however, would such inquiries require disclosure of the employee's HIV status or AIDS diagnosis.[145] Only in cases of symptomatic HIV disease resulting in interference with the employee's ability to perform the job should the issue arise.

§ 3.11 —Employer Defenses

The ADA sets forth three specific defenses that may pertain to claims of HIV-related discrimination. First, and most generally, an employer can show that application or qualification standards, tests, or selection criteria that discriminate against individuals with disabilities have "been shown to be job-related and consistent with business necessity and . . . cannot be accomplished by reasonable accommodation."[146] In general, however, circumstances in which HIV positive status cannot be accommodated would be rare. Of course, in cases in which an individual suffers from symptoms that are of such a nature or extent that basic job function cannot be met even with accommodation, the employer's actions against that individual would not violate the ADA.

Next, the ADA allows an employer to use qualification standards that include a requirement that an individual "shall not pose a direct threat to the health or safety of other individuals in the workplace."[147] *Direct threat,* in turn, is defined as "a significant risk to the health or safety of others that cannot be eliminated by

---

[142] Chai Feldblum, *Workplace Issues: HIV and Discrimination, in* AIDS Agenda: Emerging Issues in Civil Rights 286–87 (Nan D. Hunter & William B. Rubenstein eds., 1992).

[143] State laws on testing and confidentiality are discussed in **Ch. 2** and summarized in **App. A.**

[144] 42 U.S.C. § 12112(c)(4)(A).

[145] The very limited exceptions, of course, would be employment of a person as a blood or semen donor, or possibly as a paid participant in certain medical studies or experiments, where HIV status would be job-related. The testing of a blood or semen donor should be considered under the direct threat provisions of the ADA discussed in **§ 3.11.**

[146] 42 U.S.C. § 12113(a).

[147] *Id.* § 12113(b).

reasonable accommodation."[148] The Conference Committee Report emphasizes that the level of risk must be "significant" and that the employer bears the burden of showing the relevance of factors such as the "magnitude, severity, or likelihood of risk."[149] EEOC regulations interpreting the ADA direct threat defense further define its extent, in particular making clear its limited scope. The EEOC first notes that the health or safety threat may be to the "individual or others," adding a key term not included in the statute itself and thus allowing an employer to consider the risk not just to other individuals in the workplace, but also the risk to the employee in question. The regulation goes on, however, to state that "slightly increased risk" is not enough to deny employment; the "risk can only be considered when it poses a significant risk, i.e., high probability of substantial harm; a speculative or remote risk is insufficient."[150] This standard would rarely be met by an employer seeking to defend a discriminatory policy.[151] Even in regard to HIV-infected health care workers, though, an employer will have difficulty meeting the "high probability of substantial harm" standard. Although the harm may be substantial, that is, transmission of HIV, the risk of occurrence is extremely remote. Other than the health care setting, covered in § 3.12, this defense has little application in the HIV context.

Congress had previously encountered the problem of the threat of disease transmission in the workplace, and the ADA should be read in light of that history. First, in its consideration of the Civil Rights Restoration Act of 1987, Congress amended the Rehabilitation Act in regard to employment of individuals with contagious diseases.[152] That amendment sets forth a direct threat standard essentially the same as that included in the ADA. The Rehabilitation Act amendment, in turn, essentially codified the standard set forth by the Supreme Court in *School Board v. Arline*.[153] *Arline* was then applied in an AIDS discrimination case, *Chalk v. United States District Court*,[154] which ruled that in determining whether a risk is significant, the courts should not require an employee with HIV infection to disprove every theoretical possibility of harm, because "[l]ittle

---

[148] *Id.* § 12111(3).

[149] House Conference Report at 60, *reprinted in* 1990 U.S.C.C.A.N. 565, 569. The House Conference Report incorporated by reference the explanation of direct threat as set forth in S. Rep. No. 116, 101st Cong., 1st Sess. (1989).

[150] 42 C.F.R. § 1630.2(r), *reprinted in* EEOC, Americans with Disabilities Act Handbook I-47 (1991).

[151] *See* Equal Employment Opportunity Comm'n v. Prevo's Family Mkt., 5 Am. Disabilities Cas. (BNA) 1527 (D. Mich. 1996) (EEOC granted summary judgment on basis that food service worker's HIV infection did not pose direct threat).

[152] *See* 29 U.S.C. § 706(8)(D). The Rehabilitation Act also includes the direct threat standard in regard to the employment of persons whose current alcohol or drug abuse would constitute a direct threat to the property or the safety of others. *Id.* § 706(8)(C)(v).

[153] 480 U.S. 273, 287 n.16 (1987), discussed more fully in § 3.15.

[154] 840 F.2d 701 (9th Cir. 1988).

in science can be proved with complete certainty."[155] In enacting the ADA, Congress cited *Chalk* approvingly.[156]

In addition to the use of qualification standards and the direct threat defense, the ADA imposes limitations on food handlers with infectious or contagious diseases. As discussed in **§ 3.6,** this provision is a compromise between those in Congress who would have permitted exclusion of individuals with HIV from food handling employment because of customers' fears and those who wished to base such a determination on a standard of medical and scientific evidence. Persons with HIV will be affected by this defense only if they have an illness on the listing of communicable diseases issued by the secretary of Health and Human Services. Potential negative customer reaction is not a factor recognized by the ADA as an employer defense.[157] However, given the potential that persons with HIV may be at risk for other infections that may be included on the secretary's list, such as tuberculosis, the list may indirectly affect persons with HIV infection. Nevertheless, that would not give an employer the right to inquire directly about an employee's HIV status.

§ 3.12   —HIV-Infected Health Care Workers and
Risk of Transmission

After more than a decade of experience with the AIDS epidemic, public health officials in the United States have been unable to identify a single case of health-care-provider-to-patient HIV transmission, with the exception of the case of Dr. Acer, the Florida dentist who, through some means that has not been identified, infected six patients in his dental practice.[158] Because the means of transmission has not been established, the Acer case is of little, if any, value in policy formulation, although it has generated significant public controversy.

In general, HIV-infected health care workers involved in invasive procedures pose little or no risk of infection to patients or others, although they face a host of potential problems in terms of employment.[159] Many authorities believe that

---

[155] *Id.* at 707. Although *Chalk,* as a Rehabilitation Act case, discusses the employee's evidence that he did not pose a significant risk in the workplace, the burden of proving the direct threat is on the employer; it is not the employee's burden to show that he or she does not pose a direct threat.

[156] Judiciary Committee Report at 45–46, *reprinted in* 1990 U.S.C.C.A.N. 445, 468–69.

[157] Senate Comm. on Labor & Human Resources, Americans with Disabilities Act of 1989, S. Rep. No. 116, 101st Cong., 1st Sess. 24 (1989). In fact, attitudes of third parties may establish that the individual has a disability. House Labor Committee at 30–31, *reprinted in* 1990 U.S.C.C.A.N. 445, 452–53. *Compare* Farmer v. Moritsugu, 742 F. Supp. 525 (W.D. Wis. 1990) (upholding against constitutional challenge the federal prison policy of excluding inmates with HIV infection from food service employment because potential inmate reaction to such employment threatens institutional order and security).

[158] That case is discussed in **Ch. 1.**

[159] For an overview of issues confronting HIV infected health care workers, see Elise Gautier, The Legal Rights and Obligations of HIV-Infected Health Care Workers (Benjamin Schatz

adhering to infection control standards, not limiting work activities, is most effective in preventing transmission in the health care setting.[160] Nevertheless, the issue of employment of health care workers with HIV infection has been litigated in a series of cases that involve the employer's direct threat defense to the effect that the employee is not otherwise qualified for employment because of the risk of HIV transmission. Additionally, in terms of policy in this area, guidelines modeled after those of the CDC, and as required by Congress, have been promulgated on a state-by-state basis.

In response to the controversy generated by the Acer case, the CDC issued guidelines for performing "exposure-prone" invasive procedures in July 1991. The CDC then considered further revision of the guidelines for nearly a year, only to conclude in June 1992 not to undertake further revision.[161] The 1991 guidelines are reprinted in **Appendix C.** In sum, these guidelines recommend that HIV-infected health care workers who adhere to universal precautions and who practice recommended surgical or dental techniques need not modify their practices. The guidelines go on to recommend that HIV-infected health care workers who perform exposure-prone invasive procedures should know their HIV status and should not perform such procedures unless they have sought counsel from an "expert review panel." That panel's counsel may include a recommendation that the health care worker disclose his or her HIV status to patients in advance of performing an exposure-prone procedure. The CDC left the definition of exposure-prone up to health care organizations and institutions.

Spurred by concerns about the risk of transmission in this area in light of the Acer case, Congress acted by adopting an amendment (the so-called Dole Amendment) to the Treasury, Postal Service & General Government Appropriations Act of 1992, which provides:

> [E]ach State Public Health Official shall, not later than one year after the date of enactment of this Act, certify to the Secretary of Health and Human Services that guidelines issued by the Centers for Disease Control, or guidelines which are equivalent to those promulgated by the [CDC] concerning recommendations for preventing the transmission of [HIV] . . . during exposure prone invasive procedures, except for emergency situations when the patient's life or limb is in danger, have been instituted in the State.[162]

Noncompliance with this provision results in loss of funding under the Public Health Service Act.[163] Significantly, in announcing to state health officers in June

---

ed., 1993) (booklet available from the Gay and Lesbian Medical Association, 415/255-4547); web page at www.glma.org.

[160] *See, e.g.,* National Comm'n on AIDS, Preventing HIV Transmission in Health Care Settings 12–13 (1992) (recommending compliance with universal precautions and basic infection control practices).

[161] *See CDC Not Publishing Revised Guidelines on Infected Workers,* 7 AIDS Alert 113 (1992).

[162] Pub. L. No. 102-141, Title VI, § 633, 1991 U.S.C.C.A.N. (105 Stat.) 834, 876–77, *reprinted in* note to 42 U.S.C. § 300ee-2 (1994).

[163] 42 U.S.C. § 302 (1994).

1992 that the 1991 guidelines would not be further revised, the CDC stated that in determining equivalency under the Dole Amendment it would give "appropriate consideration to those states that decide that exposure-prone invasive procedures are best determined on a case-by-case basis, taking into consideration the specific procedure as well as the skill, technique, and possible impairment of the infected health care worker."[164] Accordingly, the notion that exposure-prone procedures can be identified and listed seems to have been abandoned; instead, the CDC's recommended approach is a case-by-case consideration of procedures, taking into account several factors including the skill of the individual health care worker. Currently, most cases of HIV-infected health care workers are resolved under state policies developed in response to the requirement of the Dole Amendment that state public health officials issue guidelines for prevention of HIV transmission during exposure-prone invasive procedures. Six states have implemented the CDC recommendations; the remaining states have certified adoption of guidelines equivalent to the CDC recommendations.[165]

Despite the evidence that risk of transmission is, at most, insignificant, if not nonexistent, the courts have frequently sided with employers and against health care employees with HIV when disputes have arisen in the health care employment context. The HIV-infected health care worker cases demonstrate that despite the standard set forth in nondiscrimination statutes such as the Americans with Disabilities Act that the employer bears the burden of proving that employment poses a significant risk of harm,[166] in reality the courts have shifted the burden to the employee to show that he or she poses no risk of transmission. Not surprisingly, proving the negative proposition that there is no risk is virtually impossible for the health care worker to meet.

The ruling of the Court of Appeals for the Fifth Circuit in *Leckelt v. Board of Commissioners*[167] sheds some light on how courts assess employer limitations on employing HIV-infected health care workers based on transmission risk. In that case, Kevin Leckelt, working as a licensed practical nurse, was suspected by his employer of being HIV-infected. As a result of his employer's suspicions, he was required to disclose results of a test he had previously taken to determine his HIV status. On advice of counsel, however, he refused. He was then fired, and brought suit against the hospital, alleging among other claims violation of the

---

[164] Letter of CDC Director William L. Roper to state health officials, June 18, 1992, *reprinted in* 7 AIDS Alert 115 (1992).

[165] As of Oct. 25, 1995, those states are Kansas, Maryland, Mississippi, South Carolina, Texas, and Virginia. This information is derived from materials, on file with author, provided by Centers for Disease Control and Prevention, Apr. 15, 1996, in response to Freedom of Information Act request.

[166] The ADA's direct threat standard, the same as that included in the Rehabilitation Act, is outlined in **§ 3.11.**

[167] 909 F.2d 820 (5th Cir. 1990), *aff'g* 714 F. Supp. 1377 (E.D. La. 1989). Although this case was brought under the Rehabilitation Act, the analysis of the direct threat defense is the same under the ADA.

Rehabilitation Act.[168] The court of appeals affirmed judgment in favor of the hospital, noting that Leckelt's failure to disclose the result of his test violated the hospital's infection control policy. Without knowing Leckelt's status, the court reasoned, his employer was prevented from "deciding what, if any, measures were necessary to protect the health of Leckelt, other . . . employees, and [the hospital's] patients."[169] The *Leckelt* court's ruling can certainly be assailed, particularly for its willingness to conclude that knowledge of Kevin Leckelt's HIV status was or could be legitimately related to safety in the workplace, because at the time of his termination, the hospital had not developed specific standards for employees with HIV infection. Even if Kevin Leckelt had tested positive for HIV, it is not clear that with this knowledge the hospital would or should have treated him any differently than any other employee.[170] Nevertheless, the decision in *Leckelt* demonstrates the courts' deference to health care providers' own formulation of infection control policy, aimed at eliminating any risk of HIV infection in the workplace. But in another Rehabilitation Act decision, *Doe by Lavery v. Attorney General,*[171] the court concluded that the risk of transmission was not significant in the case of a physician who was providing routine physical examinations, which included anal, vaginal, and oral cavity examinations. Although the court used a no significant risk standard, it appears that the court's conclusion is premised on the fact that compliance with infection control precautions would in fact eliminate the risk of transmission, not just reduce the risk to an insignificant level.

In other cases, the courts have relied on the risk of HIV transmission as the justification for HIV-based discrimination against health care workers. In short, in these cases, although the risk of transmission is not itself significant, the severity of the harm resulting from transmission tilts the result in favor of the employer. Thus, for example, in a case brought under both the ADA and the Rehabilitation

---

[168] 29 U.S.C. § 794 (1994). Although the ADA presents post-employment screening standards that are clearer than those articulated by the *Leckelt* court, the same result would apparently have resulted under the ADA, given the court's conclusion that Leckelt's HIV status was a job-related factor. *See* 909 F.2d at 831 n.20.

[169] 909 F.2d at 830.

[170] One factor noted in *Leckelt* is the view that health care workers do not always follow universal precautions. Thus, even if it were conceded that universal precautions would eliminate the risk of transmission, failure to observe them would allow an element of risk to exist. The question in each case, however, should be whether the employee in question has failed to observe such precautions and what are the risks resulting from that failure.

[171] 44 F.2d 715, 720, *opinion superseded by* 62 F.3d 1424 (9th Cir. 1995) (disposition without opinion), *rev'g* 814 F. Supp. 844 (N.D. Cal. 1992), *vacated and remanded sub nom.* Reno v. Doe by Lavery, 116 S. Ct. 2543 (1996), *for further consideration in light of* Lane v. Pena, 116 S. Ct. 2092 (1996). The Ninth Circuit Court of Appeals concluded that the defendant FBI was liable to the plaintiff's estate in damages; *Lane v. Pena,* however, ruled that the federal government has not waived its sovereign immunity in regard to Rehabilitation Act claims.

Act, involving the hospital privileges of an orthopedic surgeon, the court concluded that although the risk of transmission could not be precisely measured, the surgeon did pose a significant risk of transmission, and it granted the hospital employer's summary judgment motion.[172] Similarly, in *Bradley v. University of Texas M.D. Anderson Cancer Center,*[173] the court characterized the issue as that of the "probability" of transmitting HIV, which, in the case of the plaintiff surgical technologist, the court described as "small," but "not so low as to nullify the catastrophic consequences of an accident."[174] Because there was no modification of the surgical technologist position that would not involve modification of the essential job function (involvement in the surgical field), the hospital employer was not required to provide any accommodation for the plaintiff's disability. And again, in *Doe v. Washington University,*[175] although the court extended deference to what it characterized as the academic, not medical, decision to dismiss an HIV-infected third-year dental student, it concluded that even though risk of transmission from the student would be minimal, it still existed.

In *Doe v. University of Maryland Medical System Corp.,*[176] the court rejected the ADA Title II, Rehabilitation Act, and equal protection claims of a resident physician who was dismissed from a neurosurgery program. The plaintiff physician argued that because he was willing not to perform any procedures defined by the CDC as exposure-prone, his disability could be reasonably accommodated. The defendant university, however, concluded that all procedures performed by the plaintiff were exposure-prone. The court deferred to the defendant's determination on that point, ruling that "some measure of risk will always exist because of the type of activities in which Dr. Doe is engaged."[177] The court affirmed the grant of summary judgment for the defendants. The *Bradley* and *University of Maryland Medical System Corp.* cases were followed in *Mauro v. Borgess Medical Center.*[178] In that case, an operating room surgical attendant was terminated for failing either to disclose his HIV status or undergo HIV testing, or accept alternative employment providing substantially similar pay and benefits. The *Mauro* decision concluded that exclusion of an HIV-infected health care worker is lawful under the ADA's direct threat standard when the health care worker's essential job duties require him, even on an "infrequent" basis, to "place his hands in direct contact with or in the immediate vicinity of the [patient's] incision."[179]

---

[172] Scoles v. Mercy Health Corp., 63 U.S.L.W. 2415, 3 Am. Disabilities Cas. 1665, 1994 WL 686623 (E.D. Pa. Dec. 8, 1994) (not reported in F. Supp.).

[173] 3 F.3d 922 (5th Cir. 1993) (per curiam), *cert. denied,* 114 S. Ct. 1071 (1994).

[174] *Id.* at 924.

[175] 780 F. Supp. 628 (E.D. Mo. 1991).

[176] 50 F.3d 1261 (4th Cir. 1995).

[177] *Id.* at 1266.

[178] 886 F. Supp. 1349 (W.D. Mich. 1995).

[179] *Id.* at 1354.

Perhaps the leading case in this area is *Behringer Estate v. Princeton Medical Center,*[180] in which the court ruled against the claims of a surgeon with AIDS. Applying New Jersey nondiscrimination law, the court concluded that the employment posed a "reasonable probability of substantial harm."

Finally, *In re Milton S. Hershey Medical Center*[181] involved not discrimination claims but hospitals' disclosure to patients, pursuant to the Pennsylvania HIV confidentiality statute, that a resident physician was HIV-infected. The hospitals advised certain patients to seek HIV testing. Although it affirmed the ruling in favor of the hospitals, the court's opinion is significant in noting that the lack of evidence of actual risk could have justified a decision in favor of the physician.[182] The evidence showed that the hospitals identified patients as appropriate for the disclosure based on review of records of surgical procedures in which the physician merely held or was likely to have held sharp instruments.

§ 3.13   —Enforcement and Remedies

The ADA incorporates the enforcement provisions of Title VII of the Civil Rights Act of 1964.[183] Under Title VII, administrative remedies must be exhausted prior to commencing litigation, by the filing of a complaint with the Equal Employment Opportunity Commission (EEOC).[184] Although the ADA does not specify a statute of limitations for filing claims, under Title VII potential complainants have 180 days from the date of the alleged violation to file with the EEOC.[185] The EEOC has jurisdiction over the complaint for 180 days for reconciliation and investigation purposes. Upon the expiration of the 180-day period, the complainant's right to pursue the claim in court matures, upon issuance of a right to sue notice.[186] If the EEOC determines that it is probable that administrative processing of the complaint cannot be completed within the 180-day period, a right to sue notice can be issued prior to the expiration of 180 days.[187]

By incorporating the Title VII remedial provisions, it is not clear to what extent Congress has ensured that the recommendation of the Presidential Commission on the Human Immunodeficiency Virus Epidemic for "rapid and effective remedies against discrimination" is part of the ADA. The issue of timeliness of remedies is particularly important for claimants whose progressive illness may result in total disability or death in a relatively short time period of time, thus

---

[180] 592 A.2d 1251, 1276 (N.J. Super. Ct. Law Div. 1991).

[181] 634 A.2d 159 (Pa. 1993), *aff'g* 595 A.2d 1290 (Pa. Super. Ct. 1991).

[182] *Id.* at 162 n.2.

[183] 42 U.S.C. § 12117(a), *referencing* 42 U.S.C. §§ 2000e-5, 2000e-6, and 2000e-7.

[184] Pursuant to 42 U.S.C. § 12116, the EEOC has undertaken issuance of regulations interpreting the ADA. *See* 29 C.F.R. pt. 1630 (1996).

[185] *See* 29 C.F.R. pt. 1601 (1996) (current EEOC procedural regulations).

[186] *See* 29 C.F.R. § 1601.28 (1996).

[187] *Id.*

obviating the remedy of reinstatement in employment. In instances when an individual knows that an employer's discriminatory policy or practices will result in a violation of the ADA, the individual is not required by the ADA to pursue the "futile gesture" of actually applying for the position.[188] Instead, the individual can immediately pursue ADA remedies. Whether the potentially time-consuming administrative exhaustion requirement can be avoided is not clear.[189]

The ADA's remedial provisions were significantly expanded with the adoption of the Civil Rights Act of 1991,[190] which authorizes jury trials, compensatory and punitive damages in cases of intentional discrimination, and changes the order of proof in disparate impact cases.[191]

§ 3.14 Rehabilitation Act of 1973

Before the enactment of the ADA, the Rehabilitation Act of 1973[192] provided the most significant disability discrimination protection available under federal law. Even since the adoption of the ADA, the Rehabilitation Act continues to be an important source of nondiscrimination standards because it provides coverage for federal agencies, which are not covered under the ADA, even though monetary damages against federal agencies are not available.[193] Because the issue for coverage for persons with HIV infection arose under the Rehabilitation Act before the adoption of the ADA, Congress drafted the ADA in light of the history of the Rehabilitation Act.

At this point, there is no question that persons with HIV infection are covered under the Rehabilitation Act, as discussed in § 3.15.

The Rehabilitation Act provides coverage for specific workplaces, all of which have some connection with the United States government, either as agencies of the government, government contractors, or as federal financial assistance recipients. As discussed in § 3.16, the Rehabilitation Act nondiscrimination provisions in § 501 apply to federal executive agencies and the postal service. Section 503 provides coverage for private employers with contracts with the United States in excess of $10,000. Finally, § 504 applies to recipients of federal funds, which includes many educational and health care institutions.

---

[188] House Labor Report at 82–83, *reprinted in* 1990 U.S.C.C.A.N. 303, 365 (citing approvingly International Bhd. of Teamsters v. United States, 431 U.S. 324, 365–67 (1977)).

[189] *See* New Mexico Ass'n for Retarded Citizens v. New Mexico, 678 F.2d 847 (10th Cir. 1982).

[190] Pub. L. No. 102-166, 1991 U.S.C.C.A.N. (105 Stat.) 1071 (codified at 42 U.S.C. § 1981a).

[191] *See generally* H.R. Rep. No. 40, pt. 1, 102d Cong., 1st Sess., *reprinted in* 1991 U.S.C.C.A.N. 549; Henry H. Perritt, Jr., Civil Rights Act of 1991: Special Report (1992).

[192] Pub. L. No. 93-112, 87 Stat. 355, 1973 U.S.C.C.A.N. 409 (codified at 29 U.S.C. §§ 701–796i).

[193] However, because the federal government has been held immune to suit for monetary damages under section 504, Lane v. Pena, 116 S. Ct. 2092 (1996), the remedies under the Rehabilitation Act are limited.

Section 504 and its regulations define the concept of an otherwise qualified individual[194] for employment purposes, which is the same test utilized under the ADA, as discussed in **§ 3.8.** Additionally, the employer's duty to provide reasonable accommodation to a person with a disability, as required under § 504 and its regulations,[195] is discussed in the context of the ADA in **§ 3.9.** The standards are essentially the same for the two statutes.

A significant difference in wording between the ADA and the Rehabilitation Act involves the definition of the elements of an employee's proof of discrimination. The Rehabilitation Act provides that employee must prove that the disability in question was the "sole reason" for the discrimination.[196] Some courts have interpreted this language literally, concluding that if the employer can offer a nondiscriminatory reason, even without denying the discriminatory element in its decision, the employee's claim is unsuccessful.[197] In considering the adoption of the ADA, however, this reading of the Rehabilitation Act was explicitly criticized in Congress. The courts' "literal reliance" on the sole reason language was observed to lead to "absurd results."[198] The ADA, however, does not impose such an exacting standard, thus allowing for the employee's proof that the discriminatory factor was a substantial one in the employer's decision making.[199]

§ 3.15   —HIV Infection as Disability

The Rehabilitation Act prohibits discrimination against *individuals with disabilities,*[200] defined as any individual who:

---

[194] 45 C.F.R. § 84.3(k)(1).

[195] 45 C.F.R. § 84.12(b) (1995); *id.* pt. 84, app. A, subpt. B, para. 16 (1995) (analysis of final regulation).

[196] 29 U.S.C. § 794.

[197] *See* Leckelt v. Board of Commr's, 909 F.2d 820, 825 (5th Cir. 1990) (citing Norcross v. Sneed, 755 F.2d 113, 117 n.5 (8th Cir. 1985)); Buko v. American Medical Lab., 830 F. Supp. 899, 905 (E.D. Va. 1993); *compare* Pushkin v. Board of Regents, 658 F.2d 1372, 1387 (10th Cir. 1981) (holding that nondiscriminatory reasons for employment decision must be evaluated to determine whether they "encompass unjustified consideration of the handicap itself").

[198] Senate Comm. on Labor & Human Resources, Americans with Disabilities Act of 1989, S. Rep. No. 116, 101st Cong., 1st Sess. 44–45 (1989). The Senate Committee's report gives as an example of absurdity an employer who refuses to hire a qualified applicant on the basis that the applicant is both black and has a disability. Although the applicant would have a valid race discrimination claim, it could be argued that he would not have a valid disability discrimination claim because his disability was not the sole cause of the refusal to hire.

[199] *Cf.* Price Waterhouse v. Hopkins, 490 U.S. 228 (1989) (outlining standards of proof in "mixed motive" disparate treatment case under Title VII).

[200] Congress amended the Rehabilitation Act in 1992, changing references to "handicapped persons" to "individuals with disabilities." Rehabilitation Act Amendments Act of 1992, Pub. L. No. 102-569, 1992 U.S.C.C.A.N. (106 Stat.) 4344. No substantive change in meaning was intended. *See* S. Rep. No. 357, 102d Cong., 2d Sess. 13–14, *reprinted in* 1992 U.S.C.C.A.N. 3712, 3724.

1. Has a physical or mental impairment that substantially limits one or more of such individual's major life activities;

2. Has a record of such impairment; or

3. Is regarded as having an impairment.[201]

Thus, the definition of disability is the same as that of the ADA, with the exception of the ADA's extension of protection to persons with a known "relationship or association" with a person with a disability.[202] Regulations promulgated under the Rehabilitation Act provide a more detailed interpretation of the concept of disability.[203]

In examining the meaning of individual with a disability under the Rehabilitation Act, the courts have generally concluded that individuals with HIV infection are protected under either the first or third definitions of disability.[204] The same

---

[201] 29 U.S.C. § 706(8)(B).

[202] 42 U.S.C. § 12112(b)(4), discussed in **§ 3.7.**

[203] *See* 45 C.F.R. §§ 84.11–84.14 (1995) (Department of Health and Human Services regulations pertaining to § 504 employment nondiscrimination); 41 C.F.R. pt. 60-741 (1996) (Office of Federal Contract Compliance Programs implementing regulations pertaining to § 503 affirmative action obligations of federal contractors and subcontractors).

[204] Dorsey v. U.S. Dep't of Labor, 41 F.3d 1551, 1553–54 (1994) (assuming HIV infection to be disability under Rehabilitation Act, based on district court's ruling); Harris v. Thigpen, 941 F.2d 1495, 1522–24 (11th Cir. 1991) (HIV infection perceived to be handicap); Severino v. North Fort Myers Fire Control Dist., 935 F.2d 1179, 1182–83 n.4 (11th Cir. 1991) (noting perception of disability and actual impairment resulting from "AIDS infection"); Doe v. Attorney Gen., 941 F.2d 780, 797 (1991) (AIDS a disability), *subsequent opinion* 44 F.3d 715 (9th Cir. 1995); Leckelt v. Board of Comm'rs, 909 F.2d 820, 825 (5th Cir. 1990) (assuming that "seropositivity to HIV antibodies is an impairment protected under section 504"); Doe v. Garrett, 903 F.2d 1455, 1459 (11th Cir. 1990) ("it is well established that infection with AIDS constitutes a handicap," apparently referring to infection with HIV); Chalk v. United States Dist. Court, 840 F.2d 701, 705 n.6 (9th Cir. 1988) (district court's ruling that individual with AIDS is handicapped not contested on appeal); Thomas v. Atascadero Unified Sch. Dist., 662 F. Supp. 376, 381, 383 (C.D. Cal. 1987) (symptomatic HIV illness, but without discussion, Rehabilitation Act coverage deemed "inevitable conclusion"); Tanberg v. Weld County Sheriff, 787 F. Supp. 970 (D. Colo. 1992) (apparently assuming without discussion that HIV is disability); Doe v. District of Columbia, 796 F. Supp. 559, 567 n.10 (D.D.C. 1992) (asymptomatic HIV infection as disability not disputed); Local 1812, Am. Fed'n of Gov't Employees v. U.S. Dep't of State, 662 F. Supp. 50, 54 (D.D.C. 1987) (defendant conceded that great majority of persons with HIV infection are handicapped because of "measurable deficiencies in their immune systems even where disease symptoms have not yet developed"); Ray v. School Dist., 666 F. Supp. 1524 (M.D. Fla. 1987) (asymptomatic HIV covered under § 504, without discussion of precise nature of impairment); Doe v. Dolton Elementary Sch. Dist. No. 148, 694 F. Supp. 440, 443–44 (N.D. Ill. 1988) (AIDS perceived to be handicap, and interaction with others, such as attending school, noted as major life activity); District 27 Community Sch. Bd. v. Board of Educ., 502 N.Y.S.2d 325, 336–37 (Sup. Ct. Queens County 1986) (rejecting challenge to school non-exclusion policy for children with AIDS, noting in dicta that HIV and AIDS are equivalent for Rehabilitation Act purposes).

conclusion has been stated by the Department of Labor in its regulations[205] concerning federal contractor compliance under section 503. The U.S. Department of Justice as also interpreted the Rehabilitation Act to cover asymptomatic persons with HIV.[206] Some commentators have taken a different view, however.[207] In light of the congressional history in enacting the ADA, however, it is difficult to maintain that the Rehabilitation Act should be given a more limited interpretation.

The view of HIV infection as a protected disability is rooted, at least in part, in the Supreme Court's decision in *School Board v. Arline,*[208] in which the court considered a Rehabilitation Act employment discrimination claim of a public school teacher with tuberculosis. Although *Arline* explicitly purported not to rule on the issue of coverage for a person with HIV infection,[209] the Court's analysis of the issues presented by tuberculosis as an infectious disease in the disability discrimination context compels the same result regarding HIV. Gene Arline was employed as an elementary school teacher when she had her third relapse of tuberculosis within two years. As a result, the school board terminated her employment, pointing to the potentially contagious nature of her illness. The Supreme Court, however, rejected the school board's argument that because she had a contagious disease, she was not protected by the Rehabilitation Act. Instead, the Court ruled that persons with contagious diseases may be covered, but that for each such employee an "individualized inquiry" must be undertaken to determine the precise nature of the risk involved in the workplace and whether the risk of transmission can be eliminated by reasonable accommodation. The Court listed four factors to be considered in making a determination of whether an employee is otherwise qualified despite his or her infection with a contagious illness:

---

[205] *See Office of Federal Contract Compliance Procedures Directive on AIDS,* 53 Daily Lab. Rep. (BNA) D-1 (Mar. 21, 1989).

[206] Memorandum of Douglas W. Kmiec, Acting Assistant Attorney General, Office of Legal Counsel, Dep't of Justice, to Arthur B. Culvahouse, Jr., Counsel to the President (Sept. 27, 1988), *reprinted in* 8 Lab. Rel. Rep. (BNA) 405:1 *and* 195 Daily Lab. Rep. (BNA) D-1 (Oct. 7, 1988) (concluding that asymptomatic HIV infection is an impairment of the hemic or lymphatic systems, and that it substantially limits the "life activity of procreation"). This memorandum reversed the Justice Department's 1986 opinion, *reprinted in* AIDS and the Law 286 (William H.L. Dornette ed., 1st ed. 1987), that individuals with HIV infection were not covered under § 504.

[207] *See* Gary Lawson, *AIDS, Astrology, and* Arline: *Towards a Causal Interpretation of Section 504,* 17 Hofstra L. Rev. 237 (1989); *cf.* William G. Buss, *Educating Children with Human Immunodeficiency Virus, in* AIDS and the Law § 4.10 (2d ed. 1987) (conclusion that asymptomatic HIV infected individuals are covered under § 504 and the ADA is persuasive, but not inevitable); William G. Buss, *The Human Immunodeficiency Virus, the Legal Meaning of "Handicap," and Implications for Public Education Under Federal Law at the Dawn of the Age of the ADA,* 77 Iowa L. Rev. 1389 (1992).

[208] 480 U.S. 273 (1987).

[209] *Id.* at 282 n.7.

1. The nature of the risk (how the disease is transmitted);

2. The duration of the risk (how long does the condition remain transmissible);

3. The severity of the risk (what is the potential harm of transmission);

4. The probabilities the disease will be transmitted and will cause varying degrees of harm.[210]

In making this determination, the courts are to "defer to the reasonable medical judgments of public health officials."[211]

The Supreme Court's ruling that persons with contagious illnesses are protected under the Rehabilitation Act, subject to an assessment of actual risk of transmission given reasonable precautions that can be taken, was subsequently codified in amendments to the Rehabilitation Act.[212]

§ 3.16 —Extent of Workplace Coverage

Under § 501 of the Rehabilitation Act, each executive branch of the federal government must implement an affirmative action program pertaining to the employment of individuals with disabilities. The EEOC has the responsibility of promulgating standards and ensuring compliance.[213] The EEOC standards are essentially the same as those for § 504.

Section 504 covers recipients of federal financial assistance. The coverage extends to every program of the institution receiving the federal funds; the federal funds need not be received directly by the program in question.[214] Thus, even if federal funding supports only the cancer research activities of a hospital, all employees of the hospital, not just those involved in cancer research, are covered under § 504.

Section 503 imposes affirmative action requirements on employers with federal contracts in excess of $10,000.[215]

---

[210] *Id.* at 288.

[211] *Id.* (footnote omitted).

[212] Civil Rights Restoration Act of 1987, Pub. L. No. 100-259, § 9, 1988 U.S.C.C.A.N. (102 Stat.) 28, 31–32 (amending 29 U.S.C. § 706). This amendment precluded an attempt to remove contagious diseases from the definition of handicap under the Rehabilitation Act. *See* S. Rep. No. 64, 100th Cong., 1st Sess. 27-28 (1987), *reprinted in* 1988 U.S.C.C.A.N. 3, 29–30 (by vote of 2 to 14, committee defeated amendment that would have reversed *Arline* decision and ended coverage of contagious diseases under § 504).

[213] 20 C.F.R. § 1613.706 (1996).

[214] 29 U.S.C. § 794(b). This definition of coverage was clarified by the Civil Rights Restoration Act of 1987, Pub. L. No. 100-259, § 4, 1988 U.S.C.C.A.N. (102 Stat.) 28, 29 (*amending* 29 U.S.C. § 794 and *overruling* Grove City College v. Bell, 465 U.S. 555 (1984)).

[215] 29 U.S.C. § 793; *see also* 41 C.F.R. pt. 60-741 (1996) (nondiscrimination obligations of § 503 contractors and subcontractors); 29 C.F.R. pt. 1641 (1996) (procedures for processing complaints of discrimination under ADA and Rehabilitation Act § 503 against employers holding government contracts or subcontracts).

§ 3.17   —Enforcement and Remedies

The remedies available under the Rehabilitation Act vary with each section that provides coverage. Thus, under § 504, the courts have recognized a private right of action,[216] although the question of availability of punitive or emotional distress damages remains unanswered. In regard to suits against federal agencies, however, the Supreme Court has ruled that the federal government has not waived its sovereign immunity as to monetary claims.[217] Similarly, federal employees may seek a judicial remedy under §§ 501 and 504.[218] Although there is disagreement among courts ruling on the issue, the majority view appears to be that there is no private cause of action under § 503.[219]

§ 3.18   Family Medical Leave Act

The Family Medical Leave Act of 1993[220] (FMLA) requires employers to provide leave necessitated by the illness of an employee or of an employee's immediate family member. The FMLA may benefit many employees who have HIV illness or whose family member suffers from HIV illness. In essence, the FMLA requires employers to provide *unpaid* medical leave for up to 12 weeks annually, instead of terminating employees from employment because of their absence. Additionally, the employee has the right to return to his or her position, or an equivalent position, within the 12-week period. Medical and family leave policies that are more generous than required by the FMLA are not affected by it,[221] nor are state or local laws that provide more generous protection.[222] Although the FMLA was enacted by Congress to make workplaces more supportive of family

---

[216] Consolidated Rail Corp. v. Darrone, 465 U.S. 624 (1984).

[217] Lane v. Pena, 116 S. Ct. 2092 (1996). See also Reno v. Doe, 116 S. Ct. 2543 (1996), *vacating and remanding* 62 F.3d 1424 (9th Cir. 1995), for further consideration in light of *Lane v. Pena.*

[218] *See* Hall v. United States Postal Serv., 857 F.2d 1073 (6th Cir. 1988).

[219] *See* Rogers v. Frito-Lay, Inc., 611 F.2d 1074 (5th Cir. 1980); *compare* California Paralyzed Veterans Ass'n v. F.C.C., 721 F.2d 667 (9th Cir. 1983), *cert. denied,* 469 U.S. 832 (1984).

[220] Pub. L. No. 103-3, 1993 U.S.C.C.A.N. (107 Stat.) 6, 2 U.S.C. §§ 60m–60n (1994), 5 U.S.C. §§ 6381–6387 (1994), 29 U.S.C. §§ 2601, 2611–2619, 2631–2636, 2651–2654 (1994). The Department of Labor has issued regulations interpreting the FMLA. 29 C.F.R. pt. 825 (1995).

[221] 29 U.S.C. § 2653; 29 C.F.R. § 825.700.

[222] 29 U.S.C. § 2651; 29 C.F.R. § 825.701. Practitioners should consult such state and local laws. The District of Columbia, for example, provides a 16-week period of leave, compared to 12 weeks under the FMLA. D.C. Code Ann. § 36-1302(a) (1993). Additionally, the District's law does not define family member as narrowly as does the FMLA. Such protection extends to employees with whom the employee "shares or has shared, within the last year, a mutual residence and with whom the employee maintains a committed relationship." D.C. Code Ann. § 36-1301(4).

relationships, the protections it provides are far from universal given its limited coverage and narrow definition of *family.*

The FMLA's leave requirement applies only to employers of 50 employees or more,[223] although it includes both public and private employers.[224] In order to be eligible for leave under the FMLA, an employee must have worked for the employer for at least 12 months and for at least 1,250 hours during the 12-month period preceding the absence. Also, the employee must be employed at a location where there are at least 49 other employees within a 75-mile radius.[225] The FMLA provides leave for *serious health conditions,* which includes any illness or physical or mental condition that involves either "inpatient care in a hospital, hospice, or residential medical care facility" or "continuing treatment by a health care provider."[226] Therefore, there is little question that HIV illness would be covered. The serious health condition must make the employee "unable to perform the functions of the position of such employee."[227] Whether the employee can perform the functions of the position is necessarily a case-by-case inquiry.

Although the employee's absence from work is without pay,[228] the employee must be provided with the same health insurance coverage during the absence that was provided prior to it.[229] Other benefits, however, such as continued accrual of seniority or life insurance coverage, are not required. The period of leave can be up to 12 weeks per year. The leave may be taken intermittently or the work schedule itself can be reduced, if such leave is medically necessary or if it is agreeable to both employee and employer.[230] Persons with HIV disease

---

[223] 29 U.S.C. § 2611(4); 29 C.F.R. § 825.104.

[224] 29 U.S.C. § 2611(4). Special rules apply for employees of public and private elementary and secondary schools (29 U.S.C. § 2618), certain federal government employees (5 U.S.C. § 6381), and congressional employees (2 U.S.C. §§ 60m–60n).

[225] 29 U.S.C. § 2611(B)(ii).

[226] 29 U.S.C. § 2611(11). The regulations further define "continuing treatment by a health care provider" to include "the continuing supervision of, but not necessarily being actively treated by, a health care provider due to a serious long-term or chronic condition . . . which cannot be cured." 29 C.F.R. § 825.114(b)(3).

[227] 29 U.S.C. § 2612(a)(1)(D). Although the FMLA does not define these terms, the regulations reference the ADA and its regulations to define them. 29 C.F.R. § 825.115. Under the ADA, inability to perform the functions of the position may result from the need to obtain treatment for the condition, not from impairment directly interfering with the ability to do the job. In many cases, the intermittent leave rights under the FMLA would be coextensive with the reasonable accommodation requirement of the ADA. Essential job function under the ADA is discussed in § **3.8.**

[228] If the employer provides paid leave, however, the employee may be required to substitute accrued paid leave (including vacation and personal leave) for the 12-week unpaid leave required under the FMLA. *See* 29 U.S.C. § 2612(d)(2); 29 C.F.R. § 825.207.

[229] The question of the FMLA's effect on the employee's right under COBRA to continue health insurance coverage is addressed in IRS Notice 94-103, 1994-2 C.B. 569, *reprinted in* 29 C.F.R. pt. 825, app. E. Essentially, the continuation of coverage under COBRA is determined from the last day of FMLA leave.

[230] 29 U.S.C. § 2611(b)(1).

should be able to take time from work for consultation or treatment with their health care providers, assuming the absence from work is medically necessary. Upon completion of the leave, the employee is guaranteed return to work in the same position he or she held previously.[231] If the same position is no longer available, the employer is required to provide equivalent employment, that is, the same pay, benefits, and other terms and conditions.

The employee's absence to care for immediate family members includes the employee's child, spouse, or parent.[232] The term *spouse,* however, is specifically defined as "husband or wife."[233] The FMLA's restrictive concept of family thus excludes unmarried opposite-sex and same-sex couples from its coverage.[234] The term *child,* however, is defined in relation to not just biological parents, but also to adoptive, foster, and stepparents, as well as legal guardians and persons standing in loco parentis to a child.[235] Thus, for example, although grandchildren are not explicitly included within the FMLA's concept of family, in the situation in which a grandparent becomes the primary caregiver for an child orphaned by AIDS, that grandparent should be able to claim the protections of the FMLA in the event that the grandchild has a serious health condition.

In order to take FMLA leave from employment, the employee must request it. The request may be verbal and need not refer to the FMLA, as long as the request identifies an FMLA-qualified basis for the absence.[236] Accordingly, employees with HIV illness who wish to take FMLA leave would very likely need to disclose their HIV status to their employer; if they wish to obtain leave to care for a spouse, parent, or child with HIV, that family member's medical condition would very likely need to be disclosed.[237] The FMLA does not include any confidentiality provisions regarding this medical information, but it may be

---

[231] Employers may, however, deny job restoration to certain key employees. 29 U.S.C. § 2614; 29 C.F.R. §§ 825.216(c)–825.219.

[232] 29 U.S.C. § 2612(a)(C) and (D).

[233] *Id.* § 2611(13).

[234] The regulations further define *spouse* as "a husband or wife as defined or recognized under State law for purposes of marriage in the State where the employee resides, including common law marriage in States where it is recognized." 29 C.F.R. § 825.113. In promulgating this regulation, the Department of Labor (DoL) relied on the statutory language and legislative history of the FMLA and explicitly rejected inclusion of unmarried "domestic partners" in the definition, based on congressional concerns that such a definition of spouse would be ambiguous and result in difficulties in enforcement. *See* 60 Fed. Reg. 2190-91 (1995). Neither Congress nor the DoL, however, appears to have explicitly concluded that same-sex couples, if legally married, should be excluded from the FMLA.

[235] Unless the child is under 18 years of age, the child must be incapable of self-care because of a mental or physical disability. 29 U.S.C. § 2611(12).

[236] 29 C.F.R. § 825.302(c).

[237] Although the disclosure to the employer could be couched in non-HIV terms and references to the underlying HIV infection omitted (such as describing a hospitalization as treatment for pneumocystis pneumonia, without noting the underlying HIV infection), such diagnoses are often tantamount to disclosing the HIV infection itself.

protected under other federal or state laws.[238] If HIV illness is not cause for the absence, then, of course, it need not be disclosed, as would be the case, for example, if an employee with HIV infection were to request leave to obtain substance abuse treatment. If the need for leave is foreseeable, the request must be made 30 days in advance; if not foreseeable 30 days in advance, the request must be made as soon as practicable under the circumstances.[239]

Employers may require that the request for leave be documented by a health care provider's certification of the employee's condition. For employees requesting leave because of their own illness, the certification is sufficient if it includes the condition's onset date, probable duration, appropriate medical facts within the knowledge of the health care provider regarding the condition, and a statement that the employee is unable to perform the functions of his or her position. If the request is for intermittent leave or leave on a reduced leave schedule, the medical necessity for the absence must be stated as well as its expected duration. If the request is for leave to care for a family member, it must include a statement that the employee is needed to care for the family member and the expected time that the employee is needed.[240] Employers may require the employee to provide subsequent recertifications on a reasonable basis. Also, employers may require employees to obtain a second or third medical opinion, at the employer's expense, if the employer has reason to doubt the employee's certification.[241] The FMLA also allows employers to require a medical certification that the employee is able to return to work.[242]

Employers are required to notify employees regarding their rights under the FMLA in several contexts. Covered employers must maintain an FMLA notice in a conspicuous place in the workplace.[243] Civil penalties may be imposed if an employer willfully fails to post this notice,[244] but also failure to provide this notice prohibits the employer from taking any adverse action against an employee, including denial of FMLA leave, for failing to furnish the employer with advance notice of need to take such leave. Additionally, information regarding FMLA rights must be included in any written guidance to employees concerning employee benefits or rights, and when an employee requests FMLA leave, the employer must certify, in writing, whether the leave is FMLA leave or

---

[238] ADA, for example, as discussed in **§ 3.10,** provides for confidentiality for information concerning an employee's disability, which would encompass his or her HIV status. Additionally, many state HIV confidentiality laws provide for protection for subsequent disclosures of information, particularly when it is released from a health care provider, as discussed in **Ch. 2.** Employees thus may wish to have the HIV information disclosed directly from the health care provider, rather than disclosing it themselves, in order to obtain this protection.

[239] 29 C.F.R. § 825.303.

[240] 29 U.S.C. § 2613(b); *see also* 29 C.F.R. pt. 825, app. B (standard form for certification).

[241] 29 U.S.C. § 2613(c) and (d).

[242] If the employer requires a return to work certification, however, it must be uniformly required of all employees, not just those with a specific illness. 29 U.S.C. § 2614(a)(4).

[243] 29 U.S.C. § 2619(a); 29 C.F.R. pt. 825, app. C (standard employer notice of FMLA rights).

[244] 29 U.S.C. § 2619(b).

not, detailing "the specific expectations and obligations of the employee and explaining the consequences of a failure to meet these obligations."[245] If the employer fails to designate the leave as FMLA leave, the employee may then request FMLA leave in addition to that already provided by the employer. Thus, an employer's failure to notify an employee that using more than 12 weeks of unpaid leave would result in loss of re-employment rights may provide the employee with a basis to challenge the loss of those rights on the basis that he or she did not understand that leave beyond the 12-week period would have that result.[246]

The FMLA provides a private cause of action on an individual and class basis against employers for violations.[247] Damages are limited to lost salary and other benefits (not in excess of 12 weeks), actual monetary losses (such as the cost of providing care to a family member), interest, and liquidated damages in an equal amount.[248] Equitable relief (including reinstatement and promotion) and the plaintiff's attorney's fees, expert witness fees, and other costs are also available remedies.[249] The FMLA can also be enforced by administrative and civil actions, including injunctions, brought by the Department of Labor, although the initiation of civil actions by the Department of Labor may limit the right of individual employees to seek individual or class-based relief.[250]

§ 3.19 AIDS and the Armed Forces

In response to the AIDS epidemic, the U.S. Department of Defense (DOD) has promulgated a comprehensive policy of mandatory screening for persons with HIV infection,[251] very much at variance with standards regarding civilian workplaces. In essence, DOD policy has made HIV negative status a prerequisite for all persons entering military service. Although HIV-infected servicemembers can remain in the service on active duty, their assignments are significantly restricted, thus imposing a significant limitation on their potential for advancement or promotion.

This difference in standards between military and civilian is very much the result of the special requirements of the military as a workplace.[252] As the U.S. Supreme

---

[245] 29 C.F.R. § 825.301(c).

[246] *See* Fry v. First Fidelity Bancorporation, 64 U.S.L.W. 1122 (E.D. Pa., Jan. 30, 1996).

[247] 29 U.S.C. § 2617(a)(2).

[248] If the employer can show good faith and that it had reasonable grounds for believing it was not violating the FMLA, the court may, in its discretion, reduce the liability to actual damages and interest. 29 U.S.C. § 2617(a)(1)(A)(iii).

[249] 29 U.S.C. § 2617(a)(3).

[250] *Id.* § 2617(b).

[251] For an overview of military AIDS policy, see John A. Anderson et al., *AIDS Issues in the Military,* 32 Air Force L. Rev. 353 (1990).

[252] Congress has authorized the DOD to establish physical eligibility requirements for persons in the military. *See, e.g.,* 10 U.S.C. §§ 510(b) (reserve enlistees); 532(a)(4) (regular officers); 591(b) (reserve officers).

Court has ruled in determining the constitutional rights of military servicemembers, the military is a "separate society" from the civilian society with the result that constitutional protections are lessened and deference is frequently accorded to military policy.[253] Statutory protections, such as that provided by the Rehabilitation Act, have been similarly viewed by the courts as inapplicable to the military.[254]

Although the military's policy on homosexuality has been frequently challenged in court, the military has not argued exclusion of individuals with HIV as a basis for that policy. In the one case in which that issue arose, the District of Columbia Court of Appeals rejected that rationale.[255]

In addition to the policy applicable to the uniformed armed services, DOD policy addresses the rights of civilian employees of the military and the families of civilian employees.[256]

§ 3.20 —Department of Defense Policy

The DOD maintains a policy involving comprehensive, mandatory HIV testing of all servicemembers and recruit applicants.[257] Under that policy, each service

---

[253] *See, e.g.,* Goldman v. Weinberger, 475 U.S. 503 (1986); Rostker v. Goldberg, 453 U.S. 57 (1981); Greer v. Spock, 424 U.S. 828 (1976); Parker v. Levy, 417 U.S. 733 (1974).

[254] *See* Doe v. Garrett, 903 F.2d 1455 (11th Cir. 1990) (no Rehabilitation Act § 504 coverage); Smith v. Christian, 763 F.2d 1322 (11th Cir. 1985) (same); Doe v. Ball, 725 F. Supp. 1210 (M.D. Fla. 1989) (same); Aviles v. United States, 696 F. Supp. 217 (E.D. La. 1988) (constitutional and statutory damage claims against Coast Guard barred). The ADA by its explicit terms does not apply to the United States as an employer, as noted in § **3.5.**

[255] Steffen v. Aspin, 8 F.2d 57, 69 (D.C. Cir. 1993), *rev'g* 780 F. Supp. 1 (D.D.C. 1991) (court of appeals rejected district court's view that military policy was rationally related to preventing spread of HIV, stating, "Even if AIDS happens to be more prevalent today among homosexuals than among heterosexuals, justifying the [DOD policy] on this basis requires the illegitimate assumption that persons of homosexual orientation will break the rules by engaging in homosexual conduct as members of the armed forces.")

[256] Although the Rehabilitation Act is applicable to civilian employees of the DOD, as well as to employees of DOD contractors, whether statutory protections extend to employment overseas is unclear. *See* Equal Employment Opportunity Comm'n v. Arabian Am. Oil Co., 499 U.S. 244 (1991) (Title VII of Civil Rights Act does not apply extraterritorially to U.S. citizen of U.S. employer; *cf.* 42 U.S.C. §§ 12111 and 12112 (extraterritorial application of ADA).

[257] DOD Directive 6485.1, 56 Fed. Reg. 15,281 (1991), amending 32 C.F.R. pt. 58 (effective Mar. 19, 1991). This regulation was published in proposed form at 55 Fed. Reg. 38,085 (1990) and 54 Fed. Reg. 50,243 (1989). A proposed regulation covering the same policy was published at 54 Fed. Reg. 50,243 (1990), including several appendices not included in the publication of the final rule. These appendices set forth a standard clinical protocol for HIV infection (app. A), guidelines for testing and interpretation of test results (app. B), the DOD's disease surveillance and health education program (app. D), and limitations on use of information obtained from test results and during epidemiological interviews (app. G).

branch is required to promulgate its own implementing regulations on HIV. Although these regulations may vary slightly from service to service, they must conform to the general principles stated in the DOD policy.

In summary, the DOD policy provides that appointment or enlistment is denied to individuals with HIV infection, regardless of their health status, whether asymptomatic or symptomatic. Active duty servicemembers who test positive are permitted to serve the remainder of their enlistment or commission; their HIV-positive status does not bar application for reenlistment. For persons already serving on active duty in the armed forces, periodic HIV testing is mandatory.[258] Servicemembers with HIV infection are referred for medical evaluation of fitness for continued service, as would any personnel with other progressive illnesses. HIV-infected personnel are not retired or separated from service solely on the basis of their HIV status, although they can obtain discharge from the military for the convenience of the government.[259]

Military policy on HIV-infected servicemembers has been the subject of controversy. In 1996, Congress mandated that HIV-infected servicemembers be excluded from military service.[260] Initially, this legislation was vetoed by President Clinton,[261] but later he reluctantly signed a subsequent version of the legislation into law,[262] at the same time stating that the exclusion provision was unconstitutional. He took the unusual step of explaining that "[t]he Attorney General will decline to defend this provision. Instead, the Attorney General will inform the House and the Senate of this determination [of unconstitutionality] so that they may, if they wish, present to the courts their argument that the provision should be sustained."[263] Four months after its enactment, however, Congress reversed itself and repealed the ban on HIV-infected servicemembers.[264]

Reserve component members with HIV infection are denied extended active duty (active duty for more than 30 days), except under conditions of mobilization

---

[258] Servicemembers refusing to be tested are subject to criminal prosecution for their refusal. Uniform Code of Military Justice, art. 90(2) and art. 91(2), 10 U.S.C. §§ 890(2) and 891(2) (failure to follow superior's orders); *see generally* David A. Schlueter, Military Criminal Justice: Practice and Procedure § 2-4 (4th ed. 1996).

[259] *See* app. I, § B.3., to proposed amendment to 32 C.F.R. pt. 58a, published at 54 Fed. Reg. 50,251 (1989).

[260] National Defense Authorization Act for Fiscal Year 1996, H.R. 1530, § 561, 104th Cong., 1st Sess. (1995).

[261] William J. Clinton, *Message to the House of Representatives Returning Without Approval the National Defense Authorization Act for Fiscal Year 1996,* 32 Weekly Comp. Pres. Doc. 2233 (1995).

[262] Pub. L. No. 104-106, § 567, 1996 U.S.C.C.A.N. (110 Stat.) 186, 328 (amending 10 U.S.C. § 1177).

[263] William J. Clinton, *Statement on Signing the National Defense Authorization Act for Fiscal Year 1996,* 32 Weekly Comp. Pres. Doc. 260, 261 (1996).

[264] Omnibus Appropriations Act, Pub. L. No. 104-134, § 2702(a)(1), 1996 U.S.C.C.A.N. (110 Stat.) 1321, [756].

and on decision of the secretary of the military department involved. Reserve component members not on extended active duty, or not on extended full-time National Guard duty, are transferred involuntarily to the Standby Reserve only if they cannot be utilized in the Selected Reserve. As with active duty service-members, reservists are subject to fitness for continued service evaluation and are retired or separated if unfit for duty.

The DOD policy also provides standards for ensuring the safety of the blood supply, standards for complying with congressional limitations of the use of HIV data or information derived from epidemiological interviews of service-members (see § **3.21**), a disease surveillance and health education program, education and voluntary testing program for DOD healthcare beneficiaries other than servicemembers, and compliance with host-country requirements for screening civilian DOD employees (see § **3.22**).

The military policy of mandatory testing and exclusion of persons with HIV infection has, since its inception,[265] been formulated with several specific military personnel issues in mind. First, in regard to new recruits, the recruits' HIV infection is deemed a preexisting medical condition for which the DOD avoids potential medical costs by excluding the recruit. Also, the possibility that the servicemember may not complete his or her service commitment because of illness is a factor cited by the DOD in support of the policy. Third, military servicemembers may be given live-virus immunizations as part of basic training, or as part of their deployment in theaters of war that could expose them to biological weapons, and such immunizations are believed to adversely affect individuals with HIV infection. Finally, persons with HIV infection cannot participate in battlefield blood donor activities or other blood donor programs.

First promulgated in 1985,[266] the military screening policy was made possible then for the first time by the availability of FDA-approved tests for HIV antibodies. Initial court challenges to the Navy's practice of discharging, rather than retaining, new recruits who test positive for HIV within months of enlistment were successful.[267] Once the testing policy was in place, however, individuals with HIV infection were barred from entering the military, thus obviating for the future the issue presented by entry level status new recruits who test positive. Since its inception, the policy of mandatory testing and exclusion from entry,

---

[265] See *Policy on Identification, Surveillance, and Disposition of Military Personnel Infected with Human T-Lymphotropic Virus Type III (HTLV-III),* Secretary of Defense Memorandum 1-2 (Oct. 24, 1985).

[266] *Id.* This policy statement was reiterated and slightly revised in *Policy on Identification, Surveillance, and Administration of Personnel Infected with Human Immunodeficiency Virus,* Secretary of Defense Memorandum (Aug. 4, 1988). The Aug. 1988 memorandum is superseded by current policy, 32 C.F.R. pt. 58 (1996).

[267] *See* Batten v. Department of the Navy, 8 Daily Lab. Rep. (BNA) 10-A (Jan. 8, 1986) (challenge by new military recruits to entry level discharge, instead of retention under DOD policy, for testing positive for HIV antibodies).

however, has not been challenged successfully.[268] Similarly, constitutional challenges to the DOD policy by reserve servicemembers who have tested positive for HIV have not been successful.[269]

§ 3.21 —Limitations on Use of HIV-Related Information

Although the DOD policy is plainly at variance with the civilian standards of nondiscrimination against persons with HIV infection, the military policy does include several public health policy elements. The policy emphasizes the need for counselling servicemembers regarding the risks of HIV transmission, and it requires development of epidemiological data concerning the infected personnel. Because there is no physician-patient privilege between the military physician and servicemember patient,[270] however, the DOD policy of testing and followup epidemiologic interviews with servicemembers posed a problem for many servicemembers. Because servicemembers can be involuntarily separated from the service or prosecuted for unlawful drug use or homosexual acts or orientation, information provided by the servicemember could be of use in prosecution or administrative separation of the servicemember. As a result, servicemembers had a significant disincentive to participate in the followup interview, and the results of the followup interview, when given, were harmful to the servicemembers.

As a result of concern over using information derived in the course of interviewing servicemembers regarding their HIV infection, Congress imposed limitations on the use of the information in an amendment to the 1987 Defense Authorization Act:

> (1) Information obtained by the Department of Defense during or as a result of an epidemiologic-assessment interview with a serum positive member of the Armed Forces may not be used to support any adverse personnel action against the member.

---

[268] No reported cases consider the constitutionality of the military mandatory screening policy. Similar issues involving mandatory testing were decided in Local 1812, American Fed'n of Gov't Employees v. U.S. Dep't of State, 662 F. Supp. 50 (D.D.C. 1987) (upholding government policy of HIV testing and reassignment of HIV infected State Department personnel), discussed in § **3.24.**

[269] *See* Charles v. Rice, 28 F.3d 1312 (1st Cir. 1994) (upholding nondeployment rule for HIV positive Air National Guard servicemembers, constitutional challenge to policy not considered), *aff'g* 800 F. Supp. 1041 (D.P.R. 1992); Doe v. Garrett, 903 F.2d 1455 (11th Cir. 1990) (upholding discharge of Naval Reserve officer), *aff'g* 725 F. Supp. 1210 (M.D. Fla. 1989).

[270] *See* Military Rule of Evidence 501(d); DOD Directive 1332.14, enc. 3, pt. 3, § 5.3 (1982).

(2) for purposes of paragraph (1):

(A) the term "epidemiologic-assessment interview" means questioning a member of the Armed Forces for purposes of medical treatment or counseling or for epidemiologic or statistical purposes.

(B) the term "serum-positive member of the Armed Forces" means a member of the Armed Forces who has been identified as having been exposed to a virus associated with the acquired immune deficiency syndrome.

(C) the term "adverse personnel action" includes—

(i) a court-martial;

(ii) non-judicial punishment;

(iii) involuntary separation (other than for medical reasons);

(iv) administrative or punitive reduction in grade;

(v) denial of promotion;

(vi) an unfavorable entry in a personnel record;

(vii) a bar to reenlistment; and

(viii) any other action considered by the Secretary concerned to be an adverse personnel action.[271]

The confidentiality protections, however, do not extend to statements made outside a medical interview and may not cover statements made during an medical interview that does not involve HIV issues. Nor does the confidentiality provision extend to military dependents or members of their families, or to civilian employees of the military.

DOD regulations allow the use of HIV-related information for several purposes. Information obtained in the interview can be used as evidence of the servicemember's drug abuse or sexual activity for impeachment or rebuttal purposes in "any proceeding in which the evidence of drug abuse or relevant sexual activity (or lack thereof) has first been introduced by the servicemember."[272] Because HIV status is relevant to the servicemember's assignment, the confidentiality standards do not apply to the use of HIV information in "non-adverse" personnel actions, such as reassignment, including "denial, suspension, or revocation of a security clearance, suspension or termination of access to classified information" or "removal . . . from flight status or other duties requiring a high degree of stability or alertness, including explosive ordnance disposal or deep-sea diving."[273]

HIV test results cannot be used as the sole basis for separating a servicemember, nor can they be used as an independent basis for disciplinary or adverse administrative action. They can, however, be used for separation under the accession

---

[271] National Defense Authorization Act of 1987, Pub. L. No. 99-661, § 705(c), 1987 U.S.C.C.A.N. (100 Stat.) 3816, 3902, *reprinted in* note to 10 U.S.C. § 1074 (1994).

[272] 54 Fed. Reg. at 50,250 (1989) (amending 32 C.F.R. pt. 58, app. G).

[273] *Id.*

testing program applicable to all recruit applicants, in a voluntary separation for the convenience of the government, or "in any other administrative separation action authorized by DOD policy." Finally, the HIV test results can be used to establish seropositivity of a servicemember "who disregards the preventive medicine counseling or the prevention medicine order, or both, in an administrative or disciplinary action based on such disregard or disobedience" or "as an element in any permissible administrative or disciplinary action, or in any criminal prosecution, as an element of proof of an offense charged under the Uniform Code of Military Justice, or the laws of a state or the United States."[274]

Disclosure of HIV information pertaining to a member of the New Jersey National Guard was unsuccessfully challenged in *C.J. v. Viunovich*.[275] The plaintiff reported for weekend exercises and during roll call he inquired why his name had not been called. Sgt. Viunovich replied, while standing in front of the company formation, "you have AIDS and you are discharged." In his lawsuit, the plaintiff alleged that Sgt. Viunovich's actions were an invasion of his privacy and constituted intentional infliction of emotional distress; he alleged that he feared imminent death and attempted suicide as a result of Sgt. Viunovich's actions. The court rejected these claims on the basis that the National Guard and its employees are immune from suit in tort claims, and, insofar as the actions towards the plaintiff constituted discrimination under New Jersey's handicap discrimination law, federal policy regarding retention of HIV-infected Guard members preempts that state law.

§ 3.22   —Civilian Employees of DOD

Current DOD regulations prohibit HIV testing of civilian employees. The only exception is "to comply with valid host-nation requirements for screening of DOD employees."[276] DOD civilian employees include "current and prospective DOD U.S. civilian employees, including appropriated and nonappropriated fund personnel."[277] This definition does not include members of families of DOD civilian employees, or employees of or applicants for positions with contractors performing work for the DOD, or their families.

Screening standards apply both to employees currently assigned to positions in the host country and to prospective employees. As to prospective employees, "HIV-1 screening shall be considered as a requirement imposed by another nation that must be met before the decision to select the individual for a position or before approving temporary duty or detail to the host nation."[278] DOD civilian

---

[274] *Id.* HIV-related offenses under military law are covered in **Ch. 7.**

[275] 599 A.2d 548 (N.J. Super. Ct. App. Div. 1991).

[276] 32 C.F.R. § 58.4(j) and app. B (1996), promulgated at 56 Fed. Reg. 15,282 and 15,284 (1991), respectively.

[277] 32 C.F.R. § 58.3(e).

[278] *Id.* pt. 58, app. B, para. B.

employees who have volunteered for overseas assignment and who then refuse to undergo testing "shall be retained in their official position without further action and without prejudice to employee benefits, career progression opportunities, or other personnel actions to which those employees are entitled under applicable law or regulation."[279] However, those civilian employees who are obligated to host-nation service and who refuse testing "may be subjected to an appropriate adverse personnel action under the specific terms of the employment agreement or other authorities that may apply."[280] Employees who are already serving in the host nation and who accept testing, which results in a positive result, are subject to "appropriate personnel actions . . . without prejudice to employee rights and privileges."[281] Finally, employees who are not employed in a host nation and who test positive are denied the host nation assignment. They are to be retained in their current positions without prejudice. All HIV-infected employees are entitled to reasonable accommodation in employment, as provided in internal DOD standards as well as the Rehabilitation Act.[282]

Some host nations require reporting of HIV-infected DOD civilian personnel but do not bar their entry into the country. DOD policy provides that those employees will be identified to the host country only after the employee has been counseled regarding the country's reporting policy and given the option of declining the assignment while retaining their official positions without prejudice. Employees who are already in the host country may decline to have the HIV information disclosed and may request, and be provided with, early return to the U.S. at government expense.[283]

FEDERAL CONSTITUTIONAL ISSUES

§ 3.23   Constitutional Rights and HIV in the Workplace

Federal constitutional principles may be implicated by HIV policies in public-sector workplaces, such as those that mandate employee testing or establish restrictions on work assignments for persons with HIV infection. Because of statutory

---

[279] *Id.*

[280] *Id.*

[281] *Id. Cf.* Plowman v. United States Dep't of Army, 698 F. Supp. 627 (E.D. Va. 1988) (claim of HIV testing without consent resulting in coerced resignation of civilian employee), *subsequent opinion sub nom.* Plowman v. Cheney, 714 F. Supp. 196 (E.D. Va. 1989) (dismissing action on procedural grounds).

[282] *See* Burchell v. Department of Army, 679 F. Supp. 1393 (D.S.C. 1988) (Rehabilitation Act claim of civilian DOD employee).

[283] 32 C.F.R. pt. 58, app. B.

nondiscrimination protections, such as those contained in the federal Rehabilitation Act or similar state nondiscrimination laws, however, disputes concerning public employees have largely been decided on those statutory grounds, although the constitutional and statutory claims are often factually coextensive.[284] Similarly, because the ADA covers states and their political subdivisions, constitutional issues have receded further in the background for public sector employees, given the clearly enunciated statutory rights and the courts' rule of preference for statutory as opposed to constitutional decision making. In some cases, clear statutory limitations such as those of the ADA concerning an employer's testing of employees may limit employer practices with the result that potential constitutional disputes do not occur. Nevertheless, constitutional issues may arise in private as opposed to public employer workplaces when the private employer's policy is mandated by state or local law. Even when such practices are not mandated but are authorized by state or local law, and are undertaken at the discretion of the private employer, federal constitutional guarantees may be implicated.[285]

The federal constitution imposes essentially two limitations on employment policy. First, as discussed in **§ 3.24,** the Fourth Amendment limits an employer's interference with the privacy rights of employees. This constitutional guarantee is implicated most frequently, although not exclusively, by mandatory testing policies. Second, as discussed in **§ 3.25,** the guarantees of equal protection and due process of law proscribe employers' attempts to treat employees in an arbitrary fashion, thus requiring employers to formulate a policy or make employment decisions on the basis of some rational justification. Although very few cases have resulted in rulings on these constitutional issues, the cases do yield basic standards for determining the constitutionally based limits on HIV-related employment practices.

§ 3.24 —Constitutional Privacy Rights and HIV Policy

The Fourth Amendment prohibition against unreasonable governmental searches and seizures establishes some protections against intrusion into areas of an employee's privacy. Generally, however, employment-related intrusions that do not involve criminal law enforcement have been viewed as exceptions to the requirement that the search be preceded by a warrant based on a probable cause determination.[286] Thus, under Supreme Court precedents for noncriminal investigatory

---

[284] *See, e.g.,* Chalk v. United States Dist. Court, 840 F.2d 701 (9th Cir. 1988) (public employee covered under Rehabilitation Act).

[285] *See* Skinner v. Railway Labor Executives' Ass'n, 489 U.S. 602 (1989) (government's more than passive position regarding private conduct implicates Fourth Amendment search and seizure standards).

[286] This issue is discussed in more detail in **Ch. 7.**

searches,[287] the courts must assess the reasonableness of the search, by balancing the nature and quality of the intrusion of the individual's privacy interests against the importance of the government's interests alleged to justify the intrusion. The drawing of blood has been increasingly viewed as involving less than a significant violation of bodily integrity.[288] Nevertheless, in one case in the context of a mandatory employee HIV testing program, *Glover v. Eastern Nebraska Community Office of Retardation,*[289] state policy required HIV testing of certain employees who had direct contact with patients at an agency that provided services to individuals with mental retardation. The state's proffered justification for the mandatory testing program was to protect clients from the risk of HIV infection resulting from an incident in which a client might scratch or bite a staff member. The court of appeals adopted the finding of the trial court that the risk of transmission from staff to client was "extraordinarily low, approaching zero."[290] Applying a balancing test, the court of appeals concluded that the state policy would do little to protect clients, because, in reality, they were not at risk for infection. On the other hand, the intrusion on the employee's privacy interests was deemed significant. The testing policy was ruled unconstitutional. In *Local 1812, American Federation of Government Employees v. U.S. Department of State,*[291] however, the district court upheld the government's right to impose a mandatory testing program for foreign service personnel. The government's justification, that HIV-infected personnel may become ill during overseas assignments, was deemed to outweigh the employee's privacy interest, particularly because employees already undergo blood testing to comply with fitness for duty standards.[292] Similarly, in *Leckelt v. Board of Commissioners,*[293] the Fifth Circuit Court of Appeals disposed of the claim that a public hospital's requirement that an employee disclose his HIV test result violated the Fourth Amendment. The employee's expectation of privacy was viewed as diminished

---

[287] *See, e.g.,* O'Connor v. Ortega, 480 U.S. 717 (1987); New Jersey v. T.L.O., 469 U.S. 325 (1985); Camara v. Municipal Court, 387 U.S. 523 (1967).

[288] Skinner v. Railway Labor Executives' Ass'n, 489 U.S. 602, 625 (1989); *see also* Winston v. Lee, 470 U.S. 766 (1985) (disapproving surgical extraction of bullet); Schmerber v. California, 384 U.S. 757 (1966) (approving extraction of blood under exigent circumstances); Dunn v. White, 880 F.2d 1188 (10th Cir. 1989) (upholding prison policy of compulsory HIV testing of inmates); *cf.* Barlow v. Ground, 943 F.2d. 1132 (9th Cir. 1991), *cert. denied,* 505 U.S. 1206 (1992) (no exigent circumstances justify warrantless seizure of blood specimen for HIV testing from suspect accused of biting police officers).

[289] 867 F.2d 461 (8th Cir.), *cert. denied,* 493 U.S. 932 (1989), *aff'g* 686 F. Supp. 243 (D. Neb. 1988).

[290] *Id.* at 463.

[291] 662 F. Supp. 50 (D.D.C. 1986).

[292] *See also* Anonymous Fireman v. City of Willoughby, 779 F. Supp. 402, 417 (N.D. Ohio 1991) (unsuccessful constitutional challenge to municipality's "fitness for duty" annual HIV testing for firefighters); *cf.* Doe v. District of Columbia, 796 F. Supp. 559 (D.D.C. 1992) (successful Rehabilitation Act claim of firefighter with HIV).

[293] 909 F.2d 820, 832–33 (5th Cir. 1990), *aff'g* 714 F. Supp. 1377 (E.D. La. 1989). The Rehabilitation Act ruling in this case is discussed in § **3.12.**

by the employer's policy of requiring blood testing for infectious disease, particularly for those at risk for such infection; the employer's interest in knowing the employee's results was heightened, rising to a reasonable suspicion standard. The disclosure requirement was ruled constitutional.

A claimed violation of federal constitutional privacy rights was the sole issue presented at trial in *Doe v. Southeastern Pennsylvania Transportation Authority.*[294] In that case, the plaintiff employee alleged that his employer's chief administrative officer learned of his HIV infection by reviewing a report submitted to the employer by the pharmacy responsible for filling prescriptions under the self-insured employer's prescription plan. The report included employee names linked with information about their prescriptions. In the case of plaintiff John Doe, the prescription information indicated that he was taking a medication used exclusively to treat HIV illness. Although the list was subsequently destroyed, the employer's chief administrative officer showed it to the employer's medical director as well as Mr. Doe's direct supervisor. The jury awarded Mr. Doe $125,000 in damages against both the employer and the employer's chief administrative officer. Ruling on the defendants' post-trial motions, the district court concluded that the prescription information used by the employer was subject to federal constitutional protection, and that the plaintiff's evidence was adequate to support the jury's award of damages for the constitutional violation. Additionally, the court ruled that the plaintiff's claim of emotional distress upon learning that the chief administrative officer had learned of his HIV status was adequate to support the jury's award of damages. On appeal, however, the Third Circuit Court of Appeals reversed. Although the court ruled that the plaintiff's medical information was constitutionally protected and that disclosure to each employee potentially constituted a separate constitutional violation, the court ultimately concluded that the self-insured employer's interest in monitoring its health insurance plan outweighed the plaintiff's constitutional privacy interest.[295]

§ 3.25   —Equal Protection Rights and HIV Policy

Federal constitutional equal protection standards for public employment policies impose a requirement that the government employer's treatment of its employees

---

[294] 72 F.3d 1133 (3d Cir. 1995), *cert. denied,* 117 S. Ct. 51 (1996). The author of this chapter served as co-counsel to the plaintiff in the early stages of this litigation.

[295] *Id.* at 1143. The court's conclusion that the employer accessed the medical information for legitimate monitoring purposes appears to be contradicted by the district court's review of the evidence in its opinion denying the defendants' post-trial motion. 10 Indiv. Empl. Rights Cas. (BNA) 1519, 1527, 1530 (E.D. Pa. 1995) (noting that jury had reasonable basis for concluding (1) that none of the employees who had access to the information had a "business need to know" it, and (2) that review of information pertaining to John Doe was undertaken "intentionally, recklessly or with deliberate indifference" to his right to privacy). *See also* Doe v. Southeastern Pa. Transp. Auth., 886 F. Supp. 1186 (E.D. Pa. 1994) (defendant's summary judgment motion denied in part).

meet a basic test of reasonableness. Thus, the judicial standard of review of such policies or practices requires an assessment of the connection between the government's interests, which support the policy, and the objective to be obtained by that policy. The general rule, as stated by the Supreme Court, is that "legislation is presumed to be valid and will be sustained if the classification drawn by the statute is rationally related to the legitimate state interest."[296] The Supreme Court has apparently concluded that government policy affecting persons with disabilities is not subject to heightened standards of judicial scrutiny,[297] as would be the case if the policy were drawn on racial lines, for example. Nevertheless, in assessing HIV employment policies, courts will be called upon to determine if an employment policy furthers a legitimate interest and to assess the means chosen to do so; that assessment only makes sense if it actually involves a rational standard based on medical or scientific fact.[298]

The cases involving constitutional challenges to HIV employment policies demonstrate the potential lack of protection afforded under a minimum scrutiny review. Such was the case in the Fifth Circuit's ruling in *Leckelt v. Board of Commissioners,*[299] which disposed of Kevin Leckelt's claim that his employer's policy or practice of requiring his disclosure of his HIV status was not related to the government's objective of assuring provision of medical services without risk of HIV transmission from him. The fact that the hospital might have adopted alternative policies that would have affected Leckelt's rights to a lesser degree was not of concern under the court's equal protection, minimum scrutiny analysis.

STATE AND LOCAL EMPLOYMENT STANDARDS

§ 3.26 Overview of State and Local Standards

The AIDS epidemic has resulted in significant developments in local and state law, frequently, but not always, involving heightened protection for persons with HIV infection. State laws protective of persons with HIV infection are consistent with national public health strategy in response to the epidemic.[300] Although

---

[296] City of Cleburne v. Cleburne Living Ctr., 473 U.S. 432, 440 (1985).

[297] *See id.* (no heightened scrutiny of legislation affecting persons with disabilities, but nevertheless invalidating zoning ordinance on "minimal" scrutiny basis); Laurence H. Tribe, American Constitutional Law § 16-3 (2d ed. 1988) (describing "covertly heightened" level of scrutiny).

[298] *See* Scott Burris, *Rationality Review and the Politics of Public Health,* 34 Vill. L. Rev. 933 (1989) (advocating a rational medical basis test for constitutional review of public health policy).

[299] 909 F.2d 820, 831–32 (5th Cir. 1990), *aff'g* 714 F. Supp. 1377 (E.D. La. 1989) (court concluded that enforcement of infection control policy is substantial and compelling governmental interest).

[300] Relationship of employment standards and public health strategy in regard to the AIDS epidemic is discussed more fully in § **3.2.**

the adoption of the federal ADA was, in part, the result of the view that state laws did not provide clear and adequate protection for persons with disabilities,[301] in many jurisdictions, state and local law have indeed contributed significantly to the growing body of law on HIV in the workplace.[302] A majority of states has adopted nondiscrimination standards in regard to HIV, or have interpreted by court or administrative agency ruling existing laws as providing such protection. Very few states deny disability or handicap discrimination protection to persons with AIDS or HIV infection.[303]

Because of the proliferation of state and local laws, counsel must be potentially concerned with three levels of enactments (local, state, and federal) and, in some cases, with more than one enactment at each governmental level. Because state and federal law claims can be joined in one action, more than one claim may be pursued in the same action, including both statutory and common law claims. For the employer, the separate, distinct statutory provisions may appear to present compliance problems. Rarely, however, do state and federal laws require inconsistent policies; instead, the employer's problem is to identify the most stringent legal standard and comply with it. Indeed, in one case, federal and state nondiscrimination standards resulted in opposite results.[304] Conflicting results can also occur in the interpretation of the same statute in differing forums.[305]

In some localities, local legislative initiatives have been challenged as beyond the local legislature's power or as preempted by state or federal law. In *Citizens for Uniform Laws v. County of Contra Costa*,[306] for example, a taxpayer organization challenged a local law that prohibited discrimination in employment, housing, public accommodations, and county services against persons who had or were perceived to have HIV, or against persons associating with persons who had HIV. The plaintiff taxpayers argued that the local nondiscrimination

---

[301] *See* H.R. Rep. No. 485, pt. 2, 101st Cong., 2d Sess. 47, *reprinted in* 1990 U.S.C.C.A.N. 303, 329 (noting "too many states, for whatever reason, still perpetuate confusion" regarding nondiscrimination standards).

[302] *See, e.g.,* Cain v. Hyatt, 734 F. Supp. 671 (E.D. Pa. 1990) (applying Pa. law); Raytheon Co. v. Fair Employment & Hous. Comm'n, 261 Cal. Rptr. 197 (Ct. App. 1989); Cronan v. New England Tel. & Tel. Co., 41 Fair Empl. Prac. Cas. (BNA) 1273 (Mass. Super. Ct. 1986); Club Swamp Annex v. White, 561 N.Y.S.2d 609 (App. Div. 1990); Benjamin R. v. Orkin Exterminating Co., 390 S.E.2d 814 (W. Va. 1990).

[303] *See, e.g.,* Hilton v. Southwestern Bell Tel. Co., 936 F.2d 823 (5th Cir. 1991) (Texas handicap discrimination law interpreted as not covering an AIDS-related disability).

[304] *New York AIDS Discrimination Case Gets Conflicting Federal, State Rulings,* 66 Daily Lab. Rep. (BNA) A-2 (April 5, 1990) (state and federal agency rulings in conflict over medical center's refusal to hire an HIV-infected pharmacist). The conflicting rulings were subsequently resolved when the New York State Division of Human Rights concluded that the employer's discrimination against the pharmacist was a violation of New York law; previously, the Office of Civil Rights, U.S. Department of Health and Human Services, had ruled that the termination violated the Rehabilitation Act. *See In re* Westchester County Med. Ctr., 2 Empl. Prac. Guide (CCH) ¶ 5,340 (1992).

[305] *See* Leckelt v. Board of Comm'rs, 909 F.2d 820, 825 n.10 (5th Cir. 1990) (court's refusal to consider findings of administrative agency apparently contrary to its own).

[306] 285 Cal. Rptr. 456 (Ct. App. 1991).

enactment was preempted by the housing and employment nondiscrimination provisions of a California state law, the Fair Employment and Housing Act. The Court of Appeals upheld the local law, noting that its public health purpose—it had been enacted to encourage persons to seek HIV testing—removed it from the field of civil rights protection occupied by the state's Fair Employment and Housing Act. Accordingly, the local law was not preempted.

Local HIV-related ordinances have also been subject to repeal by legislative initiative. In *Citizens for Responsible Behavior v. Superior Court*,[307] a citizens' group attempted to have the Riverside City Council place a referendum on the ballot that would effectively repeal the city's ordinance prohibiting sexual orientation and HIV-related discrimination. The referendum application denial was affirmed by the California Court of Appeal on the basis that the effect of the referendum would be an unconstitutional denial of equal protection, was unconstitutionally vague, and was an invalid attempt to amend the city charter by limiting the city council's power to legislate on such issues in the future.

§ 3.27 —State and Local Statutory Claims

In each case of claimed employment discrimination, the plaintiff's counsel should assess several issues when determining coverage in regard to nondiscrimination standards. This assessment is necessary to determine both the merit of the claim, provide appropriate advice to a client, as well as choose an appropriate forum for prosecution of the claim. Analysis of state and local standards in comparison with federal standards is necessary. For example, if the statute of limitations already may have run on a case under state law, the claim could still be filed timely under federal law. The issues the attorney should consider include the following.

Private Cause of Action.   Counsel should assess the need and opportunity to have direct control over prosecution of a claim by pursuing a private cause of action, as opposed to having an administrative agency's review of the case. Depending on the availability of judicial resources, it may be possible to expedite the case if it is litigated in court, an option not available with administrative agency review. On the other hand, an administrative agency's expertise in reviewing such cases, particularly if they involve specialized medical or scientific issues of fact, and the opportunity for settlement discussions as part of the reconciliation process may result in a prompt conclusion of the case. Also, in regard to a life-threatening illness that affects a claimant, the agency may have adopted a policy of expedited consideration of such cases.

---

[307] 2 Cal. Rptr. 2d 648 (Ct. App. 1991).

Availability of Remedies. State law remedies may be as broad or broader than those available under federal law, including declaratory relief,[308] punitive damages,[309] damages for emotional distress,[310] and attorney's fees and costs.[311]

Administrative Agency Exhaustion Requirements. Many states require exhaustion of administrative complaint procedures before a claim can be pursued in court. Failure to comply with a timely filing may result in the loss of the right to litigate a state statutory claim.[312]

Exclusivity of Remedies. In some jurisdictions, the choice between state law administrative proceedings and commencement of a lawsuit is exclusive; once one option has been selected, the other is not available.[313]

Definition of Discrimination. State and federal laws have varying definitions of discrimination. As noted in **§ 3.14,** the Rehabilitation Act has been interpreted to require proof that the claimant's disability was the sole reason for the discrimination. The ADA and most state laws have no such requirement, thus allowing for proof that the discrimination was a substantial cause of the discrimination.[314]

Persons Protected. Under the ADA, even persons who associate with those with HIV infection are protected from discrimination on that basis. State standards may not be so liberal. Some states may not explicitly provide coverage on

---

[308] *See, e.g.,* "X" Corp. v. "Y" Person, 622 So. 2d 1098 (Fla. Dist. Ct. App. 1993) (per curiam) (declaratory relief sought by employer to determine application of Fla. HIV nondiscrimination law).

[309] *See, e.g.,* Cain v. Hyatt, 734 F. Supp. 671, 686–87 (E.D. Pa. 1990) (awarding plaintiff $50,000 in punitive damages under Pennsylvania Human Relations Act).

[310] *See* Club Swamp Annex v. White, 561 N.Y.S.2d 609 (App. Div. 1990) (upholding $5,000 award of compensatory damages for mental anguish).

[311] *See* Racine Unified Sch. Dist. v. Labor & Indus. Review Comm'n, 476 N.W.2d 707 (Wis. Ct. App. 1991) (upholding award of attorney's fees, including additional fees for judicial review proceeding, in litigation that successfully challenged school district policy of placing staff with AIDS on sick leave).

[312] *See, e.g.,* Finley v. Giacobbe, 827 F. Supp. 215 (S.D.N.Y. 1993) (dismissing plaintiff's state law claim for failure to comply with state notice of claim statute, but allowing federal statutory and constitutional claims to proceed); M.A.E. v. Doe, 566 A.2d 285 (Pa. Super. Ct. 1989) (claim barred for failure to exhaust administrative remedies).

[313] *See* Herman v. Fairleigh Dickinson Univ., 444 A.2d 614 (N.J. Super. Ct. App. Div.), *cert. denied,* 453 A.2d 884 (N.J. 1982) (plaintiff may choose either administrative remedy or judicial remedy, but not both).

[314] *See, e.g.,* Cain v. Hyatt, 734 F. Supp. 671, 684–85 (E.D. Pa. 1990) (noting substantial cause standard applicable under Pennsylvania law in mixed-motive termination case).

the "perceived as" disabled basis,[315] or may not protect individuals with asymptomatic HIV infection.[316]

Workplaces Covered.   Under federal standards, nondiscrimination coverage may be contingent on receipt of federal funds or number of employees employed, as is the case with the ADA, which covers only employers of 15 or more persons. State statutes or local ordinances, however, may cover smaller workplaces. On the other hand, some state statutes provide exemptions for charitable, religious, or fraternal organizations as employers. Such exemptions are limited under the ADA.

Choice of Forum.   In some cases, potential litigants may choose between federal and state courts.[317] Claims asserted under the ADA or Rehabilitation Act are not heard by juries; in some states, claims under state law may be subject to trial by jury, a potentially risky proposition for a plaintiff with AIDS or HIV infection given the potential that jurors might have substantial fears that cannot be overcome during the course of the trial.

Clarity of Governing Legal Standards.   Counsel should also consider the risks of bringing an action that may be of first impression in a jurisdiction in which legal standards are not clear.

Statute of Limitations.   Potential coverage by more than one statutory nondiscrimination standard can result in several time limits for the filing of claims, some of which may be relatively short.[318] Even though one time limit may have expired (such as the limitation for a state law statutory claim), some claims may survive under a longer limitation period (such as a common law tort claim or federal statutory claim).

Disclosure of Information.   State or local statutes prohibiting the disclosure of HIV-related information may also limit an employer's ability to disclose information regarding an employee's HIV status, and thus employer policies should

---

[315] *See* Sanchez v. Lagoudakis, 486 N.W.2d 657 (Mich. 1992) (holding that plaintiff without AIDS is protected under Mich. law in case in which employer required employee to furnish proof that she did not have AIDS), *rev'g* 457 N.W.2d 373 (Mich. Ct. App. 1990); *cf.* Rose City Oil Co. v. Missouri Comm'n on Human Rights, 832 S.W.2d 314 (Mo. Ct. App. 1992) (holding that Mo. disability nondiscrimination law does not cover individuals perceived to have HIV infection).

[316] *Compare* Burgess v. Your House of Raleigh, Inc., 388 S.E.2d 134 (N.C. 1990) (HIV infection not covered) *with* Benjamin R. v. Orkin Exterminating Co., 390 S.E.2d 814 (W. Va. 1990) (HIV infection covered); *see generally* Jeremy McKinney, Comment, *HIV, AIDS, and Job Discrimination: North Carolina's Failure and Federal Redemption,* 17 Campbell L. Rev. 115 (1995) (criticizing N.C. law in comparison to Americans with Disabilities Act).

[317] *See, e.g.,* Cain v. Hyatt, 734 F. Supp. 671, 672 (E.D. Pa. 1990) (state law claims asserted under federal diversity jurisdiction).

[318] *See, e.g.,* Beck v. Interstate Brands Corp., 953 F.2d 1275 (11th Cir. 1992) (per curiam) (AIDS employment discrimination case dismissal upheld for failure to comply with state statute of limitation).

address this issue.[319] Nondisclosure statutes may be applicable to medical service providers, and thus an employer-retained physician may be subject to these statutory provisions, which might also apply to subsequent disclosure of information from employers to third parties.[320]

Sexual Orientation Discrimination.   A recent trend has been the increasing number of state and local laws that now offer protections against sexual orientation discrimination. Although sexual orientation protection has been proposed on the federal level, it has not yet been adopted. Seven states and the District of Columbia now have statewide protection. Executive orders in other states, such as Pennsylvania and New York, provide protection to certain state employees. Furthermore, numerous municipalities, including major population areas such as Atlanta, Philadelphia, and San Francisco, have their own sexual orientation nondiscrimination ordinances.[321] As a result, many claimants may have both a disability discrimination claim and a separate claim of discrimination based on sexual orientation, with the result that the disability claim can be pursued in one forum, while the sexual orientation claim is pursued in the state or local forum.

In one case, *Racine Unified School District v. Labor & Industry Review Commission,*[322] the Racine School District's policy of mandatory sick leave or leave of absence for AIDS patients was challenged by the employee union as violative of Wisconsin's disability and sexual orientation nondiscrimination provisions. The union argued that the AIDS policy had a disparate impact on homosexual and bisexual men, given the epidemiological data indicating a disproportionately high rate of AIDS diagnosis among those individuals, thus violating Wisconsin's sexual orientation and sex nondiscrimination standards. On appeal, the court of appeals rejected the disparate impact claim because it lacked statistical substantiation in the record. The court, however, ruled favorably on the disability claim.

§ 3.28   —Common Law and Related Causes of Action

In addition to the state statutory provisions applicable to discrimination, state law may also afford rights to employees based on contract or tort doctrines. As is the case with statutory standards, these doctrines vary from state to state. They

---

[319] *See* Sharon Rennert, AIDS/HIV and Confidentiality: Model Policy and Procedures (American Bar Ass'n 1990). State confidentiality laws are summarized in **App. A** and discussed in **Ch. 2.**

[320] *See In re* Milton Hershey Medical Ctr., 634 A.2d 159 (Pa. 1993), *aff'g* 595 A.2d 1290 (Pa. Super. Ct. 1991) (state confidentiality statute governed disclosure of hospital resident's HIV status by hospital to patients).

[321] For a listing of state and local sexual orientation nondiscrimination standards, see Nan D. Hunter et al., The Rights of Lesbians and Gay Men, app. C (ACLU 3d ed. 1992).

[322] 476 N.W.2d 707 (Wis. Ct. App. 1991).

may include breach of contract claims, either express or implied.[323] These claims may result from an employer's discriminatory action towards an employee with or thought to have HIV infection, but rarely would such claims be based on the employee's HIV medical status. Instead, the employee's claim is based on the employer's breach of its obligation to the employee.

Employers may also be subjected to common law tort claims for disclosing information pertaining to the employee, under theories of invasion of privacy,[324] defamation,[325] or related tort claims, such as intentional infliction of emotional distress.[326]

WORKPLACE SAFETY STANDARDS

§ 3.29 HIV as a Workplace Hazard

Unlike the discussion of the direct threat defense under the ADA in §§ 3.11 and § 3.12, which concerned the risk posed by employees with HIV infection to others, this section concerns the issue of risk of transmission from third parties to employees in the workplace. In 1983, the CDC first identified HIV (then referred to as HTLV-III) as posing a potential risk of infection to health care workers.[327] The degree of the risk of HIV transmission in the workplace is impossible to pinpoint, but expert consensus concludes that the risk is extremely low. For example, in ruling unconstitutional a mandatory HIV testing program in a mental health facility, the court concluded that the risk of the staff's transmitting HIV to a patient was "minuscule, trivial, extremely low, extraordinarily low, theoretical, and approaches zero."[328] Documented transmission of HIV in the workplace has been a relative rarity. To date, 51 cases of health care workers'

---

[323] Breach of contract theories are discussed at length in Henry H. Perritt, Jr., Employee Dismissal Law and Practice (John Wiley & Sons, Inc. 3d ed. 1992).

[324] *See* Restatement (Second) of Torts §§ 652B, 652C, 652D, 652E (1979).

[325] *Id.* § 558.

[326] *See, e.g.,* Beck v. Interstate Brands Corp., 953 F.2d 1275 (11th Cir. 1992) (per curiam) (plaintiff in AIDS discrimination case failed to state cause of action against former employer for intentional infliction of emotional distress without allegations of extreme vindictiveness, abuse, or threats); Smith v. Dovenmuehle Mortgage, Inc., 859 F. Supp. 1138, 1143 (N.D. Ill. 1994) (employer's knowledge of employee's AIDS diagnosis put employer on notice regarding severe emotional distress that results from termination of employment); Doe v. William Shapiro, 852 F. Supp. 1246, 1253–55 (E.D. Pa. 1994) (intentional infliction of emotional distress claim barred by state workers' compensation law); Dutson v. Farmers Ins. Exch., 815 F. Supp. 349 (D. Or. 1993) (denying employer's motion to dismiss intentional infliction of emotional distress claim). Tort claims are covered in **Ch. 8.**

[327] CDC, *Acquired Immune Deficiency Syndrome (AIDS): Precautions for Health-Care Workers and Allied Professionals,* 32 MMWR 450–52 (1983).

[328] Glover v. Eastern Neb. Community Office of Retardation, 686 F. Supp. 243, 251 (D. Neb. 1988), *aff'd,* 867 F.2d 461 (8th Cir.), *cert. denied,* 493 U.S. 932 (1989).

being infected occupationally with HIV have been documented by the CDC, and 102 cases of possible infection have been documented, frequently involving the worker's failure to take appropriate precautions.[329] Nevertheless, studies have documented the potential risk of such injury's occurring, particularly when precautions are not observed.[330] OSHA similarly concluded that the risk of injury is a real one when it considered the promulgation of workplace safety standards.[331] The dire consequences of infection, however, make prevention of transmission a compelling concern when formulating workplace policy.

In some instances, however, the policy formulation may involve an intrusion on the rights of patients or others in regard to nondiscrimination and privacy of medical data. As a result, formulating a workplace policy that both protects employees or others who are potentially at risk for HIV infection in the workplace and at the same time protects the privacy and nondiscrimination interests of persons with the infection requires an examination of these potentially conflicting interests.

§ 3.30   —OSHA Standards

In 1986, the Occupational Safety and Health Administration (OSHA)[332] began considering the problem of assuring a safe workplace for employees, such as health care workers, whose jobs routinely involve their exposure to blood or other body fluids and thus, potentially, exposure to HIV. At that time, several unions

---

[329] CDC, *HIV/AIDS Surveillance Report* 15 (mid-year ed., June 1996). Beginning in July 1992, the CDC HIV/AIDS surveillance reports include figures for documented and possible occupational HIV exposure, categorized by occupation. HIV transmission in the health care setting is discussed in **Ch. 1.** *See also* 54 Fed. Reg. at 23,055–60 (summarizing studies of HIV transmission to health care workers).

[330] *Study Shows High Exposure to AIDS for Interns, Residents in San Francisco,* 17 Daily Lab. Rep. A-3 (1991) (calling for enhanced training and compliance with universal precautions, redesign of equipment, and limitations on working hours to reduce fatigue); A. Panlilio, *Blood Contacts During Surgical Procedures,* 265 JAMA 1533 (1991) (high rate of preventable exposures to patient blood); E. Wong, *Are Universal Precautions Effective in Reducing the Number of Occupational Exposures Among Health Care Workers?,* 265 JAMA 1123 (1991) (universal precautions deemed effective in preventing risk of occupational HIV exposure); Beekman, *Risky Business: Using Necessarily Imprecise Casualty Counts to Estimate Occupational Risks for HIV-1 Infection,* 11 Infection Control Hosp. Epidemiology 371 (1990) (*cited in* C. Flexner, *Management of Occupational Exposures to HIV: An Update,* 4 AIDS Med. Rep. 13 (1991)).

[331] *See* 54 Fed. Reg. at 23,053 (1989).

[332] OSHA's regulatory role in regard to workplace safety standards is defined in the Occupational Safety and Health Act of 1970 (OSH Act), 29 U.S.C. §§ 651–666 (1994), which provides broad regulatory authority to ensure that workplaces do not present a threat of serious injury to employees. The OSH Act provides in its general duty clause, 29 U.S.C. § 654(a)(1), that employers provide "employment and a place of employment which are free from recognized hazards . . . likely to cause death or serious bodily harm to [their] employees."

representing health care employees petitioned OSHA to develop a standard to protect those workers from occupational exposure to bloodborne diseases, including AIDS. OSHA declined to issue an emergency temporary standard under the Occupational Safety and Health Act (OSH Act), finding that the risk to employees did not meet the statutory grave danger standard.[333] In October 1987, however, OSHA and the Department of Health and Human Services issued a joint advisory notice pertaining both to HIV and Hepatitis B (HBV) transmission in health care settings.[334] The advisory notice alerted health care employers to the risk of HIV transmission in the workplace, emphasized the need to utilize universal precautions, and stated that OSHA would undertake inspections and enforcement activities in response to employee complaints in order to assure compliance.

Subsequently, OSHA's Office of Health Compliance Assistance issued its first instruction on uniform inspection procedures and guidelines for workplace inspections and enforcement of safety standards pertaining to health care workers potentially exposed to HIV.[335] This instruction incorporated CDC recommendations on infection control, including the use of universal precautions, as preventive measures for HIV transmission.[336]

In 1987, OSHA initiated permanent rule making on safety standards for bloodborne pathogens, which ultimately resulted in the current standard.[337] Violations of this standard may result in citation pursuant to the OSH Act.[338] The OSH Act does not include any limitation on the size of workplace covered, and thus any worksite, regardless of the number of employees, is covered under the standard.[339]

---

[333] *See* 29 U.S.C. § 655(c).

[334] *Protection Against Occupational Exposure to Hepatitis B Virus (HBV) and Human Immunodeficiency Virus (HIV)*, 52 Fed. Reg. 41,818 (1987). OSHA had previously addressed the issue of HBV transmission in the workplace in OSHA Instruction CPL 2-2.36 (1983). Compliance with that instruction, however, was voluntary on the part of employers.

[335] *See* OSHA Instruction CPL 2-2.44B (Feb. 27, 1990), which superseded Instruction CPL 2-2.44 (Jan. 19, 1988) and CPL 2-2.44A (Aug. 15, 1988). Enforcement authority for this standard is derived from 29 U.S.C. § 655(b)(7).

[336] CDC, *Update: Universal Precautions for Prevention of Transmission of Human Immunodeficiency Virus, Hepatitis B Virus, and Other Bloodborne Pathogens in Health Care Settings*, 37 MMWR 377 (1988), and *Recommendations for Prevention of HIV Transmission in Health-Care Settings*, 36 MMWR 2s (Supp. 1987) (apps. A and B, respectively, to OSHA Instruction CPL 2-2.44B).

[337] 29 C.F.R. §§ 1910.1030 (1996); *see* OSHA, *Occupational Exposure to Bloodborne Pathogens*, 54 Fed. Reg. 23,042 (1989) (proposed standard); 56 Fed. Reg. 64,175–82 (1991) (final standard effective Mar. 6, 1992, with full compliance phased in by July 6, 1992). Advance notice of this proposed rule making was published at 52 Fed. Reg. 45,438 (1987).

[338] 29 U.S.C. §§ 658–659; *see also OSHA Fines Lowell General Hospital $21,120, Alleges Inadequate Hazard Training, Education,* O.S.H. Daily (BNA) (Mar. 29, 1991) (noting citations for failure to provide safe workplace in regard to potential exposure to bloodborne diseases).

[339] 29 U.S.C. § 652(5); *see generally* Daniel E. Feld, Annotation, *Who Is "Employer" for Purposes of Occupational Safety and Health Act,* 27 A.L.R. Fed. 943 (1976 & Supp. 1996).

However, the United States and the states and their political subdivisions are not covered.[340]

Concern regarding the issue of occupational transmission of HIV predated OSHA's role in setting workplace safety standards. In 1983, the CDC reported that HIV was transmitted via blood and possibly other body fluids. As a result, the CDC recommended at that time that precautions be utilized that would protect health care workers from unnecessary exposure to blood. Public attention to the issue was focussed by the case of Veronica Prego, a medical extern at a New York City hospital, who brought suit against the hospital, alleging she was infected with HIV by a needle-stick injury from a needle used to treat an AIDS patient.[341]

Workplace safety policy has been grounded on the CDC's recommended use of *universal precautions,* that is, a method of infection control in which all human blood or other potentially infectious materials or substances[342] are assumed to be infectious, thus requiring the use of universal precautions in regard to contact with all such materials or substances. As explained by the CDC:

> Since medical history and examination cannot reliably identify all patients infected with HIV . . . blood and body fluid precautions should be consistently used for *all* patients. This approach . . . referred to as "universal blood and body fluid precautions" or "universal precautions" should be used in the care of *all* patients, especially including those in emergency-care settings in which the risk of blood exposure is increased and the infection status of the patient is usually unknown.[343]

The precautions recommended for universal use include:

1. Barrier precautions (gloves, masks, protective eyewear, face shields, gowns or aprons, as appropriate to the level of potential exposure to blood) should be used routinely to prevent exposure to skin and mucous membrane.

2. Washing hand or other skin surface immediately after exposure to blood or potentially infectious body fluids, and after removal of gloves.

---

[340] 29 U.S.C. § 652(5). Some states impose similar workplace safety standards on state or municipal workplaces as a matter of state occupational safety law. *See, e.g.,* 35 Pa. Con. Stat. Ann. § 7604 (requiring state health department to establish workplace safety guidelines, consistent with CDC standards, for workplaces not covered by OSHA).

[341] *See* Prego v. City of N.Y., 541 N.Y.S.2d 995 (App. Div. 1989).

[342] HIV transmission by various body fluids is covered in **Ch. 1.** To err on the side of safety, universal precautions were recommended for exposure to all body fluids and tissues, even though not all are thought to be infectious. *See* Joint Advisory Notice, 52 Fed. Reg. 41,819 (1987). The current regulation differentiates among infectious and noninfectious fluids, except "in situations in which it is difficult or impossible to differentiate between body fluids." 29 C.F.R. § 1910.1030 (defines "other potentially infectious materials").

[343] *Recommendations for Prevention of HIV Transmission in Health-Care Settings,* 36 MMWR 2 (Supp. 1987) (emphasis in original); *see also* 29 C.F.R. § 1910.1030(b) ("all human blood and certain body fluids are treated as if known to be infectious for HIV").

3. Precautions to prevent injury by needles, scalpels, or other sharp instruments during medical procedures, cleaning, or handling, by using proper disposal in puncture-proof containers in immediate area of use, and by not recapping needles.

4. Health care workers with abraded or broken skin should refrain from patient contact until the condition is resolved.

OSHA's current bloodborne pathogens standard incorporates the prior standards involving the use of universal precautions and workforce education. The most important change from the pre-1991 standard, however, is in regard to the scope of their application. Prior standards were applicable to workplaces identified as posing a risk of transmission, and thus health care workplaces were emphasized. The current standard, however, defines coverage by assessing the risk of transmission posed to an individual employee by looking at the employment responsibilities of the position in question. Thus, although health care workers continue to be covered, as they were under the prior standards, coverage now extends to other employees as well. *Occupational exposure* is defined as "reasonably anticipated skin, eye, mucous membrane, or parenteral contact with blood or other potentially infectious materials that may result from the performance of an employee's duties."[344] The potentially infectious materials, in addition to human blood, include: various human body fluids, including "semen, vaginal secretions, cerebrospinal fluid, synovial fluid, pleural fluid, pericardial fluid, saliva in dental procedures, any body fluid that is visibly contaminated with blood, and all body fluids in situations where it is difficult or impossible to differentiate between body fluids;"[345] unfixed human tissue or organ; HIV-containing cell or tissue cultures; organ cultures; HIV-containing culture medium; and blood, organs, or tissues from experimental animals infected with HIV.[346]

The OSHA bloodborne pathogens standard was challenged by three employer groups—dentists (represented by the American Dental Association), medical personnel employers, and home health employers—in *American Dental Association v. Martin,*[347] with only limited success. The court, in an opinion by Circuit Judge Posner, noted that its standard of review was whether the OSHA rule was rational, rejected the dental association's challenge in its entirety, but accepted in part the arguments advanced by home health employers. The dental association's primary argument was that OSHA had considered dentists in aggregate with other health care professionals, such as surgeons, who are exposed to a far greater risk of HIV infection. Instead, the dental association argued, OSHA should have developed a standard based on a "determination of the safety (or

---

[344] 29 C.F.R. § 1910.1030(b). *See also* Central Operating Co., O.S.H. Dec. (CCH) ¶ 30,704 (A.L.J. Feb. 13, 1995) (members of first aid crew covered by OSHA standard; "good samaritan" exception, which applies to unanticipated first aid, inapplicable).

[345] 29 C.F.R. § 1910.1030(b)(1).

[346] *Id.* § 1910.1030(b)(2)–(3).

[347] 984 F.2d 823 (7th Cir. 1993).

riskiness) of, at the least, each *type* of workplace."[348] The court concluded that OSHA's universal precautions approach was reasonable, however, given that OSHA had regulated the practices, as opposed to the specific workplaces, that posed a risk of transmission: "The idea behind requiring universal precautions for health care workers is to protect those workers in any situation in which there is a nontrivial risk of physical contact with a patient's blood, and these situations arise in dentist's offices as well as in doctors' offices and hospitals."[349]

Turning to the objection of the home health and medical personnel industries, the court found persuasive the argument that the standard imposed an undefined burden on those employers whose employees work off-site at a location not under the employers' control. OSHA had responded to this argument by referring to the *multi-employer worksite defense,* a defense to an OSHA charge to the effect that if the employer cannot control a hazard it is not liable for the exposure of employees to that hazard. Accordingly, the OSHA standard was vacated insofar as it applied to sites not controlled either by the employer or by a hospital, nursing home, or other entity that is itself subject to the rule. One assumes, then, that if the employee is assigned to a site (such as a nursing home) that complies with the rule in regard to its own employees, then the employer is responsible for training, but for protections like the availability of engineering controls (which are beyond the control of the employer), such as the placement of a sink for cleanup, the employer is not liable. Although the opinion does not say as much, the entity that has control of the site is also not liable, because OSHA liability can only be imposed against the employer, not a third party. This raises the question of whether the entity that controls the site could be liable for the employee's injury.

Circuit Judge Coffey concurred as to vacating the standard, but dissented, insofar as he would have invalidated the entire standard. Interestingly, he argued in dissent that the OSHA standard "was drafted partially in response to the public hysteria surrounding AIDS created by the media's failure to balance their reporting with scientific data on transmission."[350]

§ 3.31 —Employee's Right to Know versus Confidentiality Standards for HIV

In some workplaces, particularly those involved in providing health care and the concomitant risk of exposure to a patient's blood, an employee's asserted interest in knowing the HIV status of a patient or service recipient frequently conflicts with the patient's confidentiality rights. In general, in the health care setting, because the use of universal precautions provides optimal protection available to

---

[348] *Id.* at 827.

[349] *Id.*

[350] *Id.* at 831. Specifically, Judge Coffey criticized reliance on the Florida dental case of Dr. Acer as a basis for policy formulation. See **Ch. 1** and **§ 3.12.**

health care workers, the HIV status of any given patient becomes irrelevant in terms of infection control. For example, a laboratory technician handling a blood specimen for testing has no need to know whether that specimen is from an HIV-infected patient. The technician should utilize protection in regard to all specimens handled, without knowledge of an individual patient's HIV status. Thus, from an infection control point of view, disclosure of HIV status is not necessary. However, patients with HIV infection may have HIV-associated infectious illnesses, such as tuberculosis, that do require specific infection control measures beyond those routinely included in HIV precautions.[351] Given the fact that disclosure of HIV status has not been an element of infection control policy in health care,[352] disclosure of an employee's HIV status cannot be justified in non-health care employment settings.

This view is consistent with OSHA standards, which do not in general require the disclosure of a patient's HIV data. Thus, the charting of a patient's HIV status is not required under OSHA workplace safety standards as a means of alerting health care workers to the risk of infection. On the other hand, OSHA standards do not prohibit the charting of a patient's HIV data, but the charting of HIV information does not relieve the employer of its obligations under the OSHA standards. The greater risk appears to be breach of confidentiality regarding the patient's status, once that information becomes more widely known.[353]

Disclosure of HIV information may, however, be relevant to patient care issues, and, accordingly, there would be little argument that in most instances the charting of HIV information may enhance patient care. The distinction, however, is between enhancement of patient care on the one hand and protection of staff on the other.

§ 3.32   —Testing and Disclosure of Patient's HIV Status after Occupational Exposure

Workplace safety policy should also address the issue of followup procedures after an employee's potential occupational exposure to HIV, as might result from a needle-stick injury. Studies indicate that the incidence of potential percutaneous exposures is significant. Under OSHA standards, after a report of an exposure

---

[351] See CDC, *Nosocomial Transmission of Multi-Drug Resistant Tuberculosis in an Urban Hospital—Florida,* 39 MMWR 718 (1990) (noting need to observe isolation precautions with TB patients to limit infection of health care workers); D. Weber, *Management of HIV-1 Infection in the Hospital Setting,* 10 Infect. Control Hosp. Epidemiol. 3, 5 (1989) (noting need to utilize precautions against infectious diseases including respiratory precautions for pulmonary tuberculosis and herpes zoster).

[352] *Compare* Ark. Stat. Ann. § 20-15-903 (Supp. 1989) (patient has affirmative duty to disclose HIV status to any health care professional providing services to that patient); Mo. Ann. Stat. § 191.656(5) (Vernon Supp. 1990) (same).

[353] *See, e.g.,* Behringer Estate v. Princeton Medical Ctr., 592 A.2d 1251 (N.J. Super. Ct. Law Div. 1991).

incident, defined as "a specific eye, mouth, other mucous membrane, non-intact skin, or parenteral contact with blood of other potentially infectious materials that results from the performance of an employee's duties,"[354] the employer is required to identify the "source individual, unless the employer can establish that identification is infeasible or prohibited by state or local law."[355] The source individual's blood is then to be tested

> as soon as feasible and after consent is obtained in order to determine ... HIV infectivity. If consent cannot be obtained, the employer shall establish that legally required consent cannot be obtained. When the source individual's consent is not required by law, the source individual's blood, if available, shall be tested and the results documented.[356]

The results of the test are made available to the exposed employee, and the employee must then be informed "of applicable laws and regulations concerning disclosure of the identity and infectious status of the source individual."[357] The exposed employee's blood is then to be collected for baseline testing "as soon as feasible and tested after consent is obtained." If the employee consents to the collection of blood but not to baseline testing, the specimen is to be preserved for at least 90 days. Post-exposure prophylaxis and followup testing is to be provided in accordance with U.S. Public Health Service recommendations.[358]

Federal legislation also includes standards that address concerns regarding the potential occupational exposure of emergency response employees to HIV. The Ryan White Comprehensive AIDS Resources Emergency (CARE) Act of 1990,[359] amending the Public Health Service Act, required the secretary of Health and Human Services to develop a list of potentially life-threatening infectious diseases to which emergency response employees (EREs) may be exposed when responding to emergencies. The definition of ERE includes "firefighters, law enforcement officers, paramedics, emergency medical technicians, funeral service practitioners, and other persons (including employees of legally organized and

---

[354] 29 C.F.R. § 1910.1030(b).

[355] *Id.* § 1910.1030(f)(3)(ii).

[356] *Id.* § 1910.1030(f)(3)(ii)(A). If the source individual is already known to be infected with HIV, the individual need not be retested.

[357] *Id.* § 1910.1030(f)(3)(ii)(C).

[358] This issue is discussed in more detail in **Ch. 1.** In terms of post-exposure followup, according to one expert, health care workers are, not surprisingly, reassured by negative HIV antibody test results on the source patient, even when the probability of the patient's being HIV-infected is low. Determining the source patient's risk for infection is emphasized as a means of avoiding unnecessary testing (and retesting) of health care workers in cases in which likelihood of infection is remote. HIV infection should be ruled out after 6 months of antibody negative followup testing. Extending the followup testing beyond that period is noted as unlikely to detect any infections, and unnecessarily extends the health care worker's distress about the risk of infection. Julie Louise Gerberding, *Management of Occupational Exposures to Blood-Borne Pathogens,* 332 New Eng. J. Med. 444 (1995).

[359] 42 U.S.C. §§ 300ff-81 to 300ff-90 (1994).

recognized volunteer organizations, without regard to whether such employees receive nominal compensation) who, in the course of professional duties, respond to emergencies in the geographic area involved."[360] The list of life-threatening diseases includes HIV.[361]

In summary, the CARE Act provides that EREs may initiate a process to obtain information concerning a patient's status in regard to life-threatening diseases. When a designated officer (an official or officer of the ERE's employer) is notified by the ERE that the employee believes that he or she may have been exposed to an infectious disease by an emergency victim, the designated officer then determines whether there was a potential exposure, assuming the emergency victim to be infected. If the designated officer determines that there was a risk of exposure, the officer then submits a request to the facility to which the victim was transported that the facility determine, based on medical information it possesses, whether the ERE was exposed to an infectious disease on the list. The medical facility has 48 hours to respond, in writing, to the request. The designated officer then informs the ERE whether there was a risk of exposure.

The CARE Act further provides that it does not establish a cause of action for damages or any civil penalty against any designated officer or any medical facility. Nor does it require the testing of victims of emergencies for HIV or other infectious diseases.

In regard to the confidentiality rights of the emergency victims, the Act provides that in complying with the process, the medical facility is not required to disclose identifying information pertaining to the victim. The CDC's regulation clarifies the definition of *exposure* and, in particular, the concept of significant risk of exposure to HIV or other life-threatening diseases.[362] Significant exposure is defined with reference to prior legal standards, including the ADA's definition of direct threat.[363]

§ 3.33 Employer's Liability Resulting from HIV Safety Issues

An employer's liability resulting from safety issues can occur in several ways. First, as noted in **§ 3.30,** violation of OSHA standards can result in the issuance of citations and imposition of penalties. The violations may implicate state

---

[360] *Id.* § 300ff-76(4), amended by Pub. L. No. 104-146, § 2(a), 1996 U.S.C.C.A.N. (110 Stat.) 1346, 1373.

[361] CDC, *Implementation of Provisions of the Ryan White Comprehensive AIDS Resources Emergency Act Regarding Emergency Response Employees,* 59 Fed. Reg. 13,418, 13,425 (1994) (effective Apr. 20, 1994); *see also* CDC, *Proposed Implementation of Provisions of the Ryan White CARE Act Regarding Emergency Response Employees,* 57 Fed. Reg. 54,794, 54,795 (1992) (notice and request for comments).

[362] *See* 42 U.S.C. § 300ff-81(a)(2); 59 Fed. Reg. at 13,420–21 (1994).

[363] 42 U.S.C. §§ 12111(3), 12113(b), discussed in **§ 3.11.**

licensure standards, particularly if the employer is an individual, licensed practitioner. However, licensure standards may be preempted by OSHA standards, even though they potentially exceed the OSHA standard and further the state's interest in preventing transmission of HIV.[364]

Employers may be liable for the discriminatory acts of their employees, such as when an employee refuses to provide services to an individual with HIV infection. Federal nondiscrimination standards, like those contained in the Rehabilitation Act and ADA, as well as state and local standards prohibit public accommodation and access to services discrimination.[365] Enforcement agencies and the courts have increasingly read public accommodation provisions to include offices or clinics that provide health care services.[366] An employer's efforts to comply with nondiscrimination standards would be an appropriate basis for disciplinary action against an employee who refuses to provide services to persons with HIV. Thus, appropriate safety and nondiscrimination standards should be included in workplace employment policies that require employee compliance.

In some instances, employees have refused to perform their jobs because of their fear of the risk of HIV transmission. Under the applicable OSHA regulation, an employee acting in good faith can refuse to perform work because of a reasonable fear of death or serious injury, when no reasonable, less drastic alternative is available to the employee. The employer cannot discipline or terminate the employee for the refusal. However, the regulation provides that:

> the employee's apprehension of death or serious bodily injury must be of such a nature that a reasonable person, under the circumstances then confronting the employee, would conclude that there is a real danger of death or serious bodily injury and that there is insufficient time due to the urgency of the situation, to eliminate the danger through resort to regular statutory enforcement channels.[367]

In the case of HIV transmission in the workplace meeting this standard, for example, an employee who is not afforded adequate equipment or training to comply with universal precaution standards might legitimately refuse to work. In *Mendenhall v. North Carolina Department of Human Resources*,[368] for example, the

---

[364] *See* Gade v. National Solid Waste Management Ass'n, 505 U.S. 88 (1992) (OSH Act preempts any state regulation of occupational safety or health issue with respect to which a federal standard has been established, unless a state plan has been approved).

[365] *See, e.g.,* Glanz v. Vernick, 756 F. Supp. 632 (D. Mass. 1991) (refusal of hospital resident teacher to perform surgery on HIV-infected patient subjected hospital to potential liability under Rehabilitation Act); Doe v. Jamaica Hosp., 608 N.Y.S.2d 518 (App. Div. 1994) (mem.) (allowing Rehabilitation Act claims against institutional employer, even though individual employee defendant not covered by Act).

[366] Public accommodation discrimination is covered in **Ch. 4.**

[367] 29 C.F.R. § 1977.12 (1996). This regulation was upheld as a valid exercise of the secretary of Labor's statutory authority in Whirlpool Corp. v. Marshall, 445 U.S. 1 (1980).

[368] 459 S.E.2d 820 (N.C. Ct. App. 1995).

employment termination of a blind social worker for refusing to provide sharp-object-handling skills training to a blind client with AIDS was reversed, and the social worker was reinstated. Although the evidence of significant risk to the social worker was not discussed in detail and the social worker appears to have refused all contact with the client, not just the sharp-object-handling training, the court's ruling was based on the demonstrated inadequacy of the employer's infection control program. Such cases, however, should be limited primarily to employment settings, such as health care institutions, where employees routinely come in contact with patients' bodily fluids. In most workplaces, an employee's objection to working with a co-worker or other individual infected with HIV would not be based on a reasonable apprehension of an actual danger. An employer's termination or discipline of an employee who refuses to work under those circumstances does not violate OSHA standards. Similarly, an employee's action to protest unsafe working conditions may fall under the concerted activities provision of the National Labor Relations Act.[369] An employer's discipline of employees for their complaint about the risk of HIV infection on the job would violate this provision. However, unless the employer's failure to comply with infection control standards places the employees at a significant risk, the employees could be disciplined appropriately should they refuse to work on that basis.[370] As noted, such employee refusal may subject the employer to claims for public accommodation discrimination, which further supports the employer's right discipline for employee failure to provide services to persons with HIV.

Fear of disease transmission from an AIDS patient's opportunistic infections, not from HIV itself, was the basis of a nurse's refusal to work and resulting dismissal, unsuccessfully challenged, in *Armstrong v. Flowers Hospital, Inc.*[371] The plaintiff, a home care nurse, refused to work with AIDS patients during the term of her pregnancy because of her fear that the patients' opportunistic infections could harm her fetus. When assigned to a patient with HIV infection and cryptococcal meningitis, she refused the assignment and was fired. She then sued her employer, alleging that she was discriminated against on the basis of her pregnancy. The court dismissed her claim, concluding that federal nondiscrimination law in fact barred the employer from prohibiting a pregnant employee from working with AIDS patients and, at the same time, did not impose any obligation on employers to provide pregnant employees with any special or preferential treatment. The employer had shown that in the past all employees were required to work with AIDS patients or face dismissal. Only one other employee had refused to

---

[369] 29 U.S.C. § 157.

[370] *See, e.g.,* National Labor Relations Bd. v. McEver Eng'g, Inc., 784 F.2d 634 (5th Cir. 1986) (work stoppage protected as concerted activity when danger is not inherent in job; risk not assumed by employee upon acceptance of employment); National Labor Relations Bd. v. Tamara Foods, 692 F.2d 1171 (8th Cir. 1982) (employee concerted refusal to work protected when based on good faith belief regarding abnormally dangerous working condition, supported by objective evidence).

[371] 33 F.3d 1308 (11th Cir. 1994), *aff'g* 812 F. Supp. 1183 (M.D. Ala. 1993).

work with AIDS patients, and she had resigned. Other pregnant employees had worked with AIDS patients. Nor was there any allegation that the employer did not comply with OSHA workplace safety standards. On the contrary, the court noted that employees were required to comply with the CDC's universal precaution standards.

Finally, actual or risked transmission of HIV in the workplace, including fear of HIV transmission, is likely to be covered under state workers' compensation laws that provide an exclusive remedy for work-related injuries.[372] The OSH Act explicitly provides that it does not supersede or affect rights provided to employees under workers' compensation laws.[373] In such cases, the only significant issue may be whether the employee's infection was work-related or resulted from some other source of HIV infection. Employee testing at the time of the incident that risked exposure, as recommended by OSHA[374] and the CDC,[375] would provide a baseline test result from which the employee's later seroconversion can be evaluated, should it occur.

Because use of universal precautions can reduce, if not eliminate, the risk of HIV transmission, an employer may discipline or discharge employees who refuse to comply with these safety policies. An employer's actions against such an employee would not violate OSHA standards, because the employee's refusal to comply with safety standards is not the exercise of a right protected under the OSH Act.[376]

---

[372] *See, e.g.,* Arkansas Dep't of Correction v. Holybee, 878 S.W.2d 420 (Ark. Ct. App. 1994) (allowing workers' compensation claim for testing in regard to an incident that court concluded presented a risk of HIV transmission); Elliott v. Dugger, 579 So. 2d 827 (Fla. Dist. Ct. App. 1991) (dismissal of claims against state on workers' compensation exclusive remedy and state immunity grounds), *aff'g,* 542 So. 2d 392 (Fla. Dist. Ct. App. 1989); Vallery v. Southern Baptist Hosp., 630 So. 2d 861 (La. Ct. App. 1993) (workers' compensation exclusive remedy for employee's workplace injury; employee's spouse's claim for emotional distress resulting from sexual contact with potentially infected husband allowed); J.M.F. v. Emerson, 768 S.W.2d 579 (Mo. Ct. App. 1989) (workers' compensation deemed exclusive remedy for claim of workplace HIV exposure); Blythe v. Radiometer Am., Inc., 866 P.2d 218 (Mont. 1993) (workers' compensation exclusive remedy for potential HIV exposure resulting from employer's decision to use defective equipment); Jackson Township Volunteer Fire Co. v. Workmen's Compensation Appeals Bd., 594 A.2d 826 (Pa. Commw. Ct. 1991) (treatment and testing expense for potential HIV exposure covered under workers' compensation claim). One possible exception to the workers' compensation exclusive remedy doctrine in regard to occupational HIV exposure is noted in Juneau v. Humana, Inc., 657 So. 2d 457 (La. Ct. App. 1995) (co-worker alleged to have failed to inform plaintiff of patient's HIV infection, so plaintiff did not comply with infection control precautions and HIV transmission resulted; court noted that in cases in which exposure resulted from a mistake known to employer or induced by employer's misrepresentation, employee not limited to the workers' compensation remedy.). Fear of HIV transmission claims are covered in **Ch. 8.**

[373] 29 U.S.C. § 653(b)(4).

[374] OSHA standards are discussed in §§ **3.30** and **3.32.**

[375] *See* CDC, *Recommendations for Prevention of HIV Transmission in Health-Care Settings,* 36 MMWR 1, 15 (Supp. 1987).

[376] *See* 29 C.F.R. § 1977.22 (1996).

§ 3.34 —Employer's Liability to Third Parties

Recent cases involving claims of nonemployees but involving an employer's policies as a basis for the employer's liability include *Johnson v. West Virginia
University Hospitals, Inc.,*[377] in which a significant liability award was upheld
against a hospital for a security officer's fear of HIV infection as a result of
being bitten by a patient. In that case, the hospital's noncompliance with its own
policy of providing a patient-specific warning about patients with HIV or other
infectious diseases, as opposed to a universal precautions policy applicable to all
patients, was a factor in supporting the hospital's liability.

In a case similar to *Johnson* but involving an employer's liability for HIV
transmission to a nonemployee, *Doe v. New York,*[378] a New York judge awarded
$5.4 million to a hospital nurse infected with HIV as a result of a struggle with
a prison inmate who was receiving hospital care. While several nurses struggled
to restrain the uncooperative inmate, two state-employed corrections officers
stood by, offering no assistance despite the cries for help from the nurses. The
plaintiff was injured when she attempted to reattach a needle to an IV unit; in
the struggle, the needle struck her hand. The court did not indicate whether the
corrections officers' failure to act was a result of their own fear of HIV infection
from the inmate. The court rejected the state's argument that the nurse was
contributorily negligent by attempting to reconnect the needle, knowing that the
inmate was HIV-infected. On appeal, the court increased the award on the basis
that the Court of Claims had incorrectly limited recovery for the plaintiff's damages
during her lifetime.[379] New York did not contest liability, and the award was otherwise affirmed. As a result, Mrs. Doe recovered nearly $5 million, well in excess
of New York's previous offer.[380] Employers might consider whether there is any
point in disclosing HIV status of a patient, given this outcome. Such disclosure
would rarely make a difference given the assumption of underlying universal
precautions, that is, that every patient should be considered to be HIV-infected.

One issue yet to be decided in a reported case is what if any use can be made
of the OSHA workplace safety standard (see § 3.30) in determining the standard of care for purposes of negligence liability, an issue of relevance primarily
to nonemployee, third-party claims. The OSH Act[381] by its own terms does not
create a private cause of action against the employer for noncompliance resulting in an employee's injury. If a risk of transmission occurs and OSHA noncompliance is the cause, the plaintiff would certainly like the failed compliance
to be considered as evidence of the defendant's negligence, if not evidence of
negligence per se. On the other hand, if the defendant fully complied with OSHA

---

[377] 413 S.E.2d 889 (W. Va. 1991).

[378] 588 N.Y.S.2d 698 (Ct. Cl. 1992).

[379] Doe v. New York, 595 N.Y.S.2d 592 (App. Div. 1993), *rev'g in part* 588 N.Y.S.2d 698 (Ct.
Cl. 1992).

[380] *See Albany to Pay Nurse Infected with HIV,* N.Y. Times, Dec. 5, 1992, at 24 (noting New
York's offer to settle the case for $2.75 million).

[381] 29 U.S.C. § 653.

requirements, the defendant would argue that its conduct could not be considered negligent as a matter of law. The courts have considered several factors in determining whether a workplace safety rule should be admitted in evidence: (1) violation of the protective regulatory standard must be provable; (2) the regulatory standard was intended to protect the injured party; and (3) the regulatory standard was intended to protect against the risk that resulted in harm.[382] The 1991 OSHA standard, however, refers only to the employer's duty to employees, not to third parties. Certainly, this makes sense in that employees covered by the OSHA standard must receive workplace safety education; the OSHA standard thus only makes sense to those who have received that training, which, presumably, the nonemployee has not.

Although there is no discussion of the OSHA bloodborne pathogens standard in *Doe v. Doctors Bryan, Hatcher, Vick & Hastings,*[383] that standard is potentially implicated by the facts of the case. The plaintiff, a laboratory clerk, alleged that she was splashed with blood from an improperly labeled and packaged specimen sent to her laboratory by the defendant medical corporation, thus negligently causing her to suffer emotional distress. She apparently was not infected with HIV. In stating her negligence claim, she alleged that the specimen was not labeled with the appropriate biohazard warning. OSHA's bloodborne pathogens standard, reproduced in **Appendix B,** specifically addresses the issue of proper warning labels. In general, these labels must be used on all specimen containers unless universal precautions are used within the workplace in the handling of specimen containers and the container is recognizable as containing a specimen. That rule, however, does not apply when a container is shipped outside the facility. In that case, the specimen container must be appropriately labeled.

In a similar case, *Williams v. Superior Court,*[384] a nonemployee phlebotomist brought suit for HIV infection resulting from an incident in which she attempted to draw blood from the defendant's patient. None of the defendant's employees warned the phlebotomist that the patient was known to attack female health care workers. After the injury, the patient's HIV infection was disclosed to the phlebotomist. In this case, the disclosure was necessary in regard to the patient's potential for violence, not his HIV status; the facts that he was also HIV-infected and his actions resulted in infection of the phlebotomist are only relevant to the degree of harm that resulted from the failure to warn. The court noted that the warning in this situation was the same as in *Tarasoff v. Regents of the University of California:*[385] the phlebotomist was an identifiable, known, potential victim of the harm known to the defendant.

---

[382] *See* Restatement (2d) of Torts § 286 (1985); Annotation, *Violation of OSHA Regulation as Affecting Tort Liability,* 79 A.L.R.3d 962 (1977 & Supp. 1996); *Cf.* Schneider v. Union Elec. Co., 805 S.W.2d 222, 228–29 (Mo. Ct. App. 1991) (affirming admission of OSHA regulation as evidence of negligence); Wal-Mart Stores v. Seale, 904 S.W.2d 718 (Tex. Ct. App. 1995) (same).

[383] 625 So. 2d 722 (La. Ct. App. 1993).

[384] 36 Cal. Rptr. 2d 112 (Ct. App. 1994).

[385] 551 P.2d 334 (Cal. 1976).

CHAPTER 4

ACCESS TO PUBLIC SERVICES AND ACCOMMODATIONS

Julie Shapiro

David W. Webber

§ 4.1 Introduction

This chapter reviews legal protections available to HIV-infected individuals who are discriminated against when they seek to use public services or public accommodations. It examines the major federal statutes that prohibit discrimination against individuals with disabilities and their applicability to HIV-infected individuals, and it covers possible state law remedies as well.[1]

HIV-infected individuals experience discrimination when they seek access to state and local government services, such as health care, or educational or housing programs. They have been denied service, or have been offered only partial or segregated service, or have been offered service only if various special conditions are met. These acts constitute discrimination in provision of public services, and depending on the circumstance, this discrimination is unlawful.

Similarly, HIV-infected individuals have been denied service or provided only limited, segregated, or conditional service by businesses or individuals who make their services generally available to the public, such as restaurants, health clubs, hotels, or private health care providers. For example, dentists have refused to treat HIV-infected individuals, or have agreed to provide treatment only under restrictive conditions, or have agreed to provide only limited or partial treatment. These acts constitute discrimination in public accommodations and, as with discrimination in the provision of public services, may be unlawful.

Two major federal laws prohibit discrimination against individuals with disabilities in the provision of public services and accommodations. These laws apply to HIV-infected individuals. Therefore, the possibility of federal coverage should be carefully explored in any instance of discriminatory treatment of HIV-infected individuals. Additionally, state laws may prohibit these forms of discriminatory conduct and should also be researched carefully.

This chapter first reviews the federal statutory provisions and concludes with materials on state antidiscrimination laws. The more sweeping of the two federal laws is the Americans with Disabilities Act (ADA), covered in §§ **4.2** through **4.12.** The ADA was signed into law in 1990. It has two portions of particular importance for HIV-infected individuals in this context. Title II of the ADA prohibits discrimination in the provision of public services (§§ **4.4** through **4.7**). Title III prohibits discrimination in the provision of public accommodations (§§ **4.4** through **4.12**).

Sections **4.2** through **4.4** on the ADA cover topics relevant to both titles II and III of the ADA. These include the definition of disability, which is also applicable to the employment provisions of the ADA (Title I) covered in **Chapter 3,** and the provisions providing for award of attorney's fees to prevailing plaintiffs. These sections are followed by more detailed discussions of Title II (public services) in §§ **4.5** through **4.8** and Title III (public accommodations) in §§ **4.9** through **4.13.** Titles II and III differ significantly in their enforcement provisions and the remedies they provide. Specific examples of the application of Titles II and III are also provided.

---

[1] Although the emphasis in this chapter is on the litigation of claims of discrimination, practitioners should also consider alternative dispute resolution methods, which may be appropriate here as well as in the employment discrimination context and are discussed in **Ch. 3.**

The second federal law is the Rehabilitation Act of 1973, sometimes referred to as "section 504," covered in §§ **4.14** through **4.18.** The Rehabilitation Act is of more limited application. That is, it applies to fewer potential defendants. When it does apply, however, it offers broader relief to an individual plaintiff than does the ADA. Consideration of the Rehabilitation Act begins with a discussion in § **4.15** of the enforcement and remedial provisions of the statute and how they contrast to the enforcement and remedial provisions of ADA Titles II and III. **Sections 4.16** through **4.19** discuss specific definitions applicable to the Rehabilitation Act. Although the terms of the Rehabilitation Act are similar to those of the ADA, they are distinct, and care must be taken to employ the terms and definitions appropriate to the applicable statute.

§ 4.2 Americans with Disabilities Act

The Americans with Disabilities Act (ADA)[2] was enacted in 1990. The ADA is designed to eliminate discrimination against individuals with disabilities and those perceived to have disabilities. Title I of the ADA governs discrimination in employment and is covered in **Chapter 3.** Title II prohibits discrimination by public entities. Title III prohibits discrimination by private entities that fall within the definition of places of public accommodation.

The ADA is a powerful tool for HIV-infected individuals who are subjected to discrimination. However, it is a relatively new statute. Thus, some of the problems encountered in ADA litigation do not have definitive solutions. Furthermore, ADA plaintiffs may have to educate the judiciary about the provisions of the ADA as well as, in the case of discrimination based on HIV infection, the applicability of the ADA to HIV-infected individuals, transmission of HIV, and the capabilities and limitations of HIV-infected individuals.[3] Although the ADA reflects a commitment to move beyond stereotypical views of individuals with disabilities and, by extension, HIV-infected individuals, it is only through painstaking educational work that this idealistic commitment can be made real. Judges and jurors are not immune to the prejudice and ignorance that HIV-infected individuals confront throughout society.

Two key provisions of the ADA apply to the entire statute. These are the definition of disability and the entitlement to attorney's fees. **Sections 4.3** through

---

[2] Pub. L. No. 101-336, 1990 U.S.C.C.A.N. (104 Stat.) 327, 29 U.S.C. § 706, 42 U.S.C. §§ 12101–12102, 12111–12117, 12131–12134, 12141–12150, 12161–12165, 12181–12189, 12201–12213 (1994).

[3] The capabilities of HIV-infected individuals are important to establish that a plaintiff is a *qualified individual,* covered in § **4.7.** The limitations occasioned by HIV infection are relevant in establishing that HIV infection falls within the meaning of *disability,* covered in § **4.3.**

4.4 discuss these provisions, which are applicable to the public services and the public accommodation provisions as well as to the employment provisions discussed in **Chapter 3. Sections 4.5** through **4.9** discuss the particular issues implicated in public services and public accommodation cases.

§ 4.3 —Definition of Disability

The heart of the ADA is the prohibition, in varying contexts, of discrimination against individuals with a real or perceived disability. Yet, the ADA does not identify any specific conditions as disabilities, nor does it provide an inclusive or exclusive statutory listing of disabilities. Instead, in an effort to ensure broad and flexible coverage, the ADA includes a general definition of what constitutes a disability. Therefore, one necessary task in applying any part of the ADA to HIV-infected individuals is to establish that HIV disease meets the statutory criteria of a disability.

According to the ADA, a *disability* is a physical or mental impairment that substantially limits one or more of the major life activities of an individual, or having a record of such an impairment, or being regarded as having such an impairment.[4] This definition applies throughout the ADA. Thus, cases concerning the meaning of disability that arise under Title I (employment) are equally applicable to Titles II (public services) and III (public accommodations). Individuals diagnosed with AIDS, given the extent of disease progression, are clearly individuals with a disability and, hence, fall within the protections of the ADA. In addition, as discussed in **Chapter 3,** the courts have considered whether asymptomatic HIV infection constitutes a disability in Title I employment cases. The cases establish that HIV infection, even if asymptomatic, constitutes a disability. The ADA's legislative history, covered in **Chapter 3,** also points to the same conclusion. Thus, individuals with HIV disease who do not have AIDS are entitled to claim the protections of the ADA. Given the statutory structure of the ADA, which contains only a single, overarching definition of disability, these rulings are applicable to cases involving public services or public accommodations under Titles II or III.

§ 4.4 Attorney's Fees

The generally applicable provisions of the ADA state that "[i]n any action or administrative proceeding commenced pursuant to this Act, the court or agency,

---

[4] 42 U.S.C. § 12103(2). Department of Justice regulations pursuant to Titles II and III of the ADA specifically note that "HIV disease (whether symptomatic or asymptomatic)" is an impairment. 28 C.F.R. §§ 35.104 (Title II definition of disability), § 36.104 (Title III definition of disability).

in its discretion, may allow the prevailing party . . . a reasonable attorney's fee."[5] This attorney's fee provision is significantly different from the common law expectation that each side in litigation is responsible for its own attorney's fees without regard to the outcome of the litigation. The provision is specifically intended to encourage representation of plaintiffs in ADA cases by ensuring that, in meritorious cases, the attorney will be fully compensated.

This provision should be interpreted consistently with other statutory fee entitlements on which it was modeled.[6] In particular, case law has established that despite the apparent universality of the statutory language, plaintiffs and defendants do not have the same entitlement to attorney's fees. Defendants can be awarded fees only in a case deemed to be frivolous, but plaintiffs are entitled to fees whenever they attain a substantial part of the relief that they seek. Furthermore, plaintiffs are entitled to fees whether they achieve a measure of success through trial resolution or through settlement. Finally, although the award of fees appears to be discretionary, a court can refuse to award fees to a prevailing plaintiff only if there are some extraordinary circumstances. In short, in most cases in which the plaintiff achieves all or even a substantial part of his or her goals, the plaintiff is entitled to receive an award of attorney's fees from the defendant. In most cases in which the plaintiff is unsuccessful and the defendant prevails, there is no award of fees at all. Only when the court is persuaded that the entire litigation is frivolous is the defendant awarded attorney's fees from the plaintiff.[7]

§ 4.5 ADA Title II: Discrimination by Public Entities

Title II of the ADA is divided into two subparts. The first (subchapter A), and likely the more important for HIV-infected individuals, provides that "no qualified individual with a disability shall, by reason of such disability, be excluded from participation in or be denied the benefits of the services, programs or activities of a public entity."[8] The second subpart of Title II (subchapter B) specifically addresses public transportation provided by public entities. The main thrust of subchapter B is physical accessibility of transportation vehicles and facilities. Its

---

[5] 42 U.S.C. § 12205.

[6] *See, e.g.,* Civil Rights Attorney's Fee Act of 1976, 42 U.S.C. § 1988. In one regard, the entitlement to fees under the ADA is broader than that set forth in the Civil Rights Attorney's Fees Act of 1976. The ADA fee provision specifically mandates an award of fees for administrative proceedings.

[7] This interpretation of the balanced language of the statute is based on the clear congressional intent that the award of fees is designed to encourage attorneys to litigate claims under the relevant statute.

[8] 42 U.S.C. § 12132.

utility for HIV-infected individuals is untested. Accordingly, the discussion in
§§ **4.5** through **4.8** is limited to subchapter A of Title II.

Critical to understanding the scope of coverage of Title II is understanding the
term *public entity*. All state and local government bodies are public entities. In
addition, by the terms of the statute, all subdivisions and instrumentalities of
state and local government are public entities.[9] However, Title II does not apply
to entities within the executive branch of the federal government.[10] In addition,
Title II does not apply to any private, nongovernmental entities. However, at
least some private entities are covered under ADA Titles I (employment) or III
(public accommodations), or section 504 of the Rehabilitation Act.

Title II provisions are intended to prohibit a broad range of discriminatory
conduct. For example, the law obviously bars discrimination based explicitly on
a person's status as an HIV-infected individual, as when a city health clinic or
state employment training program refuses services to HIV-infected individuals.
The statute also prohibits public entities from using eligibility criteria that
screen out or tend to screen out individuals with disabilities.[11]

Title II covers "services, programs and activities" of public entities.[12] It therefore prohibits employment discrimination by public entities. In many instances,
this conduct would also be prohibited by Title I, as discussed in **Chapter 3.** But
Title II reaches all public entities, including public employers that, because they
employ less than 15 people, fall outside the scope of Title I.[13] Although the
conduct prohibited by this subpart is similar to that prohibited by section 504 of
the Rehabilitation Act (see **§ 4.14**), Title II is in one respect of significantly
broader scope: it applies to all state and local government entities, rather than
just those that receive federal financial assistance.

Unlike Titles I and III, Title II does not include a prohibition against discrimination against those who have an known relationship or association with an
individual with a disability, but who may not have a disability themselves.[14] However, the general prohibition against retaliation against individuals who oppose

---

[9] *Id.* § 12131(1).

[10] Schafer v. Wadman, No. 92 Civ. 2989, 1992 WL 350750 (S.D.N.Y. Nov. 17, 1992); Crowder
v. True, No. 91 C 7427, 1993 WL 532455 (N.D. Ill. Dec. 21, 1993). The ADA applies to
Congress and to other entities in the legislative branch of the federal government, 42 U.S.C.
§ 12209. Executive branch entities are covered by the Rehabilitation Act.

[11] 42 U.S.C. § 12132.

[12] *Id.*

[13] With respect to employment discrimination, for entities subject to both Titles I and II, Title II
adopts the standards used in Title I. For entities that fall within Title II but not Title I, Title II
adopts the standards utilized in Section 504 of the Rehabilitation Act with regard to employment discrimination. Americans with Disabilities Act of 1990, U.S. Department of Justice
Technical Assistance Manuals Titles II and III (CCH) II-4.2000 (1992).

[14] *See* 42 U.S.C. §§ 12112(b)(4) (Title I), 12182(b)(1)(E) (Title III).

unlawful discrimination applies to Title II. For example, in *Finley v. Giacobbe*,[15] the court declined to dismiss the complaint of a county hospital's former medical director who asserted that she was coerced into resigning because she attempted to make services at her hospital available to AIDS patients. Because the discrimination she opposed was a violation of Title II, her retaliation claim could be filed directly in court under Title II.

The Department of Justice issued regulations implementing Title II of the ADA in 1991.[16] The regulations require a public entity to alter programs or activities to accommodate people with disabilities. The required alterations cannot fundamentally alter the character of the program or activity.[17] Thus, a defendant may argue successfully that the alterations requested by a plaintiff would fundamentally alter the program or activity and, hence, should not be required. However, the likelihood of such a case in the context of HIV discrimination is remote.

§ 4.6 —Enforcement and Remedies

Instead of setting forth its own remedies for discriminatory conduct, Title II of the ADA incorporates the enforcement and remedial provisions of an earlier civil rights statute. Title II explicitly adopts the remedies, procedures, and rights set forth in section 505 of the Rehabilitation Act of 1974.[18] Section 505 governs enforcement and remedies for claims under the Rehabilitation Act. Questions about enforcement and remedies of Title II of the ADA must be answered by referring to the statutory provisions and case law under the Rehabilitation Act.

Unfortunately, the remedial scheme established by the Rehabilitation Act is complex and its application to claims arising within the coverage of Title II is not always clear. Section 505 of the Rehabilitation Act provides two different types of remedies, depending on which substantive provisions of the Rehabilitation Act are applicable. For violations of section 504 of the Rehabilitation Act,[19] the court uses the remedies and procedures set forth in yet another civil rights statute, Title VI of the Civil Rights Act of 1964.[20] These remedies include a private cause of action for damages. For violations of section 501 of the Rehabilitation Act,

---

[15] 827 F. Supp. 215 (S.D.N.Y. 1993). In addition to her Title II retaliation claim, the plaintiff also asserted claims under section 504 of the Rehabilitation Act and state nondiscrimination laws.

[16] 28 C.F.R. pt. 35 (1996), promulgated at 56 Fed. Reg. 35,694 (1991) (effective Jan. 26, 1992).

[17] 28 C.F.R. § 35.130(b)(7).

[18] 29 U.S.C. § 793(a), incorporated into ADA at 42 U.S.C. § 12133.

[19] 29 U.S.C. § 794.

[20] 42 U.S.C. § 2000(d), incorporated into Rehabilitation Act at 29 U.S.C. § 794(a).

section 505 references the remedies and procedures set forth in section 717 of the Civil Rights Act of 1964.[21]

Given the enforcement provisions of the Rehabilitation Act, individuals subjected to discrimination in violation of Title II of the ADA are clearly entitled to file an administrative complaint with either the federal agency that has jurisdiction over the state or local agency defendant or with the Department of Justice.[22] In addition, courts have recognized the existence of a private cause of action under Title II. Several courts have held that there is no requirement that a plaintiff exhaust administrative remedies before proceeding with an action under Title II.[23] Thus, a claim for a violation of Title II may be brought directly to federal court.

The remedies incorporated into Title II of the ADA should include a private cause of action for damages as well as for injunctive or declaratory relief. It is generally recognized that individual plaintiffs may maintain a private right of action for damages under section 504 of the Rehabilitation Act,[24] as discussed in **§ 4.15.** Given the incorporation of Rehabilitation Act remedies into Title II of the ADA, an individual asserting discrimination by a public entity should have the same options. Although the argument in favor of a private cause of action for damages under Title II of the ADA is strong, the question is not completely settled.[25] Among courts that have allowed a cause of action for damages, there are divergent views as to the availability of punitive damages under Title II.[26]

In addition to monetary damages, the remedial provisions incorporated in section 505 of the Rehabilitation Act and, by extension, in Title II of the ADA provide for the termination of federal funding for any program that discriminates in violation of the statute. This cutoff is easy to comprehend in the context of the Rehabilitation Act, which applies to entities who receive federal financial assistance. The restrictive scope of the Rehabilitation Act ensures that termination of

---

[21] 42 U.S.C. § 2000e-16, incorporated into Rehabilitation Act at 28 U.S.C. § 794(a). That section requires administrative review by federal agency employers and the Equal Employment Opportunity Commission of complaints of discrimination, which, after that review, can be filed in federal court.

[22] Department of Justice regulations specify the appropriate agency, 28 C.F.R. § 35.190, and set forth the complaint procedure, *id.* §§ 35.170–.178.

[23] *See, e.g.,* Doe v. County of Milwaukee, 871 F. Supp. 1072 (E.D. Wis. 1995); Gorsline v. Kansas, 1994 WL 129983 (D. Kan. Mar. 4, 1994); Bechtel v. East Penn Sch. Dist., 1994 WL 3396 (E.D. Pa. Jan. 4, 1994); Ethridge v. Alabama, 847 F. Supp. 903 (M.D. Ala. 1993); Finley v. Giacobbe, 827 F. Supp. 215, 219 n.3 (S.D.N.Y. 1993).

[24] *See* Consolidated Rail Corp. v. Darrone, 477 U.S. 597 (1986) (upholding private right of action for damages for employment discrimination under section 504).

[25] *See, e.g.,* Coleman v. Zatechka, 824 F. Supp. 1360 (D. Neb. 1993) (suggesting damages remedy not available under Title II).

[26] *Compare* O'Neal v. Alabama Dep't of Pub. Health, 826 F. Supp. 1368 (M.D. Ala. 1993) (generally approving punitive damages under Title II although not on facts before court) *with* Harrelson v. Elmore County, 859 F. Supp. 1464 (M.D. Ala. 1994) (holding punitive damages not available under Title II).

funding is only available against defendants who receive funding that can be terminated. By contrast, Title II applies to state and local entities, without regard to whether they received federal financial assistance. In the case of a state or local entity that does not receive any federal financial assistance, termination of such assistance would be a meaningless remedy.

Independent of specific Title II remedies, a plaintiff may seek relief under § 1983 against governmental defendants or others who, under color of law, deprive an individual of a federal statutory right.[27] To the extent Title II sets forth its own remedial scheme, courts may be reluctant to allow a plaintiff to invoke § 1983. Nonetheless, in some instances, it may be a viable path to vindicating Title II rights.[28] Section 1983 provides that claims may be brought directly to federal court. Under it, a plaintiff may receive compensatory and punitive damages as well as an award of attorney's fees.[29] In addition to damages, a successful Title II action, whether filed with an administrative agency or in court, also entitles the prevailing plaintiff to attorney's fees, discussed in § **4.4.**

As an example of recent litigation pursued under Title II of the ADA, in *Moreno v. City of Austin,*[30] a woman with HIV asserted that her performance evaluations had substantially decreased after she told her supervisor she was infected. The case was pursued in state court under Title II. The jury awarded the plaintiff $109,793 in back pay and $75,000 in compensatory damages. Attorney's fees of over $74,000 were also awarded.

§ 4.7   —Definition of Qualified Individual

Title II does not require that public entities provide services to every individual or to every HIV-infected individual. Rather, it bars public entities from discriminating against any *"qualified* individual with a disability."[31] Thus, a critical issue in many cases is whether an individual with a disability is qualified within the meaning of the ADA. The definition of disability is discussed in § **4.3** and **Chapter 3.**

A *qualified individual with a disability* is an individual who, "with or without reasonable modifications to rules, policies, or practices . . . meets the essential eligibility requirements for the receipt of services or the participation in the

---

[27] 42 U.S.C. § 1983.

[28] *See, e.g.,* Kenney v. Yarusalim, 9 F.3d 1067 (3d Cir. 1993).

[29] Section 1983 does not provide a vehicle for evading the Eleventh Amendment prohibition of actions for damages against a state. Although that statute is grounded in congressional power under the Fourteenth Amendment, the Supreme Court has held that in the absence of a explicit statement of intent to override the Eleventh Amendment, no such intent would be presumed. *See* Atascadero State Hosp. v. Scanlon, 473 U.S. 234, 242–43 (1985).

[30] No. 93-05272, Tex. Dist. Ct., 345 Jud. Dist. *cited in* Gary S. Marx & Gary G. Goldberger, Disability Law Compliance Manual SA-132 (Supp. 1996).

[31] 42 U.S.C. § 12132 (emphasis added).

programs or activities provided by a public entity."[32] Although this definition parallels the definition of "qualified individual" used in Title I of the ADA (see the employment provisions in **Chapter 3**), it is specific to Title II and hence must be separately interpreted by the courts. Nevertheless, it can be strongly argued that the meanings of qualified individual as used in Titles I and II should be consistent.

Although Title II, unlike Titles I and III, does not include a specific direct threat provision, the preamble to the Department of Justice regulations[33] defines *direct threat* by referencing the regulations under Title III.[34] An individual who poses a direct threat to the health and safety of others is not considered to be a qualified individual. Thus, that person may be excluded from programs, activities, and services that fall within Title II's coverage, or he or she may be offered only limited or segregated service. Given this potential exclusion and fears of HIV infection, care must be taken in resolving this question on behalf of an HIV-infected individual. The determination that an individual poses a direct threat to others may not be based on stereotypes or generalizations. It must instead arise from an individualized examination of the circumstances. For example, an HIV-infected individual may not be offered only restricted access to county recreation programs unless the county can show that the individual's participation would pose a significant risk to the health and safety of others that could not be mitigated by adherence to universal precautions in the event of injury. Similarly, given the precautions that should be followed routinely in dental clinics, a government-operated dental clinic cannot refuse to provide services to HIV-infected individuals, nor should it be permitted to impose any special conditions on patients who may be infected with HIV. Circumstances in which the direct threat defense applies would, like its application in the employment context, be rare. Expert testimony on both the risk presented and the degree to which any risk can be reduced is of obvious importance.

§ 4.8   —Specific Applications to Public Entities

The provisions of Title II apply to public education.[35] These claims may also fall within the coverage of the Individuals with Disabilities Education Act (IDEA), which is covered in **Chapter 5**. In general, the IDEA is more specific and detailed than the ADA. The IDEA requires administrative exhaustion as an initial matter. At least one court has held that when IDEA claims and ADA claims overlap, a plaintiff must exhaust the administrative procedures required

---

[32] *Id.* § 12131(2); 35 C.F.R. § 35.104.

[33] 28 C.F.R. pt. 35, app. A (preamble to Title II regulations, published July 26, 1991).

[34] *Id.* § 36.208 (Title III regulation on direct threat, implementing 42 U.S.C. § 12182(b)(3)).

[35] *See, e.g.,* Peterson v. Hastings Pub. Schs., 31 F.3d 705 (8th Cir. 1994), *aff'g* 831 F. Supp. 742 (D. Neb. 1993).

under the IDEA before proceeding with either claim.[36] Title II extends not only to educational programs of public schools but also to other related school activities and associations, such as sports.[37]

Health care provided under Medicaid is a service or program of a public entity (the state where the care is provided) and, hence, falls within the dictates of Title II.[38] Therefore, HIV-infected individuals who are discriminated against in the provision of health care through a Medicaid program may bring a claim against the state under Title II. However, private health care providers who serve Medicaid patients are not public entities and are not covered by Title II.[39] If an HIV-infected individual experiences discrimination in the provision of medical care funded by Medicaid, it is critical to determine whether the discrimination is attributable to the state program (in which case Title II applies), or to the individual private provider (in which case Title III applies), or both. This analysis determines not only the correct defendant but also the governing statute. Of course, it is possible to combine a Title II and Title III cause of action and sue both the individual provider and the appropriate state agency.

Various other governmental entities fall within the provisions of Title II. These include state, county, and municipal correctional facilities[40] and state boards of examiners.[41] Title II also provides a means for challenging state and local statutes or regulations that bar qualified individuals from participating in public programs. As such, it has been used successfully to enjoin state laws barring people with HIV infection from marrying.[42]

Somewhat different questions arise when the allegedly discriminatory state edict is not statutory in nature but rather arises from common law. Common law doctrines that support discrimination should fall under Title II. Under the supremacy clause of the U.S. Constitution, the ADA would control in the event of a conflict with state law, whether the state law is based on statute, administrative rule, or regulation, or is derived from common law sources. For example, a patient might bring a tort action against an HIV-infected physician and the hospital that employs the physician upon learning that the physician is HIV-infected, a fact

---

[36] Hope v. Cortines, 872 F. Supp. 14 (E.D.N.Y.), aff'd, 69 F.3d 687 (2d Cir. 1995).

[37] See Pottgen v. Missouri State High Sch. Activities Ass'n, 40 F.3d 926 (8th Cir.), rev'g 857 F. Supp. 654 (E.D. Miss. 1994); Johnson v. Florida High Sch. Activities Ass'n, Inc., 899 F. Supp. 579 (M.D. Fla. 1995).

[38] See 42 U.S.C. § 12132.

[39] They are in all likelihood covered by the provisions of Title III of ADA which govern public accommodations (see § 4.13), including medical offices that serve the public.

[40] See, e.g., Torcasio v. Murray, 862 F. Supp. 1482 (E.D. Va. 1994), aff'd, 57 F.3d 1340 (4th Cir. 1995). Many of these facilities are also governed by section 504 of the Rehabilitation Act.

[41] Argen v. New York State Bd. of Bar Examiners, 860 F. Supp. 84 (W.D.N.Y. 1994); In re Rubenstein, 637 A.2d 1131 (Del. 1994).

[42] T.E.P. v. Leavitt, 840 F. Supp. 110 (D. Utah 1993) (permanently enjoining enforcement of Utah statute).

not disclosed to the patient in advance of treatment. The patient's claims, derived from the doctrines of common law informed consent and negligent infliction of emotional distress, would be based on the fact that the physician's HIV status was not disclosed in advance of treatment.[43] If the physician did not pose a direct threat of HIV transmission to the patient,[44] however, then both the physician and hospital should be able to defend against the state tort action on the basis that the physician's employment was protected under the ADA. A Title II claim for injunctive or declaratory relief could be asserted either against the state court itself or against the plaintiff in the state law action.[45] Title II would also apply when a state court or agency prohibits adoption by HIV-infected individuals.[46]

§ 4.9   ADA Title III: Public Accommodations and Commercial Facilities

Title III of the ADA contains two sets of requirements, set forth in sections 302[47] and 303.[48] Both sections prohibit discrimination on the basis of disability by places of public accommodation,[49] but section 303 also applies to commercial facilities.[50] The Department of Justice has issued regulations implementing Title III.[51] For the most part, the requirements of section 302 are of greater importance to HIV-infected individuals than are those of section 303.

Section 302 of the ADA Title III provides that "[n]o individual shall be discriminated against on the basis of disability in the full and equal enjoyment of the goods, services, facilities, privileges, advantages, or accommodations of any place of public accommodation by any person who owns, leases (or leases to), or operates a place of public accommodation."[52] Generally speaking, public accommodations are privately owned entities that are open to the general public, such as movie theaters, doctors' offices, or hotels. The meaning of the critical

---

[43] Tort claims of this sort are covered in **Ch. 8.**

[44] The direct threat defense in the context of employment of health care workers with HIV is covered in **Ch. 3.**

[45] This example, slightly modified, is taken from Henry H. Perritt, Jr., Americans with Disabilities Act Handbook § 9.7A (Cumulative Supp. No. 2, 1996).

[46] Discrimination claims based other disabilities have been made in regard to limitations on parenting. *See, e.g., In re* Angel B., 659 A.2d 277 (Me. 1995) (termination of parental rights based on mental retardation); *In re* Welfare of A.J.R., 896 P.2d 1298 (Wash. Ct. App. 1995) (same).

[47] 42 U.S.C. § 12182.

[48] *Id.* § 12183.

[49] *Id.* § 12181(7).

[50] *Id.* § 12181(2).

[51] 28 C.F.R. pt. 36 (1996), promulgated at 56 Fed. Reg. 55,592 (1991).

[52] 42 U.S.C. § 12182(a).

term public accommodation is discussed in greater detail in **§ 4.13.** On the other hand, entities that are publicly owned or operated are governed by the public entity provisions found in Title II of the ADA.

There may be some instances in which both Titles II and III are relevant to a particular claim. For example, this would be the case if a private physician (functioning as a public accommodation under Title III) who is funded by Medicaid (a public entity under Title II) discriminated against an HIV-infected individual, or if a municipality (a Title II public entity) contracted with a privately owned gymnasium (functioning as a Title III public accommodation) that denies membership to HIV-infected individuals to operate a recreational program for the public.

Section 302 specifically requires that public accommodations make reasonable modifications in policies, practices, and procedures to accommodate individuals with disabilities.[53] However, modification is not required when it would "fundamentally alter" the nature of the goods, services, or accommodation provided.[54] Title III also explicitly identifies as a form of prohibited discrimination the use of eligibility requirements that tend to screen out individuals with disabilities.[55]

Section 303 of Title III applies to commercial facilities as well as to public accommodations. *Commercial facilities* include office buildings and factories that do not contain entities that are public accommodations, because they do not offer services to the general public. Thus, section 303 applies to a broader range of entities than does section 302. At the same time, the obligations imposed on these entities by section 303 are less far-reaching. Section 303 requires that new construction of commercial facilities and public accommodations be such as to allow full participation of individuals with disabilities.[56] These provisions are principally aimed at ensuring barrier-free physical access to facilities. The broader requirements of section 302 of the ADA do not apply to commercial facilities.

Title III includes exemptions for private clubs and religious organizations.[57] This private club exemption directly incorporates the exemption for private clubs and establishments in the Civil Rights Act of 1964. In addition, the Title III exemption provides that this portion of the ADA does not apply to "religious organizations or entities controlled by religious organizations."[58] These exemptions are limited to Title III. In particular, they do not apply to employers that fall within the coverage of Title I, which contains a more limited religious entities exception.[59]

---

[53] *Id.* § 12182(b)(2)(A).

[54] *Id.*

[55] *Id.*

[56] *Id.* § 12183.

[57] *Id.* § 12187.

[58] 42 U.S.C. § 12187.

[59] *Id.* § 12113(c).

§ 4.10   —Enforcement and Remedies

Title III explicitly adopts the procedures and remedies set forth in section 204(a), Title II of the Civil Rights Act of 1964,[60] which prohibits discrimination by public accommodations based on race and sex. Section 204(a) of the Civil Rights Act authorizes a private individual to seek injunctive relief. Thus, a private plaintiff may seek injunctive relief under Title III of the ADA. At the same time, the Civil Rights Act of 1964 does not provide for damages in private party litigation, and therefore damages are not available in private party litigation under Title III of the ADA.[61] Because only injunctive (that is, equitable) relief is available, there is in all likelihood no right to trial by jury under Title III.

Subsections of section 204 of the Civil Rights Act (other than subsection (a), which is specifically referenced in Title III of the ADA) provide for the award of attorney's fees to a prevailing plaintiff and set forth a requirement that a plaintiff exhaust administrative remedies before filing a complaint.[62] Because Title III of the ADA specifically references only section 204(a) and not the attorney's fee and exhaustion provisions, it can be argued that those provisions of the Civil Rights Act were not intended to be incorporated into Title III of the ADA. Thus, plaintiffs need not exhaust administrative remedies before pursuing their claims in court. On the other hand, their attorney's fees are authorized in the ADA itself, so reference to that provision in the Civil Rights Act is redundant. However, this interpretation has not been adopted in any reported opinion.[63] Indeed, courts tend to impose all of the procedures generally governing Civil Rights Act Title II cases when hearing ADA Title III cases. In view of this trend, it seems reasonable to assume that any future developments in remedies or procedures available under Title II of the Civil Rights Act will be reflected in the law governing remedies and procedures for Title III of the ADA.

An aggrieved individual may also proceed under Title III by filing a complaint with the Department of Justice and requesting that the department proceed on his or her behalf. Consistent with Title II of the Civil Rights Act, the attorney general may also intervene in private party lawsuits under Title III of the ADA. The department is authorized to pursue litigation only when there is evidence that a person or group has engaged in a pattern or practice of discrimination or when the alleged discrimination raises an issue of general public importance.[64]

---

[60] 42 U.S.C. § 2000a-3(a), incorporated by 42 U.S.C. § 12188(a)(1).

[61] *See* Bermudez Zenon v. Restaurant Compostela, Inc., 790 F. Supp. 41 (D.P.R. 1992).

[62] 42 U.S.C. § 2000a-3(b), (c).

[63] *See* Bechtel v. East Penn Sch. Dist., Civ. No. 93-4898, 1994 WL 3396 (E.D. Pa. Jan. 4, 1994) (Title III claims require exhaustion of administrative remedies).

[64] 42 U.S.C. § 12188(b)(1)(B)(ii).

In such cases, the attorney general may seek both monetary damages for the aggrieved individual and civil penalties.[65]

§ 4.11   —Definition of Public Accommodation

Under the ADA, places of *public accommodation* include private entities or establishments that fall into any one of 12 categories.[66] The ADA does not provide a general label for each category. Instead, each category includes an exemplary list of the type of entities that are covered. For example, one category lists "a restaurant, bar, or other establishment serving food or drink."[67]

The Department of Justice has provided general labels for these categories in its preamble to its Title III regulations. The categories identified by the Department are:

1. Places of lodging
2. Establishments serving food and drink
3. Places of exhibition or entertainment
4. Places of public gathering
5. Sales or rental establishments
6. Service establishments
7. Stations used for specified public transportation
8. Places of public display or collection
9. Places of recreation
10. Places of education
11. Social service center establishments
12. Places of exercise or recreation.[68]

The 12 categories set forth in Title III are an inclusive list of all public accommodations. An entity that does not fall within one of the 12 categories is not a public accommodation. At the same time, the entity or institution need not be specifically listed among the illustrative institutions set forth in the statute. Thus, a café or coffeehouse, although not specifically listed in the statute, falls within one of the statutory categories (an establishment serving food and drink) and is therefore a public accommodation within the meaning of the ADA.

---

[65] *Id.* § 12188(b)(2)(B) and (C) (civil penalties not to exceed $50,000 for first violation, not to exceed $100,000 for any subsequent violation); *see, e.g.,* United States v. Morvant, 843 F. Supp. 1092 (E.D. La. 1994).

[66] 42 U.S.C. § 12181(7)(A)–(L).

[67] *Id.* § 12181(7)(B).

[68] 28 C.F.R. pt. 36, app. B.

A public accommodation need not be a physical structure that individuals can physically enter. Some associations, in particular multiemployer health associations, may qualify as public accommodations.[69]

§ 4.12 —Definition of Discrimination

The concept of *discrimination* embraced by Title III is broad and is intended to cover a wide range of conduct. Prohibited conduct includes:

1. The application of eligibility requirements that screen out or tend to screen out individuals with disabilities, unless such eligibility can be shown to be necessary to the provision of the goods or services at issue[70]
2. A failure to make reasonable modifications in policies, practices, or procedures, unless the entity can show that such modifications would fundamentally alter the nature of the goods or services provided[71]
3. A failure to take necessary steps to ensure that no individual with a disability is excluded, denied services, segregated, or otherwise treated differently, unless the entity can show that those steps would fundamentally alter the nature of the goods or services provided[72]
4. A failure to remove architectural or communications barriers.[73]

Title III also prohibits discrimination against an individual because of that individual's relationship or association with an individual with a known disability.[74] This provision may be of importance to anyone who associates with HIV-infected individuals. A person may not be denied equal access to public accommodations because a member of his household or other associate is infected with HIV. This provision applies when the public accommodation accused of discrimination has knowledge of both the existence of a disability and of the relationship between the individual subjected to the discrimination and the individual with the disability.

---

[69] Car Parts Distribution Ctr., Inc. v. Automotive Wholesalers Ass'n, 57 F.3d 12 (1st Cir. 1994). This question arose because although the Title III definition of public accommodation specifically includes "insurance office, professional office of a health care provider, hospital, or other service establishment," 42 U.S.C. § 12181(7)(F), some district courts have interpreted that to restrict discriminatory conduct that occurs in those offices rather than in the plans run by those offices. *See, e.g.,* Pappas v. Bethesda Hosp. Ass'n, 861 F. Supp. 616 (S.D. Ohio 1994); Car Parts Distribution Ctr., Inc. v. Automotive Wholesalers Ass'n, 826 F. Supp. 583 (D.N.H. 1993). The Justice Department's own interpretation of ADA appears to be inconsistent with this reading of public accommodation.

[70] 42 U.S.C. § 12182(b)(2)(A)(i).

[71] *Id.* § 12182(b)(2)(A)(ii).

[72] *Id.* § 12182(b)(2)(A)(iii).

[73] *Id.* § 12182(b)(2)(A)(iv).

[74] *Id.* § 12182(b)(1)(E).

An individual may be excluded from a public accommodation when the individual's participation would pose a direct threat to the health and safety of others.[75] *Direct threat* means a significant risk to the health and safety of others that cannot be eliminated by a modification of policies, practices, or procedures.[76] Ungrounded fears of contagion do not justify excluding an HIV-infected individual from a public accommodation. Thus, a health club may not exclude an HIV-infected individual because of concerns of staff or members that HIV is a transmissible illness. In order to exclude HIV-infected individuals (and by extension, in order to justify inquiry into an individual's HIV status), a health club must show that HIV-infected individuals would pose a direct threat to the health and safety of others and that the threat could not be eliminated by providing basic education for staff and requiring certain uniform precautions in the event of injury. Given current medical knowledge, a plaintiff should be able to refute any evidence supporting a health club's direct threat defense.

If a plaintiff fails to show discriminatory treatment, the plaintiff's claim must fail. In *Toney v. U.S. Healthcare,*[77] the court granted the defendant physician's motion to dismiss on the grounds that the physician had provided appropriate care to the HIV-infected plaintiff as well as to other individuals with HIV infection. Essentially, the plaintiff failed to show that he was discriminated against because of a disability, that is, his HIV status.

§ 4.13   —Specific Title III Applications

Title III applies in several settings, including provision of health care,[78] access to services by funeral homes and morticians, and access to and participation in health clubs and other recreational or athletic facilities, that may be particularly pertinent to individuals with HIV.

Health Care Providers

Receiving adequate medical and dental care is a recurrent problem for individuals with HIV, who frequently are subjected to discrimination in this context.

---

[75] *Id.* § 12182(b)(3).

[76] 42 U.S.C. § 12182(b)(3). *See also* 28 C.F.R. § 36.208(b).

[77] 838 F. Supp. 201 (E.D. Pa. 1993).

[78] Protection against discrimination in access to hospital emergency medical services on the basis of ability to pay may be available under the Emergency Medical Treatment and Active Labor Act, 42 U.S.C. § 1395dd (1994), and the community service obligation provisions of the Hospital Survey and Construction Act of 1944 (known as the Hill-Burton Act), 42 U.S.C. § 291c(e) (1994), and the regulations thereunder, 42 C.F.R. pt. 124 (1996). Full discussion of these laws is beyond the scope of this chapter, but practitioners should be aware that although they do not provide protections that are specific to HIV, they may be relevant in cases of failure to provide services. *See* Dallas Gay Alliance v. Dallas County Hosp. Dist., 719 F. Supp. 1380 (N.D. Tex. 1989).

Medical and dental offices fall within the provisions of Title III. Thus, a doctor or dentist who refuses to treat patients with HIV because of their HIV status may be sued under the ADA. This does not necessarily mean that all doctors are required to provide all types of medical care to HIV-infected individuals. For example, a physician may limit his or her practice to a medical specialty. If an HIV-infected individual consults a specialist for care or treatment that is not within the physician's area of specialization, the physician may refuse to provide services to that potential patient. This would not be a violation of the ADA.[79]

In some instances, individual physicians who provide services in clinics or certain hospital settings may be considered employees and therefore not within the definition of public accommodation. In that case, the physician would not be covered by Title III. However, the clinic or hospital itself would be covered under Title III (a private hospital functioning as a public accommodation) or Title II (a public hospital). To the extent that discriminatory conduct could be attributed to the hospital, or to the extent hospital employees contributed to or assisted in the discriminatory conduct, the hospital itself could be liable.[80] For example, the first reported incident characterized as public accommodation HIV discrimination under the ADA arose from a physician's refusal to provide emergency treatment for a patient because the patient was infected with HIV. The physician's group practice later issued an apology to the patient, noting that the physician was no longer employed by the group and that the group had never had a policy of withholding treatment from individuals with HIV.[81]

There have been a number of reported complaints of health services discrimination under Title III, some of which have resulted in litigation.[82] In *Woolfolk v. Duncan*,[83] the court denied a defendant physician's motion for summary judgment. The court concluded that there was sufficient evidence that the physician discriminated against the plaintiff in the manner of treatment provided to him through the physician's own office. The court also permitted the case to proceed against the plaintiff's managed care provider, through which the plaintiff

---

[79] For a health care provider to argue successfully that he or she is not qualified to treat a patient because the patient is HIV-infected is not at all likely, although it has been attempted. *See, e.g.,* Beaulieu v. Clausen, 491 N.W.2d 662 (Minn. Ct. App. 1992) (rejecting dentist's defense that referring patient with HIV to another provider was appropriate given dentist's lack of knowledge about HIV disease).

[80] Aikins v. St. Helena Hosp., 843 F. Supp. 1329 (N.D. Cal. 1994). *But see* Howe v. Hull, 874 F. Supp. 779 (N.D. Ohio) (individual may constitute operator of a public accommodation, depending upon degree of control exercised as well as other factors), *subsequent opinion,* 873 F. Supp. 72 (N.D. Ohio 1994).

[81] *Health Care Provider Accused of Violating Disabilities Act,* 7 AIDS Alert 101 (1992); *Title III Update: Three Settlements, California Clinic Sued,* 1 Americans with Disabilities Act Manual (BNA) 29 (1992).

[82] For an extensive discussion of access to medical care, see Jack P. DeSario & James D. Slack, *The Americans with Disabilities Act and Refusals to Provide Medical Care to Persons with HIV/AIDS,* 27 J. Marshall L. Rev. 347 (1994).

[83] 872 F. Supp. 1381 (E.D. Pa. 1995).

obtained medical care, on the theory that the managed care entity exercised significant control over the provision of medical care. Both claims arose under Title III.

In *Howe v. Hull*,[84] the plaintiff raised claims under both Title III and section 504 of the Rehabilitation Act. In that case, the claim of discrimination arose when an individual with AIDS suffered an allergic reaction to a new medication. The emergency room doctor at the hospital he consulted determined that he should be admitted, but the defendant on-call admitting physician refused to admit him. The patient sued both the admitting physician and the hospital. He brought claims under Title III, Rehabilitation Act section 504, the Emergency Transfer and Active Labor Act (EMTALA), and state law. All claims were tried to a jury,[85] except for the Title III claim, which was tried to the court. The judge determined that, given his position of authority, the defendant physician fell within Title III of the ADA as an operator of a place of public accommodation. Finding that the patient's HIV infection had played a role in the decision to deny treatment, and that it was within the defendants' capacity to provide treatment, the court found a violation of the ADA. The court then enjoined the defendants from any future violations of the ADA.[86]

Denial of dental services is a frequent problem for people who are HIV-infected. Title III covers dental offices.[87] Under its Title III enforcement authority, the U.S. Department of Justice has commenced lawsuits against dentists who refused to provide treatment for individuals infected with HIV. In *United States v. Castle*,[88] a case initiated by the Department of Justice, the defendant dental clinic was ordered to pay $80,000 in compensatory and $20,000 in punitive damages. In *United States v. Morvant*,[89] also brought by the Department of Justice, the district court rejected the defendant dentist's argument that because he practiced dentistry as a professional corporation, he could not be sued personally. Because he controlled the operation of his practice, which was a place of public accommodation, Dr. Morvant was covered by Title III. The court also confirmed that in cases litigated by the Department of Justice, compensatory damages for individuals who have been subjected to discrimination are available.[90] In *D.B. v. Bloom*,[91] a private plaintiff raised both Title III and state statutory claims. On his state law claims he obtained a default judgment of $25,000 in compensatory

---

[84] 873 F. Supp. 72 (N.D. Ohio 1994).

[85] The jury rejected the EMTALA and state law claims but awarded $62,000 in compensatory damages and $150,000 in punitive damages against the defendant physician, and $300,000 against the hospital under section 504. *Id.* at 74.

[86] 3 Am. Disabilities Cas. (BNA) 1485 (N.D. Ohio 1994) (opinion granting injunction).

[87] 42 U.S.C. § 12181(7)(F) ("professional office of a health care provider").

[88] 63 U.S.L.W. 2216, 3 Health L. Rep. (BNA) 1343, 3 Americans with Disabilities Act Manual (BNA) 59 (S.D. Tex. Sept. 23, 1994).

[89] 843 F. Supp. 1092 (E.D. La. 1994).

[90] *Id.* at 1095–96.

[91] 896 F. Supp. 166 (D.N.J. 1995).

damages, $25,000 in punitive damages, and nearly $32,000 in attorney's fees, as well as a court order pursuant to Title III that the dentist cease his discriminatory practices and post a notice of nondiscrimination.

Finally, the plaintiff in *Abbott v. Bragdon*[92] raised claims under Title III and an analogous state statute. The defendant dentist conceded he fell within the public accommodation provisions of Title III. The district court rejected his direct threat defense and granted the plaintiff's motion for summary judgment.

Funeral Services

Complaints that funeral homes and morticians have refused to provide services or have increased charges for services for those who were infected with HIV are not uncommon.[93] Funeral homes fall within the definition of public accommodation and may not discriminate in the provision of services on the basis of a disability, such as the deceased's HIV status.[94]

In cases involving funeral homes, the application of Title III presents some potentially complex issues. The individual infected with HIV during his or her lifetime is protected by the ADA. Yet, in most cases, that person's claim of injury does not arise until after his death, at the time the funeral home refuses to handle his remains or charges a disparate fee.[95] It may be possible to pursue the claim naming the deceased's estate as plaintiff. A funeral home could argue in response that the individual infected with HIV had already died at the time of the transaction with the funeral home, and therefore he could not have a claim under the ADA, whether brought by the estate or not. Analytically, this position would appear to be correct. Perhaps the individuals who seek services could argue more effectively that they are being discriminated against because of their association or relationship with an individual with a disability, that is, the deceased. This is a proper basis for a claim under the ADA, which prohibits discrimination against an individual because he or she has a relationship or association with a person who has a disability.[96] However, the ADA uses the present tense—"has" an association or relationship—and it is not clear under the ADA whether

---

[92] 912 F. Supp. 580 (D. Me. 1996).

[93] For an overview of this problem, see Mark E. Wojcik, *AIDS and Funeral Homes: Common Legal Issues Facing Funeral Directors,* 27 J. Marshall L. Rev. 411 (1994).

[94] 42 U.S.C. § 12181(7)(F) ("funeral parlor").

[95] Title III incorporates the *futile gesture doctrine,* so if an individual knows that a funeral home engages in discrimination, the individual need not attempt to obtain those services before challenging the discriminatory policy or practice. *Id.* § 12188(a)(1). This provision might also apply when an individual seeks to prepay or make their funeral arrangements in advance directly with the provider. Also, the Justice Department is authorized to investigate and bring civil actions in cases involving a "pattern or practice of discrimination" or when the discrimination "raises an issue of general public importance." *Id.* § 12188(b)(1)(A), (B)(i)–(ii).

[96] *Id.* § 12182(b)(1)(E).

an association or relationship can continue to exist after the death of the individual with a disability. Nor is it clear, assuming that the association continues to exist, that the association continues with the person who has a disability once that person has died. No court has ruled on this point. The strongest argument may simply flow from the purposes and goals that underlie the ADA. Indeed, it is impossible to distinguish between persons discriminated against because of their association with an individual living with HIV (for example, when a moving company refuses to provide services to someone because her roommate has AIDS) and the discrimination experienced by someone who is seeking funeral services for a deceased family member.

In addition to refusing service, funeral homes have levied extra charges for services involving human remains infected with HIV. The Department of Justice has determined that it is a violation of Title III for funeral homes to charge increased fees for embalming the bodies of individuals who died of infectious diseases, including AIDS. Funeral homes have contended that protecting against HIV transmission justified such fees for cases involving known infection. The Justice Department rejected this argument, based in part on the OSHA workplace safety standard (see **Chapter 3**) that requires employees to use universal precautions, that is, to treat all individuals as though they are infected. If every person must be treated as though he or she was infected, there is no justification for any additional charge when the individual who has died is actually known to have been infected.[97]

Health Clubs and Recreational Facilities

When asked by a health club operator whether the club was permitted to deny membership to an individual who had disclosed that he was infected with HIV, the Department of Justice has responded that such discrimination is not permissible. Health clubs and similar facilities are public accommodations within the meaning of Title III.[98] As for the owner's concern that admitting an individual known to be infected with HIV will cause others to leave the club, this is properly addressed by educating staff and members as to modes of HIV transmission. Whatever the financial impact on the club, it does not justify excluding individuals with disabilities.[99]

---

[97] *See* 5 Americans with Disabilities Act Manual (BNA) 12 (1996) (settlement between Department of Justice and funeral home in which funeral home agreed to pay damages to nine families of individuals who died from AIDS and to institute universal precautions training).

[98] 42 U.S.C. § 12181(7)(L) ("gymnasium, health spa, bowling alley, golf course, or other place of exercise or recreation").

[99] ADA's legislative history, particularly in regard to the food service employee debate (**Ch.3**), makes it clear that the concerns of third parties cannot be a defense to an ADA discrimination complaint.

§ 4.14   Rehabilitation Act of 1973

The Rehabilitation Act of 1973,[100] frequently referred to as *section 504,* served as a basis for HIV discrimination litigation before the passage of ADA. It is now widely recognized that the Rehabilitation Act gives rise to a private cause of action and applies to employment (see **Chapter 3**) and the provision of services.

The Rehabilitation Act and ADA are similar. Generally speaking, conduct prohibited by the Rehabilitation Act is also prohibited by ADA. However, the Rehabilitation Act is of significantly narrower scope than ADA. For example, Title III of ADA applies to all public accommodations affecting interstate commerce, but the Rehabilitation Act applies only to entities that receive federal financial support. Thus, not all ADA plaintiffs can also bring claims under the Rehabilitation Act.

However, for those who can sue under the Rehabilitation Act, it may be highly desirable to do so. The Rehabilitation Act has been construed to entitle a private plaintiff to damages (see **Chapter 3**), whereas the ADA contains no such entitlement (see **§ 4.10**). Thus, it is advisable to carefully check whether a defendant may be subject to the Rehabilitation Act as well as ADA.

A plaintiff under the Rehabilitation Act must prove four elements to succeed:

1.   That the individual has or is perceived to have a disability
2.   That the individual is otherwise qualified for the program or activity at issue
3.   That the individual has been excluded from the program or activity solely by reason of the identified disability
4.   That the program or activity receives federal financial assistance.

The first three elements are similar to requirements imposed under portions of the ADA.[101] Because the Rehabilitation Act predated the ADA by nearly 20 years, there is an independent body of case law concerning the Rehabilitation Act elements.

Miller v. Spicer[102] is a significant case involving the Rehabilitation Act claims of an individual perceived to be HIV-infected. It illustrates both the strengths and limitations of the Rehabilitation Act. The plaintiff, Rod Miller, sought emergency services for a foot injury at the defendant Beebe Medical Center in June 1987 and required emergency surgery. The surgeon consulted about Miller's condition,

---

[100] Pub. L. No. 93-112, 87 Stat. 355, 1973 U.S.C.C.A.N. 409 (codified at 29 U.S.C. §§ 701–796i (1994)). The Rehabilitation Act is discussed generally in **Ch. 3.**

[101] Note, however, that ADA does not require the plaintiff to show that the disability was the "sole cause" for the discriminatory treatment, as some courts have ruled in cases under the Rehabilitation Act. *See, e.g.,* Leckelt v. Board of Comm'rs, 909 F.2d 820 (5th Cir. 1990); Buko v. American Medical Lab., Inc., 830 F. Supp. 899 (E.D. Va. 1993).

[102] 822 F. Supp. 158 (D. Del. 1993).

Dr. Robert Spicer, had staff privileges at the Medical Center but was not an employee there. Dr. Spicer suspected that Miller and his friends who had accompanied him to the Medical Center were gay. After closely questioning Miller about his health, Dr. Spicer asked if Miller had had an "AIDS test." Miller said he had but did not know the results. After the Medical Center and Dr. Spicer were unsuccessful in their attempt to obtain the results of Miller's test, Dr. Spicer refused to perform the necessary surgery out of fear of HIV transmission. Miller was then transferred to another facility. Miller suffered permanent injuries to his foot resulting from the delay in treatment caused by Dr. Spicer's refusal. In the subsequent lawsuit, Dr. Spicer was not subject to suit under the Rehabilitation Act because he received no federal funding.[103] However, the Medical Center did receive federal financial assistance and hence was within the coverage of the Rehabilitation Act. The district court found that the Medical Center's employees were aware of and in fact facilitated Spicer's discriminatory conduct, and therefore the Medical Center could properly be held liable. The court also found that compensatory damages were available to the plaintiff under the Rehabilitation Act.

In *Howe v. Hull*,[104] a plaintiff who alleged being denied medical care because of HIV infection was successful against a doctor and a hospital on section 504 and ADA Title III claims. Dr. Hull, the on-call admitting physician at the defendant hospital, refused to admit the plaintiff because of his HIV infection. The jury awarded compensatory damages of $62,000 and punitive damages of $150,000 against the doctor and $300,000 against the hospital under section 504. Under Title III of the ADA, the court enjoined the defendants from further discrimination.

§ 4.15 —Enforcement and Remedies

It is now widely recognized that section 504 of the Rehabilitation Act provides a private cause of action for compensatory damages.[105] Some courts have required plaintiffs to exhaust internal administrative remedies established by the defendant before turning to the courts. In Toney v. *U.S. Healthcare*,[106] the court dismissed

---

[103] If these events occurred today, Spicer would in all likelihood be liable under ADA Title III, but because Title III does not provide a damages remedy, Miller's ability to recover from Spicer would still be effectively curtailed. *See* Woolfolk v. Duncan, 872 F. Supp. 1381 (E.D. Pa. 1995) (plaintiff alleging discriminatory provision of medical care permitted to proceed under both ADA Title III and the Rehabilitation Act).

[104] 873 F. Supp. 72 (N.D. Ohio 1994).

[105] *See* Howe v. Hull, 873 F. Supp. 72 (N.D. Ohio 1994); Glanz v. Vernick, 750 F. Supp. 39 (D. Mass. 1990). *See also* Consolidated Rail Corp. v. Darrone, 477 U.S. 597 (1986) (upholding private damages action for employment discrimination in violation of section 504, although opinion focuses on other issues). Availability of punitive damages is less clear. *See* Moreno v. Consolidated Rail Corp., 99 F.3d 782 (6th Cir. 1996).

[106] 838 F. Supp. 201, 204–05 (E.D. Pa. 1993).

the plaintiff's section 504 claim because he failed to pursue an HMO's internal grievance procedure before filing his claim. The internal procedure had been devised by the HMO and its adoption was approved by the state. The process would have taken approximately two-and-one-half months. The court rejected the plaintiff's argument that resort to the grievance procedure would have been futile. *Toney* involved an internal administrative remedy established by the defendant. It does not follow that exhaustion of administrative remedies established not by the defendant but by statute is required. For example, in *Ali v. City of Clearwater*,[107] a district court judge concluded that exhaustion of administrative remedies was not required.

The Rehabilitation Act provides for the award of a reasonable attorney's fee to a prevailing party.[108] As with the Civil Rights Attorney's Fee Act of 1976,[109] the statutory language is somewhat misleading. A plaintiff who meets with reasonable success on significant issues in a case, whether at trial or at settlement, is entitled to an award of attorney's fees. Except in the case of frivolous litigation, a prevailing defendant is not entitled to attorney's fees.

§ 4.16 —Elements of Rehabilitation Act Cause of Action

To make out a claim under the Rehabilitation Act, a potential plaintiff should be prepared to plead and prove four statutory elements. First, the claimant must be an individual with or perceived to have a disability. This element is the same as that under the ADA (see § 4.3). Second, he or she must be "otherwise qualified" to receive the services or access to the program in question. This element is the same as that discussed under the ADA (see **Chapter 3** and § 4.7). Rarely would HIV status render an individual unqualified to access services or participate in any program. In any event, the defendant bears the burden of proving that the plaintiff is not otherwise qualified, based on the direct threat defense or on some other basis. Third, the alleged discrimination must be solely by reason of the disability, an element not included in the ADA, which uses a less strict concept of causation. As some courts have indicated, this language in the statute precludes success in a case in which the evidence indicates that the defendant acted with some nondiscriminatory motive combined with a discriminatory one.[110] Fourth, the defendant entity must receive federal financial assistance. This restriction to programs or activities that receive federal financial assistance substantially limits the application of the Rehabilitation Act and contrasts sharply

---

[107] 807 F. Supp. 701 (M.D. Fla. 1992).

[108] 29 U.S.C. § 794a(b).

[109] 42 U.S.C. § 1988.

[110] *See, e.g.,* Leckelt v. Board of Comm'rs, 909 F.2d 820 (5th Cir. 1990); Buko v. American Medical Lab., Inc., 830 F. Supp. 899 (E.D. Va. 1993).

with the breadth of the ADA, which applies to entities that affect commerce. However, this requirement of federal financial assistance has been broadly interpreted. Thus, the Rehabilitation Act has been interpreted to apply to programs receiving federal financial assistance of any kind,[111] including hospitals receiving Medicaid funds[112] and independent contractors who provide services to and have a close financial relationship with a federally funded employer.[113] Many state, county, and local correctional facilities receive federal monies and hence are subject to section 504.[114] The Rehabilitation Act has also been held to apply to a bank on the basis of its participation in the Small Business Administration's guaranteed loan program.[115]

§ 4.17 State Law Disability Discrimination

State nondiscrimination statutes have been frequently invoked, particularly in claims of discrimination by health care professionals, to protect the rights of individuals with HIV.[116] Unlike the ADA, however, not all state statutes are unambiguous in terms of their scope and application in the area of public accommodations. In a significant interpretation of New York law, for example, the New York Court of Appeals has clarified that the state's statutory definition of public accommodations does include professional dental offices within its scope.[117]

In a significant decision under Minnesota's Human Rights Act, the Minnesota Court of Appeals affirmed the ruling of an administrative law judge (ALJ) that a dentist's refusal to treat a patient with HIV infection was illegal, resulting in a $10,000 award to the patient for mental anguish and a $5,000 civil penalty to be paid to the Commissioner of the Department of Human Rights.[118] At the time of the discriminatory refusal to provide services, the complainant, identified in the court's opinion only by the initials "J.B.," was HIV-infected but asymptomatic. The court affirmed the ALJ's ruling that a person with asymptomatic HIV

---

[111] Jones v. Metropolitan Atlanta Rapid Transit Auth., 681 F.2d 1376 (11th Cir. 1982), *cert. denied*, 465 U.S. 1099 (1984).

[112] United States v. University Hosp., 575 F. Supp. 607 (E.D.N.Y. 1983), *aff'd*, 729 F.2d 144 (2d Cir. 1984).

[113] Frazier v. Board of Trustees, 765 F.2d 1278 (5th Cir.), *modified in unrelated part*, 777 F.2d 329 (5th Cir. 1985), *cert. denied*, 476 U.S. 1142 (1986).

[114] *See, e.g.,* Torcasio v. Murray, 862 F. Supp. 1482 (E.D. Va. 1994), *aff'd*, 57 F.3d 1340 (4th Cir. 1995).

[115] Morre v. Sun Bank, 923 F.2d 1423 (11th Cir. 1991).

[116] ADA does not preempt state nondiscrimination laws. 42 U.S.C. § 12201(b).

[117] Cahill v. Rosa, 5 Health L. Rep. (BNA) 1543, 1996 WL 625559 (N.Y. Ct. App. Oct. 15, 1996).

[118] Beaulieu v. Clausen, 491 N.W.2d 662 (Minn. Ct. App. 1992).

infection is disabled and thus protected under Minnesota's Human Rights Act, which, like the federal Rehabilitation Act and ADA, defines disability in terms of limitations on major life activities. Because of the physical limitations in areas of sexual contact, childbearing, eligibility for life, health, or disability insurance, and career choices limited by potential limitations on life expectancies, as well as limitations resulting from the social exclusion faced by persons with HIV, the court agreed with the ALJ that persons with asymptomatic HIV infection are limited in several major life activities, and thus disabled under the Minnesota act.

Turning to the discrimination issue, the court noted that J.B. received dental services from Dr. Clausen on numerous occasions between 1986 and 1990. In February 1989, J.B. informed Dr. Clausen that he was HIV-infected. Dr. Clausen then saw J.B. for routine appointments on three more occasions. J.B. made an appointment for September 1990 for an examination and cleaning, which may be invasive and which often causes bleeding. Prior to that appointment, however, Dr. Clausen cancelled the appointment and referred J.B. to a local university clinic. The court noted that Dr. Clausen referred J.B. "without any specific information" about J.B.'s condition. Dr. Clausen attempted to justify his actions by explaining that he believed referral of HIV-infected patients was appropriate in order to protect their health and because of his lack of knowledge about HIV disease. The ALJ and the court, in affirming the ALJ's finding, specifically rejected this defense. In support of Dr. Clausen's view, defense experts testified that patients with HIV infection should be treated in isolation rooms; J.B.'s experts and 1988 American Dental Association guidelines,[119] however, contradicted that view. The court also noted that at the time of the referral in 1990, the university clinic to which J.B. was referred was not treating HIV-infected patients in isolation. Significantly, the court referred to the ALJ's conclusion that although Dr. Clausen believed that referral to the clinic was appropriate in order to protect J.B.'s health, there was no medical evidence to support Dr. Clausen's conclusion. Because these beliefs were uninformed and unjustified, the court determined that the ALJ properly concluded that Dr. Clausen's explanation was not worthy of belief and was "merely a pretext for discrimination."[120]

State and local nondiscrimination administrative agencies have awarded significant damages to complainants in HIV/AIDS discrimination cases. In *Marcus Garvey Nursing Home, Inc. v. New York State Division of Human Rights*,[121] for example, the complainant's award of $150,000 was vacated and the case remanded for entry of an award not in excess of $75,000. The complainant had prevailed on his claim that because of his HIV status he had been subjected to strict isolation, including being denied the use of the public telephone on the premises, for nine-and-one-half months of his nursing home stay.

---

[119] American Dental Ass'n, Facts About AIDS for the Dental Team (2d ed. 1988).

[120] Beaulieu v. Clausen, 491 N.W.2d at 668.

[121] 619 N.Y.S.2d 106 (App. Div. 1994).

In another case of enforcing a state's HIV nondiscrimination law, a ruling and $10,000 award against a community health center for HIV-related discrimination was reversed. The state nondiscrimination commission ruled that the draping of all exposed surfaces of a treatment room during a dental procedure constituted unlawful discrimination, resulting in emotional distress and humiliation that supported the award of damages. On appeal, in which the complainant proceeded pro se, the court concluded that based on the evidence of record, the draping of surfaces was an acceptable infection control practice, and the treatment room in which the draping took place was not visible to persons other than the health center staff. Although the draping was not required as an infection control practice, the court did not find fault with using such additional precautions when treating a patient known to be HIV-infected.[122] Because the draping activity occurred only in private and only the patient and staff were aware of the practice, the damage award for public humiliation was annulled by the court.[123] In another case, the plaintiff alleged that after she tested HIV positive, she was refused treatment at the defendant hospital's high-risk prenatal care clinic and was referred to another facility for an abortion.[124] Although the court dismissed the plaintiff's Rehabilitation Act section 504 claim against an individual employee defendant, the court allowed her to proceed with claims under state nondiscrimination law.

In a case brought under the Maine Human Rights Act, *Abbott v. Bragdon,*[125] challenging a dentist's refusal to treat a patient with HIV, the court ruled that the defendant has a jury trial right as to the state law claims for civil penalties, but as to liability only; the court determines equitable relief, including the assessment of damages.

In *Phillips v. Mufleh,*[126] the court reviewed claims of discrimination, brought under a local Toledo municipal law, resulting from a hotel proprietor's excluding a customer with AIDS. The court concluded that plaintiff's emotional distress claims were included within the definition of actual damages authorized under the local law.

---

[122] *Compare* CDC, Recommended Infection-Control Practices for Dentistry (1993), which does not recommend draping environmental surfaces, but instead recommends that surfaces be cleaned and disinfected after treatment of each patient and at the completion of daily work activities.

[123] Syracuse Community Health Ctr. v. Wendi A.M., 604 N.Y.S.2d 406 (App. Div. 1993).

[124] Doe v. Jamaica Hosp., 608 N.Y.S.2d 518 (App. Div. 1994) (mem.).

[125] 882 F. Supp. 181 (D. Me. 1995).

[126] 642 N.E.2d 411 (Ohio Ct. App. 1994) (per curiam).

CHAPTER 5

SCHOOLS AND EDUCATIONAL PROGRAMS

Linda D. Headley*

§ 5.1 Introduction

HIV infection among children is becoming almost commonplace in the United States. Recent estimates of the number of children living with the disease range from 12,000 in 1994 to approximately 20,000 in 1995.[1] These children may or may not have special medical or educational requirements as they enter and progress

---

* The author acknowledges with great appreciation Penelope A. Boyd, Ira M. Fingles, Edward Haas, and Kay Henderson for their assistance in reviewing and providing research for this manuscript.

[1] Susan F. Davis et al., *Prevalence and Incidence of Vertically Acquired HIV Infection in the United States,* 274 JAMA 952 (1995); Katherine Luzuriaga & John L. Sullivan, *DNA Polymerase Chain Reaction for the Diagnosis of Vertical HIV Infection,* 257 JAMA 1360 (1996).

through the public education system. Certainly of concern to all are those children's needs to be treated with dignity, to interact with children who do not share their disability, and to maintain confidentiality. This chapter reviews the basic substantive educational entitlements of children living with HIV and the legal bases for ensuring their inclusion and privacy.

§ 5.2   Educational Implications of HIV Disease in Children[2]

Today there are really only two populations of children with HIV infection. The first is children with perinatal or birth-acquired infection. Between 15 and 30 percent of infants born to mothers with HIV infection will acquire the virus, which can be rapidly progressive in children.[3] A few children in this group, however, are *long-term survivors* who will reach school age. Although the actual number of preschool and elementary-age children with HIV infection is quite low, it can be anticipated that when treatment advances occur, this group will be surviving into the school-age years in large numbers.[4]

The second group of students with HIV infection is adolescents who acquire the virus through sexual activities or sharing of injection drug equipment, such as syringes. Most of these adolescents have "silent" infections, because so few of them are tested. Although these students are less likely to be symptomatic while still in school, they do carry the virus and may become aware that they have been infected, which may potentially lead to emotional or social problems.

The typical course of HIV disease depends upon how the virus was transmitted. For children with perinatal infection, the median latency period is 12 months, whereas those infected as a result of transfusion have a median period of 3.5 years until symptoms occur.[5] Young children have a shorter incubation period than adults, perhaps because of the immaturity of their immune systems.[6] Children with perinatal infection usually begin to show symptoms by three years of age, giving rise to the need for early intervention services to assist with developmental delays or other attendant problems.

HIV disease causes an encephalopathy in 50 to 90 percent of children with perinatal infection.[7] Symptomatic children experience a number of problems that

---

[2] This section is adapted from C.H. LeRoy et al., *Meeting Our Responsibilities in Special Education,* Teaching Exceptional Children 37–40 (Summer 1994). Used with permission.

[3] Susan F. Davis et al., *Prevalence and Incidence of Vertically Acquired HIV Infection in the United States,* 274 JAMA 952 (1995).

[4] K. Krasinski et al., *Prognosis of Human Immunodeficiency Virus Infection in Children and Adolescents,* 8 Pediatric Infectious Disease J. 216–20 (1989).

[5] Robert J. Simonds & Martha F. Rogers, *Epidemiology of HIV in Children and Other Populations, in* HIV Infection and Developmental Disabilities: A Resource for Service Providers 3–13 (Allen C. Crocker et al. eds., 1992).

[6] R. Donatelle et al., Access to Health (2d ed. 1991).

[7] L.G. Epstein et al., *Neurologic Manifestations of Human Immunodeficiency Virus in Children,* 78 Pediatrics 678–87 (1989).

are of concern to educators. Since HIV disease is a syndrome, this means that a group of symptoms develops. Typical symptoms associated with childhood HIV disease include: attention difficulties, cardiac disease, central nervous system damage, cognitive deficits, cold sores, coughing, acute and chronic diarrhea, emotional problems, fine and gross motor difficulties, hearing problems, frequent viral and bacterial infections, seizures, shortness of breath, speech and language delays, visual problems, weakness, and weight loss.

It has been suggested that HIV disease may become the largest cause of mental retardation and brain damage in children, with 75 to 90 percent of infected children having significant developmental problems.[8] Further complicating the educational environment is the fact that children follow an erratic course of neurological deterioration, possibly stable for months with rapid deterioration over a few weeks.[9]

§ 5.3 Individuals With Disabilities Education Act

Congress addressed the problem of educating children with disabilities in 1966 and 1970 by establishing grant programs to serve as incentives to the states to expand educational opportunities for children with disabilities. The second of these, the Education of the Handicapped Act,[10] was amended in 1975 by the Education for All Handicapped Children Act (EAHCA).[11] The EAHCA for the first time established specific guidelines for the use of federal monies, and it required participating states to guarantee a free, appropriate, public education to children with disabilities.[12] Subchapter II, commonly referred to as Part B,[13] is the current embodiment of this congressional drive to integrate children with disabilities into the public school system and to ensure the availability of appropriate programs for children aged 3 to 21.[14]

---

[8] Gary W. Diamond & Herbert J. Cohen, *Developmental Disabilities in Children with HIV Infection, in* HIV Infection and Developmental Disabilities: A Resource for Service Providers 33–42 (Allen H. Crocker et al. eds., 1992); M.L. Batshaw & Y.M. Perret, Children with Disabilities: A Medical Primer (1992).

[9] J. Byers, *AIDS in Children: Effects on Neurological Development and Implications for the Future,* 23 J. Special Educ. 5–16 (1989).

[10] Pub. L. No. 91-230, Title VI, 84 Stat. 175, 1970 U.S.C.C.A.N. 198.

[11] Pub. L. No. 94-142, 1975 U.S.C.C.A.N. (89 Stat.) 773.

[12] *See* Board of Educ. v. Rowley, 458 U.S. 176 (1982).

[13] 20 U.S.C. §§ 1411–1420 (1994).

[14] The statute contains a grandfather clause relieving states of the obligation to serve children either between the ages of 3 and 5, or 18 and 21, based on existing state law. 20 U.S.C. § 1412(2)(B). At present, all children in the three-to-five age group are eligible for services. Children in the vast majority of states, territories, and possessions, as well as those served by the Bureau of Indian Affairs in the Department of the Interior, can receive services either to or through age 21. Some states provide education for longer periods. Services are available in Utah through age 22 and in Michigan until age 25. However, Florida, Indiana, and Montana only serve individuals through age 18; Hawaii terminates services after age 19; and Delaware, Kentucky, Mississippi, and Missouri educate through age 20. Office of Special Educ. Programs, U.S. Dep't of Educ., FAPE Entitlement and Due Process Hearing System (1994).

The 1986 amendments to the law added a new Part H to assist in the establishment of coordinated, statewide early intervention service delivery systems for infants and toddlers.[15] Congress intended to create universal access to services for children outside of the traditional school-age range,[16] building on the successes realized from an incentive grant program initiated in 1983.[17] This created a national system of services for children with disabilities from birth through age 21. In 1990 the statute was renamed the Individuals with Disabilities Education Act (IDEA).[18]

In adopting IDEA, Congress initially sought to address the needs of millions of children with disabilities who were excluded from the public school system or whose need for special education and related services was either undetected or not fully met.[19] The Act addresses these problems by: requiring that all children with disabilities be identified, located, and evaluated for their need for special education and related services;[20] requiring that states have in effect a policy that assures the right to a free, appropriate, public education to all children with disabilities residing within the state;[21] establishing a presumption of inclusion of children with disabilities in the regular educational environment;[22] establishing strong procedural protections;[23] and mandating ongoing training and education of personnel providing services under the Act.[24]

The addition of assistance to states to provide early intervention services to infants and toddlers with disabilities was predicated on a congressional finding of "an urgent and substantial need" to enhance their development, reduce long-term educational costs, prevent institutionalization, and assist families to meet the challenge of raising an exceptional child.[25] Both the Part B and Part H programs provide services in accordance with an individualized program developed in consultation with parents and based upon professional evaluations, establish a single line of authority for development and implementation of those programs, and contain procedural safeguards for children and parents.

---

[15] 20 U.S.C. §§ 1471–1485 (1994).

[16] S. Rep. No. 315, 99th Cong., 2d Sess. 3 (1986).

[17] *Id.* at 4–5.

[18] Pub. L. No. 101-476, § 901(a)(1), 1990 U.S.C.C.A.N. (104 Stat.) 1441, *amending* 20 U.S.C. § 1400(a).

[19] 20 U.S.C. § 1400(b).

[20] This is the *child find obligation* of IDEA, codified at 20 U.S.C. § 1412(2)(C).

[21] 20 U.S.C. § 1412(1).

[22] *Id.* § 1412(5)(B).

[23] *Id.* § 1415.

[24] *Id.* § 1413(a)(3).

[25] *Id.* § 1462(a).

§ 5.4   IDEA Part B Services for Children Aged Three to Twenty-One

In order to qualify for Part B services under IDEA, a child must have a disability that meets a two-pronged test.[26] First, there must be a disability as defined in the Act. Second, the disability must result in a need for special education and related services.

The definition of *disability* is categorical, rather than functional. It lists the following conditions: mental retardation, hearing impairments including deafness, speech or language impairments, visual impairments including blindness, serious emotional disturbance, orthopedic impairments, autism, traumatic brain injury, other health impairments, or specific learning disabilities.[27] A child with HIV infection who does not have one of the other listed conditions will not automatically be considered to have a disability.[28] Should the child meet the second prong of the definition by needing services because of the infection, the child will qualify as having an "other health impairment." For example, a developmentally delayed child with HIV disease who requires frequent hospitalizations—necessitating a program that includes tutoring, home instruction and a modified testing schedule in addition to specialized instruction—would qualify under this second prong. The statute is somewhat broader for preschoolers. States have the option of expanding the definition to serve three- to five-year-olds who are experiencing developmental delays in physical, cognitive, communication, social or emotional, or adaptive development.[29]

§ 5.5   —Free, Appropriate, Public Education

A child with a disability is entitled to receive a free, appropriate, public education emphasizing special education and related services designed to meet his or her unique needs.[30] *Free, appropriate, public education* is defined as special

---

[26] 20 U.S.C. § 1401(a)(1)(A).

[27] *Id.* § 1401(a)(1)(A)(i). The definition of *specific* learning disabilities intentionally excludes children who experience problems because of "environmental, cultural or economic disadvantage." S. Rep. No. 168, 94th Cong., 1st Sess. 10 (1975), *reprinted in* 1975 U.S.C.C.A.N. 1425, 1435.

[28] Doe v. Belleville Pub. Sch. Dist., 672 F. Supp. 342 (S.D. Ill. 1987). *See* Sandra E. McNary-Keith, *AIDS in Public Schools: Resolved Issues and Continuing Controversy,* 24 J. L. & Educ. 69, 73 (1995) (*citing* Maureen M. Murphy, *Special Education Children with HIV Infection: Standards and Strategies for Admission to the Classroom,* 19 J. L. & Educ. 345, 353 (1990)).

[29] 20 U.S.C. § 1401(a)(1)(B).

[30] 20 U.S.C. § 1400(c).

education and related services that: (1) are provided without charge, at public
expense, and under public supervision; (2) meet state standards; (3) include
preschool, elementary, and secondary school education; and (4) are provided in
accordance with an individualized education program.[31] The interpretation of
this provision has been the subject of extensive litigation over the years.

IDEA does not on its face create a substantive standard. It instead references
state standards in its definition of what constitutes a free, appropriate, public
education. In 1982, the Supreme Court rejected the interpretation that IDEA
requires an agency to maximize a child's development. The Court construed this
provision to require only that a child receive an education through an individual
education program "reasonably calculated to enable the child to receive educational benefits," as long as the procedural requirements of the statute have been
followed.[32] Subsequent lower court decisions, although continuing to reject the
concept of maximizing educational potential, have interpreted the provision to
require that the benefit must be "meaningful."[33]

§ 5.6 —Individualized Education Program

The success or failure of programming for a special needs student lies in the
development and implementation of an effective individualized education program, known commonly as an IEP,[34] a document that has been characterized as
"the cornerstone of contemporary special education."[35] IDEA requires, as a
condition of participation, that each child with a disability have an IEP in effect[36]

---

[31] *Id.* § 1401(a)(18).

[32] Board of Educ. v. Rowley, 458 U.S. 176 (1982) (child with deafness who was making
academic progress not entitled to sign language interpreter services in the classroom).

[33] Board of Educ. v. Diamond, 808 F.2d 987, 991 (3d Cir. 1986) (the law requires a plan in
which educational progress is likely, not trivial or merely preventing regression); *accord* Polk
v. Central Susquehanna Intermediate Unit 16, 853 F.2d 171, 184 (3d Cir. 1988), *cert. denied,*
488 U.S. 1030 (1989); *but see* Swift v. Rapides Parish Pub. Sch. Sys., 812 F. Supp. 666, 672
(W.D. La. 1993) (law guarantees meaningful access to allow some educational benefit).

[34] The Department of Education has issued a Notice of Interpretation of its regulations regarding individual education programs (IEPs) that answers the most common questions about the
entire IEP process. *See* 34 C.F.R. pt. 300, app. C (1995).

[35] Daniel P. Morgan, A Primer on Individualized Education Programs for Exceptional Children:
Preferred Strategies and Practices 1 (2d ed. 1981); *see* Honig v. Doe, 484 U.S. 305, 311
(1988) (IEP is "centerpiece of the statute's education delivery system"); *see also* School
Comm. v. Department of Educ., 471 U.S. 359, 368 (1985) (IEP is *"modus operandi"* of
IDEA).

[36] In order to be "in effect," the IEP must: (1) have been developed properly; (2) be regarded by
the agency and the parents as appropriate in terms of the child's needs, goals, and objectives,
and the services to be provided to assist in the attainment of those goals and objectives; and
(3) be implemented as written. 34 C.F.R. pt. 300, app. C, question 3.

at the beginning of each school year, and that it be reviewed and revised at least annually.[37]

The IEP was viewed by Congress as both "the logical extension and the final step of the evaluation and placement process" and "an extension of procedural protections" afforded to parents.[38] By definition, a child is not receiving a free, appropriate, public education unless it is provided in conformity with an IEP meeting the standards of the statute.[39]

Consistent with IDEA's goal that every child with a disability receive an education tailored to meet his or her individual needs, there must be a full evaluation of those needs before initial placement[40] and at least every three years thereafter.[41] Minimum standards for evaluation include assessment of all areas related to the suspected disability by a multidisciplinary team, using validated tests and procedures. Suggested assessment areas include, as appropriate, "health, vision, hearing, social and emotional status, general intelligence, academic performance, communicative status, motor abilities,"[42] and the need for assistive technology devices and services.[43] Additional procedures exist for evaluating a child for the existence of a specific learning disability.[44] Prescribed components of the evaluation process are that testing be performed in a child's native language[45] and that it be done in a way that accurately reflects aptitude and skills.[46]

Within 30 calendar days following a decision that a child is eligible for Part B services, a meeting must be held to develop an IEP, with subsequent meetings at least once per year or more frequently, as appropriate, to review and revise it.[47] The IEP conference and resulting document are "not intended to be the evaluation process itself."[48] Instead, the conference serves as the forum for development of

---

[37] 20 U.S.C. § 1414(a)(5).

[38] S. Rep. No. 168, 94th Cong., 1st Sess. 11 (1975), *reprinted in* 1975 U.S.C.C.A.N. 1425, 1435. Although the statute ultimately required that once an initial IEP has been developed, it is subject to review and appropriate revision "periodically but not less than annually," 20 U.S.C. § 1414(a)(5), the Senate version required review at least three times per year.

[39] 20 U.S.C. §§ 1401(a)(18), (20), 1414(a)(5).

[40] 34 C.F.R. § 300.531 (1996).

[41] *Id.* § 300.534.

[42] *Id.* § 300.532.

[43] 20 U.S.C. § 1401(a)(26)(A); 34 C.F.R. § 300.6(a); *see* Letter to Seiler, 20 Indivs. Disabilities Educ. L. Rep. (LRP) 1216 (Office Spec. Educ. Programs 1991); Letter to Anonymous, 18 Indivs. Disabilities Educ. L. Rep. (LRP) 627 (Office Spec. Educ. Programs 1991); Letter to Goodman, 16 Educ. Handicapped L. Rep. (LRP) 1317 (Office Spec. Educ. Programs 1990).

[44] 34 C.F.R. §§ 300.540–300.543.

[45] This includes other modes of communication, such as sign language or the use of augmentative communication devices.

[46] 20 U.S.C. § 1412(5)(C); 34 C.F.R. § 300.532.

[47] 34 C.F.R. § 300.343.

[48] S. Rep. No. 168, 94th Cong., 1st Sess. 11 (1975), *reprinted in* 1975 U.S.C.C.A.N. 1425, 1435.

a document that the Department of Education views as serving multiple functions: a commitment of resources,[49] management tool, a compliance and monitoring document, and an evaluation device.[50] The document is a statement of:

1. Present levels of educational performance
2. Annual goals, including short-term instructional objectives
3. Specific educational services to be provided, and the extent of participation in regular educational programs
4. Transition services needed for children before leaving the school setting, including interagency responsibilities or linkages[51]
5. The projected date of initiation and anticipated duration of services
6. Objective criteria and evaluation procedures and schedules to determine whether instructional objectives are being achieved.[52]

Since the inception of the IEP process, there has been tension between the dual needs to systematically approach the unique educational needs of children with disabilities and to preserve flexibility and creativity in the educational process.[53] When the spirit as well as the letter of the law are followed, the IEP process develops an educational plan—as a result of full collaboration among a child's parents and educators—tailored to meet the student's unique educational needs.[54] The child's needs drive the service plan.[55] When attention is paid merely to the need to have an IEP in order to be in compliance with the black letter of the law, all too often the result is "a paper exercise characterized by fragmented objectives,

---

[49] An agency must provide all services a child needs, as determined through evaluations, either directly or by contract, or other arrangements. *See* 34 C.F.R. pt. 300, app. C, questions 44–46.

[50] 34 C.F.R. pt. 300, apps. C, I.

[51] Transition planning must begin for pupils not later than when they reach age 16. However, when appropriate, planning should begin at age 14 or younger. 20 U.S.C. § 1401(a)(20).

[52] *Id.*

[53] *See* Daniel P. Hallahan & James M. Kauffman, Exceptional Children: Introduction to Special Education 38–39 (6th ed. 1994) [hereinafter Hallahan & Kauffman]; *cf.* Joan F. Goodman & Lori Bond, *The Individualized Education Program: A Retrospective Critique,* 26 J. Special Educ. 408, 413–17 (arguing that "the IEP makes it harder for teachers to maintain flexibility in goals and objectives . . . and channels teacher efforts into 'scripted instruction' rather than 'opportunistic' learning" . . . thus often defeating the intended goal of providing individualized instruction) (citation omitted)); *but see* Daniel P. Morgan, A Primer on Individualized Education Programs for Exceptional Children 23 (2d ed. 1981) ("[W]ithout written goals and objectives instruction tends to be poorly formulated, disorganized, impossible to evaluate objectively, and simply not as effective in terms of student learning.").

[54] Hallahan & Kauffman at 38.

[55] Spielberg v. Henrico County Pub. Schs., 853 F.2d 256 (4th Cir. 1988) (placement decision before developing IEP violates letter and spirit of the law except in rare circumstances in which private school by regulation must assist in IEP process).

lower expectations, and instructional irrelevance."[56] An advocate for a child with HIV disease should pay close attention to the development of the IEP to ensure that it is, in fact, a useful educational tool.

The local educational authority (LEA) or intermediate unit responsible for providing services to the child's area of residence is generally charged with developing the IEP.[57] This is true regardless of whether the LEA or a private or public school or facility directly implements it.[58] In the case of private school placements, the LEA may in its discretion allow the private school or facility to perform subsequent reviews and revisions.[59] However, the state has ultimate responsibility for making sure that every child who requires an IEP has one. The state must develop all necessary interagency policies or agreements to accomplish this end.[60]

Consistent with the congressional purpose of ensuring that parents have a pivotal role in developing their child's educational program, IDEA establishes strong procedural safeguards in the IEP process. The language is mandatory, rather than permissive, throughout the regulations implementing the relevant sections of the Act, dictating that agencies "ensure" parental participation.[61] Meetings conducted for the development, review, or revision of an IEP are to include one or both parents,[62] and the agency initiating the meeting must "take steps to ensure . . . that they are present . . . or are afforded the opportunity to participate."[63] Those steps include early notification[64] of meetings and scheduling at a mutually agreed upon time and place.[65] In the event that neither parent can attend, the agency is to use other means to ensure participation, including individual or conference telephone calls.[66] The agency must also "take whatever action

---

[56] U.S. Dep't of Educ., Individuals with Disabilities Education Act Amendments of 1995: Reauthorization of the Individuals with Disabilities Education Act (IDEA) 16 (1995); see also Hallahan & Kauffman at 39.

[57] 20 U.S.C. § 1414(a)(1)(A), (a)(5).

[58] 34 C.F.R. § 300.348(a)(1).

[59] Id. § 300.348(b). When a student is in a parochial or private school and receiving special education and related services, but was not placed by the public agency, this responsibility cannot be delegated. Id. § 300.349.

[60] 34 C.F.R. pt. 300, app. C, question 1.

[61] The regulations do recognize that parents cannot always be convinced to participate and a meeting may be conducted without them. If that happens, the burden remains with the agency to keep records of its attempts to arrange for meetings at a mutually convenient time and place, including telephone calls, correspondence, and visits to the parent's home or place of employment. 34 C.F.R. § 300.345(d).

[62] Id. §§ 300.343(a), 300.344(a)(3).

[63] Id. § 300.345(a).

[64] Notices must specify the purpose, time, location, and persons attending the meeting. 34 C.F.R. § 300.345(b)(1).

[65] Id. § 300.345(a)(1), (2).

[66] Id. § 300.345(c).

is necessary to ensure that the parent understands the proceedings," including arranging for interpreter services for persons who are deaf or for whom English is not their native language.[67]

Other participants at IEP meetings should include the child if appropriate, the child's teacher, and a public agency representative qualified to provide (or supervise) special education. At least one of the agency representatives within this core group should have expertise regarding the child's particular disability and must, in the case of a child who is initially being admitted to services, at least be familiar with the evaluation techniques that were used.[68] In addition, particular care should be taken to guarantee that the agency has at least one representative present with authority to commit necessary resources to ensure that the IEP will be implemented, rather than "vetoed at a higher administrative level."[69] The Department of Education has recently recommended adding a child's general education teacher to this group in order to help redirect the focus of IEP meetings away from "access to special education (and toward) access to an overall high-quality education."[70]

Either the parents or the agency may include other individuals,[71] such as persons with professional expertise, lay advocates, or attorneys, and the meetings should be of a size and length conducive to a full discussion of all relevant issues.[72] They may also be tape recorded.[73]

The statute merely requires that the IEP be a written statement and does not deal with the mechanics of its execution or implementation. Many key issues have been clarified by its implementing regulations and their interpretive guidance. Parental signatures are not required, but do constitute consent to placement if they are secured.[74] Parents have a right to a copy of the IEP, on request, and it is recommended that they be advised of this right or automatically given a copy within a reasonable time after the meeting.[75] The document must contain a list of all specific special education and related services needed by a child, including the amount of each service.[76] Placement decisions are to occur during the IEP meeting; therefore, a completed document can not be presented to the

---

[67] *Id.* § 300.345(e).

[68] *Id.* § 300.344 and accompanying n.1.

[69] 34 C.F.R. pt. 300, app. C, question 13.

[70] U.S. Dep't of Educ., Individuals with Disabilities Education Act Amendments of 1995: Reauthorization of the Individuals with Disabilities Education Act (IDEA) 15 (1995).

[71] 34 C.F.R. § 300.344(a)(5).

[72] 34 C.F.R. pt. 300, app. C, questions 10, 17.

[73] *Id.,* question 12.

[74] *Id.,* questions 29, 30.

[75] *Id.,* question 31.

[76] *Id.,* questions 44, 51.

parents at its outset.[77] Finally, as a general rule, "no delay" is acceptable between the completion of the IEP and commencement of services.[78]

§ 5.7 —Special Education and Related Services

Special education and related services are the constituent elements of a free, appropriate, public education. *Special education* is "specially designed instruction . . . to meet the unique needs of a child with a disability," including physical education.[79] IDEA provides that this instruction can occur in a variety of settings, including but not limited to the classroom, home, hospitals, and institutions.[80] An educational agency may be required to fund residential and extended school-year placements as part of its responsibilities.[81]

Regardless of the setting required to provide a child with an appropriate education, the Act contains a clear directive for inclusion. This is most clearly stated in the requirement that states have:

> procedures to assure that, to the maximum extent appropriate, children with disabilities, including children in public or private institutions or other care facilities, are educated with children who are not disabled, and that special classes, separate schooling, or other removal of children with disabilities from the regular educational environment occurs only when the nature or severity of the disability is such that education in regular classes with the use of supplementary aids and services can not be achieved satisfactorily.[82]

The educational authority bears the burden of demonstrating that a child cannot be appropriately educated in an inclusive environment.[83]

---

[77] *Id.,* questions 8, 55.

[78] 34 C.F.R. pt. 300, app. C, question 4.

[79] 20 U.S.C. § 1401(a)(16).

[80] *Id.* § 1401(a)(16)(A).

[81] *Id.* § 1401(a)(9)–(10); 34 C.F.R. § 300.302; *see* Abrahamson v. Hershman, 701 F.2d 223 (1st Cir. 1982) (youth functioning at preschool level required residential placement); Kruelle v. New Castle County Sch. Dist., 642 F.2d 687 (3d Cir. 1981) (education for children with severe disabilities broadly defined to include basic life skills); Battle v. Pennsylvania, 629 F.2d 269 (3d Cir. 1980), *cert. denied,* 452 U.S. 968 (1981) (application of state policy of 180-day school year to children requiring special education violates the Act); M.C. & G.C. *ex rel.* J.C. v. Central Regional Sch. Dist., 22 Indivs. Disabilities Educ. L. Rep. (LRP) 1036 (D.N.J. 1995) (youth with severe mental retardation and behavior disorders required residential placement to make educational progress).

[82] 20 U.S.C. § 1412(5)(B).

[83] Oberti v. Board of Educ., 995 F.2d 1204 (3d Cir. 1993); *but see* Briggs v. Board of Educ., 882 F.2d 688, 692 (2d Cir. 1989) (parents bear burden to show needs could be met in more integrated setting).

Courts have tended to follow two lines of authority in determining whether an educational authority fulfills its inclusion obligations. The first, which has been questioned, is limited to determining whether required services that would make a proposed segregated placement superior could feasibly be provided in an inclusive setting.[84] The second adopts a two-part test, determining first whether a child's education "can be achieved satisfactorily" with aids and services. If it cannot, the court will still address whether mainstreaming occurs "to the maximum extent appropriate."[85]

School districts have the duty to provide for a *continuum of alternative placements,* including the use of supplementary services such as itinerant teachers or resource rooms provided along with regular classroom instruction.[86] Placements are assumed to be in the school a child would normally attend unless otherwise provided for in the IEP, and in any event they should be "as close as possible" to home.[87]

These requirements also apply to preschoolers. Public agencies operating preschool programs for nondisabled children are to abide by the general policy of providing education in the local school. Recognizing that not all jurisdictions provide public education for children under six, the regulations implementing the inclusion provisions of the statute do not require that programs be created. Districts instead have a variety of options, from creating a program for children with disabilities and housing it in a regular elementary school, to serving children in other public programs such as Head Start or in private school preschool programs.[88]

IDEA provides that a child is also to receive the services he or she needs in order to benefit from the special education. By statute, these related services are:

> transportation, and such developmental, corrective and other supportive services (including speech pathology and audiology, psychological services, physical and occupational therapy, recreation, including therapeutic recreation, social work services, counseling services, including rehabilitation counseling, and medical services, except that such medical services shall be for diagnostic and evaluation purposes only) as may be required to assist a child with a disability to benefit from special education, and includes the early identification and assessment of disabling conditions in children.[89]

---

[84] Ronker v. Walter, 700 F.2d 1058 (6th Cir. 1983); *see also* A.W. v. Northwest R-1 Sch. Dist., 813 F.2d 158, 163 (8th Cir. 1987).

[85] Daniel R.R. v. State Bd. of Educ., 874 F.2d 1036 (5th Cir. 1989); Oberti v. Board of Educ., 995 F.2d 1204 (3d Cir. 1993).

[86] 34 C.F.R. § 300.551.

[87] *Id.* § 300.552.

[88] *Id.* § 300.552 note.

[89] 20 U.S.C. § 1401(a)(17).

The regulations also list school health services, school social work services, and parent counseling and training.[90] These statutory and regulatory lists are not exhaustive; other types of services should be available, such as art and cultural programs or art, music, and dance therapies.[91]

The majority of conceivable related services that might be required by a child with HIV disease are specifically listed and clearly defined. With one exception, disputes are only likely to arise with respect to whether a particular child needs a listed service in order to benefit from special education. This exception is the need for medical services, an area of continuing controversy in special education law.

As children with perinatal HIV disease enter the school system in increasing numbers, it is probable that there will be a concomitant increase in the demand for health-related assistance. Significant numbers of these children are likely to need to have medication administered during school hours or physical assistance of the type often provided by a nurse or other trained health care professional.

IDEA excludes medical services, except those necessary to evaluate or diagnose a disability, from the definition of *related services.*[92] The implementing regulations for this provision limit the scope of permissible medical services to "services provided by a licensed physician to determine a child's medically related disability that results in the child's need for special education and related services."[93] The regulations do, however, recognize that children with disabilities may have health needs that must be met during the course of a school day. The regulations include *school health services* within their definition of related services.[94] These are defined as services "provided by a qualified school nurse *or other qualified person.*"[95]

Courts have struggled with the interpretation of the medical services exclusion in the statute. The first definitive interpretation occurred in *Irving Independent School District v. Tatro,*[96] when the Supreme Court held that in-school, clean, intermittent catheterization services needed by a child with spina bifida, which could be provided by a school nurse or a trained layperson, were not excluded medical services because "Congress plainly required schools to hire various specially trained personnel to help handicapped children."[97] In addition to individuals from commonly needed disciplines such as speech or occupational therapy, those persons may include "other appropriately trained personnel." The court noted that "transportation services and access requirements

---

[90] 34 C.F.R. § 300.16.

[91] *Id.* § 300.16 note.

[92] 20 U.S.C. § 1401(a)(17).

[93] 34 C.F.R. § 300.16(b)(4) (emphasis added).

[94] *Id.* § 300.16(a).

[95] *Id.* § 300(16)(b)(11) (emphasis added).

[96] 468 U.S. 883 (1984).

[97] *Id.* at 893.

are specifically required by the Act" and concluded that services like catheterization services that permit a child to remain at school during the day "are no less related to the effort to educate than are services that enable the child to reach, enter or exit the school."[98]

The majority of courts have declined to interpret *Tatro* as establishing a bright-line rule of physician versus nonphysician. Instead, relying upon the Court's assertion that the medical services exclusion is "designed to spare schools from an obligation to provide a service that might well prove unduly expensive and beyond the range of their competence,"[99] courts have commonly considered the extent and nature of the services performed, not solely the professional or occupational status of the person performing the service.

Although the issue of catheterization is fairly settled, these are highly individualized determinations. Litigation continues over psychological or psychiatric services, and tracheotomy and/or gastrostomy care. Placements in which psychiatrists supervise therapy or medications[100] have been ordered under the Act, as has reimbursement for psychotherapy conducted by a psychiatrist.[101] Contrary decisions turn in part on the characterization of the facility—primarily medical or not—and have refused to require payment under IDEA of residential costs of a program with a psychiatric component.[102]

The provision of tracheotomy care has only been considered in a handful of cases. In several brought either in connection with children with multiple, severe disabilities or in the case of a state statute's requiring the care by a medical professional, services were deemed to be excluded under IDEA.[103] However, in

---

[98] *Id.* at 891; *accord* Tokarcik v. Forest Hills Sch. Dist., 665 F.2d 443 (3d Cir. 1981), *cert. denied,* 458 U.S. 1121 (1982).

[99] Irving Indep. Sch. Dist. v. Tatro, 468 U.S. 883, 892 (1984).

[100] Taylor *ex rel.* Taylor v. Honig, 910 F.2d 627 (9th Cir. 1990) (residential placement with psychiatrist on call); T.G. v. Board of Educ., 576 F. Supp. 420 (D.N.J.), *aff'd* 738 F.2d 420 (3d Cir. 1983), *cert. denied,* 469 U.S. 1086 (1984) (milieu therapy under supervision of psychiatrist).

[101] Max M. v. Illinois State Bd. of Educ., 629 F. Supp. 1504 (N.D. Ill. 1986).

[102] *See* Clovis Unified Sch. Dist. v. California Office of Admin. Hearings, 903 F.2d 635, 645–46 n.4 (9th Cir. 1990); Darlene L. v. Illinois State Bd. of Educ., 568 F. Supp. 1340, 1345 (N.D. Ill. 1983).

[103] Neely v. Rutherford County Schs., 68 F.3d 965 (6th Cir. 1995), *cert. denied,* No. 95-212, 64 U.S.L.W. 3690 (U.S. Apr. 15, 1996) (absent nursing care for a tracheotomy, child could not attend school and would not receive special education designed for her benefit as proposed in her IEP; care for child's tracheotomy denied because state law requires licensed professional to provide care); Detsel v. Board of Educ., 820 F.2d 587 (2d Cir. 1986), *cert. denied,* 484 U.S. 981 (1987) (7-year-old with severe disabilities required constant respirator assistance and a continuous supply of 40 percent oxygen); Bevin H. v. Wright, 666 F. Supp. 71, 75 (W.D. Pa. 1987) (cost of nursing service was $18,500 annually for child with severe broncho-pulmonary dysplasia, profound mental retardation, and blindness, with tracheotomy

other situations, courts have ordered such care, finding it to be a supportive service not subject to the medical services exclusion.[104]

§ 5.8 IDEA Part H Services for Children from Birth Through Age Two

Recognizing that "even very young infants [are] capable of participating in complex interactions with their world,"[105] Congress added a new part H to IDEA in 1986. The program has since been characterized as the "new paradigm for the delivery of all services and supports to individuals with special needs and their families in our communities."[106] It is predicated on an approach geared toward eliminating the need for parents to master the labyrinth of health, education, and social services programs—each with unique requirements—required by an infant or a toddler with a disability. This program is particularly important for a child with HIV infection and his or her family, because it can immediately provide developmental services and support and assistance to the family in identifying and securing other necessary services.

Part H is the foundation of a congressional scheme to provide "seamless" services for children from birth through age five and their families, with early intervention services available through age two, and a "smooth transition"[107]

---

tube and gastrostomy tubes, requiring chest physical therapy during classroom hours); Granite Sch. Dist. v. Shannon M., 787 F. Supp. 1020, 1027 (D. Utah 1992) (child confined to wheelchair and needing assistance with respiration, nasogastric feeding tube, pain, and positioning, as well as tracheotomy tube, also required occasional tube changes and portable ventilator to open her lungs; cost of care for the school year was $30,000).

[104] Department of Educ. v. Katherine D., 727 F.2d 809, 812 (9th Cir. 1983), *cert. denied,* 471 U.S. 1117 (1985) (tracheotomy care by qualified person not within medical services exclusion); *compare* Special Sch. Dist. No. 6, 23 Indivs. Disabilities Educ. L. Rep. (LRP) 119 (Minn. 1994) (child with multiple disabilities provided suctioning in nurse's office rather than classroom); *see also* Macomb County Intermediate Sch. Dist. v. Joshua S., 715 F. Supp. 824 (E.D. Mich. 1984) (applying bright-line test to require district to transport medically fragile child with an aide when school had already conceded its responsibility to provide tracheotomy suctioning in the classroom); Cedar Rapids Community Sch. Dist., 22 Indivs. Disabilities Educ. L. Rep. (LRP) 278 (Iowa 1994) (finding services by trained individual in classroom to assist child with multiple disabilities appropriate related service under all current interpretations of the law). These decisions are in accord with the policy under Part H of IDEA, which includes clean, intermittent catheterization, tracheostomy care, tube feeding, and changing dressings and colostomy collection bags among required health services. *See* 34 C.F.R. § 303.13(b)(1).

[105] H.R. Rep. No. 860, 99th Cong., 2d Sess. 4 (1986), *reprinted in* 1986 U.S.C.C.A.N. 2401, 2405.

[106] S. Rep. No. 84, 102d Cong., 1st Sess. 23 (1991).

[107] H.R. Rep. No. 198, 102d Cong., 1st Sess. 4 (1991), *reprinted in* 1991 U.S.C.C.A.N. 310, 313.

to Part B education programs at age three.[108] In contrast to Part B, the focus of Part H is the family. The program calls for states to develop and implement "[a] statewide system of coordinated, comprehensive, multidisciplinary, interagency programs providing appropriate early intervention services to all infants and toddlers with disabilities and their families," and to establish a state interagency coordinating council.[109] Congress identified key system features:

1. the state definition of *developmentally delayed*
2. timetables for making all appropriate services available
3. timely comprehensive multidisciplinary evaluations for each disabled infant and toddler
4. an individual family service plan (IFSP) for each disabled infant and toddler
5. a comprehensive child-find system with referrals to service providers
6. a public awareness program
7. a central directory of services, resources, experts, and research and demonstration projects
8. a system of personnel development
9. a single line of authority in a lead agency designated or established by the governor
10. a policy on contracting with local providers
11. procedures for timely reimbursement of Part H funds
12. standards to ensure that personnel are sufficiently trained to implement the program
13. a data collection system
14. procedural safeguards.[110]

States electing to participate in the program were given a period in which to phase in full service delivery but were required to have a fully functioning system in place by their fifth year of participation.[111] This requirement was strictly

---

[108] A series of policy letters from the Office of Special Education Programs discusses the interplay between Parts H and B as a child turns three. *See* Letter to Bradley, 22 Indivs. Disabilities Educ. L.Rep. (LRP) 975 (Office Spec. Educ. Programs 1995); Letter to Gill, 22 Indivs. Disabilities Educ. L. Rep. (LRP) 983 (Office Spec. Educ. Programs 1995); Letter to Anonymous, 22 Indivs. Disabilities Educ. L. Rep. (LRP) 980 (Office Spec. Educ. Programs 1993).

[109] 20 U.S.C. §§ 1476(a), 1482. The council acts in an advisory capacity to the lead agency and the state educational agency.

[110] 20 U.S.C. § 1476; *see* H.R. Rep. No. 860, 99th Cong., 2d Sess. 10–12 (1986), *reprinted in* 1986 U.S.C.C.A.N. 2401, 2410–12.

[111] 20 U.S.C. § 1475(c).

construed in *Marie O. v. Edgar,*[112] the only reported judicial decision under part H. In *Marie O.,* the District Court awarded summary judgment in favor of a class of eligible children who were not receiving early intervention services in Illinois during its eighth year of participation in the program. It acknowledged and rejected the defenses of lack of both funding and trained personnel, finding that "Congress expressly chose to frame Part H in definite, explicit terms" and that "[m]eaningful compliance by the state, at the very least, should be required by the state's fifth year."[113]

§ 5.9 —Eligibility for Part H

A child is eligible for early intervention services either because of developmental delay or a condition that has a high probability of causing a developmental delay.[114] A regulatory note lists congenital infection (such as HIV) as an example of a diagnosed condition that results in a high probability of developmental delay.[115] *Developmental delay* is not defined, because Congress allowed each state flexibility to adopt its own definition, as long as the definition addresses functional levels in five basic areas:[116] cognitive development; physical development; communication development;[117] psychosocial development; or self-help skills.[118] A child may also be eligible for services if he or she is at risk of having a substantial developmental delay if services are not provided, in states that choose to include such children.[119] A child with HIV infection may be eligible for service under any of these criteria.

---

[112] 23 Indivs. Disabilities Educ. L. Rep. (LRP) 709 (N.D. Ill. 1996).

[113] *Id.*

[114] 20 U.S.C. § 1472(1)(A), (B).

[115] 34 C.F.R. § 303.16 n.1.

[116] H.R. Rep. No. 860, 99th Cong., 2d Sess. 7 (1986), *reprinted in* 1986 U.S.C.C.A.N. 2401, 2407.

[117] The 1986 statute used the term *language and speech development* throughout. The 1991 amendments retained that term in the definitions in § 1472, but substitute *communication development* elsewhere. This is intended to reflect current terminology, rather than effect a substantive change. The term includes acquiring communication skills (including spoken, nonspoken, and sign language, and use of augmentative devices); oral-motor development; and auditory awareness. H.R. Rep. No. 198, 102d Cong., 1st Sess. 12 (1991), *reprinted in* 1991 U.S.C.C.A.N. 310, 321.

[118] Similarly, the 1991 amendments also retained the terms *psychosocial development* and *self-help skills* in § 1472, but substituted *social or emotional development* and *adaptive development,* respectively, in their stead throughout to reflect current usage. H.R. Rep. No. 198, 102d Cong., 1st Sess. 12 (1991).

[119] 20 U.S.C. § 1472(2).

§ 5.10 —Early Intervention Services

The unique feature of this program is the breadth of assistance available to a child and his or her family. Early intervention services are provided under public supervision and are designed to meet developmental needs in one or more of the functional areas discussed in § 5.9.[120] Services include but are not limited to:[121] family training and counseling, special instruction, speech pathology and audiology, occupational and physical therapy, psychological services, medical services for diagnosis or evaluation, early identification screening and assessment, social work, vision services, health services to enable a child to benefit from other early intervention services, assistive technology services and devices, transportation and related costs, and service coordination.[122]

Service coordination may be the singularly most important feature of this program for a child with HIV disease and his or her family, according to one of the three federal officials primarily responsible for oversight of Part H.[123] Although the statute uses the term *case management* in its definitional section, all remaining references were changed to *service coordination* by the 1991 amendments.[124] Service identification and coordination are at the heart of the Part H program. The legislative history demonstrates Congress's intent that this be "an active, on-going process of continuously seeking the appropriate services or situations to benefit the development" of a child "for the duration of . . . eligibility."[125] The service coordinator, the "single point of contact" for a family, is responsible for coordinating services among agencies and programs,[126] and must be "able to effectively carry out [his or her duties] on an interagency basis."[127]

The service coordinator has duties beyond assisting a family to identify and access traditional early intervention services. The coordinator's role extends to coordination of those services with other services (such as medical services), assisting a family to identify providers, monitoring service delivery, and advising a family about the availability of advocacy services.[128] The coordinator, who

---

[120] 20 U.S.C. § 1472(2)(A), (C).

[121] H.R. Rep. No. 860, 99th Cong., 2d Sess. 8 (1986), *reprinted in* 1986 U.S.C.C.A.N. 2409; Letter to Renne, 23 Indivs. Disabilities Educ. L. Rep. (LRP) 437 (Office Spec. Educ. Programs 1995).

[122] 20 U.S.C. § 1472(2)(E); 34 C.F.R. § 303.12(d).

[123] Telephone conversation with Dr. Bobbi Stetner-Eaton, Education Program Specialist, U.S. Dep't of Educ., Mar. 1996.

[124] H.R. Rep. No. 198, 102d Cong., 1st Sess. 12 (1991), *reprinted in* 1991 U.S.C.C.A.N. 310, 321.

[125] H.R. Rep. No. 860, 99th Cong., 2d Sess. 8 (1986), *reprinted in* 1986 U.S.C.C.A.N. 2401, 2408.

[126] 34 C.F.R. § 303.22(a)(2).

[127] *Id.* § 303.22(c)(2).

[128] *Id.* § 303.22(b).

may be a parent,[129] also assists in the development of the individualized family service plan and plan for transition to preschool.[130]

Expedition is the watchword of Part H. As part of the comprehensive child-find system of IDEA, a child who has been identified by a primary referral source as potentially eligible for Part H must be referred for evaluation and assessment within two working days, after which a service coordinator shall be assigned "as soon as possible."[131] Evaluation and assessment of the child, and the child's family (on a voluntary basis), must be completed and an individual family service plan (see § 5.11) meeting held within 45 days of the referral.[132] Services are to begin "as soon as possible" after the meeting,[133] and those that are "needed immediately" may begin earlier with the consent of the family.[134]

Like Part B services, early intervention services must meet state standards;[135] unlike Part B, they are provided at no cost except when federal or state law allows for payments by families.[136] Part H funds are to be used as a last resort and cannot be used to pay for services that would be funded from another public or private source.[137] However, funds may be used to prevent delay in services, except for medical or well-baby health care, pending reimbursement from the appropriate payor.[138]

Of particular import to a child with HIV disease is the requirement that services be provided in natural environments, to the maximum extent appropriate.[139] The regulations foster the maximum opportunity for integration with children without disabilities, recognizing that "the appropriate location of services for some infants and toddlers might be in a hospital setting [only] during the period in which they require extensive medical intervention."[140] Otherwise, a child should receive early intervention services "in natural environments (e.g., the home, child care centers, or other community settings) to the maximum extent appropriate to the needs of the child."[141] Although preschool and child-care are not early intervention services, according to interpretive guidance by

---

[129] H.R. Rep. No. 198, 102d Cong., 1st Sess. 19 (1991), *reprinted in* 1991 U.S.C.C.A.N. 310, 328.

[130] 34 C.F.R. § 303.22(b)(2), (7).

[131] *Id.* § 303.321(d).

[132] *Id.* § 303.321(d)(2).

[133] *Id.* § 303.344(f)(1).

[134] *Id.* § 303.345.

[135] 20 U.S.C. § 1472(2)(D).

[136] *Id.* § 1472(2)(B).

[137] *Id.* § 1481; 34 C.F.R. § 303.527(a).

[138] 34 C.F.R. § 303.527(b).

[139] 42 U.S.C. § 1472(2)(G); 34 C.F.R. § 303.12(b).

[140] 34 C.F.R. § 303.344 n.1.

[141] *Id.*

the Office of Special Education Programs, those costs should be assumed by Part H to the extent they are necessary to supply otherwise covered services.[142]

§ 5.11 —Individual Family Service Plan

Part H services are furnished as a result of an individual family service plan (IFSP).[143] The IFSP follows the IEP model in many respects; it is a written plan developed by a multidisciplinary team following assessments of a child's unique strengths and needs and the services to meet those needs.[144] An IFSP is broader in terms of service identification than an IEP, however, and is family-directed. It should address all of a child's service needs—regardless of whether they will be provided under Part H—and their funding sources.[145] A voluntary family assessment by trained personnel, based on a personal interview "to determine the resources, priorities, and concerns . . . related to enhancing the development of the child," is a precursor to the IFSP,[146] and assists in ensuring that the family, rather than a professional team, shapes the service plan.

An IFSP is developed at a meeting attended by the parents, an advocate and family members requested by the parents, the service coordinator, individuals involved in the evaluations and assessments of the child and the family, and service providers, if appropriate.[147] As with the IEP meeting for the Part B program, the meeting must occur at a time and place convenient to the parents, on adequate written notice, and be conducted in their native language.[148] The plan should be reviewed at least every six months and evaluated annually.[149]

The plan itself is to be drafted with particularity, although it can be "a brief outline with appropriate attachments."[150] It should include:

1. Information based on "professionally acceptable objective criteria" about the child's current levels of development

---

[142] Letter to Dicker, 22 Indivs. Disabilities Educ. L. Rep. (LRP) 464 (Office Spec. Educ. Programs 1995); Letter to Zimenoff, 23 Indivs. Disabilities Educ. L. Rep. (LRP) 439 (Office Spec. Educ. Programs 1995).

[143] 20 U.S.C. § 1472(2)(H); 34 C.F.R. § 303.12(a)(3)(iii).

[144] 20 U.S.C. § 1477.

[145] 34 C.F.R. § 303.344. Note 3 to the regulation clarifies that the service coordinator is authorized to assist a child and the family to obtain other services "related to enhancing the development of the child," in addition to early intervention services.

[146] 34 C.F.R. § 303.322(d).

[147] Id. § 303.343.

[148] Id. § 303.342(d).

[149] Id. § 303.342.

[150] Id. § 303.343 n.4.

2. Family information—with their agreement—about resources, priorities, and concerns

3. Expected outcomes and the criteria and timeframes for their evaluation

4. Specific early intervention services to be provided

5. Other needed services, as appropriate

6. The dates services will be started and the length of time they will be provided

7. The name of the service coordinator

8. A transition plan from Part H to Part B or other services.[151]

§ 5.12 Procedural Protections

Part B and Part H of IDEA both contain strong procedural protections. Part B guarantees to a parent or guardian the rights to: (1) examine records and obtain an independent educational evaluation; (2) receive adequate written prior notice when there is a proposed change or refusal to change a child's identification, evaluation, placement, or free appropriate public education; and (3) an impartial due process hearing.[152] The traditional rights to counsel, to present evidence, to cross-examine and compel the attendance of witnesses, to a verbatim record, and to written factual findings and decisions are afforded to the parties, who may also be accompanied by individuals with special knowledge about children with disabilities.[153]

Under Part B, a child is entitled to "stay-put," that is, to remain in his or her current educational placement or be admitted to an initial placement, while an appeal is pending.[154] The impartial hearing process may have one or two levels, determined by the practice within a state. The statute allows the initial hearing to be conducted either by the local educational authority or intermediate unit, subject to review by the state educational agency, or by the state educational agency itself.[155] The initial hearing decision must be mailed within 45 days of the hearing request; in a state that has a review mechanism, that decision must be mailed within 30 days.[156] Appeal from the final administrative decision is made by filing an action in state or federal district court. This appeal is an independent review of the administrative record, with the parties' having the opportunity to

---

[151] *Id.* § 303.344.

[152] 20 U.S.C. § 1415.

[153] *Id.* § 1415(d).

[154] *Id.* § 1415(e)(3); 34 C.F.R. § 300.513. *See* Honig v. Doe, 484 U.S. 305 (1988). The only exception to this provision is for a child who has brought a firearm to school.

[155] 20 U.S.C. § 1415(b), (c).

[156] 34 C.F.R. § 300.512.

present additional evidence.[157] Attorney's fees may be awarded to a parent or guardian who prevails.[158]

Part H has similar protections, granting access to records, ensuring adequate prior written notice of significant agency actions to parents, requiring that there be a mechanism for "timely administrative resolution of complaints by parents," subject to judicial review, and providing for stay-put pending complaint resolution.[159] In addition, a parent or guardian must give express consent before services begin and may decline any offered service without affecting the right to other services.[160]

§ 5.13   Exclusion and Segregation

Today it is generally accepted that a child with HIV infection should be educated in whatever setting is otherwise appropriate: regular or special classes dictated by professional judgment regarding the child's educational needs. This was not the case during the early years of the HIV epidemic, when fear of possible contagion in school settings caused many communities to act on their unfounded

---

[157] 20 U.S.C. § 1415(e). Although the statute provides that the reviewing court base its decision on a preponderance of evidence, it does not give specific direction about the treatment of the record below or supplementation of the record. Accordingly, these issues have been the source of significant litigation, with markedly different results among the circuits. The Supreme Court has directed reviewing courts to accord "due weight" to the administrative decision to avoid "substitut[ing] their own notions of sound educational policy for those of the school authorities which they review." Board of Educ. v. Rowley, 458 U.S. 176, 206 (1982). Interpretations vary from the narrow approach, Roland M. v. Concord Sch. Comm., 910 F.2d 983, 984 (1st Cir. 1990) (reviewing court should be "thorough yet deferential"), to the expansive, Oberti v. Board of Educ., 995 F.2d 1204 (3d Cir. 1993) (court to review the administrative record but make independent findings). Similarly, there are varying interpretations of the extent to which additional evidence will be received at the request of a party under 20 U.S.C. § 1415(e)(2). Town of Burlington v. Department of Educ., 736 F.2d 773, 790 (1st Cir. 1984) ("the [IDEA] contemplates that the source of the evidence generally will be the administrative hearing record, with some supplementation at trial"), aff'd on other grounds, 471 U.S. 359 (1985); Susan N. v. Wilson Sch. Dist., 70 F.3d 751, 759 (3d Cir. 1995) (characterizing Burlington approach as "restrictive").

[158] 20 U.S.C. § 1415(e)(4)(B). The law does contain restrictions on the amount of fees, as well as disincentives to rejecting good faith written offers of settlement. Id. § 1415(e)(4)(C), (D).

[159] Id. § 1480. The regulations permit a state to meet its due process obligations under this part either by adopting the Part B procedures of 34 C.F.R. §§ 300.506–300.512 and ensuring the availability of stay-put, or implementing a separate system, in which case a final decision must be mailed within 30 days of the receipt of a parent's complaint. See id. §§ 303.420–303.425. The explanatory notes to the regulations also encourage the use of mediation in the interest of expediting dispute resolution.

[160] 20 U.S.C. § 1480(3); 34 C.F.R. § 303.404.

prejudices and exclude infected children from their schools,[161] or to segregate them in a solitary modular classroom or behind a glass wall.[162]

In 1985, the Centers for Disease Control issued guidelines for the management of children with HIV in schools, day care, and foster care. The CDC recommendations were prefaced by findings that "[b]ased on current evidence, casual person-to-person contact as would occur among schoolchildren appears to pose no risk," and "a theoretical potential for transmission" existed with younger children and children who lacked control over bodily functions.[163] The CDC made three recommendations. First, decisions about an educational setting should be made by a team, including a child's parents or guardian, the child's doctor, public health personnel and personnel from the proposed placement, and that the team should weigh the risks and benefits to the child and others. Second, "most infected school-age children" should not be restricted from regular school

---

[161] The courts invariably responded to these community actions by requiring that children be allowed to attend school. *See* Thomas v. Atascadero Unified Sch. Dist., 662 F. Supp. 376 (C.D. Cal. 1987) (permanent injunction entered in favor of kindergarten student with AIDS who had been excluded from school after biting another child); Doe v. Dolton Elementary Sch. Dist. No. 148, 694 F. Supp. 440 (N.D. Ill. 1988) (preliminary injunction issued in favor of 12-year-old, requiring his admission to regular academic and extracurricular programs except for contact sports, imposing medical monitoring, and requiring confidentiality and HIV education for school personnel); Ray v. School Dist., 666 F. Supp. 1524 (M.D. Fla. 1987) (preliminary injunction entered in favor of three children with HIV disease, mandating return to an integrated educational program, prohibiting participation in contact sports, imposing medical monitoring for the children and their immediate family, requiring sex education for the children and HIV education for all parents in the district, and providing for alternative educational programs during any proper removal from the integrated setting); Parents of Child, Code No. 870901W v. Group I, 676 F. Supp. 1072 (E.D. Okla. 1987) (preliminary injunction entered on behalf of child with HIV disease, requiring placement in special education class in accordance with IEP and enjoining certain defendants from proceeding with state court action to compel exclusion); Phipps v. Saddleback Valley Unified Sch. Dist., 251 Cal. Rptr. 720 (Ct. App. 1988) (affirming entry of permanent injunction requiring HIV-infected 11-year-old to be admitted to public schools and awarding attorney's fees); District 27 Community Sch. Bd. v. Board of Educ., 502 N.Y.S.2d 325 (Sup. Ct. 1986) (application for permanent injunction requiring exclusion of child with AIDS from public schools denied). *See also* Child v. Spillane, 866 F.2d 691 (4th Cir. 1989) (discussing development of policy on admission after temporary exclusion from kindergarten of child with HIV and vacating award of attorneys' fees); Board of Educ. v. Cooperman, 523 A.2d 655 (N.J. Super. Ct. 1987) (upholding regulations establishing procedures for education of children with HIV infection).

[162] Martinez v. School Bd., 692 F. Supp. 1293 (M.D. Fla.), *vacated and remanded,* 861 F.2d 1502 (11th Cir. 1988), *opinion on remand,* 711 F. Supp. 1066 (M.D. Fla. 1989); Robertson v. Granite City Community Unit Sch. Dist. No. 9, 684 F. Supp. 1002 (S.D. Ill. 1988); *see* Monte L. Betz, Kindergartner with AIDS and the Glassroom Barrier (1992).

[163] CDC, *Education and Foster Care of Children Infected with Human T-Lymphoıropic Virus Type III/Lymphadenopathy-Associated Virus,* 34 MMWR 519 (1985).

attendance. Third, infected preschoolers and those with lack of control over bodily secretions or with "uncoverable oozing lesions" and those who bite should be restricted until there was more information about the risk of transmission.[164] These recommendations were echoed by the American Academy of Pediatrics the next year.[165]

The safety of allowing children with HIV infection to attend school was also widely publicized by Surgeon General C. Everett Koop in 1986. The *Surgeon General's Report on Acquired Immune Deficiency Syndrome* discussed the fact that exposure that could cause transmission in a school setting is "highly unlikely," and that "[c]asual social contact between children and persons infected with the AIDS virus is not dangerous."[166] Nevertheless, the mid- to late-1980s saw a brief firestorm of litigation over the rights of children with HIV infection to attend school with their peers.

The nondiscrimination provision of the Rehabilitation Act of 1973, commonly known as section 504,[167] served as the primary defense against this prejudice.[168] Section 504 is a succinct yet potentially powerful statute, stating simply:

No otherwise qualified individual with a disability in the United States, as defined in [29 U.S.C. § 706(8)], shall, solely by reason of her or his disability, be excluded from the participation in, be denied the benefits of, or be subjected to discrimination under any program or activity receiving Federal financial assistance or under any program or activity conducted by any Executive agency or by the United States Postal Service.[169]

All of the operations of local educational agencies, vocational education, and other school systems are specifically identified as covered programs or activities.[170]

The thorny questions under section 504, during the period in which the law was developing in this area, were: (1) whether an asymptomatic child infected with HIV has a handicap; (2) whether a child with HIV disease is an "otherwise qualified" person; and (3) whether such children pose a threat in the classroom so significant as to justify their segregation or exclusion.

---

[164] *Id.*

[165] *See* Thomas v. Atascadero Unified Sch. Dist., 662 F. Supp. 376, 378 (C.D. Cal. 1987). The American Academy of Pediatrics eliminated its recommendation to restrict children who cannot control bodily secretions in 1988, following the CDC update on the use of universal precautions, which stated that precautions only need be taken with secretions containing visible blood. *See* Martinez v. School Bd., 711 F. Supp. 711, 720 (M.D. Fla. 1989).

[166] U.S. Pub. Health Serv., Surgeon General's Report on Acquired Immune Deficiency 23–24 (n.d.) (issued Oct. 1986). *See* C. Everett Koop, Koop: Memoirs of America's Family Doctor 213 (1991).

[167] Section 504 is codified at 29 U.S.C. § 794.

[168] Rehabilitation Act claims are discussed in more detail in **Chs. 3** and **4.**

[169] 29 U.S.C. § 794(a) (1994).

[170] *Id.* § 794(b)(2)(B).

Today the law is settled. The U.S. Department of Education regulations implementing section 504, together with policy interpretations by the Office of Civil
Rights, remove all doubts about whether a child with HIV is an "otherwise
qualified individual with a disability" under the law. Early opinions adopting the
section 504 analyses of *School Board of Nassau County v. Arline*[171] and *Chalk v.
United States District Court*[172] disposed of the safety question.[173]

The Department of Education regulations follow the Rehabilitation Act and
define an *individual with a disability* as someone who has a physical or mental
impairment that substantially limits one or more major life activities, who has a
record of such an impairment, or who is regarded as having such an impairment.[174] The third prong is broadly interpreted. A child will be covered even
when the impairment's limitation is substantial "only as a result of the attitudes
of others toward such impairment."[175] A child with HIV disease is *qualified* for
educational services merely by being of school age or by being eligible for
IDEA.[176]

The Office on Civil Rights (OCR) within the Department of Education issued
a memorandum in 1990 to guide its staff "in addressing situations where school
districts have a formal or informal policy regarding the placement of children
with HIV infection."[177] First establishing that "[n]o case law has been identified
. . . in which a person with [HIV infection] was not considered handicapped"
under section 504, OCR discusses placement, procedural safeguards, and confidentiality.[178] The memorandum specifies that children can attend school in the
regular classroom, unless there is a current risk of contagion due to opportunistic
infections or weeping lesions. This is in accord with the regulatory requirement that
a child receive an education in "the most integrated setting appropriate" to their
needs.[179] If there appears to be a need for a different placement and/or related

---

[171] 480 U.S. 273 (1987).

[172] 840 F.2d 701 (9th Cir. 1988). A more detailed discussion of issues involved in risk of HIV
transmission as a defense to claims of discrimination is provided in **Ch. 3.**

[173] *See, e.g.,* Ray v. School Dist., 666 F. Supp. 1524 (M.D. Fla. 1987); Doe v. Dolton Elementary Sch. Dist., 694 F. Supp. 440 (N.D. Ill. 1988).

[174] 34 C.F.R. § 104.3(j) (1996); *see* 29 U.S.C. § 706(8)(B). Although the Rehabilitation Act
was amended in 1992 to substitute *individual with a disability* for *handicapped individual,*
the cited regulation has not been similarly amended. However, there is no difference in
meaning between the two terms.

[175] 34 C.F.R. § 104.3(j)(2)(iv)(B).

[176] *Id.* § 104.3(k)(2).

[177] William H. Smith, U.S. Dep't of Educ., OCR Staff Memo., 16 Educ. Handicapped L. Rep.
(LRP) 712 (1990) [hereinafter OCR Memorandum].

[178] *Id. Cf.* Ennis v. National Ass'n of Business & Educ. Radio, Inc., 53 F.3d 55, 60 (4th Cir.
1995) (implying in dicta that fact of child's HIV infection alone, without other evidence,
may not be adequate to prove substantial limitation on major life activity under Americans
with Disabilities Act).

[179] 34 C.F.R. § 104.4(b)(2); *see id.* § 104.34 (child shall be placed for academic and non-
academic purposes with children who do not have disability to maximum extent appropriate).

services, a child should be evaluated and placement decisions made by a multi-disciplinary group with access to "the latest reliable public health information" about the disease.[180]

Procedural safeguards attach to identification, evaluation, and placement actions by an educational authority under section 504.[181] Among these are the rights to notice, to review records, and to an impartial hearing and review.[182] Although these procedural safeguards are available, there is no requirement to exhaust administrative remedies when a child is challenging exclusion or segregation because of his or her HIV status.[183] Although section 504 and to a lesser extent IDEA have formed the basis for preventing exclusion or segregation on the basis of HIV status, the Americans With Disabilities Act and state human rights laws also prevent such actions and can reach entities that are not recipients of federal funds.[184]

An illustrative case in this area involved a school district's policy of excluding children with HIV from the classroom. An administrative complaint, alleging violation of section 504 of the Rehabilitation Act, was filed with the Office of Civil Rights (OCR), U.S. Department of Education, against the Fairfax County (Virginia) School District regarding its AIDS/HIV policy.[185] The policy provided that students with HIV could be "excluded from school until it is determined that

---

[180] OCR Memorandum at 716; *see* 34 C.F.R. § 104.35 (requirements for preplacement evaluation, evaluation procedures, and placement procedures). In addition to the expected treatment of nondiscrimination on the basis of disability, Department of Education regulations create an entitlement to a free, appropriate, public education regardless of the nature or severity of the disability. *Id.* § 104.33(a). Accordingly, the regulations include some of the framework for identification, evaluation, and placement found in IDEA.

[181] *Id.* § 104.36.

[182] *Id.*

[183] Robertson v. Granite City Community Unit Sch. Dist. No. 9, 684 F. Supp. 1002 (S.D. Ill. 1988) (preliminary injunction granted to direct placement in regular classroom rather than segregated "modular classroom" for child with AIDS-Related Complex, finding that no administrative remedy existed under IDEA because child did not require special education and related services); *accord* Doe v. Belleville Indep. Sch. Dist. No. 118, 672 F. Supp. 342 (S.D. Ill. 1987). Note, however, that if issue relates to provision of free, appropriate, public education and is cognizable under both IDEA and § 504 "or other Federal statutes protecting the rights of children and youth with disabilities," exhaustion under IDEA is required. 20 U.S.C. § 1415(f).

[184] The Americans with Disabilities Act and state law nondiscrimination standards are discussed more fully in **Ch. 4.**

[185] Fairfax County (Va.) Pub. Sch., 19 Indivs. Disabilities Educ. L. Rep. (LRP) 649 (1993). Other school districts have revised their policies to avoid liability under nondiscrimination laws, as was the case in Chicago in 1996. *See* Chicago Board of Educ., Rescind Board Report 94-0824-PO1 and Establish a Comprehensive AIDS Policy of the Chicago Public Schools (Mar. 27, 1996) (copy on file with author); Michael Martinez & Tracy Dell'Angela, *City School Policies on HIV Are Revised,* Chi. Trib., Apr. 2, 1996, § 2 (Metro), at 1 (noting that previous policy may have violated the Americans with Disabilities Act).

students' attendance at school does not pose an unreasonable risk to the health and welfare of themselves or others." The OCR concluded that the policy of exclusion violated its regulations, which require that an individual evaluation be conducted before any action is taken with respect to initial placement or any subsequent change in placement of a handicapped child who is believed to need special education or related services.[186] In December 1992, apparently in response to the OCR complaint, the school district revised its policy to provide that any student with HIV will remain in regular placement unless his or her health status requires otherwise. It set forth a procedure providing that any temporary exclusion is not to exceed 10 days. The revised policy was deemed to be lawful, as consistent with regulations mandating placement of children with handicaps in regular classrooms and providing adequate procedural protections for determining when there is a health risk to the child or others.

Many states have also responded to the need to have policies in place that deal with public fears about persons with HIV disease. The approaches vary. For instance, one of the best is a comprehensive manual developed in Connecticut which addresses clinical, educational, and legal issues related to serving students with special health care needs.[187] Michigan has issued a communicable disease control policy generally prohibiting the exclusion of persons with HIV or other diseases not spread by casual contact, requiring individualized assessments when a threat of transmission is suspected, and establishing extensive procedural safeguards.[188] Tennessee recently adopted a specific HIV policy for school employees and students that explicitly prohibits discrimination against those with the disease.[189] At least one state has HIV-specific regulations governing school attendance of infected students or adults.[190] The National Association of State Boards of Education has also published a guide to education policies on HIV.[191]

---

[186] See 34 C.F.R. § 104.35(a).

[187] Connecticut Dep't of Educ., Serving Students with Special Health Care Needs (1992). The 250-page manual provides substantive information and policies and identifies employee responsibilities.

[188] Michigan State Bd. of Educ., Model Communicable Disease Control Policy (1991).

[189] Tennessee State Bd. of Educ., HIV-AIDS Policy for Employees and Students of Tennessee Public Schools (1995).

[190] N.J. Admin. Code tit. vi, § 29-2.4 (1995). The New Jersey Department of Education regulations address students and employees, providing that neither may be excluded on the basis of HIV status. They cross-reference and defer to regulations adopted by the New Jersey Department of Health to establish the only permissible grounds for exclusion: the presence of weeping skin lesions that cannot be covered or other conditions that would necessitate exclusion from a school setting.

[191] James F. Bogden et al., Someone at School has AIDS: A Complete Guide to Education Policies Concerning HIV Infection (1996).

§ 5.14   Confidentiality

A key concern of families and students with HIV infection is the protection of information which directly or indirectly discloses their disability. There are several independent legal bases that require that such information remain confidential. Foremost among these are myriad federal and state statutory, regulatory, and policy provisions. Protection of personal information is also grounded in constitutional privacy interests and common law.

In addition to these rights, students attending public and private educational institutions funded by the U.S. Department of Education[192] are entitled to privacy of personal information. The Family Educational Rights and Privacy Act of 1974 (FERPA),[193] commonly known as the Buckley Amendment, and its implementing regulations[194] establish strong procedural protections for student records. FERPA guarantees the rights of parents and eligible students[195] to have access to records[196] and generally to prevent disclosure to third parties of personally identifiable information from educational records absent prior written consent.[197] With the exception of some records maintained by postsecondary institutions,[198] the right of inspection is limited only when records contain information about more than one student.[199]

There are, however, several situations in which information may be disclosed without prior written consent. Three are potentially troublesome for students with HIV infection. Personal information may be disseminated without prior consent in a health or safety emergency,[200] in response to a judicial order or subpoena,[201] or to the alleged victim of a crime.[202]

Disclosures can also be made to state and local officials pursuant to state laws predating the effective date of FERPA.[203] So-called directory information, such as a pupil's name and address, may be released as long as an institution has given

---

[192] A limited number of programs administered by the Secretary of Education are exempted from FERPA, such as those administered by the Commissioner of the Rehabilitation Services Administration and the Director of the National Institute on Disability and Rehabilitation Research. *See* 34 C.F.R. § 99.1(b).

[193] Pub. L. No. 93-380, Title V, § 513, 88 Stat. 484, 571, 1974 U.S.C.C.A.N. 541, 647 (codified at 20 U.S.C. § 1232g).

[194] 34 C.F.R. pt. 99 (1995).

[195] *Eligible students* are 18 years old or are attending a postsecondary institution. 20 U.S.C. § 1232g(d).

[196] 20 U.S.C. § 1232g(a)(1)(A); 34 C.F.R. § 99.10.

[197] 20 U.S.C. § 1232g(b)(1), (b)(2)(A); 34 C.F.R. § 99.30.

[198] 20 U.S.C. § 1232g(a)(1)(B); 34 C.F.R. § 99.12(b).

[199] 20 U.S.C. § 1232g(a)(1)(A); 34 C.F.R. § 99.12(a).

[200] 34 C.F.R. § 99.31(10).

[201] *Id.* § 99.31(9).

[202] *Id.* § 99.31(13).

[203] *Id.* § 99.31(5).

public notice of the right to refuse permission to release it.[204] Information may circulate among school officials having "legitimate educational interests"[205] and may be disclosed to other educational agencies or institutions in connection with enrollment,[206] for federal and state program purposes,[207] and in connection with accreditation.[208]

Parents and the student may be given information without prior written consent.[209] Information can also be released to organizations conducting certain educational studies[210] or in connection with a student's financial aid.[211]

FERPA provides a mechanism to contest the content of educational records, including to challenge information that is "inaccurate, misleading, or in violation of the student's rights of privacy or other rights."[212] Parents or an eligible student may request an amendment[213] and are entitled to a hearing before an individual who does not have a direct interest in its outcome.[214]

FERPA does not create a private right of action,[215] although its violation may form the basis of a claim under 42 U.S.C. § 1983.[216] Complaints must be filed with the Family Policy Compliance Office of the U.S. Department of Education within 180 days of an alleged violation.[217] Remedies include withholding payments, terminating eligibility to receive funding, and issuing a complaint to compel compliance.[218] There are also confidentiality regulations applicable to Parts B and H of IDEA that guarantee the privacy of a child with HIV infection; in large part, they mirror the requirements of FERPA.[219] Finally, although § 504 does not have a specific confidentiality provision, the OCR policy discussed in

---

[204] *Id.* §§ 99.3, 99.31(a)(11), 99.37.

[205] *Id.* § 99.31(a)(1).

[206] 34 C.F.R. § 99.31(a)(2).

[207] *Id.* § 99.31(a)(3).

[208] *Id.* § 99.31(7).

[209] *Id.* § 99.31(8), (12).

[210] *Id.* § 99.31(6).

[211] 34 C.F.R. § 99.31(4).

[212] 20 U.S.C. § 1232g(a)(2).

[213] 34 C.F.R. § 99.20.

[214] *Id.* §§ 99.21, 99.22.

[215] Tarka v. Cunningham, 917 F.2d 890 (5th Cir. 1990); Tombrello v. USX Corp., 763 F. Supp. 541, 545 (N.D. Ala. 1991).

[216] Tarka v. Cunningham, 917 F.2d 890 (5th Cir. 1990).

[217] 34 C.F.R. §§ 99.63, .64. The 180-day limitation may be extended by the Office in its discretion.

[218] *Id.* § 99.67.

[219] *See id.* §§ 300.560–.576, 303.460. The Part H program provides an added measure of protection, requiring parental consent to release information for the purpose of transition to Part B services. *See* Letter to Shipp, 23 Indivs. Disabilities Educ. L. Rep. (LRP) 442 (Office Spec. Educ. Programs 1995); Letter to Ackerhalt, 23 Indivs. Disabilities Educ. L. Rep. (LRP) 346 (Office Spec. Educ. Programs 1995).

§ **5.13** states that "singling out children handicapped with AIDS for treatment that differs from that provided to nonhandicapped children or children with other handicaps with respect to confidentiality would constitute different treatment on the basis of handicap," violating the regulation prohibiting the provision of "different or separate aids, benefits or services."[220]

---

[220] OCR Memorandum; *see* 34 C.F.R. § 104.4(b)(iv).

CHAPTER 6

AIDS AND HOUSING

Karen L. Black

David W. Webber

---

§ 6.1   Introduction

Individuals with HIV infection often experience difficulty in obtaining and, on becoming symptomatic, maintaining housing on the private market. There are numerous reasons for these difficulties. Discrimination by housing providers, real estate professionals, and residents of the community account for a large portion of the problem. Financial distress, increased need for on-site medical assistance, and other problems only indirectly connected with HIV also cause difficulties. Substance abuse or mental illness, either as a result of dementia caused by HIV illness or as an unrelated condition, may exacerbate the problem of obtaining housing. Finally, overcoming bureaucratic hurdles to obtain needed housing assistance is a daunting task for homeless persons and their advocates.

This chapter begins by addressing the most extreme result of this problem, homelessness among individuals with HIV, in **§ 6.2,** and congressional efforts to ameliorate it, in § **6.3. Sections 6.4** through **6.11** discuss strong federal, state, and local nondiscrimination laws that prohibit discrimination against home seekers, tenants, and others with HIV, and provide victims of discrimination with the ability to obtain or remain in their chosen home and to collect monetary damages to compensate them for any loss they suffered as a result of the discrimination.[1] **Section 6.12** covers the legal issues involved in disclosure of HIV information in real estate transactions involving properties that may be stigmatized by association with someone with HIV/AIDS. Finally, § **6.13** considers the legal issues that can arise when one owner of shared housing must succeed another, typically as the result of the death of one co-owner.

§ 6.2   The Problem of Homelessness and HIV

The lack of affordable and appropriate housing was termed an "acute crisis" for persons with HIV illness in the 1992 report on the subject by the National Commission on AIDS.[2] According to the commission, although the exact number of homeless persons in the United States is unknown, one to three million people are estimated to be without housing. Seroprevalence studies among the homeless indicate a high rate of HIV infection: 15 percent of these individuals have been estimated to be HIV-infected. Estimates also indicate that as many as one-third to one-half of the persons with HIV infection in the United States are homeless.

The resulting cost in human suffering is inestimable. Additionally, this lack of housing frequently results in extended hospitalization for patients with AIDS who would be appropriate for discharge if they had homes to return to, thus adding to the cost of medical care.[3]

§ 6.3   Federal Housing Assistance and AIDS/HIV

In response to the problem of providing housing to homeless persons with AIDS in 1990, Congress enacted the AIDS Housing Opportunity Act, a subtitle of the Cranston-Gonzalez National Affordable Housing Act.[4] That legislation established

---

[1] Harassment or exclusion of persons with HIV may also violate landlord-tenant law and the lease or sales agreement that governs the property transfer. This chapter does not attempt to cover these various laws because they differ in each locality, are very extensive, and because any act that violates such laws or contracts with the intent to exclude or harm persons with HIV would also fall under the Fair Housing Act, which offers much greater protection than either contract law or landlord-tenant ordinances.

[2] National Comm'n on AIDS, Housing and the HIV/AIDS Epidemic: Recommendations for Action 7 (1992).

[3] *See* Peter Arno, *Housing, Hopelessness, and the Impact of HIV Disease, in* The AIDS Reader: Social, Political, and Ethical Issues 177–89 (Nancy F. McKenzie ed., 1991).

[4] Pub. L. No. 101-625, Title VIII, §§ 851–863, 1990 U.S.C.C.A.N. (104 Stat.) 4079, 4375 (codified at 42 U.S.C. §§ 12901–12912 (1994)).

the Housing Opportunities for Persons with AIDS (HOPWA) program, the primary congressional response to the housing needs of persons with AIDS.[5] HOPWA is intended to assist states and local governmental units in providing housing to persons with AIDS and related medical conditions. HOPWA's definition of AIDS and related diseases includes "any conditions arising from the etiologic agent for acquired immunodeficiency syndrome."[6] In 1992, Congress amended the definition of persons eligible for HOPWA assistance to include the families of persons with AIDS.[7]

HOPWA is administered by the Department of Housing and Urban Development (HUD), which provides grants for housing assistance and supportive services for eligible low-income individuals. Income eligibility standards are promulgated by the secretary of HUD consistent with the statutory definition.[8] Program services are without charge to eligible individuals, although fees may be charged of other individuals, based on the individual's income and resources.[9] HUD has issued regulations governing the administration of the HOPWA program.[10]

HOPWA Grant Allocation Standards

As a prerequisite to funding under HOPWA, states and cities must have an approved, comprehensive, housing affordability strategy pursuant to the National Affordable Housing Act.[11] Additionally, metropolitan areas must establish or designate a governmental agency or organization for receipt of grants.

HOPWA grants are allocated by two means: a formula system of grants (90 percent of appropriated funds) and nonformula, competitive grants (remaining 10 percent of funds). The formula system provides that 90 percent of the total appropriated funds are divided and distributed such that 75 percent are allocated to cities and states. The recipient cities must be in a metropolitan statistical area (MSA) with a population greater than 500,000 and more than 1,500 cases of AIDS outside of the MSA; recipient states must have more than 1,500 cases of AIDS. The remaining 25 percent of the formula funding is allocated among cities that are greater than 500,000 in population, the most populous in an MSA, and that have more than 1,500 cases of AIDS as well as a "higher than average

---

[5] A complete discussion of all federal housing assistance programs as they pertain to individuals with HIV is beyond the scope of this section. For an excellent introduction to this subject, see Betsy Lieberman & Donald P. Chamberlain, Breaking New Ground: Developing Innovative AIDS Care Residences (1993). This and other publications are available from AIDS Housing of Washington, 2025 First Avenue, Suite 420, Seattle, Washington 98121; telephone (206) 448-6242.

[6] 42 U.S.C. § 12902(1).

[7] Pub. L. No. 102-550, Title VI, § 606(j)(1), 1992 U.S.C.C.A.N. (106 Stat.) 3810.

[8] 42 U.S.C. § 12902(3).

[9] *Id.* § 12905(d).

[10] 24 C.F.R. pt. 574 (1995).

[11] 42 U.S.C. § 12705.

per capita incidence of AIDS."[12] The number of cases of AIDS is that "reported to and confirmed by" CDC as of March 31 of the fiscal year immediately preceding the fiscal year for which the amounts are appropriated.[13] Cities may receive funds under both categories. Cities that receive funds under the formula allocation must provide assurances that funds will address the needs within the MSA, including areas that are not within the jurisdiction of the city itself. The formula grants are subject to a minimum grant amount of $200,000. The minimum grant amounts are factored into the formula, and grant amounts in excess of the minimum are reduced on a pro rata basis to assure funding at the minimum level.

The competitive, nonformula grants are awarded to states that do not qualify for the formula allocations and to states, local governments, and nonprofit organizations for "special projects of national significance."[14] The competitive selection is based on relative numbers of AIDS cases reported and per capita AIDS incidence, local housing needs, extent of local planning and coordination of housing programs, and the likelihood of the continuation of state and local efforts.

The HOPWA program imposes several restrictions on grantees. To be certain that receipt of federal funds does not result in concomitant reduction in state funding, grantees are forbidden from substituting HOPWA funding for "other amounts made available or designated by State or local governments."[15] Grantees are prohibited from charging fees to eligible persons.[16] Grantees are required to maintain the confidentiality of the "name . . . and any other information regarding individuals receiving such assistance."[17] Administrative costs of grantees are limited to 3 percent of the grant amount; project sponsors' administrative costs are limited to 7 percent,[18] and annual reports to HUD are required.[19]

HOPWA grants are available for "eligible activities" supporting an array of housing and housing-related services in six statutorily defined areas. First, HOPWA funds housing information and coordination of services activities, including counseling, information, and referral services to assist eligible persons locate, acquire, finance, and maintain housing, and to identify, coordinate, and develop housing assistance resources, including preliminary research and making expenditures necessary to determine the feasibility of housing-related initiatives.[20] Second, HOPWA supports both short-term housing (shelter services) and supportive services. *Supportive services* may include health, mental health,

---

[12] *Id.* § 12903(c)(1)(B).

[13] *Id.* § 12903(c)(2).

[14] *Id.* § 12903(c)(3).

[15] *Id.* § 12905(a).

[16] *Id.* § 12905(d).

[17] 42 U.S.C. § 12905(e).

[18] *Id.* § 12905(g).

[19] *Id.* § 12911.

[20] *Id.* § 12906.

assessment, permanent housing placement, drug and alcohol abuse treatment and counseling, day care, and nutritional services. However, the supportive services are limited to persons with AIDS, not family members who do not have AIDS. Third, HOPWA funds rental assistance for shared housing as provided under the low-income housing assistance provision,[21] but this is not limited to elderly individuals. Fourth, HOPWA provides rental assistance for or development of single room occupancy (SRO) dwellings, consistent with 42 U.S.C. § 1437f(n). Providers are required to assist any individual who requires more care than is available in SRO housing to locate an appropriate care provider. Fifth, HOPWA funds the development of community residences, involving multi-unit residences as an alternative to more costly institutional care and providing permanent or transitional residential settings with appropriate services for persons who are unable to live independently. Recipients of these housing services may be required to pay rent consistent with 42 U.S.C. § 1437a(a) for low-income families, by a formula determined by the secretary of HUD, determined by the income and resources of the resident. HOPWA allows that "Section 8" funding[22] may be used in conjunction with a community residence. The program is specifically intended to delay or prevent the placement of residents in hospitals or other institutions. Sixth, funding may be used to "carry out other activities that the Secretary develops in cooperation with eligible states and localities," but such activities are funded only under the projects of national significance funding stream.

§ 6.4 Fair Housing Act

The Fair Housing Act (FHA), when first enacted in 1968, prohibited discrimination in housing based on race, color, religion, and national origin.[23] In 1974, the FHA was amended to prohibit discrimination based on gender,[24] and in 1988 it was extended further to prohibit discrimination against families with children and handicapped persons.[25]

The 1988 amendments also strengthened the enforcement mechanisms of the FHA by providing victims of discrimination with the possibility of unlimited punitive damages, free government legal counsel, and other redress designed to

---

[21] *Id.* § 1437f(p).

[22] *Id.* § 1437f.

[23] Pub. L. No. 90-284, Title VIII, §§ 801–819, and Title IX, § 901, 82 Stat. 73, 81, 1968 U.S.C.C.A.N. 89, 99 (codified at 42 U.S.C. §§ 3601–3619, 3631 (1994)).

[24] Housing and Community Development Act of 1974, Pub. L. No. 93-383, Title VIII, § 808, 88 Stat. 633, 729, 1974 U.S.C.C.A.N. 713, 829 (1974).

[25] Fair Housing Amendments Act of 1988, Pub. L. No. 100-430, § 6, 1988 U.S.C.C.A.N. (102 Stat.) 1619, 1620–23 (amending 42 U.S.C. §§ 3604–3606). The amendments were effective March 12, 1989.

enhance enforcement of a law that had been previously viewed as well meaning but weak. As a result, the FHA has emerged as one of the strongest and most expansive civil rights laws in existence today, broadly prohibiting discriminatory acts and offering extensive remedies to victims of discrimination.

§ 6.5 —Persons Protected

A *handicapped*[26] individual within the meaning of the FHA is a person with: "(1) a physical or mental impairment which substantially limits one or more of such person's major life activities; (2) a record of having such an impairment; or (3) being regarded as having such an impairment."[27] The FHA's definition of *handicap* is same as the definition of disability contained in the Rehabilitation Act of 1973 (see **Chapters 3** and **4**), and in the Americans with Disabilities Act of 1990 (ADA) (see **Chapters 3** and **4**). Thus, like both the Rehabilitation Act and the ADA, the FHA does not specifically make reference to HIV infection or any specific condition or impairment, but there is no question that HIV infection is covered by the statutory definition of handicap. The legislative history of the FHA's handicap amendments in 1988, the interpretive regulations, and the rulings of federal courts that have considered the question have all supported this interpretation.

First, the legislative history of the 1988 FHA amendments supports the conclusion that HIV infection was intended to be included, as indicated by the actions of the House Judiciary Committee in amending and then reporting the final version of the bill, H.R. 1158, before its enactment. The House Judiciary Committee report is the only congressional committee report accompanying H.R. 1158. It notes that the bill, as recommended for passage, differed from the introduced bill in that the handicap provisions "do not require that a dwelling be provided to any person whose tenancy poses a direct threat to the health or safety of others," language that was added by an amendment in the nature of a substitute.[28] After the direct threat amendment was agreed to, the House Judiciary Committee considered but rejected another amendment that would have excluded from coverage as a handicap "any infectious, contagious or communicable disease whether or not such disease causes any other impairment which would be a direct threat to the property, health or safety of others," an amendment intended to exclude HIV.[29] Moreover, the Judiciary Committee's report provides an example of unlawful discrimination: "[p]eople with [AIDS]

---

[26] Although the term "disability" is now preferred to "handicap," as evidenced by the usage in ADA and other federal and state statutes, this chapter generally uses "handicap," consistent with the usage of the FHA.

[27] 42 U.S.C. § 3602(h).

[28] H.R. Rep. No. 711, 100th Cong., 2d Sess. 12, *reprinted in* 1988 U.S.C.C.A.N. 2173, 2173 [hereinafter House Judiciary Report].

[29] House Judiciary Report at 28, *reprinted in* 1988 U.S.C.C.A.N. 2173, 2189.

and people who test positive for the AIDS virus have been evicted because of an erroneous belief that they pose a health risk to others."[30] The Judiciary Report explains that the direct threat amendment paralleled that of the Civil Rights Restoration Act of 1988,[31] which was enacted just months before the Judiciary Report was issued with the intention that HIV infection be included as a handicap under the Rehabilitation Act.[32] Additionally, the Judiciary Report refers approvingly to *Chalk v. United States District Court*[33] in terms of applying the direct threat defense.

In interpreting the FHA in its regulations, the Department of Housing and Urban Development concluded that for purposes of defining handicap, "physical or mental impairment includes . . . Human Immunodeficiency Virus infection."[34]

In light of the legislative history and administrative agency interpretation, the courts have consistently concluded that AIDS is a handicap for FHA purposes. In *Support Ministries for Persons with AIDS v. Village of Waterford*,[35] for example, the court found the defendants' claim that persons with AIDS were not handicapped to be incredible and rejected it. In *Stewart B. McKinney Foundation v. Town Plan & Zoning Commission*,[36] the court noted that despite frequent congressional references to people with AIDS (not HIV infection), "it appears clear that Congress intended to refer to HIV-infected persons as well" and that Congress's failure to do so was the result of a "prevalent 'nomenclature' problem." In any event, most cases in this area have involved the housing rights of persons with AIDS and not just persons with asymptomatic HIV infection, although both symptomatic and asymptomatic HIV infection come within the coverage of the statute.

Consistent with its disability discrimination enactments in other areas, Congress extended protection not just to individuals who are in fact handicapped but also to individuals perceived to be handicapped.[37] This is essential in addressing discrimination based on stereotyped views of individuals thought to have or be at risk for HIV. Thus, for example, if discrimination against a gay man is based on the perception that he is HIV-infected or at risk for HIV infection, he would be protected under the FHA, without regard to whether there is any legal protection against discrimination based on his sexual orientation. In addition, discrimination

---

[30] House Judiciary Report at 18, *reprinted in* 1988 U.S.C.C.A.N. 2173, 2179 (footnote omitted) (citing N.Y. Comm'n on Human Rights, Report on Discrimination Against People with AIDS (1987)).

[31] Pub. L. No. 100-259, 1988 U.S.C.C.A.N. (102 Stat.) 28 (amending 29 U.S.C. § 706).

[32] House Judiciary Report at 29, *reprinted in* 1988 U.S.C.C.A.N. 2173, 2190.

[33] 840 F.2d 701 (9th Cir. 1988) (treating AIDS as a handicap under Rehabilitation Act).

[34] 24 C.F.R. § 100.201 (1996).

[35] 808 F. Supp. 120, 128–30 (N.D.N.Y. 1992); *see also* Association of Relatives & Friends of AIDS Patients v. Regulations & Permits Admin., 740 F. Supp. 95, 103 (D.P.R. 1992); Baxter v. City of Belleville, 720 F. Supp. 720, 728–30 (S.D. Ill. 1989).

[36] 790 F. Supp. 1197, 1210 n.8 (D. Conn. 1992).

[37] 42 U.S.C. § 3602(h)(3).

based on the handicap of any person who associates with the buyer or renter (or sublessee of the renter) is prohibited.[38] The fact that a tenant is visited in the rental unit by persons with AIDS would bring the tenant within the protection of the FHA if discrimination results from such visits, even though the tenant himself is not a person with a handicap.[39]

It is important to note that the only handicapped individuals not protected by the FHA are those who are currently using or involved in the distribution or manufacture of illegal drugs.[40] However, alcoholics, persons who have completed a drug-addiction recovery program, or those who use drugs prescribed by a physician are protected.

The FHA also protects housing providers, realtors, and rental agents who comply with the law from retaliation by their employers or clients.[41] They benefit from the same protection afforded by the FHA against coercion, threats, or intimidation as an individual with HIV or AIDS.[42]

§ 6.6 —Direct Threat Defense

The FHA provides a direct threat defense: "[n]othing in [the FHA] requires that a dwelling be made available to an individual whose tenancy would constitute a direct threat to the health or safety of other individuals or whose tenancy would result in substantial physical damage to the property of others."[43] Individuals with HIV are protected under the FHA because they do not pose a direct threat to the health and safety of others. The legislative history of the FHA reflects a disbelief that a person with HIV could pose such a threat,[44] and no court has held that an HIV or AIDS-infected person poses such a substantial health risk.[45] Consequently, a housing provider who wishes to utilize this exclusion has a substantial burden to demonstrate that the individual tenant's conduct creates a direct threat to the health or safety of the other tenants, and may not merely assert general concerns about HIV illness. As stated in the House Report:

---

[38] *Id.* § 3604(f)(1)(C), (2)(C).

[39] *See* Beasley v. Ken Edwards Enters., Inc., No. 91-CV-1348, AIDS Litig. Rep. (Andrews Pubs.) 6526 (N.D. Ga., complaint filed June 11, 1991) (exclusion of tenant's guest with AIDS from swimming pool resulted in FHA lawsuit).

[40] 42 U.S.C. § 3602(h), referencing the Federal Crimes Code, 21 U.S.C. § 802, definition of *controlled substance.*

[41] 24 C.F.R. § 100.400(c)(3) (1996); *see, e.g.,* Wilkey v. Pyramid Constr. Co., 619 F. Supp. 1453 (D. Conn. 1985); *see also* Favors v. MAQ Management Corp., 753 F. Supp. 941 (N.D. Ga. 1990) (applicant for employment with real estate management firm protected).

[42] 42 U.S.C. § 3617.

[43] *Id.* § 3604(f)(9).

[44] House Judiciary Report at 28, *reprinted in* 1988 U.S.C.C.A.N. 2173, 2189–90.

[45] Baxter v. City of Belleville, 720 F. Supp. 720, 729 (S.D. Ill 1989); Association of Relatives & Friends of AIDS Patients v. Regulations & Permits Admin., 740 F. Supp. 95, 103 (D.P.R. 1990).

Generalized assumptions, subjective fears, and speculation are insufficient to prove the requisite direct threat to others. In the case of a persons with a mental illness, for example, there must be objective evidence from the person's prior behavior that the person has committed overt acts which caused harm or which directly threatened harm.[46]

Even if a housing provider shows that a tenant with HIV poses such a threat, the provider is then required to rent to that person if a reasonable accommodation can be made which eliminates the risk.[47]

§ 6.7 —Prohibited Conduct

The FHA makes it unlawful "[t]o discriminate in the sale or rental, or to otherwise make unavailable or deny, a dwelling to any buyer or renter because of a handicap."[48] This prohibition extends to a broad range of housing options. The FHA refers to *dwelling,* which is defined as "any building, structure, or portion thereof which is occupied as, or designed or intended for occupancy as, a residence by one or more families."[49] Although the FHA covers single or multiple family dwellings, this does not limit its protection to only families, because the definition of *family* includes "single individual,"[50] and thus transactions involving housing intended for an individual renter or buyer are covered. In addition to buildings, "vacant land that is offered for sale or lease for the construction or location thereon" is included in the definition of *dwelling.*[51] Not included is the sale or rental of space for office or commercial use, not involving use as a residence.[52] But in that regard, the renter's or buyer's intended future use, as opposed to the current nonresidential use, should prevail.[53] Commercial or nonresidential transactions, however, may be covered under state or local laws, as discussed in § 6.11. Similarly, hotels, motels, and other temporary housing arrangements would not be covered,[54] although they would be covered under the Title III public accommodation provisions of ADA.[55]

---

[46] House Judiciary Report at 28, *reprinted in* 1988 U.S.C.C.A.N. 2173, 2189–90.

[47] 42 U.S.C. § 3604(f)(3)(B). House Judiciary Report at 29, *reprinted in* 1988 U.S.C.C.A.N. 2173, 2190.

[48] 42 U.S.C. § 3604(f)(1).

[49] 42 U.S.C. § 3602(b).

[50] *Id.* § 3602(c).

[51] *Id.* § 3602(b).

[52] *Id.*

[53] *See* Baxter v. City of Belleville, 720 F. Supp. 720, 731 (S.D. Ill. 1989) (former office building is "dwelling" within meaning of FHA based on tenant's construction of kitchen, indicating intended use as residence).

[54] *See* Patel v. Holley House Motels, 483 F. Supp. 374 (S.D. Ala. 1979) (motel not designed, occupied, or intended for use as residence was not "dwelling" within meaning of FHA).

[55] 42 U.S.C. § 12165(7)(A). ADA's Title III provisions are covered in **Ch. 4.**

The FHA has also been applied to nursing care facilities. In *Doe v. Camargo Manor, Inc.,*[56] a nursing care facility refused to accept the plaintiff as a resident because of his HIV status. In settling the resulting lawsuit, the defendant nursing home paid $10,000 in damages, in addition to attorneys' fees and costs. The defendant also agreed to end its exclusionary practices, institute staff training, impose mandatory discipline on employees who fail to comply with nondiscrimination standards, notify local hospitals of their willingness to accept persons with HIV, and report for three years to the Department of Justice on all applications of persons with HIV/AIDS.

The FHA also prohibits discrimination with respect to the terms, conditions, privileges, services, and facilities attendant to housing.[57] In *Doe v. Carrollan Gardens Condominium Ass'n,*[58] for example, the court found an FHA violation when a landlord failed to provide maintenance and parked a giant dumpster in front of the tenant's apartment after becoming aware that the tenant was HIV positive.

The FHA includes a broad prohibition against interference or retaliation:

> It shall be unlawful to coerce, intimidate, threaten, or interfere with any person in the exercise or enjoyment of, or on account of his having exercised or enjoyed, or on account of his having aided or encouraged any other person in the exercise or enjoyment of, any right granted or protected [under the FHA].[59]

The FHA exempts persons who own three or fewer single family homes and do not transfer more than one within 24 months or who live in the same dwelling as housing they rent to others with less than four units.[60] There is no exemption once a real estate agent is involved or when an unlawful advertisement is used to attract prospective renters or buyers.

Criminal sanctions are available for violations of the FHA, as the courts have emphasized in response to community opposition to housing initiatives for persons with AIDS.[61] Derogatory statements intended to frighten are sufficient to

---

[56] No. C-1-90-107 (S.D. Ohio 1991), consent decree on file with authors.

[57] 42 U.S.C. § 3604(f)(2). These clauses are virtually identical to those protecting persons faced with discrimination based on race, national origin, religion, age, gender, and familial status, except that the language does not preclude providing housing specifically for persons with handicaps.

[58] Fair Hous.-Fair Lending Cas. (P-H) ¶ 18,171 (Md. Ct. Spec. App. 1995) (per curiam). *See also* Joel Truitt Management v. District of Columbia Comm'n on Human Rights, 646 A.2d 1007 (D.C. 1994) (per curiam) (failure to provide plumbing services to tenant with AIDS absent a "certification from a qualified health authority" that it is safe to enter apartment resulted in affirmance of award of $35,000 under analogous D.C. law).

[59] 42 U.S.C. § 3617.

[60] No exemption is allowed under civil rights statutes if racial discrimination is involved, 42 U.S.C. §§ 1918, 1982.

[61] 42 U.S.C. §§ 3617, 3631. *See* Association of Relatives & Friends of AIDS Patients v. Regulations & Permits Admin., 740 F. Supp. 95, 108 n.15 (D.P.R. 1990) (noting that "court will not tolerate" any violation of federal law and will direct U.S. attorney to investigate and, if necessary, prosecute any apparent violation resulting from opposition to group housing for persons with AIDS).

violate the FHA, even if they are not accompanied by any threat of force.[62] Some cases of harassment have resulted in significant recoveries for plaintiffs with HIV. In one particularly egregious case, the court found that a landlord had harassed a tenant with HIV for over 18 months by turning off his electricity, burglarizing his apartment, leaving threatening phone messages, and informing his employer about his HIV status. The court awarded the tenant $125,000 in damages, explaining that "an agenda of spite, malice and bias, acted upon over an extended period of time, resulting in the severe emotional and mental abuse of a tenant, seriously ill with AIDS, will not be met with half-hearted sanctions or 'slaps on the wrist'."[63] In another case, *United States v. Short*,[64] a landlord harassed residents with AIDS, resulting in a $16,000 settlement and extensive injunctive relief.

The FHA prohibits discrimination in any term or condition of a residential real estate transaction, such as making or purchasing loans, providing homeowners insurance, or providing other financial assistance for purchasing, constructing, improving, repairing, or maintaining a dwelling.[65] Mortgage lending institutions cannot discriminate on the basis of HIV when making mortgage loans. Lenders are also prohibited from discriminating in making consumer or other loans that are secured by real estate. Although a lender might take into account the limited income of a homeowner who is receiving disability benefits as a result of HIV illness, the illness itself cannot be used as a basis for assuming that earning capacity would be limited in the future, thus rendering the applicant ineligible, for example, for mortgage refinancing. In addition, the lender cannot refuse to make the loan because of the source of income. Disability insurance payments, 401K accounts, and pensions that have vested must all be considered within the income-debt ratios used by the lender. If this is not a standard practice for the lender, the applicant is entitled to a reasonable accommodation and should request one (see **§ 6.9**).

Also, although no case appears to have considered the question, appraisals of real estate cannot discriminate on the basis of handicap, and thus an appraisal of a home of a person with AIDS (or one that is to be purchased by a person with AIDS), at a value lower than it would otherwise be if the owner or purchaser did not have AIDS would be unlawful because that valuation would not be based on any actual threat of HIV transmission (or other defect in the property that reduced its value), but instead would be on the appraiser's unreasonable fear or the anticipated response of future buyers.[66]

---

[62] *See* People Helpers Found. v. City of Richmond, 781 F. Supp. 1132 (E.D. Va.), *subsequent opinion,* 789 F. Supp. 725 (E.D. Va. 1992).

[63] *In re* 119–121 East 97th St. Corp., AIDS Litig. Rep. (Andrews Pubs.) 15,825 (N.Y. App. Div. 1996) (citing Velazquez v. Salinas Realty Corp., Compl. No. GA-00299061190-H (1992) (awarded $75,000 to plaintiff for mental anguish caused by his landlord's numerous menacing and discriminatory comments about his HIV status and refusal to make requested repairs)).

[64] Fair Hous.-Fair Lending Cas. (P-H) ¶ 15,838 (W.D. Pa. 1993).

[65] 42 U.S.C. § 3605.

[66] *See* 24 C.F.R. § 100.135 (1996) (appraisal of residential real estate may not take handicap into account). The related problem of disclosing HIV information pertaining to properties is discussed in **§ 6.12.**

Municipal authorities are prohibited from acting to exclude or make it more difficult for individuals with HIV to live in the community of their choice by excluding group homes, hospices, or other care facilities for individuals with HIV illness.[67] Typically, municipalities apply zoning laws that purport to restrict the use of properties or to limit the number of individuals who may reside at the property as a means to limit access to their communities. In enacting the 1988 handicap amendments to the FHA, Congress specifically stated its intention that the prohibition against discrimination towards persons with handicaps apply to zoning decisions and practices. The FHA is intended to prohibit "the application of special requirements through land-use regulations, restrictive covenants, and conditional or special use permits that have the effect of limiting the ability of such individuals to live in the residence of their choice in the community."[68] In several cases, persons with HIV have successfully challenged attempts by municipalities to impose special procedural burdens on housing transactions that establish community living arrangements for persons with HIV. In *Stewart B. McKinney Foundation v. Town Plan & Zoning Commission*,[69] the court enjoined a town zoning commission from requiring a community living arrangement for HIV-infected persons to obtain a special exception to use a two-family residence. The court held that not only was the township intentionally discriminating but the requirement also had a disparate impact on persons with disabilities:

> The court finds requiring the plaintiff to apply for a special exception has a discriminatory impact on HIV-infected persons because it holds the future tenants up to public scrutiny in a way that seven unrelated non-HIV infected persons would not be. In addition, the process has the potential of being burdensome and, based on the previous public hearings dealing with this case, could be quite controversial and unpleasant and further inflame public opposition to the Foundation's plans. If the exception were granted and the neighbors took an appeal, it could also be expensive for the plaintiff.[70]

Similarly, in *Association of Relatives & Friends of AIDS Patients v. Regulations & Permits Administration*,[71] the court enjoined a government agency from denying a special use permit for a hospice on the grounds that the agency had relied in part on certain discriminatory comments from community members in making its decision. In *Support Ministries for Persons with AIDS, Inc. v. Village of*

---

[67] Courts have recognized the importance of community living arrangements for persons with HIV illness or AIDS who require additional supports and medical assistance. Hill v. Community of Damien of Molokai, No. 21,715, AIDS Litig. Rep. (Andrews Pubs.) 15,233, 15,240 (N.M. 1996); Oxford House, Inc. v. Town of Babylon, 819 F. Supp. 1179, 1183 (E.D.N.Y. 1993); Support Ministries for Persons with AIDS v. Village of Waterford, 808 F. Supp. 120, 132 (N.D.N.Y. 1992).

[68] House Judiciary Report at 24, *reprinted in* 1988 U.S.C.C.A.N. 2173, 2185.

[69] 790 F. Supp. 1197 (D. Conn. 1992).

[70] *Id.* at 1197.

[71] 740 F. Supp. 95 (D.P.R. 1990).

Waterford,[72] the court found that the village changed its zoning ordinance specifically to stop the creation of a group home for HIV-positive persons and found that behavior unlawful. The case settled and Support Ministries received $140,000. Similarly, a case filed against the city of Charlotte, North Carolina, by the Department of Justice and Taylor Homes, a housing provider, asserting that city zoning laws were written and interpreted to deny persons with AIDS the opportunity to live in residentially zoned, group home settings, settled and Taylor Homes received $135,000.[73]

In other cases, courts have found that zoning requirements, although not intentionally discriminatory, may have a disparate effect on handicapped persons and are therefore unlawful. For instance, courts have found unlawful ordinances that defined family in terms of "blood" and "marriage" relationships, or that imposed stringent safety requirements on group homes without distinguishing between different disabilities,[74] or that excluded group homes from single-family residential districts.[75]

Zoning ordinances that limit occupancy to a certain number of unrelated individuals have also been successfully challenged.[76] Although the FHA allows "reasonable local, State, or Federal restrictions regarding the maximum number of occupants permitted to occupy a dwelling,"[77] the Supreme Court recently held, in *City of Edmonds v. Oxford House,*[78] that these restrictions cannot distinguish between families and unrelated persons. If a structure is too small to hold a certain number of individuals, the limitation must apply regardless of the legal relationship between the occupants. The FHA permits restrictions that apply

---

[72] 808 F. Supp. 120 (N.D.N.Y. 1992).

[73] United States v. City of Charlotte, No. 3:94-CV-394-MCK, AIDS Litig. Rep. (Andrews Pubs.) 2621 (W.D.N.C. 1994).

[74] Marbrunak, Inc. v. City of Stow, 974 F.2d 43, 46–48 (6th Cir. 1992).

[75] *In re* Millcreek Township Zoning Ordinance 4, Pa. D. & C.4th 449, 457–61 (C.P. Erie County 1989).

[76] *See* Oxford House, Inc. v. Township of Cherry Hill, 799 F. Supp. 450 (D.N.J. 1992) (township enjoined from enforcing single-family residential zoning rule against group home); Oxford House-Evergreen, Inc. v. City of Plainfield, 769 F. Supp. 1329 (D.N.J. 1991) (successful challenge to six-person limit on group home); United States v. Borough of Audubon, 797 F. Supp. 353 (D.N.J. 1991) (zoning citation for failure to apply for change of use from house to boarding home violated FHA), *aff'd without opinion,* 968 F.2d 14 (3d Cir. 1992); Oxford House, Inc. v. City of Albany, 819 F. Supp. 1168 (N.D.N.Y. 1993) (challenge to zoning restrictions against group home); Oxford House v. Town of Babylon, 819 F. Supp. 1179 (E.D.N.Y. 1993) (challenge to eviction of group home residents under single family zoning ordinance); Support Ministries for Persons with AIDS v. Village of Waterford, 808 F. Supp. 120 (N.D.N.Y. 1992); Association of Relatives & Friends of AIDS Patients v. Regulations & Permits Admin., 740 F. Supp. 95 (D.P.R. 1990) (successful challenge to denial of special use permit for AIDS hospice).

[77] 42 U.S.C. § 3607(b)(1).

[78] 115 S. Ct. 1776 (1995). *Cf.* Oxford House-C, Inc. v. St. Louis, 64 U.S.L.W. 2536 (8th Cir. 1996) (eight-person limit on group home occupancy not violation of FHA).

"numerical ceilings that serve to prevent overcrowding in living quarters," not rules designed to preserve the "family" character of a neighborhood.[79]

§ 6.8 —Prohibited Inquiries Regarding HIV

Regulations of the U.S. Department of Housing and Urban Development (HUD) specifically prohibit inquiries about whether a housing applicant, resident, or guest has a handicap, and its nature or severity.[80] This is true even when the landlord seeks to use the information to assess whether a prospective resident can live independently[81] or has "antisocial tendencies."[82] A landlord may ask questions about an applicant's ability to pay the rent and meet the obligations of tenancy if the landlord asks these questions of all applicants.[83]

In only one case has a judge found an inquiry into a tenant's HIV status to be permissible. In *HUD v. Williams,*[84] the administrative law judge (ALJ) recognized that "permitting landlords to ask a tenant whether they [sic] have diseases that pose no threat to others, would make a mockery of the [FHA]'s premise that handicapped people are to be treated with the same dignity as non-handicapped people in the United States housing market."[85] However, the ALJ's view that the tenancy posed a direct threat because of the risk of HIV transmission is largely speculative. To the extent that the threat actually existed, it could have been eliminated by simple safety precautions that should have been observed in housekeeping activities for all tenants, not just for the tenant known to have HIV. The ALJ then went on, however, to find an exceptional case when a specific tenancy produced a direct threat to the health and safety of others because the landlords' minor children were responsible for cleaning the bathroom of the tenant with HIV who was a known drug user. Nevertheless, the ALJ found that the FHA was violated because of the harassing manner in which the landlord questioned the tenant.

§ 6.9 —Reasonable Accommodation

Under the FHA, a landlord is required to permit a tenant to make reasonable modifications to the rental property, but the tenant must do so at his or her own

---

[79] City of Edmonds v. Oxford House, 115 S. Ct. at 1782.

[80] 24 C.F.R. § 100.202(c) (1996). The related question of disclosure of HIV information in real estate transactions is covered in **§ 6.12.**

[81] *See* Cason v. Rochester Hous. Auth., 748 F. Supp. 1002, 1008–09 (W.D.N.Y. 1990).

[82] 24 C.F.R. subch. A, app. I, at 742 (1996) (discussion of 24 C.F.R. § 101.202).

[83] *See* Cason v. Rochester Hous. Auth., 748 F. Supp. 1002, 1008–09 (W.D.N.Y. 1990).

[84] Fair Hous.-Fair Lending (P-H) ¶ 25,007 (A.L.J. 1991).

[85] *Id.* at 25,115 n.30.

expense. In addition, the landlord may require the tenant to restore the premises to their prior condition, with the exception of normal wear and tear.[86] The landlord may also require the tenant to deposit monies in escrow for the restorations.[87]

The FHA also requires housing providers "to make reasonable accommodations in rules, policies, practices, or services, when such accommodations may be necessary to afford such persons equal opportunity to use and enjoy a dwelling."[88] A reasonable accommodation requires more than nondiscriminatory treatment. It requires a housing provider to change or make an exception to a rule or policy generally applied to all tenants in order "to make its burden less onerous on the handicapped individual."[89] It is important that the individual who is seeking the accommodation make a written request to the housing provider stating his need for the accommodation and suggesting a reasonable method for satisfying that need. Unlike a claim of disparate impact or treatment, the remedy is not system-wide change. Instead, a reasonable accommodation is based on the assumption that the rule itself is lawful, but that a change in the rule is necessary to allow a handicapped individual a full opportunity to live in his or her chosen home. Common cases involve the need for a parking space for a mobility-impaired tenant or a dog for a visually impaired tenant,[90] but there does not need to be a causal nexus between the handicap and the restriction, and it does not need to have a direct adverse impact on the handicapped individual. For example, a federal court ordered the city of Philadelphia to accommodate a property owner who was creating a group home for handicapped individuals by permitting a side yard to satisfy a rear yard zoning requirement.[91] In another case, the U.S. Department of Justice filed suit in California alleging that a senior citizen mobile home park violated the FHA when it refused a reasonable accommodation requested by a tenant to allow her son, who had AIDS, to live with her.[92]

A reasonable accommodation should be granted if any rule, policy, or restriction adversely affects, directly or indirectly, any handicapped individual,[93] and the requested accommodation does not impose an undue financial or administrative burden or a fundamental alteration of the program or zoning scheme.[94] For example, it is reasonable to accommodate a group home for persons with AIDS

---

[86] 42 U.S.C. §§ 3604(f)(3)(A).

[87] 24 C.F.R. § 100.203(b).

[88] The premise of a reasonable accommodation was borrowed from section 504 of the Rehabilitation Act, 29 U.S.C. § 794.

[89] North Shore-Chicago Rehabilitation, Inc. v. Village of Skokie, 827 F. Supp. 497, 508 (N.D. Ill. 1993).

[90] 24 C.F.R. § 100.204(b)(1).

[91] United States v. City of Phila., 838 F. Supp. 223, 229–30 (E.D. Pa. 1993).

[92] United States v. R.&M. Shorecliffs, Ltd., No. SACV 96-549, AIDS Litig. Rep. (Andrews Pubs.) 15,849 (C.D. Cal. 1996).

[93] *Id.*

[94] Oxford House v. Town of Babylon, 819 F. Supp. 1179, 1186 (N.D.N.Y. 1993).

by not enforcing a restrictive covenant limiting the use of residential lots to families, because allowing the group home to operate would not impose any financial burden on neighboring homeowners and nonenforcement of the ordinance would not fundamentally alter the nature of the restrictions.[95]

§ 6.10 —Enforcement and Remedies

Enforcement of the FHA involves proof of either intentional discrimination or disparate impact discrimination. To prove intentional discrimination, a plaintiff must show that HIV status was at least a partial factor in the discriminatory decision making. HIV status need not be the sole or even a primary reason for the refusal.[96] Consequently, circumstantial evidence of intent, most often in the form of evidence that the neutral, stated reason for refusing an application or evicting a tenant is pretextual and is actually based on dislike or fear towards persons with HIV, is essential. In *United States v. Short*,[97] the court found intent based on the defendant's statements to reporters after the filing of the lawsuit about his attitude towards persons with AIDS. In *HUD v. Elroy R. & Dorothy Burns Trust*,[98] the ALJ found intent when the tenant was evicted the day after the landlord became aware that he had AIDS, without the normal procedures regarding written warnings prior to eviction.[99]

The courts have clearly stated the requisite elements of a viable housing discrimination claim under the FHA.[100] The plaintiff's prima facie case in the context of HIV-based discrimination includes: (1) the tenant or buyer has or is perceived to have HIV, and the landlord or seller knew or reasonably should have known this fact; (2) discrimination has occurred in some form, such as rejection of a qualified prospective tenant or buyer, or a qualified tenant or buyer was prevented from applying for the dwelling by the landlord, owner, or agent; and (3) the property remained available for sale or lease. Of course, the specific factual elements are not absolute and have been modified appropriately in cases that asserted discrimination against a guest or friend who has AIDS, a rejection of a mortgage or refinancing application with a lender, and many other situations. Once the prospective buyer or tenant has proven these elements, the property owner must rebut the appearance of discriminatory intent by proffering valid, nondiscriminatory reasons for its actions. The tenant or buyer then has the opportunity to demonstrate that the reasons proffered are pretextual, that is, not

---

[95] Hill v. Community of Damien of Molokai, No. 21,715, AIDS Litig. Rep. (Andrews Pubs.) 15,233, 15,240 (N.M. 1996).

[96] Metropolitan Hous. Dev. Corp. v. Village of Arlington Heights, 558 F.2d 1283, 1290 (7th Cir. 1977), *cert. denied,* 434 U.S. 1025 (1978).

[97] Fair Hous.-Fair Lending (P-H) ¶ 15,838 (W.D. Pa. 1993).

[98] Fair Hous.-Fair Lending (P-H) ¶ 25,073 (A.L.J. 1994).

[99] *Id.* at 25,681.

[100] Betsy v. Turtle Creek Assocs., 736 F.2d 983, 985–88 (4th Cir. 1984).

the real reason for the property owner's refusal to sell or rent. For example, in *HUD v. Elroy R. & Dorothy Burns Trust,*[101] the ALJ found pretextual the landlord's explanation that a tenant with HIV was evicted for causing noise and property damage; the alleged incidents occurred more than a year prior to the eviction, and the landlord took no contemporaneous action to address the problems.

In terms of disparate impact discrimination, the FHA prohibits a property owner from implementing facially neutral, apparently nondiscriminatory leasing or selling policies that nonetheless have an adverse impact on handicapped individuals. A tenant or buyer who has suffered disparate impact discrimination does not need to prove any intent or motive to discriminate. It should be proven in accordance with a four-step test enunciated in *Metropolitan Housing Development Corp. v. Village of Arlington Heights.*[102] In the context of HIV discrimination, these steps involve analysis of (1) whether the policy has a greater impact on persons with HIV than on others; (2) whether there is any evidence of discriminatory intent;[103] (3) whether there are legitimate, nonpretextual reasons for the policy or action, or whether it benefits a governmental interest in protecting the public welfare or a private interest; (4) the extent of the relief that the plaintiff is seeking (for example, compelling the property owner to convey the property or merely to cease interference with the rights of the residents with HIV).

Any aggrieved person may file a complaint for a violation of the FHA. A person is aggrieved for the purposes of the FHA when he has been injured by a discriminatory housing practice or will be injured by a discriminatory housing practice that is about to occur.[104] Also, testers,[105] fair housing organizations,[106] real estate brokers who have lost a commission because a sales transaction was not completed,[107] or housing providers who have been prevented from renting or selling to a homeseeker with AIDS,[108] have been deemed to have standing to challenge discriminatory practices under the FHA.[109]

Fair housing advocacy organizations are an important resource for individuals who may have suffered housing discrimination. These organizations are devoted to ending housing discrimination by investigating the alleged discrimination and

---

[101] Fair Hous.-Fair Lending (P-H) ¶ 25,073 (A.L.J. 1994).

[102] 558 F.2d 1283, 1290–93 (7th Cir. 1977), *cert. denied,* 434 U.S. 1025 (1978).

[103] The *Arlington Heights* court held that this was the least important factor. *Id.* at 1292.

[104] 42 U.S.C. § 3602.

[105] Havens Realty Corp. v. Coleman, 455 U.S. 363 (1980).

[106] *Id.*

[107] Crumble v. Blumthal, 549 F.2d 462 (7th Cir. 1977).

[108] *See* Old W. End Ass'n v. Buckeye Fed. Sav. & Loan Ass'n, Fair Hous.-Fair Lending Cas. (P-H) ¶ 15,548 (N.D. Ohio 1986) (sellers have standing against lender who allegedly discriminated against buyers on basis of race).

[109] Standing under the FHA is defined as broadly as permitted by the U.S. Constitution. Trafficante v. Metropolitan Life Ins. Co., 409 U.S. 205, 209 (1992); Gladstone Realtors v. Village of Bellwood, 441 U.S. 91, 102–09 (1979).

confirming or disaffirming its existence, often by using fair housing testers. Fair housing testers pose as renters or buyers of residential property and attempt to rent or purchase a house from a housing provider suspected of discriminatory practices. Two testers with similar income, credit history, and housing needs are paired together. The only difference between the testers' profiles is that only one has the characteristic that is believed to be the reason for the discrimination. Fair housing organizations also provide education and counseling to landlords, sellers, and even entire communities to allay their fears and concerns about renting or selling to a person with HIV. Perhaps most importantly, however, fair housing organizations have standing to file a lawsuit under the FHA in their own name.[110] For individuals with HIV who may not want to file a lawsuit because of their desire for anonymity or because of their unwillingness to invest time and energy in litigation, this means that they can provide the evidence of discrimination to the fair housing organization, which may then bring the lawsuit in the organization's name.

Regardless of whether individuals who suspect that they have been unlawfully discriminated against intend to sue, testing for differential treatment based on HIV status may provide important answers about the legality of the housing provider's practices. Testing for discrimination based on HIV is more difficult than the more common testing for racial discrimination, but it is not impossible. A test coordinator should develop a profile similar to the complainant's for one of the testers. For example, if the landlord discovered that an applicant had HIV because he attends an HIV treatment program at a nearby hospital, the tester could also state that he is interested in the apartment because of its proximity to the hospital's program. If possible, however, the tester profile should be modified and should not exactly duplicate the original applicant's profile. If the profiles are too similar to the actual case, it may arouse suspicions, particularly in a community in which fair housing testing is well known.

Anyone who commits one of the prohibited acts may be sued for violating the FHA. This includes brokers, agents and their principals (that is, homeowners, employers, corporate officers, shareholders, or franchisors), lenders, insurers, appraisers, landlords, neighbors, and local governments. When an employee discriminates within the scope of his employment, the business owner is liable. The duty not to discriminate is nondelegable, and it does not matter whether the business owner practiced the discrimination herself or even had knowledge of it.[111]

---

[110] Havens Realty Corp. v. Coleman, 455 U.S. 363 (1980).

[111] City of Chicago v. Matchmaker Real Estate Sales Ctr., 982 F.2d 1086, 1096–97 (7th Cir. 1992), *cert. denied,* 113 S. Ct. 2961 (1993) (real estate agent liable for conduct of employees without knowledge they were discriminating and regardless of having provided training on nondiscriminatory procedures); Walker v. Crigler, 976 F.2d 900, 904 (4th Cir. 1992) (property owner liable for discriminatory acts of agent even without owner's knowledge or intent).

Any person who has suffered housing discrimination may sue in federal court for up to two years after the alleged discrimination occurred.[112] An aggrieved individual can also file with the Department of Housing and Urban Development (HUD) or a substantially equivalent state or city agency within one year from the last incident of discrimination.[113] In cases in which the state or local agency is substantially equivalent to HUD, which means that the rights, procedures, and remedies are substantially equivalent to those created by the FHA, the case is referred to that agency. Filing with an administrative agency, rather than the courts, is preferable in cases in which initially there is insufficient evidence of discrimination to produce a prima facie case. HUD or the local agency investigates the matter and determines whether discrimination was the cause of the negative treatment. The agency finds either probable cause to believe discrimination exists or no probable cause. Either finding is admissible in a court of law.[114] Although state and local adjudication procedures may differ, if the complaint remains with HUD, as opposed to being referred to a state or local agency, HUD investigates and is then required to issue a finding within 100 days.[115] However, HUD often fails to issue a finding within 100 days, and many local and state agencies may take up to two years to make a determination. Another disadvantage of this process is that the complainant has virtually no control over the quality of the investigation or the content of the final report.

Upon a finding of probable cause, either party has the option of proceeding to federal court.[116] For the aggrieved party, the advantage is a federal trial with free representation by the Department of Justice. The disadvantage is that the department's client is the United States, not the individual complainant. The aggrieved individual may intervene with her own attorney.[117] If neither party elects to proceed in federal court, the case after discovery is heard by an ALJ, who should issue a decision within 120 days. The ALJ may award injunctive relief, compensatory damages, and civil penalties, which, unlike court-awarded punitive damages, go to the government rather than to the complainant. At any point prior to a final finding, an action may also be brought in state or federal court. The two-year statute of limitations does not include the time during which an administrative proceeding is pending.

---

[112] When there is a continuing violation over many years, the two-year statute of limitation does not commence until the last incident of discrimination.

[113] 42 U.S.C. § 3604(f)(3)(A).

[114] Douglas v. Chase Management Co., Fair Hous.-Fair Lending Cas. (P-H) ¶ 15,669 (N.D. Ga. 1990).

[115] Kelly v. HUD, 3 F.3d 951 (6th Cir. 1993); Baumgardner v. HUD, 960 F.2d 572 (6th Cir. 1992); HUD v. Elroy R. & Dorothy Burns Trust, Fair Hous.-Fair Lending (P-H) ¶ 25,073 (A.L.J. 1994).

[116] 42 U.S.C. § 3612; 24 C.F.R. § 103.410 (1996).

[117] 42 U.S.C. § 3614(e).

Successful FHA plaintiffs can obtain compensatory damages, including out-of-pocket expenses as well as damages for intangible injuries, such as humiliation and embarrassment.[118] Under the FHA, the plaintiff's testimony alone is sufficient to support a claim for emotional damages, and the testimony of a psychologist or other medical expert is not required.[119] Compensatory damages may also include the costs of searching for a new home and moving,[120] the difference between the refused housing and the rent or purchase price for other housing the plaintiff ultimately found, estimates on the value of features lost within the residence, and even the cost of a longer commute[121] or a move to a less desirable school district for the plaintiff's children.

A plaintiff may also obtain injunctive and other equitable relief on an emergency basis or at the resolution of her case. In emergency situations, a preliminary injunction may be obtained, for example, to allow a plaintiff facing eviction to remain in her home, or to prevent the sale or rental of the housing in which the plaintiff resides or desires to reside until a final ruling by the court. This obviously imposes a burden on a landlord or owner/seller, who faces significant potential economic loss, and thus it would be ordered by the court only when there is substantial likelihood that the plaintiff will prevail on the merits. Other common forms of injunctive relief include fair housing education for the defendant's employees, requiring objective selection criteria for the processing of all applicants, mandating marketing and advertising the availability of all housing in a manner in which the individuals formerly discriminated against could be reached, and monitoring by a fair housing organization of all selection decisions made with respect to property transfers.[122]

Punitive damages are also available to punish the defendant. Punitive damages may be awarded if the defendant has acted maliciously, knowingly, or with reckless disregard of the plaintiff's rights.[123] They are awarded to punish the defendant and to serve as an example and warning to others not to engage in similar behavior. Unlike compensatory damages, punitive damages are based on the defendant's financial status and degree of wrongdoing rather than the actual extent of the plaintiff's damages. When the Department of Justice prosecutes an FHA case, a civil penalty can be assessed for the same reasons as punitive damages, that is, to punish and deter.

---

[118] Hamilton v. Svatik, 779 F.2d 383, 388–89 (7th Cir. 1985); Phillips v. Hunter Trails Community Ass'n, 685 F.2d 184, 190 (7th Cir. 1982).

[119] United States v. Balistrieri, 981 F.2d 916, 931–33 (7th Cir. 1992), *cert. denied,* 114 S. Ct. 58 (1993).

[120] Woods-Drake v. Lundy, 667 F.2d 1198, 1203 (5th Cir. 1982).

[121] HUD v. Elroy R. & Dorothy Burns Trust, Fair Hous.-Fair Lending (P-H) ¶ 25,073 (A.L.J. 1994).

[122] For other examples, see Fair Hous.-Fair Lending (P-H) § 19,300 (Consent Decrees); John Relman, Housing Discrimination Litigation Practice Manual (1992).

[123] Phiffer v. Proud Parrot Motor Hotel, 648 F.2d 548, 553 (9th Cir. 1980).

Finally, the FHA provides for attorney's fees and costs to be paid by the defendant if the plaintiff prevails.[124]

§ 6.11   State and Local Nondiscrimination Laws

In addition to the remedies provided by the Fair Housing Act (FHA) discussed in §§ **6.4** through **6.10,** practitioners should consider the protections provided by state and local laws. The FHA does not preempt state or local fair housing laws.[125] In several respects, local laws may provide protections that are not available under federal law. In particular, because the FHA's coverage is limited to residential housing opportunities, nonresidential use of space may be covered under state or local law (or, under ADA, covered in **Chapter 4**). In New York, for example, nondiscrimination laws extend to the leasing of commercial properties for use as professional offices, with the result that discrimination against a tenant who intended to provide services to persons with AIDS was successfully challenged.[126] The majority of states, and many localities as well, have nondiscrimination laws that extend to persons with HIV infection. These state statutes frequently parallel the federal disability discrimination definition, with the result that HIV infection is covered. Thus, like federal law, some states prohibit "handicap" or "disability" discrimination, terms that have been interpreted to include HIV infection, whether asymptomatic or symptomatic. The judicial interpretations of disability under the ADA are discussed in **Chapter 3**. Also, reference to decisions involving more frequently reported employment discrimination cases is important insofar as those cases interpret terms that apply not just in the employment context, but in that of housing as well.[127]

As is the case with federal law, many state and local laws prohibit discrimination on the basis of "perceived" disability. Even in state statutes that do not include the perceived as having a disability standard, the courts have interpreted the statute to include this category as necessary to effectuate the legislature's intent. For example, in *Poff v. Caro,*[128] the court held that a landlord's refusal to

---

[124] United States v. City of Taylor, 798 F. Supp. 442, 447–48 (E.D. Mich. 1992).

[125] 42 U.S.C. § 3615.

[126] Seitzman v. Hudson River Assocs., 542 N.Y.S.2d 104 (Sup. Ct. N.Y. County 1989) (successful discrimination claim of physicians whose practice included AIDS patients).

[127] *See, e.g.,* Joel Truitt Management v. District of Columbia Comm'n on Human Rights, 646 A.2d 1007, 1009 n.2 (D.C. 1994) (referencing employment guideline for definition of AIDS as a handicap in housing discrimination case).

[128] 549 A.2d 900 (N.J. Super. Ct. 1987). *See also* Sanchez v. Lagoudakis, 486 N.W.2d 657 (Mich. 1992) (disability discrimination law extends to persons perceived to have AIDS, but who do not in fact have the disease), *rev'g* 457 N.W.2d 373 (Mich. Ct. App. 1990); Petri v. Bank of N.Y. Co., 582 N.Y.S.2d 608, 611 (Sup. Ct. N.Y. County 1992) (asymptomatic HIV infection, whether perceived or actual, is disability under New York nondiscrimination law).

rent to gay tenants, based on the landlord's view that they had or would contract AIDS, brought them within the protection of the handicap discrimination statute.

Several states and localities have specifically added AIDS, HIV infection, or similar terms as conditions explicitly protected from discrimination.[129] Many localities have also adopted such protections.[130]

§ 6.12 Disclosure of HIV Information in Real Estate Transactions

Selling a home in which a person with HIV or AIDS has lived may present the problem that potential buyers, acting out of fear or distaste, may regard the property with disapproval and offer only a fraction of the property's fair market value. On the other hand, if sellers and their agents do not disclose that a former owner or resident had HIV and that information subsequently becomes available to a new owner, the owner may perceive that the property's value is lower than the amount paid and assert a claim against the seller or seller's agent for failing to disclose the information. Alternatively, if the broker discloses the information, the broker may fear that the owner will make a claim of discrimination under federal or state housing nondiscrimination laws. Properties in this circumstance are sometimes referred to as "psychologically impacted," referring to the fact that the so-called defect is not a physical aspect of the property or its surroundings, but instead is simply the psychological impact or stigmatizing effect that the information regarding a former resident has on the buyer. Not insignificantly, properties that have AIDS in their histories are often grouped with properties in which there has been a murder or suicide, or that are rumored to be haunted by ghosts. This issue has received repeated critical commentary.[131] Despite the views of commentators in favor of a rule of disclosure, many states

---

[129] *See, e.g.,* N.H. Rev. Stat. Ann. 354-A:10 (1995) (prohibiting eviction on basis of AIDS or perception of AIDS); R.I. Gen. Laws § 23-6-22 (1995) (nondiscrimination in housing on "basis of positive AIDS test result"); Mo. Ann. Stat. §§ 191.665, 213.010 (protecting against discrimination on basis of HIV infection or AIDS in housing) (Vernon 1996).

[130] *See, e.g.,* Phillips v. Mufleh, 642 N.E.2d 411 (Ohio Ct. App. 1994) (per curiam) (affirming award of punitive damages under Toledo municipal ordinance in case in which hotel proprietor excluded a customer with AIDS).

[131] *See, e.g.,* Robert M. Washburn, *Residential Real Estate Condition Disclosure Legislation,* 44 DePaul L. Rev. 381, 447 n.465 (1995) (noting that enactment of shield laws for sellers or brokers in regard to disclosure of AIDS information goes against general trend of disclosure legislation); Ross R. Hartog, Note, *The Psychological Impact of AIDS on Real Property and a Real Estate Broker's Duty to Disclose,* 36 Ariz. L. Rev. 757 (1994) (recommending legislation that makes disclosure of AIDS material to transaction, thus no liability to seller for broker's disclosure); Sharlene A. McEvoy, *Caveat Emptor Redux: "Psychologically Impacted" Property Statutes,* 18 W. St. U. L. Rev. 579 (1991) (contending that shield statutes for nondisclosure of AIDS information improperly withhold material facts regarding the transaction); Marianne M. Jennings, *Buying Property from the Addams Family,* 22 Real Est. L.J. 43 (1993).

have addressed the problem of these AIDS-stigmatized properties by statutes that protect sellers and brokers from liability for withholding such information.

The seminal case in this area of the law, *Reed v. King*,[132] held that the seller and the seller's agent could be liable for withholding information that multiple murders had occurred in the home some 10 years earlier. The same result might have been viewed as appropriate in the case of a property in which a person with AIDS has resided. However, three years later the ruling in *Reed* was reversed by the California legislature in regard to HIV.[133] Intentional misrepresentation, however, is prohibited.[134] Conceptually, the buyer's action in offering less than the fair market value of a property because the property is stigmatized is a form of discrimination, similar to that prohibited by the FHA. In a similar vein, the Texas attorney general ruled that a Texas statute requiring disclosure of AIDS in real estate transactions violates the Fair Housing Act,[135] and that statute was subsequently repealed.[136]

Similar legislation has been adopted in other states.[137] These laws simply define AIDS or HIV information as immaterial to the transaction and thus not subject to disclosure, but they do not prevent a buyer from inquiring about such circumstances. If a buyer asks and the statute does not specify that a truthful response must be provided, it is unclear whether the seller or broker would need to provide one, because the seller could subsequently argue that the information was statutorily defined as immaterial, and thus the buyer could not have relied on it as a matter of law.[138]

§ 6.13 Succession of Rights in Shared Housing

If individuals with HIV are gay men or low-income persons living in nontraditional relationships and not related by blood or lawful marriage, problems can

---

[132] 193 Cal. Rptr. 130 (Ct. App. 1983).

[133] Cal. Civ. Code § 1710.2 (West 1996) (protecting both seller and agent).

[134] Cal. Civ. Code § 1710.2(d).

[135] Tex. Atty. Gen. Op. No. JM-1093 (1989).

[136] Tex. Rev. Civ. Stat. Ann. art. 6573a, § 15E (West 1996) (no duty to inquire about, disclose, or release information related to AIDS, HIV-related illnesses, or HIV infection, or death on property by natural causes, suicide, or accident unrelated to the condition of the property).

[137] *See, e.g.,* Colo. Rev. Stat. Ann. § 38-35.5-101 (West 1995) (psychological impact facts or suspicions are not material, including HIV/AIDS "or any other disease which has been determined by medical evidence to be highly unlikely to be transmitted through the occupancy of a dwelling place"; no cause of action against seller's agent); Conn. Gen. Stat. § 20-329cc (West 1996) (same, but references owner as well as agent); Utah Code Ann. § 57-1-1 (Supp. 1993) (defining stigmatized property as dwelling place of person infected or suspected of being infected with HIV or other infectious disease that the Health Department determines cannot be transferred by occupancy).

[138] *But see* Van Camp v. Bradford, 623 N.E.2d 731 (Ohio C.P., Butler County 1993) (noting that nondisclosure statutes do not authorize seller or agent to make any misrepresentation in response to buyer's inquiry).

arise when the person listed on the lease of the shared housing dies. As a practical matter, this circumstance can be avoided by adding at least one other resident to the lease, although this may have the disadvantage of obligating the other resident for the rent in the event the first tenant defaults. Alternatively, if the lease provides that the lease is held by the tenant as well as the tenant's heirs, then leaving the leasehold to the surviving resident by will or other testamentary document would protect the second tenant's right to the apartment. In some cases a landlord may simply agree to execute a new lease for the surviving tenant, but in jurisdictions in which rental units are subject to rent control or stabilization programs, landlords have a significant incentive to negotiate a new lease at a significantly increased rent, not subject to rent stabilization or control. The unmarried partner may not be protected under rent control regulations, which are limited to married spouses or blood relatives.

In *Two Associates v. Brown,*[139] however, the court ruled that New York City's rent stabilization regulations were unconstitutional insofar as they failed to extend the same rights to unmarried couples as were granted to married couples. Another case, *Braschi v. Stahl Associates Co.,*[140] ruled that New York City's rent control program's definition of family should include "two adult life-time partners whose relationship is long-term and characterized by an emotional and financial commitment and interdependence." Following and expanding the *Braschi* rationale, the New York Division of Housing and Community Renewal issued new regulations for rent-controlled and rent-stabilized apartments and expanded the definition of family to include unmarried partners.[141] In other jurisdictions, these issues may be addressed by the adoption of domestic partnership legislation that recognizes same-sex and other unmarried relationships on a par with legally married opposite-sex couples.[142]

---

[139] 502 N.Y.S.2d 604 (Sup. Ct. N.Y. County 1986).

[140] 543 N.E.2d 48, 54 (N.Y. 1989).

[141] N.Y. City Rent Regs., tit. 9, subtit. S, subchs. A & B (1990), *upheld in* Rent Stabilization Ass'n v. Higgins, 562 N.Y.S.2d 962 (App. Div. 1990).

[142] For a discussion of the history of these issues in New York City and San Francisco, two areas with significant impact from the epidemic, see National Research Council, The Social Impact of AIDS in the United States 219–36 (Albert R. Jonsen & Jeff Stryker eds., 1993).

CRIMINAL LAW

David L. McColgin
Elizabeth T. Hey*

* Mr. McColgin authored the substantive law and fair trial and post-conviction sections, §§ 7.1
through 7.12, 7.19 through 7.22; Ms. Hey authored the sections on search and seizure law,
§§ 7.13 through 7.18. Both authors acknowledge the extensive research assistance provided
by Dina Chavar, Paralegal, Defender Association of Philadelphia, Federal Court Division,
and third-year student at Temple University School of Law.

§ 7.1   The Problems Inherent in a Criminal Justice Response to an Epidemic

The HIV epidemic has provoked a criminal justice response of historic proportions. Prosecutors have brought high-publicity cases against HIV positive people under attempted murder[1] and assault statutes,[2] as well as under recently enacted laws specifically criminalizing conduct thought to create a risk of HIV

---

[1] *See, e.g.,* State v. Smith, 621 A.2d 493 (N.J. Super. Ct. 1993); Tom Hester, *Appeals Court Upholds Conviction of HIV-Infected Inmate Who Bit Guard; Judges Rule Defendant's Intent Outweighs Scientific Evidence,* Star Ledger (Trenton, N.J.), Feb. 18, 1993, *available in* Westlaw Allnews file (case discussed in § **7.2**).

[2] *See, e.g.,* United States v. Moore, 846 F.2d 1163 (8th Cir. 1988); Bill Deener, *AIDS Fight Moving into Nation's Courtrooms; Criminal Cases Target Carriers Who Knowingly Spread Virus,* Dallas Morning News, Aug. 24, 1987, *available in* Westlaw, Allnews file (case discussed in § **7.3**).

In one of the most publicized cases of criminal prosecution of a person with AIDS, the defendant, Edward Savitz, after a year in jail, died just before his case was to come to trial. Mr. Savitz had been charged with sexual contact with four males aged 13 to 16. In the criminal prosecution against Savitz, there was no allegation that his activities posed any risk of HIV infection. After his arrest, however, Philadelphia District Attorney Lynne Abraham called a press conference to announce the arrest and the fact that the defendant had AIDS, for the purpose of informing those who had had sexual contact with Savitz that they may have been put at risk for HIV. At the same time, Abraham refused to disclose the identity of the defendant, purportedly because Pennsylvania law protected such information from disclosure, although the news media had no difficulty in identifying the defendant. A storm of publicity followed, and the district attorney made a series of appearances on national television shows, including *Today, Larry King Live,* and *Nightline.* Mr. Savitz's bail, set initially at $3 million and then increased to $20 million, prevented his pretrial release. After his health declined to such an extent that it was not possible for him to be tried, he was released to an AIDS hospice, where he died a week later. Barnaby C. Wittels & Stephen Robert LaCheen, *The Persecution of Ed Savitz,* Phila. Inquirer, May 12, 1993, at A11. *See also* Lynne M. Abraham, *Ed Savitz Was No Victim, No Icon of Virtue,* Phila. Inquirer, June 1, 1993, at A13 (arguing that the pretrial publicity was not the fault of the prosecutor but instead was generated by the defense attorneys and also by dozens of young boys who "gleefully" told the press of their sexual contacts with Savitz); Loren Feldman, *The Trials of Abraham,* Phila. Mag., July 1996, at 68, 71 (in interview, Philadelphia District Attorney Lynne Abraham stated that "if we didn't announce that [Savitz] was AIDS-infected, we would be accused of hiding evidence").

transmission.[3] Never before have states sought to enact criminal laws and use criminal prosecutions so aggressively in an effort to fight an epidemic and quell public fears of a disease.[4] Some politicians and prosecutors evidently believe that criminal prosecutions and criminal laws can supplement the efforts of public health authorities. A look at history, however, shows that compulsory measures have in the past been ineffective in controlling diseases.

During World War I, the United States implemented a largely coercive program to control venereal disease. The program required the closing of houses of prostitution, the mandatory testing and incarceration of prostitutes, and punishment for servicemen who became infected.[5] Over 20,000 prostitutes were held in camps and local jails.[6] These compulsory measures constituted the "most concerted attack on civil liberties in the name of public health in American history."[7] Yet, despite their widespread popular appeal, these measures did nothing to stem the tide of venereal disease, particularly in the absence of a cure. Instead, the incidence of venereal disease actually increased during the war.[8] During World War II, in contrast, the federal government implemented a program that emphasized noncompulsory measures such as condom distribution in the military, massive education, and rapid treatment of infected service members without punishment. These noncompulsory measures were highly successful and rates of venereal disease went down.[9] No doubt the discovery in 1943 that penicillin could effectively treat venereal diseases such as syphilis contributed greatly to the dramatic reduction in levels of venereal diseases over the next decade. However, even before the discovery of penicillin, noncompulsory measures such as voluntary confidential testing during the 1930s led to a decline in

---

[3] *See, e.g.,* State v. Stark, 832 P.2d 109 (Wash. Ct. App. 1992); *Port Angeles Man Guilty of Exposing Woman to AIDS Virus,* Portland Oregonian, June 7, 1990, at C2 (case discussed in **§ 7.8**).

[4] J. Kelly Strader, *Criminalization as a Policy Response to a Public Health Crisis,* 27 J. Marshall L. Rev. 435, 445 (1994).

[5] Stephen V. Kenney, Comment, *Criminalizing HIV Transmission: Lessons from History and a Model for the Future,* 8 J. Contemp. Health L. & Pol'y 245, 255 (1992).

[6] Allan M. Brandt, *AIDS in Historical Perspective: Four Lessons from the History of Sexually Transmitted Diseases,* 78 Am. J. Pub. Health 367, 370 (1988). For an in-depth historical analysis of the efforts to control venereal disease in the United States since 1880, see Allan M. Brandt, No Magic Bullet: A Social History of Venereal Disease in the United States Since 1880 (1987).

[7] Allan M. Brandt, *AIDS: From Social History to Social Policy,* 14 Law Med. & Health Care 231, 233 (1988).

[8] Allan M. Brandt, *AIDS in Historical Perspective: Four Lessons from the History of Sexually Transmitted Diseases,* 78 Am. J. Pub. Health 367, 370 (1988).

[9] Allan M. Brandt, *The Syphilis Epidemic and Its Relation to AIDS,* 239 Science 375, 379 (1988).

rates of infection in certain urban areas (like Chicago) which implemented these measures. Conversely, when the federal government in the 1950s and 1960s greatly reduced funding for venereal disease programs (which included public education, case-finding, tracing, and diagnostics), rates of venereal disease went up, in spite of the widespread availability of antibiotics. Thus, history shows that whether or not a "cure" is available, noncompulsory public health measures are a crucial part of any campaign to reduce sexually transmitted diseases.[10]

The lesson to be learned from these past efforts is that, in spite of their popularity, compulsory measures such as criminal sanctions do not work to control an epidemic. Instead, such measures may actually be counterproductive.[11] Public health authorities today agree that the most effective means of stopping the spread of HIV is widespread confidential or anonymous testing combined with counseling and education programs and the availability of condoms and needle

---

[10] *Id.* at 379–80. *See also* John C. Cutler & R.C. Arnold, *Venereal Disease Control by Health Departments in the Past: Lessons for the Present,* 78 Am. J. Pub. Health 372, 374–75 (1988) (concluding that past experience demonstrates the effectiveness of noncompulsory public health measures such as public education encouraging "self-protective sexual behavior and practices such as condom usage and discrimination in patterns of sexual behavior").

Although there clearly are lessons to be learned from the history of venereal disease programs in deciding how best to address the HIV epidemic, there are also important differences between venereal disease and HIV. HIV is far more stigmatizing and thus it is much more likely to result in discriminatory treatment. For this reason, although an approach like mandatory name reporting might be appropriate for venereal disease, it is counterproductive for HIV because the fear of discrimination is likely to drive those at risk for HIV away from public health authorities. *See* New York State Soc'y of Surgeons v. Axelrod, 572 N.E.2d 605 (N.Y. 1991) (articulating New York state health commissioner's reasons for deciding not to add HIV to list of diseases subject to reporting, mandatory testing, and contact tracing). Accordingly, public health strategies addressing venereal disease and those addressing HIV are not comparable in all respects.

[11] J. Kelly Strader, *Criminalization as a Policy Response to a Public Health Crisis,* 27 J. Marshall L. Rev. 435, 447 (1994) ("The HIV/AIDS epidemic can be contained by more effective and less costly means than enacting and enforcing new criminal statutes."); Mark H. Jackson, *The Criminalization of HIV, in* AIDS Agenda 239, 241 (Nan D. Hunter & William B. Rubenstein eds., 1992) (the use of coercive measures to fight the HIV epidemic would be impossible to implement, ineffective, and counterproductive to public health efforts to encourage testing and treatment); Larry Gostin, *The Politics of AIDS: Compulsory State Powers, Public Health, and Civil Liberties,* 49 Ohio St. L.J. 1017, 1020 (1989) ("compulsory state powers have little place in fighting a disease epidemic"); Allan M. Brandt, *AIDS in Historical Perspective: Four Lessons from the History of Sexually Transmitted Diseases,* 78 Am. J. Pub. Health 367, 370 (1988) (compulsory measures will not control the HIV epidemic); Kathleen M. Sullivan & Martha A. Field, *AIDS and the Coercive Power of the State,* 23 Harv. C.R.-C.L. L. Rev. 139, 156–62, 186–97 (1988) (quarantine and criminalization are poor approaches to the HIV epidemic). *But see* David Robinson, *Criminal Sanctions and Quarantine, in* AIDS and the Law § 8.2 (2d ed. 1992) (noting that the goal of criminal sanctions against transmission of HIV is to "isolate offenders from the general population to reduce the spread of a lethal virus"); Jacob A. Heth, *Dangerous Liaisons: Criminalizing Conduct Related to HIV Transmission,* 29 Willamette L. Rev. 843 (1993) (arguing that due to the severe consequences of HIV infection, criminalizing conduct likely to transmit the virus is justified).

exchange programs.[12] If, however, the states aggressively pursue criminal prosecutions under traditional criminal laws or newly enacted HIV transmission statutes, the very people at highest risk for HIV may, as some commentators have argued, have an incentive not to get tested and to avoid public health programs.[13] They may fear that testing positive could create a risk of criminal liability. Moreover, high publicity prosecutions for conduct that poses no risk of HIV transmission such as spitting or biting not only waste judicial resources but may also further public misconceptions about how HIV is spread. Such prosecutions thus can undermine public education efforts.[14]

For these reasons, the Presidential Commission on the Human Immunodeficiency Virus Epidemic, which was established by President Reagan to recommend ways of slowing the spread of HIV, found that "traditional criminal laws are not well suited to prevention of HIV transmission."[15] The Commission expressed its "concern that criminal sanctions will undermine public health goals by diverting attention and resources from effective prevention policies such as education, testing, [and] counseling . . . [and will also] inhibit people from seeking testing."[16]

Criminal prosecutions, therefore, should not be viewed as part of a public health strategy to stop the spread of HIV. Instead, criminal prosecution should be reserved for only the most egregious cases—those involving intentional or reckless conduct that deserves punishment because it creates a genuine risk of HIV transmission. The following are proposed prosecutorial guidelines for when and how HIV-related criminal charges could justifiably be brought. These guidelines would help prevent criminal prosecutions from interfering with public health efforts to fight the HIV epidemic:

---

[12] John C. Cutler & R.C. Arnold, *Venereal Disease Control by Health Departments in the Past: Lessons for the Present,* 78 Am. J. Pub. Health 372, 374–75 (1988) (advocating public education efforts that promote condom usage and safe sex practices and concluding that a "judgmental, moralistic attitude" is not helpful; the authors are retired Assistant Surgeons General, U.S. Public Health Service); National Research Council, *Preventing HIV Transmission; The Role of Sterile Needles and Bleach* (Jacques Normand et al. eds., 1995) (finding that needle-exchange programs are an effective component of a comprehensive strategy to prevent transmission of HIV and recommending that the Surgeon General certify that federal funds be made available to support such programs); National Comm'n on AIDS, Report: The Twin Epidemics of Substance Use and HIV 10–11 (1991). *See generally* **Ch. 2.**

[13] J. Kelly Strader, *Criminalization as a Policy Response to a Public Health Crisis,* 27 J. Marshall L. Rev. 435, 443–47 (1994); Mark H. Jackson, *The Criminalization of HIV, in* AIDS Agenda 239, 251–52 (Nan D. Hunter & William B. Rubenstein eds., 1992). Although commentators such as Strader and Jackson have argued that criminal sanctions are counterproductive to public health efforts, no studies have been done to establish whether or to what extent compulsory measures such as criminal sanctions actually do discourage people at risk for HIV from being tested or receiving treatment.

[14] Harlon L. Dalton, *Criminal Law, in* AIDS Law Today 242, 256 (Scott Burris et al. eds., 1993).

[15] Report of the Presidential Commission on the Human Immunodeficiency Virus Epidemic 130 (1988).

[16] *Id.*

1. The case must involve either force, coercion, a victim whose consent is inadequate because of age or other capacity, or affirmative deceit regarding HIV status. This guideline would bar prosecution in cases involving sexual conduct if the sexual partner of the accused assumed some risk of infection through a consensual relationship in which there was no affirmative deceit by the accused regarding his or her HIV status. It is interesting to note that, outside of the military courts (discussed in § **7.9**), all the reported HIV-related prosecutions appear to have complied with this guideline insofar as they have all involved some degree of force or affirmative deceit (see §§ **7.2** through **7.4**).

2. The accused must have known prior to the offense conduct that he or she was infected with HIV, but the prosecution's proof of this knowledge must not be derived from confidential medical or social service sources. This guideline would prevent the prosecution of HIV-related criminal cases from discouraging people at risk for HIV from being tested.[17]

3. The accused must have been aware of the risk of HIV transmission posed to the victim by the offense conduct. This guideline would require proof either that the accused received counseling regarding the risks of HIV transmission, or that he or she made a statement indicating awareness of the risk.

4. The offense's conduct must have posed a clear and medically significant risk of transmission of HIV (not merely a theoretical risk), and the accused must have failed to employ reasonable prophylactic measures (such as use of a condom) to prevent transmission of HIV. This guideline would eliminate prosecutions, like the spitting cases discussed in § **7.2,** in which there is no medically significant risk of HIV transmission. Also, by barring prosecution in cases in which the accused did, for example, use a condom, the guideline would encourage people to follow the safer sex guidelines advocated by public health institutions.

5. The accused must be clearly capable of engaging in similar behavior in the future. The purpose of this guideline would be to avoid the pointless prosecution of people who are either about to die from HIV or are too sick and incapacitated to pose any real danger to the community.

6. The prosecution must not seek to publicize the case before trial, and the identity of the accused should not be revealed in public or in any court records open to the public. The purpose of this guideline is to prevent the prejudicial pretrial publicity that can accompany the filing of charges in an HIV-related case. Also, because infection with HIV can be very stigmatizing, it

---

[17] *See* State v. J.E., 606 A.2d 1160, 1162 (N.J. Super. Ct. Law Div. 1992) (holding that interests of HIV positive inmates in maintaining privacy of medical records outweighed interests of complainant and public in disclosure of that information: "[I]f confidentiality of AIDS records is not maintained, inmates may elect not to report their HIV status to correctional authorities. . . . This reluctance to seek treatment and counselling can logically result in the disease being spread further either within an institution or beyond.").

is important to maintain the anonymity of the accused because that is the only way to maintain the confidentiality of the accused's HIV status during a trial. See § **7.18**. The government's interest in deterring similar crimes can best be served by waiting until after the trial and then publicizing the conviction, if there is one.[18]

7. The penalties imposed should be proportionate both to the actual risk of HIV transmission posed by the accused's conduct and to penalties for other crimes creating a comparable risk of injury.

This chapter begins with an analysis of traditional criminal laws and their use to prosecute those who create a risk of HIV transmission. **Section 7.2** analyzes prosecutions under homicide and attempted homicide statutes. **Section 7.3** looks at the use of assault statutes, and § **7.4** looks at the use of reckless endangerment statutes. **Sections 7.5** through **7.7** examine, respectively, the use of sodomy statutes, prostitution statutes, and communicable disease control statutes, concluding that all three are poorly suited to fighting the spread of HIV. **Section 7.8** then examines an alternative to the traditional criminal statutes: the slew of recently enacted laws specifically criminalizing conduct that might cause transmission of HIV. These new laws generally suffer from vagueness and over-inclusiveness. **Sections 7.9** through **7.12** review how the military courts have been treating prosecutions for HIV transmission. **Section 7.20** analyzes the defenses of diminished capacity, insanity, and incompetency and their applicability to HIV-infected defendants.

Sections 7.13 through **7.18** address the involuntary testing of criminal defendants for HIV and the extent of the government's authority to obtain and use a defendant's HIV-related medical information. **Section 7.14** outlines search and seizure law as it pertains to involuntary testing in general. **Section 7.15** applies that law in the context of HIV testing for purposes of prosecuting the defendant for a crime, including bail, trial, and sentencing purposes. **Sections 7.16** and **7.17** apply search and seizure law to the issue of testing for purposes of notifying a complainant of the defendant's HIV status. **Section 7.18** examines the issues relating to the disclosure of a defendant's HIV-related medical records, including access to medical records and the use by the prosecution of test results that were originally gathered just for purposes of complainant notification.

The last sections of the chapter address how HIV infected criminal defendants are treated in the courts. **Section 7.19** discusses bail and fair trial issues such as the use of prejudicial and unnecessary precautions during the trial of an HIV infected defendant. **Section 7.21** addresses sentencing issues, including the relevance of a defendant's HIV status as a mitigating or an aggravating factor. Lastly, § **7.22** examines motions to vacate a plea or sentence that may be filed by a defendant who discovers only after conviction that he or she is infected with HIV.

---

[18] *See* People v. Anonymous, 582 N.Y.S.2d 350 (Monroe County Ct. 1992) (allowing HIV testing and release of medical records for defendant accused of biting two people, but requiring that defendant's name be kept confidential).

HIV AND SUBSTANTIVE CRIMINAL LAW

§ 7.2 Homicide and Attempted Homicide

Prosecutors have charged HIV-infected people with attempted homicide in cases involving sexual conduct[19] as well as in cases involving spitting[20] and biting.[21] Most of these cases illustrate the danger that in an atmosphere of AIDS hysteria, draconian criminal sanctions may be imposed for conduct that in fact poses no significant risk of HIV transmission. Indeed, several courts have ruled that as long as there is evidence that the defendant believed his or her actions could transmit the virus, it does not matter that the actual risk of transmission may have been negligible.[22] In other cases, so-called experts have persuaded juries, contrary to the mainstream of scientific opinion, that actions such as spitting could transmit the virus, and convictions have resulted.[23] Such convictions do nothing to educate the public about behaviors that really do create a risk of HIV transmission; instead, they merely advance common misconceptions and incarcerate defendants for harmless conduct.

Criminal laws in the United States are primarily enacted and enforced on the state and local levels. As a result, the definitions of offenses vary from state to state. Most states, however, have revised their criminal codes in recent years, usually guided by the American Law Institute's Model Penal Code,[24] and thus some degree of generalization is possible.

Under the Model Penal Code a homicide can either be *murder* (a homicide committed purposely, knowingly, or with extreme recklessness),[25] *manslaughter* (a reckless homicide),[26] or *negligent homicide* (a homicide committed negligently).[27] Primarily for two reasons, however, there have been no prosecutions for homicide resulting from HIV transmission. First, prosecution for homicide obviously requires the death of the victim, and death from HIV is unlikely to occur until many years after the act of transmission.[28] By that time the HIV-infected

---

[19] *E.g.,* State v. Hinkhouse, 912 P.2d 921, *modified,* 915 P.2d 489 (Or. Ct. App. 1996).

[20] *E.g.,* Weeks v. State, 834 S.W.2d 559 (Tx. Ct. App. 1992).

[21] *E.g.,* State v. Smith, 621 A.2d 493 (N.J. Super. Ct.), *cert. denied,* 634 A.2d 523 (N.J. 1993).

[22] *E.g., id.*

[23] *E.g.,* Weeks v. State, 834 S.W.2d 559 (Tx. Ct. App. 1992).

[24] *Definition of Specific Crimes, Offenses Involving Danger to the Person,* Model Penal Code, pt. II (1985).

[25] Model Penal Code §§ 210.2 (1985).

[26] *Id.* § 210.3.

[27] *Id.* 210.4. *See also id.* § 2.02 (general requirements of culpability: definitions of "purposely," "knowingly," "recklessly," "negligently").

[28] Only about 50 percent of people infected with HIV will develop AIDS within 10 years of infection. Moreover, even after an AIDS diagnosis, particularly with the advent of medications to treat opportunistic infections, people can continue to live for years, as is more fully discussed in **Ch. 1.**

transferor is also likely be dead. In about half the states, moreover, there is a requirement that the victim's death occur within a year and a day of the criminal act,[29] thus making any prosecution for homicide even more unlikely.

Second, the prosecution in a homicide case has to prove causation, that it was the accused who actually infected the deceased victim with HIV. Proof of causation is extremely difficult, especially because most people infected with HIV may have contracted the virus from any number of different sources. Ruling out all conceivable sources other than the accused is close to impossible, especially once the victim is dead and unavailable to testify regarding his or her lifestyle and risk factors. In addition, laboratory tests matching the strain of HIV present in the victim with the strain of the virus in the accused are very expensive, and the tests are not 100 percent reliable, particularly if much time has elapsed between the alleged transmission and the testing.[30] It is thus very unlikely that there will ever be a successful prosecution for homicide resulting from HIV transmission.

There have, however, been several prosecutions for attempted homicide. The crime of attempted homicide is much easier to prove than homicide because it avoids problems of proof; the victim need not have died, and there is no need to prove causation because the victim need not have actually been infected with HIV. Attempted homicide does require proof, however, that the accused acted with the intent or purpose to cause the death of the victim.[31] This element often is a major stumbling block for the prosecution because in most cases it would be difficult to prove specific intent to kill absent some express statement by the defendant. In addition, it is hard to understand why anyone truly intending to kill someone would choose HIV infection as the means, because HIV is unlikely to result in death for many years. Aside from the element of specific intent, the prosecution typically must also prove that the accused engaged in some conduct that he or she believed would result in the death of the victim.[32]

Several of the prosecutions for attempted homicide have arisen from an HIV-infected person's having unprotected sex. In *State v. Hinkhouse,*[33] for example, the defendant was convicted in the state of Oregon of 10 counts of attempted murder based on his having had unprotected vaginal sexual intercourse with several different women over a period of years. Hinkhouse had been on probation, and when he tested positive for HIV, his probation officer repeatedly told him to use condoms. The officer also told him that infecting someone else with HIV would be murder. When Hinkhouse nonetheless continued having unprotected sex with women, his probation officer had him sign an agreement that he would not engage in any unsupervised contact with women without express

---

[29] Wayne R. LaFave & Austin W. Scott, Criminal Law 611 (2d ed. 1986).

[30] *See generally* Gerald Myers, *Molecular Investigation of HIV Transmission,* 121 Annals Internal Med. 889, 890 (1994).

[31] Model Penal Code § 5.01(b) (1985).

[32] *Id.* §§ 5.01(1)(b) (attempted homicide), 210.2 (murder).

[33] 912 P.2d 921, *modified,* 915 P.2d 489 (Or. Ct. App. 1996) (eliminating reference in original opinion to hearsay statement regarding defendant's threat to spread HIV).

permission from the officer. Still, Hinkhouse continued to have unsafe sex, refusing to use condoms even when women requested that he do so, and telling the women that he was not HIV-infected. One of his sexual partners was a 15-year-old girl who later tested positive for HIV. Hinkhouse eventually, however, met a woman whom he hoped to marry. He did inform her of his HIV infection, and when they had sex he always used a condom.[34]

On appeal, the defense argued that Hinkhouse, who suffered from attention deficit disorder, did not have the specific intent to murder but instead was acting recklessly and did not think about the consequences of his actions. The state appeals court, however, upheld the convictions, finding there was sufficient evidence of specific intent to murder. The court reasoned that the evidence that Hinkhouse had been advised not to have unprotected sex, that he had recruited sex partners over a period of years and not only lied to them about his HIV status but also refused to use condoms, showed a specific intent to kill people by infecting them with HIV. The court also found that Hinkhouse's unsafe sexual behavior was not merely for his own sexual gratification because he did use condoms with the one woman he planned to marry.[35]

This case is an egregious example of a defendant's persisting in unsafe sexual conduct. Most likely it was these bad facts that persuaded the appellate court to find that the evidence of specific intent was sufficient to uphold the attempted murder convictions, even though the evidence was equally consistent with a purely reckless state of mind. A more appropriate conviction in this case would have been for reckless endangerment, discussed in § **7.4.**

In a case factually analogous to *Hinkhouse,* Maryland's highest court held in *Smallwood v. State*[36] that the state's evidence was insufficient to prove intent, and the court reversed the defendant's convictions for attempted murder. The court held that the mere fact the defendant, Smallwood, knew he was infected with HIV when he raped three women was not sufficient to prove that he had the intent to kill them. Smallwood had tested positive while in prison, and, like Hinkhouse, he had been counseled on the importance of using condoms. Smallwood told his social worker that he had only one sexual partner and that he always used condoms. After his release from prison, Smallwood raped and robbed three women at gunpoint, each on separate occasions. In each instance Smallwood threatened to kill the woman if she did not cooperate, and he did not use condoms during any of the rapes. Smallwood was convicted of attempted murder, assault with intent to murder, rape, robbery, and reckless endangerment.[37]

On appeal, Smallwood challenged his convictions for attempted murder and assault with intent to murder on the ground that he did not have the specific intent to kill. The state argued that Smallwood's acts of unprotected sex while HIV positive were equivalent to firing a loaded gun at a person. Because it is

---

[34] *Id.* at 922–23.

[35] *Id.* at 924–25.

[36] 680 A.2d 512 (Md. 1996).

[37] *Id.* at 513–14.

well established that intent to kill can be inferred from the act of firing a deadly weapon at a person's body, the state argued that the same inference could be drawn here: Smallwood knew he was HIV positive, he knew that HIV could ultimately lead to death, and he knew that he would be exposing his victims to the risk of infection by having unprotected sex with them. Therefore, the state argued, it could be inferred that Smallwood had the intent to kill his rape victims by infecting them with HIV.[38]

The appeals court rejected the state's argument, reasoning that the magnitude of the risk to the victim must be considered. Although it is permissible to infer that "one intends the natural and probable consequences of his act," the state must show "that the victim's death would have been a natural and probable result of the defendant's conduct" before an intent to kill can be inferred.[39] Because firing a deadly weapon at a person creates a high probability of death, it is reasonable to infer that a defendant who shoots a gun at someone has an intent to kill. The court concluded, however, the state's evidence regarding the probability of death from AIDS was insufficient:

> While the risk to which Smallwood exposed his victims when he forced them to engage in unprotected sexual activity must not be minimized, the State has presented no evidence from which it can reasonably be concluded that death by AIDS is a probable result of Smallwood's actions to the same extent that death is the probable result of firing a deadly weapon at a vital part of someone's body.[40]

The court in *Smallwood* concluded that Smallwood's actions could be fully explained by his intent to rape and rob the women, and thus his acts failed to prove that he also had an intent to kill.[41]

Although *Smallwood* involved rape, and *Hinkhouse* involved consensual sex, the two cases are in other respects comparable. In both cases the defendants had been counseled on the importance of safe sex, and both defendants did use condoms

---

[38] *Id.* at 514.

[39] *Id.* at 516.

[40] *Id.* The prosecution, it should be noted, could never have proven that death by AIDS was probable because studies suggest that the per contact HIV infectivity rate during sexual intercourse between an HIV infected male and a female is as low as two per 1,000. Lawrence O. Gostin et al., *HIV Testing, Counseling, and Prophylaxis after Sexual Assault,* 271 JAMA 1436 (1994). The per contact infectivity rate for receptive anal intercourse between gay men is estimated at two per 100 contacts. *Id.* at 1437. "The risk of HIV transmission is highly variable, with some individuals infected after the first encounter, while others remain uninfected after hundreds of unprotected sexual contacts." *Id.* Factors that may affect the infectiousness of an assailant include the clinical stage of HIV infection, the presence of genital ulcerative sexually transmitted diseases, and the virulence of the viral strain. Unlike anal and vaginal intercourse, receptive oral exposure to ejaculate has been associated with HIV seroconversion only in very rare cases. *Id.*

[41] Smallwood v. State, 680 A.2d 512, 516 (Md. 1996). The reversal of Smallwood's attempted murder convictions, for which he had received concurrent thirty-year sentences, was a hollow victory for Smallwood since his sentence on the rape convictions, which were not challenged, was life in prison. *Id.* at 514.

with their primary girlfriends. On these facts, the court in *Hinkhouse* strained to conclude that the defendant there had an intent to kill, whereas the court in *Smallwood* correctly concluded that more evidence would be needed of the intent to kill in order to uphold the attempted murder convictions.

Some attempted homicide prosecutions have been for conduct like spitting or biting, which present no real threat of HIV transmission. In accordance with the Model Penal Code, however, in most states it is not a defense that under the circumstances of the case the murder would have been factually impossible.[42] Thus, several courts have ruled that it is irrelevant whether conduct such as spitting and biting can actually transmit HIV, as long as the accused believed that the conduct could cause transmission. The problem with these decisions is that they allow the prosecutor to make a serious crime out of essentially harmless behavior.[43] An HIV-positive person who spits on someone while thinking he will transmit HIV is essentially no more dangerous than a believer in voodoo who sticks needles into a doll while thinking that his actions will cause his intended victim pain and death.

In *State v. Haines,*[44] for example, the defendant, who was HIV positive, attempted suicide by slashing his wrists. When the police and emergency medical technicians arrived, Haines screamed at them that he had AIDS and should be left alone. As the police tried to restrain Haines, he threatened to use his wounds to give them AIDS and he said he would show everyone what it was like to have the disease and die. He then began spitting at them and biting and scratching them. He also sprayed blood on one of the officers and struck the officer in the face with a bloody wig. Haines was convicted on three charges of attempted murder, but the trial judge dismissed the charges on the ground that the state did not prove that AIDS could be spread by the conduct in this case.[45]

The appeals court reinstated the attempted murder charges, ruling that impossibility is not a defense. The court held that when a defendant has done all that he believes is necessary to commit a crime, regardless of what is possible, he has committed an attempt. The court also observed that some jurisdictions had recognized the defense of *inherent impossibility*. Under this defense, charges may be dismissed if the defendant's actions were so inherently unlikely to result

---

[42] Model Penal Code § 5.01(1)(b). Some states, however, have retained the common law defense of impossibility, and, thus, in those states the defense could argue that the means by which the defendant attempted to transmit the virus were inherently unlikely to succeed. *See, e.g.,* Ark. Stat. Ann. § 5-3-101 (1977) (affirmative defense to charge of criminal attempt that defendant's conduct is "inherently unlikely to result" in commission of a crime and "neither the conduct nor the defendant presents a public danger warranting imposition of criminal liability").

[43] Larry Gostin, *The Politics of AIDS: Compulsory State Powers, Public Health, and Civil Liberties,* 49 Ohio St. L.J. 1017, 1020 (1989) (arguing that compulsory state powers have little place in fighting a disease, and that especially in spitting and biting cases criminal sanctions have no public utility).

[44] 545 N.E.2d 834 (Ind. Ct. App. 1989).

[45] *Id.* at 835–37.

in commission of the crime that the action would not "present a public danger."[46] But the medical evidence at the trial established that there was at least some risk of HIV transmission through blood splattering, and the court ruled that this risk was not so speculative or purely theoretical as to be inherently unlikely.[47]

The court in *State v. Smith*[48] reached the same result in a case involving a bite wound. The defendant, Smith, was an HIV positive inmate in a county jail in New Jersey. On several occasions Smith threatened to kill jail guards by biting them or spitting at them. One day, while he was being treated in an emergency room, he became enraged at the treatment he was receiving and began struggling with the jail guards. He again threatened to bite them and give them AIDS, and while the guards tried to restrain him, he bit one of the guards, leaving puncture wounds that bled. The guard did not become infected, but Smith was convicted of attempted murder and related charges and was sentenced to 25 years in prison.[49] The appeals court found that the scientific evidence was inconclusive as to whether HIV could be transmitted by a bite, but because impossibility is not a defense, the court ruled that the conviction could be upheld based on the evidence that Smith subjectively believed he could transmit HIV through a bite.[50]

In *Scroggins v. State,*[51] the court reached the same result as the courts in *Smith* and *Haines.* In *Scroggins,* the defendant, while struggling with a police officer, sucked up excess sputum into his mouth and then bit the officer, leaving a full mouth bite wound. Scroggins later told a nurse he was HIV positive, and when the officer asked him if he really was infected with HIV, Scroggins laughed. Scroggins had in fact tested positive for HIV two months earlier. Based on this

---

[46] *Id.* at 839. Some states have followed the Model Penal Code, which provides in § 5.05(2) that the court has the power to dismiss charges or reduce the penalty if "the particular conduct charged to constitute criminal attempt . . . is so inherently unlikely to result or culminate in the commission of a crime that neither such conduct nor the actor presents a public danger."

[47] State v. Haines, 545 N.E.2d at 841. *See also* State v. Caine, 652 So. 2d 611 (La. Ct. App.), *writ denied,* 661 So. 2d 1358 (La. 1995) (conviction for attempted second degree murder upheld. After saying, "I'll give you AIDS," defendant had stabbed a store clerk with a syringe containing a clear liquid. The evidence showed that Caine tested positive for HIV three months after the incident, and that he had track marks on his arm, indicating that he had a history of injection drug use. Court held that specific intent to kill could be inferred from Caine's statement and actions, and although the syringe was not recovered and therefore could not be tested, court ruled that impossibility was not a defense. In addition, court found there was a strong possibility that the needle was infected with HIV in view of Caine's HIV positive status after the incident and the evidence that he used needles.). A used syringe can transmit HIV when the needle contains blood infected with the virus, as is discussed in **Ch. 1.**

[48] 621 A.2d 493 (N.J. Super. Ct.), *cert. denied,* 634 A.2d 523 (N.J. 1993).

[49] *Id.* at 496–98.

[50] *Id.* at 505. The court also rejected the defense argument, based on the Model Penal Code, that biting was such an "absurd" means for Smith to try to murder the officer that there was good ground for doubting that Smith really planned to commit murder. Model Penal Code § 5.01 commentary at 315 (1985).

[51] 401 S.E.2d 13 (Ga. Ct. App. 1990).

evidence, Scroggins was convicted of aggravated assault with intent to murder. On appeal, the court ruled that there is no defense of impossibility under Georgia law, and thus it was irrelevant whether HIV could in fact be transmitted by a bite as long as Scroggins believed he could transmit it in this manner. Regarding the mental element of the crime, the court ruled that under state law a wanton and reckless state of mind could be equivalent to a specific intent to kill, and Scroggins' act of biting the officer while knowing he was HIV infected was sufficient to establish a wanton or reckless disregard for whether he might transmit the virus.[52]

Similarly, in *Weeks v. State*,[53] a court in Texas upheld an attempted murder conviction and sentence of life in prison for an HIV positive inmate who spit on a guard, causing saliva to land on the guard's glasses, lips, and nose. The inmate had threatened the guard, stating that he had AIDS and would take as many people with him as possible. Unlike other states, Texas does allow an impossibility defense. The Texas attempt statute requires proof that the defendant, acting with specific intent to commit the offense, did an act tending, but failing, to effect the commission of the offense. The Texas courts, however, interpret the word *tends* to mean could, and thus the question on appeal was whether the state had shown that the defendant could have transmitted HIV by spitting on the guard.[54] The court upheld the conviction based on questionable expert testimony presented by the prosecution that spitting does pose a risk of HIV transmission.[55] A defense expert testified, on the other hand, that although HIV is present in saliva, it is inactive, and that the chance of transmitting HIV through saliva would be "the lowest in theoretical possibility."[56] The jury's decision to believe the prosecution's experts, whose opinions were contrary to mainstream scientific opinion on the issue, illustrates the danger that in an age of AIDS-phobia, juries may be inclined to convict defendants in HIV spitting cases based on junk science.[57]

---

[52] *Id.* at 18–19.

[53] 834 S.W.2d 559 (Tex. Ct. App. 1992), *petition for habeas corpus denied sub nom.* Weeks v. Scott, 55 F.3d 1059 (5th Cir. 1995) (holding evidence sufficient to establish that act of spitting could transmit HIV and cause death).

[54] *Id.* at 562.

[55] *Id.* at 562–65. The court relied in part on testimony that people with HIV often have gum disease which can cause bleeding, and when blood is mixed in with spit, the risk of HIV transmission is greater. *Id.* at 564. However, even though there was evidence that Weeks did have gingivitis, there was no direct evidence that his spit contained blood. *Cf.* **Ch. 1,** discussing the virtually nonexistent risk of HIV transmission through saliva.

[56] *Id.* at 565.

[57] In the related context of the employment of a person with a contagious disease, the Supreme Court has emphasized the importance of basing legal decisions "on reasonable medical judgments given the state of medical knowledge" and not on "unfounded fear." School Bd. v. Arline, 480 U.S. 273, 288 (1987) (holding that school teacher infected with tuberculosis could not be fired unless evidence established that she posed a "significant risk" to the health of others).

It should be noted that in biting cases, some juries have acquitted HIV-positive defendants of attempted murder, convicting them instead of assault.[58]

§ 7.3 Assault and Assault with a Deadly Weapon

In several jurisdictions, prosecutors have charged HIV-infected people with assault and assault with a deadly weapon based on conduct thought to create a risk of HIV transmission. Jurisdictions following the Model Penal Code define *simple assault* as an attempt to cause, or purposely, knowingly, or recklessly causing bodily injury to another. The crime also includes negligently causing bodily injury to another with a deadly weapon.[59] The crime becomes an *aggravated assault* if the actor causes or attempts to cause "serious" bodily injury, or if he or she knowingly or purposely causes or attempts to cause bodily injury with a deadly weapon.[60] In addition, some states have aggravated sexual assault statutes which apply to sexual assaults in which the accused causes or attempts to cause serious bodily injury or death.[61]

Under the Model Penal Code, the consent of the victim can be a defense to a charge such as assault only if the bodily harm caused by the defendant is not serious.[62] Thus, the Model Penal Code would appear to exclude a consent defense in cases involving the actual transmission of HIV, because HIV is potentially fatal. However, for the reasons discussed in **§ 7.2,** proof of actual transmission of HIV usually is impossible, and thus assault prosecutions for the actual transmission of HIV are very unlikely. The Model Penal Code also disallows a consent defense if the bodily harm "threatened by the conduct consented to" is serious.[63] This limitation would apply to attempts to cause serious bodily injury

---

[58] *See, e.g.,* Brock v. State, 555 So. 2d 285 (Ala. Ct. App. 1989); Commonwealth v. Brown, 605 A.2d 429 (Pa. Super. Ct. 1992). Both cases are discussed in **§ 7.3.** *See also* Mary Jo Layton, *Woman Indicted in Biting Incident Escapes Charge of Attempted Murder,* Record, Northern New Jersey, Oct. 15, 1992, *available in* Westlaw, Allnews file (grand jury voted not to indict HIV infected woman on attempted murder charge for saying "I got AIDS, man," and then biting a man during struggle in supermarket; woman indicted instead only for robbery and terroristic threats).

[59] Model Penal Code § 211.1(1) (1985).

[60] *Id.* § 211.1(2).

[61] *E.g.,* Tex. Penal Code Ann. § 22.021 (West 1994) (aggravated sexual assault). *See* Zule v. State, 802 S.W.2d 28 (Tex. Ct. App. 1990) (court upheld the defendant's conviction under Texas aggravated sexual assault statute based on evidence that defendant, knowing he was HIV positive, had anal intercourse with a 15-year-old boy who himself later tested positive for HIV. Defendant was sentenced to life in prison.).

[62] Model Penal Code § 2.11(2) (1962). Presumably, in any jurisdiction in which consent could be a defense, only "informed" consent would suffice. For example, in a case involving sexual conduct by an HIV infected defendant, the defendant's sexual partner would have to have consented to the sex after having been informed of the defendant's HIV positive status. *See* Model Penal Code § 2.11(3)(d) (consent ineffective if induced by deception).

[63] *Id.* § 2.11(2)(a).

(aggravated assault). It is unlikely, however, that the issue of consent would ever arise in such cases. To be guilty of an attempt to cause serious bodily injury, the defendant would have to specifically intend to cause the injury through HIV infection. It would be most unusual for a defendant with such an intent to seek to obtain the informed consent of the intended victim before attempting to transmit the virus. Outside of the military (see § 7.9), there have not been any reported cases of HIV-related prosecutions in which the defense of informed consent was raised.[64]

There have been several assault prosecutions of HIV-positive prison inmates for biting guards. In *Brock v. State,*[65] the defendant, who was in the AIDS unit of an Alabama prison, was charged with attempted murder and assault after he bit a prison guard on the arm during a scuffle. The guard did not become infected with HIV. There was no evidence that Brock made any statements indicating what his intent was, and the jury acquitted him of the attempted murder charges. The jury did convict him, however, of the lesser included offense of assault in the first degree, which in Alabama requires proof that the defendant had the intent to cause, and did in fact cause, serious bodily injury by means of a deadly weapon or instrument. The appeals court, noting that the prosecutor had presented no evidence on the nature of AIDS or how it could be transmitted, held that the evidence was insufficient to prove that Brock intended to cause or did in fact cause serious bodily injury. The court also held, in line with the majority of courts, that teeth cannot be considered a "deadly weapon."[66] The court, therefore, reversed the conviction for assault in the first degree and reduced the charge to the lesser included offense of assault in the third degree.[67]

Contrary to the majority rule, two federal circuit courts have held that teeth, under certain circumstances, can constitute a deadly weapon. The two courts have reached opposite conclusions, however, regarding the danger of a bite wound's transmitting HIV. In *United States v. Moore,*[68] an HIV-positive inmate was convicted of assault with a deadly weapon after he bit two prison guards. He told a nurse that he had wanted to kill the guards and hoped their wounds were bad enough for them to contract HIV. At the trial, an expert testified that there was no evidence HIV could be transmitted by a bite, but that human bite wounds are still very dangerous because serious infection can result. Based on this testimony, the

---

[64] *See, e.g.,* United States v. Morris, 30 M.J. 1221 (A.C.M.R. 1990) (holding that informed consent of partner to unprotected sexual intercourse was not a defense to charge of conduct prejudicial to good order and discipline in military in view of the risk of serious bodily harm to partner).

[65] 555 So. 2d 285 (Ala. Crim. App. 1989).

[66] *Id.* at 287 (citing Vitauts M. Gulbis, Annotation, *Parts of the Human Body Other Than Feet as Deadly or Dangerous Weapons for Purposes of Statutes Aggravating Offenses Such as Assault and Robbery,* 8 A.L.R.4th 1268, 1269 (1981) ("the main line of authority . . . is to the effect that in no circumstances can fists or teeth be dangerous weapons within the meaning of applicable statutes")).

[67] *Id.* at 286–88.

[68] 846 F.2d 1163 (8th Cir. 1988).

Eighth Circuit Court of Appeals ruled that the evidence was not sufficient to show that HIV could be transmitted through saliva or bite wounds:

> Although there is sufficient evidence in the record that the human mouth and teeth may be used as a deadly and dangerous weapon, we nevertheless wish to emphasize that the medical evidence in the record was insufficient to establish that AIDS may be transmitted by a bite. The evidence established that there are no well-proven cases of AIDS transmission by way of a bite; that contact with saliva has never been shown to transmit the disease; and that in one case a person who had been deeply bitten by a person with AIDS tested negative several months later. Indeed, a recent study has indicated that saliva actually may contain substances that *protect* the body from AIDS. *New York Times,* May 6, 1988, at A 16, col. 4. While Dr. Gastineau testified "in medicine everything is conceivable," in a legal context the possibility of AIDS transmission by means of a bite is too remote to support a finding that the mouth and teeth may be considered a deadly and dangerous weapon in this respect.[69]

Nonetheless, the court upheld the assault conviction, ruling that regardless of whether the assailant is infected with HIV, the mouth and teeth are a deadly weapon because of the danger of other serious infections. Moore was sentenced to five years in prison, to run consecutively to the seven years he was already serving at the time of the incident.

Similarly, in *United States v. Sturgis,*[70] an inmate bit two prison guards, causing profuse bleeding. Sturgis said that he knew he was HIV positive and that he hoped to infect the guards. Following the *Moore* decision, the appeals court upheld the defendant's conviction for assault with a dangerous weapon, the weapon again being the defendant's teeth. But contrary to *Moore,* the Fourth Circuit in *Sturgis* found, based on the prosecution's expert witness, that HIV could be transmitted by saliva and a bite wound.[71] The defense evidently did not present any expert testimony to show, as is well established,[72] that the chances of transmitting HIV through saliva or a bite are practically nonexistent. This case illustrates once again the importance of presenting accurate expert testimony in cases in which the risk of HIV transmission is at issue.

State v. Hinkhouse[73] is an example of an assault prosecution arising from a defendant's sexual activity. Hinkhouse was charged with multiple counts of attempted assault (along with attempted murder) based on his having had unprotected sex with several different women without informing them of his HIV infection. The attempted assault charges, like the attempted murder charges, were

---

[69] *Id.* at 1167–68.

[70] 48 F.3d 784 (4th Cir. 1995).

[71] *Id.* at 789. Sturgis was sentenced to 14 years in prison. *See also* Commonwealth v. Brown, 605 A.2d 429 (Pa. Super. Ct. 1992) (upholding conviction for aggravated assault for defendant who was infected both with HIV and Hepatitis B and who threw fecal matter on guard's face).

[72] Risk of HIV transmission through saliva and bite wounds is discussed in **Ch. 1.**

[73] 912 P.2d 921, *modified on reconsideration,* 915 P.2d 489 (Or. Ct. App. 1996). See § **7.2.**

upheld on appeal on the ground that the evidence showed that Hinkhouse had an intent to infect the women with HIV.

§ 7.4   Reckless Endangerment

Many states have followed the Model Penal Code in enacting criminal statutes prohibiting recklessly endangering another person. Under these statutes, one commits a misdemeanor if one "recklessly engages in conduct which places or may place another person in danger of death or serious bodily injury."[74] *Recklessness* is defined as a conscious disregard of a substantial and unjustifiable risk.[75] Further, "[t]he risk must be of such a nature and degree that, considering the nature and purpose of the actor's conduct and the circumstances known to him, its disregard involves a gross deviation from the standard of conduct that a law-abiding person would observe in the actor's situation."[76]

To the extent that any criminal statute is to be used to prosecute those whose conduct creates a serious risk of HIV transmission, this statute would be the best choice.[77] The statute does not require proof of a purpose or intent to transmit HIV, and it does not require proof that HIV was in fact transmitted. Instead it only requires proof that the accused consciously disregarded a substantial and unjustifiable risk that his or her conduct would result in transmission of the virus. The conscious disregard element, however, should require proof that the accused not only knew he or she was infected with HIV, but also that he or she had been counseled regarding HIV and was aware of what behaviors could create an unjustifiable risk of transmission.[78] But prosecutions for reckless endangerment in all but the most egregious cases could be counterproductive to public

---

[74] Model Penal Code § 211.2 (1985). Consent is not a defense to reckless endangerment because, under the Model Penal Code, consent can only be a defense when the threatened harm is "not serious." Model Penal Code § 2.11(2)(a). *See* Commonwealth v. Mathis, 464 A.2d 362, 366 (Pa. Super. Ct. 1983) (consent not a defense to crime of reckless endangerment in Pennsylvania).

[75] Model Penal Code § 2.02(2)(c).

[76] *Id.*

[77] Some commentators have argued that a misdemeanor reckless endangerment charge is too minor an offense for someone who has created a serious risk of HIV transmission in view of the fatal nature of the disease. *See, e.g.,* Donald H.J. Hermann, *Criminalizing Conduct Related to HIV Transmission,* 9 St. Louis U. Pub. L. Rev. 351 (1990). However, because even a short prison sentence can amount to a "life" term for someone living with HIV because of shorter life expectancy, the deterrent and punitive effect of a misdemeanor conviction for an HIV positive person should be similar to a more serious conviction for someone who does not have a life-threatening illness.

[78] One commentator has argued that reckless endangerment prosecutions would be problematic because the recklessness standard could be met by someone who was at high risk for HIV but who was never tested and yet continued engaging in unsafe sex. *See* Larry Gostin, *The Politics of AIDS: Compulsory State Powers, Public Health, and Civil Liberties,* 49 Ohio St. L.J. 1017,

health goals: widespread fear of prosecution would discourage people at high risk of HIV from getting tested and receiving counseling.[79]

In the reported cases to date, there have not been any convictions for this offense standing alone. Instead, reckless endangerment has been included as a lesser included offense of more serious charges such as attempted murder and assault.[80]

1051–52 (1989) (arguing that prosecutions under reckless endangerment statutes of people in high risk groups who have not been tested for HIV would cast far too wide a prosecutorial net and would further stigmatize already disfavored populations such as gays and injection drug users). However, no such cases have been reported. In the absence of proof that a defendant did test positive and did receive safe sex counseling, it would be very difficult for a prosecutor to prove that the defendant had an actual awareness of an unjustifiable risk. *See In re* Gribetz, 605 N.Y.S.2d 834, 836 (Rockland County Ct. 1994) (granting prosecutor's motion for disclosure of defendant's HIV test results in biting case on ground that in order for prosecutor to prove reckless endangerment, he must prove at a minimum that defendant knew she was HIV positive).

An additional concern with prosecutions for reckless endangerment is the question of what constitutes an "unjustifiable risk." There is a small chance of transmission of HIV even if condoms are used during sexual intercourse. Would "safer sex" therefore be considered by courts and juries to be an unjustifiable risk? Because public health authorities have spent much time and energy actively encouraging people to employ safer sex techniques such as using condoms, a strong argument could be made that as long as one follows public health advice, one has not grossly deviated from acceptable societal standards and has not created an unjustifiable risk. *In re* Gribetz, 605 N.Y.S.2d at 836. Support for this position can be found in an attempted murder case in which the court held that it was the defendant's failure to use condoms during sexual intercourse that created the risk of HIV transmission. State v. Hinkhouse, 912 P.2d 921, 925, *modified on reconsideration,* 915 P.2d 489 (Or. Ct. App. 1996). See **Ch. 8.**

[79] Joint Subcommittee on AIDS in the Criminal Justice Sys. of the Comm. on Corrections and the Comm. on Criminal Justice Operations and Budget of the Ass'n of the Bar of the City of N.Y., AIDS and the Criminal Justice System: A Final Report and Recommendations 186 (July 1989) ("prosecutions for reckless endangerment should be limited to . . . [situations] . . . where risk-creating behavior is committed by someone who knows he or she is infected"). *See also* Kathleen M. Sullivan & Martha A. Field, *AIDS and the Coercive Power of the State,* 23 Harv. C.R.-C.L. L. Rev. 139, 195–96 (1988) (HIV-related prosecutions for reckless endangerment run "the risk of jury arbitrariness and discrimination" in applying the concept of recklessness; "even the best medical knowledge remains uncertain about the precise degree of risk of AIDS transmission attached to particular sexual acts and the degree to which precautions can reduce that risk.")

[80] *See* Smallwood v. State, 680 A.2d 512 (Md. 1996) (HIV positive defendant who, during robberies, raped three women without using condoms was found guilty of rape, robbery, and reckless endangerment) (discussed in **§ 7.2**); Commonwealth v. Brown, 605 A.2d 429 (Pa. Super. Ct. 1992) (defendant's convictions for assault and reckless endangerment upheld based on evidence that he threw fecal matter in guard's face, knowing that he was infected with HIV and Hepatitis B). *See also* People v. Hawkrigg, 525 N.Y.S.2d 752 (Suffolk County Ct. 1988) (defense motion to dismiss indictment charging third-degree sodomy, reckless endangerment, and endangering the welfare of a child denied because of evidence sufficient to show that defendant engaged in deviate sexual intercourse with a youth knowing that he, the defendant, had AIDS and knowing that such conduct could transmit HIV).

§ 7.5 Sodomy

The definition of *sodomy* varies from state to state, but generally includes anal and oral sexual intercourse.[81] Of the minority of states that still have enforceable sodomy statutes, six have statutes that apply only to homosexual sodomy, and 14 have statutes that on their face apply to both homosexual and heterosexual sodomy.[82]

Sodomy statutes are not effective as a means of inhibiting the spread of HIV for several reasons. First, sodomy statutes are so rarely enforced that they certainly cannot serve as much of a disincentive to engage in anal or oral sex. In *Bowers v. Hardwick*,[83] for example, the state declined to prosecute defendant Michael Hardwick even though a police officer caught him in the act of having sex with another man. The state of Texas, moreover, actually defended its sodomy law on the ground the law "has not been, and in all probability, will not be, enforced."[84] However, although unenforced, sodomy statutes do serve to buttress discrimination against gays and lesbians. The laws thereby inhibit people from getting tested for HIV and from truthfully acknowledging risky behavior to their doctors. Sodomy laws thus run counter to public education efforts and campaigns in favor of voluntary testing, which public health officials agree are key to limiting the spread of HIV.[85]

---

[81] *See, e.g.,* Ga. Code Ann. § 16-6-2 ("(a) A person commits the offense of sodomy when he performs or submits to any sexual act involving the sex organs of one person and the mouth or anus of another. . . . (b) A person convicted of the offense of sodomy shall be punished by imprisonment for not less than one nor more than 20 years.").

[82] Lambda Legal Defense & Education Fund, "Sodomy" Laws State-By-State as of July 1995, available from LLDEF, Inc., 666 Broadway, 12th Floor, New York, NY 10012, (212) 995-8585.

[83] 478 U.S. 186 (1986).

[84] Texas v. Morales, 869 S.W.2d 941, 943 (Tex. 1994). *See* Gilbert Geis et al., *Reported Consequence of Decriminalization of Consensual Adult Homosexuality in Seven American States,* 1 J. Homosexuality 419 (1976) (study showed decriminalization of sodomy had no effect on prevalence of homosexual behavior).

[85] J. Kelly Strader, *Constitutional Challenges to the Criminalization of Same-Sex Sexual Activities: State Interest in HIV-AIDS Issues,* 70 Denv. U. L. Rev. 337, 355–56 (1993). *See also* Brief of *Amicus Curiae* American Public Health Association in Support of Plaintiffs/Appellees, Campbell v. Sundquist, 926 S.W.2d 250 (Tenn. Ct. App. 1996) (arguing that Tennessee sodomy statute is counterproductive to public health goals because the statute (1) does not deter behavior through which HIV may be spread, (2) it discourages gay men, who may be at high risk for HIV, from cooperating fully and openly with public health workers, and (3) it interferes with education efforts designed to encourage safer sex practices). *See generally* David G. Ostrow & Norman L. Altman, *Sexually Transmitted Diseases and Homosexuality,* 10 Sexually Transmitted Diseases 208, 212 (1983) (societies that impose severe penalties for sodomy have poorer records of reporting and treating sexually transmitted diseases); Jeffrey D. Fisher, *Possible Effects of Reference Group-Based Social Influence on AIDS-Risk Behavior and AIDS Prevention,* 43 Am. Psychologist 914, 919 (1988) (fear of prejudice and discrimination could have negative effects on AIDS prevention).

Second, sodomy statutes are both overinclusive and underinclusive as a means of stopping the spread of HIV, and as a result the statutes bear no rational relationship to public health goals.[86] The statutes are overinclusive in that they cover conduct, such as cunnilingus and fellatio with use of a condom, which poses virtually no risk of HIV transmission. Conversely, they are underinclusive because they do not cover certain high risk sexual behaviors, such as vaginal sexual intercourse without use of a condom. When the statutes were originally enacted, moreover, there was no HIV epidemic, and thus the statutes clearly were not intended historically to be a means of preventing disease transmission.[87] Sodomy statutes, therefore, cannot be justified in any manner as a public health measure.

Most courts that have considered the constitutionality of sodomy statutes have not accepted as a rationale for the statutes the argument that they help prevent HIV transmission. In *Bowers v. Hardwick*,[88] for example, in which the Supreme Court by a five-to-four margin[89] upheld Georgia's sodomy statute, the Court did not adopt the HIV-related justifications for the statute put forward by the state and amicus.[90] The Court only ruled that sodomy statutes do not violate the federal constitutional right to privacy or the right to due process,[91] although it did not address the question of whether sodomy statutes may be invalid as violations of the Equal Protection Clause or the First Amendment.[92] The strength of *Bowers* as precedent is doubtful, however, in light of the Supreme Court decision in *Romer v. Evans*.[93] In *Romer*, the Court majority, without any mention of the *Bowers* decision, struck down as violation of equal protection a Colorado constitutional amendment which precluded all legislative, executive, or judicial action designed to protect lesbians and gays from discrimination.

---

[86] J. Kelly Strader, *Constitutional Challenges to the Criminalization of Same-Sex Sexual Activities: State Interest in HIV-AIDS Issues*, 70 Denv. U. L. Rev. 337, 353–54 (1993).

[87] *Id.*

[88] 478 U.S. 186 (1986).

[89] After his retirement from the Court, Justice Powell, who had been in the five justice majority in *Hardwick*, declared that he "probably made a mistake" in voting to uphold the statute and that the dissent in that case had the better argument. Marcus, *Powell Regrets Backing Sodomy Law*, Wash. Post, Oct. 26, 1990, at A3.

[90] Brief for Petitioner at 37, Bowers v. Hardwick, 478 U.S. 186 (1985); Brief of David Robinson, Jr., as Amicus Curiae at 5, Bowers v. Hardwick, 478 U.S. 186 (1985).

[91] Bowers v. Hardwick, 478 U.S. at 190–95.

[92] *See* Laurence H. Tribe, American Constitutional Law 1616 (2d ed. 1988) (arguing that homosexuals fulfill the criteria for status as a protected class under equal protection analysis); Note, *The Tradition of Prejudice Versus the Principle of Equality: Homosexuals and Heightened Equal Protection Scrutiny after* Bowers v. Hardwick, 31 B.C. L. Rev. 375 (1990) (same). *See also* David Cole & William N. Eskridge, *From Hand-Holding to Sodomy: First Amendment Protection of Homosexual (Expressive) Conduct*, 29 Harv. C.R.-C.L. L. Rev. 319 (1994) (arguing that sodomy laws and the military's ban on homosexual conduct violate the First Amendment right to freedom of expression).

[93] 116 S. Ct. 1620 (1996). *See* Nabozny v. Podlesny, 92 F.3d 446, 458 n.12 (7th Cir. 1996) (noting that *Romer* eclipses *Bowers* in the area of equal protection).

State courts have reached differing results regarding the validity of sodomy statutes. Six years before *Bowers,* the highest court in New York struck down the state's sodomy statute in *People v. Onofre,*[94] on the ground that it violated the federal constitutional right to privacy. In *People v. Uplinger,*[95] the New York high court followed its decision in *Onofre* and struck down a state statute prohibiting loitering for the purpose of engaging in or soliciting deviate sexual intercourse. Similarly, in another pre-*Bowers* decision, the Pennsylvania Supreme Court in *Commonwealth v. Bonadio*[96] struck down a state sodomy statute on the ground that it violated both the state and federal equal protection clauses. Two jurisdictions have upheld state sodomy statutes.[97] However, only three courts have discussed the impact sodomy statutes may have on controlling the spread of HIV. In *State v. Walsh,*[98] the Supreme Court of Missouri upheld a state sodomy statute that applies only to homosexual sex, finding that the statute does not violate rights of privacy or equal protection, and that it was rationally related to the state's interest in promoting public morality and "protecting the public health."[99] Even though the statute had been enacted well before anyone was aware of AIDS, the court, with very little analysis, concluded that the statute could be upheld as a means of inhibiting the spread of AIDS and other sexually communicable diseases. The court further held that it was reasonable for the statute to single out homosexual sex because of "the general promiscuity characteristic of the homosexual lifestyle."[100] The court reached these questionable conclusions without benefit of any expert witness testimony at the trial.

The Supreme Court of Kentucky came to an opposing conclusion in *Commonwealth v. Wasson.*[101] The court held that the Kentucky sodomy statute, which only applied to homosexual sex, was invalid as a violation of the rights of privacy and equal protection in the Kentucky state constitution.[102] The court dismissed as "simply outrageous" the state's attempt to justify the statute on the ground that "homosexuals are more promiscuous than heterosexuals" and that "homosexuals enjoy the company of children."[103] The court found that the only

---

[94] 415 N.E.2d 936 (N.Y. 1980), *cert. denied,* 451 U.S. 987 (1981).

[95] 447 N.E.2d 62 (N.Y. 1983).

[96] 415 A.2d 47 (Pa. 1980).

[97] State v. Lopes, 660 A.2d 707 (R.I. 1995) (upheld state sodomy statute on ground that neither right to privacy nor right to equal protection applies to "private unnatural copulation" between unmarried adults), *cert. denied,* 116 S. Ct. 934 (1996); Christensen v. State, 468 S.E.2d 188 (Ga. 1996) (upheld state statutes prohibiting sodomy and solicitation of sodomy).

[98] 713 S.W.2d 508 (Mo. 1986) (en banc).

[99] *Id.* at 511–12.

[100] *Id.* at 512.

[101] 842 S.W.2d 487 (Ky. 1992).

[102] The *Wasson* court was careful to limit the grounds for its decision to the state constitution. Nonetheless, the court noted its disagreement with the Supreme Court's decision in *Bowers,* stating that it viewed that decision "as a misdirected application of the theory of original intent." *Id.* at 497.

[103] *Id.* at 501.

justification for the statute that had even "superficial validity" was the state's argument that infectious diseases such as AIDS are more readily transmitted through anal sex than through other forms of sexual activity. The court rejected this justification, however, because the statute was both overinclusive and underinclusive: the statute was not limited to anal sex, and the state's reasoning would apply just as strongly to male-female anal sex, which the statute did not cover, as to male-male anal sex. The medical evidence before the court showed that there was no distinction between homosexual and heterosexual anal sex as a means of transmitting AIDS.[104] The defense at trial had also presented extensive expert testimony showing that the sodomy statute could not help prevent the spread diseases such as AIDS, and that it could actually have an adverse impact on public health because it could create a "barrier to getting accurate medical histories."[105]

A court of appeals in Tennessee followed the *Wasson* decision in *Campbell v. Sundquist.*[106] The court struck down the state sodomy statute on the ground that it violated the right to privacy under the Tennessee state constitution. As in *Wasson,* one of the justifications for the statute advanced by the state was that it would help prevent the spread of infectious disease. The court rejected this argument on the ground that the statute was not narrowly tailored to advance this interest. The court went on to state:

> Moreover, the appellees and the American Public Health Association, as amicus curiae, forward a compelling argument that the statute is actually counterproductive to public health goals. The appellees introduced evidence that due to fear of prosecution, some homosexual individuals infected with sexually transmitted diseases do not seek medical treatment for the infection or report the infection, and that others are reluctant to be tested to determine if they are infected.[107]

---

[104] *Id.*

[105] *Id.* at 490. The amicus brief submitted in the *Wasson* case on behalf of the American Public Health Association and other public health organizations stated,

> Criminal prosecution of sodomy not only is an ineffective means of controlling AIDS, but actually is counterproductive to public health goals. . . . The stigma of criminal prohibition and the threat of prosecution actually harm the public health effort by driving the disease underground. The legal condemnation of same-sex activity leads individuals to refrain from being frank with their doctors, impedes the flow of preventive information from public health experts to the general population, and renders the disease more difficult to study and contain.

Amicus Brief of the American Public Health Association et al. at 2, Commonwealth v. Wasson, 842 S.W.2d 487 (Ky. 1992). *See also* Equality Found. of Greater Cincinnati, Inc. v. City of Cincinnati, 860 F. Supp. 417, 425 (S.D. Ohio 1994) (relating testimony of Dr. Marcus Connant that Cincinnati charter amendment revoking a nondiscrimination law for lesbians and gays would be counterproductive to public health efforts because it would thwart public health efforts to prevent HIV infection and encourage the early diagnosis and treatment of HIV), *aff'd in part and rev'd in part,* 54 F.3d 261 (6th Cir. 1995), *vacated,* 116 S. Ct. 2519 (1996) (remanding to circuit court for reconsideration in light of Romer v. Evans, 116 S. Ct. 1620 (1996)).

[106] 926 S.W.2d 250 (Tenn. Ct. App. 1996).

[107] *Id.* at 263–64.

Thus, when courts have had the benefit of accurate expert testimony, as they did in both *Wasson* and *Campbell,* they have found that sodomy statutes simply cannot be justified as a public health measure. Indeed, because sodomy statutes are counterproductive to public health goals, the state interest in fighting the spread of HIV actually militates against sodomy statutes, rather than in favor of them.

§ 7.6   Prostitution

Laws against *prostitution,* which is defined in the Model Penal Code as "engag[ing] in sexual activity as a business,"[108] constitute yet another criminal justice approach advocated by some as a means of limiting the spread of HIV.[109] To the extent that prostitutes and their patrons do not follow safe sex practices, prostitution may indeed be one avenue through which HIV is spread. Although it is difficult to obtain reliable data on sero-prevalence among prostitutes, studies indicate that anywhere from 0 to 65 percent of prostitutes in various localities in the United States are HIV positive.[110] The primary risk factor for prostitutes, however, is not sexual contact but injection drug use.[111]

Laws that prohibit prostitution are of questionable value in fighting the spread of HIV. It is widely recognized that prostitution laws have done little to stop prostitution.[112] Instead they have only driven the practice of prostitution underground,[113] thus making it even more difficult to educate prostitutes and their patrons regarding safe sex practices and to regulate their behavior. In addition, the laws criminalize prostitution regardless of whether the sexual conduct in question creates any risk of HIV transmission. In this respect they are over-inclusive and do nothing to encourage safe sex practices. Accordingly, like

---

[108] Model Penal Code § 251.2 (1962) (Prostitution and Related Offenses).

[109] Report of the Presidential Commission on the Human Immunodeficiency Virus Epidemic 131 (1988) (stating in recommendation 9-51, "Prostitution laws should be strictly enforced").

[110] Michael J. Rosenberg & Jodie M. Weiner, *Prostitutes and AIDS: A Health Department Priority?,* 78 Am. J. Pub. Health 418, 420 (1988).

[111] *Id.*

[112] *See* Carol Hauge, *Prostitution of Women and International Human Rights Law: Transforming Exploitation Into Equality,* 8 N.Y. Int'l L. Rev. 23 (1995) (observing that criminalization has not been an effective means of ending prostitution in any society); Julie Pearl, *The Highest Paying Customers: America's Cities and the Costs of Prostitution Control,* 38 Hastings L.J. 769, 789 (1987) (cost-benefit analysis of prostitution laws concludes that enforcement of prostitution laws is disproportionately costly and labor-intensive, and that "even the most vigorous police battles against prostitution yield Pyrrhic victories at best").

[113] *See* Arlene Carmen & Harold Moody, *Working Women: The Subterranean World of Street Prostitution* 189 (1985).

sodomy laws (discussed in **§ 7.5**), laws against prostitution run counter to the public education efforts that are at the center of the effort to stop the spread of HIV.[114]

Nevada is the only state that has legalized and regulated prostitution for the purpose of controlling sexually transmitted diseases. Counties within Nevada have the option of licensing "houses of prostitution,"[115] and it is a misdemeanor for anyone to engage in prostitution except in a licensed house of prostitution.[116] State regulations[117] require that before starting work, prostitutes must be tested for HIV and sexually transmitted diseases. (Mandatory HIV testing for those arrested for sex offenses is discussed in **§§ 7.13** through **7.18.**) In addition, while working, prostitutes continue to be tested periodically, including monthly tests for HIV. The state regulations also require prostitutes to wear latex condoms during sexual intercourse. One sign that legalization and regulation of prostitution may be effective in slowing the spread of HIV is the fact that there have been no instances of licensed prostitutes in Nevada testing positive for HIV.[118]

Nevada imposes severe penalties on prostitutes who continue working after being notified that they are HIV positive. By statute, any prostitute, whether licensed or not, who continues working after having been notified of HIV positive test results is guilty of a class B felony and shall be imprisoned for between

---

[114] *See* Michael J. Rosenberg & Jodie M. Weiner, *Prostitutes and AIDS: A Health Department Priority?*, 78 Am. J. Pub. Health 418, 422 (concluding that "educational approaches" are most effective for lowering the risk of HIV transmission among prostitutes).

As the National Commission on AIDS has noted, one type of prostitution that is especially problematic from the public health standpoint is the "growing practice of trading drugs, especially crack (the smokeable form of cocaine), for sex." The Commission offered this example from testimony presented at its hearings:

One particular crack dealer . . . in our adolescent clinic in Newark revealed that in the month of August he had sex with 30 different women in trade for crack. In addition, he carried on a sexual relationship with his girlfriend who did not use drugs. All of this activity occurred without the benefit of the protection of condoms. In that month, he and his girlfriend, and his girlfriend's new boyfriend, and his girlfriend's new boyfriend's alternative sexual partner, all became infected with gonorrhea and chlamydia.

National Comm'n on AIDS, Report: The Twin Epidemics of Substance Use and HIV 6 (1991). A criminal law enforcement approach to this sort of sex-for-drugs "prostitution" will not be effective, and, not surprisingly, the Commission does not recommend it.

[115] Nev. Rev. Stat. § 244.345.

[116] *Id.* § 201.354.

[117] Nev. Admin. Code ch. 441A, §§ 800–815.

[118] Nevada Bureau of Disease Control and Intervention Services, HIV/AIDS Program Office, Quarterly Sexually Transmitted Disease (STD) Report—Brothels (1995) (from 1989 to third quarter of 1995 no "line workers" in legal brothels have tested positive for HIV). *See also* Michael A. Lerner, *A Move To Ban Bordellos,* Newsweek, June 13, 1988, at 34 (9,000 tests of licensed prostitutes in Nevada had not turned up a single HIV positive test result).

two and ten years.[119] Other states have adopted similar statutes imposing higher sentences on prostitutes who continue working after testing positive for HIV.[120]

In the one reported case of a prosecution under the Nevada statute, *Glegola v. State*,[121] the defendant, Glegola, was arrested for solicitation for prostitution after she solicited an undercover police officer. She was convicted of engaging in prostitution being notified she was HIV positive, based on testimony of several witnesses that she knew her HIV status. Glegola was sentenced to 15 years in prison. The Nevada Supreme Court upheld the conviction and sentence, ruling that the fact that the Glegola was likely to die of an AIDS-related illness during her 15 years in prison did not make the sentence cruel and unusual punishment.[122]

From a public health policy standpoint, there is a serious problem with imposing such severe sentences on prostitutes who continue working after learning that they are infected with HIV. Severe sentences in these cases create a powerful

---

[119] Nev. Rev. Stat. § 201.358. All those arrested for engaging in illegal, unlicensed prostitution must submit to an HIV test under § 201.356.

[120] *See* Cal. Penal Code § 1202.6 (upon first conviction for prostitution defendant must submit to HIV testing, the results of which are reported to the sentencing court and the State Department of Health); Cal. Penal Code § 647(f) (raises prostitution offense to a felony for any person previously convicted of prostitution and tested under § 1202.6 who tested positive, was aware of the result, and subsequently engaged in prostitution); Colo. Rev. Stat. Ann. § 18-7-201.5 (any person convicted of prostitution must submit to HIV testing); Colo. Rev. Stat. Ann. § 18-7-201.7 (grading as class 5 felony commission of act of prostitution with knowledge of HIV positive status); Colo. Rev. Stat. Ann. § 18-7-205.7 (grading as class 6 felony patronizing a prostitute with knowledge of HIV positive status); Fla. Stat. Ann. § 796.08(3) (mandating HIV testing for anyone convicted of prostitution); Fla. Stat. Ann. § 796.08(5) (grading as felony in third degree committing crime of prostitution after having been previously convicted of prostitution and after having tested HIV positive); Ga. Code Ann. § 16-5-60 (grading as a felony subject to 10-year prison sentence act of soliciting and performing sex for money without disclosing HIV positive status); Ky. Rev. Stat. Ann. § 529.090(3)–(4) (grading as class D felony act of prostitution by one who knows he or she has tested positive for HIV); Nev. Rev. Stat. Ann. § 201.356 (requiring that all those arrested for prostitution submit to HIV test); Nev. Rev. Stat. Ann. § 201.358 (grading as felony punishable by up to 10 years in prison engaging in prostitution with knowledge of HIV positive status); Okla. Stat. Ann. tit. 21, § 1031 (grading as felony punishable by up to five years in prison crime of engaging in prostitution with knowledge of being infected with HIV); 18 Pa. Cons. Stat. Ann. § 5902 (grading as third-degree felony engaging in prostitution while knowing of HIV positive status); S.C. Code Ann. § 44-29-145(2) (grading as felony punishable by up to 10 years in prison engaging in prostitution with knowledge of HIV positive status); Tenn. Code Ann. § 39-13-516 (grading as class C felony engaging in prostitution with knowledge of HIV positive status); Tenn. Code Ann. § 39-13-521 (requiring that all those arrested for prostitution submit to HIV testing); Utah Code Ann. § 76-10-1309 (grading as third-degree felony engaging in prostitution or patronizing a prostitute while knowing of HIV positive status); Utah Code Ann. § 76-10-1311 (requiring HIV testing for anyone convicted of prostitution).

[121] 871 P.2d 950, 952–53 (Nev. 1994).

[122] *Id.* at 953. Before the statute was amended in 1995, § 201.358 allowed for a maximum sentence of up to 20 years.

incentive for unlicensed prostitutes to avoid HIV testing. The *Glegola* case sends unlicensed prostitutes in Nevada a message they are unlikely to ignore. If they continue working knowing they are infected with HIV, they face a felony conviction and a sentence of what could amount to life in prison. If they avoid getting tested, however, the worst they face is a misdemeanor conviction for being an unlicensed prostitute and a sentence of no more than six months in the county jail.[123] The Nevada legislature's decision after *Glegola* to lower the maximum sentence from 20 to 10 years indicates at least some concern for avoiding extremely harsh prison sentences for this offense.[124]

§ 7.7 Communicable Disease Control Statutes

Many states have long had criminal statutes prohibiting the spread of communicable diseases. Some states have broad public health statutes which prohibit the transmission of any "communicable" or "contagious" disease, without referring to any disease specifically.[125] Most of the disease control statutes, however, only prohibit transmitting or creating a risk of transmitting venereal diseases, and they do not specifically define venereal disease as including HIV or AIDS.[126] At least two states, however, have amended their venereal disease statutes to include HIV.[127] All of these disease control statutes have gone largely unenforced ever since

---

[123] Nev. Rev. Stat. § 193.150.

[124] *Id.* § 201.358 (as amended in 1995).

[125] *See, e.g.,* Minn. Stat. Ann. § 145.36 (prohibiting the wilful exposure of anyone affected with a contagious or infectious disease in any public place); Utah Code Ann. § 26-6-5 (prohibiting the wilful or knowing introduction of any communicable or infectious disease into any community).

[126] *See, e.g.,* Ala. Code § 22-11A-21 (prohibiting knowingly transmitting or creating the risk of transmitting a sexually transmitted disease); Cal. Health & Safety Code § 120600 (prohibiting anyone infected with venereal disease from marrying, engaging in sexual intercourse, or exposing any person to or infecting any person with the venereal disease); La. Rev. Stat. Ann. § 1062 (same); Mont. Code Ann. § 50-18-112 (prohibiting knowingly exposing another to a sexually transmitted disease); N.Y. Pub. Health Law § 2307 (prohibiting anyone knowingly infected with an infectious venereal disease from having sexual intercourse with another); S.C. Code Ann. § 44-29-60 (prohibiting knowingly exposing another to a sexually transmitted disease); S.D. Codified Laws Ann. § 34-23-1 (prohibiting the exposure of another to venereal disease); Tenn. Code Ann. § 68-10-107 (prohibiting exposure of another to sexually transmitted disease); Vt. Stat. Ann. tit. 18, § 1106 (prohibiting anyone knowingly infected with gonorrhea or syphilis in a communicable stage from engaging in sexual intercourse); W. Va. Code § 16-4-20 (prohibiting anyone with an infectious venereal disease from exposing another to infection).

[127] Fla. Stat. Ann. § 384.24 (prohibiting anyone infected with HIV or other sexually transmitted diseases, who has been informed that the disease may be transmitted by sexual intercourse, from having sexual intercourse with another, unless the other person has given informed consent); Idaho Code § 39-601 (designating HIV and AIDS as venereal diseases and prohibiting those infected with venereal disease from knowingly exposing others to infection). See § **7.8.**

World War I, when the statutes were used as part of a campaign to incarcerate prostitutes in what proved to be an ineffective effort to stop the spread of syphilis.[128]

The disease control statutes are problematic when applied to people whose conduct risks the spread of HIV. First, those statutes that simply refer to venereal diseases without specifically defining the term to include HIV would appear not to apply at all to people infected with HIV, because HIV is not generally classified as a sexually transmitted disease.[129] In New York, for example, the state commissioner of health expressly decided not to add HIV to the list of communicable and sexually transmissible diseases, and this decision was upheld by the state's highest court.[130] Thus, any attempt to prosecute people for risking transmission of HIV under these statutes would probably fail on due process grounds because the statutes do not provide fair notice that they cover HIV.[131] Second, the statutes that do expressly cover HIV have been criticized as being both underinclusive and overinclusive,[132] as discussed in § 7.8.

The disease control statutes, in sum, were enacted long before the advent of HIV, and their applicability to HIV is doubtful. They have been ineffective in controlling diseases in the past, and there is no reason to think they would be any more helpful now in controlling HIV.

---

[128] See § 7.1. *See also* Stephen V. Kenney, *Criminalizing HIV Transmission: Lessons from History and a Model for the Future,* 8 J. Contemp. Health L. & Pol'y 245, 256 (1992).

[129] Larry Gostin, *The Politics of AIDS: Compulsory State Powers, Public Health, and Civil Liberties,* 49 Ohio St. L.J. 1017, 1041 (1989).

[130] New York State Soc'y of Surgeons v. Axelrod, 572 N.E.2d 605 (N.Y. 1991). This case arose from a suit brought by four medical organizations whose membership consisted of New York state physicians. The medical organizations sought to compel the New York State Commissioner of Health to add HIV to the list of communicable and sexually transmitted diseases pursuant to a state public health law. The addition of HIV to the list would have triggered statutory provisions relating to reporting, mandatory testing, and contact tracing. The Commissioner of Health had determined based on policy considerations that it would be counterproductive to add HIV to the list. Contact tracing is only useful in stemming the spread of those communicable diseases which, unlike HIV, have a short incubation period and are readily discoverable through symptoms that appear soon after infection. In addition, the commissioner had determined that mandatory testing and contact tracing would discourage many people infected with HIV, who already fear stigmatization, from cooperating with public health officials. The New York Court of Appeals found that these determinations were rationally based and upheld the commissioner's decision. 572 N.E.2d at 609–10. *See also* Plaza v. Estate of Wisser, 626 N.Y.S.2d 446, 452 (App. Div. 1995) (holding that New York public health law classifying as misdemeanor an act of having sexual intercourse while infected with venereal disease implicitly excludes HIV from definition of venereal disease).

[131] A penal statute fails to give fair notice of what conduct is prohibited if on its face it forbids "the doing of an act in terms so vague that men of common intelligence must necessarily guess at its meaning and differ as to its application." Connally v. General Constr. Co., 269 U.S. 385, 391 (1926); *see also* Kolender v. Lawson, 461 U.S. 352, 357 (1983) ("the void-for-vagueness doctrine requires that a penal statute define the criminal offense with sufficient definiteness that ordinary people can understand what conduct is prohibited and in a manner that does not encourage arbitrary and discriminatory enforcement").

[132] Kathleen M. Sullivan & Martha A. Field, *AIDS and the Coercive Power of the State,* 23 Harv. C.R.-C.L. L. Rev. 139, 171 (1988).

§ 7.8   HIV-Specific Criminal Statutes

Many states recently have enacted HIV-specific criminal statutes. These new statutes are partially in response to the perceived difficulties with using traditional criminal statutes to prosecute conduct that poses a risk of HIV transmission, and partially in response to political pressures to do something about the epidemic. These statutes have pushed the criminalization of HIV transmission to historic levels. Never before has a single disease been the focus of such a panoply of serious criminal laws.[133] Although in some states these statutes have the advantage of providing very detailed definitions of the conduct they prohibit, they just as frequently present problems because of their vagueness.

Since 1989, 19 states[134] plus the federal government[135] have passed HIV-specific criminal statutes, and most have classified the crime as a felony. These statutes

---

[133] *See* J. Kelly Strader, *Criminalization as a Policy Response to a Public Health Crisis,* 27 J. Marshall L. Rev. 435, 441 (1994) (legislative response of criminalizing HIV has exceeded the more restrained past responses of legislatures to outbreaks of contagious diseases such as syphilis); Michael L. Closen et al., *Criminalization of an Epidemic: HIV-AIDS and Criminal Transmission Laws,* 46 Ark. L. Rev. 921, 923 n.8 (1994) ("Commentators have observed that the HIV-specific criminal laws were hastily conceived for political expedience.").

[134] Ark. Code Ann. § 5-14-123 (class A felony: "exposes another person to [HIV] infection through the parenteral transfer of blood or blood products or engages in sexual penetration with another person without first having informed the other person of the presence of [HIV]"); Cal. Health & Safety Code § 1621.5 (felony: donates blood, body organs, semen, or breast milk knowing that he or she is infected with HIV); Fla. Stat. Ann. § 384.24 (first-degree misdemeanor: has sexual intercourse knowing of infection with HIV or other sexually transmitted diseases, having been informed of risk of transmission, and without informed consent of partner); *id.* § 381.0041(11)(b) (third-degree felony: donates blood, plasma, organs, skin, or other human tissue knowing of infection with HIV and having been informed or risk of transmission of HIV through donation); Ga. Code Ann. § 16-5-60 (felony: knowing of HIV infection and without disclosing that fact, engages in sexual intercourse or sex acts involving sex organs of one person and mouth or anus of another person, or shares hypodermic needle, or donates blood or other body fluids); Idaho Code § 39-608 (felony: knowing of HIV infection, "exposes another in any manner" to HIV or transfers or attempts to transfer his or her body fluid, body tissue or organs to another person); Ill. Ann. Stat. ch. 720, para. 5/12–16.2 (class 2 felony: knowing of HIV infection, "engages in intimate contact with another," donates blood, tissue, organs, or exchanges or transfers non-sterile intravenous drug paraphernalia); Ind. Code Ann. § 35-42-1-7 (class A felony: recklessly, knowingly, or intentionally donates blood or semen containing HIV); Kan. Stat. Ann. § 21-3435 (class A misdemeanor: knowing of infection with a "life threatening communicable disease," and with intent to expose others to that disease, engages in sexual intercourse or sodomy, sells or donates blood, semen or organs, or shares hypodermic needles); Ky. Rev. Stat. Ann. §§ 214.454, 214.990(7) (class D felony: donates blood while being infected with HIV or "at high risk for infection" with HIV); La. Rev. Stat. Ann. § 43.5 (felony: intentionally exposes another to HIV through "sexual contact" or through "any other means or contact" without the knowing and lawful consent of the victim); Md. Health-Gen. Code Ann. § 18-601.1 (misdemeanor: knowingly transferring or attempting to transfer HIV to another); Mich. Comp. Laws Ann. § 333.5210 (felony: knowing of HIV infection, "engages in sexual penetration with another person" without informing the other of the HIV infection); Mo. Ann. Stat. § 191.677 (class D felony: knowing of HIV infection, donates or

vary greatly in content. They range from simple prohibitions against the knowing or intentional transfer or attempted transfer of HIV to another person,[136] to
very detailed statutes that attempt to delineate the exact conduct proscribed.[137]
Although the United States Congress recommended that states impose criminal
sanctions only for those acting with a specific intent to expose others to HIV,[138]
only four states require specific intent.[139] The majority of states merely require
that the defendant acted knowing that he or she was infected with HIV. Of the
states requiring mere knowledge of one's HIV infection, only two states require

---

attempts to donate blood, organ, sperm or tissue, or "deliberately create[s] a grave and
unjustifiable risk of infecting another with HIV through sexual or other contact" while
knowing he or she is creating that risk); N.D. Cent. Code § 12.1-20-17 (class A felony:
knowing of HIV infection, "willfully transfers any of that person's body fluid [defined as
semen, blood or vaginal secretion] to another person"); Ohio Rev. Code Ann. § 2927.13
(felony of the third degree: knowing of HIV infection, sells or donates blood with knowledge that the blood is being accepted for purpose of transfusion to another person); Okla.
Stat. Ann. tit. 21, § 1192.1 (felony: knowing of HIV infection, and with intent to infect
another, engages in "conduct reasonably likely to result in the transfer of the person's own
blood, bodily fluids containing visible blood, semen or vaginal secretions into the bloodstream of another, or through the skin or other membranes of another person" without the
informed consent of the other person); S.C. Code Ann. § 44-29-145 (felony: knowing of
HIV infection, engages in sexual intercourse with another person without first informing
that person of his HIV infection, or sells or donates blood semen tissue or organs, or forcibly
engages in sexual intercourse without the consent of the other person, or shares a hypodermic needle with another without informing that person of his HIV infection); Va. Code
Ann. § 32.1-289.2 (class 6 felony: donates or sells blood or bodily fluids, organs or tissues,
knowing of HIV infection and having been instructed that such donations may transmit
HIV); Wash. Rev. Code Ann. § 9A.36.021 (class B felony: "with intent to inflict bodily
harm, exposes or transmits" HIV).

135 18 U.S.C. § 1118 (1994) applies only to those who, knowing they have tested positive for
HIV, "donate or sell blood, semen, tissues, organs or other bodily fluids for use by another,
except as determined necessary for medical research or testing." Conviction carries a penalty
of not less than one year and up to 10 years in prison. The constitutionality of this law may
be open to challenge under the Commerce Clause of the United States Constitution. *See*
United States v. Lopez, 115 S. Ct. 1624 (1995) (striking down as a violation of the Commerce Clause the Gun-Free School Zones Act, which forbids possession of a gun in a school
zone but does not require that the firearm have any nexus with interstate commerce).

136 *See* Md. Health-Gen. Code Ann. § 18-601.1; Wash. Rev. Code Ann. § 9A.36.021.

137 *See, e.g.,* Ark. Code Ann. § 5-14-123 (defining *sexual penetration* to mean "sexual intercourse, cunnilingus, fellatio, anal intercourse, or any other intrusion, however, slight, of any
part of a person's body or of any object into the genital or anal openings of another person's
body, but emission of semen is not required"). The Arkansas statute has been criticized for
being both under- and overinclusive and for being inconsistent with public policy. Michael
L. Closen, *The Arkansas Criminal HIV Exposure Law: Statutory Issues, Public Policy
Concerns, and Constitutional Objections,* 1993 Ark. L. Notes 47 (1993).

138 42 U.S.C. § 300ff-47 (1994) (CARE Act).

139 *See* Kan. Stat. Ann. § 21-3435; La. Rev. Stat. Ann. § 214.454; Okla. Stat. Ann. tit. 21,
§ 1192.1; Wash. Rev. Code Ann. § 9A.36.021.

proof that the defendant knew of the infection as a result of an HIV positive blood test.[140] The other states fail to define the knowledge element at all.[141] Only two states require proof that the defendant had previously been informed of the risk of transmitting HIV.[142]

Although most statutes cover sexual acts, needle sharing, and blood donation,[143] the federal government and some states have chosen to criminalize only the act of blood donation by HIV-infected persons,[144] and one state has only criminalized sexual acts by infected individuals that may risk HIV transmission.[145] Most of the statutes expressly permit the defendant to raise as a defense the claim that he or she informed the victim regarding the HIV infection and the victim consented to the exposure.[146] Only one state, North Dakota, requires that in addition to obtaining the victim's informed consent, the defendant must also use a condom or other "appropriate prophylactic device."[147] None of the states allow the fact that the defendant used a condom to be a complete defense by itself.

---

[140] Ark. Code Ann. § 5-14-123 ("knows he or she has tested positive for [HIV]"); Cal. Health & Safety Code § 1621.5 ("knows that he or she has [AIDS], as diagnosed by a physician and surgeon, or who knows that he or she has tested reactive to the etiologic agent of AIDS or to the antibodies to that agent"); *see also* 18 U.S.C. § 1118 ("after testing positive for . . . [HIV] and receiving actual notice of that fact").

[141] Fla. Stat. Ann. §§ 384.24, 381.0041(11)(b); Ga. Code Ann. § 16-5-60; Idaho Code § 39-608; Ill. Ann. Stat. ch. 720, para. 5/12-16.2; Ind. Code Ann. § 35-42-1-7; Ky. Rev. Stat. Ann. §§ 214.454, 214.990(7); Md. Health-Gen. Code Ann. § 18-601.1; Mich. Comp. Laws Ann. § 333.5210; Mo. Ann. Stat. § 191.677; N.D. Cent. Code § 12.1-20-17; Ohio Rev. Code Ann. § 2927.13; S.C. Code Ann. § 44-29-145; Va. Code Ann. § 32.1-289.2.

[142] Fla. Stat. Ann. §§ 381.0041(11)(b), 384.24; Va. Code Ann. § 32.1-289.2.

[143] *See* Ark. Code Ann. § 5-14-123; Ga. Code Ann. § 16-5-60; Idaho Code § 39-608; Ill. Ann. Stat. ch. 720, para. 5/12-16.2; Kan. Stat. Ann. § 21-3435; Md. Health-Gen. Code Ann. § 18-601.1; Mo. Ann. Stat. § 191.677; Okla. Stat. Ann. Tit. 21, § 1192.1; S.C. Code Ann. § 44-29-145; Wash. Rev. Code Ann. § 9A.36.021.

[144] *See* 18 U.S.C. § 1118; Cal. Health & Safety Code § 1621.5; Ind. Code Ann. § 35-42-1-7; Ky. Rev. Stat. Ann. § 214.454; Ohio Rev. Code Ann. § 2927.13; Va. Code Ann. § 32.1-289.2.

[145] Mich. Laws Ann. § 333.5210.

[146] The following state statutes include the lack of informed consent as an element that the prosecution must prove as part of its case: Ark. Code Ann. § 5-14-123; Fla. Stat. Ann. § 384.24; Ga. Code Ann. § 16-5-60; La. Rev. Stat. Ann. § 43.5; Mich. Comp. Laws Ann. § 333.5210; Okla. Stat. Ann. tit. 21, § 1192.1; S.C. Code Ann. § 44-29-145. In Idaho, Illinois, and North Dakota, informed consent may be raised by the defendant as an affirmative defense. *See* Idaho Code § 39-608; Ill. Ann. Stat. ch. 720, para. 5/12-16.2; N.D. Cent. Code § 12.1-20-17. The states of Maryland, Missouri, Ohio, Virginia, and Washington do not expressly provide for any defense of informed consent. *See* Md. Health-Gen. Code Ann. § 18-601.1; Mo. Ann. Stat. § 191.677; Ohio Rev. Code Ann. § 2927.13; Va. Code Ann. § 32.1-289.2; Wash. Rev. Code Ann. § 9A.36.021.

[147] N.D. Cent. Code § 12.1-20-17(3).

Commentators have argued that HIV-specific criminal statutes have several advantages over traditional criminal statutes.[148] The primary advantage is the elimination of the burden of proving the problematic elements of intent and causation, elements that usually must be proven under traditional criminal laws, as discussed in §§ **7.2** through **7.4.** Instead, under most HIV-specific statutes, the prosecution need only prove that the defendant knew he or she was infected and then engaged in acts that created some risk of transmission, even if transmission did not actually result.

A second advantage is that the HIV-specific statutes, if narrowly written, can give the public clear warning as to exactly what behavior is prohibited. The traditional criminal statutes, on the other hand, are too general to provide any specific warning, and it is left up to the prosecutors to determine what acts create a sufficient risk of transmission to warrant prosecution. Through passage of HIV-specific statutes then, the legislators, rather than individual prosecutors, assume the responsibility for defining the crime.[149]

The third advantage of HIV-specific statutes is that those statutes which provide a defense of informed consent serve to encourage people who are infected with HIV to disclose that fact to their sexual or drug partners before engaging in risky behavior. Such disclosure would further the public health goal of encouraging people to take precautions to prevent HIV transmission.

The impetus for passage of HIV-specific criminal statutes came in part from the federal government. In 1988, the Presidential Commission on the Human Immunodeficiency Virus Epidemic recommended the enactment of such statutes, but it cautioned that "criminal sanctions for HIV transmission must be carefully drawn" and "must be directed only towards behavior which is scientifically established as a mode of transmission."[150] Congress followed up on this recommendation when it passed The Ryan White Comprehensive AIDS Resources Emergency (CARE) Act of 1990.[151] The CARE Act conditions the award of certain federal AIDS-related funds to each state on the state's certifying that its criminal laws are adequate to prosecute any HIV-infected person who, knowing of the infection, and with intent to expose others to HIV, donates blood, semen, or breast milk, engages in sexual activity, or shares hypodermic needles.[152] The CARE Act permits states to allow for the defense of informed consent.[153] Importantly, the CARE Act does not actually require states to enact

---

[148] *See* Donald H. J. Hermann, *Criminalizing Conduct Related to HIV Transmission,* 9 St. Louis U. Pub. L. Rev. 351 (1990); Jacob A. Heth, Note, *Dangerous Liaisons: Criminalizing Conduct Related to HIV Transmission,* 29 Willamette L. Rev. 843 (1993).

[149] *See* Harlon L. Dalton, *Criminal Law, in* AIDS Law Today 242, 251 (Scott Burris et al. eds., 1993).

[150] Report of the Presidential Commission on the Human Immunodeficiency Virus Epidemic 130 (1988).

[151] 42 U.S.C. § 300ff-47 (1994).

[152] *Id.* § 300ff-47(a).

[153] *Id.* § 300ff-47(b).

HIV-specific criminal statutes but allows states, in the alternative, to certify that existing criminal laws accomplish the objectives set out in the Act.[154]

The HIV-specific statutes as written have not lived up to the expectations of their proponents. First, most of the statutes are both vague and overinclusive.[155] Instead of providing clear warning, the statutes create confusion regarding what conduct is prohibited, and they appear to criminalize conduct that poses no real risk of transmitting HIV. The Washington state statute, for example, simply states that a person is guilty if he or she, "with intent to inflict bodily harm, exposes or transmits" HIV.[156] The statute does not define the term *exposes*. Thus, people infected with HIV in the state of Washington are left to wonder whether they are barred from engaging in any sexual activity whatsoever, or whether they are permitted to engage in safer sex activities such as kissing, mutual masturbation, or sexual intercourse with the use of a condom.

In *State v. Stark,*[157] however, an appellate court rejected a vagueness challenge to the statute in the case of a defendant who repeatedly engaged in unprotected sexual intercourse with three different women. The defendant, Stark, had previously tested positive for HIV and had been counseled regarding safe sex, the risk of spreading HIV, and the importance of informing his partners of his HIV infection before engaging in sex. The court found that as applied to the facts of the case, the term "expose" was not unconstitutionally vague because an ordinary person would understand that it covered unprotected sexual intercourse. The court stated,

> Any reasonably intelligent person would understand from reading the statute that the term ["expose"] refers to engaging in conduct that can cause another person to become infected with the virus. Stark engaged in unprotected sexual intercourse with other human beings after being counselled on several occasions that such conduct would expose his partners to the virus he carries. He was not forced to guess at what conduct was criminal.[158]

---

[154] *Id.* § 300ff-47(c).

[155] As the Supreme Court has held, criminal statutes that are vague offend the Due Process Clause of the Fourteenth Amendment to the United States Constitution. The Court set forth the standards for evaluating vagueness in Grayned v. City of Rockford, 408 U.S. 104, 108–09 (1972):

> First ... we insist that laws give the person of ordinary intelligence a reasonable opportunity to know what is prohibited, so that he may act accordingly. Vague laws may trap the innocent by not providing fair warning. Second, if arbitrary and discriminatory enforcement is to be prevented, laws must provide explicit standards for those who apply them. A vague law impermissibly delegates basic policy matters to policemen, judges, and juries for resolution on an ad hoc and subjective basis, with the attendant dangers of arbitrary and discriminatory application.

[156] Wash. Rev. Code Ann. § 9A.36.021.

[157] 832 P.2d 109 (Wash. Ct. App. 1992).

[158] *Id.* at 116. To the extent that this decision defines expose as "conduct that can cause another person to become infected" with HIV, it still does not cure the vagueness of the statute. By

The court also found that the requirement of specific intent "to inflict bodily harm" in the statute tended to make the remaining terms less vague.[159] The court found the evidence sufficient to prove intent to inflict bodily injury based on testimony that Stark, when confronted by a neighbor about his sexual activity, said, "I don't care. If I'm going to die, everybody's going to die." The fact that this sort of flippant comment could be sufficient to prove an intent to inflict bodily harm, as opposed to establishing merely reckless indifference, shows how little proof of intent is needed to satisfy juries and courts in cases involving HIV-specific criminal statutes.

It is important to note, however, that because the court only considered the vagueness argument "as applied" to the facts of this case, and not as applied to other conduct, defendants in factually dissimilar cases might have the statute struck down as unconstitutionally vague. When the courts examine a statute for vagueness, as long as the statute does not impinge on First Amendment freedoms, it will only be struck down if it is vague "as applied" to the facts of that case. In other words, the court will only look to see whether the defendant in that case had sufficiently clear warning in the statute that the specific acts he is accused of committing were forbidden. As a result, the courts will not consider whether the statute might be vague "on its face," as applied to other hypothetical cases.[160]

Even the HIV statutes that attempt to be specific and to delineate the prohibited conduct tend to suffer from vagueness problems. The Illinois statute, for example, states in part that a "person commits criminal transmission of HIV when he or she, knowing that he or she is infected with HIV, engages in intimate contact with another."[161] The statute fails to define *knowing,* and thus it is unclear whether it covers only actual knowledge or constructive knowledge as well.[162] The statute does define *intimate contact with another* as "the exposure of the body of one person to a bodily fluid of another person in a manner that

---

"can cause" does the court mean theoretically capable of causing or likely to cause? For example, although HIV has been isolated in saliva, and thus it would be theoretically possible to transmit HIV through kissing, the chances of such transmission are so remote that kissing is considered safe. See **Ch. 1.**

[159] *Id.* at 115–16.

[160] *See* Village of Hoffman Estates v. Flipside, Hoffman Estates, Inc., 455 U.S. 489, 494–95 n.7 (1982); Parker v. Levy, 417 U.S. 733, 756 (1974).

[161] Ill. Ann. Stat. ch. 720, para. 5/12-16.12(1).

[162] *See* Michael L. Closen & Jeffrey S. Deutschman, *A Proposal to Repeal the Illinois HIV Transmission Statute,* 78 Ill. B.J. 592, 594–95 (1990) (if constructive knowledge is sufficient under the Illinois statute, then a person might be found to "know" he or she is infected with HIV if the person's lover is infected, or if the person belongs to a high risk group such as sexually active gay men, intravenous drug users, or hemophiliacs). *See also* Cooper v. State, 539 So. 2d 508, 511 (Fla. Dist. Ct. App. 1989) (holding that enhanced sentence for gay man convicted of sexual battery was justified because defendant, who tested positive for HIV just prior to sentencing, should have known "because of his lifestyle" that he had been exposed to HIV and might expose the victim).

could result in the transmission of HIV."[163] The term *bodily fluid,* however, is not defined, and there is no indication whether the phrase "could result in transmission" includes all theoretical possibilities of transmission. As one commentator has pointed out, this statute on its face appears to make it a felony for a person infected with HIV to shake hands if his palms are sweaty, or to swim in a public swimming pool, although both behaviors pose no realistic threat of HIV transmission.[164] The statute would also appear to require that a pregnant woman have an abortion if, after becoming pregnant, she discovered that she was infected with HIV. If the woman were to carry the child to term she would risk exposing the child to HIV-infected body fluids, and thus an abortion would be the only way for her to avoid committing a felony.[165]

Closely related to the problems of vagueness and overinclusiveness is the concern that HIV-specific statutes may violate the right to privacy.[166] Although the United States Supreme Court has adopted a narrow interpretation of the right to privacy,[167] the state courts are free to adopt a broader interpretation under their state constitutions, and several have done so. Thus, some state courts have held under their state constitutions that the right to privacy includes the right of adults to engage in private, noncommercial, consensual sexual conduct.[168]

---

[163] Ill. Ann. Stat. ch. 720, para. 5/12-16.2(b).

[164] Michael C. Closen & Jeffrey S. Deutschman, *A Proposal To Repeal the Illinois HIV Transmission Statute,* 78 Ill. B.J. 592 (1990). Like the Washington statute, the Illinois statute has withstood constitutional vagueness challenges. In each case, however, the court only determined that the statute was not vague as applied in that case. People v. Russell, 630 N.E.2d 794, 796 (Ill.), *cert. denied,* 115 S. Ct. 97 (1994) (two defendants in two separate cases, each knowing they were infected with HIV, had sexual intercourse with others without disclosing their HIV status); People v. Dempsey, 610 N.E.2d 208, 222–24 (Ill. App. Ct. 1993) (defendant, who had been informed by a doctor that he was infected with HIV and who had been counseled regarding the risks of transmission, had oral sex with and ejaculated in the mouth of victim).

[165] Michael C. Closen & Jeffrey S. Deutschman, *A Proposal To Repeal the Illinois HIV Transmission Statute,* 78 Ill. B.J. 592 (1990). The risk of a mother's transmitting HIV to a fetus is estimated to be between 30 and 50 percent. See **Ch. 1.**

[166] One can also argue that in addition to the right to privacy, the First Amendment right to freedom of expression is infringed by restrictions on private consensual sexual conduct since sexual activity is expressive and communicative. *See* David Cole & William N. Eskridge, Jr., *From Hand-holding to Sodomy: First Amendment Protection of Homosexual (Expressive) Conduct,* 29 Harv. C.R.-C.L. L. Rev. 319, 325–37 (1994). Courts in Washington and Illinois, however, have without any analysis rejected the argument that HIV-specific criminal statutes in those states impinge on freedom of expression. People v. Russell, 630 N.E.2d 794, 796 (Ill. 1994); State v. Stark, 832 P.2d 109, 115 (Wash. Ct. App. 1992).

[167] Bowers v. Hardwick, 478 U.S. 186, 190–92 (1986).

[168] *See, e.g.,* Campbell v. Sundquist, 926 S.W.2d 250 (Tenn. Ct. App. 1996) (striking down state sodomy statute on ground that it violates state constitutional right to privacy, which includes right of adults "to engage in consensual and noncommercial sexual activities in the privacy of that adult's home" with adults of the same gender); Commonwealth v. Wasson, 842 S.W.2d 487, 496–97 (Ky. 1992); People v. Onofre, 415 N.E.2d 936 (N.Y. 1980), *cert. denied,* 451 U.S. 987 (1981); Commonwealth v. Bonadio, 415 A.2d 47 (Pa. 1980).

When a state statute regulates conduct in a way that infringes on a fundamental right, such as the right to privacy, the courts subject the statute to strict scrutiny.[169] Under strict scrutiny analysis, the statute may be upheld only if it furthers compelling state interests, and if it is narrowly tailored to meet those interests.[170] To be sure, the prevention of the spread of HIV is a compelling state interest. But to the extent that an HIV statute is overinclusive and criminalizes private, adult, consensual sexual conduct that poses little or no risk of HIV transmission, the statute is not narrowly tailored to prevent HIV transmission. Such a statute therefore could be challenged as an unconstitutional infringement of the right to privacy,[171] or may violate the right to equal protection.[172]

The strongest argument against HIV-specific criminal statutes is one of public health policy. No matter how well written the statutes are, they run counter to public education efforts because they discourage people from getting tested for HIV or informing their sexual partners if they do test positive.

The statutes that do not provide for a defense of informed consent, for example, in effect tell people that if they test positive for HIV, they will be forbidden from engaging in most sexual activities, even if their partner knowingly consents and even if they always use a condom to minimize the risk of transmission. Thus, anyone in a high risk group would have a powerful incentive to avoid getting tested: they would know that if they test positive, even safer sex activities could lead to prosecution for a felony. If, nonetheless, they do get tested and find they are infected with HIV, they certainly would not want to tell their sexual partners. They would fear that whatever safe sex precautions they take, they could still face criminal prosecution if an angry or spurned lover reports them to the police.

The statutes that do provide for a defense of informed consent are also counterproductive from a public health point of view. Like all HIV-specific criminal statutes, they discourage people from getting tested for HIV by raising the threat of criminal sanctions. Some people, already reluctant to find out if they are infected with HIV, would be further discouraged by the knowledge that if they do test positive, their sex lives will be governed by strict criminal laws.[173] Moreover, although these statutes do provide some incentive for people who have tested positive for HIV to inform their sexual partners of their status, this incentive to

---

[169] Laurence. H. Tribe, American Constitutional Law 1454–65 (2d ed. 1988).

[170] Id.

[171] Cf. Colautti v. Franklin, 439 U.S. 379, 394–401 (1979) (abortion control statute invalidated on its face as violation of right to privacy even though it could conceivably have had some valid application).

[172] See R. Brian Leech, *Criminalizing Sexual Transmission of HIV: Oklahoma's Intentional Transmission Statute: Unconstitutional or Merely Unenforceable?*, 46 Okla. L. Rev. 687 (1993) (arguing that Oklahoma statute has a discriminatory impact on homosexuals and violates equal protection).

[173] One commentator has argued that whatever discouraging effect criminal statutes may have on people's willingness to get tested, it will be counteracted by the desire to have early access to drug therapies which may be most effective when given early in the course of HIV disease. Donald H. J. Hermann, *Criminalizing Conduct Related to HIV Transmission,* 9 St. Louis U. Pub. L. Rev. 351 (1990). The flaw in this argument is that it assumes people will

disclose exists only prior to their first sexual encounter with their partner. If an HIV-infected person fails to obtain informed consent before the first encounter, the incentive thereafter would be for him or her not to tell the partner at all. To inform the partner any time after their first sexual encounter would be to admit to having committed a felony. Because, as a matter of public health, late disclosure is better than no disclosure at all, this effect of discouraging late disclosure runs counter to an important public health goal.

All of the HIV-specific statutes, in addition, discourage testing because prosecution inevitably breaches the confidentiality of the test results. Once criminal charges have been brought, the charges are a matter of public record[174] and the accused may even discover that his or her HIV positive status is widely publicized in the press. The courts, moreover, have not been willing to suppress evidence of test results that are obtained in apparent violation of confidentiality statutes.[175] Thus, HIV-specific statutes tend to undermine the assurances of public health officials that HIV test results will remain confidential.[176]

Because HIV-specific criminal statutes are so counterproductive from a public health standpoint, numerous commentators have argued against them.[177] And four

---

rationally balance the costs and benefits of the HIV test. Some people will and some people will not, especially because getting an HIV test raises emotionally charged issues related to life-style, sex and death. Moreover, because the value of early treatment for HIV is still speculative, some people may decide that the danger of having the criminal justice system intrude on their private lives outweighs any benefits the HIV test may offer.

[174] *See, e.g.,* Doe v. Alton Tel., 805 F. Supp. 30 (C.D. Ill. 1992) (holding that state AIDS confidentiality law is not applicable to publication of information relating to court order that a defendant convicted of prostitution undergo HIV testing if that information was already contained in public court files); *cf.* People v. Anonymous, 582 N.Y.S.2d 350 (Monroe County Ct. 1992) (allowing HIV testing and release of medical records for defendant accused of biting two people, but requiring that defendant's name be kept confidential).

[175] *See, e.g.,* United States v. Jessup, 966 F.2d 1355 (10th Cir. 1992) (holding that exclusionary rule did not apply when FBI agents illegally disclosed defendant's HIV status to a witness so as to obtain names of other sexual assault victims); State v. Stark, 832 P.2d 109 (Wash. Ct. App. 1992) (holding that state confidentiality statute was not violated by prosecutor who obtained information regarding defendant's HIV status from county health official). *But see* State v. J.E., 606 A.2d 1160 (N.J. Super. Ct. 1992) (rejecting prosecutor's request for disclosure of defendant's medical records).

[176] *See* Report of the Presidential Commission on the Human Immunodeficiency Virus Epidemic 126 (1988) ("Rigorous maintenance of confidentiality is considered critical to the success of the public health endeavor to prevent the transmission and spread of HIV infection."). *See also* American Bar Ass'n No. 115A, *Summary of the House of Delegates, 1988 Mid-Year Meeting* § III (Feb. 8–9, 1988) (Report to House of Delegates) (ABA described confidentiality as "a sine qua non for testing" and observed that almost all federal and state public health officials agree that strict confidentiality protections are necessary to encourage people to voluntarily receive HIV testing.).

[177] *See, e.g.,* Kathleen M. Sullivan & Martha A. Field, *AIDS and the Coercive Power of the State,* 23 Harv. C.R.-C.L. L. Rev. 139, 196 (1988) (arguing that the disadvantages of HIV specific statutes outweigh the advantages because the statutes run counter to public health efforts to encourage testing, threaten the privacy of sexual relationships, and increase risk of official harassment and abuse of groups at risk for HIV that are already stigmatized in our society); Harlon L. Dalton, *Criminal Law, in* AIDS Law Today 242, 250–56 (Scott Burris et

of the five states with the highest levels of HIV infection have wisely chosen not to enact any HIV-specific statutes criminalizing sexual activity.[178] The most effective public health response to the HIV epidemic is massive public education to encourage testing among those at high risk and to encourage safer sex practices and needle exchange programs that will reduce the risk of transmission. Because criminalization of HIV may only undercut the public education approach, it should be avoided. Instead, only the most egregious cases involving a genuine risk of HIV transmission should be prosecuted, and they can be prosecuted under traditional criminal statutes, such as reckless endangerment, rather than HIV-specific statutes.

§ 7.9   Military Offenses

The military is the jurisdiction that has seen by far the most HIV-related criminal prosecutions. This large number of prosecutions results not from a high percentage of HIV-infected people in the military—all applicants are tested for HIV and those who test positive are not admitted—but from the universal mandatory testing of all military personnel. All active duty, reserve, and national guard service members are tested for HIV periodically, and all positive test results are reported to the military authorities. See **Chapter 3.** The military command generally issues

---

al. eds., 1993) (arguing that HIV-specific criminal statutes are not justified by theories of deterrence or retribution and tend to undermine public health response to HIV); Mark H. Jackson, *The Criminalization of HIV, in* AIDS Agenda: Emerging Issues in Civil Rights 239, 240–42 (Nan D. Hunter & William B. Rubenstein eds., 1992) (arguing that coercive criminal measures against the spread of HIV are "both impossible to implement and ineffective in fighting the spread of the disease" and that the approach of criminalization "largely contradicts and undermines current public health strategies"); Larry Gostin, *The Politics of AIDS: Compulsory State Powers,* 49 Ohio St. L.J. 1017, 1054–57 (1989) (arguing that HIV-specific criminal statutes will tend to exacerbate public health problems, and that the statutes will "further stigmatize carriers and raise apprehension among the public"). *See also* Joint Subcommittee on AIDS in the Criminal Justice System, *AIDS and the Criminal Jus.ice System: Executive Summary of the Final Report,* 144 Rec. of Ass'n of Bar of City of N.Y. 601, 621 (Oct. 1989) (recommending against proposals to enact HIV-specific criminal statutes).

[178] The five states with the highest number of reported AIDS cases as of June 1995 were New York, California, Florida, Texas, and New Jersey. These five states account for 60% of the reported AIDS cases in the United States. *See* CDC, HIV/AIDS Surveillance Report 5 (1995). Of these five states, only Florida has an HIV-specific statute that criminalizes (as a misdemeanor) sexual activity that may risk transmission of HIV. *See* Fla. Stat. Ann. § 384.24. California does have an HIV-specific criminal statute relating to donation of blood, body organs, and semen, Cal. Health & Safety Code § 1621.5, but the state does not have any statute specifically criminalizing HIV transmission through sexual conduct. Traditional criminal statutes cover HIV transmission in Texas, and in 1993 the legislature repealed its 1989 HIV-specific statute, Tex. Code Ann. § 22.012, repealed by Acts 1993, 73d Leg., ch. 900, § 1.01.

specific orders to HIV positive personnel prohibiting unsafe sexual activity, and violation of these orders can lead to criminal prosecution.

The criminal prosecutions in the military relating to transmission of HIV may be divided into three categories: 1) prosecutions for violations of safe sex orders; 2) prosecutions for conduct prejudicial to good order and discipline; and 3) prosecutions for assault. The first two are uniquely military in nature; the third is analogous to civilian prosecutions for assault.[179]

§ 7.10 —Violations of Safe Sex Orders

The typical safe sex order issued to an HIV positive service member directs him or her, at a minimum, to inform all sexual partners of his or her HIV positive status prior to sexual relations, and requires the service member to use condoms during sexual intercourse.[180] The military courts have upheld these orders, ruling that they serve the valid military purpose of preventing the spread of disease, and that they do not violate the right of privacy.[181] Violation of a safe sex order is prosecuted under Article 90 of the Uniform Code of Military Justice, which provides for the court martial of anyone who willfully disobeys a lawful order.[182]

United States v. Womack[183] provides an example of an overbroad safe sex order that was upheld in spite of the fact that the order covered activity that involved no real risk of transmission of HIV. Womack, who was serving in the Air Force, tested positive for HIV and was counseled on safe sex practices. His

---

[179] *See generally* David A. Schlueter, Military Criminal Justice: Practice and Procedure 99–107 (4th ed. 1996) (surveying the military's various types of HIV-related prosecutions); Elizabeth Beard McLaughlin, *A "Society Apart?" The Military's Response to the Threat of AIDS,* Army Law. 3, 6–16 (Oct. 1993) (same).

[180] *See, e.g.,* United States v. Womack, 29 M.J. 88, 89 (C.M.A. 1989).

[181] *Id.;* United States v. Dumford, 30 M.J. 137 (C.M.A.) (upholding conviction for violation of safe sex order by service member who engaged in unprotected consensual heterosexual sex without informing partner of his HIV infection), *cert. denied,* 498 U.S. 854 (1990); United States v. Sargeant, 29 M.J. 812, 814–17 (A.C.M.R. 1989) (same); United States v. Negron, 28 M.J. 775, 776–79 (A.C.M.R.) (upholding conviction for violation of safe sex order by service member who did wear a condom during heterosexual intercourse but did not inform partner of his HIV infection), *aff'd,* 29 M.J. 324 (C.M.A. 1989). The military courts have not yet addressed the question whether the safe sex orders may constitutionally be applied to sex within the marital relationship. The Army's version of the order does not apply to marital relations, but the Air Force's version does apply. *See* Elizabeth Beard McLaughlin, *A "Society Apart?" The Military's Response to the Threat of AIDS,* Army Law. 3, 10 (Oct. 1993). One commentator has argued that because of the strength of the right to privacy in the context of marriage, a successful prosecution for informed, consensual, but unprotected sex with one's spouse would be unlikely. David A. Schlueter, Military Criminal Justice: Practice and Procedure 106 (4th ed. 1996).

[182] 10 U.S.C. § 890(2) (1983).

[183] 29 M.J. 88 (C.M.A. 1989).

base commander then issued a six-part order requiring Womack, in part, to take affirmative steps "during any sexual activity to protect your sexual partner from coming in contact with your blood, semen, urine, feces, or saliva."[184]

Womack's prosecution arose from an act of nonconsensual sex with another service member. An airman who had fallen asleep on the floor in Womack's room awoke to find Womack performing fellatio upon him. The airman fled the room and later reported the incident to the authorities. Womack was convicted of violating the safe sex order as well as of committing "forcible sodomy."[185] The lack of consent clearly justified the conviction for forcible sex. But Womack's performance of fellatio upon the airman, which merely brought Womack's saliva in contact with the skin on the airman's penis, involved no risk of transmission of HIV, and thus the safe sex order was plainly overbroad as applied to this conduct. In the lower military appellate court (the Air Force Court of Military Review), the judges upheld the ban on contact with saliva based on the testimony of two military doctors that "it was possible but not very likely that one could transmit the virus through his saliva incident to an act of fellatio."[186] The judges acknowledged, however, that as more is learned about HIV, future safe sex orders would have to be adjusted "to reflect current knowledge."

§ 7.11 —Conduct Prejudicial to Good Order

The second category of uniquely military prosecutions for HIV transmission consists of those prosecutions brought under the *general article,* Article 134 of the Uniform Code of Military Justice. Article 134 criminalizes all conduct "to the prejudice of the good order and discipline in the armed forces" and "all conduct of a nature to bring discredit upon the armed forces."[187] Despite the lack of specificity in this language, the military courts have upheld prosecutions under this article for HIV-infected people who engage in unsafe sex. The courts have reasoned that the safe sex counseling all HIV positive service members receive provides sufficient notice of the conduct forbidden by Article 134.[188]

---

[184] *Id.* at 89. The order's requirement that Womack notify all health care professionals (which would appear to include even a nurse taking his temperature) was certainly overbroad and be no need for an HIV positive person to inform any health care worker, unless it is directly relevant to his treatment or diagnosis. The issue of HIV transmission in the health care setting is discussed in **Chs. 1** and **3.**

[185] *Id.* at 88–89.

[186] *Id.* at 89. The lack of evidence for HIV transmission by saliva is discussed in **Ch. 1.**

[187] U.C.M.J. art. 134, 10 U.S.C. § 934 (1983). The Supreme Court has upheld this article as being neither unconstitutionally vague nor overbroad in the context of military society and its justice system. Parker v. Levy, 381 U.S. 479 (1965).

[188] *See, e.g.,* United States v. Woods, 28 M.J. 318, 319 (C.M.A. 1989) (upholding prosecution under Article 134 on the grounds that unsafe sex by an HIV-infected person is an act that is "palpably and directly prejudicial to the good order and discipline of the service" and that an accused is on "fair notice" that such conduct is forbidden based on training sessions concerning Article 134 and individual counseling given to HIV infected service members regarding safe sex practices); United States v. Morris, 30 M.J. 1221 (A.C.M.R. 1990).

In *United States v. Morris,*[189] for example, an HIV-infected serviceman was charged with an Article 134 violation for engaging in sexual intercourse with a woman on numerous occasions and using a condom only about 25 percent of the time. The serviceman, who had been counseled on safe sex practices, had informed the woman of his HIV infection, and she had consented to the unprotected sex knowing that she might contract HIV. The court held that in view of the risk of great bodily harm to the woman, her consent was not a defense and the unprotected sex constituted a crime under Article 134.[190]

§ 7.12   —Prosecutions for Assault

The third category of military prosecutions consists of aggravated assault charges brought under Article 128. This article defines *aggravated assault* as an assault committed with a means "likely to produce death or grievous bodily harm."[191] In a series of cases, however, the military courts have stretched the interpretation of the term *likely to produce* so as to include even that conduct which is not likely to transmit HIV.

In *United States v. Johnson,*[192] an HIV-positive serviceman engaged in consensual sex with a 17-year-old civilian without informing him that he was HIV positive. The serviceman attempted to have anal intercourse with the civilian without using a condom but abandoned the attempt before achieving penetration. The serviceman had been counseled on safe sex practices, but he had not received any safe sex order. The military charged him with aggravated assault and sodomy. Because the crime of assault under Article 128 includes attempts to cause bodily harm,[193] the fact that the serviceman did not actually have intercourse with the civilian was not a defense to the assault charge. The court focussed its analysis on the question of "How likely is 'likely?' "—whether unprotected anal intercourse constitutes a means likely to produce death or grievous bodily harm.[194] The court decided that "likely" need only be "more than

---

[189] 30 M.J. 1221 (A.C.M.R. 1990).

[190] *Id.* at 1228. Morris was sentenced to a bad-conduct discharge, forfeiture of $400 pay per month for three months, and restriction to the limits of his base. *See also* United States v. Bygrave, 40 M.J. 839 (N.M.C.M.R. 1994) (holding that knowing consent to unprotected sexual intercourse with an HIV-infected service member is not a defense to the charge of aggravated assault).

[191] U.C.M.J. art. 128, 10 U.S.C. § 928 (1994).

[192] United States v. Johnson, 27 M.J. 798, 801 (A.R.C.M.R. 1988), *aff'd,* 30 M.J. 53 (C.M.A.), *cert. denied,* 498 U.S. 919 (1990).

[193] The first element of assault under Article 128 is "that the accused attempted to do, offered to do, or did bodily harm to a certain person." United States v. Johnson, 30 M.J. at 56 (citing The Manual for Courts-Martial, United States ¶ 54b(4)(a)(i), pt. IV (1984)).

[194] *Id.* at 57. It is interesting to note that although the serviceman did perform fellatio upon the civilian during the consensual sex, the military correctly did not charge that this sexual conduct presented any risk of HIV transmission. Instead, the military charged that the aggravated assault consisted of the attempt to have unprotected anal intercourse. Anal intercourse without the use of a condom does in fact present a risk of HIV transmission, as

merely a fanciful, speculative, or remote possibility," and it therefore held that unprotected anal intercourse "would have been likely to transmit a disease which can ultimately result in death."[195]

In *United States v. Joseph,*[196] the Court of Military Appeals provided another interpretation of the term *likely* which further diluted its meaning. Joseph, who had tested positive for HIV and had been counseled on safe sex practices, had sexual intercourse with a woman on one occasion without first informing her of his HIV infection. The woman herself later tested positive for HIV. Joseph claimed that during their sexual encounter he had used a condom with a lubricant containing nonoxynol-9, a spermicide added to some lubricants and found to have some anti-HIV effect.[197] At trial, a medical expert testified that the chances of transmitting HIV in a single sexual encounter were small, and that use of a condom could be extremely effective in reducing the risk further. The expert also testified, however, that condoms are not 100 percent effective in preventing transmission.

The Court of Military Appeals, faced with evidence that transmission of HIV in this case would not have been likely, ruled that "the question is not the statistical probability of HIV invading the victim's body, but rather the likelihood of the virus causing death or serious bodily harm if it invades the victim's body. The probability of infection need only be 'more than merely a fanciful, speculative, or remote possibility.'"[198] The court analogized the risk of HIV infection to the risk of a rifle bullet causing injury: "If we were considering a rifle bullet instead of HIV, the question would be whether the bullet is likely to inflict death or serious bodily harm if it hits the victim, not the statistical probability of the bullet hitting the victim."[199] The court thus entirely abandoned any requirement that the risk of HIV transmission itself be likely in order for the conduct to meet the definition of aggravated assault. Accordingly, the court held that even ostensibly protected sexual intercourse was an assault "with a means likely to cause death or grievous bodily injury."[200]

discussed in **Ch. 1.** United States v. Johnson, 27 M.J. at 801. *Cf.* United States v. Womack, 29 M.J. 88 (C.M.A. 1989) (holding that HIV positive serviceman performing fellatio violated safe sex order directing him to prevent his saliva from having contact with any sex partners).

[195] United States v. Johnson, 30 M.J. at 57. Johnson was sentenced to confinement for six years, total forfeitures, reduction in rank, and dishonorable discharge. *Id.* at 54.

[196] 37 M.J. 392 (C.M.A. 1993).

[197] *Id.* at 394. Joseph's testimony regarding the condom was disputed. The woman with whom he had sex testified that Joseph had been reluctant to use a condom, and that the condom he did use appeared dry and unlubricated. She also testified that the condom broke during intercourse. *Id.*

[198] *Id.* at 397 (quoting United States v. Johnson, 30 M.J. 53, 57 (C.M.A. 1990). 37 M.J. 392, 396 (C.M.A. 1990)).

[199] *Id.* at 396.

[200] *Id.* at 397. *See also* United States v. Schoolfield, 40 M.J. 132 (C.M.A. 1994) (holding that HIV positive service member who had unwarned and unprotected sex with a woman on five occasions was guilty of aggravated assault, and that there was no need for proof of a specific

The court's holding with regard to protected sexual intercourse is particularly disturbing because it runs counter to the military's own safe sex orders and safe sex counseling. Joseph had been issued a four-page counseling sheet which explained that sexual intercourse would be safer if he used a condom with nonoxynol-9. The sheet also stated, however, that the only "absolute way" to prevent transmission of HIV was not to have sex at all. The court interpreted this counseling sheet as providing notice that even protected sex was "unsafe."[201] A more reasonable interpretation of the safe sex instructions, however, would be that condoms, although not 100 percent effective, do reduce the risk of transmission to an acceptable level. Why else would the counseling sheet encourage the use of condoms? The court's strained rationale appears to have been a means of affirming the conviction of aggravated assault because the victim had tested positive for HIV, and the court concluded that Joseph, in spite of whatever precautions he took, must have been the one who infected her despite the apparent inadequacy of the record on that issue.[202] This case illustrates the truth of the adage that bad cases make bad law.[203]

---

intent to infect, but only a general intent to have unprotected sex), *cert. denied,* 115 S. Ct. 1162 (1995); United States v. Stewart, 29 M.J. 92 (C.M.A. 1989) (holding that service member who had unprotected and unwarned sex with a woman on numerous occasions, apparently resulting in the woman's contracting HIV, was guilty of aggravated assault in view of the probability that death would result from HIV infection); United States v. Goldsmith, No. ACM 31172, 1995 WL 730266 (A.F.C.C.A. Nov. 20, 1995) (holding that service member who repeatedly had unprotected and unwarned sex with two women, but who claimed he withdrew before ejaculating, was guilty of aggravated assault even if the probability of transmission was only 1 in 1000 in each instance of sexual intercourse); United States v. Bygrave, 40 M.J. 839 (N.M.C.M.R. 1994) (holding that the informed consent of the partner is not a defense to aggravated assault if the service member did not use any protection during the sexual intercourse). *Cf.* United States v. Perez, 33 M.J. 1050 (A.C.M.R. 1991) (holding that evidence was insufficient to support conviction for aggravated assault because there was no evidence that defendant, who had had a vasectomy, could transmit HIV).

A question arises as to whether the holding in *United States v. Johnson,* that use of condoms is not a defense, can be combined with the holdings in United States v. Morris, 30 M.J. 1221 (A.C.M.R. 1990), and United States v. Bygrave, 40 M.J. 839 (N.M.C.M.R. 1994), that informed consent is not a defense? If so, it would appear that the military courts could come to the manifestly unjust conclusion that a service member who follows a safe sex order perfectly, both informing his partners of his infection and using condoms, could still be prosecuted for aggravated assault or for conduct prejudicial to good order and discipline. On the other hand, the military courts could read both these cases more narrowly and hold that use of condoms is not a defense only when there is *no* informed consent, and conversely, that consent is not a defense only when condoms are *not* used. Under this interpretation, the combination of informed consent plus use of condoms would constitute a defense.

[201] United States v. Joseph, 37 M.J. at 393.

[202] *Id.* The court simply noted that the victim became infected "apparently as a result of the sexual contact" with Joseph. Joseph was sentenced pursuant to a pretrial agreement to six months' confinement, dishonorable discharge, total forfeitures, and reduction in rank. *Id.* at 393 n.1.

[203] Richard A. Givens, Manual of Federal Practice § 8.34 (4th ed. 1991).

HIV TESTING AND DISCLOSURE

§ 7.13 Involuntary HIV Testing of Criminal Suspects and Defendants

More and more frequently, persons charged with or suspected of crime are being asked or ordered to submit to HIV testing.[204] Legislation has proliferated over the past few years to the point that now all but about 10 states by statute authorize courts to order persons suspected or convicted of certain crimes to undergo HIV testing. **Sections 7.13** through **7.18** address governmental authority to obtain, compel disclosure of, and/or use HIV-related information in the context of a criminal prosecution. Generally speaking, authority to require testing is provided by statute. Nonetheless, if a state does not have a statute governing involuntary testing, a court might still order testing under its inherent authority.[205] Other courts have determined that statutory authority is required, especially if the test would result in disclosure prohibited by a confidentiality statute.[206]

A few introductory comments are in order with respect to the utility of the antibody test used to detect HIV infection.[207] If the issue is notice to a crime victim of the alleged perpetrator's status, the real focus is not whether the suspect is HIV positive but whether the complainant is. In this respect, limitations in testing technology play a significant role. If a test is available to reliably inform a complainant as to his or her HIV status at the time of the test (that is, it

---

[204] *See, e.g.,* Bell v. Wolfish, 441 U.S. 520, 535–40 (1979) (pretrial detainees may be subject to reasonable conditions and restrictions); Harris v. Thigpen, 941 F.2d 1495 (11th Cir. 1991) (prison policy of isolating HIV positive inmates, resulting in disclosure of status, did not violate constitutionally protected privacy rights).

[205] *See, e.g.,* Government of V.I. v. Roberts, 756 F. Supp. 898, 900 (D.V.I. 1991) (general authority to obtain nontestimonial evidence); Doe v. Burgos, 638 N.E.2d 701, 703–04 (Ill. App. Ct. 1993) (court had authority to order testing of inmate who had bitten corrections officer despite lack of statutory authority because prison had broad power to test inmates for medical purposes); People v. Cook, 532 N.Y.S.2d 940 (App. Div.) (no statutory authority cited; held trial court did not violate constitutional rights of defendant convicted of rape by ordering HIV testing on request of complainant), *appeal denied,* 533 N.E.2d 676 (N.Y. 1988); People v. Thomas, 529 N.Y.S.2d 429 (Schoharie County Ct. 1988) (on motion for testing of defendant who pleaded guilty to attempted rape with evidence to grand jury that showed repeated acts of penetration, court had inherent authority to order testing "simply because it is the intelligent, humane, logical, and proper course of action under the circumstances); *see also* Syring v. Tucker, 498 N.W.2d 370 (Wis. 1993) (in a civil case, court had equitable authority to require assault defendant to submit to HIV testing even though contrary to state confidentiality law).

[206] *See, e.g.,* Doe v. Connell, 583 N.Y.S.2d 707 (App. Div. 1992); Shelvin v. Lykos, 741 S.W.2d 178, 184–85 (Tex. Ct. App. 1987) (court did not have inherent authority to order testing and disclosure of defendant detained on charges on sexual assault in absence of authorizing statute).

[207] For a discussion of the limitations inherent in the antibody tests, see **Ch. 1.**

does not have a "window period"), testing of a suspect would be a moot exercise. But because infection cannot yet be detected immediately after possible exposure, testing of the suspect is requested. Once antigen tests, as opposed to antibody tests, become more reliable and more widely available, testing defendants for notification purposes should die a natural death.

Given the window period involved in antibody testing, however, a complainant's negative result may be of little comfort, because he or she may have an undetected infection. Thus, the complainant may want to know the suspect's status to determine whether transmission was possible. However, similar problems of utility arise with testing the suspect. The test may not reveal the suspect's HIV status at the time of the test, and thus a negative result could give a complainant false comfort. More problematic, if the test occurs some time after the alleged crime took place, is that a positive result is not proof of the suspect's status at the time of that event. The question whether involuntary testing is constitutionally permissible despite these limitations is discussed in **§§ 7.16** and **7.17.**

Testing for purposes related to prosecution, as opposed to notification purposes, may seek to use the suspect's HIV status, for example, to set bail conditions. More typically, however, the test is sought to answer a different question, such as in a prosecution charging a suspect with attempt to transmit HIV. Such prosecutions, as discussed in **§§ 7.2** through **7.12,** require the prosecution to prove the defendant's knowledge that he or she was infected with HIV at the time of the alleged crime. The suspect's status, as subsequently determined, is of limited relevance to that question.

Certainly, there are many benefits to testing, both personal and societal.[208] If properly counseled as to the test's limitations, negative results from a test of either a suspect or complainant can be reassuring and retesting can be sought. If a complainant's test is negative but a suspect tests positive, the complainant can be encouraged to take greater care not to engage in high risk behavior and to be retested as indicated. And anyone whose own test result is positive can begin to explore treatment options and counseling to adjust to the significant changes that accompany living with HIV. These benefits are balanced by the potentially devastating social and emotional consequences of disclosure of positive results.

This discussion concerns testing when a suspect does not agree to testing and/or disclosure. If the suspect consents to the test and to disclosure, and no coercion is involved, no legal analysis is required. A waiver may also occur when a suspect has disclosed his or her positive status.[209] An inadvertent waiver

---

[208] *See generally* Lawrence O. Gostin et al., *HIV Testing, Counseling, and Prophylaxis after Sexual Assault,* 271 JAMA 1436 (1994); Lucinda L. Bryant & Tracey A. Hooker, National Conference of State Legislatures, State Legislative Report: Testing Sex Offenders for HIV (1991).

[209] *See, e.g., In re* Gribetz, 605 N.Y.S.2d 834, 836–37 (Rockland County Ct. 1994); People v. Anonymous, 582 N.Y.S.2d 350 (Monroe County Ct. 1992), People v. Durham, 553 N.Y.S.2d 944, 947 (Queens County Ct. 1990); People v. Hawkrigg, 525 N.Y.S.2d 752 (Suffolk County Ct. 1988); Syring v. Tucker, 498 N.W.2d 370, 376 (Wis. 1993).

can have devastating consequences, however. For example, in a case in which the defendant had voluntarily revealed his HIV positive status, the court ruled that the lack of a blood test verifying the defendant's HIV status did not prevent a sentencing enhancement based on the defendant's positive status.[210] A warrantless search through which authorities had obtained the defendant's blood had been held unlawful and the evidence suppressed, leaving the government without physical proof of the defendant's positive status.

§ 7.14 —Search and Seizure Framework

The purpose of this section is not to undertake a fully detailed analysis of the Fourth Amendment; rather, it is to provide a basic framework of analysis.[211] Reliable HIV results depend on blood tests, and therefore this section speaks primarily of blood testing as a means of learning whether a person is HIV positive. Saliva and urine screening tests have been FDA-approved, but they do not produce reliable results and must be followed up by blood testing. Authorities might seek to compel saliva or urine testing rather than a blood test, perhaps to establish probable cause that a blood test would reveal evidence of infection or to minimize the physical intrusion of the test. Nevertheless, the use of urine or saliva versus blood testing does not alter the search and seizure analysis.[212]

An involuntary blood test, for whatever purpose, is unquestionably a search and seizure within the meaning of the Fourth Amendment,[213] which states in part that "[t]he right of the people to be secure . . . against unreasonable searches and seizures, shall not be violated." "What is reasonable depends on all of the

---

[210] People v. Shoemake, 20 Cal. Rptr. 2d 36, 40–43 (Ct. App. 1993).

[211] The subject is taken up in much greater detail in the following sources: Paul H. MacDonald, Note, *AIDS, Rape, and the Fourth Amendment: Schemes for Mandatory AIDS Testing of Sex Offenders*, 43 Vand. L. Rev. 1607 (1990); Christine M. Stevenson, Note, *In the Matter of Juveniles A, B, C, D, E: Analyzing the Rights of Individuals by Junkyard Standards*, 11 J. Contemp. Health L. & Pol'y 281 (1994); Mary C. Morgan, *The Problems of Testing for HIV in the Criminal Courts*, 29 Judge J. 22 (1990); Bernadette Pratt Sadler, Comment, *When Rape Victims' Rights Meet Privacy Rights: Mandatory HIV Testing, Striking the Fourth Amendment Balance*, 67 Wash. L. Rev. 195 (1992); Barbara Danko, Comment, *The Fourth Amendment's Challenge to Mandatory AIDS Testing of Convicted Sexual Offenders—Has the AIDS Virus Attacked Our Constitutional Right to Privacy?*, 4 Seton Hall Const. L.J. 279 (1993).

[212] *See, e.g.,* Skinner v. Railway Labor Executives' Ass'n, 489 U.S. 602, 616–17 (1989) (both blood and urine collection are searches under the Fourth Amendment); United States v. Nicolosi, 885 F. Supp. 50 (E.D.N.Y. 1995) (government had to obtain warrant to compel saliva sample).

[213] Skinner v. Railway Labor Executives' Ass'n, 489 U.S. 602, 619 (1989) (quoting United States v. Montoya de Hernandez, 473 U.S. 531, 537 (1985)). *See also* Delaware v. Prouse, 440 U.S. 648, 654 (1979).

circumstances surrounding the search or seizure and the nature of the search or seizure itself," and "is judged by balancing its intrusion on the individual's Fourth
Amendment interests against its promotion of legitimate governmental interests."[214] Traditionally, "[i]n most criminal cases we strike this balance in favor
of the procedures described by the Warrant Clause of the Fourth Amendment."[215]
That clause states that "no Warrants shall issue, but upon probable cause, supported by Oath or affirmation, and particularly describing the place to be searched,
and the persons or things to be seized." Therefore, determining the constitutionality of any involuntary test should begin with an analysis of the Fourth Amendment or a state constitutional equivalent.[216] To determine the legality of a search,
it must first be asked whether the traditional warrant/probable cause requirement, or the *special needs test,* which dispenses with both the warrant and probable cause requirements, is the appropriate standard.

Generally, searches and seizures must be pursuant to a warrant supported
by probable cause that the person has committed a crime, and that the place
searched will reveal evidence of crime. This means that prior to making the
search the government must obtain a warrant by convincing a neutral and de-
tached magistrate that probable cause exists that the search will uncover evidence of crime. In this context, application of the traditional test means that the

---

[214] Skinner v. Railway Labor Executives' Ass'n, 489 U.S. at 619.

[215] *See* Schmerber v. California, 384 U.S. 757, 767 (1966) ("Such testing procedures [blood
withdrawal and test for alcohol] plainly constitute searches of 'persons,' and depend ante-
cedently upon seizures of 'persons,' within the meaning of [the Fourth] Amendment.").

[216] Other constitutional grounds for challenges include the right to privacy, equal protection,
and due process. These challenges were made and rejected in the following cases: Love v.
Superior Court, 276 Cal. Rptr. 660, 666–67 (Ct. App. 1990) (due process and equal protection); Johnetta v. Municipal Court, 267 Cal. Rptr. 666, 683 (Ct. App. 1990) (privacy under
state law); Fosman v. State, 664 So. 2d 1163, 1166 (Fla. Dist. Ct. App. 1995) (privacy under
state constitution); People v. Adams, 597 N.E.2d 574, 584–86 (Ill. 1992) (equal protection);
In re A, B, C, D, E, 847 P.2d 455, 462–63 (Wash. 1993) (privacy); State v. Farmer, 805 P.2d
200, 208–09 (Wash.) (privacy), *modified,* 812 P.2d 858 (Wash. 1991). Religious or other
First Amendment objections have not yet been put forward. *See* Government of V.I. v.
Roberts, 756 F. Supp. 898, 900 (D.V.I. 1991) (upheld constitutionality of testing of defendant to inform complainant, notes that "defendant does not complain that the requested
blood test is uniquely offensive to him for religious or other reasons").

Challenges based on the prohibition against ex post facto laws, in which the statute
authorizing the test was enacted after the alleged criminal act occurred, have also been
rejected on the theory that testing is not punitive. *See* People v. McVickers, 840 P.2d 955
(Cal. 1992); People v. Doe, 642 N.Y.S.2d 996, 1002–03 (Nassau County Ct. 1996).

As a general matter, the Fifth Amendment privilege against self-incrimination does not
provide a basis upon which to refuse to provide blood samples. *See generally* Pennsylvania
v. Muniz, 496 U.S. 582, 588–89 (1990) (citing California v. Schmerber, 384 U.S. 757,
761–62, 764 (1966)); *see also* Mace v. Morris, 851 S.W.2d 457 (Ky. 1993) (state constitution did not prohibit order compelling rape defendant to provide blood, hair, and saliva
samples for comparison with evidence obtained from complainant).

government must show that there is a fair probability (1) that the suspect committed a crime (in this discussion, had sexual contact with another knowing he or she was infected); and (2) that the blood test will provide evidence of infection.[217]

The Supreme Court has created an exception to these traditional requirements if the evidence to be seized is required for some reason other than use in a criminal prosecution. Thus, if "special needs, beyond the normal needs of law enforcement, make the warrant and probable-cause requirement impracticable," the Supreme Court has been willing to dispense with these requirements.[218] The special needs analysis has been approved in the following contexts:

Drug and alcohol testing of railroad employees involved in accidents or safety incidents[219]

Drug and alcohol testing of U.S. Customs Service employees who carry firearms, are directly involved in drug interdiction, or hold sensitive information[220]

Search of probationers' homes[221]

Search of premises of highly regulated business[222]

Search of offices of public employees[223]

Search of student property to maintain security and order in schools[224]

Body cavity searches of prison inmates following visits.[225]

If the special needs analysis applies, the government can compel a search without a warrant based on probable cause, which very significantly reduces the

---

[217] The degree of probability necessary to establish probable cause is not specifically defined. "[P]robable cause is a fluid concept—turning on the assessment of probabilities in particular factual contexts—not readily, or even usefully, reduced to a neat set of legal rules." Illinois v. Gates, 462 U.S. 213, 232 (1983). Certainly, probable cause is something less than the proof beyond a reasonable doubt required in a criminal trial, or even proof by a preponderance of the evidence required in a civil trial. "The task of the issuing magistrate is simply to make a practical, commonsense decision whether, given all the circumstances set forth in the affidavit before him, . . . there is a fair probability that . . . evidence of a crime will be found." Id. at 238.

[218] Griffin v. Wisconsin, 483 U.S. 868, 873 (1987) (quoting New Jersey v. TLO, 469 U.S. 325, 351 (1985) (Blackmun, J., concurring)); see also Skinner v. Railway Labor Executives' Ass'n, 489 U.S. 602, 619 (1989); National Treasury Employees Union v. Von Raab, 489 U.S. 656, 665–66 (1989).

[219] Skinner v. Railway Labor Executives' Ass'n, 489 U.S. 602 (1989).

[220] National Treasury Employees Union v. Von Raab, 489 U.S. 656 (1989).

[221] Griffin v. Wisconsin, 483 U.S. 868 (1987).

[222] New York v. Burger, 482 U.S. 691 (1987).

[223] O'Connor v. Ortega, 480 U.S. 709 (1987).

[224] New Jersey v. T.L.O., 469 U.S. 325 (1985).

[225] Bell v. Wolfish, 441 U.S. 520 (1979).

government's burden. So long as the person falls within the group of people to which the special needs apply, the search may be compelled.[226]

Does HIV testing in the criminal context present a "special need beyond the normal needs of law enforcement?" If the purpose of the test is law enforcement-related, discussed in § 7.15, the traditional probable cause/warrant analysis applies. The more difficult question is whether testing for notification purposes falls within the special needs category, which is addressed more fully in §§ 7.16 and 7.17. If there are enforceable protections against disclosure of the results other than to the complainant and the suspect, and if testing is limited to situations in which there is probable cause that the suspect committed a crime that carries a risk of transmission, then the special needs analysis will apply and the testing will be constitutional.

§ 7.15 —Testing for Prosecution Purposes

Testing for prosecution purposes includes use of test results for evidence at trial, as a condition of or to deny bail, or for sentence enhancement. If the test results are to be used for prosecution purposes, then the normally applicable probable cause test controls rather than the special needs test. Accordingly, the government must obtain a warrant based on (1) probable cause that the person committed a crime (which will presumably be met if the person has been formally charged or held after a preliminary hearing), and (2) probable cause that the test will provide evidence of crime, that is, that the person was infected at the time of the alleged crime. If probable cause of either is lacking, the search is illegal and the test results would be inadmissible against the suspect. For example, in a case in which police officers were bitten during an arrest and then withdrew blood from the arrestee without a warrant, the Court of Appeals for the Ninth Circuit held that the warrantless search was illegal.[227]

With regard to the question of whether there is probable cause that the test will reveal evidence of infection, presumably any reliable information concerning

---

[226] If a testing statute requires a hearing and/or court order prior to testing, a warrant requirement may be redundant. *See* State v. Superior Court, No. 1 CA-SA 95-0340, 1996 WL 408688, at *2–3 (Ariz. Ct. App. July 23, 1996). The element of probable cause is a separate question and may still be required.

[227] Barlow v. Ground, 943 F.2d 1132 (9th Cir. 1991), *cert. denied,* 505 U.S. 1206 (1992). In the underlying prosecution the California Court of Appeal vacated the lower court's grant of a warrant to draw and test the arrestee's blood. Barlow v. Superior Court, 236 Cal. Rptr. 134 (Ct. App. 1987) (rehearing denied). The purpose for the warrant was to provide evidence of intent to kill. The court of appeal, applying a straightforward probable cause analysis, held that there was no probable cause that the test would disclose evidence that a crime was committed. The California Court of Appeal's opinion reflects that the California Supreme Court, upon denying rehearing in the case, ordered that the Court of Appeal's opinion not be officially published, which may have the effect under local rule of removing the opinion's precedential value.

whether the suspect is infected, including risk group and infection rates, is relevant to the probable cause analysis. However, the cases have not focused on this issue to any great degree, and what is necessary to meet the probable cause burden is not yet settled.

If testing is sought some time after the alleged criminal event, a positive result will not tell the complainant whether the suspect was infected at the time of the event. Also, if the test results are offered as evidence of crime in a trial, the question is not HIV status but whether the suspect committed an act knowing he or she was HIV positive. A subsequent test for HIV is of only limited relevance to that question. And finally, if the suspect does not fall into any established group at risk for contracting HIV, probable cause to believe that the suspect is infected may be lacking.[228] Thus, whether the probable cause test can be met will require a case-by-case analysis.[229]

One can hypothesize various scenarios in which a prosecutor might seek evidence of a suspect's HIV status. For example, suppose a rape suspect is arrested, and the police want to test him for HIV so they can charge him with an HIV-transmission crime. Assuming there is probable cause supporting the inference that the suspect is the actual perpetrator, the next question is whether the police can obtain a warrant based on probable cause that the suspect is HIV positive. Unless the suspect has made a statement that he is HIV positive, probable cause is probably lacking. If the suspect falls into any documented risk groups for HIV infection, such as evidence that he is a long-time injecting drug user or a hemophiliac, the court must decide whether that evidence raises a fair probability that the person is infected. That will be a difficult burden to meet, because infection rates are generally not so high as to establish a fair probability that someone falling into even a well-recognized risk group is infected.

Also, assuming the suspect has not admitted to being HIV positive, is his positive HIV status probative of his knowledge of his status? If the police are unable to meet the probable cause standard, they might seek to have the blood drawn and withhold testing until some later date at which time they could meet

---

[228] *See, e.g., In re* Harry G., 599 N.Y.S.2d 425 (Broom County Fam. Ct. 1993) (denied complainant's guardian motion to discover the person's blood for HIV testing pursuant to the applicable criminal discovery statute, because there was no showing that defendant was HIV positive or of a nexus between allegations in petition and need for testing). *See also* Barlow v. Ground, 943 F.2d 1132, 1138–39 (9th Cir. 1991) (warrantless seizure of blood after suspect bit officer held unconstitutional in part because of very low likelihood that bite could transmit HIV), *cert. denied,* 505 U.S. 1206 (1992). Other courts have paid no attention to the problem and simply ordered testing to uncover evidence of crime. *E.g., In re* Anonymous, 549 N.Y.S.2d 308 (App. Div. 1989) (upheld trial court's order requiring defendant to submit to HIV testing for evidence in attempted murder prosecution), *aff'd,* 559 N.E.2d 670 (N.Y. 1990).

[229] If probable cause is established, the court must still undertake a balancing analysis, and if the suspect's interests in privacy and bodily integrity outweigh the public's interest in the information, the test cannot be compelled. Winston v. Lee, 470 U.S. 753, 760 (1985) (government's interest in obtaining evidence in criminal trial did not outweigh defendant's interest in bodily integrity that would be infringed by surgical removal of bullet).

the probable cause standard. This would deprive a suspect from later arguing that he was infected after the incident occurred. The police may also want the blood tested so that in the event of a future crime there is evidence that the person was informed that he was HIV positive. The testing of the blood is a search entirely separate from the seizure of the blood and itself must be justified. See § **7.17.**

Therefore, in both of these situations future use of the test would not be a valid basis for drawing or testing blood, unless the government can establish probable cause that the suspect is currently HIV infected.

Involuntary HIV testing in the criminal context is typically addressed in specific statutes separate from other HIV-related statutes. They are referred to as *involuntary testing statutes,* to distinguish them from provisions protecting HIV-related information from disclosure (confidentiality statutes) and those setting forth the proper procedures for conducting HIV tests. The involuntary testing statutes are listed in § **7.16,** because the majority of these statutes are primarily directed to testing for notification purposes. The salient points of those statutes as they relate to testing for prosecution purposes are summarized here.

Some involuntary testing statutes specifically permit disclosure of the results of a court-ordered HIV test to a prosecutor for the purposes of evidence at trial or for future charges.[230] Others specifically prohibit use of the results of the test as evidence in the case from with the offense arose, although they contain no bar to nonevidentiary or future use.[231] Virginia may be unique in specifically providing that the results are not admissible in any criminal proceeding.[232]

---

[230] *E.g.,* Cal. Penal Code §§ 1202.1, 1202.6 (results of test available to prosecutor for sentence enhancement or for charging later prostitution case as felony); Colo. Rev. Stat. § 18-7-205.5 (results reported to prosecutor who shall keep results confidential unless charge is for prostitution or patronizing prostitute with knowledge of being HIV infected and results were positive); Fla. Stat. Ann. §§ 775.0877, 796.08 (results of testing of convicted persons not admissible in proceeding arising out of offense, but subsequent convictions are enhanced); Ill. Comp. Stat. Ann. § 5/5-5-3(g), (h) (court shall grant prosecutor's petition to obtain results if relevant to prosecution criminal transmission of HIV); Ky. Rev. Stat. Ann. § 529.090(2)–(4) (person who commits prostitution-related offense after testing positive for HIV and being informed of risk of communicating disease is guilty of crime); Tenn. Code Ann. § 39-13-521(a)(2)(G), (e) (test results of all persons arrested for listed sexual offenses shall be available to the district attorney prosecuting the case; district attorney may review test results of person convicted of prostitution offense for sole purpose of determining whether to prosecute for aggravated prostitution).

   Some statutes take great pains to inform the defendant of any positive results, suggesting that such notice could potentially be used against the defendant at a later time. *E.g.,* Nev. Rev. Stat. § 201.356 (person arrested for prostitution offense who tests positive must be notified and shall appear in court to determine if notice was made; no notification required if results are negative).

[231] Md. Code Ann. art. 27, § 765(I) (results not admissible as evidence of guilt or innocence in criminal proceeding arising out of alleged offense); Tex. Code Crim. Proc. Ann. art. 21.31 (state may not use results in any criminal proceeding arising out of alleged offense).

[232] Va. Code Ann. § 18.2-62 (regarding testing in cases of sexual offenses). In contrast, Virginia provides that results of testing in prostitution cases shall not be admissible in any criminal proceeding related to prostitution. *Id.* § 18.2-346.1.

Some statutes directly address whether the information obtained can be used for bail[233] or sentencing[234] purposes. At least one court has held that testing for the purpose of sentence enhancement, on the ground that a defendant committed a sexual offense knowing he or she was infected, is improper because the test cannot be related back to the time of the offense.[235]

Testing can also be used as a negotiation tool, without any statutory authorization or court involvement. For example, a prosecutor might condition a guilty plea on the suspect's being tested, thus avoiding the significant legal hurdles to obtaining court-ordered testing.[236] Depending on the circumstances, such testing should not be considered voluntary and should be examined and authorized under the principles set forth here.[237]

A potentially analogous situation to the use of HIV information in a criminal prosecution is the warrantless and involuntary blood testing of persons convicted of sex offenses for DNA typing for use in future prosecutions. The weight of the caselaw on that issue is that involuntary testing is constitutional, even without a

---

[233] *E.g.,* Mo. Ann. Stat. § 191.663(4) (defendant charged with sexual offense shall be required to post bond for release prior to trial in amount sufficient to cover cost of post-conviction HIV testing); Okla. Stat. Ann. tit. 63, § 1-524(B) (testing ordered at arraignment; defendant detained until results of test known); W. Va. Code § 16-3C-2(f)(5) (person convicted must undergo immediate testing and shall not be released from custody or bail shall be revoked until testing performed).

One court has held that testing as a condition of release on bail, where not authorized by statute, was an abuse of discretion. People v. McGreevy, 514 N.Y.S.2d 622 (Sup. Ct. 1987).

[234] *E.g.,* Colo. Rev. Stat. § 18-3-415 (fact that person voluntarily submitted to HIV test shall be admissible in mitigation of sentence); Ga. Code Ann. § 17-10-17(e) (submitting to test may be condition to suspending or probating any part of person's sentence); Ind. Code § 35-38-1-10.5(c) (if test is positive, probation department must prepare presentence report to obtain medical reports and determine whether person previously received risk counseling); Iowa Code § 709B.3(7)–(9) (defendant's voluntary disclosure to complainant not a basis to reduce plea or sentence; results shall not be used to enhance sentence in case flowing from incident); Ky. Rev. Stat. Ann. § 529.090(1) (person convicted of prostitution-related offense who tests positive must submit to treatment and counseling as condition of release from probation or incarceration); Mont. Code Ann. § 46-18-256 (statement of intent to 1993 amendment: "This bill is intended to be a benefit to public health and safety [and i]t is not intended to add additional sanctions or penalties for conviction . . . or to make criminals of the complainants of disease."); Tenn. Code Ann. § 39-13-521(c), (d) (court shall review test results prior to sentencing and may consider positive result as an enhancement factor at sentencing); Utah Code Ann. § 76-5-502 (court shall order convicted offender to submit to testing upon sentencing or as condition of probation).

[235] State v. Farmer, 805 P.2d 200, 209 (Wash.), *modified,* 812 P.2d 858 (Wash. 1991) (testing was not conducted pursuant to the involuntary testing statute; rather, prosecutor had requested and obtained an order for testing for the specific purpose of sentence enhancement).

[236] Susan Hendricks, *Problems and Issues in Criminal Prosecutions, in* AIDS Practice Manual: A Legal and Educational Guide § 13.3(3) (Paul Albert et al. eds., 3d ed. 1991).

[237] In this respect, analogy might be made to cases examining the voluntariness and thus the enforceability of a defendant's release of authorities from suit in exchange for dismissal of criminal charges. *See, e.g.,* Town of Newton v. Rumery, 480 U.S. 386 (1987).

warrant.[238] These cases have not been applied by courts addressing the use of HIV evidence in a prosecution.

§ 7.16   —Testing for Purposes Other Than Prosecution

The most common reason for court-ordered involuntary HIV testing is, at least ostensibly, complainant notification. The proliferation of statutes authorizing testing for this purpose was in response to a 1992 federal statute conditioning certain funding on the availability of such testing. Under 42 U.S.C. § 3756(f), 10 percent of certain funds under the Drug Control and System Improvement Grant Program are conditioned on a state's having in effect and enforcing

> a law that requires the State at the request of the victim of a sexual act (A) to administer, to the defendant convicted under State law of such sexual act, a test to detect in such defendant the presence of the etiologic agent for acquired immune deficiency syndrome; (B) to disclose the results of such test to such defendant and to the victim of such sexual act; and (C) to provide to the victim of such sexual act counseling regarding HIV disease, HIV testing, in accordance with applicable law, and referral for appropriate health care and support services.

The term *sexual act* is defined in § 3756(f)(3)(B) by reference to 18 U.S.C. § 2246(2)(A) and (B) as:

> (A) contact between the penis and the vulva or the penis and the anus, and . . . contact involving the penis occurs upon penetration, however slight; [and] (B) contact between the mouth and the penis, the mouth and the vulva, or the mouth and the anus.

Forty-one states have passed statutes permitting court-ordered or involuntary HIV testing of certain criminal suspects, defendants, or convicts.[239] Typically, more

---

[238] *See, e.g.,* Rise v. State of Oregon, 59 F.3d 1556 (9th Cir. 1995), *cert. denied,* 116 S. Ct. 1554 (1996); Vanderlinden v. Kansas, 874 F. Supp. 1210 (D. Kan. 1995); Ryncarz v. Eikenberry, 824 F. Supp. 1493 (E.D. Wash. 1993); People v. Wealer, 636 N.E.2d 1129 (Ill. App. Ct. 1994); State v. Olivas, 856 P.2d 1076 (Wash. 1993).

[239] Ala. Code § 22-11A-17; Ariz. Rev. Stat. Ann. § 13-1415; Ark. Code Ann. § 16-82-101; Cal. Penal Code §§ 1202.1, 1202.6; Cal. Health & Safety Code §§ 121050, 121055; Colo. Rev. Stat. §§ 18-3-415, 18-7-205.5; Conn. Gen. Stat. §§ 54-102a, -102b; Fla. Stat. Ann. §§ 775.0877, 796.08, 960.003; Ga. Code Ann. § 17-10-15; Ill. Comp. Stat. ch. 730, § 5/5-5-3 (amended by Public Act 89-462, Art. 2, § 280 (eff. May 29, 1996)); Ind. Code § 35-38-1-10.5; Iowa Code § 709B.1-3; Kan. Stat. Ann. § 38-1692; 1996 Kan. Sess. Laws ch. 215 (H.B. 2586), §§ 4–5 (repealing Kan. Stat. Ann. § 22-2913); Ky. Rev. Stat. Ann. §§ 510.320, 510.090; La. Rev. Stat. Ann. § 15:535; La. Code Crim. Proc. art. 499; Me. Rev. Stat. Ann. tit. 5, §§ 19203-A, 19203-F; Md. Ann. Code art. 27, § 765; Mich. Comp. Laws § 333.5129; Minn. Stat. §§ 144.765, 611A.19; Miss. Code Ann §§ 99-19-201, 203, 43-21-623 (amended

than one statute bears on the question of court-ordered testing. Thus, in addition to the specific statutes listed and discussed in this section, state confidentiality statutes, listed in **Appendix A,** should also be consulted. The federal government has enacted a testing statute,[240] although it does not yet contain the list of crimes that trigger authorization for testing and thus has not yet been used. No model statute has been employed, so each state's statute is unique and thus should be considered individually. This section summarizes the primary features of many of these statutes.

Under most statutes, testing procedures are triggered upon a complainant's request. Some schemes give the court discretion to order a test without a complainant's request, and then require the court to order the test if a complainant does request it.[241] Statutes that authorize across-the-board testing without a complainant's request or that do not allow for complainant notification[242] raise concerns that the true purpose for the test is prosecution related, which could result in the application of the probable cause analysis rather than the more lenient special needs analysis.

Another key issue is whether the person tested must be convicted of a crime or only charged with a crime. The federal statute conditions funding on testing

---

by 1994 Miss. Laws ch. 504, S.B. 2815 (Mar. 23, 1994)); Mo. Ann. Stat. § 191.663; Mont. Code. Ann. § 46-18-256; Neb. Rev. Stat. § 29-2290; Nev. Rev. Stat. §§ 201.356, 441A.320; N.H. Rev. Stat. Ann. §§ 632-A:10-b, 141-F:5; N.J. Rev. Stat. §§ 2A:4A-43.1, 2C:43-2.2; N.M. Stat. Ann. § 24-2B-5.1; N.Y. Crim. Proc. Law § 390-15; N.Y. Family Law Act § 347.1; N.D. Cent. Code § 23-07-07.5; Ohio Rev. Code Ann. § 2907.27; Okla. Stat. Ann. tit. 63, §§ 1-524, 525; Or. Rev. Stat. § 135.139; 35 Pa. Cons. Stat. Ann. §§ 521.11a, 7608; R.I. Gen. Laws §§ 11-34-10, 11-37-17, 21-28-4.20; S.C. Code Ann. §§ 16-3-740, 16-15-255 (both amended by Act 340, S.B. No. 914 (May 27, 1994)); Tenn. Code Ann. §§ 39-13-521, 68-10-116; Tex. Code Crim. Proc. Ann. art. 21.31; Utah Code Ann. § 7605-502; Va. Code Ann. §§ 18.2-62, 18.2-346.1; Wash. Rev. Code §§ 70.24.330, 70.24.105; W. Va. Code §§ 16-3C-2(f), 16-3C-3, 16-4-5; Wis. Stat. §§ 252.15, 968.38.

[240] 42 U.S.C. § 14011 (1994).

[241] *E.g.,* Ark. Code Ann. § 16-82-101 (prior to conviction, court is prohibited only from ordering testing it finds to be inappropriate; testing becomes mandatory if complainant requests it, once defendant has been convicted); 1996 Kan. Sess. Laws ch. 215 (H.B. 2586), § 4 (court must order testing upon complainant's request after arrest; after conviction court may order testing and must order testing if complainant requests).

[242] *E.g.,* Cal. Penal Code § 1202.1 (all persons convicted of listed sexual offenses must be tested regardless of whether person sentenced to incarceration, and results are available to complainant); Miss. Code Ann. § 99-19-203 (persons convicted of sex offense and sentenced to incarceration, probation or given suspended sentence or other disposition shall be tested; positive results shall be reported to complainant, offender, and their spouses); N.D. Cent. Code § 23-07-07.5 (testing of all persons convicted of crime and sentenced to 15 days or more, and of certain sexual and substance offenders regardless of sentence); Ohio Rev. Code Ann. § 2907.27(B) (testing of all persons charged with sexual offenses; court shall inform complainant of right to be informed of results); Okla. Stat. Ann. tit. 63, § 1-524(B), (C) (testing of all persons arrested for prostitution or sex offenses; results can be disclosed to complainant on request); Wash. Rev. Code § 70.24.340(1) (all persons convicted of listed offenses shall be tested as soon as possible after sentencing).

of *convicted* persons;[243] most state statutes do require conviction, but many authorize testing of persons who are only arrested or charged.[244] Others provide for different procedures, or for mandatory testing once the person has been convicted, or have different requirements based on the type of offense.[245] Some give the court discretion to order testing upon the suspect's being charged but require the court to do so upon the person's conviction.[246] If probable cause existed that the crime was committed and the statute provides for testing based on that alone, subsequent acquittal may not invalidate the testing order.[247]

Another potential problem, in view of the very limited modes of HIV transmission, is how the statutes define the types of conduct that trigger involuntary testing. The majority, like the federal funding statute, target only specific sexual offenses or contacts that are most likely to result in HIV exposure. Some even require an actual possibility of transmission.[248] However, a significant number

---

[243] 42 U.S.C. § 3756(f)(2)(A) (1994).

[244] *E.g.,* Ark. Code Ann § 6-82-101(b); Colo. Rev. Stat. § 18-3-415; Fla. Stat. Ann. § 960.003; Ga. Code Ann. § 17-10-15(b); 1996 Kan. Sess. Laws ch. 215 (H.B. 2586) § 4(a); Nev. Rev. Stat. §§ 201.356, 441A.320; N.J. Rev. Stat. § 2C:43-2.2(a); Ohio Rev. Code Ann. § 2907.27(B); Okla. Stat. Ann. tit. 63, § 1-524(B), (C); Tenn. Code Ann. § 39-13-521(a); Tex. Code Crim Proc. Ann. art. 21.31(a); Wis. Stat. § 968.38(3), (4).

[245] *E.g.,* Ariz. Rev. Stat. § 13-1415 (prior to conviction, complainant can request prosecutor to request voluntary testing; testing becomes mandatory after conviction); Cal. Penal Code § 1202.1 (testing of persons charged with sex offenses), *cf.* Cal. Health & Safety Code § 121055 (providing for testing of persons convicted of prostitution); Colo. Rev. Stat. § 18-3-415 (testing of persons bound over for trial for sexual offense, *cf.* § 18-7-205.5 providing for testing of persons convicted of patronizing prostitute); Ga. Code Ann. § 17-10-15 (complainant may request and court may order testing of person arrested for sexual offense or other offense involving significant exposure; testing mandatory upon conviction for "AIDS transmitting crime"); Mich. Comp. Laws § 333.5129 (1), (3) & (4) (testing of persons arrested and charged with prostitution offense, held to stand trial on criminal sexual conduct charge, or convicted of crime involving intravenous use of controlled substances); Nev. Rev. Stat. § 201.356 (testing of persons arrested for prostitution offense), *cf.* §441A.320 (providing for testing of persons detained for commission of sexual offense); Va. Code Ann. § 18.2-62 (testing upon finding of probable cause offense committed), *cf.* § 18.2-346.1 (providing for testing upon conviction); *id.* § 18.2-62(A) (testing upon arrest for sexual offense), *cf.* § 18.2-346.1 (providing for testing upon conviction for prostitution offenses); Wis. Stat. § 968.38 (testing in criminal action for listed sexual offenses upon finding of probable cause of significant exposure; no finding necessary for testing after conviction).

[246] *E.g.,* Ark. Code Ann. § 16-82-101; Conn. Gen. Stat. §§ 54-102a, 102b; Ga. Code Ann. § 17-10-15; La. Rev. Stat. Ann. § 15:535; La. Code Crim. Proc. art. 499; Md. Ann. Code art. 27, § 765(b), (c).

[247] State v. Parr, 513 N.W.2d 647, 651–52 (Wis. Ct. App. 1994) (applying Wis. Stat. § 968.38 to defendant convicted of child enticement and child sexual assault, upheld testing even though defendant was acquitted of sexual intercourse count).

[248] *E.g.,* Ind. Code §§ 35-38-1-10.5, 35-38-1-7.1(b)(8), (9)(A), (e), (f) (sex or substance crime involving sharp object where offense created epidemiologically demonstrated risk of transmission); 1996 Kan. Sess. Laws ch. 215 (H.B. 2586), § 4 (any crime involving likelihood of transmission of body fluids); Neb. Rev. Stat. § 29-2290(a) (offense involving sexual penetration or sexual contact where circumstances demonstrate possibility of transmission of HIV);

cover undefined sexual contact, or incorporate definitions of sexual contact that require no potential exchange of fluids.[249] Even if the statute specifically lists the offenses that warrant testing, some courts have gone beyond that list if the evidence suggests conduct that is the same as that listed in the specified statutes.[250] Thus, if a defendant were to plead guilty to a charge that is not listed in the testing statute, testing might still be ordered. On the other hand, conviction for an attempt to commit one of the enumerated offenses has been held insufficient for involuntary testing.[251]

N.M. Stat. Ann. § 24-2B-5.1 (listed sexual contacts in which court determines there was likelihood of transmission of blood, semen, or vaginal secretions). The 1994 amendment to South Carolina's testing statutes removed this requirement and now requires testing of all person convicted of the listed offenses. S.C. Code Ann §§ 16-3-740, 16-15-255 (as amended by Act 340, S.B. No. 914 (May 27, 1994)).

[249] *E.g.,* Ala. Code § 22-11A-17 (incorporating sexual offenses as defined in § 13A-6-60 *et seq.,* which define *sexual contact* as "any touching of the sexual or intimate parts"); La. Rev. Stat. Ann. §§ 15:535, 14:42-43.4 (offenses include sexual battery, defined as the touching of anus or genitals using any object or body part); Mont. Code Ann. § 46-18-256 (incorporating definition of sexual offense in § 46-23-502, which in turn incorporates sexual assault in § 45-5-503(3) including any sexual contact); N.H. Rev. Stat. Ann. § 632-A:10-b (testing of persons convicted of offenses under chapter 632-A, which include offenses for sexual penetration, defined to include intrusion of object or nonsexual body part, and sexual contact, defined to include touching of intimate parts or clothing covering such parts); N.J. Rev. Stat. §§ 2C:43-2.2, 2C:14-2, :14-1 (testing of person charged with sexual assault, defined as sexual penetration, including insertion of nonsexual body part or object, and sexual contact, including touching intimate body part or clothing of complainant or self); N.D. Cent. Code § 23-07-07.5(1)(b) (incorporating definitions and offenses under ch. 12.1-20, which include offenses involving sexual act, defined to include contact between an object and the complainant's sexual parts, or sexual contact, defined to include touching of intimate parts); Okla. Stat. Ann. tit. 63, § 1-524(B) (testing of persons arrested for other sex crimes not specified); Tenn. Code Ann. § 39-13-521(a) (crimes listed include crimes involving sexual penetration, defined at § 39-13-501(7) as any intrusion of any body part or object into complainant's sexual openings); Tex. Code Crim. Proc. Ann. art. 21.31(a) (crimes listed involve sexual contact with child, defined at Tex. Penal Code Ann. § 21.01 as any touching of sexual parts of complainant); Utah Code Ann. § 76-5-502(1)(a) (listed sexual crimes, including child sex offenses, defined at § 76-5-407 to include any touching even if accomplished through clothing); Va. Code Ann. § 18.2.62 (sexual assault offenses, which include sexual battery and object penetration); Wash. Rev. Code § 70.24.340 (sexual offenses, including offenses involving sexual contact, defined at § 9A.44.010(2) to include any touching of intimate parts); Wis. Stat. § 968.38 (listed crimes include sexual contact as defined in § 940.225(5)(b) as any intentional touching directly or through clothing by body part of object or other's intimate parts).

[250] *See* People v. Doe, 642 N.Y.S.2d 996, 998–1001 (Nassau County Ct. 1996) (construed statute, which required that offense have sexual intercourse as essential element, to include other offenses if evidence demonstrated that intercourse occurred); People v. Frausto, 42 Cal. Rptr. 2d 540 (Ct. App. 1995) (defendant pleaded no contest to rape while acting in concert under Cal. Pen. Code § 264.1; upheld testing under § 1202.1 even though offense not listed where defendant at plea admitted that he personally raped complainant); People v. Thomas, 529 N.Y.S.2d 429 (Schoharie County Ct. 1988) (testing authorized upon conviction for attempted offense because there was probable cause that sexual penetration occurred).

[251] People v. Jillie, 11 Cal. Rptr. 2d 107 (Ct. App. 1992).

In addition to sexual offenses, many statutes also provide for testing in prostitution cases[252] and/or hypodermic needle offenses.[253] Some authorize testing for other crimes if potential exposure was involved.[254] Virtually all apply to juvenile as well as adult suspects.

Some statutes provide for hearing procedures, or at least for the holding of a hearing, at which the court determines whether the factors necessary for an order are present.[255] Most make no mention of a hearing, and some appear to mandate testing without even any court involvement.[256] A strong argument exists that a hearing can be demanded by the suspect in any event, in view of the important Fourth Amendment concerns.[257] A suspect who is served with a subpoena or other process without a hearing should file a motion to quash or other appropriate motion to request a hearing on the issue. Nevertheless, some courts have determined that hearing procedures are not necessary. For example, a Florida appellate court held that, in view of the special needs test, the fact that the statute lacked procedures for a hearing did not render it unconstitutional.[258]

Some statutes require that the suspect first be asked to voluntarily submit to the test before it is ordered.[259] Also, some states have recognized the problems

---

[252] *E.g.*, Ark. Code Ann. § 16-82-101(b)(1); Colo. Rev. Stat. § 18-7-205.5; Fla. Stat. Ann. §§ 775.0877(1)(k), 796.08; Ill. Comp. Stat. ch. 730, § 5/5-5-3(g); Ky. Rev. Stat. Ann. § 529.090(a); Mich. Comp. Laws § 333.5129(1); Nev. Rev. Stat. § 201.356; Okla. Stat. Ann. tit. 63, § 1-524(B); R.I. Gen. Laws § 11-34-10; Tenn. Code Ann. § 39-13-521(e); Va. Code Ann. § 18.2-346.1; Wash. Rev. Code § 70.24.340(1)(b).

[253] *E.g.*, Ill. Comp. Stat. ch. 730, § 5/5-5-3(h); Ind. Code § 35-38-1.10.5 (a)(2); Mich. Comp. Laws § 333.5129(4); N.D. Cent. Code § 23-07-07.5(1)(c); R.I. Gen. Laws § 21-28-4.20; Wash. Rev. Code § 70.24.340(1)(c).

[254] *E.g.*, Minn. Stat. § 611A.19(1)(a) (testing in context of other violent crime when evidence exists that broken skin or mucous membrane of complainant was exposed to offenders's semen or blood in a manner demonstrated epidemiologically to transmit HIV).

[255] *See, e.g.*, Iowa Code § 709B.2(2)–(5) (providing for notice and hearing and giving petitioner burden of proof by preponderance of evidence); N.Y. Pub. Health Law § 2785(4) (providing for notice and opportunity to be heard unless public health officer shows clear and imminent danger); Md. Code Ann. art. 27, § 765(c)(2) (if test requested prior to conviction, court shall hold hearing to determine if probable cause exists that exposure occurred); N.Y. Crim. Proc. Law § 390.15(5) (court shall hold hearing only if necessary to determine if applicant is victim of offense); N.Y. Family Court Act § 347.1(5) (same); Wis. Stat. § 968.38 (hearing necessary for testing prior to conviction to determine if there is probable cause of significant exposure).

[256] *E.g.*, Mont. Code Ann. § 46-18-256 (person convicted must be tested; county attorney must make arrangement for test and disclose results); Nev. Rev. Stat. §§ 201.356, 441A.320 (health authority shall test person arrested); N.H. Rev. Stat. Ann. § 632-A:10-b (state shall administer test to convicted person).

[257] *See In re* J.G., 674 A.2d 625, 629 (N.J. Super. Ct. App. Div. 1996) (rejecting government's argument that the trial judge should not have conducted an evidentiary hearing).

[258] Fosman v. State, 664 So. 2d 1163, 1166 (Fla. Dist. Ct. App. 1995). In that case, the trial court had in fact held a hearing.

[259] *E.g.*, Ga. Code Ann § 17-10-15; Iowa Code § 709B.2(1)(b), (5)(b)–(c); Or. Rev. Stat. § 135.139(2); Va. Code Ann. § 18.2-62 (defendant must first be requested to submit to voluntary test prior to conviction; no request necessary for testing after conviction).

associated with the window period and specifically provide for retesting if an initial test result is negative.[260] Others place time limits on requests for court-ordered testing.[261]

If a suspect challenges testing under one of these statutes for purposes of notification, will the court apply a traditional search and seizure analysis (probable cause/warrant) or a special needs analysis? The answer determines whether the government will have to make a showing of probable cause that the test would reveal evidence of infection, that is, that the person is HIV positive.

The most recent pronouncements by the Supreme Court as to the appropriate circumstances for the special needs analysis are the 1989 companion cases of *Skinner v. Railway Executives' Ass'n*[262] and *National Treasury Employees Union v. Von Raab*.[263] In *Skinner*, regulations issued by the Federal Railroad Administration required blood and urine tests for drugs and alcohol for employees involved in rail accidents and for those alleged to have violated certain safety rules. Labor organizations sued to enjoin enforcement of the regulations, and the Supreme Court, applying a special needs analysis, determined that the regulations were reasonable under the Fourth Amendment. Because (1) the purpose of the testing was not to assist in a criminal prosecution; (2) the government had a justifiable interest in protecting passengers from harm caused by accidents contributed to by drugs and alcohol; (3) requiring a warrant would not further the warrant's purpose in having a neutral magistrate review evidence; and (4) requiring a warrant would frustrate the government's purpose because the substances dissipate quickly from the body, the Court ruled that neither a warrant nor probable cause was necessary.[264] In light of *Schmerber v. California*,[265] the Court held that the intrusion occasioned by a forced withdrawal of blood for alcohol testing was "not significant."[266] This was especially so because the testing was in the context of employment in an already heavily regulated industry.

Certain language in the Court's opinion suggests a rational relationship standard while other language suggests a stricter standard. The Court ultimately concluded

---

[260] *E.g.,* Iowa Code § 709B.3(6); Ohio Rev. Code Ann. § 2907.27(B); Or. Rev. Stat. § 135.139(4); Tex. Code Crim. Proc. Ann. art. 21.31 (court may order subsequent test after conviction); W. Va. Code § 16-3C-2(f)(10).

[261] *E.g.,* Me. Rev. Stat. Ann. tit. 5, § 19203-F(2) (complainant may petition court to order testing of convicted offender any time before sentencing or not later than 80 days after conviction); Pa. Cons. Stat. Ann. § 521.11a(b) (tests results shall be released to complainant if complainant made request within six weeks of conviction; otherwise complainant must seek disclosure under confidentiality statute).

[262] 489 U.S. 602 (1989).

[263] 489 U.S. 656 (1989). The Supreme Court may be issuing a new opinion on this issue. In October 1996 the Court granted review of an Eleventh Circuit decision upholding the constitutionality of a Georgia statute that required candidates to high public office to submit to drug testing. Chandler v. Miller, 73 F.3d 1543 (11th Cir.), *cert. granted,* 117 S. Ct. 38 (1996).

[264] 489 U.S. at 620–23.

[265] 384 U.S. 757, 771 (1966).

[266] Skinner v. Railway Labor Executives' Ass'n, 489 U.S. at 625.

that the court of appeals had erred in ruling that the regulations were not reasonably related to the government's objectives. On the other hand, the Court concluded that the government's interest in testing without a showing of individualized suspicion was "compelling."[267] Also, the Court held that the blood and urine tests were "highly effective" means of ascertaining on-the-job substance use and illegal drug use and were "accurate in the overwhelming majority of cases."[268]

In *Von Raab,* the Court upheld the U. S. Customs Service's requirement that employees who carried firearms or were involved in the direct interdiction of drugs at the border submit urine samples for drug analysis. Under the testing program, test results could not be turned over to prosecutors or anyone else without the employee's consent. The Court again rejected the traditional probable cause analysis, because the tests were not "peculiarly related to criminal investigation."[269] Similar to the Court's analysis in *Skinner,* on balance the Court found that the Customs Service's special need outweighed the limited intrusion of the urine drug test. And because the testing program "bears a close and substantial relation" to the goal of deterring drug users from seeking sensitive job positions, the testing was constitutional.[270] Other courts have picked up on this language and held that testing is constitutional so long as it "bears a close and substantial relationship to a legitimate end."[271]

Obviously, the application of the *Skinner* and *Von Raab* principles to a given program for mandatory HIV testing will depend on a balancing undertaken in the specific context of that program and the available technology at the time.[272] Nevertheless, a few distinctions between the involuntary HIV testing scenario and the testing addressed in *Skinner* and *Von Raab* merit discussion.

§ 7.17   —Testing as a Separate Search

Although the law is settled that the physical withdrawal of the blood (or even saliva or urine, although these procedures are arguably less intrusive) and routine

---

[267] *Id.* at 628.

[268] *Id.* at 632 n.10.

[269] National Treasury Employees Union v. Von Raab, 489 U.S. at 667.

[270] 489 U.S. at 676.

[271] *See, e.g.,* State v. Superior Court, No. 1 CA-SA 95-0340, 1996 WL 408688, at *3–5 (Ariz. Ct. App. July 23, 1996).

[272] *See, e.g.,* Winston v. Lee, 470 U.S. 753, 760 (1985) ("The reasonableness of surgical intrusions beneath the skin depends on a case-by-case approach, in which the individual's interest in privacy and security are weighed against society's interests in conducting the procedure."); Bell v. Wolfish, 441 U.S. 520, 559 (1979) ("[E]ach case . . . requires a balancing of the need for the particular search against the invasion of personal rights that the search entails. Courts must consider the scope of the particular intrusion, the manner in which it is conducted, the justification for initiating it, and the place in which it is conducted."); Camara v. Municipal Court of San Francisco, 387 U.S. 523, 536–37 (1967) ("[T]here can be no ready test for determining the reasonableness [of a search] other than by balancing the need to search against the invasion which the search entails.").

attendant procedures present only minimal intrusions on a person's interest in privacy and bodily integrity,[273] the interest in freedom from physical invasion is not the only interest at stake. The subsequent analysis of the blood, and the information that is disseminated as a result, is a separate, constitutionally cognizable interest.[274] And the Supreme Court has not addressed a test the results of which can be so devastating to an individual. If positive results are revealed, the person becomes subject to severe stigma and discrimination in all areas of his or her life. These effects make an involuntary HIV test far more intrusive on privacy and dignity rights than a test for the presence of alcohol or even illegal drugs. Also, negative results of an HIV test can give false comfort without proper counseling as to the test's limitations.

Similarly, the greater the extent to which the information can be disseminated beyond the individual and the party directing the test, the greater the intrusion on the individual's privacy rights. For this reason, the extent of the potential disclosure by the complainant or by anyone else of the information should play an important role in the balancing.[275]

Also, it is not clear that requiring compliance with the normal warrant and probable cause regimen would frustrate the purpose of the test. Typically, as in *Schmerber* and *Skinner*, the test must be done immediately or the evidence dissipates. In the HIV context, in contrast, there is less reason not to wait the small amount of time necessary until a determination of probable cause is made and a warrant obtained. On the other hand, it can also be argued that any delay be kept to a minimum so that intervening events do not cloud any interpretation of positive results.

Another distinguishing factor is the utility of the test for providing the information sought. In the line of cases upholding blood tests, typically for the presence of alcohol or drug metabolites, the test was highly reliable and directly correlated to the physiological state being tested. For example, in *Skinner*, the blood tests were "highly effective means of ascertaining on-the-job impairment

---

[273] Schmerber v. California, 384 U.S. 757, 771 (1966). ("Such tests are commonplace in these days of periodic physical examination and experience with them teaches that the quantity of blood extracted is minimal, and that for most people the procedure involves virtually no risk, trauma, or pain.") (footnote omitted); *see also* Skinner v. Railway Labor Executives' Ass'n, 489 U.S. 602, 616 (1989).

[274] Skinner v. Railway Labor Executives' Ass'n, 489 U.S. at 616 ("The ensuing chemical analysis of the sample to obtain physiological data is a further invasion of the tested employees' privacy interests."). *See also* Winston v. Lee, 470 U.S. 753, 761 (1985) ("Another factor [beyond the risk to health and safety as a result of the procedure] is the extent of intrusion upon the individual's dignitary interests in personal privacy and bodily integrity.").

[275] Disclosure issues are discussed further in § **7.18.** Some courts have reasoned that the effects of disclosure are not relevant to the determination of whether the blood test and analysis themselves are lawful under the Fourth Amendment. Rather, if the test and analysis are lawful, then disclosure must be made consistent with the Fourth Amendment and other interests of the suspect. *See* Government of V.I. v. Roberts, 756 F. Supp. 898, 901–02 (D.V.I. 1991) (recognizing devastating consequences of disclosure but upholding involuntary testing and limited disclosure to defendant, complainant, and their doctors).

and of deterring the use of drugs," and were "accurate in the overwhelming majority of cases."[276] The same cannot be said for the current antibody tests for HIV. Because of the delay in the body's development of detectable antibodies, the test may not be "highly effective" in revealing whether the person was infected with HIV at the time of an alleged crime.[277] The question is even more problematic if testing is sought at some time after the event occurred, because, if the results are positive, the infection could have been contracted after the event.

Finally, frequently the alleged event that precipitated the test involves only a minimal or undetermined risk of transmission. On this basis, the United States Court of Appeals for the Eighth Circuit, in a pre-*Skinner* case, concluded that the mandatory testing of employees working with mentally retarded individuals was unreasonable under the Fourth Amendment because the risk of transmission was negligible.[278] In contrast, some courts have relied on the fast pace at which discoveries in HIV research are being made to justify testing even if there is only a theoretical possibility of infection, especially when there is a difference of expert opinion.[279]

The last two factors, utility of the test and risk of transmission, can be analogized to one of the groups of employees in *Von Raab*.[280] Although the Supreme Court approved testing of two groups of Customs Service employees, those who carry firearms and those who were involved in the direct interdiction of drugs at the border, it came to a different conclusion with respect to testing of a separate group of employees. The Customs Service had also sought to test employees handling "sensitive information," and the Court did not disagree that those persons, if they could be properly identified, could be constitutionally subject to the testing procedures. But the Court remanded, because it was not clear from the record "whether the category defined by the Service's testing directive encompasses *only those* Customs employees likely to gain access to sensitive information."[281] The Court instructed the lower court on remand to examine whether the category was defined "more broadly than is necessary to meet the purposes."[282] By analogy, HIV testing statutes may be overbroad if the group subject to testing is not limited to only those likely to have committed a crime. Also, the program may be overbroad if not limited to conduct capable of resulting in infection.

---

[276] Skinner v. Railway Labor Executives' Ass'n, 489 U.S. at 632 & n.10.

[277] At least one court has relied on the window period to deny disclosure of HIV-related medical records when the disclosure was sought eight months after the incident. *See* State v. J.E., 606 A.2d 1160 (N.J. Super. Ct. 1992).

[278] Glover v. Eastern Neb. Community Office of Retardation, 867 F.2d 461 (8th Cir.), *cert. denied,* 493 U.S. 932 (1989).

[279] *See, e.g.,* Johnetta v. Municipal Court, 267 Cal. Rptr. 666, 681 (Ct. App. 1990); *In re* J.G., 674 A.2d 625, 633 (N.J. Super. Ct. App. Div. 1996) ("Because the field is not static, a court should be very hesitant to rule that a legislative scheme of mandated testing is medically or psychologically useless to the victim or the treatment community.").

[280] National Treasury Employees Union v. Von Raab, 489 U.S. 656 (1989).

[281] *Id.* at 678 (emphasis added).

[282] *Id.*

Based on these considerations, there may be circumstances in which the Supreme Court's special needs analysis would allow involuntary testing without a warrant or probable cause. That is, if the evidence suggests that there was conduct associated with transmission, but disclosure is limited to notification for health purposes, testing is constitutional. If, however, the conduct alleged is not associated with transmission, or if there are insufficient protections against unauthorized disclosure beyond the suspect and the complainant, especially disclosure for prosecution-related purposes, the traditional warrant/probable cause analysis should apply.

Statutes in Arizona, California, Florida, Illinois, New Jersey, New York, and Washington have been directly challenged by criminal defendants objecting to involuntary testing. Each has been upheld under the special needs analysis, primarily on the theory that the purpose of the test was not to punish but to notify a complainant and that, on balance, the complainant's interest in knowing the defendant's HIV status outweighed the defendant's privacy and bodily integrity interests.[283] The only federal court to address the constitutionality of involuntary testing has reached the same conclusion.[284]

---

[283] State v. Superior Court, No. 1 CA-SA 95-0340, 1996 WL 408688 (Ariz. Ct. App. July 23, 1996) (upheld testing of juvenile convicted of child molestation where evidence showed juvenile attempted anal intercourse); Johnetta v. Municipal Court, 267 Cal. Rptr. 666 (Ct. App. 1990) (challenge to predecessor to current statute upheld testing of defendant charged with biting officer; probable cause of transmission not necessary); Love v. Superior Court, 276 Cal. Rptr. 660 (Ct. App. 1990) (upheld testing of defendant convicted of soliciting prostitution under Cal. Penal Code § 1202.6, and also upheld portion of statute authorizing disclosure to prosecutor for purposes of preparing counts and enhanced sentence in subsequent prosecution; fact that transmission may not have occurred not relevant because defendant was member of risk group); Fosman v. State, 664 So. 2d 1163 (Fla. Dist. Ct. App. 1995) (upheld testing of defendant charged with armed sexual battery pursuant to Fla. St. Ann § 960.003 because there was probable cause to believe defendant transmitted bodily fluids to complainant and results were disclosed only to complainant and public health authorities); People v. Adams, 597 N.E.2d 574 (Ill. 1992) (upheld testing of defendant convicted of prostitution pursuant to Ill. Rev. Stat. ch. 38, ¶ 1005-5-3(g) without any showing of individualized suspicion because disclosure of results could be made only upon court order); People v. C.S., 583 N.E.2d 726 (Ill. App. Ct. 1991) (upheld testing of defendant convicted of unauthorized possession of hypodermic needle pursuant to Ill. Rev. Stat. ch. 38, ¶ 1005-5-3(h) and disclosure of results to jail personnel and police supervisor, but disclosure to prosecutor was abuse of discretion), *appeal denied,* 602 N.E.2d 461 (Ill. 1992); People v. Thomas, 580 N.E.2d 1353 (Ill. App. Ct. 1991) (upheld testing of defendant convicted of unlawful possession of hypodermic needle pursuant to Ill. Rev. Stat. ch. 38, ¶ 1005-5-3(h)), *appeal denied,* 587 N.E.2d 1023 (Ill. 1992); In re J.G., 674 A.2d 625 (N.J. Super. Ct. App. Div. 1996) (held N.J. Rev. Stat. §§ 2A:4A-43.1, 2C:43-2.2 constitutional as applied to defendants convicted of aggravated sexual assault), *rev'g,* 660 A.2d 1274 (N.J. Super. Ct. 1995); People v. Doe, 642 N.Y.S.2d 996, 1001–02 (Nassau County Ct. 1996) (ordered testing of person convicted of attempted sexual abuse because evidence demonstrated sexual intercourse occurred); In re Juveniles A, B, C, D, E, 847 P.2d 455 (Wash. 1993) (upheld testing of juvenile defendants found to have committed sex offenses, some limited to saliva exposure, pursuant to Wash. Rev. Code § 70.24.340(1)(a), because results could not put defendants at risk for new conviction or longer sentence, although disclosure could be made to probation department and prison).

[284] Government of V.I. v. Roberts, 756 F. Supp. 898 (D.V.I. 1991) (recognizing "devastating consequences" of disclosure of HIV test results, held testing constitutional under Fourth

Some of these decisions are in conflict with the analysis set forth here. For example, the decision in *Love v. Superior Court*[285] in California upheld the testing without a probable cause analysis, even though the results could be used as evidence in a prosecution. Also, *In re Juveniles A,B,C,D,E*[286] in Washington and *People v. Adams*[287] in Illinois raise concerns in that they upheld testing even though the conduct alleged carried a negligible, if any, risk of transmission. Both reasoned, however, that because the behavior established by the evidence showed that the person was high risk for being HIV positive, there was no need to show actual risk of transmission.[288] This rationale is consistent with the Eighth Circuit's reasoning in *Glover v. Eastern Nebraska Community Office of Retardation*,[289] which determined that employees could not be required to submit to mandatory AIDS testing because the risk of transmission to mentally retarded clients was negligible.

Despite the differences between the Supreme Court's special needs cases and the HIV testing context, the courts are approaching consensus that testing for purposes of complainant notification falls under the Supreme Court's special needs analysis, and that therefore testing for such purposes can be compelled without a warrant and showing of probable cause.[290] Nevertheless, a determination in a given case will still depend on the particular factors present, most significantly the potential disclosure and uses of the information. In particular, if there are no protections against use of the information for purposes of punishment, for instance, if the results could be used as evidence in a prosecution for transmission of HIV, or to determine eligibility for bail, to enhance a convicted

---

Amendment because disclosure limited to defendant, complainant, and their doctors for purposes of treatment).

[285] 276 Cal. Rptr. 660 (Ct. App. 1990) (upheld testing of defendant convicted of soliciting prostitution under Cal. Penal Code § 1202.6, also upheld portion of statute authorizing disclosure to prosecutor for purposes of preparing counts and enhanced sentence in subsequent prosecution; fact that transmission may not have occurred not relevant because defendant was member of group at high risk for AIDS).

[286] 847 P.2d 455 (Wash. 1993).

[287] 597 N.E.2d 574 (Ill. 1992).

[288] People v. Adams, 597 N.E.2d at 581–84 (statute has public health purpose of targeting at-risk groups, testing of persons convicted of crimes involving high risk behavior not unreasonable); *In re* Juveniles A, B, C, D, E, 847 P.2d at 461–62 (legislature reasonably determined that sex offenders, even when offense did not involve transmission of bodily fluids, are a high risk group for exposing others to AIDS). *See also* Love v. Superior Court, 276 Cal. Rptr. 660, 666 (Ct. App. 1990).

[289] 867 F.2d 461 (8th Cir.), *cert. denied,* 493 U.S. 932 (1989).

[290] *See* Wayne R. LaFave, Search and Seizure: A Treatise on the Fourth Amendment § 5.4 at nn.41–51 and corresponding text (3d ed. 1996) (agreeing with cases that apply special needs analysis in the context of involuntary testing of defendants).

A New Jersey trial court's decision had for a time caused a split in authority in holding testing unconstitutional, reasoning that because a test of the defendant's blood could not inform the complainant as to her own status, the test did not bear a close and substantial relationship to the government's compelling interest in assisting the complainant. *In re* J.G., 660 A.2d 1274 (N.J. Super. Ct. 1995). The Appellate Division reversed, concluding that *Skinner* and *Von Raab* do not require a narrowly tailored scheme, so the limited utility of the test was not fatal. *In re* J.G., 674 A.2d 625 (N.J. Super. Ct. App. Div. 1996).

defendant's sentence, or for some other prosecution-related purpose, a warrant based on probable cause should be obtained prior to the search.[291]

There may be times when a criminal suspect may want to know whether the complainant in a case has tested positive for HIV. For example, in an assault case in which a defendant was charged with biting the complainant, defense counsel was inadvertently provided discovery disclosing that the complainant was HIV positive.[292] On the government's motion to prohibit defense counsel from disclosing the information to her client, the court ruled that the defendant could be informed that he was potentially exposed, but that counsel could not identify the source.[293]

§ 7.18 —Release of Existing Medical Information and Other Disclosure Issues

Disclosure, with its potential for harm, is arguably the most salient concern for persons objecting to involuntary testing. Unfortunately, there is no uniformity either in how disclosure is addressed in the statutes authorizing involuntary testing or in judicial approaches to the issue. As a general matter, most statutes limit disclosure to the suspect, complainant, and public health officials and, in some cases, prison authorities, and direct that confidentiality is to otherwise be maintained. Some prohibit disclosure to the court or law enforcement authorities,[294] and some go on to provide for civil or criminal penalties for unauthorized disclosure.[295] Others permit further disclosure or specifically grant the court discretion

---

[291] *See, e.g.,* Barlow v. Ground, 943 F.2d 1132 (9th Cir. 1991) (officers bitten during arrest withdrew blood for testing without warrant; search held unlawful where no exception to warrant requirement existed), *cert. denied,* 505 U.S. 1206 (1992).

[292] People v. Pedro M., 630 N.Y.S.2d 208 (Kings County Ct. 1995).

[293] *Id.* at 213. *But see* State v. Brewster, 601 So. 2d 1289 (Fla. Dist. Ct. App. 1992) (in absence of statutory authority and compelling need for order requiring complainant to submit to HIV test, complainant's right to privacy outweighed defendant's need for information sought).

[294] *E.g.,* Minn. Stat. § 611A.19(2) (no reference to test may appear in criminal record, and after results reported to complainant, data must be removed from medical records); N.Y. Crim. Proc. Law § 390.15(1)(a) (results not disclosed to court, in contrast to N.Y. Public Health Law § 2785, which permits court to disclose upon showing of compelling need for adjudication of civil or criminal proceeding); N.Y. Family Court Act § 347.1(1)(a) (same); N.Y. Public Health Law § 2785-a(1) (same); Tex. Code Crim. Proc. Ann. art. 21.31 (results available to health authority and complainant and defendant; nothing in section would allow court to release result to anyone else).

[295] *E.g.,* Md. Code Ann. art. 27, § 765(h) (complainant may disclose to others to protect health of complainant or complainant's sexual partner or family, but anyone who knowingly discloses in violation of section subject to fine and imprisonment); Or. Rev. Stat. § 135.139(5), (10) (results disclosed only to complainant or parent/guardian, physician, health division and defendant; otherwise results are confidential and violation is a Class C misdemeanor).

to disclose.[296] Iowa may be unique in prohibiting disclosure to a suspect who has elected against disclosure.[297]

The scope of disclosure should be critical to the search and seizure analysis, because the testing of the blood and dissemination of that information is an intrusion wholly separate and apart from the withdrawal of the blood.[298] If a confidentiality statute bars the disclosure and the testing statute does not specifically limit the applicability of the confidentiality statute, it may be argued that the confidentiality statute bars the disclosure.[299] Moreover, further disclosure by someone authorized to receive the results, such as the complainant or the complainant's family, is a concern, and all persons to whom the information is disclosed should be instructed against further disclosure. For example, in authorizing involuntary testing, the District Court for the Virgin Islands, after reviewing the litany of social harms visited upon a person perceived to be infected with HIV, limited disclosure to the defendant, the complainant, and their doctors, and specifically ruled that the government would not receive the results and that the results would not be aired at any proceeding.[300] Other courts that have upheld testing have placed similar restrictions on disclosure.[301]

If test results are to be admitted during a court proceeding, the court should take steps to protect the suspect's confidentiality rights, either by sealing the case file and proceeding in camera, and/or by using a pseudonym or other means

---

[296] *E.g.,* Ill. Comp. Stat. Ann. § 5/5-5-3(g)(h) (court has discretion "acting in accordance with the best interests of the public" to determine to whom the results may be revealed); N.J. Rev. Stat. § 2C:43-2.2(f) (results may not be further disclosed except as otherwise authorized by law or court order); 1996 Kan. Sess. Laws Ch. 215 (H.B. 2586) § 4(c) (disclosed to "such other persons as the court determines have a legitimate need to know . . . in order to provide for their protection"); Wash. Rev. Code § 70.24.105(2)(f) (court may grant access upon showing of good cause); W. Va. Code § 16-3C-3(a)(9) (disclosure upon compelling need). Some of the statutes further protect persons who reveal information in good faith from liability. *E.g.,* Ind. Code § 35-38-1-10.5(d)–(f).

[297] Iowa Code § 709B.3(5).

[298] Skinner v. Railway Labor Executives' Ass'n, 489 U.S. 602, 616 (1989).

[299] Some legislatures have specifically limited the applicability of confidentiality statutes in the context of HIV testing to warn or protect complainants of potential exposure. *E.g.,* Cal. Health & Safety Code § 121050 (purpose of chapter to protect workers put at risk; intent of chapter to supersede confidentiality and other laws in conflict). Others specifically refer to confidentiality limitations to bar further disclosure. *E.g.,* Iowa Code § 709B.3(4), (14), (15) (informed consent required for disclosure beyond those authorized; civil penalty for knowing or reckless violations).

[300] Government of V.I. v. Roberts, 756 F. Supp. 898, 902 (D.V.I. 1991).

[301] *See, e.g.,* People v. C.S., 583 N.E.2d 726, 730–32 (Ill. App. Ct. 1991) (permitting disclosure in trial judge's discretion to prison and law enforcement personnel for protection in future interaction with defendant convicted of unlawful needle possession, but reversing order permitting disclosure to prosecutor's office), *appeal denied,* 602 N.E.2d 461 (Ill. 1992). The court in *C.S.* suggested that if a prosecution were initiated in the future, the prosecutor could seek disclosure of the results of the test. 583 N.E.2d at 731.

of protecting the suspect's identity.[302] Similar procedures are required by statute in many states.[303]

If a suspect has previously been tested for HIV, a complainant or prosecutor may seek release of that medical information, either through subpoena or request for a warrant or court order. All of the same concerns weighing for and against testing discussed in §§ **7.15** through **7.17** would come into play in this context as well. In addition, it could be argued that a suspect has a less compelling interest in this situation than in the context of a request for involuntary testing because the information already exists without the coercion of law enforcement, that is, the blood has already been withdrawn and tested. On the other hand, additional interests that weigh against disclosure may come into play, including the physician- or psychotherapist-patient relationship and the interest in promoting voluntary testing and its associated public health benefits.[304]

Generally speaking, the same principles that apply to a court-ordered test should apply to court-ordered disclosure of medical records. That is, if the purpose of the disclosure is to notify a complainant of the suspect's HIV status, and further disclosure is limited, the search and seizure may be authorized without a warrant under the special needs analysis. But if the records are to be used, or could be made available in the future, for prosecution-related purposes, the government should have to obtain a warrant based on probable cause, as outlined in § **7.15.**

Release of HIV-related information is addressed in the confidentiality and testing statutes of many states, and these statues should be consulted in determining whether information pertaining to a criminal suspect can be released.[305]

---

[302] *See, e.g.,* State v. Gamberella, 633 So. 2d 595, 600 (La. Ct. App. 1993) (in upholding trial court's denial of motion to suppress results of HIV test, appellate court noted trial court's order sealing the record and holding disclosure hearings in camera), *cert. denied,* 640 So. 2d 1341 (La. 1994); People v. Anonymous, 582 N.Y.S.2d 350 (Monroe County Ct. 1992).

[303] *See, e.g.,* Colo. Rev. Stat. § 18-3-415; Iowa Code § 709B.2(4)(d); W. Va. Code § 16-3C-3(a)(9).

[304] *See, e.g.,* State v. J.E., 606 A.2d 1160 (N.J. Super. Ct. 1992) (in absence of statutory authorization for disclosure of medical records for purpose of notifying complainant, sexual assault defendant's interest in confidentiality in physician-patient relationship outweighed need for disclosure); People v. Hawkrigg, 525 N.Y.S.2d 752 (Suffolk County Ct. 1988) (in absence of waiver or statutory exemption, improper to admit medical records before grand jury; court found waiver in defendant's disclosure of HIV status to sexual partners prior to alleged offense).

[305] For example, the New York statute authorizes disclosure of confidential HIV information based on, among other grounds, a showing of a "compelling need for disclosure of the information for the adjudication of a criminal or civil proceeding." N.Y. Pub. Health Law § 2785(2). This provision has been interpreted to permit disclosure of a defendant's HIV test results in order to provide evidence that he committed a crime. People v. Gribetz, 605 N.Y.S.2d 834 (Rockland County Ct. 1994); *see also* People v. Anonymous, 582 N.Y.S.2d 350 (Monroe County Ct. 1992). Similar statutes include N.J. Rev. Stat. § 26:5C-9(a), (b) (disclosure of AIDS records permitted on showing of good cause or to investigate crime).

For general discussions of orders for the release of medical records, see **Ch. 2.**

Some courts will stretch the language of these statutes to justify disclosure to a prosecutor even if a person was assured at the time of testing that the results would be kept confidential.[306]

As noted in § **7.13,** if a suspect has already disclosed his or her HIV status during the offense or proceeding, some courts have held that the suspect's interest in the privacy of medical records containing such information has been waived. If the question is whether a test obtained illegally can be later used in a prosecution for transmission of HIV, the answer may turn on whether the party seeking to use the information participated in the illegal conduct and whether the test could have been ordered via legal procedures.[307]

FAIR TRIAL AND POST-CONVICTION ISSUES

§ 7.19 Bail, Fair Trial Issues, and HIV

When an HIV positive person is a defendant in a criminal case, his or her HIV status generally ought not to have any effect on issues such as bail or the way judges, lawyers, and courtroom personnel treat the defendant during the proceedings. However, especially in the 1980s, false notions of how HIV was transmitted often resulted in the use of prejudicial and unnecessary courtroom procedures in cases involving HIV positive defendants.[308] The press has reported discrimination in courts against people actually infected or thought to be infected with HIV, including the use of face masks, gowns, and rubber gloves by court personnel, and long delays in transportation to court.[309] In Florida, a defendant was sentenced in 1987 via closed circuit television because the judge, lawyers, and clerks

---

[306] See State v. Stark, 832 P.2d 109 (Wash. Ct. App. 1992) (upheld denial of motion to suppress in prosecution for exposing sexual partners to HIV because statute "as a whole" contemplates that prosecutors may "at some point" have access to otherwise confidential information).

[307] For example, in State v. Gamberella, 633 So. 2d 595 (La. Ct. App. 1993), *cert. denied,* 640 So. 2d 1341 (La. 1994), the defendant had donated blood and been informed that his blood tested positive for HIV. He was charged with intentionally exposing a sexual partner with the virus. Without first going through the statutorily required procedures, the government obtained by subpoena the results of the test performed by the blood donation center. The court of appeal held that the government obtained the test results illegally, but nonetheless permitted admission of the results at trial, reasoning that under state law the government would have been entitled to obtain them legally, and that in any event the state's interest in prosecution outweighed the defendant's confidentiality interest. 633 So. 2d at 600–01.

[308] See Thomas R. Schuck & Lawrence K. Hoyt, *AIDS and the Criminal Justice System, in* AIDS and the Law § 9.2 (Wiley Law Publications Ed. Staff eds., John Wiley & Sons, Inc. 2d ed. 1992).

[309] *Increasing Reports of AIDS Discrimination in Justice System,* UPI, Aug. 12, 1987, *available in* LEXIS, Nexis Library, UPI File.

were afraid of contracting AIDS.[310] In Texas, an arrested man suspected of having AIDS was arraigned in his cell because of fears that the courtroom and staff would be contaminated.[311] In New York, a 1989 report by the New York Bar Association found that some court officers in the state were refusing to bring HIV positive defendants into the courtroom, forcing judges to hold hearings in the holding pens.[312] Other HIV positive defendants were not even brought to the courthouse for their hearings, and judges at times actively encouraged attorneys to waive their clients' presence in court. In one extreme case, an HIV positive defendant had no contact with his attorney or the court for 17 months.[313]

As lawyers, judges, and court personnel have become better educated about HIV,[314] the instances of disparate treatment for HIV positive defendants have decreased.[315] The American Bar Association in 1989 approved a policy of non-discrimination relating to HIV positive defendants. The policy states that defendants who are HIV positive should be treated no differently than any other defendant, and that "[n]o unusual safety or security precautions should be employed, unless the defendant is violent or poses a demonstrated risk of escape."[316] The report accompanying the ABA's AIDS policy notes that an epidemiologist with the Centers for Disease Control stated, "We [the CDC] have not recommended special precautions for courtroom proceedings where one or more of the participants had AIDS. I know of no usual courtroom proceedings that would result in the transmission of [HIV]."[317] Likewise, the New York Bar Association report states:

> Defendants infected with HIV pose no medical risk to others in the courtroom. Therefore, for purposes of establishing courtroom procedures, there is no medical justification for, and thus no compelling state interest in, inquiring about a defendant's HIV status or in revealing that status to others . . . There is also no justification for plastic handcuffs, plastic gloves, gowns, masks, or restraining bars unless

---

[310] *Convict with AIDS Sentenced by TV,* UPI, Jan. 14, 1987, *available in* LEXIS, Nexis Library, UPI File.

[311] Evan Thomas, *The New Untouchables,* Time, Sept. 23, 1985, at 24 (describing San Antonio arraignment).

[312] Joint Subcomm. on AIDS in the Criminal Justice Sys. of the Comm. on Corrections and the Comm. on Criminal Justice Operations and Budget of Ass'n of Bar of City of N.Y., AIDS and the Criminal Justice System: A Final Report and Recommendations 161–63 (1989).

[313] *Id.* at 163–64. The deliberate exclusion of a defendant from a courtroom based on his HIV positive status would be clearly an unconstitutional violation of the confrontation clause of the Sixth Amendment, which provides that "[i]n all criminal prosecutions, the accused shall enjoy the right . . . to be confronted with the witnesses against him." The confrontation clause also guarantees the accused the right to be present in the courtroom at every stage of the trial. Illinois v. Allen, 397 U.S. 337, 338 (1970).

[314] See **Ch. 1** (describing modes of HIV transmission).

[315] Patricia Hurtado, *AIDS Tests and the Limits of Courts,* Newsday, June 18, 1989, at 6.

[316] American Bar Ass'n Policy on AIDS and the Criminal Justice System 1 (adopted by ABA House of Delegates, Feb. 7, 1989).

[317] *Id.* at 13.

and until a violent situation arises, or for permitting court personnel to stand back a distance of 10 feet from an HIV-infected defendant.[318]

In addition, some state supreme courts, in their supervisory role, have adopted guidelines that bar discriminatory and unusual courtroom procedures for defendants or witnesses who are HIV positive.

For example, in *State v. Mercer*,[319] the Connecticut Supreme Court noted that it had promulgated the following guidelines:

> POLICY REGARDING ACQUIRED IMMUNODEFICIENCY SYNDROME (AIDS) . . . With respect to the activities and conduct of nonemployees (jurors, attorneys, criminal defendants, parties to civil litigation, witnesses, juvenile detainees, visitors to a courthouse) in a facility of the Judicial Department, no special treatment (privilege or restriction) may be ordered solely on the basis of a diagnosis that the nonemployee has AIDS, ARC, or a positive HTLV-III/LAV [now called HIV] antibody blood test, unless it is based on a recommendation of a physician or is required to allow the Department to comply with a law or regulation concerning communicable diseases.

Similarly, the Delaware Supreme Court issued a directive barring lawyers from discriminating against people with HIV by refusing to represent them.[320]

HIV positive defendants also should not be subject to discriminatory treatment in the setting of bail. The primary purpose of bail is to assure the presence of the defendant at trial.[321] The federal Bail Reform Act of 1984[322] permits preventative detention if the judge finds "that no condition or combination of conditions will reasonably assure the appearance of the person as required and the safety of any other person and the community." Preventative detention is limited, however, to cases involving serious crimes of violence, offenses carrying a sentence of life in prison, serious drug offenses, or cases involving a serious risk of flight or serious risk of obstruction of justice.[323] Moreover, the preventative detention provisions cannot be invoked to guard against harms unrelated to

---

[318] Joint Subcomm. on AIDS in the Criminal Justice Sys. of the Comm. on Corrections and the Comm. on Criminal Justice Operations and Budget of Ass'n of Bar of City of N.Y., AIDS and the Criminal Justice System: A Final Report and Recommendations 166–67 (1989). *See also* A. Laszlo & M. Ayres, AIDS: Improving the Response of the Correctional System 68 (1990) (sponsored by National Institute of Corrections, U.S. Department of Justice) (guidelines for court personnel state no special precautions are needed when HIV-infected persons are brought before them).

[319] 544 A.2d 611, 613 n.1 (Conn. 1988).

[320] Bureau of Nat'l Affairs, 28 Government Employee Relations Report No. 1374, at 956 (1990).

[321] Stack v. Boyle, 342 U.S. 1, 5 (1951); *see also* United States v. Salerno, 481 U.S. 739, 753 (1987) ("a primary function of bail is to safeguard the courts' role in adjudicating the guilt or innocence of defendants" by preventing the flight of defendants or intimidation of witnesses by defendants).

[322] 18 U.S.C. § 3142(e) (1994).

[323] 18 U.S.C. § 3142(f). United States v. Himler, 797 F.2d 156, 159 (3d Cir. 1986).

the charges at issue in the bail hearing.[324] Thus, a defendant's HIV status will rarely if ever be relevant to the issue of bail.[325] Accordingly, judges at bail hearings should not inquire about a defendant's HIV status, or require a defendant to submit to HIV testing as a condition of bail.[326] In one of the only reported cases on the subject, a court in New York held that it was improper for a judge, in setting bail for a defendant charged with rape, to condition the defendant's release on bail on a negative HIV test result.[327] The court held that such a condition effectively denied bail and violated the presumption of innocence.[328] In some cases, however, a defendant may make his or her HIV status relevant to the bail determination by arguing that health concerns and need for special treatment require release on bail.[329] For instance, in a much publicized case,[330] an HIV positive criminal defendant, Edward Savitz, was effectively denied bail by the imposition of bail conditions that were virtually impossible to meet. Savitz was charged with numerous counts of sexual abuse of children, criminal solicitation, involuntary deviate sexual intercourse, and prostitution. These charges arose from allegations that Savitz had engaged in various sex acts with young men below the age of consent. Bail was initially set at $20 million, but was later reduced to $200,000 with conditions. These conditions included the requirement that Savitz voluntarily commit himself to a private mental health facility in Philadelphia County which had a secure lock-up unit and that Savitz be segregated from contacts with all other patients. Although Savitz argued that none of the mental health facilities in Philadelphia could meet these conditions, the bail conditions were nonetheless upheld by state and federal courts on the ground that Savitz was a danger to the community.

Court opinions have generally rejected the use of unusual courtroom security procedures for HIV-infected defendants. In *State ex rel. Callahan v. Kinder,*[331] for

---

[324] United States v. Ploof, 851 F.2d 7 (1st Cir. 1988) (defendant's threat to kill girlfriend's husband could not be considered at detention hearing unless it could be connected to the case).

[325] Joint Subcomm. on AIDS in the Criminal Justice Sys. of the Comm. on Corrections and the Comm. on Criminal Justice Operations and Budget of Ass'n of Bar of City of N.Y., AIDS and the Criminal Justice System: A Final Report and Recommendations 155–56 (1989).

[326] *Id.* The report of the New York City Bar Association notes that for a period of time some judges had a practice of asking counsel and prosecutors about defendants' HIV status at arraignment in New York City. The report also notes, however, that under New York's HIV Testing and Confidentiality Law, N.Y. Pub. Health Law § 2781, enacted in 1989, HIV testing may not be ordered for purposes such as setting bail. *Id.*

[327] People *ex rel.* Glass v. McGreevy, 514 N.Y.S.2d 622, 623 (Sup. Ct. Rensselaer County 1987).

[328] *Id.*

[329] *See* United States v. Scarpa, 815 F. Supp. 88 (E.D.N.Y. 1993) (granting bail to terminally ill defendant with AIDS who was charged with murder and racketeering, on condition that defendant reside in hospice under 24-hour guard, to be paid for by defendant).

[330] United States *ex rel.* Savitz v. Gallagher, 800 F. Supp. 228, 233 (E.D. Pa. 1992). Savitz was not released on bail, and he ultimately died shortly before his trial was to take place. See **§ 7.1.**

[331] 879 S.W.2d 677 (Mo. Ct. App. 1994).

example, the court struck down a discriminatory local rule adopted by the judges in a county in Missouri. The local rule required the county jails and state Department of Corrections to give the judges the medical records of HIV positive defendants prior to any court appearances. In a comprehensive opinion, the court held that the local rule violated the state HIV confidentiality statute, Missouri Revised Statutes § 191.656.1, as well as the right to privacy as it relates to medical records. Noting the "stigma that attaches with the disease" of HIV, the court found that information relating to HIV status "is deserving of a high degree of protection."[332] The court also observed that the CDC had found that the risk of infection through saliva or urine is "extremely low or nonexistent."[333] Furthermore, the court stated, "There is no hint criminal courtroom activity, present or past, presents any danger resulting from an inmate who is HIV positive."[334] Any risk of transmission of HIV through blood could, the court found, be safely addressed through the use of "universal precautions such as wearing rubber gloves to clean blood spills."[335] The court concluded that the state had not shown a compelling interest in obtaining the inmate's medical records.

For similar reasons, the court in *Commonwealth v. Martin*[336] reversed convictions for rape, assault, and burglary after finding that the trial court erred in having the defendant, Martin, who was HIV positive, shackled and separated from his attorney during the latter part of his trial. Martin had gone into a rage on the second day of his trial as he was being led into a holding cell, complaining that his trial was not going well and that "he wasn't going to spend the rest of his life in jail for something he did not do."[337] Soon afterwards, a court officer noticed blood on Martin's hand. Martin explained that it was just a cut. The court officer reported the incident to the judge, suggesting that in his opinion Martin was planning to escape by using his blood as a weapon. The judge leapt to the conclusion that Martin was planning to use his HIV-infected blood to cause a mistrial, and he ordered that Martin be shackled with leg irons and that the irons be covered so the jury could not see them. He also directed that Martin be seated at a table alongside the defense table and separated from his attorney by a row of law books so as to give the attorney "some distance in the event [Martin] acts up."[338] The appeals court found that there was no evidence Martin planned to escape or be disruptive in the courtroom, and it held that the unusual security precautions were unnecessary and had unfairly prejudiced Martin.[339]

---

[332] *Id.* at 681–82 (quoting Faison v. Parker, 823 F. Supp. 1198, 1201–02 (E.D. Pa. 1993)). *See also* Doe v. Borough of Barrington, 729 F. Supp. 376, 384 (D.N.J. 1990).

[333] State *ex rel.* Callahan v. Kinder, 879 S.W.2d at 680.

[334] *Id.* at 681.

[335] *Id.*

[336] 660 N.E.2d 670 (Mass. App. Ct. 1996).

[337] *Id.* at 675.

[338] *Id.* at 676.

[339] *Id.* at 676–77. The Supreme Court has ruled that the legality of unusual security precautions should be determined by weighing the prejudice to the defendant against the need for their use. *See* Estelle v. Williams, 425 U.S. 501 (1976); Illinois v. Allen, 397 U.S. 337 (1970).

The use of rubber gloves by court officers was likewise found unnecessary and prejudicial in *Wiggins v. State*.[340] The trial court heard rumors that the defendant, Wiggins, might be HIV positive and, without further investigation, permitted the court officers to wear rubber gloves while escorting Wiggins to and from the courtroom and while standing behind him in court. The appellate court found that this unusual treatment must have aroused the jurors' curiosity and concern, and it probably led them to speculate that Wiggins had AIDS.[341] As a result, the "specter of the dread disease AIDS hovered over the trial . . . [and the] trial judge refused to exorcise it."[342] The court held that the trial judge erred both in failing to determine whether Wiggins was in fact infected with HIV and by assuming, contrary to the prevailing expert view, that HIV could be transmitted by casual contact.[343]

HIV has also become an issue in some cases through the questioning of witnesses and the court's instructions to the jury. In *Commonwealth v. Martin*,[344] for example, Martin claimed in his defense to the rape and sexual assault charges that the complainant had consented to having sex. The prosecution presented as evidence of lack of consent the complainant's testimony that Martin had told her sometime before the incident that he had tested positive for HIV. The appellate court ruled that the testimony was relevant, because it did make it less likely that the complainant would have consented.[345] But the court also held that the unfair prejudicial effect was great because of the widespread lack of knowledge about HIV and the "deep anxieties, and considerable hysteria, about the disease and those that suffer from it."[346] For this reason the court ruled that the complainant's testimony that Martin was HIV positive should only have been admitted if it were coupled with cautionary instructions to the jury to minimize the prejudice.[347] Because the trial judge did not give these instructions, the admission of the testimony was error.

---

[340] 554 A.2d 356 (Md. 1989).

[341] *Id.* at 359–60.

[342] *Id.* at 357.

[343] *Id.* at 359–60, 362 n.5. *Cf.* People v. Bonaventura, 563 N.Y.S.2d 465, 466 (App. Div. 1990) (holding that court officers' use of surgical gloves at trial in handling defendant's clothing introduced into evidence did not prejudice defendant because judge instructed jury that it "is the rule" for court officers to wear gloves whenever handling a defendant's clothing).

[344] 660 N.E.2d 670 (Mass. App. Ct. 1996).

[345] *Id.* at 674. *See also* State v. Deal, 459 S.E.2d 93 (S.C. Ct. App. 1995) (holding that charge of exposing another to HIV was properly tried together with sexual assault charges because (1) all the charges arose from the same incident, (2) the complainant's knowledge of defendant's HIV status was relevant to the issue of consent, and (3) the prejudicial effect of the testimony about the defendant's HIV status did not outweigh its probative value).

[346] Commonwealth v. Martin, 660 N.E.2d at 674–75.

[347] The appellate court stated that the judge should have instructed the jury to consider the statement the defendant allegedly made only on the issue of the complainant's state of mind at the time of the alleged rape and assault and not to allow themselves to become prejudiced against the defendant based on his HIV status. *Id.* at 675. It is doubtful, however, that jurors

The judge in *Martin* compounded the error of admitting the prejudicial testimony by the instructions he gave to the jurors regarding their handling of several items of evidence. The judge said he would not send the rape kit out with the jurors during their deliberations because of "some concerns that I might have, and I think you might have concerning the handling of it." The judge similarly expressed doubt over whether handling the complainant's clothing would be "safe," and offered to provide gloves to the jurors if they did want to handle the clothes or if they insisted on seeing the rape kit.[348] The appellate court found that these comments in effect told the jury that Martin did have AIDS, even though there was no evidence of his being infected aside from the complainant's testimony. The judge thus vouched for the credibility of the complainant, thereby exacerbating the risk that the jurors would believe Martin had AIDS and be prejudiced against him.[349]

Attorneys have several options for dealing with the danger that the issue of HIV may cause unfair prejudice during the criminal trial process. First, it is very important for counsel to make a complete record of any HIV-related discrimination so that the issue can be raised on appeal. Counsel must insist that HIV-infected defendants and witnesses be treated normally and that no unusual precautions be taken. Defense counsel should be in contact with the defendant's physician and confirm that the defendant is medically able to attend court appearances. If the defendant is barred from the courtroom or not produced from the jail, counsel should insist that the judge make an inquiry into the reasons for the defendant's absence.[350]

Second, if HIV will be a relevant issue during the trial, or if through pretrial publicity jurors may know the defendant is HIV positive, counsel should conduct a thorough voir dire regarding the potential jurors' beliefs and attitudes towards HIV and AIDS. The American Bar Association recommends that judges permit extensive voir dire in such cases,[351] and several courts have held that thorough voir dire can be an effective method of mitigating the prejudice from

---

truly will banish their prejudices from their minds just because a judge has told them to do so. As the Supreme Court has stated, "The naive assumption that prejudicial effects can be overcome by instructions to the jury . . . all practicing lawyers know to be unmitigated fiction." Bruton v. United States, 391 U.S. 123, 129 (1968) (quoting Krulewitch v. United States, 336 U.S. 440, 453 (1949) (Jackson, J., concurring)).

[348] Commonwealth v. Martin, 660 N.E.2d at 677.

[349] *Id.* at 678. Similar issues of balancing relevance against prejudicial effect have arisen in the context of questioning witnesses about their HIV status. *See* Kirk v. Commonwealth, 464 S.E.2d 162, 166 (Va. Ct. App. 1995) (holding that evidence that defendant's alibi witness was defendant's homosexual lover and had AIDS was probative of bias, and probative value outweighed the prejudicial impact).

[350] Susan Hendricks, *Problems and Issues in Criminal Prosecutions, in* AIDS Practice Manual 13-6 (Paul Albert et al. eds., 1991).

[351] American Bar Ass'n Policy on AIDS and the Criminal Justice System 2 (Recommendation B,4,(b)) (adopted by ABA House of Delegates Feb. 7, 1989).

the HIV issue.[352] Individual voir dire would be preferable to group or panel voir dire because in a group or panel, prejudicial answers by one of the prospective jurors may influence the others. At the same time, however, counsel must be sure to maintain confidentiality and not divulge a defendant's HIV status without the defendant's express (and preferably written) consent.

Third, whenever counsel suspects that opposing counsel may ask prejudicial and irrelevant questions about HIV or AIDS, counsel should make a motion in limine asking the court to explicitly bar those questions.[353] Finally, counsel must become knowledgeable on HIV medical issues so as to be able to educate the court and court personnel and prevent discriminatory measures from being taken.

§ 7.20 HIV Dementia and Defenses to Criminal Charges

Apart from giving rise to criminal charges, a defendant's HIV positive status may also come into play in a criminal prosecution as a defense. HIV infection can cause dementia, an insidious mental impairment that may cause cognitive degeneration and lead to legally inappropriate behavior.[354] Known broadly as *HIV dementia*,[355] this impairment may in some cases be severe enough to constitute

---

[352] *See* State v. Mercer, 544 A.2d 611, 614–17 (Conn. 1988) (holding that by permitting unrestricted individual voir dire on AIDS issue, trial court, which had without objection disclosed defendant's HIV status to the potential jurors, ensured defendant received a fair trial before an unbiased jury); State v. Van Straten, 409 N.W.2d 448, 451–53 (Wis. Ct. App. 1987) (holding that in case for which there had been statewide media coverage that defendant had AIDS and had splattered blood on jailers, extensive voir dire was the only way to ensure a fair trial).

[353] If counsel waits until after a question about HIV is asked, even if the court sustains counsel's objection, the jury will already have heard the question and will have been prejudiced by it. In such situations, unless the prejudice is extreme, appellate courts are reluctant to reverse the conviction. *See, e.g.,* State v. Mastracchio, 612 A.2d 698, 702–04 (R.I. 1992) (holding that prosecutor's question to defense witness regarding whether he was HIV positive was clearly improper in view of question's lack of relevance and highly sensitive nature of AIDS; but since witness did not answer question and trial judge sustained defense's objection, prosecutor's misconduct did not rise to level of due process violation); Farmah v. State, 789 S.W.2d 665, 673–74 (Tex. Ct. App. 1990) (holding that prosecutor's question to complainant during punishment phase of sexual assault case as to whether she was worried about possibility of contracting AIDS was prejudicial, but witness did not answer question and trial judge cured error by instructing jury to ignore question).

[354] Debra J. Balek, *AIDS Dementia Complex: A New and Necessary Insanity Defense,* Med. Trial Tech. Q. 467, 468–69 (1994) [hereinafter Balek, *AIDS Dementia*].

[355] HIV dementia is also known as HIV-1-associated dementia complex, HIV encephalopathy, subacute encephalitis, AIDS encephalopathy, and AIDS dementia complex. Justin C. McArthur, *Neurological and Neuropathological Manifestations of HIV Infection, in* Neuropsychology HIV Infection 56, 61 (Igor Grant & Alex Martin eds., 1994) [hereinafter McArthur, *Neurological Manifestations*].

a defense to criminal charges in the form of the defenses of insanity, diminished capacity, or automatism. Also, a defendant suffering from HIV dementia may be legally incompetent and therefore incapable of standing trial at all.

HIV dementia is a result of the direct and indirect effects of HIV infection on the central nervous system. Some people with HIV may also suffer from dementia caused not by HIV itself but by opportunistic infections.[356] HIV dementia has been divided into four stages of severity:

Stage 1 (mild): Able to perform most activities of daily life, but with evidence of functional intellectual or motor impairment.

Stage 2 (moderate): Unable to work or maintain more demanding aspects of daily life.

Stage 3 (severe): Major intellectual incapacity or motor disability.

Stage 4 (end stage): Nearly vegetative.[357]

It is recognized as a mental disorder by the American Psychiatric Association in its *Diagnostic and Statistical Manual of Mental Disorders*.[358] In its more severe stages, dementia may be characterized by hallucinations, delusions, aggression, and personality changes.[359] People suffering from dementia may begin to disregard normal rules of social conduct. Although most will become socially withdrawn, some may become abusive or physically assaultive, or they may engage in inappropriate behavior such as extravagant shopping sprees.[360] HIV dementia is rare in people with HIV who are asymptomatic, but it may affect 7.5 to 27 percent of people in the late stages of HIV disease.[361]

HIV dementia is difficult to diagnose. Particularly in its early stages, it may easily be overlooked or confused with other psychiatric complaints or the effects of psychoactive drugs.[362] There are no tests that are specific to HIV dementia, but instead the diagnosis is one of exclusion.[363] Any HIV positive criminal defendant whose behavior suggests the possibility of dementia should receive a

---

[356] *Id.* at 56.

[357] *Id.* at 62.

[358] American Psychiatric Ass'n, Diagnostic and Statistical Manual of Mental Disorders (DSM-IV) 148 (4th ed. 1994) (294.9 Dementia Due to HIV Disease).

[359] James T. Becker et al., *The Dementias and AIDS, in* Neuropsychology of HIV Infection 133, 141 (Igor Grant & Alex Martin eds., 1994).

[360] Balek, *AIDS Dementia* at 471.

[361] David M. Simpson & Michele Tagliati, *Neurologic Manifestations of HIV Infection,* 121 Annals Internal Med. 769, 771 (1994).

[362] McArthur, *Neurological Manifestations* at 62–63.

[363] David M. Simpson & Michele Tagliati, *Neurologic Manifestations of HIV Infection,* 121 Annals Internal Med. 769, 771 (1994).

battery of tests and obtain a professional psychiatric diagnosis from an expert familiar with HIV dementia.[364]

In its more severe stages, HIV dementia may provide the basis for an insanity defense. Under the *McNaghten* test for insanity, the defendant must, at the time of the crime, have been suffering from such a defect of reason from disease of the mind that the defendant did not know what he or she was doing, or did not know that the act was wrong.[365] The Model Penal Code formulation of the insanity defense incorporates the *McNaghten* test and adds a volitional prong: "[A] person is not responsible for criminal conduct if at the time of such conduct as a result of mental disease or defect he lacks substantial capacity either to appreciate the criminality [wrongfulness] of his conduct or to conform his conduct to the requirements of the law."[366] Most jurisdictions use either the Model Penal Code test or a modified version of the *McNaghten* test.[367] The federal insanity defense reads:

> (a) Affirmative defense.—It is an affirmative defense to a prosecution under any federal statute that, at the time of the commission of the acts constituting the offense, the defendant, as a result of a severe mental disease or defect, was unable to appreciate the nature and quality or wrongfulness of his acts. Mental disease or defect does not otherwise constitute a defense.
>
> (b) Burden of proof.—The defendant has the burden of proving the defense of insanity by clear and convincing evidence.[368]

To raise a successful insanity defense, counsel for a defendant with dementia must show the existence of the dementia, that the dementia impaired the defendant to a legally significant degree, and that, but for the impairment, the defendant would not have committed the crime.[369] A successful insanity defense, however, leads to the automatic initiation of involuntary commitment proceedings. Under these proceedings, the person remains committed as long as he or she continues to be insane and dangerous.[370]

If a defendant is unable to meet the test for insanity, the defense of diminished capacity may be available. Under the Model Penal Code, evidence that a defendant suffered from a mental disease or defect at the time of his offense may be

---

[364] In addition to a mental status exam, the following lab tests and procedures are recommended in order to make a diagnosis of HIV dementia: lumbar puncture (spinal tap); computed tomographic (CT) scan; magnetic resonance imaging (MRI); single-photon emission computed tomography (SPECT); positron emission tomography (PET). McArthur, *Neurological Manifestations* at 64–66.

[365] Rollin M. Perkins & Ronald N. Boyce, Criminal Law 959 (3d ed. 1982).

[366] Model Penal Code § 4.01 (1985).

[367] Balek, *AIDS Dementia* at 474.

[368] 18 U.S.C. § 17 (1994).

[369] Balek, *AIDS Dementia* at 476.

[370] *Id.* at 481.

admitted to disprove the mental element of the offense.[371] In other words, if an element of the crime is, for example, premeditation, or purposeful or knowing conduct, the defense can argue that the defendant's dementia was severe enough to negate this required mental state. Depending on the crime charged, however, the defendant may still be guilty of a lesser offense requiring proof of a less stringent mental element.[372]

Another possible defense arising from HIV dementia is that of *automatism*. It is a fundamental principle of criminal law that people can be found guilty only for conduct that is voluntary. Thus, under the common law defense of automatism, if the defendant committed the offense while in a state of virtual unconsciousness, like an automaton, then the crime was committed without voluntariness and therefore without intent or free will.[373] This defense was used with some success in a first-degree murder and robbery trial, resulting in an acquittal on these two charges and a conviction on the lesser charge of second-degree murder.[374] In this case, which is unreported, the defendant, Robert Braga, was diagnosed with both syphilis and AIDS. He allegedly went to the business of a friend to get some money. There, he stabbed the friend and ran away, leaving the money neatly stacked on a counter. Braga refused to plead insanity, so defense counsel raised the defense of automatism instead. The defense presented to the jury neurologists and other medical experts who testified regarding HIV dementia and its effects on Braga's cognitive functioning. The defense also showed the jury two MRIs (magnetic resonance images), one taken five years before the offense, and one taken shortly after the arrest. Projected onto a screen side-by-side, the two MRIs showed graphically the extensive shrinkage of Brag's cortex.

Related to these defenses of mental incapacity is the issue of the defendant's competence to stand trial. Unlike the defenses, however, the competence issue focuses not on the defendant's mental status at the time of the offense, but on his or her mental status at the time of the judicial proceedings. A defendant may not be tried, convicted, or sentenced if during the criminal proceedings, as a result of a mental disease or defect, he or she does not have the capacity to understand the nature and object of the proceedings or to assist in his or her defense.[375] The

---

[371] Model Penal Code § 4.01(1) (1962). *See also* United States v. Westcott, 83 F.3d 1354, 1358 (11th Cir.) (enactment of 1984 Insanity Defense Reform Act, 18 U.S.C. § 17, did not abolish defense of diminished capacity, which may be used to show that defendant lacked required intent for element of crime charged), *cert. denied,* 117 S. Ct. 269 (1996); United States v. Pohlot, 827 F.2d 889, 897 (3d Cir. 1987) (same), *cert. denied,* 484 U.S. 1011 (1988).

[372] Balek, *AIDS Dementia* at 477.

[373] *Id.* at 478.

[374] *Id.* at 490–93.

[375] Joshua Dressler, Understanding Criminal Law 310 (2d ed. 1995); *see* Cooper v. Oklahoma, 116 S. Ct. 1373 (1996) ("the criminal trial of an incompetent defendant violates due process"); Dusky v. United States, 362 U.S. 402, 402 (1960) (test for competence is that the defendant must have "sufficient present ability to consult with his lawyer with a reasonable degree of rational understanding . . . [and] a rational as well as factual understanding of the proceedings against him").

competence issue is typically a question of law for the judge to decide on the basis of psychiatric evidence, and its resolution is legally independent of the question of whether the defendant may have a defense to the charges. If the judge finds the defendant incompetent to stand trial, the defendant is generally committed to a mental health facility until competence is restored, or until it becomes clear that the defendant will never be competent.[376]

HIV dementia thus may provide a defense to criminal charges, or it may render a defendant incompetent to stand trial. Even if a defendant's dementia does not rise to this level of seriousness, however, it may still be relevant as a mitigating factor during the sentencing. See § **7.21.**

§ 7.21 Sentencing Issues

Judges across the United States have taken differing positions on the relevance of a defendant's HIV infection to sentencing. Some judges have lowered the sentences for HIV positive defendants, particularly in cases in which the defendants were in the advanced stages of AIDS. Other judges, however, have ruled that HIV infection alone is simply irrelevant to sentencing. Still others, in cases in which the defendant's crime may have risked infecting other people, have imposed enhanced sentences for HIV positive defendants.

Of all the courts, the federal courts have provided the most complete analysis of when HIV status is a valid basis for a reduced sentence. The federal sentencing guidelines, which apply to all federal crimes committed after November 1, 1987, set out a narrow range for sentencing in each case based on a point system that factors in the nature of the crime, some common aggravating or mitigating circumstances, and the defendant's criminal history. The judge is required to sentence within the "guideline range" unless he or she finds there are special circumstances that make the case unusual and warrant an upward or a downward departure from the guideline range.[377] Under the federal sentencing guidelines, a court may impose a sentence below the guideline range when the defendant has "an extraordinary physical impairment . . . *e.g.,* in the case of a seriously infirm defendant, home detention may be as efficient as, and less costly than, imprisonment."[378] Accordingly, several federal circuit courts of appeal have held that AIDS is a basis for a sentence below the guideline range when the disease "has progressed to such an advanced stage that it could be characterized as an 'extraordinary physical impairment.'"[379] Similarly, one federal circuit appeals court has

---

[376] Joshua Dressler, Understanding Criminal Law 311 (2d ed. 1995). If the judge determines that the defendant will not be restored to competence in the foreseeable future, the defendant must be released or committed pursuant to civil commitment proceedings, which requires proof that the defendant is dangerous. *Id.*

[377] U.S. Sentencing Comm'n, Federal Sentencing Guidelines Manual § 1B1.1 (1995).

[378] *Id.* § 5H1.4.

[379] United States v. Rabins, 63 F.3d 721, 728 (8th Cir. 1995) (upholding denial of sentence below guideline for HIV positive defendant who was not taking medications for any AIDS-related ailments and who did not offer any evidence that prison would worsen his condition

ruled that HIV infection may be a basis for a reduced sentence if the defendant has a "related serious physical complication."[380] The defense, of course, would have to introduce the defendant's medical records and produce medical experts to testify on this issue at time of sentencing.

Another ground for reduced sentences under the federal sentencing guidelines is the provision allowing for downward departures based on mitigating circumstances "of a kind or to a degree, not adequately taken into consideration by the Sentencing Commission in formulating the guidelines."[381] For example, if an HIV positive defendant is receiving new or experimental treatments that are not available in prison, this would certainly be a factor not considered by the Sentencing Commission and could justify a sentence of house arrest instead of imprisonment.

Another mitigating factor not adequately considered by the Sentencing Commission is that typically crowded prison conditions create an especially unhealthy environment for HIV positive people because their immune systems are compromised. HIV positive inmates are not only more susceptible to various illnesses prevalent in prisons, but they are far more likely to die from them. As a result, studies have found that people living with HIV who are imprisoned live only half as long as those who remain in the general population.[382] Tuberculosis (TB), particularly the multi-drug resistant strain, has in recent years become common in some prisons, and it is highly contagious in prison conditions.[383] In

---

or that he required special care), *cert. denied,* 116 S. Ct. 1031 (1996) (quoting United States v. Woody, 55 F.3d 1257, 1275 (7th Cir.), *cert. denied,* 116 S. Ct. 234 (1995)). *See also* United States v. Thomas, 49 F.3d 253, 261 (6th Cir. 1995) (upholding denial of sentence below guideline for HIV positive defendant who had not yet developed AIDS, reasoning that although defendant did have a life expectancy of about one-half his 9-year prison sentence, defendant's physical condition at time of sentencing was not serious enough to warrant a downward departure).

[380] United States v. Schein, 31 F.3d 135, 138 (3d Cir. 1994) (remanding for resentencing and for judge to consider whether the defendant, who was HIV positive, was suffering from a related serious physical complication that could warrant a downward departure); *see also* United States v. Streat, 22 F.3d 109, 112 (6th Cir. 1994) (noting that AIDS may be a proper basis for a lower sentence under certain circumstances).

[381] U.S. Sentencing Comm'n, Federal Sentencing Guidelines Manual § 5K2.0 (1995); 18 U.S.C. § 3553(b) (1994).

[382] Faith Colangelo & Mariana Hogan, *Jails and Prisons—Reservoirs of TB Disease: Should Defendants with HIV Infection (Who Cannot Swim) Be Thrown into the Reservoir?,* 20 Fordham Urb. L.J. 467, 480–81 (1993); People v. Jimmie E., N.Y.L.J., Apr. 4, 1991, at 21 (Sup. Ct. N.Y. County) (witness Dr. Stephen Sorrell, found to be an expert in the field of AIDS diagnosis and treatment, testified that statistically people with AIDS who are incarcerated live only half as long as those in the general population); William Gaunay & Rosemary L. Gido, *Acquired Immune Deficiency Syndrome, A Demographic Profile of New York State Inmate Mortalities 1981–1985* at 32 (New York State Commission of Correction 1986) (reporting that the average time period from confirmation of AIDS to death among inmates with AIDS in the New York State correctional system was 5.3 to 6.3 months).

[383] Faith Colangelo & Mariana Hogan, *Jails and Prisons—Reservoirs of TB Disease: Should Defendants with HIV Infection (Who Cannot Swim) Be Thrown into the Reservoir?,* 20 Fordham Urb. L.J. 467, 479–84 (1993).

comparison to the general population, people with HIV are not only more easily infected with TB, but they are also less easily diagnosed because immune suppression often causes them to test negative for TB even when they are infected. In addition, TB treatments for people with HIV are much less effective than for people not infected, and people with HIV die of TB much more quickly.[384] Thus, the threat of infection with diseases prevalent in prisons, particularly TB, is a mitigating factor not adequately considered by the Sentencing Commission and could justify a sentence below the guideline range.[385]

The reduced life expectancy of people with HIV is also a mitigating factor that should be considered at sentencing. Even if HIV infection has not progressed to the point of causing physical impairment, life expectancy with HIV is, in general, substantially lower than life expectancy without HIV. Thus, for a person with HIV, a sentence of 10 years could well be a life sentence. Simple fairness supports a reduced prison sentence for such a defendant so that the term of imprisonment would be proportional to the predicted number of years remaining in the defendant's life. For example, an Arizona state appellate court has held that the reduced life expectancy of an HIV positive person can be a basis for a reduced sentence. In *State v. Ellevan*,[386] the court stated, "Positive HIV status is material to informed plea bargaining and sentencing because it can transform into a life sentence a term of years that would otherwise end well within the recipient's probable life span." The defendant in *Ellevan* had not learned of his HIV infection until after his sentencing. He then moved for post-conviction relief on the ground that his HIV status constituted newly discovered evidence that could have mitigated his sentence if known at the time of sentencing. The lower court denied the motion, but the appeals court reversed and remanded for resentencing, finding that the defendant had met his burden of showing that he probably was HIV positive at the time of sentencing.[387]

Because the federal sentencing guidelines do not consider the issue of reduced life expectancy, this factor was not adequately taken into account by the federal Sentencing Commission, and it is a mitigating factor that warrants a downward departure from the guideline range.[388]

---

[384] *Id.*

[385] *See also* John D. Nelson, *Jails Microbes, and the Three-foot Barrier,* 335 New Eng. J. Med. 885, 886 (1996) (observing that prison conditions provide a milieu which fosters the "exchange of skin and mucosal flora and outbreaks of disease"); Jordan W. Tappero et al., *Meningococcal Disease in Los Angeles County, California, and Among Men in the County Jails,* 335 New Eng. J. Med. 833 (1996) (concluding that outbreaks of meningococcal disease in county jails were most likely the result of crowding and prolonged or repeated exposure to county jails).

[386] 880 P.2d 139, 140 (Ariz. Ct. App. 1994).

[387] *Id.* at 141–42.

[388] The argument that reduced life expectancy is a mitigating factor not adequately considered by the federal Sentencing Commission was rejected with scant analysis in United States v. Thomas, 49 F.3d 253, 260–61 (6th Cir. 1995). There, the court held that although the defendant, who was sentenced to nine years in prison, had a life expectancy of only 5.8 years,

Several state courts have approved reduced sentences for defendants with HIV. In *State v. E.R.*,[389] for example, the defendant, who had pleaded guilty to possession of pipe bombs and drugs, had AIDS, and his predicted life expectancy was six months. The sentencing judge originally imposed a sentence of seven years in prison, but later reduced it to five years' probation. The judge reasoned that imprisonment would be an excessive hardship on the defendant, and that in view of his medical condition, he was no longer a risk to society. Incarceration, therefore, was not required for the purpose of deterrence.[390] The appellate court affirmed the judge's reasoning and rejected the state's argument that this decision would open the floodgates to thousands of other HIV positive inmates seeking to avoid prison terms. The court found that the defendant's condition had deteriorated to the point that his condition was extraordinary and "idiosyncratic."[391]

Note that if a defendant's condition deteriorates after sentencing while the defendant is in federal prison, the director of the Bureau of Prisons may request that the sentencing court reduce the sentence under 18 U.S.C. § 3582(c)(1), which permits a reduction if there are "extraordinary and compelling reasons."[392] Similarly, in New York, an inmate's HIV status may allow for early parole. By statute, the State Parole Board has the power to release on medical parole any inmate "suffering from a terminal condition, disease or syndrome" who is "so debilitated or incapacitated as to create a reasonable probability that he or she is physically incapable of presenting any danger to society."[393]

---

this factor was taken into account in § 5H1.4 of the Federal Sentencing Guidelines Manual, which allows for a downward departure if the defendant is suffering from an extraordinary physical impairment. The *Thomas* court failed to recognize, however, that the issue of physical impairment is distinct from the issue of reduced life-expectancy caused by an incurable illness. There is nothing in § 5H1.4 of the Federal Sentencing Guidelines Manual to indicate that the Sentencing Commission gave any consideration to the reduced life expectancy of defendants living with life-threatening and incurable diseases such as HIV. Accordingly, reduced life-expectancy ought to be a basis for a sentence below the federal sentencing guidelines.

[389] 641 A.2d 1072 (N.J. Super. Ct. App. Div. 1994).

[390] *Id.* at 1077.

[391] *Id.* at 1078. *See also* Brogdon v. State, 781 P.2d 1370, 1371 (Alaska Ct. App. 1989) (judge suspended two years of a five year sentence in view of HIV positive defendant's physical and emotional condition; appellate court held further reduction of sentence not required); State v. Ellevan, 880 P.2d 139, 140 (Ariz. Ct. App. 1994) (holding that HIV positive status may be mitigating factor justifying reduced sentence).

[392] *See* United States v. Rabins, 63 F.3d 721, 729 n.15 (8th Cir. 1995), *cert. denied,* 116 S. Ct. 1031 (1996).

[393] N.Y. Exec. Law 259-r. The statute exempts certain violent offenses such as murder and manslaughter from its application. *See also* Newton E. Kendig et al., *The Maryland Division of Correction Medical-Parole Program: A Four-Year Experience, 1991–1994,* 11 AIDS & Pub. Pol'y J. 21, 25 (1996) (concluding, based on review of Maryland's medical-parole program, that early release for inmates with terminal illnesses, including AIDS, "can be accomplished expeditiously and with minimal impact on public safety").

The downside of any sentencing argument that involves disclosing the defendant's HIV positive status is, of course, that it requires the defendant to give up the confidentiality of the HIV test results and related medical information. Defense counsel needs to review carefully with the defendant the advantages and disadvantages of such a course of action. If the defendant chooses to disclose his or her HIV status for sentencing purposes, counsel should obtain from the defendant a written waiver permitting the disclosure.[394] Defense counsel could, however, limit the extent of the disclosure of confidential information by moving to have all sentencing papers and documents discussing the defendant's medical condition filed under seal.

The Committee on Criminal Law and Probation Administration of the Judicial Conference of the United States has issued guidelines regarding disclosure of a defendant's HIV status in pretrial services reports (which are used for setting bail in federal court) and presentence reports (on which federal district court judges rely in determining the sentence)

> without the defendant's written, informed consent unless it is relevant to the offense charged, such as a sexual assault. However, the court may require the officer to disclose all known medical information about the defendant in order to determine its relevancy in the disposition of the case. In this situation, the officer should advise the court, confidentially, pursuant to the provisions of Fed. R. Crim. P. 32(c)(3)(A), of the individual's positive HIV test results and current symptomatic status and of the defendant's refusal to give consent for disclosure of this information.[395]

Applewhite v. United States[396] illustrates one of the risks defendants face in disclosing their HIV status to the court. Applewhite, who was an injecting drug user, disclosed his HIV infection to the judge during a violation of probation hearing in hopes of receiving more lenient treatment. Defense counsel requested that court place Applewhite under house arrest, instead of in prison, so that he could receive outpatient treatment at a clinic specializing in the treatment of people with HIV. The judge, however, concerned that Applewhite might spread HIV to others in the community by sharing intravenous needles, revoked his probation

---

[394] See **App. A.**

[395] Memorandum from the Committee on Criminal Law and Probation Administration of the Judicial Conference of the United States to Judges, United States District Courts, United States Probation Officers and United States Pretrial Services Officers, Guidelines for U.S. Probation Officers and U.S. Pretrial Services Officers Supervising Clients Who Have Been Exposed to the Human Immunodeficiency Virus (HIV) or Who Have Acquired Immune Deficiency Syndrome (AIDS) 5 (Sept. 30, 1988) (on file with author). *Cf.* Faison v. Parker, 823 F. Supp. 1198 (E.D. Pa. 1993) (holding in prisoner civil rights action that disclosure in state court presentence report of confidential medical and mental health information did not violate prisoner's state or federal rights of privacy in view of the safeguards against disclosure of the report and the state's compelling interest in providing this information to the sentencing judge).

[396] 614 A.2d 888 (D.C. 1992).

and required him to complete his five-year sentence. Although other factors also supported the judge's revocation of probation, the appellate court upheld the judge's reliance on the risk of HIV transmission as the primary basis. Thus, in some cases, the decision to disclose the defendant's HIV positive status to the court can backfire.

Some state courts have held that HIV positive status and shortened life expectancy are not grounds for a reduced sentence. In *Commonwealth v. O'Neil*,[397] for example, a Pennsylvania appellate court upheld a four- to ten-year sentence for an HIV positive defendant convicted of burglary. The court reasoned that sentencing a defendant to a term of imprisonment that may exceed his life expectancy is not per se cruel and unusual punishment.[398] Similarly, the state appellate courts in New York have all held that HIV positive status alone is not relevant to sentencing.[399] These decisions provide little in the way of reasoning and none addresses the arguments that support treating HIV infection as a mitigating factor at sentencing. It should be noted, however, that although the New York courts do not permit consideration of HIV status at sentencing, a defendant's HIV infection may support a *Clayton* motion, that is, a motion to dismiss the charges in the "interests of justice."[400] The availability of the *Clayton* motion in

---

[397] 573 A.2d 1112, 1115 (Pa. Super. Ct. 1990).

[398] *Id.* at 1115. *See also* People v. Baca, 852 P.2d 1302, 1309–10 (Colo. Ct. App. 1993) (holding that 45-year prison sentence for defendant convicted of murder was not excessive simply because the defendant was HIV positive); State v. Sherrill, 611 So. 2d 728, 731 (La. Ct. App. 1992) (holding that sentence of 15 years at hard labor for defendant convicted of manslaughter was not excessive and that defendant's HIV positive status was not a mitigating factor); Glegola v. State, 871 P.2d 950, 953 (Nev. 1994) (upholding 15-year sentence for prostitute convicted of solicitation for prostitution after notice of positive HIV test; "the fact that [defendant] is likely to die of an AIDS related illness during those 15 years does not make the sentence cruel and unusual punishment"); State v. Wright, 534 A.2d 31, 34–35 (N.J. Super. Ct. App. Div. 1987) (holding that HIV positive defendant was not entitled to early release from prison because there was not sufficient evidence showing that continued imprisonment for a few more months until parole eligibility would cause defendant's condition to worsen).

[399] *See, e.g.,* People v. Shuman, 624 N.Y.S.2d 299 (App. Div.) (holding that sentence of 20 years to life for murder was not excessive despite defendant's HIV positive status), *appeal denied,* 655 N.E.2d 718 (N.Y. 1995); People v. Alvira, 619 N.Y.S.2d 126 (App. Div. 1994) (holding that defendant's HIV infection was not basis for reducing otherwise valid sentence); People v. Branham, 616 N.Y.S.2d 968 (App. Div.) (same), *appeal denied,* 645 N.E.2d 1230 (N.Y. 1995); People v. King, 585 N.Y.S. 503, 504 (App. Div.) (same), *leave denied,* 602 N.E.2d 238 (1992).

[400] People v. Clayton, 342 N.Y.S.2d 106 (App. Div. 1973) (setting out guidelines for granting motion to dismiss in interests of justice under N.Y. Crim. Proc. § 210.40). *See* People v. Herman L., 639 N.E.2d 404, 405 (N.Y. 1994), *aff'g* People v. Lawson, 603 N.Y.S.2d 311, 312–13 (App. Div. 1993) (court upheld dismissal in interests of justice of drug sale charges against homeless, HIV-infected drug addict. While on bail, Lawson had not committed any new offenses, he had enrolled in a clinical HIV study and a methadone treatment program, and his physical condition had deteriorated noticeably. Court found that "the prosecution of Herman Lawson while accomplishing little if anything to promote in any real way either public safety or the rule of law, will predictably succeed only in blighting what remains of

New York may explain why the New York courts have not seen any need to consider HIV status as a mitigating factor at sentencing.

Just as some courts have ruled that HIV status alone cannot be a basis for a lower sentence, some courts have ruled that it cannot be a basis for an enhanced sentence. In *Brooks v. State,*[401] for example, a judge sentenced a prostitute convicted of theft to a sentence above the state sentencing guideline range because she had AIDS. The appellate court reversed the sentence because the crime of theft had nothing to do with the spread of HIV. In *People v. Dempsey,*[402] the court reversed an enhanced sentence imposed on an HIV positive defendant because the sentencing judge had based the sentence on his own unfounded fears and prejudice regarding HIV. Dempsey had been convicted of sexual assault and criminal transmission of HIV arising from a sexual encounter he had with his nine-year-old brother. In imposing a sentence of 33 years in prison, the judge compared people with HIV to people with scarlet fever, suggesting the need for quarantine. He also compared people with HIV to rabid dogs, mad dogs, and lepers. The appellate court found that the judge was "so prejudiced by fear of the disease" that a remand for resentencing in front of a different judge was necessary.[403]

In cases in which the crime may have created a risk of transmission of HIV, the defendant's awareness of being HIV positive at the time of the offense has been a basis for imposing a higher sentence. Especially in rape and sexual assault cases, the courts have ruled that the defendant's HIV positive status is a valid aggravating factor that may be considered at sentencing.[404]

Mr. Lawson's drastically abbreviated existence. Such a pointlessly harsh result is, we think, precisely what the discretion afforded pursuant to [N.Y. Crim. Proc.] § 210.40 was designed to avoid."). *See also* People v. Wong, 642 N.Y.S.2d 396, 397 (App. Div. 1996) (upholding dismissal in interests of justice of burglary charges against HIV positive defendant in part because defendant's medical records showed that he would not survive the minimum term of imprisonment mandated for burglary); People v. Camargo, 516 N.Y.S.2d 1004, 1006 (Sup. Ct. 1986) (granting dismissal in interests of justice for defendant charged with drug sale who was bedridden with AIDS and had only three to four months left to live). *Cf.* United States v. Leonard, 817 F. Supp. 286, 305 (E.D.N.Y. 1992) (denying motion to dismiss federal drug distribution charges pending against defendant with AIDS).

[401] 519 So. 2d 1156 (Fla. Dist. Ct. App. 1988).

[402] 610 N.E.2d 208 (Ill. App. Ct. 1993).

[403] *Id.* at 225–27. *See also* State v. Stark, 832 P.2d 109, 117 (Wash. Ct. App. 1992) (reversing exceptional sentence of 10 years in prison for HIV positive defendant convicted of exposing others to HIV through sexual intercourse; appellate court found there was no evidence that defendant actually infected anyone, nor were there any other aggravating factors).

[404] *See, e.g.,* State v. Lewis, 848 P.2d 394, 410 (Idaho 1993) (upholding sentence of life in prison for offense of lewd conduct with minor based in part on fact that defendant was HIV positive at time of offense); State v. Sebasky, 547 N.W.2d 93, 101 (Minn. Ct. App. 1996) (upholding triple upward departure sentence in part based on defendant's knowledge that he was HIV positive at time of sexual offenses); State v. Guayante, 783 P.2d 1030, 1031–32 (Or. Ct. App.) (holding that judge could consider as aggravating factor at sentencing that defendant knew he was HIV positive at time he attempted to rape 13 year old girl), *review*

Only one court, however, has gone so far as to hold that an HIV positive defendant's sentence could be enhanced even in the absence of proof that the defendant knew he was HIV positive at the time of the crime. In *Cooper v. State*,[405] the defendant was convicted of sexual battery upon a 17-year-old boy who was in his custody. Just before trial, Cooper tested positive for HIV. The judge departed above the guideline range of 12 to 17 years to impose a sentence of 30 years in prison, in part because of the likelihood that the defendant had exposed the boy to HIV. The appellate court upheld the sentence, stating that "because of his life-style, Cooper knew or should have known that he had been exposed to the AIDS virus."[406] By the term *life-style,* the court was referring to the fact that Cooper was gay. This decision thus rests on the unwarranted assumption that all gay men should know that they have been exposed to HIV. A dissenting judge pointed out accurately that there was simply no evidence in the record to support the conclusion that merely being gay means that one knows or should know that one is HIV positive.[407] The *Cooper* case was wrongly decided, and it has not been followed in other jurisdictions.

Several states have passed statutes providing for aggravated sentences for HIV positive defendants in cases involving offenses such as sexual assault.[408] Similarly, many states have statutes providing for aggravated sentences for prostitutes

---

denied, 789 P.2d 1383 (Or. 1990); Hunter v. State, 799 S.W.2d 356, 360 (Tex. Ct. App. 1990) (holding that issue of whether defendant was infected with HIV was relevant to punishment phase in trial for aggravated sexual assault); State v. Farmer, 805 P.2d 200, 209 (Wash. 1991) (upholding exceptional sentence of seven and one-half years in prison for defendant convicted of sexual exploitation of minors; defendant knew at time of sexual encounters that he was HIV positive, and thus his actions were "deliberate, cruel and malicious" and could have resulted in the death of the minors). *See also* Morrison v. State, 673 So. 2d 953, 954 (Fla. Dist. Ct. App. 1996) (upholding upward departure resulting in sentence of 10 years in prison for defendant convicted of aggravated robbery, based in part on fact that defendant, who was HIV positive, bit victim's arm to the bone, and victim later tested HIV positive).

[405] 539 So. 2d 508 (Fla. Dist. Ct. App. 1989).

[406] *Id.* at 511.

[407] *Id.* at 512 (Shivers, J., dissenting).

[408] *See, e.g.,* Cal. Penal Code § 12022.85 (providing three-year enhancement for committing specified sex offenses with knowledge of HIV infection); People v. Shoemake, 20 Cal. Rptr. 2d 36, 41–44 (Ct. App. 1993) (upholding sentence for rape and related charges that was enhanced on basis of defendant's statements that he was HIV positive); Ind. Code Ann. § 35-38-1-7.1(b)(8) and (9) (listing as aggravating factor for sentencing that defendant, after learning that he or she was HIV positive and after being counseled on safe sex practices, committed a sex offense or drug offense that created "an epidemiologically demonstrated risk of transmission" of HIV); Lockhart v. State, No. 34A05-9511-CR-432, 1996 WL 566998, at *10 n.5 (Ind. Ct. App. Oct. 7, 1996) (improper to consider risk of transmitting HIV as aggravating factor for sentence in child molestation case in which there was no evidence that defendant was HIV positive, knew he was HIV positive, or had received risk counseling); Ridenour v. State, 639 N.E.2d 288, 297 (Ind. Ct. App. 1994) (improper for judge to cite risk of transmission of HIV as aggravating factor for death penalty when there was no evidence defendant was HIV positive).

who, after testing positive for HIV, continue to engage in prostitution.[409] The usefulness of enhanced sentences for HIV positive prostitutes is doubtful because prostitutes have not been found to be a major vector of HIV transmission.[410] Also, as discussed in § 7.6, compulsory measures such as sentence enhancement statutes are likely to be counterproductive because they discourage prostitutes from being tested voluntarily.[411] The prostitution sentence enhancement statutes, moreover, make no distinction between sexual acts that create a real risk of HIV transmission and those that do not, and thus they are overinclusive and fail to encourage safe sex practices. Educational efforts emphasizing safe sex practices are far more likely to be an effective means of preventing the spread of HIV than are sentence enhancement statutes that scapegoat prostitutes.

§ 7.22   HIV and Motions to Vacate Plea or Sentence

The courts are divided over whether a defendant's discovery after a guilty plea or after sentencing that he or she is HIV positive can be a ground for vacating the plea or the sentence. In *State v. Dockery*,[412] an Arizona appellate court considered the case of a defendant who discovered after he had pleaded guilty to theft that he had AIDS and would probably die before he finished serving his negotiated sentence of seven and one-half years. The court held that these circumstances entitled the defendant to withdraw his plea. The court reasoned that "[w]hen, before sentencing, the defendant discovers that his assumption that he will outlive the sentence he bargained for is incorrect, it is manifestly unjust not to allow him to withdraw from the bargain."[413]

The U.S. Sentencing Commission, after studying the issue of the intentional spread of HIV through sexual activities, did not see any need to adopt an HIV-specific sentencing standard. In its review of 235 criminal cases sentenced in fiscal year 1993, the Commission found that HIV was mentioned in only four cases; in only one of those cases, which was not a sexual abuse case, was intentional transmission an issue. The Commission concluded that the guidelines' general departure provision (U.S. Sentencing Commission, Federal Sentencing Guidelines Manual § 5K2.0), which allows for an upward departure from the guideline range for aggravating circumstances, would be the most appropriate way to handle such rare cases. U.S. Sentencing Commission, Report to Congress: Adequacy of Penalties for the Intentional Exposure of Others Through Sexual Activity to the Human Immunodeficiency Virus 4 (1995).

[409] See § 7.6. In the only reported case of an enhanced sentence for an HIV positive prostitute, Glegola v. State, 871 P.2d 950, 952 (Nev. 1994), the court upheld the sentence of 15 years in prison, finding that it did not constitute cruel and unusual punishment.

[410] William A. Rushing, The AIDS Epidemic 202 (1995). Among female prostitutes, the primary risk factor for contracting HIV is not sexual contact but drug use. Michael J. Rosenberg & Jodie M. Weiner, *Prostitutes and AIDS: A Health Department Priority?*, 78 Am. J. Pub. Health 418, 420 (1988) (concluding that compulsory efforts to control HIV among prostitutes are counterproductive).

[411] *Id.* at 422.

[412] 821 P.2d 188 (Ariz. Ct. App. 1991).

[413] *Id.* at 190.

Similarly, in *State v. Cooper,*[414] another Arizona appellate court held that a defendant's discovery after sentencing that he was HIV positive could constitute newly discovered evidence entitling the defendant to a new sentencing hearing. The defendant in *Cooper* had pleaded guilty to several counts of burglary and theft in exchange for a negotiated sentence of 15 years in prison. Over six months after his sentencing, Cooper discovered he was HIV positive when he participated in a blood donor program. The court held that a defendant's health is a factor to be considered at sentencing and that the severity of Cooper's illness may have altered his sentence. Thus, the court held that if Cooper could show he probably was infected with HIV at the time of his sentencing, he would be entitled to a new sentencing hearing.[415]

Appellate courts in New York, on the other hand, have held that a defendant's discovery after pleading guilty that he is HIV positive is not a ground to vacate the plea.[416] The courts have not provided any reasoning, other than to cite to a case in which the court held that HIV status alone is not a basis to lower a defendant's sentence.[417] It should be noted that the courts in New York hold inconsistent positions on the significance of a defendant's HIV status. On the one hand, they have held that HIV infection alone is not relevant either to sentencing or to plea withdrawal;[418] on the other hand, they have held that shortened life expectancy as a result of HIV infection can support a *Clayton* motion to dismiss the charges "in the interests of justice."[419] If HIV infection is relevant to the question of whether charges should be dismissed, then surely it should also be considered relevant to less drastic relief, such as sentence reduction or a motion to vacate a guilty plea. To date, however, the courts in New York have not addressed this inconsistency. Thus, the availability of relief to defendants who discover their HIV status after plea or sentencing depends on the jurisdiction.

---

[414] 800 P.2d 992 (Ariz. Ct. App. 1990).

[415] *Id.* at 996–97. *See also* State v. Ellevan, 880 P.2d 139, 140 (Ariz. Ct. App. 1994) (holding that petitioner was entitled to post-conviction relief on ground that his diagnosis with HIV after sentencing constituted newly discovered evidence that could have mitigated his sentence).

[416] People v. Santiago, 621 N.Y.S.2d 327 (App. Div. 1995); People v. Torres Rentas, 598 N.Y.S.2d 206 (App. Div.), *leave to appeal denied,* 622 N.E.2d 323 (N.Y. 1993).

[417] *See* People v. Howard, 559 N.Y.S.2d 572 (App. Div.), *appeal denied,* 564 N.E.2d 679 (N.Y. 1990).

[418] *Id.*

[419] People v. Herman L., 639 N.E.2d 404 (N.Y. 1994).

CHAPTER 8

NEGLIGENCE AND INTENTIONAL TORTS

Jean R. Sternlight

§ 8.1   Introduction

Persons who have been infected or placed in fear of infection with HIV may bring a civil action in tort against the person they feel is responsible for the injury.[1] Although some tort law is statutorily defined, most tort law is common law, made by courts on a case-by-case basis. Because that law is developed primarily by under state law standards, it may vary somewhat from jurisdiction to jurisdiction.

---

[1] W. Page Keeton et al., Prosser and Keeton on the Law of Torts 2 (5th ed. 1984) [hereinafter Prosser & Keeton].

To determine whether a defendant is liable for the harm, courts decide whether the defendant owed a duty of care to the plaintiff, whether the defendant breached that duty, and whether the breach caused harm to the plaintiff.[2] Recognizing that it would be impractical and undesirable to require compensation for every single hurtful look or thoughtless comment, tort law generally provides for compensation only when the defendant has acted deliberately or "unreasonably" as compared to how a reasonably prudent person would act in a similar situation.[3] Similarly, tort law requires compensation only for those injuries that may fairly be said to have been caused by the tortious act.[4] If the causal connection is too remote, no liability will be found.[5]

Tort law is intended to serve several purposes. First, personal injury lawsuits can provide an injured party with compensation for the harm he has suffered. Second, by holding wrongdoers liable for their acts, tort law is designed to encourage people to act with more regard for one another. Third, it is hoped that by requiring those who cause injury to pay for the harm they cause, tort law will encourage a more efficient distribution of societal resources.[6]

The AIDS epidemic has spawned many different types of tort claims in many different factual contexts. Individuals who have become infected or perhaps merely fear infection have, for example, brought claims against sexual partners; against third parties they believe deliberately exposed them to the virus; against

---

[2] *Id.* at 4.

[3] *Id.* at 6. Strict liability in tort law is an exception to the general tenet of judging conduct in terms of negligence based on a reasonable person standard. *Id.* at 536 (stating that in some cases, defendant may be held liable though charged with no moral wrongdoing nor departure from a reasonable standard of intent or care).

[4] *Id.* at 263. Causation is typically broken down into two distinct elements: "cause in fact," which looks simply at whether the injury would have occurred absent the wrongful act; and "proximate cause," which limits liability for social reasons to "those causes which are so closely connected with the result and of such significance that the law is justified in imposing liability." *Id.* at 264.

[5] To resolve issues of both duty and proximate cause, the courts make decisions of social policy as to the appropriate scope of a person's liability. In fact, it is well recognized that the line distinguishing these two decisions is both blurry and confusing. *Id.* at 273–75, 284–86 (discussing *Palsgraf v. Long Island R.R.*). It is also somewhat unclear which of these decisions should be made by the judge, and which by the jury. As one court explained: "Whether a legal duty existed between respondent and appellant is generally an issue of law to be resolved by the court . . . . Cases involving close questions of foreseeability are for the jury to determine, while those with clear issues of foreseeability should be resolved by the court as a matter of law." C.A.U. v. R.L., 438 N.W.2d 441, 443 (Minn. Ct. App. 1989).

[6] *See generally* Guido Calabresi, The Costs of Accidents (1970) (addressing question of which activities that cause accidents should be limited on the grounds that their social cost exceeds their social value, and also discussing fairness and justice rationales underlying tort law); George P. Fletcher, *Fairness and Utility in Tort Theory,* 85 Harv. L. Rev. 57 (1972) (contrasting individually-oriented paradigm of compensating nonreciprocal risks with societally oriented paradigm of reasonableness); Richard A. Posner, *The Concept of Corrective Justice in Recent Theories of Tort Law,* 10 J. Legal Stud. 187 (1981) (arguing that corrective theory of justice is a component of the economic theory of law).

medical personnel, hospitals, employers, or public facilities they believe exposed them to HIV; against doctors for making incorrect diagnoses; and against a variety of persons for falsely or perhaps truthfully publicizing the fact of their HIV infection.

It is not at all clear that the tort system is actually deterring socially undesirable behavior with respect to HIV. Considering the huge number of persons who have now been infected with HIV in the United States, relatively few tort actions have been brought.[7] Moreover, it is far from obvious that the lawsuits that have been brought actually deter many individuals from engaging in risky behavior. HIV is most often spread through sexual behavior, and rational risk assessment of the likelihood of being sued may not play a very important role in most individuals' decision making about that behavior.[8]

This chapter surveys the various types of tort actions brought in connection with HIV. It looks first at those claims that may be brought when one person intentionally or negligently causes another to become infected, in §§ 8.2 through 8.6. Section 8.9 examines claims that may be brought by a person who, although not testing positive for HIV, seeks compensation for her fear that she may in fact be infected. The chapter provides some practical tips for both plaintiffs and defendants with respect to claims involving transmission of HIV in §§ 8.7 through 8.8. Finally, in §§ 8.10 through 8.11 the chapter examines claims resulting from disclosure or release of information regarding an individual's infection with HIV.

CAUSES OF ACTION FOR HIV TRANSMISSION

§ 8.2 Battery

Battery is defined in most states as the intentional, harmful, or offensive and unprivileged contact with the person of another.[9] Persons who have become infected with HIV have brought battery claims in two very different kinds of situations. First, some persons have brought battery claims against a defendant who they allege violently and without their consent set out to infect them with

---

[7] As discussed in § 8.7, because these actions are quite difficult to win, it is understandable that few people would attempt to use the tort system to secure compensation, particularly when the potential plaintiffs are likely to be ill and focusing on preserving their health.

[8] *Compare* Tomas J. Philipson & Richard A. Posner, Private Choices and Public Health: The AIDS Epidemic in an Economic Perspective (1993) (arguing that rationality governs sexual and other behavior in the HIV context), *and* Richard A. Posner, Sex and Reason (1992) (arguing more generally that sexual activity is rational), *with* David Charny, *Economics of Death,* 107 Harv. L. Rev. 2056 (1994) (reviewing and critiquing rationality thesis).

[9] Restatement (Second) of Torts §§ 13, 18 (1985); Prosser & Keeton at 39. "Privilege," as used in this sense, is synonymous with consent. If a supposed victim has genuinely consented to be touched, the person who touched her cannot be held liable for committing a battery.

HIV. This battery claim might be brought against a rapist or against a person who deliberately bit or used an infected needle on another. Although there have been accounts of persons who, upon finding out they had AIDS, deliberately set out to infect others,[10] in fact it appears such scenarios are quite rare.

The second type of battery scenario is much more common and thus more significant. A touching may be categorized as a battery if, although the person who was touched consented to be touched, he would not have consented had he been fully aware of the facts. In particular, the tort of battery may apply to acts between consensual sexual partners, when one partner causes the other to become infected.[11] A woman who claimed to have been infected as a result of having sex with professional basketball player Earvin "Magic" Johnson brought suit against him after he announced he was HIV-infected. Johnson sought to have the battery claim dismissed on the ground that the sexual contact could not constitute a battery, because at the time the couple had sex he did not know that he was infected with HIV. The court ruled that when a person engages in sexual contact with knowledge that risk of HIV transmission is a "substantial certainty," a claim for battery is stated.[12] The court found that because plaintiff had alleged that Johnson had such substantial certainty when he engaged in sexual relations with the plaintiff, the court could not dismiss the complaint as a matter of law.[13]

The difficult issue courts must therefore seek to resolve is when a person should reasonably know that he is putting another person at risk of HIV infection. One court faced the question of whether a homosexual man, who had symptoms including headaches, spots on his legs, weakness, and fatigue, reasonably should have known he was HIV-infected in March 1985. The court refused to impute such knowledge to the defendant, stating that based on the physicians' affidavits and on the information available to the public in March 1985, "it was not reasonable for respondent to have constructive knowledge he might have AIDS, or that he was capable of transmitting the disease to appellant."[14] Similarly, a court found that a mortician, who sued a hospital, physician, and others

---

[10] *See, e.g.,* James F. Clarity, *Irish Priest's Tale Stirs Furor about AIDS and Unprotected Sex,* N.Y. Times, Sept. 14, 1995, at A12 (priest claims that an HIV infected woman tried to avenge her illness by having unprotected intercourse with numerous partners); Randy Shilts, And the Band Played On 251–52 (1988) (implying that Gaetan Dugas, the so-called Patient Zero, deliberately risked infecting others by having sexual relationships without disclosing his diagnosis with AIDS).

[11] Now that most states have eliminated spousal immunity, one spouse can often sue the other for infecting them with HIV. *See generally* Carl Tobias, *Interspousal Tort Immunity in America,* 23 Ga. L. Rev. 359 (1989). **Section 8.9** discusses claims for fear of AIDS that can be brought even where the exposed partner has not tested positive for HIV.

[12] Doe v. Johnson, 817 F. Supp. 1382, 1396–97 (W.D. Mich. 1993) (applying Mich. law). *See also* Douglas W. Baruch, *AIDS in the Courts: Tort Liability for the Sexual Transmission of Acquired Immune Deficiency Syndrome,* 22 Tort & Ins. L.J. 165, 176 (1987).

[13] 817 F. Supp. at 1396.

[14] C.A.U. v. R.L., 438 N.W.2d 441, 444 (Minn. Ct. App. 1989). *See also* Doe v. Johnson, 817 F. Supp. 1382, 1393 (W.D. Mich. 1993) (no duty exists to disclose possible HIV infection solely based on fact that defendant has engaged in frequent, unprotected sex).

for failing to inform him that the deceased had HIV, could not state a claim for battery because he could not allege that the defendants intended to cause harm, as required under West Virginia law.[15] Yet, in the case of Magic Johnson, as noted above, the court held that a person could potentially be held liable for battery even if he had not yet tested positive for HIV.[16]

Persons who have been infected by HIV somewhat less directly, such as by sharing an infected needle or receiving an infected blood transfusion, cannot likely win a battery suit. They would not be able to show that they were unlawfully touched by the defendant. They might, however, have other recourse, such as a claim for fraud (§ 8.3) or negligence (§ 8.4).

§ 8.3 Fraud and Deceit

A defendant will be found to have committed a fraud or engaged in deceit when he or she: (1) knowingly or without reasonable basis (2) made an untruthful statement (3) with the intention that the plaintiff rely on that misrepresentation, (4) if the plaintiff reasonably relied on that misrepresentation, and (5) thereby caused damage to the plaintiff.[17] For example, if an HIV-infected person lied to a potential sexual partner, claiming to be HIV negative when in fact he knew he was not, the partner could sue for fraud if she was injured as a result of the contact. For example, a woman claiming to have had a sexual relationship with Earvin "Magic" Johnson sued, among other claims, for fraud, alleging that Johnson had committed fraud by failing to inform her that he was HIV-infected when he knew he had HIV or should have known he had HIV based on his symptoms.[18] The court allowed the fraud claim to proceed but rejected the plaintiff's claim that Johnson committed fraud simply by failing to inform her of his sexually active lifestyle.

As with battery, the defendant would not be liable for fraud unless the plaintiff could show that defendant was lying and not merely mistaken when she claimed to be disease-free. Nor would the defendant be liable if she could show that the plaintiff was already so high on drugs or so in love that she could not understand or react to the defendant's misstatement. That is, the defendant would win if she could show that the plaintiff did not "rely" on the misstatement.

Fraud cases are relatively difficult to prove. First, it is difficult to show that a person deliberately as opposed to merely negligently exposed another to HIV.

---

[15] Funeral Servs. by Gregory Inc. v. Bluefield Community Hosp., 413 S.E.2d 79 (W. Va. 1991). The mortician, who repeatedly tested negative for HIV following the embalming, was also unable to allege physical injury. He had in fact been wearing proper protective gear during the embalming. *Id.* at 81. Although *Gregory* was overruled in part on statute of limitation grounds in Courtney v. Courtney, 437 S.E.2d 436 (W. Va. 1993), and Bramer v. Dotson, 437 S.E.2d 773 (W. Va. 1993), these cases do not challenge the holding of *Gregory* on the merits.

[16] Doe v. Johnson, 817 F. Supp. 1382, 1396–97.

[17] Restatement (Second) of Torts § 525 (1985). *See also id.* §§ 526–545, 552 (further defining various components of tort of fraudulent or negligent misrepresentation).

[18] Doe v. Johnson, 817 F. Supp. 1382, 1387–95 (W.D. Mich. 1993).

Second, fraud cases may often come down to one person's word against another's. It is rare that someone would record a lie in a letter, for example, that might be submitted in evidence. Thus, most actions for fraud concerning HIV also include claims for negligence or other torts.

One need not necessarily test positive in order to recover in a fraud action. For instance, upon proving that movie star Rock Hudson had falsely claimed to be uninfected with HIV, his former lover Marc Christian recovered $5.5 million in compensatory and punitive damages reduced from a jury verdict of $21.75 million.[19] Although Christian did not test positive, the jury found he was entitled to substantial compensation for the emotional suffering he had endured as a result of the misrepresentation.[20]

§ 8.4   Negligence

A person can be held liable for committing a negligent act when he breaches a duty of care to another by engaging in conduct in which a similarly situated reasonable person would not engage.[21] That is, to win, the plaintiff need not show that the defendant intended to cause harm, but only that defendant engaged in conduct that was unreasonable.

This very broad standard can encompass many different types of fact situations pertaining to HIV/AIDS. One lover might sue another;[22] a hospital patient might sue her doctor and/or hospital for negligently exposing her to an infected employee;[23] an employee or patient might sue a hospital for negligently exposing her to an infected hypodermic needle;[24] one drug addict might sue another for negligently exposing her to a dirty needle;[25] a doctor might sue her patient for

---

[19] *Christian Still Feels "Vindicated" Despite Award Cut in Hudson Case,* L.A. Times, Apr. 23, 1989, pt. 2, at 5 (reporting that judge reduced jury's award of punitive damages from $7.25 million to $500,000 and reduced compensatory damages from $14.5 million to $5 million).

[20] Aetna Casualty & Sur. Co. v. Sheft, 989 F.2d 1105 (9th Cir. 1993) (Christian prevailed on claims of intentional misrepresentation, intentional concealment, and intentional infliction of emotional distress). Claims for fear of HIV infection are discussed in **§ 8.9.**

[21] Restatement (Second) of Torts §§ 282–283 (1985). *See also* Prosser & Keeton at 173–76.

[22] *E.g.,* Doe v. Johnson, 817 F. Supp. 1382, 1393, 1395 (W.D. Mich. 1993) (denying motion to dismiss claims for negligent transmission when defendant allegedly had actual knowledge he was HIV infected, had symptoms of HIV disease, or had knowledge that a prior sex partner had been diagnosed as HIV-infected; court noted, however, that mere allegations that Johnson had engaged in "high risk" sexual activities in the past or was a member of a "risk group" for HIV infection were not alone sufficient to support a claim for negligent transmission); *In re* Estate of Casey, 583 N.E.2d 83 (Ill. App. Ct. 1991) (noting claim against estate for decedent's failure to disclose HIV status, resulting in transmission to plaintiff).

[23] Faya v. Almaraz, 620 A.2d 327 (Md. 1993) (allowing patients to recover in claim against surgeon).

[24] Carroll v. Sisters of St. Francis Health Servs., Inc., 868 S.W.2d 585 (Tenn. 1993).

[25] Although theoretically possible, it is unlikely this particular suit would be economically viable, and no such decisions have been reported.

negligently exposing the doctor to the patient's disease;[26] a recipient of blood might sue a blood bank; and an athlete might sue her team for exposing her to another player who was HIV-infected.[27]

Each of these types of claims, involving very different sets of facts, turn on the same basic questions: did the defendant have a duty of care toward the plaintiff, did the defendant act unreasonably, and did the defendant's unreasonable act cause harm to the plaintiff? For example, with respect to the question of duty, a court analyzing the claim brought against Magic Johnson found that although a person has a duty to inform a sexual intimate that he knows himself to be HIV-infected, has recognizable symptoms, or that a prior sexual partner was HIV-infected, the person has no duty to reveal the mere fact that he is quite sexually active and therefore in a high risk group.[28]

To establish that certain damages were caused by another's negligent acts, one must show both that such acts were the *cause in fact,* in that the damage would not have occurred but for the act, and also that the act was the *proximate cause* of the injury, in that the damage was reasonably foreseeable.[29]

§ 8.5   Medical Malpractice

Plaintiffs have brought four major types of claims related to HIV against medical personnel. First, plaintiffs have sued claiming they either were infected or came to fear infection because medical personnel were negligent in failing to follow applicable medical standards of care.[30]

---

[26] *See, e.g.,* A. Samuel Oddi, *Reverse Informed Consent: The Unreasonably Dangerous Patient,* 46 Vand. L. Rev. 1417 (1993).

[27] *See generally* Paul M. Anderson, Comment, *Cautious Defense: Should I Be Afraid to Guard You?,* 5 Marq. Sports L.J. 279 (1995) (discussing employment but not tort issues in the context of professional sports). Employees may well seek to sue their employers, as well, for negligently exposing them to HIV by failing to take proper precautions or provide proper instructions. The vast majority of such cases, however, will be covered by workers' compensation rather than by tort principles. *See, e.g.,* Stout v. Johnson City Medical Ctr. Hosp., No. 03501-9504-CV-00031, 1995 WL 599708 (Tenn. Oct. 11, 1995).

[28] Doe v. Johnson, 817 F. Supp. 1382, 1393–95 (W.D. Mich. 1993) (weighing public health advantages of mandating disclosure against invasiveness of requiring disclosures). *See also* C.A.U. v. R.L., 438 N.W.2d 441 (Minn. Ct. App. 1989) (affirming summary judgment on ground defendant had no actual or constructive knowledge that he had AIDS at time he had sexual relationship with fiance).

[29] Doe v. United States, 737 F. Supp. 155, 159 (D.R.I. 1990) (doctor's negligence in performing tonsillectomy was both cause in fact and proximate cause of child's becoming HIV-infected from blood transfusions) (citing Prosser & Keeton at 41–42).

[30] *See, e.g.,* Doe v. United States, 737 F. Supp. 155 (D.R.I. 1990) (a 12-year-old plaintiff showed that the doctor's negligence in employing certain procedures caused him to need massive blood transfusions as a result of which he developed AIDS); Howard v. Alexandria Hosp., 429 S.E.2d 22 (Va. 1993) (plaintiff sued for physical and emotional injuries resulting from hospital's failure properly to sterilize its instruments). See also § **8.9,** discussing claims for fear of HIV.

Second, plaintiffs have sued doctors for failing to secure the plaintiff's informed consent before conducting an operation by failing to inform plaintiff of the likelihood that he might become HIV-infected in connection with surgery.[31] In another variety of informed consent claim, patients have sued HIV-infected doctors for failing to reveal their infected status. For example, in *Brzoska v. Olsen,*[32] a group of 38 plaintiffs sued their former dentist, who had died of AIDS, alleging that in failing to inform them of his status he had committed battery, fraudulent misrepresentation, and made false pretenses, and that he had acted negligently in failing to obtain his patients' informed consent.[33]

Third, some patients have brought suit against medical personnel for making inaccurate diagnoses of HIV. Most traditionally, a patient might sue a doctor for failing to realize that the patient's symptoms stemmed from HIV infection.[34] More unusually, several suits have been brought by persons who were told that they were HIV-infected when in fact they were not. One such woman appeared on a *60 Minutes* segment, achieving national publicity.[35] Victims of such misdiagnoses have sought to recover for their medical costs as well as their substantial emotional distress as a result of the misdiagnosis. Courts have varied in their response to such cases. Some have accepted plaintiffs' claims of emotional distress,[36] but others have rejected such claims, essentially holding that plaintiffs should simply have been happy they were not in fact HIV-infected.[37] One court ruled that the plaintiff could recover on a claim for negligent misdiagnosis

---

[31] Doe v. Johnston, 476 N.W.2d 28 (Iowa 1991) (affirming verdict for defendant).

[32] No. 92C-06-142, 1994 Del. Super. LEXIS 230, at *7 (Del. Super. Ct. May 2, 1994) (rejecting claims on summary judgment because patients could not show actual exposure).

[33] *See also* Faya v. Almaraz, 620 A.2d 327 (Md. 1993) (holding two patients could recover for their fear of acquiring AIDS because their surgeon did not disclose his HIV-positive status although patients did not contract HIV). *But see* K.A.C. v. Benson, 527 N.W.2d 553 (Minn. 1995) (rejecting patient's suit for emotional damages against HIV-positive gynecologist who examined patient while gynecologist had open sores on his hands and forearms); Gentzler v. Atlee, 660 A.2d 1378 (Pa. Super. Ct. 1995) (allowing doctor to bring action for wrongful use of civil procedure against plaintiff in dismissed action, because doctor had no personal role in operation and thus no duty to provide informed consent). *See generally* Mary K. Logan, *Who's Afraid of Whom? Courts Require HIV-Infected Doctors to Obtain Informed Consent of Patients,* 44 DePaul L. Rev. 483 (1995); Jody B. Gabel, *Liability for "Knowing" Transmission of HIV: The Evolution of a Duty to Disclose,* 21 Fla. St. U. L. Rev. 981 (1994); Jane H. Barney, Comment, *A Health Care Worker's Duty to Undergo Routine Testing for HIV/AIDS and to Disclose Positive Results to Patients,* 52 La. L. Rev. 933 (1992).

[34] *See, e.g.,* Doe v. McNulty, 630 So. 2d 825 (La. Ct. App. 1993) (affirming jury verdict of $700,000 in general damages and reducing special damages award from $314,000 to $76,337 in case in which defendants negligently failed to diagnose plaintiff as being HIV-infected).

[35] *60 Minutes* (CBS television broadcast, Jan. 1, 1995).

[36] Bramer v. Dotson, 437 S.E.2d 773 (W. Va. 1993) (rejecting defendants' motions for summary judgment when plaintiff claimed he had suffered major depression and anxiety due to misdiagnosis that he was HIV-infected). *See also* Chizmar v. Mackie, 896 P.2d 196 (Alaska 1995) (plaintiff may recover for emotional distress if she can show severe or serious distress arising out of breach of doctor's duty of care).

[37] Heiner v. Moretuzzo, 652 N.E.2d 664 (Ohio 1995).

with HIV only if he could show he had suffered a resulting physical impact, such as treatment with AZT.[38]

Finally, patients who are HIV-infected may bring malpractice actions against medical personnel who, because of their negligence, fail to treat the infection properly. For example, in *Hoffman v. Brandywine Hospital*,[39] the plaintiff alleged that her doctor was negligent in failing to send her to an infectious disease specialist once she was diagnosed with HIV, thereby delaying administration of anti-viral medications and hastening the onset of opportunistic infection. Although the court ultimately rejected the plaintiff's claim on the ground that the plaintiff's expert's testimony on causation was too speculative, the court certainly recognized the theoretical viability of such a claim.[40]

§ 8.6 Damages and Other Relief Available to Plaintiff Infected with HIV

Individuals who become ill with HIV disease as a result of the intentional or negligent acts of another may seek to recover various types of financial compensation.[41] Clearly, they may seek compensation for the immediate out-of-pocket effects of their illness: medical bills and any lost income.[42] A person who becomes HIV-infected or ill with HIV disease may also seek compensation for the emotional distress endured as a result of becoming ill, as well as for loss of consortium. Although it is obviously not easy to put a dollar figure on someone's emotional suffering, judges and juries are frequently called upon to make just such a calculation.[43]

A person with HIV who is asymptomatic may nonetheless bring suit to recover for damages he expects to incur in the future. Similarly, a person who is suffering from certain symptoms of AIDS but who will, in the future, endure additional problems, can sue for future as well as present damages. Although courts instruct juries not to award damages that are merely speculative, it is well established that future damages may be awarded.[44] If future damages were not available, plaintiffs

---

[38] R.J. v. Humana of Fla., Inc., 652 So. 2d 360 (Fla. 1995). *See also* Jones v. Dep't of Health & Human Rehabilitation Servs., 661 So. 2d 1291 (Fla. Dist. Ct. App. 1995).

[39] 661 A.2d 397 (Pa. Super. Ct. 1995).

[40] *Id.* at 401–02.

[41] In addition, certain persons who were close relatives of a person who died from HIV disease may be able to state actions for loss of consortium or companionship, or wrongful death. *See generally* Prosser & Keeton at 931–39, 940–61.

[42] Doe v. State, 595 N.Y.S.2d 592 (App. Div. 1993) (awarding $1,700 in past medical expenses and $43,850 in loss of wages). Courts generally do not set off payments plaintiffs have recovered from collateral sources like medical insurance. *E.g.,* Doe v. United States, 737 F. Supp. 155, 162 (D.R.I. 1990).

[43] Doe v. State, 595 N.Y.S.2d 592, 594 (App. Div. 1993) (awarding $750,000 for past pain and suffering).

[44] *Id.*

would either have to forgo full recovery, keep bringing lawsuit after lawsuit, or wait until the verge of death to bring a claim. These options are particularly unrealistic for individuals with advanced-stage AIDS. Future damages might, as before, include lost income, medical bills, and compensation for emotional distress.[45] To obtain future damages it generally is necessary for the plaintiff to call several expert witnesses. An expert medical witness could testify as to the likely path the illness might take and treatment costs. An economist might help present evidence on likely future loss of income. Some economists also attempt to provide a basis to juries for calculating the less tangible compensation for emotional distress.

Persons who win claims for intentional tort may also be allowed to recover punitive damages, in excess of the money necessary to compensate them for the harm that they incurred, if the defendant's conduct was sufficiently outrageous.[46] To recover punitive damages, the plaintiff must show not only that the defendant acted intentionally, but also that the defendant's actions were outrageous.[47] The purpose of punitive damages is to provide financial disincentives to deter persons from acting in an intentionally harmful or outrageous fashion.[48]

In addition to or sometimes in lieu of awarding monetary compensation, courts at times order injunctive relief, for example, requiring that a person undergo HIV testing.[49] Plaintiffs may also request that the defendant be required to provide medical monitoring of their condition. In the context of certain diseases including cancer, courts have sometimes ordered defendants to pay for such monitoring,[50] however, this sort of award is probably not necessary in HIV/AIDS cases because the cost of testing for HIV is generally less than $100.

§ 8.7 Plaintiffs' Practical Problems in Suing for Infection with HIV

Plaintiffs face numerous practical problems in suing someone for intentionally or negligently exposing them to HIV.

---

[45] *See, e.g.,* Doe v. United States, 737 F. Supp. 155, 162–63 (D.R.I. 1990) (calculating lost earning capacity of 12-year-old boy with AIDS as $229,895 and current and future pain and suffering as $800,000).

[46] *See, e.g.,* Doe v. Roe, 599 N.Y.S.2d 350 (App. Div. 1993), *leave to appeal dismissed,* 627 N.E.2d 519 (N.Y. 1993) (reinstating plaintiff's claim for punitive damages because doctor released HIV information to plaintiff's employer pursuant to subpoena).

[47] Prosser & Keeton at 9–10.

[48] *Id.* at 9.

[49] *See, e.g.,* Doe v. Burgos, 638 N.E.2d 701 (Ill. App. Ct.), *appeal denied,* 645 N.E.2d 1357 (Ill. 1994) (court affirmed order that prisoner who had bitten guard be compelled to be tested). *See also* Syring v. Tucker, 498 N.W.2d 370 (Wis. 1993) (compelling testing of woman who bit security guard at Department of Social Services).

[50] *See generally* Akim F. Czmus, *Medical Monitoring of Toxic Torts,* 13 Temp. Envtl. L. & Tech. J. 35 (1994).

Difficult to prove source of infection. Given the long latency period of the disease, it may be extremely difficult for a plaintiff to prove when and how she became infected. A plaintiff may realize she has HIV only when she develops symptoms six to ten years after being infected. A plaintiff looking back at that point may often be able to identify many possible opportunities for infection in the preceding years.[51] A plaintiff who had sexual relations exclusively with just a few people and who had no other risk factors for infection may be able to trace the source of the disease, but many plaintiffs may not.[52]

The long latency period of HIV disease may also give rise to statute of limitations problems. Most state statutes of limitation are triggered by the discovery of injury, not by mere exposure to a possibility of injury.[53] Thus, a plaintiff's discovery that she is HIV-infected may well be enough to start the running of the statute, even if she has not yet suffered any physical symptoms. If the plaintiff therefore files her case, the action may well be resolved before she has developed AIDS, making damages somewhat difficult to evaluate. Although a court would probably recognize the fact that a person who has HIV will eventually die of AIDS, the details of a plaintiff's future damages in terms of life expectancy, number of hospitalizations, future employability, and future emotional stress will be unknown. Faced with this speculative difficulty, a court would likely award a plaintiff a sum less than the damages she will actually incur. Yet, if the plaintiff instead waits to file the lawsuit until she has developed AIDS, she may find the action barred by the statute of limitations.[54]

Slow legal process. Given the slow pace of civil litigation in most courts in this country, an HIV-infected potential plaintiff must face the gruesome prospect that she or the defendant may become seriously ill or even die before the case might be heard in court. Given this risk some courts have granted expedited status to cases in which a plaintiff showed sufficiently serious symptoms.[55]

---

[51] Although the fact that there are multiple strains of the virus may help plaintiff identify the source of her infection, viruses can not be identified as precisely as could, for example, a strain of DNA. *See* Gerald Myers, *Molecular Investigation of HIV Transmission,* 121 Annals Internal Med. 889 (1994).

[52] Plaintiffs who are unable to identify a particular source of their HIV infection may attempt to rely on cases like Summers v. Tice, 199 P.2d 1 (Cal. 1948), to argue that multiple potential sources of the virus should be required to share liability. *See generally* Richard C. Schoenstein, Note, *Standards of Conduct, Multiple Defendants, and Full Recovery of Damages in Tort Liability for the Transmission of Human Immunodeficiency Virus,* 18 Hofstra L. Rev. 37, 63–72 (1989). No reported cases have been found that make use of this theory in regard to sexual transmission of HIV.

[53] *See, e.g.,* Casarez v. NME Hosps., 883 S.W.2d 360 (Tex. Ct. App. 1994) (Tex. statute of limitations runs from receipt of positive test result).

[54] *Cf.* Large v. Bucyrus-Erie Co., 524 F. Supp. 285, 289 (E.D. Va. 1981), *aff'd,* 707 F.2d 94 (4th Cir. 1983) (in an asbestos case, court found "the limitations period begins to run when the initial injury, even if relatively slight, is sustained, and the manifestation of more substantial injuries at a later date does not extend the limitations period").

[55] *See, e.g.,* Sanfilippo v. Carrington's, Inc., 601 N.Y.S.2d 663 (Sup. Ct. 1993) (although plaintiff had not been diagnosed with AIDS, court found his HIV illness to be sufficiently severe to warrant expedited treatment).

Certain claims may survive the plaintiff's death and thus could be brought by the plaintiff's estate, but other claims may be deemed personal to the plaintiff and thus not survive her death.[56]

When the defendant dies prior to completion of the litigation, the plaintiff may continue litigation against the estate of the deceased.[57] However, some states place restrictions on suits against estates, including a prohibition on punitive damages.[58]

Loss of privacy. Plaintiffs face the practical problem that by bringing suit for exposure to HIV they will reveal their own illness or potential illness to the public. Lawsuits filed in court are public documents, and newspapers may even have reporters stationed at the courthouse to read every new complaint that is filed. Although judges may allow plaintiffs to file lawsuits on an anonymous basis, it is still fairly likely that a plaintiff's identity will be revealed or uncovered by the press during the course of the litigation. For example, in *Doe v. Shady Grove Adventist Hospital,*[59] the plaintiff alleged that, without obtaining his permission, the defendant hospital had revealed his AIDS diagnosis to his family. When he sought to bring the action anonymously, a local newspaper intervened, asserting a First Amendment right to obtain and publish the identities of the parties. Balancing the plaintiff's privacy interests against the public's right to know, the court approved the use of a pseudonym for the plaintiff but left the records open to the public. The court found that the plaintiff had not waived his privacy interest by anonymously publicizing his plight and found that ruling otherwise would force plaintiff to abandon his privacy challenge.[60]

Thus, the plaintiff who sues for battery or negligence must recognize that by doing so she will likely call attention to her own condition. Unfortunately, although

---

[56] *See, e.g.,* Benson v. Minnesota Bd. of Medical Practice, 526 N.W.2d 634 (Minn. Ct. App. 1995) (statutory privacy claim does not survive decedent).

[57] *See, e.g.,* Christian v. Sheft, No. C574153 (Cal. Super. Ct. Feb. 17, 1989), *cited in* Aetna Casualty & Sur. Co. v. Sheft, 989 F.2d 1105, 1106 (9th Cir. 1993); Plaza v. Estate of Wisser, 626 N.Y.S.2d 446 (App. Div. 1995); Klein v. Deveney, 203 N.Y.L.J. 22 (Sup. Ct. N.Y. County Jan. 23, 1990) (suit against estate of lover who died of AIDS); Flynn v. Doe, 553 N.Y.S.2d 288 (Sup. Ct. N.Y. County 1990) (same). In one fairly unusual action, the man who would normally have been the plaintiff had already died, and his parents sued the former lover of the deceased in a wrongful death action. Rorie Sherman, *In Novel AIDS Suit, Wrongful Death Is Alleged,* Nat'l L.J., June 22, 1992, at 10.

[58] *See generally* Scott A. Hennis, *Exemplary Damages—Survival Statute—Recovery of Exemplary Damages from the Estate of a Tortfeasor Is Permitted under the Texas Survival Statute,* 16 St. Mary's L.J. 731, 741 (1985) (majority of jurisdictions do not permit punitive damages to be awarded against the estate of a decedent tortfeasor).

[59] 598 A.2d 507 (Md. Ct. Spec. App. 1991).

[60] *See also In re* Marriage of R.E.G., 571 N.E.2d 298 n.1 (Ind. Ct. App. 1991) (allowing use of initials instead of names because of "sensitive matters" involved, specifically allegations of HIV transmission in a divorce case involving a bisexual husband). The vast number of "Doe" cases involving HIV demonstrates that judges are generally sympathetic to plaintiffs' pleas for anonymity.

federal and state laws prohibit discrimination on the basis of HIV status, the reality is that publicizing one's status may jeopardize one's ability to maintain employment, housing, access to services, and even one's personal relationships.

Potential plaintiffs must also face the unpleasant reality that the defendant will likely effectively put the plaintiff's personal past on trial. In an attempt to show that plaintiff could have been infected by someone other than the defendant, the defendant may pry into the plaintiff's medical and sexual history, as well as any past use of intravenous drugs that might have involved syringe-sharing activity.[61] If the case goes to trial, the judge may permit the defendant to introduce evidence on some or all of these matters, thereby laying open the plaintiff's private life to the public. Plaintiffs who fear they have AIDS but have not yet been tested, perhaps dreading the results, also face the prospect that they may be forced to take an HIV test if they wish to pursue the litigation. The court might specifically require the plaintiff to be tested, perhaps in response to a discovery request by the defendant. Moreover, the court might effectively require the plaintiff to be tested by ruling that the plaintiff could not prevail in her action unless she could produce evidence that she was HIV-infected.

Defendant's inability to pay damage award.   The plaintiff must also consider the question of whether, even if she were to win a lawsuit, she could collect a sufficient judgment to make the lawsuit worthwhile. If the defendant who exposed the plaintiff to the virus is herself ill, the defendant may well not have sufficient resources left to pay a substantial judgment. AIDS treatments are quite expensive, and persons who are in the final stages of AIDS generally are not working and thus have no income. Although the estates of certain decedents, such as Rock Hudson's, might be sufficiently large to pay a substantial verdict, the more typical defendant with AIDS is poor if not completely indigent. Homeowners' or other personal liability insurance may sometimes provide coverage[62] but may exclude claims for intentional injury or sexually transmitted disease.[63] Moreover, state statutes may sometimes be interpreted to preclude insurance payments for inherently harmful acts.[64]

---

[61] Although a court may issue a protective order to preclude discovery requests that are unduly intrusive, a court would be likely to allow discovery relevant to prove another possible source of the infection. *Cf.* Agosto v. Trusswal Sys. Corp., 142 F.R.D. 118 (E.D. Pa. 1992) (allowing defendant in products liability suit to obtain plaintiff's medical records).

[62] *See* North Star Mut. Ins. Co. v. R.W., 431 N.W.2d 138 (Minn. Ct. App. 1988) (insurance company had duty to defend against allegation of negligent transmission of genital herpes when only applicable exclusion was for intentional conduct); Austin C. Wehrwin, *Homeowner Policy Pays Herpes Claim,* Nat'l L.J., July 15, 1985, at 3.

[63] Cynthia Gorney, *The New Laws of Love: The Courts, Sexually Contracted Diseases and a Partner's Right to Know,* Wash. Post, Nov. 14, 1985, at C1.

[64] Aetna Casualty & Sur. Co. v. Sheft, 989 F.2d 1105 (9th Cir. 1993) (applying Cal. statute to protect insurance company from having to indemnify or defend Rock Hudson's estate against claims of former lover, Marc Christian).

Third-party suits.   To enhance their opportunity for monetary recovery, plaintiffs often attempt to sue a third party, with significant assets or insurance, other than or in addition to the person who actually infected them with HIV. A patient might therefore sue a hospital for using negligent procedures, as well as the doctor who more directly posed the risk of infection to the patient.[65] A plaintiff infected through a sexual relationship might sue the doctor who had treated the woman with whom the plaintiff became intimate for failing to inform the woman she was HIV-infected or at risk for infection.[66] A medical technician who was pricked by a possibly infected needle might bring a products liability suit against the manufacturer of the sharps disposal container, rather than against an individual who failed properly to dispose of the needle.[67] A prison guard might similarly sue the state over its negligent training, rather than suing the prisoner who was the direct source of the infection.[68]

Some third-party actions present very attenuated theories of causation and are rejected on that basis. In *Levitt v. Lenox Hill Hospital,*[69] for example, the court rejected the medical malpractice claim of an HIV-infected plaintiff who asserted that his HIV infection was the result of his medical care providers' negligence in prescribing an addictive pain medication, which caused him to become re-addicted to drugs and, in turn, to engage in criminal behavior resulting in incarceration, as a result of which he shared a needle and became HIV-infected.[70]

Prejudice against individuals with HIV.   One final problem that plaintiffs must confront is the fact that many people maintain a prejudice against individuals with HIV, taking the position that those who were infected must have brought the disease on themselves by engaging in sinful sexual activity or using illegal drugs. Although the existence of some large jury verdicts in favor of persons with HIV demonstrates that such prejudice can be avoided or surmounted, attorneys representing persons with HIV must carefully select a geographic forum and use the voir dire process to ensure that the claim will be treated fairly.

---

[65] *See* Barrett v. Danbury Hosp., 654 A.2d 748 (Conn. 1995) (hospital sued for causing patient to fear transmission of HIV); Doe v. Surgicare, 643 N.E.2d 1200 (Ill. App. Ct. 1994) (same).

[66] Reisner v. Regents of Univ. of Cal., 37 Cal. Rptr. 2d 518 (1995).

[67] Burk v. Sage Prods., Inc., 747 F. Supp. 285 (E.D. Pa. 1990).

[68] *See* Ordway v. County of Suffolk, 583 N.Y.S.2d 1014 (Sup. Ct. Suffolk County 1992) (surgeon unsuccessfully sued county for failing to disclose patient's HIV status in advance of surgery); Hare v. State, 570 N.Y.S.2d 125 (App. Div. 1991) (x-ray technician sued state for exposing him to HIV-infected patient/prisoner and for failing to protect him).

[69] 585 N.Y.S.2d 401 (App. Div. 1992) (claim dismissed for lack of proximate cause).

[70] *Cf.* King v. Best W. Country Inn, 138 F.R.D. 39 (S.D.N.Y. 1991) (personal injury action alleging transfusions subsequent to injury caused AIDS); Shoemaker v. Workmen's Compensation Appeal Bd., 604 A.2d 1145 (Pa. Commw. Ct.), *appeal denied,* 618 A.2d 403 (Pa. 1992) (allowing workers' compensation claim to claimant who developed AIDS following transfusion necessitated by work-related accident).

§ 8.8 Practical Suggestions for Defendants Sued for Causing Exposure to HIV

A defendant who is sued for exposing a plaintiff to HIV should consider the availability of the following five defenses. First, the defendant may deny that he is actually the source of the plaintiff's HIV. It is often quite difficult for the plaintiff to establish, by a preponderance of the evidence, that the defendant is the one who infected her.

Second, a defendant may often be able to raise a statute of limitations defense. Although tort statutes of limitations vary from state to state, typically a plaintiff has just two years from the time she reasonably should have become aware of her injury to bring her lawsuit.[71] The issue, of course, is when the plaintiff should reasonably have become aware she was HIV-infected.[72]

Third, a defendant may argue that the plaintiff shares part of the blame for her own injury, thereby limiting if not entirely eliminating the defendant's liability. In Alabama, Maryland, North Carolina, Virginia, and the District of Columbia, if a defendant can show that the plaintiff herself acted unreasonably and was thus contributorily negligent, the defendant may be able to avoid liability altogether.[73] A defendant might, for example, argue that the plaintiff acted negligently in cleaning up a blood spill without putting on protective clothing. Forty-six states, however, employ a comparative negligence concept, in which case the jury would be asked to assess both the plaintiff's and defendant's negligence and to divide the liability accordingly.[74] Alternatively, the defendant could also introduce the concept of mutual fault by arguing that the plaintiff assumed the risk of her injury and thus is entitled to no compensation at all. For example, a defendant could argue that by having unprotected sex with a stranger, the plaintiff assumed the risk of HIV transmission.[75]

---

[71] The statute of limitations for medical malpractice claims may be even shorter. *See generally* Restatement (Second) of Torts § 899 cmt. E (1985) (medical malpractice claims often have very short statutes of limitation of one year or at most two).

[72] *See* Murray v. Hamot Medical Ctr., 633 A.2d 196 (Pa. Super. Ct. 1993), *appeal denied,* 658 A.2d 796 (Pa. 1994) (discussing statute of limitations defense in detail).

[73] *See* Marilyn Minzer et al., Damages in Tort Actions 48-10 to 48-11 (1993).

[74] *Id.* In states that employ a "pure" comparative negligence concept, plaintiff's recovery is reduced in proportion to her share of the negligence. In those states that employ a "modified" comparative negligence standard, plaintiff's liability is reduced proportionately except that plaintiff may not recover at all if her liability is greater than that of the defendant. Victor Schwartz, Comparative Negligence §§ 3.1–3.5 (3d ed. 1994).

[75] Although the estate of Rock Hudson attempted to show that Marc Christian was partially liable for having engaged in unprotected sex with Rock Hudson, the jury was not persuaded, instead awarding $21.75 million (later reduced to 5.5 million) to Marc Christian. Commenting on the award, an attorney for National Gay Rights Advocates said, "I think the case is troubling because it sends people a message that if they contract AIDS through unprotected sex, it's someone else's fault and not their own." Edward J. Boyer, *Rock Hudson's Male Lover Is Awarded $14.5 Million,* Wash. Post, Feb. 15, 1989, at A1.

A fourth and related type of defense a defendant might raise is that the plaintiff violated a statute or public policy when she became infected with HIV and is thus not entitled to recover for her injuries. For example, in states that criminalize certain consensual sexual acts, a defendant might argue that a plaintiff who was infected with HIV by engaging in an illegal sexual act should not be allowed to recover, even if the defendant intentionally or negligently caused the plaintiff to become infected.[76] This illegality defense is troubling, however, in that it allows tortfeasors to escape liability for their wrongful action, which is particularly questionable when both the plaintiff and defendant have engaged in the same illegal act.

Fifth, a defendant may argue that even if she should be held liable, certain of the damages the plaintiff seeks to recover are too speculative and therefore impermissible. As discussed in **§ 8.6,** a plaintiff may often seek to recover not only the medical expenses she has incurred, income she has lost, and emotional suffering she has endured but also such expenses and suffering she expects to incur in the future as the result of the injury. Because of recent advances in treating HIV disease, it may become increasingly difficult to predict the limitation on life expectancy resulting from infection with HIV. A defendant may successfully argue, however, that the plaintiff's evidence is too speculative to the extent she seeks compensation for specific costly or painful medical treatments.[77]

CAUSE OF ACTION FOR FEAR OF AIDS

§ 8.9 Claims for Fear of HIV/AIDS

Some plaintiffs who are not proven to be HIV-infected nonetheless bring claims contending they are entitled to compensation for the emotional distress they have incurred as a result of their fear that they were infected and will develop AIDS.[78] Because the tests most frequently used to determine whether a person is

---

[76] *See, e.g.,* Oberlin v. Upson, 95 N.E. 511, 512 (Ohio 1911) (woman who committed crimes of adultery and fornication "cannot be heard to complain of a wrong which she helped to produce"); Zysk v. Zysk, 404 S.E.2d 721 (Va. 1990) (transmission of herpes not actionable because plaintiff participated in crime of fornication). Criminal prohibitions against sexual activities as a response to the AIDS epidemic are discussed in **Ch. 7.**

[77] Although it seems counterintuitive, it is nonetheless true that courts often award less to compensate a death than they award to compensate the pain and suffering of the living. Randall R. Bovbjerg et al., *Valuing Life and Limb in Tort: Scheduling "Pain and Suffering,"* 83 Nw. U. L. Rev. 908, 911 (1989).

[78] *See, e.g.,* Vance A. Fink, *Emotional Distress Damages for Fear of Contracting AIDS: Should Plaintiffs Have to Show Exposure to HIV?,* 99 Dick. L. Rev. 779 (1995); James C. Maroulis, *Can HIV-Negative Plaintiffs Recover Emotional Distress Damages for Their Fear of AIDS?,* 62 Fordham L. Rev. 225 (1993); Victoria L. Rees, Comment, *AIDSPHOBIA: Forcing Courts to Face New Areas of Compensation for Fear of a Deadly Disease,* 39 Vill. L. Rev. 241 (1994);

HIV-infected look for the presence of the HIV antibody, which may not be detectable for approximately six months following transmission, a person who fears he is infected may not be able to obtain an immediate determination as to whether or not he is in fact infected.[79]

Plaintiffs may fear exposure to AIDS as a result of a variety of factual scenarios: having engaged in sexual relations with a person known or feared to be HIV-infected;[80] having been bitten by a person known or feared to be HIV-infected;[81] having been treated or operated on by a doctor known or feared to be HIV-infected;[82] or having been pricked by a hypodermic needle known or feared

---

Mandana Shahvari, Comment, *AfrAIDS: Fear of AIDS as a Cause of Action,* 67 Temp. L. Rev. 769 (1994); Ivan Yip, Note, *AIDSPHOBIA and the "Window of Anxiety": Enlightened Reasoning or Concession to Irrational Fear?,* 60 Brook. L. Rev. 461 (1994).

[79] HIV antibody testing is discussed in **Ch. 1.** Antibodies generally appear within one to four weeks of infection. Viral detection by polymerase chain reaction or other methods may be possible even earlier.

[80] The best known such action is probably that filed by Marc Christian, the former companion of Rock Hudson, against Hudson's estate. Although Christian had tested negative for HIV 19 times, the jury awarded him $21.75 million for his emotional distress, which award the judge reduced to a "mere" $5.5 million. *See* Philip Hager, *Hudson AIDS Suit Is Settled,* L. A. Times, Aug. 29, 1991, at B3; Christian v. Sheft, No. C574153 (Cal. Super. Ct. Feb. 17, 1989), *cited in* Aetna Casualty & Sur. Co. v. Sheft, 989 F.2d 1105, 1106 (9th Cir. 1993). *See also* Billman v. Indiana Dep't of Corrections, 56 F.3d 785 (7th Cir. 1995) (prisoner raped by HIV-infected cellmate could bring civil rights claim seeking damages, among other things, for fear of AIDS); Baranowski v. Torre, No. CV90-0236178, 1991 WL 240460 (Conn. Super. Ct. Nov. 8, 1991); Tischler v. Dimenna, 609 N.Y.S.2d 1002 (Sup. Ct. Suffolk County 1994) (refusing to grant summary judgment to girlfriend who claimed fear of AIDS); Doe v. Doe, 519 N.Y.S.2d 595 (App. Div. 1987) (refusing to allow wife to state claim for AIDSphobia in connection with divorce for fear of opening a "Pandora's box"); Mason v. Calhoun, 20 Fam. L. Rep. (BNA) 1356 (Sup. Ct. N.Y. County 1994) (denying summary judgment to decedent's estate because even though plaintiff tested negative, issue of possible future medical damages was for jury, not court).

[81] Hare v. State, 570 N.Y.S.2d 125 (App. Div.), *appeal denied,* 580 N.E.2d 1058 (N.Y. 1991) (x-ray technician bitten by prison inmate); Johnson v. West Va. Univ. Hosps., 413 S.E.2d 889 (W. Va. 1991) (university security guard bitten by hospital patient could recover for fear of AIDS).

[82] Macy's Cal. Inc. v. Superior Ct., 48 Cal. Rptr. 2d 496 (Ct. App. 1995) (lower court's denial of summary adjudication reversed for shopper who was stuck by needle in jacket she tried on); Kerins v. Hartley, 33 Cal. Rptr. 2d 172 (Ct. App. 1994) (affirming grant of summary judgment against patient who could show only slight risk of exposure); Brzoska v. Olsen, No. 284,1994, 1995 WL 558413 (Del. Super. Ct. Sept. 8, 1994) (rejecting on summary judgment claims of dental patients who could prove no actual exposure); Faya v. Almaraz, 620 A.2d 327 (Md. 1993) (limiting recovery of former patient who sued AIDS-infected surgeon to "window of anxiety"); K.A.C. v. Benson, 527 N.W.2d 553 (Minn. 1995) (affirming summary judgment granted against patient who could not prove actual exposure, ruling that when gloved doctor performed gynecological exam patient was beyond "zone of danger"). *See also* Ordway v. County of Suffolk, 583 N.Y.S.2d 1014 (Sup. Ct. Suffolk County 1992) (summary judgment granted to defendant when surgeon sued defendant county for allowing him to operate on AIDS-infected patient without disclosing patient's condition).

to contain HIV.[83] Such lawsuits are sometimes referred to as claims for fear of AIDS or AIDS-phobia.[84] Plaintiffs sometimes bring such fear of AIDS claims as an independent cause of action, arguing that the defendant either intentionally or negligently inflicted emotional distress upon them. Plaintiffs may also raise the fear of AIDS issue as an element of damages in one of the tort actions discussed in §§ **8.2** through **8.5**. For example, a plaintiff who has not tested HIV positive[85] might sue a sexual partner for negligently exposing her to the virus and then argue that the damages consist of her fear of AIDS.

Fear of AIDS claims, whether brought independently or in conjunction with another tort action, are quite troubling from a policy standpoint in that allowing these claims may heighten prejudice against persons who are HIV-infected. AIDS can be a very frightening disease. It is particularly frightening to people who do not understand the limited ways in which HIV can be communicated.

---

[83] Marchica v. Long Island R.R., 31 F.3d 1197 (2d Cir. 1994), *cert. denied,* 115 S. Ct. 727 (1995) (railroad employee pricked by discarded needle); Burk v. Sage Prods., Inc., 747 F. Supp. 285 (E.D. Pa. 1990) (paramedic stuck by needle that protruded from receptacle); Herbert v. Regents of Univ. of Cal., 31 Cal. Rptr. 2d 709 (Ct. App. 1994) (mother could not recover when son played with needles in hospital because she could not show, based on reliable scientific information, that it was more likely than not that her son would develop HIV); Doe v. Surgicare of Joliet, 643 N.E.2d 1200 (Ill. App. Ct.), *appeal denied,* 645 N.E. 2d 1357 (Ill. 1994) (rejecting motion to dismiss claim of patient stuck with needle which technician had previously used on himself); Castro v. New York Life Ins. Co., 588 N.Y.S.2d 695 (Sup. Ct. N.Y. County 1991) (cleaning worker pricked by discarded needle); Carroll v. Sisters of St. Francis Health Servs., Inc., 868 S.W.2d 585 (Tenn. 1993) (visitor to hospital stuck by needle when she placed her hand inside a used-needle receptacle that resembled a towel dispenser); Stout v. Johnson City Medical Ctr. Hosp., No. 03S01-9504-CV-00031, 1995 WL 599708 (Tenn. Oct. 11, 1995) (affirming nurse's worker's compensation award for emotional distress although she did not become HIV infected from needle prick). *See also* Cotita v. Pharma-Plast, USA, Inc., 974 F.2d 598 (5th Cir. 1992) (nurse pricked by defectively packaged needle and thereby exposed to blood on his gloves sued manufacturer of needle packaging in products liability action).

[84] "Fear of" claims were initially brought in connection with diseases other than HIV/AIDS, such as cancer. *See, e.g.,* Herbert v. Johns-Manville Corp., 785 F.2d 79 (3d Cir. 1986) (shipyard worker entitled to recover for emotional distress from fear of developing cancer when exposure to asbestos led to pleural thickening in lungs); Laxton v. Orkin Exterminating Co., 639 S.W.2d 431 (Tenn. 1982) (plaintiffs, whose drinking water was contaminated with chlordane, a possible carcinogen, permitted to recover for fear of cancer because they had ingested an unknown amount of the chemical). *See generally* David Carl Minneman, Annotation, *Future Disease or Condition or Anxiety Relating Thereto, as Element of Recovery,* 50 A.L.R.4th 13 (1986); Fournier J. Gale III & James L. Goyer III, *Recovery for Cancerphobia and Increased Risk of Cancer,* 15 Cumb. L. Rev. 723 (1985); Corey Scott Cramin, Comment, *Emotional Distress Damages for Cancerphobia: A Case for the DES Daughter,* 14 Pac. L.J. 1215 (1983).

[85] At least one court has held that a plaintiff who brings an AIDSphobia claim cannot be required to undergo an HIV test. Brown v. New York City Health & Hosps. Corp., 624 N.Y.S.2d 768 (App. Div. 1995).

Even some health care providers have refused to treat or deal with persons who were HIV-infected for fear that they, too, might catch the disease.[86] Today, although much more is known about how HIV in fact is spread than was known at the beginning of the epidemic, many lay persons continue to believe that HIV can be transmitted through food, silverware, handshakes, and toilet seats.[87] Legislation has been passed prohibiting discrimination in employment, public accommodations, and other areas to fight precisely such irrational fears. It has long been recognized that a business should not be allowed to discriminate merely because its customers, out of ignorance, wish that the business would discriminate, that is, irrationally founded customer preferences cannot justify an employer's discriminatory acts.[88]

If persons can obtain compensation for their fear of AIDS, it must be decided which fears are compensable. Should a person be compensated for fears which, although entirely unrealistic from a scientific perspective, in fact affect the person very significantly? A person who truly believes HIV may be communicated through a handshake may suffer significant physical and emotional trauma as a result of shaking hands with a person whom he subsequently learns was HIV-infected. Unfortunately, courts have not responded uniformly to fear of AIDS claims. Applying the legal doctrines developed in other contexts involving claims for intentional and negligent infliction of emotional distress, courts have failed to focus adequately on the unique aspects of actions pertaining to HIV/AIDS.

Tort principles generally do not support recovery if the plaintiff suffers from unrealistic, baseless fears. Because scientific evidence has established that HIV cannot be transmitted through a handshake, an HIV-infected person cannot be said to have acted negligently or unreasonably in shaking the hand of someone who

---

[86] Randy Shilts, And the Band Played On 321–22 (1988).

[87] *See generally* Gerald Friedland et al., *Additional Evidence for Lack of Transmission of HIV Infection by Close Interpersonal (Casual) Contact,* 4 AIDS 639, 642 (1990) (citing survey showing large percentage of population believe they could be infected through using public toilet, sharing eating utensils, or working with an infected person). It was even reported that White House security personnel in 1995 insisted on wearing rubber gloves to meet a delegation of gay and lesbian politicians for fear that the visitors might transmit HIV. *Time to Take the Gloves Off,* Chi. Trib., June 17, 1995, at 18 (editorial).

[88] Cain v. Hyatt, 734 F. Supp. 671 (E.D. Pa. 1990) (prohibiting discrimination against an employee with AIDS because co-employees or clients would prefer not to have contact with the employee). *See also* Gerdom v. Continental Airlines, Inc., 692 F.2d 602 (9th Cir. 1982), *cert. denied,* 460 U.S. 1074 (1983) (alleged customer preference for slim flight attendants held insufficient to justify discriminatory weight requirements); Rucker v. Higher, 669 F.2d 1179 (7th Cir. 1982) (employer forbidden to refuse to hire prospective employee for racial reasons on grounds that its customers do not like employee's race). Also, customer preference was rejected in the congressional debate regarding food service employee provisions in the Americans with Disabilities Act, as discussed in **Ch. 3.**

is not HIV infected.[89] In determining the scope of damages, courts often follow a principle known as the eggshell skull rule, such that a defendant who commits the wrong of hitting someone on the head may be held liable for the death of a particularly vulnerable plaintiff and not merely for the bump on the head that defendant may have anticipated causing.[90] However, this rule should not result in liability if the defendant's actions could not realistically be expected to cause any harm to anyone. Nor should plaintiffs be allowed to recover for fears which, although real, are based solely on stereotypes and prejudices rather than on medical actuality. In fact, allowing plaintiffs to recover for their totally unrealistic fears would undercut the principles of nondiscrimination and would encourage society's irrational fears.

It is generally extremely difficult to prevail on a claim for intentional infliction of emotional distress. To do so, the plaintiff must prove that:

1. The defendant's conduct was extreme and outrageous, defined by the *Restatement (Second) of Torts* as conduct that exceeds "all possible bounds of decency, and [is] regarded as atrocious, and utterly intolerable in a civilized community."[91]
2. The defendant intended to cause severe emotional distress to the plaintiff
3. The defendant caused the plaintiff to suffer emotion distress
4. The emotional distress the defendant caused the plaintiff to suffer was severe.[92]

Courts have often interpreted the phrase *extreme and outrageous* quite narrowly.[93] Thus, it is not easy for a plaintiff to establish that a defendant intentionally put him at risk for HIV/AIDS in order to cause the plaintiff severe emotional distress.[94] Because few persons would *deliberately* cause another emotional harm due to fear of AIDS, AIDSphobia claims are more frequently pursued under negligence theories.

---

[89] Nor would a court hold such a defendant liable for proximately causing plaintiff to fear developing HIV. Courts use the doctrine of proximate cause to determine, as a matter of social policy, when defendants should and should not be held liable for consequences of a particular wrongful act. Prosser & Keeton at 264, 272–300.

[90] Prosser & Keeton at 290–92.

[91] Restatement (Second) of Torts § 46 cmt. d (1985).

[92] *See generally* Prosser & Keeton at 60.

[93] *See, e.g.,* Burgess v. Perdue, 721 P.2d 239, 243 (Kan. 1986) (physician did not act outrageously in informing mother of deceased patient that he kept son's brain in jar for autopsy purposes).

[94] *See, e.g.,* Moore v. Johnson, 826 F. Supp. 1106 (W.D. Mich. 1993) (court rejected claim for intentional infliction of emotional distress brought by child of plaintiff who claimed a sexual partner had infected plaintiff with HIV, concluding that because child was not present during sexual encounter, child could not bring a claim for intentional infliction of emotional distress). *But see* Aetna Casualty & Sur. Co. v. Sheft, 989 F.2d 1105 (9th Cir. 1993) (Rock Hudson's companion recovered on claim of intentional infliction of emotional distress).

Courts vary substantially in their approach to claims for negligent infliction of emotional distress. Traditionally, courts were hostile to such claims. They feared an onslaught of claims, saw the unfairness of imposing a heavy burden on a defendant for remote consequences, and recognized the difficulty of determining the fact and extent of mental injuries. Thus, historically some courts allowed recovery for emotional distress only if a plaintiff had also suffered some physical injury.[95] Other courts imposed a somewhat more lax requirement that the plaintiff have endured a physical impact, but did not necessarily require physical injury.[96] Today, many courts have loosened the requirement further, allowing recovery if the plaintiff was a close family member in the "zone of danger" and exposed to similar injury as the victim.[97] Finally, some courts have now liberalized the rule substantially to permit recovery if the defendant breached a duty of care owed to the plaintiff and thereby caused the plaintiff to suffer emotional distress.[98]

Given the confusion in the underlying doctrine, as well as substantial public fear and controversy relating to HIV/AIDS, it is not surprising that courts' determinations in fear of AIDS claims have proved both confusing and contradictory. The majority of courts have limited recovery to those situations in which the plaintiff showed a likelihood or at least a realistic possibility that he could have become infected with HIV. For example, in *Burk v. Sage Products, Inc.*,[99] the court granted summary judgment against a paramedic who had stuck his hand on a used syringe needle. The court emphasized that the plaintiff was unable to establish an actual risk of HIV transmission because he could not "prove that the needle with which he was stuck was a needle that was used on an AIDS patient."[100] The court further observed that in light of the fact that the plaintiff had tested negative on five occasions, the last of which was more than a year after he was allegedly stuck by the needle, "it has become substantially likely that he will not develop the illness."[101] Similarly, in *Funeral Services by Gregory Inc. v. Bluefield Community Hospital*,[102] a mortician sought to recover

---

[95] *See* Prosser & Keeton at 363; Wisniewski v. Johns-Manville Corp., 759 F.2d 271, 274 (3d Cir. 1985), *subsequent opinion*, 812 F.2d 81 (1987) (plaintiffs who sustained no physical injury not permitted to recover for fear of cancer).

[96] Prosser & Keeton at 363.

[97] *E.g.*, Asaro v. Cardinal Glennon Memorial Hosp., 799 S.W.2d 595, 596 (Mo. 1990) (en banc). This theory, which has been applied to automobile and other similar accidents, appears to have little direct relevance to claims for fear of AIDS.

[98] Prosser & Keeton at 364–65.

[99] 747 F. Supp. 285, 288 (E.D. Pa. 1990).

[100] *Id.* at 286.

[101] *Id.* at 287. The court also noted "it is extremely unlikely that a patient who tests HIV-negative more than six months after a potential exposure will contract the disease as a result of that exposure," *id.* at 288 (citing CDC, *Interpretation and Use of the Western Blot Assay for Serodiagnosis of Human Immunodeficiency Virus Type 1 Infections*, 38 MMWR 1 (Supp. 7, 1989)).

[102] 413 S.E.2d 79 (W. Va. 1991), *overruled in part on other grounds by* Courtney v. Courtney, 437 S.E.2d 436 (W. Va. 1993).

damages for his fear of AIDS when he discovered that the body he had embalmed was HIV-infected. The court found that the plaintiff had failed to establish actual exposure to HIV, in light of the fact that he had worn protective gear and tested negative for HIV on four separate occasions following the embalming.[103] One court rejected a plaintiff's claim on somewhat different grounds, ruling in responding to a motion for summary judgment that the plaintiff had failed to submit sufficient evidence of emotional distress.[104]

Other courts, however, have permitted recovery in situations in which the plaintiffs' fears appeared to be totally unrealistic. For example, in *Johnson v. West Virginia University Hospitals,*[105] the court found that the plaintiff, a police officer who was bitten by an unruly hospital patient who had stated he was HIV-infected, had a reasonable and compensable fear of AIDS, three years after exposure, even though he had repeatedly tested negative for HIV. Affirming the jury's verdict of $1.9 million in favor of the plaintiff, the court stated that the plaintiff's continuing emotional trauma was "reasonable" in light of his exposure

---

[103] *Id. See also* Rothschild v. Tower Air, Inc., No. Civ. A. 94-2656, 1995 WL 71053 (E.D. Pa. Feb. 22, 1995) (refusing to allow woman who pricked finger on needle in plane to present evidence of fear of AIDS because there was no proof of exposure to HIV); Macy's Cal. Inc. v. Super. Ct., 48 Cal. Rptr. 2d 496 (Ct. App. 1995) (lower court's denial of summary adjudication reversed for shopper who was stuck by needle in jacket she tried on, on ground that mere needle stick, absent proof that hazardous foreign substance entered body and caused detrimental change to body, is not "harm" sufficient to support emotional damages); Barrett v. Danbury Hosp., 654 A.2d 748 (Conn. 1995) (motion to dismiss appropriate because plaintiff could not show that hospital's conduct, in performing rectal exam on patient found sitting in blood later found to be that of another patient, involved an unreasonable risk that might result in illness or bodily harm); Doe v. Surgicare of Joliet, 643 N.E.2d 1200 (Ill. App. Ct. 1994) (rejecting on motion to dismiss claim of patient stuck with needle previously used on medical technician); *In re* Marriage of R.E.G., 571 N.E.2d 298 (Ind. Ct. App. 1991) (reversing trial court's judgment which awarded wife 60 percent of marital assets and attorney's fees because homosexual husband allegedly had put her at risk for HIV exposure); Kaufman v. Physical Measurements Inc., 615 N.Y.S.2d 508 (App. Div. 1994) (reversing lower court's finding that postal clerk, who was pricked by hypodermic needle but who subsequently tested negative five times over 18 months, could state a claim for emotional distress when neither needle nor patient from whom blood was extracted tested positive for HIV); Doe v. Doe, 519 N.Y.S.2d 595 (Sup. Ct. Kings County 1987) (dismissing claim of wife who claimed that husband's failure to disclose prior homosexual relationship gave rise to reasonable fears, where husband had tested HIV negative and wife refused to be tested); Lubowitz v. Albert Einstein Medical Ctr., 623 A.2d 3, 5 (Pa. Super. Ct. 1993) (concluding that fear of AIDS without a rational basis is not a legally cognizable injury, denied recovery to a woman who in connection with an in vitro fertilization program received donated placental blood that initially tested positive for HIV but ultimated proved not to be infected). *Cf.* Martin v. Vaughn, No. Civ. A. 92-3828, 1995 WL 458977 (E.D. Pa. May 30, 1995) (dismissing prisoners' Eighth Amendment claim based on exposure to HIV-infected inmates because medical evidence does not support claim).

[104] J.B. v. Bohonovsky, 835 F. Supp. 796 (D.N.J. 1993).

[105] 413 S.E.2d 889, 895 (W. Va. 1991).

to HIV.[106] Similarly, in *Marchica v. Long Island Railroad*,[107] the court held that the plaintiff's employer could be held liable for the plaintiff's continuing emotional trauma, as a result of his having pricked himself on a hypodermic needle he feared but did not know contained HIV, even though the plaintiff had tested negative for the virus six months after the incident and had not tested positive by several years after the alleged exposure.[108] In *Carroll v. Sisters of St. Francis Health Services, Inc.*,[109] the court similarly allowed the plaintiff to pursue an action for fear of AIDS from a needle prick without evidence of actual exposure and despite numerous negative tests, citing a doctor's testimony that "AIDS testing is not susceptible of the same degree of certitude as is testing for other pathogens." This decision was reversed on appeal, with the Tennessee Supreme Court's ruling that the plaintiff could pursue her claim for fear of AIDS only if she had evidence of actual exposure to HIV.[110]

Finally, in the workers' compensation setting, a court awarded compensation to a critical care nurse who had pricked her finger on a needle previously used to anesthetize an HIV-infected patient, even though the court concluded the nurse had no rational basis for her fears. The court found that although the nurse had tested negative for HIV long past the time when infection would have appeared, the nurse nonetheless continued to suffer real and severe psychological distress as a result of the exposure, saying, "To her, perception is reality."[111]

---

[106] The court also noted that plaintiff "considers himself a social outcast" and presented testimony that he "is shunned by co-workers and superiors." *Id.* at 892. *See also* Marchica v. Long Island R.R., 810 F. Supp. 445, 447 (E.D.N.Y. 1993), *aff'd*, 31 F.3d 1197 (2d Cir. 1994) (noting evidence that plaintiff was shunned by his co-workers and his supervisor after having been pricked by used syringe), *cert. denied*, 115 S. Ct. 727 (1995).

[107] 810 F. Supp. 445 (E.D.N.Y. 1993), *aff'd*, 31 F.3d 1197 (2d Cir. 1994), *cert. denied*, 115 S. Ct. 727 (1995).

[108] *Id.* at 447, 453. *See also* Christian v. Sheft, No. C574153 (Cal. Super. Ct. Feb. 17, 1989) (awarding Marc Christian $5 million for fear of contracting AIDS even though he had tested HIV negative at least 16 times in the four years between his last exposure to the AIDS virus and 1989) *cited in* Aetna Casualty & Sur. Co. v. Sheft, 989 F.2d 1105, 1106 (9th Cir. 1993); Castro v. New York Life Ins. Co., 588 N.Y.S.2d 695, 698 (Sup. Ct. N.Y. County 1991) (denying defendant employer's motion to dismiss when a cleaning worker was pricked by a discarded hypodermic needle not proven to contain HIV, and two years after incident plaintiff had not tested positive, on ground that "the AIDS disease is still not completely understood by the medical profession [and] is known to have a dormant quality which may not manifest itself in its victims for many years after a person is exposed to the HIV virus"). *See generally* Susan Adams, *Money for Fear: Why a Jury Awarded $21.75 Million to Rock Hudson's Lover*, Am. Law., July–Aug. 1989, at 136, 137–38.

[109] 1992 WL 276717 (Tenn. Ct. App. Oct. 12, 1992).

[110] 868 S.W.2d 585 (Tenn. 1993). *See also* Williamson v. Waldman, 677 A.2d 1179 (N.J. Super. Ct. App. Div. 1996) (allowing fear of infection claim without proof of exposure; plaintiff need only prove exposure was possible as result of defendant's negligence).

[111] Stout v. Johnson City Medical Ctr. Hosp., No. 03501-9504-CV-00031, 1995 WL 599708 (Tenn. Oct. 11, 1995).

A third set of courts has adopted a compromise position. Refusing to allow plaintiffs to recover for irrational fears on a long-term basis, these courts have nonetheless allowed plaintiffs to recover for their actual fears during the "window period" between the moment of feared exposure (or knowledge of potential exposure) and the receipt of negative test results indicating that infection has not occurred.[112] Although courts that adopt this window approach must answer such questions as the length of the reasonable anxiety period, this approach certainly places a significant limit on a plaintiff's potential recovery.

In light of the fear of AIDS cases decided, it is clear that courts around the country have not yet arrived at a uniform way in which to analyze claims for fear of AIDS. Courts should rationalize this difficult area of law by focusing on the plaintiff's ability to prove that the fear has a rational basis, given current medical evidence. If the risk of exposure is remote, either because the plaintiff cannot prove contact with an HIV-infected bodily fluid or because the particular form of contact raises no or virtually no risk of infection, the claim should be rejected.

Courts' compromise approach of allowing a plaintiff to recover for irrational fears during the window of anxiety is a good first step toward dealing with fear of AIDS cases but not a good total solution.[113] If there is no factual or medical evidence at all supporting a plaintiff's fears, then the plaintiff should not be permitted to recover for those fears, even if they are actual.[114] On the other hand, if a plaintiff has at least some factual evidence of exposure and some medical

[112] *See, e.g.,* Kerins v. Hartley, 21 Cal. Rptr. 2d 621, 631–32 (Ct. App. 1993) (emotional distress claim became unreasonable once plaintiff obtained surgical records containing no note of exposure, negative HIV test results, and counseling regarding improbability of being HIV-infected); Faya v. Almaraz, 620 A.2d 327, 337 (Md. 1993) (denying defendant's motion to dismiss but holding that plaintiffs could recover for fear of HIV only for period between which they learned of surgeon's illness and when they received test results showing they were not HIV-infected); De Milio v. Shrager, 666 A.2d 627, 636 (N.J. Super. Ct. 1995) (plaintiff who was impaled by dental instrument while collecting dentist's trash and who had tested negative for HIV for five years following incident was allowed to seek compensation for his severe emotional distress from time of possible exposure until he knew or should reasonably have known he was not HIV-infected); Madrid v. Lincoln County Medical Ctr., 909 P.2d 14 (N.M. Ct. App. 1995) (denying medical center's motion for summary judgment against plaintiff who was splashed with medical samples she feared but did not know were HIV-infected, but allowing plaintiff to recover at most for six-month period prior to receiving negative test results), *cert. denied,* 5 Health L. Rep. (BNA) 1379 (N.M. 1996); Brown v. New York City Health & Hosp. Corp., 65 U.S.L.W. 2335, 5 Health L. Rep. (BNA) 1581 (N.Y. Sup. Ct. App. Div. 1996) (allowing recovery only for first six months after exposure unless plaintiff can prove actual infection).

[113] It should be noted that with improved viral detection methods, as noted in **Ch. 1,** individuals who fear infection can determine whether or not they are infected without having to wait for any significant period of time, as has been required for antibody detection in the past. Accordingly, the reasonable window of anxiety period may be extremely short.

[114] This approach was taken by the court in Vogelsang v. Yeh, No. C-940793, 1995 WL 675991 (Ohio Ct. App. Nov. 15, 1995) (woman who had requested to receive bone graft from own body and was instead given bone graft from state tissue bank denied recovery for fear of AIDS because there was no evidence she was in fact exposed to HIV). For discussion of this issue with particular regard to fear of HIV transmission in the health care setting, see Wendy K. Mariner, *AIDS Phobia, Public Health Warnings, and Lawsuits: Deterring Harm or Rewarding*

evidence that that exposure can lead to infection, then she should be permitted to recover for her emotional suffering, but only during the window period, unless she ultimately tests positive for HIV. In other words, courts should focus on whether a plaintiff's fears are reasonable in light of current medical evidence. Although it is initially reasonable for a plaintiff pricked by an HIV-contaminated needle to fear becoming infected with HIV, the plaintiff's fears become unreasonable once the plaintiff tests negative, even within several weeks after the potential exposure. Similarly, it is never reasonable for a plaintiff to fear infection because she was kissed on the cheek by a person who was HIV-infected or otherwise had only casual contact that poses no risk of transmission. If courts instead allow plaintiffs to recover for their actual but objectively unreasonable fears, courts will fuel society's irrational fears about AIDS.

CAUSES OF ACTION FOR RELEASING INFORMATION

§ 8.10   Defamation

Defamation is a false written or oral communication that tends to injure the claimant's reputation or standing in the community.[115] *Snipes v. Mack*[116] illustrates a simple example of defamation. Mr. Snipes posted several large signs at major intersections around town. These signs stated in red letters that one Frances Mack had AIDS. The jury determined the statement was false, found Mr. Snipes liable for defamation, and awarded Ms. Mack general damages of $100,000.[117] It is less commonly known, but also true, that a person may be liable for defamation if he merely repeats a false statement initially made by someone else.[118]

If a person falsely accuses another person of suffering from a "loathsome disease," the accuser is said to have engaged in *defamation per se*. This is significant in that a plaintiff must usually prove actual damages resulting from a defamatory statement, but in a defamation per se claim, damages are presumed.[119]

Ignorance?, 85 Am. J. Pub. Health 1562 (1995) (arguing that AIDS phobia claims should be denied in all cases unless actual transmission has occurred).

[115] Prosser & Keeton at 771, 774, 839. Traditionally defamation has been divided into two categories: libel (written statements); and slander (oral statements).

[116] 381 S.E.2d 318 (Ga. Ct. App. 1989).

[117] *See also* McCune v. Neitzel, 457 N.W.2d 803 (Neb. 1990) (neighbor held liable in defamation for spreading false rumor that plaintiff had AIDS).

[118] Prosser & Keeton at 799 (repetition may be defamatory even if repeater states the source, says merely "it is alleged," or even makes it clear that she herself does not believe the derogatory remark is true).

[119] *See, e.g.,* Hunter v. Enquirer/Star, Inc., 619 N.Y.S.2d (App. Div. 1994) (libelous per se to accuse plaintiff of having had sex with person who was HIV-infected). *See generally* Prosser & Keeton at 790.

In general, a defendant may be found liable for defamation if the defendant merely acted negligently in making the false statement.[120] However, if the person who claims to have been defamed was a public official or public figure or if the statement involved a matter of public concern, the Supreme Court has held under the First Amendment that a defendant may be held liable only if he knew that the statement was false or if he acted with "reckless disregard" as to whether the statement was true or false.[121]

Although truth is generally a complete defense to a claim for defamation,[122] a statement that merely has some basis in truth may be found defamatory.[123] A plaintiff who was merely seropositive, therefore, argued that a hospital and newspaper had defamed him by implying he had AIDS, but the court rejected the claim.[124] Further, as discussed in **§ 8.11,** a person who distributes a statement that is entirely true may also be subject to liability for invasion of privacy. Thus, every effort must be made by those who possess HIV-related information both to ensure that the information is accurate and to ensure that it is not inappropriately communicated.

In certain circumstances, however, the disclosure of inaccurate information is privileged and thus may not constitute defamation. Most states recognize an absolute privilege to disclose information in the context of a judicial proceeding. Thus, if the inaccurate information were properly disclosed pursuant to a subpoena, the disclosure would be privileged.[125] Similarly, if a newspaper accurately reports a false allegation of AIDS that was made in connection with a judicial proceeding, the newspaper should not be liable for defamation.[126]

---

[120] The Supreme Court, in New York Times v. Sullivan, 376 U.S. 254 (1964), left to each state the determination of whether negligently making a false statement regarding a person who is not a public figure or official is defamatory.

[121] Dun & Bradstreet, Inc. v. Greenmoss Builders Inc., 472 U.S. 749 (1985); Gertz v. Robert Welch Inc., 418 U.S. 323 (1974); New York Times v. Sullivan, 376 U.S. 254 (1964).

[122] Lee v. Calhoun, 948 F.2d 1162 (10th Cir. 1991) (truth is absolute defense to patient's defamation claim against physician for reporting AIDS diagnosis to newspaper without obtaining patient's authorization).

[123] Prosser & Keeton at 117 (Supp. 1988).

[124] Anderson v. Strong Memorial Hosp., 531 N.Y.S.2d 735 (Sup. Ct. 1988), *aff'd,* 542 N.Y.S.2d 96 (App. Div. 1989) (mem.). *See also* Cruz v. Latin News Impacto Newspaper, 627 N.Y.S.2d 388 (App. Div. 1995) (newspaper may not be held liable for defamation for stating that HIV-infected person had AIDS even though pursuant to then-current CDC definiton person did not in fact have AIDS).

[125] *See, e.g.,* Doe v. Southeastern Pa. Transp. Auth., 72 F.3d 1133 (3d Cir. 1995) (self-insured employer did not violate employee's privacy right when it disclosed nature of drug taken by employee to persons who had a need to know of drug in order to monitor health plan expenses); Gilson v. Knickerbocker Hosp., 116 N.Y.S.2d 745 (App. Div. 1952) (disclosure of confidential medical records containing false statement about patient's alcohol consumption was privileged because produced pursuant to subpoena).

[126] Dorsey v. National Inquirer, Inc., 952 F.2d 250 (9th Cir. 1991) (newspaper's apparently untrue report that Engelbert Humperdinck had AIDS was not defamatory because it was a "fair and true" report of an allegation made by plaintiff in course of child custody proceeding).

Most states also recognize a qualified privilege covering a good faith publication if a public or private interest is served.[127] To be covered by the qualified privilege, one court has stated that a defendant must prove that "the disclosure was necessary to prevent spread of disease, that the communication was to one who, it was reasonable to suppose, might otherwise be exposed, and that he himself acted in good faith, with reasonable grounds for his diagnosis, and without malice."[128] Courts have applied this doctrine in the HIV context, for example, holding that a supervisor who informed a personnel supervisor that an employee was thought to be HIV-infected was covered by intracorporate immunity.[129] Several states have now codified this common law rule, at least with respect to physicians, authorizing physicians to notify a patient's sexual partners of the patient's HIV status if the patient, upon counseling, refuses to make the notifications.[130]

§ 8.11 Invasion of Privacy

Although disclosure of information that is entirely accurate is not defamatory, it may result in liability for invasion of privacy or for violation of state HIV confidentiality statutes. As one noted scholar of constitutional law has observed, AIDS "has created the most controversial context in which the right of record privacy arises today."[131] Although it might be argued that the First Amendment of the Constitution should protect all truthful statements, the Supreme Court, in *Time, Inc. v. Hill*,[132] recognized the possibility of allowing a tort action for truthful publications by stating that "revelations may be so intimate and so unwarranted in view of the victim's position as to outrage the community's notion of decency."[133] The Supreme Court's subsequent decision in *Cox Broadcasting Corp v. Cohn*[134] raised a question as to whether the Court might be receptive to a future constitutional challenge to such invasion of privacy limitations on truthful

---

[127] *See generally* Prosser & Keeton at 824–25 (qualified privilege when public interest supports allowing spokesperson some latitude for making mistakes).

[128] Simonsen v. Swenson, 177 N.W. 831, 832 (Neb. 1920) (disclosure by physician to hotel owner that guest had "contagious disease," when in fact he may have been disease-free, was covered by qualified privilege).

[129] Blake v. May Dep't Stores Co., 882 S.W.2d 688 (Mo. Ct. App. 1994).

[130] *See* Cal. Health & Safety Code § 121015 (West 1995); Fla. Stat. § 455.2416 (West 1994); Ga. Code Ann. § 24-9-47(g) (Michie 1995); Haw. Rev. Stat. § 325-101(a)(4) (1995); Ky. Rev. Stat. Ann. § 311.282 (1995). See also **Ch. 2.**

[131] Laurence H. Tribe, American Constitutional Law § 15-16, at 1394 (2d ed. 1988).

[132] 385 U.S. 374 (1967).

[133] *Id.* at 383 n.7.

[134] 420 U.S. 469 (1975) (state may not impose sanctions for publication of truthful information contained in official records open to public inspection). *See* Alfred Hill, *Defamation and Privacy Under the First Amendment,* 76 Colum. L. Rev. 1205 (1976).

statements. Nonetheless, the common law doctrine of invasion of privacy still appears alive and well today.[135]

The common law tort of invasion of privacy is generally defined as including five elements: (1) public disclosure of (2) private facts, (3) if such a disclosure would be highly offensive to (4) a person of reasonable sensitivities and (5) there exists no public interest in disclosing the information.[136] In addition, many states have now adopted legislation that protects privacy interests with respect to HIV information.[137]

Whether under statute or common law, claimants have sued insurance companies, neighbors, police officers, physicians, and health center employees for allegedly disclosing to inappropriate persons the fact that the claimant had AIDS or was HIV-infected.[138] The news media are subject to liability as well. In *Multimedia WMAZ v. Kubach,*[139] the Georgia Court of Appeals upheld a jury verdict of $500,000 in general damages against a television station that broadcast a seven-second image of a man with AIDS.[140] Although the plaintiff had agreed to the broadcast of a digitally altered image, the digitalization equipment malfunctioned, resulting in broadcast of a recognizable image.

In some states there may be an issue as to whether the statement was made to a sufficient number of persons to constitute publication of the statement. With respect to defamation, it is well established that making the defamatory statement to even a single person is enough to establish defamation. However, some courts have held that publicizing private information to a small number of persons does not support liability on an invasion of privacy claim.[141]

---

[135] Moreover, Professor Tribe has argued that government disclosure of accurate but private information might itself be unconstitutional. Laurence H. Tribe, American Constitutional Law § 15-16, at 1395–96 (2d ed. 1988).

[136] Restatement (Second) of Torts § 652D (1965).

[137] State HIV confidentiality statutes are discussed in **Ch. 2.**

[138] *See, e.g.,* Doe v. Prime Health, No. 88-C5149 (Johnson County Dist. Ct. Kan. injunction issued May 17, 1988), (*reported in* 3 AIDS Pol'y & L. 8 (1988)) (HMO enjoined from disclosing HIV lab test results to patient's estranged wife); Doe v. Borough of Barrington, 729 F. Supp. 376 (D.N.J. 1990) (officer and borough held to have violated family members' privacy rights by informing neighbors that they were HIV-infected); Doe v. Roe, 599 N.Y.S.2d 350 (App. Div. 1993) (physician's disclosure of patient's HIV status to employer pursuant to subpoena issued in workers' compensation action violated state HIV confidentiality statute). *Cf.* Beck v. Interstate Brands Corp., 953 F.2d 1275 (11th Cir. 1992) (per curiam) (plaintiff failed to state claim for invasion of privacy because complaint alleged only that employer "published information regarding the dread nature" of AIDS and not that employer had published information about plaintiff's own AIDS status).

[139] 443 S.E.2d 491 (Ga. Ct. App. 1994).

[140] The appeals court reversed the award of $100 in punitive damages on the ground that the plaintiff had failed to establish intentional misconduct on the part of the station but held that the $500,000 awarded in general damages was identifiable, separable, and supported by the evidence. *Id.* at 495.

[141] *See, e.g.,* Doe v. Methodist Hosp., 639 N.E.2d 683 (Ind. Ct. App. 1994) (no invasion of privacy found when defendant told only two co-workers, one of whom already knew, that plaintiff was HIV-infected). *See also* McNemar v. Disney Stores, Inc., 91 F.3d 610 (3d Cir. 1996).

Invasion of privacy claims often turn on the question of whether the persons to whom the information was deliberately released had a need to know that information. Although it may be justifiable to release an AIDS diagnosis to hospital employees directly involved in the patient's care, to patients or co-workers of an infected physician,[142] or in connection with a criminal investigation,[143] it would often be actionable to release such information more broadly. For example, in *Doe v. Town of Plymouth*,[144] the court held that the plaintiff stated a claim when a police officer had communicated the fact that she was HIV-infected to various neighbors.[145] Similarly, a court found that when medical professionals conveyed a patient's HIV status to an attorney for the plaintiff's employer, they violated his privacy expectation. Although there was no doctor-patient privilege, in that the examination was pertinent to a workers' compensation claim, the defendants were still obligated to respect the patient's privacy right by conveying the HIV-related information only to those persons with a need to know.[146]

Individuals and institutions must also be careful not to negligently allow the release of private information. In *Behringer Estate v. Princeton Medical Center*,[147] the defendant hospital was held liable for failing to establish a charting policy to protect the privacy of its patients. Instead, the charting policy was such that, within hours of his release from the hospital for treatment of an AIDS-related opportunistic infection, the plaintiff, a plastic surgeon who also operated at the hospital, received phone calls from numerous well-wishers who indicated an awareness of his condition.[148]

Defendants are not held responsible for invasion of privacy if the plaintiff has waived the right to privacy. For example, in *Lee v. Calhoun*,[149] the Tenth Circuit held that the plaintiff waived his right to privacy with respect to his HIV status when he sued his physician for $38 million in a medical malpractice action. Faced with this action, the doctor gave an interview to the *Daily Oklahoman* in which he explained that he was justified in performing a temporary colostomy

---

[142] *In re* Milton S. Hershey Medical Ctr., 634 A.2d 159 (Pa. 1993) (approved lower court ruling permitting hospital to inform other physicians at hospital of infected physician's status and to notify patients of status without identifying physician by name).

[143] Andreini v. Dufek, No. 2:93-CV-277, 1995 U.S. Dist. LEXIS 11296, at *28 (W.D. Mich. July 22, 1995) (intrusive statement about plaintiff's HIV status protected when made by police officer in connection with execution of facially valid search and arrest warrants pertaining to plaintiff's allegedly having sought to infect other persons).

[144] 825 F. Supp. 1102 (D. Mass. 1993).

[145] *See also* Doe v. Borough of Barrington, 729 F. Supp. 376 (D.N.J. 1990) (claim stated against police officers who informed neighbors of plaintiff's HIV status); Hillman v. Columbia County, 474 N.W.2d 913 (Wis. 1991) (prisoner stated claim when jailers released information broadly throughout prison).

[146] Urbaniak v. Newton, 227 Cal. Rptr. 354 (Ct. App. 1991).

[147] 592 A.2d 1251 (N.J. Super. Ct. 1991).

[148] The court found that the hospital's general confidentiality policy was not sufficient to restrict access to HIV test results or charts containing such results.

[149] 948 F.2d 1162 (10th Cir. 1991).

instead of the appendectomy consented to by the plaintiff, given the fact that he was "a carrier of the AIDS virus."[150] The court found that by filing his suit, the plaintiff waived any right he may have had to retain his privacy regarding his medical condition.[151] On the other hand, in *Multimedia WMAZ, Inc. v. Kubach,*[152] the court found that the plaintiff did not waive his right to sue a television station for invasion of privacy by telling approximately 60 of his friends and relatives that he was HIV-infected. In short, the waiver question is determined on a highly fact-specific basis.

---

[150] *Id.* at 1164.

[151] The decision is rather puzzling in that, from a medical standpoint, it is not clear how the plaintiff patient's HIV status related to his medical condition. Although the defendant physician stated that the plaintiff was incorrectly diagnosed as suffering from appendicitis rather than a perforated colon, in fact, a perforated colon is not an HIV-related condition.

[152] 443 S.E.2d 491 (Ga. Ct. App. 1994).

CHAPTER 9

PUBLIC BENEFITS FOR PERSONS WITH HIV

Irwin E. Keller

REFERENCE MATERIALS

§ 9.1   Introduction

Becoming disabled from HIV disease can be a tremendous physical and emotional ordeal. Making health care decisions and coping with the fact of progressive illness are sufficient challenges in and of themselves. Add to that recipe dealing with government bureaucracies, in order to secure enough income not to be evicted or to secure health care coverage so that there will actually be health care decisions to make, and you have a true nightmare. An effective advocate can lift the burden of securing income and health care off the shoulders of someone with disabling HIV. To a professional accustomed to reading statutes, regulations, and other such governmental esoterica, navigating these public benefits systems is certainly frustrating, but it definitely is manageable. To someone without that familiarity, the project of obtaining and retaining public benefits can be a bewilderment.

This chapter provides a practitioner-oriented overview of the most important federal benefits programs. These include disability benefits: Social Security Disability Insurance (§ **9.2**), Supplemental Security Income (§ **9.3**), and those for veterans (§§ **9.28** through **9.35**); as well as health care programs, such as Medicaid (§§ **9.36** through **9.45**) and Medicare (§§ **9.46** through **9.47**). Although laypeople commonly merge these various programs in their minds, they are in fact distinct, with widely differing eligibility criteria and benefits. This chapter will not discuss state or local benefits (such as state-administered short-term disability insurance, or county health programs) that may also be available to people disabled with HIV. Advocates should consult local resources to learn more about the existence of and eligibility for such programs.

This chapter should enable practitioners to begin doing simple initial claim and appeals advocacy for people with HIV. It covers eligibility, procedure (§§ **9.4** through **9.8**), and ways to use the programs more effectively once entitled (§§ **9.24** through **9.27**). It also gives some practice pointers which can dramatically smooth the rough spots in the journey (§§ **9.20** through **9.23**).[1]

---

[1] Practitioners may wish to consult the *Social Security Advisory Service,* a looseleaf technical support manual; telephone: (415) 388-2400. Several nonprofit advocacy organizations may also be valuable resources to practitioners. The National Health Law Program provides technical support on health care issues, including Medicare and Medicaid, telephone: (310) 204-6010;

For the attorney who does not plan to do public benefits advocacy, it is nevertheless important to have a basic understanding of these programs, how they fit into the landscape of the client's life, and how they affect the representation of the client in other matters. For instance, if the client receives SSI or Medicaid, and the attorney is litigating a matter that will result in a settlement or judgment in the client's favor, advance planning is necessary or else the receipt of those funds could cause the client to lose his or her access to income and health care. This would be a misfortune for the client that far outweighs the benefit of having received the settlement to begin with.

DISABILITY INCOME PROGRAMS

§ 9.2 Social Security Disability Insurance (SSDI)

Social Security Disability Insurance, referred to variously as SSDI, SSD, SSA, or simply as Social Security, under Title II is best described as a government-sponsored disability insurance program. Working people pay premiums in the form of Social Security contributions (FICA payroll deductions or self-employment taxes). Individuals who have made sufficient contributions and who meet Social Security's standard of disability may collect a monthly benefit. Some individuals may qualify for both SSDI and Supplemental Security Income, discussed in § 9.3.

Eligibility

In order to be eligible for SSDI, a claimant for benefits must be disabled according to the regulations issued by the Social Security Administration (SSA),[2] have a lawful immigration status, and have sufficient work history (that is, be "fully insured"). Disability is evaluated by means of a complex regulatory scheme, discussed in detail in §§ 9.9 through 9.14. Sufficient work history means having paid Social Security taxes in enough quarters, either through the FICA payroll deduction or through self-employment tax. The formula for the number of quarters one must have contributed is gauged according to age.[3] At age 31 or older,

---

the National Organization of Social Security Claimants' Representatives (NOSSCR) is a membership organization, providing a newsletter and advice line, among other services, telephone: (800) 431-2804; National Senior Citizens Law Center provides technical support on Social Security and Medicare issues, telephone: (213) 236-3890; the National Veterans' Legal Services Program provides technical support on veterans' issues, telephone: (202) 265-8305; the Western Center on Law and Poverty provides technical support on poverty law, including welfare benefits in general, telephone: (213) 487-7211.

[2] Further information pertaining to the Social Security Administration is available on the Internet at http://www.ssa.gov; gopher.ssa.gov; ftp.ssa.gov.

[3] 20 C.F.R. § 404.130 (1996).

taxes must have been paid for at least 20 of the last 40 quarters. The quarters need not have been consecutive. At ages 24 through 30, taxes must have been paid for at least half of the quarters between the 21st birthday and the onset of disability. Under age 24, taxes must have been paid for at least 6 quarters during the three years before the disability commenced.

Because SSDI is not a means-tested benefit, other income generally has no effect on one's eligibility to receive SSDI. The exception to this rule is when a person is simultaneously receiving either workers' compensation or state disability insurance (if this is available). In that case, the SSA will reduce the SSDI level so that the combined benefits do not exceed 80 percent of the individual's final working income. Specifically, the SSA looks at the highest annual earnings the individual received in the last five years. That amount is divided by 12 months to determine *average current earnings* (ACE). The monthly SSDI award will be reduced so that, in combination with either state disability insurance or workers' compensation, it will not total more than 80 percent of the ACE.[4] Practitioners have noted, though, that this adjustment is not made to retroactive SSDI awards.

Benefit

If one is *fully insured,* the right to be a beneficiary of the SSDI program accrues on the date one becomes disabled by SSA's standards. There is, however, a waiting period of five full calendar months before benefits become payable. If approval for SSDI occurs after the sixth month of disability, SSA will make a retroactive payment. There is no deadline for how long a person may wait to apply for SSDI benefits. An applicant may not, however, collect retroactive benefits dating back more than 12 months prior to the filing of the application.[5]

The monthly benefit level is a function of the amount of earnings, age at the onset of disability, and date of disability. An estimate of benefits can be obtained by sending a completed Form SSA-7004 (Request for Earnings and Benefit Estimate Statement) to a regional processing office.

An individual's monthly SSDI benefit can range from under $100 to over $1000, depending on length of work history. Once an individual begins to receive an SSDI benefit, payments continue until death or until the individual is no longer disabled. The dependent married spouse or minor children of an SSDI recipient are also entitled to a monthly benefit.

Relevance for Health Care

A disabled individual who has received SSDI for 24 months is automatically entitled to Medicare coverage. Because there is a five-month waiting period for SSDI to begin, Medicare entitlement (§ **9.46**) will actually begin 29 months

---

[4] 20 C.F.R. § 404.408.

[5] *Id.* § 404.621.

after the onset of disability. Although some SSDI recipients may also be eligible for Medicaid, there is no automatic link between the two programs.

SSDI entitlement also affects continuation of private health insurance in some cases. An individual who leaves work because of a disability, or who becomes disabled within 60 days after leaving employment, is entitled to 29 months, not the usual 18, of extended health insurance coverage (COBRA), to be paid by the former employee at the group, not individual subscriber, rate.[6] The purpose of this extension is to bridge from private insurance coverage to Medicare entitlement. Note, however, that this extension is only available if the individual receives a disability determination from SSA and provides it to the former employer within 60 days of receiving it, and under no circumstances after the initial 18 months have elapsed. The disability award letter must indicate a disability onset date of no later than 60 days after termination of employment. If the SSA award indicates a date later than that, it may be worth considering appealing the SSA determination in order to argue for an earlier onset date.

SSDI and Immigration Status

Despite recent attacks on the availability to immigrants of means-tested benefits such as SSI, anyone with a lawful immigration status may still apply for SSDI benefits, if the individual has enough work history to support a claim.[7] If in the past the claimant had worked using a fictitious Social Security number or another person's Social Security number, the record can be corrected by filing a Form SSA-7008 once a lawful immigration status has been granted.[8]

Also, note that some countries, such as Canada, Great Britain, France, and Italy, have reciprocal Social Security agreements with the United States, whereby work credits acquired in those countries will be honored by SSA.

§ 9.3 Supplemental Security Income (SSI)

Supplemental Security Income (SSI) is a need-based or "welfare" program administered under Title XVI by the Social Security Administration (SSA). SSI provides benefits to low-income individuals who are disabled, blind, or over 65 years old.

---

[6] This health insurance extension, if applicable, is required under the 1985 Consolidated Omnibus Budget Reconciliation Act (COBRA), as amended. *See* 29 U.S.C. § 1162(2)(A) (1994); Health Insurance Portability and Accountability Act of 1996, Pub. L. No. 104-191, Title IV, § 421, 1996 U.S.C.C.A.N. (110 Stat.) 1936, 2087–89, *amending* 29 U.S.C. § 1162(2) *and* 42 U.S.C. § 300bb-2(2). Note also that if an individual is eligible for neither SSDI or SSI (because lack of work history and excess income or assets), SSA, under an agreement with the Department of Labor, will make a disability determination for the sole purpose of the COBRA extension. COBRA disability determinations are made at the federal DDS in Baltimore and not at the state agency. *See* SSA, Program Circular on Disability #92-15 (1992).

[7] Personal Responsibility and Work Opportunity Reconciliation Act of 1996, Pub. L. No. 104-193, Title IV, § 401(b)(2), 1996 U.S.C.C.A.N. (110 Stat.) 2105, 2261–62.

[8] 20 C.F.R. § 404.821.

A basic SSI benefit level is set federally by the SSA. State governments have the option to increase that amount for SSI recipients in their state by adding a State Supplemental Payment (SSP). Total SSI benefit levels, therefore, vary from state to state and are sensitive to both federal and state budgeting processes.

Eligibility

SSI eligibility is based on three factors: disability, financial need, and citizenship.[9] Disability is determined exactly as it is in the case of SSDI and is discussed in §§ **9.9** through **9.14.** Financial need is based on tests of both income and resources.

To be financially eligible for SSI, an individual must have monthly *countable income* that is less than that state's SSI benefit level. For instance, in a state where the SSI benefit level is $600 for an unmarried individual, a claimant's monthly countable income must be under $600. The benefit level is higher for married couples who, in order to be eligible for SSI, must have monthly countable income under the married couple benefit amount. Income, for SSI purposes, may be earned income, unearned income, or in-kind gifts and services, such as food, clothing, or shelter.

SSI financial eligibility also takes into account one's available assets. An unmarried claimant may not have available resources exceeding $2000. A married couple may not have available resources exceeding $3000. Some property is not considered an available resource, for instance, a home the claimant lives in, or a car under $4500 in value or that is used for medical purposes.[10] Because of these limitations, a client's benefit is jeopardized by the sudden receipt of any lump sum disbursements, such as settlements, inheritances, or court judgments, which are considered income in the month they are received and resources every month thereafter. Before the client receives any large sums, therefore, it is important to consider ways of protecting the award, such as through a *special needs trust* (see § **9.44**). Although there are no SSI penalties for giving away money after it is received in order to maintain SSI eligibility, there can be some serious consequences with respect to Medicaid entitlement, as discussed in § **9.42.**

Unlike the income limitations which vary according to each state's current benefit level, the asset limitations apply uniformly in all states.

These financial tests of SSI eligibility are relevant not only at the application phase but also on an ongoing basis. Countable income or available assets over the permissible SSI amounts will result in ineligibility for benefits during any month in which such income is received or such assets are held.[11]

---

[9] For an overview of nondisability issues, including income and resource rules, and overpayment, work incentive, and representative payee issues, see National Senior Citizens Law Center, SSI Nondisability Issues (3d ed. 1993) (available from National Senior Citizens Law Center, telephone: (202) 887-5280).

[10] *See* 20 C.F.R. §§ 416.1201.

[11] Due to SSA's method of *retroactive monthly accounting* (RMA), the effect of receiving excess income will not be felt for two months. If, for instance, a claimant's countable income in January exceeds the SSI benefit level, SSA will not receive notice of that fact until February, and so will schedule the SSI benefit to stop in March.

Benefit

Entitlement to SSI accrues as of the first of the month following the application date[12] or the onset of the disability, whichever is later. Unlike SSDI, there is no waiting period, so the benefit becomes payable as of the accrual date.

The monthly SSI benefit level varies from state to state, depending on how large a supplement a particular state adds to the monthly SSI check. Unlike SSDI, spouses and dependent children of an SSI recipient do not receive a benefit unless they, too, are disabled. Note, though, that the disability of one or both parents might entitle the remaining family members to welfare benefits through Temporary Assistance for Needy Families (TANF).[13]

A claimant's living arrangements may affect the amount of the SSI benefit. A disabled individual who lives in someone else's home and does not pay a fair share of the rent will receive SSI at a lower level. The basic federal benefit level drops one-third, regardless of the actual amount of discount or support the claimant receives. Some states, such as California, increase the SSI level for homeless individuals or others who do not have access to a working kitchen, in order to accommodate a higher food cost.

The SSI benefit level discussed here is the amount claimants receive if they have no other income. If they do have other *unearned* income, such as another small disability benefit, all of that income except $20 is considered *countable*. This $20 is referred to as the *set aside* or disregard. SSA pays the difference between the countable income and that state's SSI level. For individuals who have earned income through working even though they are disabled, SSA considers less than half of the earned income to be countable. This more lenient treatment of earned income is called the *earned income exclusion,* discussed in § 9.27.

The following example illustrates how SSI benefits are calculated. Manny is an unmarried man disabled by HIV, living in the state of Fredonia, where the monthly SSI level is $625. Manny has enough work history to receive $550 per month of SSDI. He will receive an additional SSI check of $95.00 every month:

$550.00	monthly SSDI check
−20.00	set aside
$530.00	countable income

---

[12] If an applicant makes first contact with SSA by calling 1-800-772-1213, the date of that call is considered the *protective filing date* and benefits will accrue as of the first day of the subsequent month. *See* Personal Responsibility and Work Opportunity Reconciliation Act of 1996, Pub. L. No. 104-193, Title II, § 204(a), 1996 U.S.C.C.A.N. (110 Stat.) 2105, 2187–88, *amending* 42 U.S.C. § 1382(c)(7)(A) and (B).

[13] This program replaced Aid to Families with Dependent Children (AFDC) as part of the Personal Responsibility and Work Opportunity Reconciliation Act of 1996, Pub. L. No. 104-193, Title I, 1996 U.S.C.C.A.N. (110 Stat.) 2105, 2110–85.

$625.00	state SSI level
– 530.00	countable income
$ 95.00	monthly SSI check

Be aware that this discussion relates to *ongoing* SSI eligibility after initial entitlement. At the application stage, monthly wages of over $500 are considered to constitute *substantial gainful activity* and, as discussed in § **9.10,** will likely undermine the entire disability claim.[14] For current benefit levels in a particular state, contact a local SSA office, or call 1-800-772-1213.

Presumptive Benefits

Some disabilities are so severe and obvious that SSA acknowledges that there is a high probability the claim will be approved and that the claimant should not be deprived of support while the claim is pending. In these cases, presuming the claimant is financially eligible, SSA will issue SSI (but not SSDI) benefits to the claimant for up to six months while the claim is being processed.[15] If the claim is subsequently denied, the claimant is under no obligation to pay the money back.[16]

Technically, presumptive benefits are only available when the claim involves a *listing level impairment* (§ **9.12**). In the case of HIV infection, a completed Medical Report (Form 4814-F5), in which the claimant's physician indicates that the disability criteria are met, qualifies the claimant for presumptive SSI payments. The claimant must still submit evidence supporting the disability claim in the application process so that SSA's evaluators can make a final determination.

Relevance for Health Care

Recipients of SSI in many states are categorically eligible for Medicaid. In other states, an SSI recipient must independently apply for Medicaid. In those states, however, an SSI recipient will automatically meet the criteria for disability. Medicaid eligibility and coverage are discussed in §§ **9.37** through **9.41.**

An SSI award extends COBRA benefits to 29 months, the same as an SSDI award. SSI recipients receiving COBRA coverage should check with their state Medicaid program to determine if Medicaid will pay the COBRA premiums, as discussed in § **9.41.**

---

[14] *See* 20 C.F.R. §§ 416.1100–416.1112 (effect of income on benefit level). The effect of income at the application level is discussed in 20 C.F.R. §§ 404.1574, 416.974.

[15] *Id.* §§ 416.931–416.934.

[16] If presumptive benefits are paid but were inappropriate for a nonmedical reason, for instance because the claimant is in prison or does not have a proper immigration status, the recipient will be required to pay that money back. *Id.* § 416.537(b).

SSI and Immigration Status[17]

Since the passage of the Personal Responsibility and Work Opportunity Reconciliation Act of 1996,[18] most noncitizens are categorically barred from receiving SSI benefits. The few narrow exceptions include:

1. Refugees, but only for the first five years after admission
2. Persons granted asylum, but only for the first five years after the granting of asylee status
3. Persons whose deportation has been withheld under § 243(h) of the Immigration and Nationality Act, but only for the first five years after the date that status is official
4. Individuals lawfully present in the United States who are U.S. veterans with honorable discharges or on active duty, along with their spouses or unmarried dependents
5. Individuals who have worked in the United States for at least 10 years, contributing at least 40 quarters under Title II, and who did not receive any federal means-tested public benefit, except Medicaid, during any quarter beginning after December 31, 1996.

In other words, a noncitizen immigrant must contribute twice as much to the Social Security system to receive SSI as he or she has to in order to be entitled to SSDI.

Although for all immigrants other than these exceptions there is a total SSI ban, some of those individuals may still be eligible for other means-tested programs, such as Medicaid, as discussed in § **9.37.**

Even if a noncitizen falls into one of the exceptions listed above, he or she should speak with an immigration advocate prior to applying for SSI, in order to carefully consider the public charge risk that receipt of benefits might pose to any upward adjustment of immigration status.[19]

SOCIAL SECURITY PROCEDURE

§ 9.4   Initial Claims

Individuals apply for SSI or SSDI benefits by filing their claims at a Social Security district office either in person or by telephone by calling 1-800-772-1213. The

---

[17] Immigration and public benefits availability are discussed in **Ch. 11.** For an overview of issues in this area, see National Immigration Law Center, Guide to Alien Eligibility for Federal Programs (2d ed. 1993) (available from the National Immigration Law Center, telephone: (213) 938-6452).

[18] Pub. L. No. 104-193, Title IV, §§ 400–451, 1996 U.S.C.C.A.N. 2105, 2260–77.

[19] The public charge issue is discussed in **Ch. 11.**

date of the phone call is the *protective filing date* and is considered the application date for the purpose of SSI or SSDI retroactive payments.

Although SSA is experimenting with ways of using community organizations to assemble more of the application file, currently the district office puts together a file for use by the disability analysts. The district office collects several forms from the claimant. They are:

- Disability Report (Form SSA-3368), eliciting data about the claimant's condition, medical records, activities, education, and past work
- Vocational Report (Form SSA-3369), eliciting information about work history and job duties
- Medical Release Forms (Form SSA-827), authorizing the claimant's physician to provide medical information to SSA (always file at least enough for each medical provider, plus several extra).

A worker in the district office then interviews the claimant and completes an Initial Application, which reviews the claimant's financial, citizenship, and residential eligibility.

If an SSI claimant submits a completed Form 4814-F5 (Medical Report) at this time indicating that listing-level HIV disability criteria are met, the district office has the authority to award *presumptive SSI payments.* An individual applying for SSDI may also submit a Form 4814-F5, but it will only be used as a piece of medical evidence, because no presumptive benefits are available under the SSDI program, although an SSDI applicant who is also SSI eligible may receive presumptive SSI benefits pending approval of the SSDI application.

When the claimant informs the district office worker that HIV is a factor in the claim, the case should be expedited as a TERI (terminal illness) case. As a matter of practice, every form filed on the claimant's behalf should have "AIDS" or "HIV" written in large letters across the top, in order to speed the process. Also, as a matter of practice, a completed, well-documented file will move through the system faster. With the initial application materials, the claimant should ideally include medical records (so that the disability analysts will not have to request them) as well as a Medical Report (Form 4814-F5). If the claimant needs to demonstrate functional impairment, statements by friends, relatives, roommates, or social workers who are aware of the disabling effects of the claimant's condition should be submitted.

§ 9.5   State Agency Disability Evaluation

When the key pieces of the application have been assembled (Disability Report, Vocational Report, and Initial Application or Claim Form), the file is forwarded from the district office to a state agency that evaluates disability claims under a contract with SSA. At the state agency, the file is assigned to a disability analyst.

The analyst is a sort of claims adjustor who manages the file until a decision is made by one of the state agency's medical consultants. The disability analyst requests medical records from all sources mentioned in the Disability Report. In some jurisdictions, the state agency may have special HIV-related question-naires which are sent to treating physicians. The disability analyst also has the authority to require a claimant to undergo a consultative examination by an agency physician or psychotherapist, but only if the claimant's physician is unable or unwilling to give sufficient evidence.[20] If the disability analyst feels there is not sufficient information in the file relating to the claimant's ability to function, the analyst may request additional information from the claimant. In some jurisdictions, the state agency relies on its own daily activities question-naire.

Analysts are frequently willing to discuss a claim with the claimant's autho-rized representative and to tell the advocate what additional documentation is necessary in order to complete the evaluation. When all information is in, the analyst submits the package to the medical consultant who evaluates the claim using the 5-step sequential evaluation described in detail in §§ **9.9** through **9.14.** Unlike the analysts, medical consultants rarely are willing to talk to advocates. State agency analysts also have the authority to award presumptive SSI pay-ments if the district office neglected to do so.

Successful claims are the minority at the application level. In 1992, 43 percent of disability claims were allowed at the application level; 57 percent were denied.[21] This is in part a result of the fact that claimants often do not work with advocates at the application level.

§ 9.6   Reconsideration

Reconsideration is the first level of appeal when an initial claim is denied. It is a de novo review of the file by another analyst at the state agency.[22]

If an initial claim is denied, the claimant must request reconsideration within 60 days of receipt of the denial notice. Receipt of the denial notice is presumed to be five days after it was sent, so the claimant in reality has at least 65 days from the date of the notice. A late filing may be excused upon showing good cause.

To initiate reconsideration, the district office assembles a file including new report forms and medical authorizations. To speed matters, the claimant or advocate should immediately file any new medical records.

---

[20] 42 C.F.R. § 404.1517.

[21] Social Security Advisory Serv., Apr. 1993.

[22] SSA, as part of its reengineering process, intends to eliminate reconsideration probably sometime after the year 1999. Initial claims at that time will be appealable directly to the ALJ level of appeal, discussed in § **9.7.** SSA believes that with sufficient reform of the initial application and determination process, far more correct disability determinations will be made and the need for a reconsideration level of review will plummet.

The district office again sends the file to the state agency where it is assigned to a different analyst than the one who processed the original claim. Again, the advocate may work with the analyst to supplement the file. The medical consultant may choose to grant the claim but with a later disability date, if it appears that the claimant's health has deteriorated in the interim, or may allow the case from the application date if new medical evidence can be developed supporting that finding.

Although the Request for Reconsideration form offers the option of a conference, these are not available for reconsideration solely on the issue of disability. They are, however, available on reconsideration of nondisability issues, such as assessment of overpayment or financial eligibility.

§ 9.7 Administrative Law Judge Hearing

If upon reconsideration the claim is again denied, the claimant has 60 days from receipt of the denial to appeal the case. The district office yet again assembles a file of new report forms and medical authorizations. Again, the claimant or advocate should submit any additional medical evidence available at that time.

The district office forwards the file to the Office of Hearings and Appeals (OHA). OHAs usually serve a number of counties. At the OHA, the claim is assigned to an administrative law judge (ALJ) and scheduled for a hearing.

The hearing provides the claimant a high chance of reversal. In 1992, 68 percent of disability claims that were appealed to the hearing level were allowed.[23] This success rate is much higher than at the initial and reconsideration stages and is attributable to several factors. First, far more claimants have advocates at the hearing level than they do at the application or reconsideration levels. Also, at a hearing the claimant finally has the opportunity to speak with a decision maker face to face. Finally, although allowances can be reviewed by the Appeals Council on its own motion, ALJs are more likely to risk reversal if they deny a claim, because the claimant has the right to appeal.

Having an advocate, though not mandatory, is critical to success at this phase. In addition to representing the claimant at the hearing (including examining and cross-examining witnesses), the advocate can contact the ALJ's clerk or the supervising attorney at the OHA in order to discuss the case and determine what additional evidence the ALJ would like to see. The representative need not be a licensed attorney.

At the time of filing for a hearing, it is highly advisable to request a *decision on the record*. If the evidence in the file is insufficient for the ALJ to make a favorable decision, the claim will not be denied. Instead, the claimant will be scheduled for a hearing as if this paper review had never happened.[24] The

---

[23] Social Security Advisory Serv., Apr. 1993.

[24] 20 C.F.R. §§ 404.948, 416.1448.

opportunity for a decision on the record is especially important considering the fact that, nationally, OHAs can have a backlog of hundreds of thousands of cases at any given time.[25] Through the reengineering process, the OHA will come to have adjudication officers who can make decisions on the record without having to involve the ALJ.[26] Attorney advisors have already been granted the authority to issue wholly favorable decisions.[27] These various changes are intended to free ALJs up for the most difficult cases.

If the denial at the reconsideration stage was not a result of insufficient evidence but rather because of regulations that may be unconstitutional, the ALJ hearing may be bypassed so that the federal district court can hear the constitutional question.[28]

§ 9.8   Further Appeals

Appeals Council.   If the claim is denied at the hearing level, the claimant may request review by the Appeals Council by filing a Request for Review of Hearing Decision/Order (Form HA-520). The Appeals Council does not hold a new hearing, although it may grant oral argument on request. Review is generally limited to: errors of law; abuse of discretion by the ALJ; the ALJ's action, findings, or conclusions are not supported by substantial evidence; or when there is a broad policy or procedural issue that may affect the general public interest. New and material evidence also is considered. The Council may uphold the ALJ's decision, reverse the decision, or remand to the ALJ for another hearing.

As part of its reengineering, SSA will substantially eliminate the Appeals Council level of review. The Appeals Council may accept some cases, but this level of appeal will no longer need to be exhausted in order to proceed to federal court.

Judicial review.   A denial at the Appeals Council level may be appealed to federal district court. Issues not raised at the Appeals Council may be barred at the district court appeal.[29] The court can reverse an ALJ decision if there was an error of law or if the decision is not based on substantial evidence.[30] Courts may

---

[25] Remarks of OHA Associate Commissioner Skoler at the June 1993 convention of the National Organization of Social Security Claimants' Representatives, reported in Social Security Advisory Serv., July 1993.

[26] Pilot programs testing various approaches to processing claims at the ALJ level are currently in place in localities across the county. 60 Fed. Reg. 20,023 (1995).

[27] 20 C.F.R. §§ 404.942, 416.442 (1995).

[28] *See* Expedited Appeals, 20 C.F.R. §§ 404.923, 416.1423.

[29] Paul v. Shalala, 29 F.3d 208, 210 (5th Cir. 1994).

[30] *Id.* at 210; Muse v. Sullivan, 925 F.2d 785, 789 (5th Cir. 1991).

consider additional evidence outside the record only for the purpose of remand and only if the evidence is "material" and there is "good cause" for the failure to incorporate such evidence into the record in prior administrative proceedings.[31]

SOCIAL SECURITY'S DISABILITY EVALUATION

§ 9.9   Sequential Evaluation of Disability Claims

All evaluators of disability claims use a five-step *sequential evaluation process* in determining disability. The evaluation is based on the Social Security Act's definition of *disability* as "the inability to engage in any substantial gainful activity by reason of any medically determinable physical or mental impairment which has lasted or can be expected to last for a continuous period of not less than 12 months [or result in death]."[32]

The evaluators using the sequential evaluation might be state agency medical consultants (in cooperation with the disability analysts), administrative law judges, or Appeals Council panels. For the sake of simplicity, they will be referred to collectively in this section as evaluators. The sequential evaluation is charted in **Figure 9–1.** Its purpose is to address, one by one, the minimum requirements for disability under the Act and its regulations.

§ 9.10   —Substantial Gainful Activity (SGA)

The threshold question of the disability evaluation is whether the claimant is currently engaging in *substantial gainful activity* (SGA). In other words, is the claimant currently working? Claimants who are working will be found to be *not disabled.*[33]

Substantial gainful activity involves the performance of significant physical or mental duties, or both, which are productive in nature. The work does not have to be full-time to be substantial; part-time can be enough. *Gainful activity* means work typically performed for pay or profit, whether it is actually profitable in this case or not. So, for instance, school attendance is not considered to be substantial gainful activity, because it is not typically done for pay.[34]

---

[31] 42 U.S.C. § 405(g) (1994); Key v. Heckler, 754 F.2d 1545, 1551 (9th Cir. 1985).

[32] 42 U.S.C. §§ 423(d)(1) [SSDI], 1382c(a)(3)(A) [SSI]. *See also* 20 C.F.R. § 404.1505.

[33] As discussed in § **9.27,** however, claimants may work under some circumstances and remain eligible for benefits, as long as the work is not deemed to be substantial gainful activity.

[34] For more details on what constitutes substantial gainful activity, see 20 C.F.R. §§ 404.1572–404.1576, 416.971–416.976.

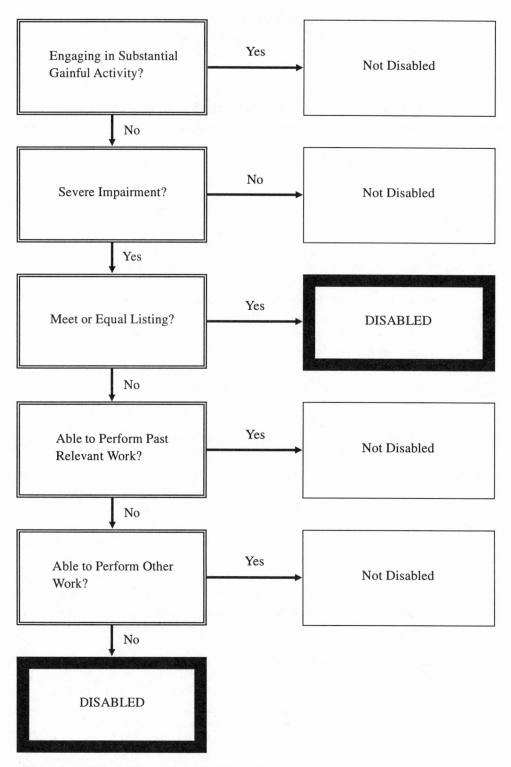

Figure 9–1. Sequential evaluation of disability.

There is a rebuttable presumption that monthly earnings of $500 or more constitute substantial gainful activity.[35] If a benevolent employer keeps a disabled employee with HIV on the payroll, despite the fact that the employee either cannot be productive or requires constant help in order to do work, SSA will consider only the portion of the claimant's salary that relates to actual productivity. Anything above that is considered a subsidy and is not counted as income in determining substantial gainful activity.[36]

If the evaluator determines that the claimant is not engaging in substantial gainful activity, the process moves to Step 2 of the sequence, involving determination of the existence of an impairment.

§ 9.11 —Severe Impairment

Step 2 evaluates whether the claimant suffers from a severe impairment that is expected to last 12 months or result in death. In legal terms, this step is analogous to a motion to dismiss on the part of SSA. It is not meant to determine disability in and of itself, but simply that there is enough of an impairment to warrant continuing with the evaluation. In order to establish severe impairment, the claimant must show three elements: impairment, severity, and duration.

Under the regulations, an *impairment* must "result from anatomical, physiological, or psychological abnormalities which can be shown by medically acceptable clinical and laboratory diagnostic techniques."[37]

The regulations indicate that to be considered *severe,* the impairment must significantly limit the claimant's physical or mental ability to do basic work activities. The Supreme Court, however, has ruled that a claimant's impairment is severe enough for this stage of the inquiry when medical evidence establishes even a "slight abnormality" that has more than "a minimal effect" on the claimant's ability to work.[38]

Occasionally, SSA will find that an impairment has not lasted and is not expected to last 12 months, in which case the durational requirement is not met. It is, therefore, important to document exactly when the claimant began suffering from the impairment, in order to meet this burden. However, if a claimant with documented HIV has a listing-level impairment (see § 9.15), the durational requirement is deemed to have been met.[39]

If the claimant cannot show the existence of a severe impairment, the evaluation stops and the claimant is found to be not disabled. If the claimant can demonstrate a severe impairment, the evaluator moves on to Step 3 of the sequence.

---

[35] 20 C.F.R. §§ 404.1574, 416.974.

[36] *Id.*

[37] 20 C.F.R. § 404.1508.

[38] Bowen v. Yuckert, 482 U.S. 137 (1987).

[39] SSR 93-2p, 58 Fed. Reg. 52,973 (1993).

§ 9.12 —Meeting or Equalling the Listings

This crucial stage of the evaluation, Step 3, is the first at which the claimant has the potential to win the claim. In legal terms, it is analogous to a claimant's motion for summary judgment. Here, the claimant attempts to prove a specific condition included in a list of impairments that SSA has previously deemed to be disabling.[40] Claimants who meet the listings will be found disabled without further inquiry. If a claimant's condition is not actually included in the listings but is of similar severity and duration as a listed condition, a claimant may be considered to have "equalled" the listings, and will be found disabled without further analysis.[41]

Specific listings for HIV infection were not adopted until July 1993. These HIV listings are rather complex and are discussed in detail in §§ **9.15** through **9.17.** Some claimants with HIV may also meet the listings based on non-HIV factors. For instance, psychological disorders and, in a few limited instances, substance addiction may provide grounds for a disability determination.[42]

The advocate should assess all potential medical grounds for a disability determination and document them as exhaustively as possible, along with the functional impairment they cause. A successful claim may be based on many medical and psychological conditions in combination. The advocate should also, whenever possible, submit a memo or brief detailing exactly how the evidence relates to the applicable listings. Remember, if the claimant is found to have an impairment that meets or equals a listing, the claimant is found disabled at this step and no further evaluation is necessary.

If the claimant's medical condition is not found to meet or equal a listing, the evaluator moves on to Step 4 of the sequence.

§ 9.13 —Past Relevant Work

Claimants who do not have an impairment that meets or equals the listings must next prove that they cannot perform any past relevant work. Generally, *past relevant work* is defined as any work that a claimant has done in the last 15 years.

---

[40] These conditions are listed in 20 C.F.R. pt. 404, subpt. P, app. 1, commonly referred to as *the listings.*

[41] The method for determining medical equivalence is discussed in 20 C.F.R. § 404.1526.

[42] Although substance addiction was, for many years, a legitimate basis for a disability claim, drug addiction and alcoholism were specifically excluded from consideration as of March 29, 1996, pursuant to the Contract with America Advancement Act of 1996, Pub. L. No. 104-121, § 105(a)(1), 1996 U.S.C.C.A.N. (110 Stat.) 847, 852 (to be codified at 42 U.S.C. § 423(d)(2)(C)). Diagnosable physical or psychological effects of the drug or alcohol use (as opposed to the addiction itself) should still be considered.

The SSA evaluates the claimant's ability to perform past relevant work by considering the functional limitations the claimant currently experiences in performing work-like activities and comparing those to the duties of the claimant's past work. To determine the relevant limitations, the evaluator reviews the medical evidence and determines the claimant's physical *residual functional capacity* (RFC). The RFC assessment classifies a claimant as capable of doing "sedentary," "light," "medium," "heavy," or "very heavy" work.[43] This assessment must also take into consideration "non-exertional" impairments such as mental difficulties, pain not related to physical exertion, balance, and sensitivity to environmental conditions. After the claimant is classified in one of these categories, the claimant's RFC is compared to the requirements of relevant former jobs. In performing this analysis, the medical consultant (MC) fills out a form evaluating the claimant's physical RFC. The MC may also choose to complete a form evaluating the claimant's mental RFC, if mental impairment is alleged or uncovered in the development of the claim.

Claimants who are found to be capable of performing past relevant work are found to be not disabled. In the case of claimants who have met their burden of proving that they cannot engage in past relevant work, the evaluator moves on to the final step of the sequential evaluation.

§ 9.14   —Other Work

Once the claimant has proven that he or she cannot perform any past relevant work, the burden shifts to SSA to prove that the claimant is nonetheless capable of adjusting to other work that exists in the national economy.[44] At this stage, vocational factors such as age, education, and work experience are considered. In determining if an individual can perform other work, the evaluator uses a set of guidelines known as *the grids.*[45]

The grids are designed to assess vocational potential based on physical factors alone. Therefore, if a claimant has been determined to have nonexertional impairments, the grids cannot be used to deny the claim. This is especially important for young claimants, because under the grids, young people are considered more adaptable to new work environments. It is, therefore, important that claimants include evidence of nonexertional impairments, for example, mental difficulties, pain not related to physical exertion, balance, or sensitivity to environmental conditions.

If SSA proves that the claimant is able to do other work, the claim is denied. Otherwise, there is a finding of disability.

---

[43] 20 C.F.R. § 416.967.

[44] 20 C.F.R. § 416.920(f).

[45] *Id.* pt. 404, subpt. P, app. 2.

SOCIAL SECURITY'S LISTINGS FOR
HIV DISABILITY

§ 9.15   Listings for HIV Disability

In July 1993, the SSA issued—for the first time since the beginning of the AIDS epidemic—final regulations describing what an individual with HIV must prove in order to meet a disability listing. Before these regulations were issued, many people living with HIV experienced inordinate delays in the processing and approval of their disability claims. In many instances, these delays resulted in the claimant's death before a penny of disability money was paid.

In the early days of the AIDS epidemic, SSA simply relied on the surveillance definition of AIDS promulgated by the CDC.[46] Individuals with an AIDS diagnosis were considered to have met the listings; those without that diagnosis did not. Because the CDC issued its definition of AIDS for broad epidemiological purposes and not for the purpose of determining the functionality of particular individuals, there was a significant lack of fit between an AIDS diagnosis and actual disability. Many individuals with an AIDS-defining illness were quite functional. Others were severely impaired by a variety of opportunistic infections, none of which were AIDS-defining. Moreover, because the CDC developed its AIDS definition based on information from health care providers, "AIDS" as a diagnosis was shaped by who had access to health care to begin with. Of those individuals infected with HIV, the most likely to have ready access to health care were relatively affluent, employed, gay white men. This had the effect of obscuring the particular ways HIV disease presents in men of color and in women. Because many HIV manifestations in women are not unique to HIV (even though they may be profoundly more severe or resistant to therapy when HIV is present), women were consistently misdiagnosed. This inherent bias in the AIDS definition was then absorbed into SSA's disability evaluation, through the adoption of the CDC's AIDS definition.[47]

Over the years, SSA officially advised its evaluators of additional ways that HIV could be disabling. However, the suggestions fell short of establishing listings for HIV disability to which evaluators had to defer and upon which claimants could rely. This translated into a perpetuation of a system in which CDC AIDS diagnoses resulted in disability awards, whereas other HIV manifestations required an inordinate amount of medical and functional assessment and documentation. Not surprisingly, the populations less likely to have access to medical care also had less access to advocates who could assist in navigating SSA's waters.

---

[46] *See* Interim Regulation, 50 Fed. Reg. 5573 (1985).

[47] For a more detailed discussion of the CDC's AIDS definition in relation to public benefit programs, see Carol Levine & Gary L. Stein, *What's in a Name? The Policy Implications of the CDC Definition of AIDS,* 19 L. Med. & Health Care 278, 282–84 (1991).

In December 1991, SSA released proposed HIV listings, which were adopted as an interim regulatory scheme.[48] The interim regulations set up a remarkably complex methodology for meeting a listing. Although the interim regulations were theoretically decoupled from the CDC AIDS definition, the interim scheme continued to privilege conditions that, at that time, constituted formal AIDS diagnoses, by treating them as disabling per se. For the remainder of HIV conditions, claimants had to make additional showings in order to meet the listings. These included demonstrating a level of functional impairment usually required by SSA for claims based on psychological factors, in which there are no significant physical symptoms. To many, this seemed to reveal SSA's deep, institutional disbelief in the physically disabling nature of HIV disease.

In July 1993, SSA released final listings for HIV disability.[49] These new regulations, incorporated as Listings 14.08 (adults) and 114.08 (children),[50] replace the interim regulations as the standard for proving disability based on HIV disease. The 1993 HIV listings are, at least on paper, a significant improvement over all the regulatory schemes that preceded it, by allowing HIV-based disability to be described (and the listing to be met) by use of a far more open-ended inquiry than has ever been used in a listing of any sort. As a practical matter, it still tends to disserve lower income claimants who may have little medical documentation of their repeated manifestations of HIV disease.

§ 9.16 Disability Standard for Adults with HIV

Under the HIV listings, an adult claimant may qualify as disabled by HIV in one of two ways: (1) a diagnosis of any one of 41 stand alone conditions (set forth in § 9.49); or (2) a series of repeated manifestations of HIV disease accompanied by functional impairment. Regardless of which approach is used, claimants must first document their HIV status itself. This can be done using results of antibody tests, antigen tests, or through a diagnosis of an opportunistic infection that has no known cause other than HIV.[51]

Opportunistic and Indicator Diseases
(Stand-Alone Conditions)

The first method of demonstrating disability involves showing medical documentation of one of 41 severe HIV conditions, presenting in the particular way

---

[48] 56 Fed. Reg. 65,498, 65,702 (1991).

[49] 58 Fed. Reg. 36,008 (1993), *amending* 20 C.F.R. pt. 404.

[50] The stand-alone disabling conditions of Listing 14.08 are reprinted in § **9.49,** and those of Listing 114.08 are reprinted in § **9.50.**

[51] 20 C.F.R. pt. 404, subpt. P, app. 1, § 14.00 D.3.; 58 Fed. Reg. 36,053 (1993). The regulations state that a low T-cell (CD4) count is not, in and of itself, a sufficient indicator of HIV infection.

described in the listing. Although for some conditions there are no qualifiers (for instance pneumocystis carinii pneumonia is considered disabling per se), others must be located at particular body sites, be resistant to therapy, or involve particular symptoms in order to be considered automatically disabling. One noticeable improvement in the HIV listings is the inclusion of more conditions that are specific to women. Although 41 items certainly constitute a substantial list, many of the conditions are described quite restrictively. Nonetheless, manifestations of HIV conditions that do not quite meet the qualifications of the stand-alone list may still be used in the repeated manifestations inquiry.

Because the mere diagnosis of a condition may not satisfy the particular terms of the stand-alone listing, the claimant's physician should be supplied with a copy of the new listings, or Form 4814-F5, so that the medical assessments can closely track the specific requirements of the listing.

Repeated Manifestations plus Functional Impairment

Claimants who do not have any of the 41 stand-alone indicator diseases as specifically defined in the regulations have another opportunity to demonstrate disability by listing other manifestations of HIV infection and providing evidence of functional impairment. This alternative method of meeting the HIV listings creates an open-ended opportunity to report on the many conditions one may be experiencing. As SSA notes in its preamble to the new regulations:

> We decided that instead of expanding the list of manifestations, we could respond to the commenters' concerns by abandoning the finite list of HIV-related manifestations and referring instead to "manifestations of HIV infection" in general. This allows for consideration of any manifestations, whether identified in the listing or not. . . . We had hoped to include in the listings [by means of this provision] a group of individuals whom we believed would be very difficult to describe in strictly medical terms—individuals who become ill then improve, only to repeatedly become ill again, either with the same manifestation of HIV infection or with different manifestations.[52]

The repeated manifestations approach constitutes, at least on paper, a significant achievement in SSA's recognition of what HIV disability often looks like: an endless series of different medical problems, none of which would be disabling in and of itself, but which, in combination and rapid succession, can make it impossible to do just about anything.

A claimant will meet the listings upon a showing of three manifestations of HIV infection in the course of one year, resulting in significant, documented symptoms or signs (for example, fatigue, fever, malaise, weight loss, pain, night sweats), *and* a marked level of one of the following: (1) restrictions of activities of daily living; (2) difficulties in maintaining social functioning; or (3) difficulties in

---

[52] 58 Fed. Reg. 36,016–17 (1993).

completing tasks in a timely manner because of deficiencies in concentration, persistence, or pace.

Under the first prong of the repeated manifestations analysis, the claimant must provide evidence of repeated manifestations of HIV infection. These manifestations can include conditions listed in the stand alone section whose exact terms were not met or any other condition attributable to HIV. To be sufficient, the claimant must document the following severity: (1) at least three episodes within one year, each episode lasting at least two weeks; (2) substantially more than three episodes within one year, each episode lasting less than two weeks; or (3) less than three episodes within one year, each episode lasting substantially more than two weeks. These episodic occurrences of HIV conditions, although referred to in the regulations as repeated manifestations, do not have to be recurrences of the same condition. Three distinct HIV manifestations will suffice. So, for instance, two episodes of diarrhea each lasting two weeks and one episode of a bacterial infection lasting two weeks should meet the first prong of the test.

Although this formula represents the minimum number of episodes necessary to prove disability, there is no limit on how many manifestations may be included in the disability claim. The claimant's physician should be encouraged to list as many manifestations of HIV disease as possible and to submit additional paperwork if necessary. It may be useful to create a repeated manifestations worksheet for the physician to fill out, because the SSA 4814-F5 form only gives three lines to list these conditions.

The second prong of the analysis is a functional limitations inquiry. The claimant must show marked functional impairment in one of three categories of life function: activities of daily living, social functioning, or completing tasks in a timely manner. Evaluators are instructed to take all the facts into consideration in determining whether the claimant is functionally impaired:

> Important factors to be considered in evaluating the functioning of individuals with HIV infection include, but are not limited to: symptoms, such as fatigue and pain; characteristics of the illness, such as the frequency and duration of manifestations or periods of exacerbation and remission in the disease course; and the functional impact of treatment for the disease, including the side effects of medication.[53]

Functional impairment can be very subjective and difficult to document. Practice pointers to help with this task can be found in § **9.20.**

Irrelevance of CD4 Counts

The last significant feature of the new regulations is the exclusion of T-helper lymphocyte, or CD4, counts from direct consideration as an indication either of

---

[53] *Id.* at 36,054.

HIV infection or of disability. CD4s are the white blood cells that are taken to be a marker of the body's immune function. A CD4 count of 200 per cubic millimeter or less constitutes an AIDS diagnosis, as defined by the CDC.[54] Although such a low CD4 count is considered to indicate the body's susceptibility to disease, many individuals with low CD4s remain asymptomatic.

As part of its decoupling from the CDC definition of AIDS, SSA has taken the position that if someone with under 200 CD4s experiences significant functional impairment, the impairment is likely attributable to some diagnosable condition or some manifestation of a diagnosable condition.

Despite this decision by SSA, many state agency analysts seem to continue looking at CD4 counts, at least informally, which may have favorable or unfavorable effect on the claim, depending on the count. In addition, a decrease in CD4 levels may have some prognostic value. If the claimant's physician finds the numbers meaningful, they should be included as evidence, regardless of the fact that there is no neat, regulatory niche for them to fill. A period of rapidly dropping T-cells could, at the very least, be included in the list of repeated manifestations, in order to point out that there is currently some actual, detrimental change happening within the body.

The results of viral load tests also have no official role in the HIV disability determination, because they were not in common use during the drafting of the regulations. Nonetheless, it would not hurt to include a period of steep increase of viral load within a longer list of repeated manifestations.

§ 9.17 Disability Standard for Children with HIV

Children with HIV infection may be eligible for SSI if they qualify as disabled and their parents meet the SSI financial restrictions. Children may also be eligible for SSDI if they have earned sufficient income.[55] As of the summer of 1996, proving a child's disability has become more difficult. Under the previous comparable severity rule of *Sullivan v. Zebley,*[56] children could demonstrate that their inability to engage in age-appropriate activities was comparable to an adult level of functional impairment. However, SSA may no longer make such an "individualized functional assessment" of children to determine functional impairment, leaving children largely subject to the more restrictive medical listings. It

---

[54] The CDC's definition of AIDS is discussed in **Ch. 1.**

[55] Proving disability for children may now be harder, because Congress replaced the comparable severity rule, which formed the basis of Sullivan v. Zebley, 493 U.S. 521 (1990), with new statutory language requiring that a child have a "medically determinable physical or mental impairment which results in marked and severe functional limitations" of substantial duration. Pub. L. No. 104-193, Title II, § 211, 1996 U.S.C.C.A.N. (110 Stat.) 2105, 2188–89; *see* H. Conf. Rep. No. 725, 104th Cong., 2d Sess. 328, *reprinted in* 1996 U.S.C.C.A.N. 2649, 2716. It is unclear how this new definition of disability will affect or interact with the children's HIV listings.

[56] 493 U.S. 521 (1990).

is unclear how this will affect disability under the HIV-specific listings for children which, as seen below, incorporate an individualized functional assessment standard.

The children's listings are similar to the listings for adults. A child may qualify in one of two ways: (1) a diagnosis of any one of 47 stand alone illnesses (set forth in § 9.50); *or* (2) any other manifestation along with one category of functional impairment (for children up to age three) or marked impairment in two categories of functioning (for children ages 3 to 18).

Opportunistic and Indicator Diseases (Stand Alone Conditions)

The listings include a variety of stand alone categories for children, including specific listings that address physical growth and neurological development. These items explicitly consider children's estimated growth for their age, so that not only weight loss but also the absence of expected growth for two months or longer are indicative of HIV disability. The stand alones also include neurological manifestations that result in the loss of previously acquired intellectual ability or the development of a new learning disability.

As in the case of the adult listings, the children's stand alones are often so restrictively defined that only severely disabled children will be able to meet them. However, as in the case of the adult listings, an open-ended alternative is available.

Other Manifestations plus Functional Impairment

Unlike the adult listings, the other manifestations approach to disability does not require that manifestations be repeated (one manifestation will do) or that they have a particular duration. They do, however, still entail the satisfaction of a functional impairment test.

The functional impairment requirement is age-specific. As mapped out on the Form SSA 4815-F6, and as set forth in § 9.51, children up to age one need only exhibit some functional impairment in one of the infant categories. Children ages one to three need only exhibit some functional impairment in one of the toddler categories. Children ages three to 18 must exhibit "marked" impairment in two of four categories specific to that age group. Ironically, for children of that age group, the functional limitations test is, at least formally, harsher than that faced by adults.

Of course, like adults, children need to demonstrate that their disability stems from HIV. Advocates should pay careful attention to the regulations setting out acceptable HIV testing methods, especially for children under age two who may be harboring their mother's HIV antibodies. The regulations include alternative means of demonstrating the presence or probable presence of HIV in children.[57]

---

[57] 20 C.F.R. pt. 404, subpt. P, app. 1, Listing 114.00 D.3.; 58 Fed. Reg. 36,056 (1993).

SOCIAL SECURITY'S DISABILITY STANDARD FOR MENTAL ILLNESS AND SUBSTANCE ABUSE

§ 9.18   Disability Based on Mental Illness

A claimant may, in addition to documenting HIV infection, seek a disability determination based on mental illness. As in all disability claims, one must not be engaging in substantial, gainful activity and must demonstrate the existence of a medically determinable impairment that is expected to last at least 12 months.

Once the listings phase of the sequential evaluation has been reached, the claimant must not only meet clinical criteria for a particular disorder but also must exhibit marked restriction in two of four categories of activity, three of four for some disorders. This is a stricter standard of functional impairment than that required by the repeated manifestations inquiry of the HIV listings.

The exact clinical criteria that must be met vary from diagnosis to diagnosis.[58] As in all disability evaluations, claimants who do not meet or equal the specific listings will still be evaluated for residual functional capacity to determine their ability to engage in relevant past work or other work. In assessing residual functional capacity, psychological factors constitute nonexertional impairments (§§ **9.13** to **9.14**). SSA evaluates psychological disorders using the Psychiatric Review Technique, Form SSA-2506-BK.

§ 9.19   Disability Based on Substance Abuse

Since early 1996, drug addiction and alcoholism (DAA) are not considered grounds for a finding of disability. Federal case law previously permitted individuals with severe addiction to receive disability benefits if they were unable to voluntarily cease their drug use and the addiction made it impossible to work.[59] Benefits are no longer available, however, unless the effects of the claimant's chemical dependency or alcoholism manifest in a diagnosable physical or behavioral condition: organic mental disorder, depressive syndrome, anxiety disorder, personality disorder, peripheral neuropathy, liver damage, gastritis, pancreatitis, or seizures—in other words, a physical or psychological condition that meets a listing in its own right.[60]

If DAA is a *material factor* in a disability claim (in other words, if the claimant would not be found disabled but for the DAA evidence), the claim will not be allowed. Unfortunately, drug and alcohol addiction may not be so easily separable

---

[58] The listings for mental illness begin at 20 C.F.R., pt. 404, subpt. P., app. 1, Listing 12.00.

[59] *See, e.g.,* Cooper v. Bowen, 815 F.2d 557, 560 (9th Cir. 1987); Johnson v. Harris, 625 F.2d 311, 312 (9th Cir. 1980).

[60] 20 C.F.R. pt. 404, subpt. P, app. 1, Listing 12.09 (substance addiction disorders).

from other physical and psychological symptoms that the claimant is experiencing. It is still unclear whether in practice the mere inclusion of DAA evidence will have a detrimental effect on the claim.

PRACTICE POINTERS FOR
PROVING DISABILITY

§ 9.20   Thorough Intake, Developing Medical
Evidence, and Persuasive Writing

Although Social Security is a public entitlement program, it is, for all intents and purposes, inaccessible to the public. The process itself is complicated and the documentation required is nearly impossible to compile without professional support. For this reason it is advisable for claimants to work with benefits counselors from the beginning of the process. It is also crucial for advocates, such as attorneys, to be available to lend their skills at the appeals level.

Intake Interview

The intake must be thorough and should include a frank discussion of the process and what tasks will be necessary in order for the client to prevail on his or her claim. At the first appointment, the client should sign an Appointment of Representative Form, SSA-1696, along with medical releases for all health care providers, specifically authorizing the attorney or advocate to obtain information relating to HIV, substance use, and mental health. The client should inform his or her doctors that the advocate will be contacting them, and the client should urge them to cooperate with the advocate. Also, inquire whether the client ever served in the Armed Forces, because he or she may be eligible for Veterans disability benefits.

The attorney should attempt to develop evidence of functional impairment in all three of the areas set out in the repeated manifestations portion of the HIV listings: daily activities; social functioning; and concentration, persistence, and pace.

In order to elicit information about daily activities, it is more valuable to ask questions based on "a day in the client's life" than to ask broader, open-ended questions about activities. For instance, "What are your hobbies?" might produce a response of "carpentry and jujitsu." But it also might be that the client has not been able to engage in either of those activities for a year. Instead, start at the beginning of a typical day and work forward. For instance, ask the client "What time do you get up? Do you sleep well? Do you eat breakfast? Do you make your own breakfast or does someone make breakfast for you?" Each answer the client gives should elicit at least one followup question. For instance, if the client answers that he has cold cereal for breakfast, the attorney can follow up by asking what he used to have for breakfast. If he says omelets, find out if cooking is now too fatiguing. Making these comparisons with past, pre-illness activity levels is extremely useful and should be done for every question relating to daily activities.

The day in the life approach should also turn up evidence relating to social functioning and concentration. If it does not, be sure to specifically ask about the client's contact with friends and family and how that may have changed during the course of the illness. Ask the client whether and what he reads, and whether he watches television. Changes in reading habits or choices of television programs may be connected to a decreased ability to concentrate.

Identify friends, social workers, or social service "buddies" who could write informal statements or letters to the evaluator describing the client's condition. Talking to these people (with the client's permission) is also important because the client might be in denial about his or her current low level of activity or might not recognize how impaired he or she is. Friends or buddies might have a better idea than the client of what household tasks have fallen on their shoulders.

Working with Physicians

The strongest piece of the client's claim is the medical file. If it seems that there is insufficient medical information in the file, it may be fruitful to have the client consult specialists, including psychologists who can do neuropsychological testing for AIDS-related dementia if the client is complaining of mental, emotional, or memory problems. A comprehensive statement from the treating physician is the best evidence a claimant can offer, because great weight is given to the treating physician's opinion.[61] Work with the physician to create a statement that carefully tracks the HIV or other relevant listings.

The attorney should also make sure that the client keeps track of symptoms, reports them all to the doctor, and that they are included in the chart. If the physician is not willing to do this, the attorney should help the client find a new physician. It is especially important for the repeated manifestations inquiry of the HIV listings to have medical records of all complaints, including duration of each symptom.

When drafting a release in order to obtain these and other medical records, the authorization should include specific reference to HIV (as well as mental illness and substance use), or else the facility may withhold that information, depending on the state's medical and HIV confidentiality laws. If a health care facility

---

[61] Information from the treating physician is considered prior to any other evidence. 42 U.S.C. § 423(d)(5)(B). Consultative exams may be ordered only if the primary medical source cannot or will not give sufficient evidence. 42 C.F.R. § 404.1517. If contradicted by another doctor, the treating physician's opinion can only be rejected by an ALJ for "specific and legitimate reasons supported by substantial evidence in the record." Lester v. Chater, 81 F.3d 821, 830 (9th Cir. 1995).

refuses to permit access to the client's medical records, it may be in violation of federal law and possibly state law, depending on the type of facility.[62] If representing the client on a pro bono basis, the attorney may try requesting a waiver of the medical record copying charge, depending on the provider and the size of the medical file. In addition to the physician, there may be medical records that are available through a workers' compensation claim or a personal injury lawsuit.

Persuasive Writing

Once thorough information about the client's condition and daily activities has been obtained, the attorney must communicate that information effectively to the evaluators. The arguments may be structured differently, depending on whether they are in a written letter to state agency disability analysts or in a hearing brief for an ALJ. But in either case, the arguments should be written as descriptively as possible, helping the reader to visualize the client's situation and empathize with the client's experience. The best way to vividly communicate the client's condition is by using adjectives. "Constant throbbing pain" communicates much more than simply "pain." "Frequent explosive diarrhea" communicates far more than merely "diarrhea." The descriptive phrases should force the reader to make the connection between the symptom and the effect it has on an individual's life, work, and dignity. (Loss of dignity is, of course, not relevant to SSA, but it may still impress a decision maker.)

The attorney should also include her own observations and experience from working with the client in the description of the client's disability. For instance, if the attorney gave the client an SSA disability form to fill out, and it took two hours to do so when the form estimates 15 minutes, or if the client needs the attorney to do the writing, this is evidence of functional impairment that can be given to the analyst.

When advocating to the evaluator at the initial or reconsideration level, the attorney should cite to SSA's *Program Operation Manual System* (POMS) rather than the *Code of Federal Regulations* (CFR) or *Federal Register* cites. The POMS provides a great amount of detail about the substantive and procedural requirements of disability claimants, including those with HIV. Local SSA offices have the POMS and will allow an attorney to review it upon making an appointment to do so.[63] Also, when working with state agency evaluators, you can refer to the HIV disability forms, SSA 4814-F5 and SSA 4815-F6. For instance, you may reference pneumocystis carinii pneumonia as "4814-F5, stand alone condition number 15." In contrast, when advocating before an ALJ, it is appropriate to use official federal cites.

---

[62] Law governing access to medical records can be found in 42 U.S.C. §§ 1395i-3(c)(1)(A)(iv) (skilled nursing facilities) and 42 C.F.R. § 483.10(b)(2) (long-term care). More general statutes regarding access to medical records can be found at the state level.

[63] For instructions on evaluation of HIV disability for the purpose of granting presumptive SSI, see POMS, DI 11055.241.

§ 9.21   Working with SSA and State
Agency Personnel

When a claim is denied, either at the initial application or reconsideration level, the attorney should check the denial notices (there will be separate notices for SSDI and SSI) to make sure that all the treating doctors or hospitals are listed. If they are not, the attorney must submit missing evidence along with any new evidence she has.

At this point, the attorney should copy the client's file at the SSA district office. Often, there are notes between the disability analyst and the medical consultant that provide the exact reasons for the denial. Also, she should see if there are written assessments from any consultative exams performed on the client. Finally, the lawyer should see if there was medical evidence in the file that is not listed in the denial letter, in other words evidence that was present but was not looked at.

Once an initial claim or reconsideration has been submitted, the lawyer should wait about one week, then contact the state agency reviewing the client's claim. She should identify and contact the disability analyst to find out what additional information would be desirable, then submit it directly to that analyst. After submitting the new evidence, she should check in periodically with the analyst to see if a decision has been made on the claim. If the analyst says that the determination is negative, the attorney should try to submit additional evidence before the decision is final. Success at the reconsideration stage will spare the client months of waiting for a hearing and a subsequent decision.

If the client's claim is denied at the reconsideration stage, the client has 60 days to request a hearing before an ALJ. Shortly after submitting the request for hearing, the attorney should check with the Office of Hearings and Appeals (OHA) to verify receipt of the request for hearing and the client's file and also request a decision on the record. She should ask if there is a special procedure for an accelerated paper review. A decision on the record could, without any risk, save the client months of waiting for the hearing. In the meantime, the attorney must continue to gather and submit medical evidence to the OHA.

The attorney should receive a notice identifying the ALJ and stating that the client's hearing file is available for inspection and copying. If that notice has not arrived within a few weeks of submitting the request for hearing, the lawyer must call the OHA and make sure the case has not fallen through the cracks, making an appointment to inspect the file and copy anything in it that is not already in the attorney's possession, such as analyst's notes or evaluations by SSA physicians or psychiatrists. The lawyer must make sure that everything that was previously in the file is there; if any evidence is missing, additional copies should be submitted directly to the OHA.

§ 9.22 Advocacy at Hearings

The attorney should receive a notice of the hearing date. If the date needs to be changed, it should be done immediately. The attorney should confirm the date with any potential witnesses (for example, the client's doctor, social worker, or practical support "buddy"). The advocate must continue to gather additional medical evidence and declarations and submit them directly to the OHA.

A memorandum summarizing the evidence and making legal arguments must be prepared. It is easy to check with the judge's staff to ascertain whether all materials, including memos, must be submitted in advance. Some judges hold the record open for up to 30 days after the hearing for submission of a memo or additional medical evidence. A memo that reviews in detail the evidence (with appropriate record cites) and relates the evidence to the sequential evaluation and the listings can be very effective.

Prepare Direct Examination

ALJs vary as to how much direct examination they conduct. Therefore, the attorney should prepare an extensive direct examination that covers work history (including the date the client last worked), a history of illness, all symptoms (in detail, separately for each ailment), the client's daily activities (or lack of activities, including questions about any assistance the client receives in performing these activities, and how the activities compare to the "old days"), and functional limitations (for example, sitting, standing, walking, lifting, carrying, concentrating). Also, the lawyer should prepare the direct examination of any witnesses who will be called, but be aware that ALJs may prefer to limit the hearing to one hour, so the examination should be brief without leaving out crucial information.

Prepare Cross-Examination

Cross-examination will only be necessary if the notice of hearing states that a medical or vocational expert will be present at the hearing. If an expert witness appears without notice having been provided, the objection must be stated on the record. In most cases, medical experts will never have met the client. They are probably not immunologists, infectious disease specialists, or HIV experts. In fact, they may not have any clinical experience with HIV. They may testify for SSA very frequently and in a majority of cases find claimants to be not disabled. All those facts should be brought out on cross-examination.

It is often very effective to construct a hypothetical question for a vocational expert by adding symptoms one at a time, after each one asking if someone with those symptoms would be able to work. Eventually the vocational expert will admit that the hypothetical individual is disabled. The attorney then points out that the hypothetical describes her client, as substantiated by the medical records. If the vocational expert never gives in on the hypothetical, he or she will lose credibility.

Prepare the Client

The hearing is an excellent opportunity for claimants to tell their story face to face. Many claimants will be hesitant to discuss their illness with a stranger or may be embarrassed about their degree of functional impairment. For some it may be important never to be negative about their condition. In response, it is necessary to emphasize that on this one day, for this one hour, it is crucial for claimants to express what they feel like at their worst. The client must understand that it is his worst day—not the best or even an average day—that keeps him from being able to work.

Post-Hearing

If the client receives a favorable decision, it might expedite the processing of benefits to mail a copy of the ALJ's decision to the local SSA office. Claimants who are awarded SSI will be notified to appear for an appointment to establish eligibility based on the nondisability requirements (income and resources). The claimant must not miss this meeting; it will delay payment and SSA may close the file despite the favorable ruling. The client should receive a notice of the amount of monthly benefits, as well as retroactive benefits.

A claimant who receives an unfavorable decision has 60 days to request an Appeals Council review of the decision. Again, the attorney should submit any new evidence she wishes to have considered by the Appeals Council with the request for review. Upon request, the Appeals Council will give the claimant and all other parties an opportunity to file briefs about the facts and law relevant to the case, usually not more than 30 days after the OHA forwards a tape of the proceedings and a copy of all the evidence.

Attorney's Fees

SSA permits attorneys to charge up to 25 percent of a claimant's retroactive SSI and SSDI benefits. The attorney who is handling the case on a pro bono basis must fill in the fee waiver portion of the appointment of representative form (SSA-1696) as well as the various appeal forms, and should also write a letter to the address on the notice, saying that the attorney does not intend to claim fees, remind the ALJ at the hearing, and even included this in the memo to the ALJ. Otherwise a portion of the client's retroactive SSDI award may be withheld for the attorney, which could slow down the overall processing of the client's benefits.

The attorney who is charging fees should execute a fee agreement with the client and attach a copy of it to the appointment of representative form when it is first submitted. At the hearing, the ALJ should issue an approval of the fee agreement, making sure that the client is not being charged above the 25 percent limit.

The method of payment depends on whether the client's claim is either SSI or SSDI, or both concurrently. SSI retroactive awards are paid to claimants in full by the local SSA office, and the client will then have to pay the attorney's fee. SSDI retroactive awards, on the other hand, are processed in Baltimore, where the attorney's fee is deducted and sent to the attorney, and the balance is sent to the client.

In the case of concurrent claims, the combined retroactive payment is paid out by the local office right away as if it were only an SSI claim (that is, without attorney's fees deducted). Baltimore subsequently processes the SSDI portion, essentially to properly allocate that payment between the SSI and SSDI funds. At that time, a check for 25 percent of the SSDI portion of the retroactive payment is deducted and issued to the attorney. If the attorney has already collected 25 percent directly from the client, and then receives this additional SSDI piece, it is known as "attorney fee windfall." In that instance, the attorney must turn that 25 percent over to the client, because under no circumstance may an attorney collect more than 25 percent of the total retroactive award, even if it is coming from two different sources.

Another complicating twist occurs when a claimant was receiving general assistance through the county of residence while awaiting an SSI ruling. In many jurisdictions, SSA directly reimburses the county welfare department for its outlay of general assistance funds, and then pays the balance to the client. In those jurisdictions, attorneys should be able to petition the county for 25 percent of that reimbursement.

An attorney may also charge the client for actual costs (this should be in the fee agreement) and may attempt to collect costs whether or not the claim is won.

§ 9.23   Working with Chemically Dependent Clients

Because SSI and SSDI claims can no longer be based substantially on drug and alcohol use, this evidence should not be included except perhaps as it functions as a causative agent of the client's physical or psychological condition. Caution is warranted, however. Even in the past when disability claims could be based on substance addiction, many evaluators did not like awarding benefits to addicts. If it is obvious from the medical records that the client uses drugs or alcohol, the lawyer should try also to include evidence of any treatment the client is undergoing, even if it is self-help or peer-supported, such as Alcoholics Anonymous. Evidence of the client's efforts may help mitigate the effects of Social Security's anti-addict bias.

If the client has a long history of addiction, it may prove difficult to assemble supportive statements. The client simply might not be liked. He or she may be so used to manipulating others to get drug money that everyone in his or her life (perhaps including the attorney) ultimately feels like they are being "worked." It is important in those instances for the lawyer to keep in mind that the client's behaviors are part of the addiction disorder, and that those behaviors, though not considered a valid basis of disability by SSA, and difficult as they may be to bear, are part of why the client cannot hold a job.

This does not mean that the attorney has no right to address the client's treatment of her. If for no other reason than the credibility of the evidence being developed, the attorney should not work with the client when she perceives the client is high. She may need to find out from the client or (with permission) from the client's social worker what is the best time of day to catch the client clear and relaxed and make appointments for that time of day. The client should also be involved in the process to the extent he or she is capable. For instance, the client may be able to do some of the footwork in getting third-party statements or records. It may be personally empowering to the client and may have the effect of cultivating greater cooperation.

If the attorney has qualms about arguing for benefits when the money may likely be used for drugs or alcohol, it is important to keep in mind that SSA may require the client to engage a representative payee to handle the client's money. The lawyer should help the client find a payee who can be trusted to use the money for clothes, shelter, and housing, and perhaps a community-based AIDS social service organization can act as representative payee.

Perhaps most important is that the attorney ought to take care of herself in these situations. The lawyer who feels anxious about the client or the relationship with the client must get support. A counselor or a legal support center can give the lawyer ideas about how best to handle the situation. The lawyer must be sure, however, not to breach the duty of confidentiality.

SOCIAL SECURITY POST-ENTITLEMENT ISSUES

§ 9.24   Overpayments

An SSI or SSDI recipient has the same appeal rights as those discussed earlier in this chapter (reconsideration, ALJ hearing, Appeals Council, federal court) with respect to any adverse action taken by SSA, such as suspension of benefits, reduction in amount, or assessment of overpayment. During a reconsideration of nondisability issues, conferences are available with the decision maker. Usually, if an appeal is undertaken within 10 days of a notice of an adverse action, the full benefit amount will continue to be paid while the appeal is pending.[64]

An assessment of overpayment occurs when SSA has reason to believe that an individual should not have been receiving benefits during a period when that person actually did receive them. If an overpayment is assessed, SSI or SSDI recipients not only have the right to appeal the action if they believe the assessment to have been incorrect, but they also have the right to request a *waiver of overpayment*.[65] An appeal of the assessment of overpayment must be filed within 60 days. A petition for waiver of overpayment, on the other hand, may be filed at any time during which SSA is withholding any portion of benefits in order to recover the overpayment. Filing a waiver petition may prevent SSA from reducing the benefit until the waiver issue has been decided.

Two factors must be shown before SSA will waive an overpayment. First, recipients must show that they were "without fault." This does not simply mean that the overpayment was SSA's mistake. Not returning a check that one reasonably knew one should not have received will lead to being found to be at fault. Second, the individual must show one of two things: either that recovery of the overpayment by SSA would defeat the purpose of the program (for instance, it would mean the person's inability to meet ordinary and necessary living expenses), or that recovery of the overpayment would be "against equity and good conscience" (for instance, if one relinquished a valuable right in reliance on a notice that one would be receiving a certain amount of benefit).

If the recipient does not contest the overpayment, or loses on appeal, SSA will recoup the overpayment by reducing the monthly benefit. The method of recoupment is different for SSDI and SSI. An SSDI overpayment will result in a complete withholding of the monthly benefit. If the individual is without fault and withholding would render the individual incapable of meeting ordinary and necessary living expenses, SSA may elect to withhold only a portion of the monthly benefit, but at least $10 per month.[66] If the overpayment is determined to be the result of any sort of fraud on the part of the recipient, no leniency is available. It is important to note that if one's SSDI is withheld to recoup an overpayment, it is still counted for SSI purposes. In other words, one cannot expect one's SSI to increase in order to make up for the reduction of SSDI.[67] An SSI overpayment is recovered by a monthly reduction of benefit equal to 10 percent of the individual's total monthly income (for example, SSI plus other

---

[64] 20 C.F.R. § 416.1336(b) sets forth the usual procedure regarding suspension of SSI benefits. For suspensions based on medical improvement, see **§ 9.26.**

[65] 20 C.F.R. §§ 404.506–404.512, 416.550–416.556.

[66] *Id.* § 404.502. If the SSDI recipient is also entitled to Medicare, instead of withholding the entire monthly benefit, SSA will reduce it to the amount of the monthly Medicare premium and will apply that amount directly to the premium, so Medicare coverage does not lapse.

[67] *Id.* § 416.1123(b)(1).

earned or unearned income), or the full SSI benefit, whichever is less.[68] As with SSDI, this limitation does not apply if SSA determines that the overpayment is a result of the individual's fraud.

§ 9.25 Representative Payee Problems

In certain cases, SSA may refuse to pay the claimant directly. SSA will demand the appointment of a *representative payee* for claimants who are not physically or mentally capable of managing their finances, for claimants who are minors, and for claimants who have a history of substance use.[69] In choosing a representative payee, SSA gives preference to qualified community-based organizations, governmental agencies, and relatives. The payee then receives the payments directly and is responsible for using them in the disabled individual's best interests.

Although SSA does a cursory investigation of the person nominated to be representative payee, many claimants find themselves dealing with a payee who turns out to be unscrupulous and uses benefit money for his or her own purposes. Individuals who have this experience should immediately contact SSA to have payments redirected and should request an investigation. If an advocate believes that SSA should never have approved a payee who does steal a client's benefits, the advocate should demand that SSA reimburse any missing funds to the client.

§ 9.26 Continuing Disability Review (CDR)

Recipients of disability benefits are reviewed periodically to determine if they are still disabled. The frequency of this review varies; for individuals whose condition is considered to be permanent, continuing disability review (CDR) occurs on a five- to seven-year cycle. However, if SSA learns of changes (for instance, that the recipient has returned to work or earnings have been reported to her wage record), a continuing disability review will be precipitated regardless of how much time has passed.[70]

If SSA rules that benefits should stop because of the claimant's medical improvement, the full benefit amount will continue to be paid pending the outcome of the appeal if the individual files for reconsideration or hearing within 10 days.[71]

---

[68] *Id.* § 416.571.

[69] 20 C.F.R. §§ 404.2010 (SSDI), 416.610 (SSI).

[70] 20 C.F.R. § 404.1590.

[71] *Id.* §§ 404.1597a(f), 416.996.

§ 9.27 Returning to Work

SSA has several programs designed to help disabled individuals who receive benefits reenter the work force. As medical advances in treating HIV illness continue to accelerate and the ranks of long-term survivors of HIV disease increase, it is important for advocates to be able to support their clients' wishes to be active, launch projects, and attempt to return to work. In order to do so, it is essential to have a working knowledge of work incentive programs.[72]

Trial Work

An incentive program that can be of great use to claimants who receive SSDI is called *trial work*.[73] Under this program, an SSDI recipient can work for up to nine months (not necessarily consecutively) and still receive a full monthly SSDI benefit. There is no upward cap on what the individual may earn each month from the work. However, monthly wages must be at least $200 in order for the activity to be considered trial work. For a self-employed person, any month in which one works at least 40 hours counts as a trial work month, regardless of that month's income.

After nine months of trial work, the SSDI recipient will be reevaluated for disability. If earnings exceeded $500 per month, the trial work will have constituted *substantial gainful activity* (see **§ 9.10**), and the individual will no longer be considered disabled. The SSDI monthly benefit will continue for an additional three-month grace period, and then it will stop. However, SSA provides a safety net after these benefits are stopped, by means of the *extended period of eligibility*.[74]

The extended period of eligibility is a consecutive 36-month period during which an individual's SSDI benefits will be reinstated for any month in which he or she does not work at the substantial gainful activity level ($500). The benefit will resume without a having to undertake a new application, disability determination, or waiting period.

An SSDI recipient who was entitled to Medicare can receive 39 months of free hospital and medical insurance after the trial work period, regardless of earnings or whether the individual is still considered disabled by SSA.[75] After the 39 months, one can elect to continue Medicare coverage by paying premiums. For an SSDI recipient who was not already Medicare-eligible, the Medicare clock will continue to tick during the extended period of eligibility, even

---

[72] For a simple overview of all the programs, see Social Security's free publication, Working While Disabled (SSA Pub. No. 05-10095).

[73] 20 C.F.R. § 404.1592.

[74] 20 C.F.R. § 404.1592a.

[75] 42 U.S.C. § 426(b).

though there have been no SSDI cash benefits. Once 29 months have elapsed since the onset of disability, Medicare entitlement will begin.

Earned Income Exclusion

The *earned income exclusion* is SSI's substitute for trial work. Under this program, earned income is counted at a highly discounted rate in evaluating financial need for SSI. This allows an individual to continue to be eligible for SSI (and consequently Medicaid) despite significant earnings.

The formula works as follows. In addition to allowing the usual $20 set-aside, SSA will subtract $65 from the wages earned as an earned income exclusion, and then divide the remainder in half in order to arrive at the individual's countable income. The individual's SSI benefit is the difference between the current benefit rate and the countable income. For example, María is an unmarried resident of the state of Fredonia who is disabled by HIV. She has started a small consulting business at home that earns her $550 every month. She will end up receiving a monthly SSI benefit of $371:

$550.00	earned income
− 20.00	set aside
530.00	
$530.00	
− 65.00	earned income exclusion
465.00	
$465.00	
− 232.50	one half of remainder
232.50	countable income
$625.00	state SSI level
− 232.50	countable income
$392.50	monthly SSI check, rounded up to $393

If you compare this example to that of Manny in § 9.3, María, whose $550 income comes exclusively from earnings, nets out much better than Manny, whose $550 income is exclusively SSDI. María brings in $942.50 per month, whereas Manny brings in only $645. If the individual receives both earned and unearned income, the $20 set-aside would apply to the unearned income. The earned income would be reduced by $65 and divided in half. These two components added together total the individual's countable income. Doing the formula backwards (that is, current SSI benefit level × 2 + $65 + $20), one can see that the break-even point in the state of Fredonia is \$1335. That means that if all of one's non-SSI income is from wages, one can earn up to \$1334 per month and still collect a cash SSI benefit of one dollar. Only at the break-even point would SSI benefits stop.

Extended Medicaid Eligibility

SSI recipients who begin to earn over the break-even amount and whose SSI cash benefits therefore stop may still retain a special SSI status for the exclusive purpose of categorical Medicaid eligibility.[76] This is sometimes referred to as *1619(b) extended Medicaid.*

In order to be initially eligible for extended Medicaid, one must be able to:

1. Continue to have a disabling impairment
2. Have been eligible to receive an SSI check at some point during the previous 12 months
3. Have used Medicaid within the last 12 months, or expect to use it within the next 12 months, or be unable to pay unexpected medical bills without Medicaid
4. Have annual income below that state's threshold amount[77]
5. Have unearned income less than the SSI limits and
6. Have resources within the SSI available resource limits.

Extended Medicaid is a Social Security program, not a Medicaid program, because it is merely a calculus to treat more individuals as SSI recipients for the purpose of categorical Medicaid eligibility. Processing would therefore be done by the SSA district office, not by Medicaid. In order to avoid potential loss of benefits, Social Security should be informed regarding the claimant's eligibility for extended Medicaid before earnings are reported.

Impairment-Related Work Expenses (IRWE)

If, because of one's disability, special equipment is necessary in order to work, the reasonable cost of those items may be deducted from earnings for both the

---

[76] 20 C.F.R. §§ 416.265–416.269; the SSA internal operations manual has significantly more detail on eligibility. *See* POMS, SI A02302.030.

[77] This sum is calculated on the basis of the state's break-even point and Medicaid costs per person. In 1993, for example, California's threshold was \$21,877, New York's was \$25,082. One can also create an individualized threshold higher than the state's general threshold, depending on what other expenses are involved in continuing to work.

purpose of determining if one is engaging in substantial gainful activity and for determining the amount of SSI benefit (as well as determining an individualized threshold for extended Medicaid, discussed above).[78]

The item need not be medical equipment; it could, for instance, be a computer if one can demonstrate that it is needed because of the impairment. The item can also be used for nonwork purposes, as long as it is also used for work purposes.

Plan for Achieving Self-Support (PASS)

An individual who is receiving disability benefits (either SSDI or SSI) can submit a plan to SSA, describing a strategy for achieving self-sufficiency.[79] A PASS plan may address education, vocational training, or starting a business. If the plan is approved by SSA, the individual can set aside some income each month, as well as some assets, in order to meet the plan's expenses. SSA will disregard those funds when determining countable income and available resources for the purpose of calculating SSI benefits. This will allow an SSI recipient to receive a larger SSI check, or an SSDI recipient to begin receiving SSI (and thus Medicaid).

Individuals who succeed in their plan to become self-sufficient may also be able to take advantage of the other work incentives, such as trial work or earned income exclusion. They also may be able to bridge into ongoing § 1619(b) extended Medicaid coverage by means of a PASS plan.

The following hypothetical case illustrates how a PASS plan can benefit a claimant. Susan is disabled by HIV and can no longer do her former work as a locksmith, because she can no longer respond to calls 24 hours a day. She receives an $800 monthly SSDI benefit and has no health insurance. Her only asset is a $3000 savings account. She has decided to try to become a graphic designer, because she could work at home and set her own hours. To do so, she will need a computer and will need to attend classes for six months.

Susan submits a PASS plan to SSA. In her PASS budget, she allocates $1000 of her savings to go toward purchase of the computer. She designates $100 per month to pay her tuition and $100 per month for the next year to go toward the purchase of software and a printer.

Under her PASS plan, Susan will begin to receive a $45.00 monthly SSI benefit, which will bring with it categorical eligibility for Medicaid. If Susan is able to make a go of her business, she will be able to use both the earned income exclusion and trial work programs to help support her in the early months.

Once Susan is out of the trial work period and her monthly SSDI check of $800 is discontinued, she may be eligible for extended Medicaid if her earnings

---

[78] 20 C.F.R. §§ 404.1576, 416.976. *See also* Social Security Ruling SSR 84-26.

[79] 20 C.F.R. §§ 416.1180–416.1182.

exceed the break-even point. This will allow her to bridge from disability back into the job market without the risk of being uninsured.

Susan's PASS Plan Budget		
Susan's Resources:		
	$3000.00	current savings
	−1000.00	set aside for computer purchase
	2000.00	"available resources"
Susan's Income (and SSI Benefit Calculation):		
	$800.00	SSDI monthly benefit
	− 20.00	offset
	780.00	
	$780.00	
	− 200.00	set aside for tuition and printer
	580.00	countable income
	$625.00	SSI benefit level (in Fredonia)
	− 580.00	countable income
	$ 45.00	monthly SSI check

VETERANS' DISABILITY AND HEALTH BENEFITS

§ 9.28   Who Is a Veteran?

Many people with HIV served in the military at some point and may be eligible for disability benefits from the Department of Veterans Affairs (VA). For purposes of disability benefits, a *veteran* is a person who served in the active military, naval, or air service and who was discharged under conditions other than dishonorable.[80] The discharges that qualify as "other than dishonorable" are honorable, general, and under honorable conditions. Discharges that are less than honorable may be upgraded by the military itself, or (the easier alternative) the veteran may request the VA to make a Character of Service Determination. The determination would be binding only on the VA, but that would be sufficient to meet this eligibility criterion.

---

[80] 38 U.S.C. § 101 (1994).

There are two basic entitlement programs for disabled veterans: service-connected compensation[81] and nonservice-connected pension.[82]

§ 9.29   Service-Connected Compensation

Monthly service-connected compensation payments are available for a disability incurred or aggravated in the line of duty in the active military, naval, or air service. The disabling condition does not need to be the result of an injury. A disability arising out of VA health care also qualifies. HIV infection through a transfusion in a VA hospital is a likely example. The amount of the benefit is calculated on a percentage basis to compensate the veteran to the degree of service-connected disability. The minimum disability to receive compensation is 10 percent. These benefits are tax-free and are available regardless of the veteran's financial status.

HIV infection and AIDS-related conditions may be service-connected, if there is evidence that the exposure occurred during military service. HIV-related symptoms need not have appeared during active service, as long as evidence indicates the exposure did.[83] The U.S. Court of Veterans Appeals has been asked, and has declined, however, to establish a specific presumption that an HIV-related disability arising within 15 years of separation from the military is necessarily service-connected.[84]

§ 9.30   Nonservice-Connected Pension

A nonservice-connected pension is the VA's equivalent to the SSI program. It is a monthly payment for veterans who are permanently and totally disabled, financially eligible, and who have served for at least 90 days of active duty, at least one of which occurred during wartime.[85] The disability does not have to be related to the military service. Financial eligibility involves both income and net worth limits. In evaluating income, the VA will deduct unreimbursed "unusual medical expenses," those which exceed 5 percent of the claimant's annual income.[86]

---

[81] *Id.* § 1110.

[82] *Id.* § 1521; 38 C.F.R. § 3.3 (1996).

[83] ZN v. Brown, 6 Vet. App. 183, 194 (1994).

[84] Kern v. Brown, 4 Vet. App. 350, 352 (1993).

[85] Qualifying wartimes currently include World War II, Korea, Vietnam, and the Gulf War. Veterans of the conflicts in Grenada and Panama would not be eligible for nonservice-connected pensions. 38 U.S.C. § 101; 38 C.F.R. § 3.3(a)(3) (1995).

[86] 38 C.F.R. §§ 3.262(1), 3.271. The 1996 monthly benefit level is $687 for a veteran with no dependents.

Veterans entitled to both service-connected compensation and nonservice-connected pension may receive only one. The VA will award whichever benefit is greater.

§ 9.31   Special Monthly Pension

Some additional benefits may be available to a veteran upon request.[87] The VA will grant them automatically if a veteran is rated 100 percent disabled. The benefits include *housebound benefits,* available to pension recipients who are permanently housebound, and *aid and attendance,* available to pension recipients who need regular assistance to perform the functions of everyday living. Aid and attendance benefits require a greater degree of disability than housebound benefits. The standard is met per se if the veteran is in a nursing home.

§ 9.32   Special Issue of HIV and Willful Misconduct

Disabilities arising during military service are presumed to be service-connected unless they arise out of a veteran's willful misconduct.[88] *Willful misconduct* has been held to be "an act involving . . . [a] known prohibited action."[89] The most common disabilities for which the VA denies service-connected compensation are drug/alcohol addiction and venereal disease. Substance addiction could be compensable if it is service-connected, for instance, if the veteran can prove it is the result of post-traumatic stress disorder.

Although HIV exposure during military service is generally not considered by the VA to be the result of willful misconduct, a concurring opinion in *ZN v. Brown*[90] suggests that it should be taken into consideration. The majority in that case remanded the service-connected disability claim to the Board of Veterans Appeals with instructions on how to weigh the medical evidence, but the concurring opinion argued that the means of HIV exposure also be considered on remand. In the view of that opinion, exposure stemming from same-sex sexual contact during military service must be considered to be the result of willful misconduct because "Congress has clearly stated that homosexual acts of sodomy are proscribed conduct within the military."[91] The opinion goes on to suggest that the VA make an inquiry into the mode of transmission by which the veteran became infected with HIV. Although this minority view is dictum, it may reflect a growing viewpoint.

---

[87] 38 U.S.C. § 1502.

[88] 38 U.S.C. § 105(a); 38 C.F.R. §§ 3.1(m), 3.301(a)–(b).

[89] Smith v. Derwinski, 2 Vet. App. 241, 243–44 (1992).

[90] 6 Vet. App. 183 (1994).

[91] *Id.* at 196.

§ 9.33 Relationship of VA Income to SSDI/SSI

SSDI benefits are not reduced on receipt of VA compensation. VA benefits are, however, considered income for SSI accounting purposes. These federal agencies share information; one should presume that information reported to Social Security is reported to the VA. Regardless, the veteran has an ongoing duty to report changes in income to the VA. Be careful to advise SSI recipients about the impact of VA income. Offsets can be confusing and may result in an overpayment to the recipient, which would have to be repaid.

§ 9.34 Procedure

For disability benefits, veterans apply to the Department of Veterans Affairs, Regional Office (1-800-827-1000). Because the VA benefits bureaucracy can be as difficult to negotiate as SSA's, it is advisable to speak first with a VA benefits counselor (some VA hospitals have specific HIV benefits counselors) or with a service organization, such as Disabled American Veterans or Swords to Plowshares. Because benefits vest as of the application date, it is important to apply as early as possible. There is no official expedited track for HIV disability evaluations, and no presumptive benefits are available. During the evaluation, it is useful to be in contact with the VA medical examiners. The ratings board that makes the ultimate determination, however, is not accessible to advocates.

An appeal of an adverse decision about income benefits must be made to the Regional Office. To appeal a denial of medical care, the claimant must get the denial in writing and appeal to the Director of Medical Services at the medical center where the benefits were denied (although one may wish to simultaneously file protective notice with the regional office).[92]

§ 9.35 Veterans' Health Care Programs

Some HIV-positive individuals may be eligible for health care through Department of Veterans Affairs (VA) hospitals and clinics.[93] The VA may not discriminate in the provision of health care on the basis of HIV status.[94] Hospital care must be provided (and nursing home care may be provided) by the VA to certain categories of veterans, including: (1) those who have a service-connected disability; (2) those who have a disability resulting from VA medical care; (3) those

---

[92] The sources of law useful in handling an appeal include: Title 38, United States Code; Title 38, Code of Federal Regulations; Veterans Appeals Reporter (West); VA General Counsel Opinions (available on Westlaw, databases FMIL-VA and FMIL-VAGC); and VA Adjudication Manual Procedure, M21-1 (available at VA regional offices through FOIA requests).

[93] 38 U.S.C. §§ 1710, 1712.

[94] 38 U.S.C. § 7333(a); 38 C.F.R. § 17.48.

who have a nonservice-connected disability who are unable to pay for care and who meet a limited income and assets test; (4) any other veterans, on a fee-for-service basis, if "resources and facilities are available" to that veteran.[95]

Outpatient care must be provided to certain categories of veterans, including those: (1) with service-connected disability (for treatment of that disability); (2) with service-connected condition rated at 50 percent or more, for treatment of any disability; (3) with disability resulting from VA care.[96] Service-connected and nonservice-connected here have the same meanings as they do in the disability program context, discussed in §§ **9.29** and **9.30.**

The VA may furnish outpatient care to certain other veterans on a limited basis. The VA may charge some of those veterans a fee for its services. Veterans with discharges under less than honorable conditions may receive VA care for any disability incurred or aggravated in the line of duty unless there is a statutory bar to benefits.[97] The VA will also reimburse for non-VA care in some emergency situations, if the veteran has a service-connected disability rating 50 percent or more.[98] To apply for medical benefits, veterans should contact a VA hospital, medical center, or outpatient clinic.

MEDICAID

§ 9.36 Program Structure and Legislative Changes

Medicaid is a federal program that acts as health insurer to some of the neediest Americans, including persons with HIV disease.[99] Already in 1990, 40 percent of adults with AIDS and 90 percent of children with AIDS were covered by Medicaid.[100] This crucial program is administered jointly by the federal government, through the Health Care Financing Administration (HCFA), and by each state, which selects its own agency to operate the program. The federal government sets minimum standards that states must meet in providing health care assistance through the Medicaid program. These standards relate to eligibility, scope of services, and procedural requirements. Some standards are required uniformly for all states; others are in the form of options among which states may choose. States may also provide, at their own expense, greater coverage than is

---

[95] 38 U.S.C. § 1710.

[96] *Id.* § 1712.

[97] 38 C.F.R. § 3.360.

[98] *Id.* §§ 17.50, 17.80.

[99] The program was established by Title XIX of the Social Security Act, 42 U.S.C. § 1396. For an overview of this program, see National Health Law Program, An Advocate's Guide to the Medicaid Program (rev. ed. 1993) (available from National Health Law Program, telephone: (310) 204-6010).

[100] J. Green & P. Arno, *The Medicaidization of AIDS,* 264 JAMA 1261 (1990).

required by any of the federal options. States may also request waivers from HCFA to permit them to establish pilot programs to explore other avenues for health care delivery. For instance, a waiver of the federal freedom of choice provision would permit states to require that all Medicaid recipients enroll in a managed care program through a health maintenance organization that the state program has contracted with. For all these reasons, the Medicaid program can look radically different from state to state.

Medicaid is a costly program, both for the federal government and for the states. For this reason, along with growing public sentiment against social programs that assist the poor, the Medicaid program is repeatedly under attack in a variety of ways. In the states, legislatures often attempt to move the state toward the least expensive options of care that federal Medicaid law permits them. States may also attempt to obtain federal waivers to allow them to experiment with more inexpensive ways of providing care, such as encouraging or requiring enrollment of Medicaid recipients in managed care systems.

On the federal level, Congress can always reduce appropriations to the program. The states have spearheaded legislative moves to eliminate the "amount, duration and scope" requirements of the Medicaid law, thus eliminating the minimal guarantees of what Medicaid care will look like from state to state. There have also been movements to "block grant" the Medicaid program to the states, again allowing the states far greater discretion to run the program as they see fit, possibly reducing or eliminating certain types of coverage.

The Personal Responsibility and Work Opportunity Reconciliation Act of 1996,[101] though severely limiting eligibility for other federal means-tested benefits, left the Medicaid machinery relatively intact. The new law leaves discretion to the states to decide whether to continue providing Medicaid benefits to "qualified immigrants."[102] Noncitizens whose entitlement to SSI has been severed may remain eligible for Medicaid if they qualify independently under their state's Medicaid rules, both in terms of immigration status and income and asset restrictions.

§ 9.37   General Eligibility Standards

Individuals will only be eligible for Medicaid if they meet all five of the following criteria: linkage, income, resources, residency, and immigration status.

Linkage

In order to receive Medicaid, the beneficiary must be linked in some way to the program, either through participation in other designated programs or by meeting a certain profile. The most common linkage is a *categorical linkage*. In other

---

[101] Pub. L. No. 104-193, Title I, § 114, 1996 U.S.C.C.A.N. (110 Stat.) 2105, 2177–80.

[102] *Id.* § 402(b), 1996 U.S.C.C.A.N. 2105, 2264–65.

words, one's eligibility for another public benefits program creates automatic eligibility for Medicaid. Disabled individuals are categorically eligible for Medicaid in the vast majority of states if they receive SSI. In most of those states, an SSI award automatically triggers the Medicaid machinery, and the beneficiary simply receives a Medicaid card in the mail. In a handful of states, the SSI beneficiary is instead required to take the SSI award letter to the welfare office that administers Medicaid. In states that consider SSI to be a categorical link to Medicaid coverage, the state must provide coverage to individuals receiving "presumptive" SSI benefits (see **§ 9.3**) or who are receiving conditional SSI pending disposal of excess resources.[103]

Currently, 12 states, known as 209(b) states, have opted to create more stringent standards of disability or more restrictive financial eligibility criteria than those of the SSI program.[104] In those states, SSI eligibility does *not* create categorical Medicaid eligibility. Instead, an SSI recipient must independently apply for Medicaid and meet that state's disability and financial standards in order to qualify. In counting income to establish financial eligibility, 209(b) states are required to deduct certain amounts, including SSI payments received and medical expenses incurred.[105]

Among the others who are categorically eligible for Medicaid in all states are families who would have been eligible to receive Aid to Families with Dependent Children (AFDC) on July 16, 1996.[106] Families who are eligible for Temporary Assistance to Needy Families (TANF) are not categorically entitled to Medicaid as they would have been under the predecessor AFDC program.

Under the federal poverty level (FPL) programs, pregnant women and children under 12 may categorically qualify for Medicaid if they fall within various levels of the federal poverty guidelines. Pregnant women (and up to 60 days post-partum) are eligible for Medicaid for pregnancy-related care if their household income is under 200 percent of the federal poverty level (a pregnant woman counts as two in calculating financial eligibility). In addition, children under one year of age are eligible for Medicaid for medically necessary care if their family income is under 200 percent of the FPL. Medicaid's resource restrictions are waived for participants under the 200 percent program. Children aged one to six are eligible for FPL Medicaid if their family income is within 133 percent of the federal poverty level. Children through age 11 are eligible for Medicaid if their family income is within the federal poverty level itself. There is no monthly spend-down requirement under the 100 and 133 percent FPL programs, although the Medicaid resource restrictions do apply.

---

[103] 42 C.F.R. § 435.120.

[104] 42 U.S.C. § 1396a(f). The program was created by Pub. L. No. 92-603, § 209(b), 86 Stat. 1329, 1972 U.S.C.C.A.N. 1548, 1613, hence the name. The current 209(b) states are: Connecticut, Hawaii, Illinois, Indiana, Minnesota, Missouri, New Hampshire, North Carolina, North Dakota, Ohio, Oklahoma, and Virginia.

[105] 42 C.F.R. § 435.121(b).

[106] Pub. L. No. 104-193, § 114, 1996 U.S.C.C.A.N. (110 Stat.) 2105, 2177–80.

States have the option of providing categorical coverage for other groups, including individuals who would be eligible for AFDC or SSI, except for certain characteristics that disqualify them from receiving benefits through those programs, for instance people who would be eligible for SSI except that they are institutionalized and thus ineligible for a cash benefit. Also, states may offer categorical connection to Medicaid for individuals who have enough other income so that they do not receive federal SSI, but only the state SSP portion, as described in § 9.3.

States have the option and 209(b) states are required to provide Medicaid coverage to the *medically needy*. These are individuals who would be eligible for SSI or AFDC but for the fact that their incomes are too high, in other words, individuals or families that look like categorically linked people (including limited resources) except for their incomes. Many individuals with HIV qualify for Medicaid through the medically needy program: they have a disability (based on the Social Security standard of disability) and fall within Medicaid's resource limitations, but their income (usually SSDI) exceeds the SSI limit.

Typically, states set a monthly income amount above which the Medicaid beneficiary is required to contribute to his or her own health care. In California, for instance, this *medically needy income level* is $600 for an individual, and beneficiaries' monthly countable income above that amount are considered a deductible which Medicaid will not pay.

In all states with medically needy programs, individuals have the option to "spend down" each month, by incurring sufficiently high debts on medical expenses (see § 9.38).

States have the option of creating additional categories of linkage to permit financially eligible individuals access to health care. There is no federal contribution toward care for these individuals. Instead, the state will bear the cost of care. Only a few states have created a *medically indigent* category, such as California, which considers all financially eligible pregnant women to be medically indigent and thus eligible for health services under the Medicaid program.

Income and Resources

For individuals who are categorically linked to the Medicaid program through SSI or AFDC, Medicaid does not do an independent counting of income, but rather it relies on the individual's ongoing eligibility for the other program to ensure financial eligibility for Medicaid. For medically needy Medicaid recipients, however, any countable income above their state's established *maintenance need* ($600 in California, for instance) does not disqualify the individual, but instead constitutes a *share of cost*. A share of cost acts as a monthly deductible (see § 9.38).

Medicaid beneficiaries whose eligibility is linked to SSI entitlement can begin to earn income at a level that would disqualify them for SSI, but they can still continue to be eligible for Medicaid, through what is called the 1619(b) program (see § 9.27).

Although individuals can have income in excess of SSI levels and still qualify for Medicaid as medically needy, having available resources above the levels permitted is cause for disqualification from the Medicaid program. A Medicaid beneficiary's "available" resources must be under $2000 for an unmarried individual or $3000 for a household of two (husband and wife or parent and child). The limit increases to $3150 for a family of three; $3300 for four; $3450 for five; and $3600 for six or more.

Not all of an individual's material resources are considered to be available for Medicaid purposes. The *exempt resources* not counted by Medicaid include a home (as long as the Medicaid recipient lives in it or, if currently in a long-term care facility, states an intention to return to it), a car of any value, clothing, household goods, musical instruments, work tools, wedding rings, or heirlooms. Medicaid also does not consider burial funds, burial trusts or contracts up to $1500 in value, or burial trusts of any value if they are irrevocable. Funds held in certain trusts, known as *special needs trusts,* may also be exempt (see § **9.44**).

Residence

States may limit Medicaid coverage only to residents of that state. Federal regulations, however, define residence rather broadly. Non-institutionalized adults are considered residents of the state in which they live and intend to stay permanently or indefinitely.[107] Children are generally residents of the state in which their caretaker relative or legal guardian lives.[108]

Immigration Status

Noncitizens may be eligible for some or all Medicaid services, depending on their immigration status and the rules set out by the state. Note, however, that regardless of immigration status, all other elements of eligibility (linkage, income, and resources) must be met. States must, at the very least, provide undocumented immigrants and others who do not fall into a full-scope Medicaid category with treatment for emergencies (presuming, again, that they are otherwise eligible).[109]

§ 9.38   Spend-Down or Share of Cost

A medically needy Medicaid recipient is responsible for spending down to the *medically needy income level* (MNIL) in order for Medicaid to begin paying.

---

[107] 42 C.F.R. § 435.403(i)(1), (4).

[108] *Id.* § 435.403(h)(2), (3), and (4)(i)–(iii).

[109] 42 U.S.C. § 1396b(v)(2).

States may choose the length of the spend-down period, which may range from one month to six months. In California, for example, the spend-down period is one month, and the MNIL is $600 per month for an unmarried individual. In that state, a Medicaid recipient with countable monthly income of $700 must demonstrate $100 of medical debt each month before the state will assume the costs of health care for that month. This amount is known as the individual's *share of cost.* By federal law, the debt only needs to be incurred, not necessarily paid, in order to count towards the spend-down.[110] Old bills that are still due may be used toward the spend-down. Also, the bills may be for medical services not covered by the Medicaid program. Private health insurance premiums also count toward the spend-down.

In some states, individuals may satisfy the spend-down by making partial or whole payments directly to the state Medicaid program.[111] In no state are individuals obligated to meet the spend-down requirement in this manner.

§ 9.39   General Coverage and Scope of Services

Medicaid requires that states pay for certain medically necessary care. For categorically eligible individuals, this includes inpatient hospital services, outpatient hospital services, lab and x-ray services, nursing facility services, family planning services and supplies, physician services, services furnished by a nurse-midwife, and home health services.[112] If a state plan offers care to medically needy individuals, the care must include at least prenatal care, ambulatory services for some individuals, and home health services to individuals entitled to skilled nursing facility services.[113] States have the option under the Medicaid program to pay for additional services, such as dental services, physical therapy, prescription drugs, hospice care, some psychiatric care, case management services, and alcohol and drug treatment.[114] The individual state's Medicaid office should be contacted to determine what specific HIV-related procedures and prescriptions are covered.

Medicaid generally does not pay for experimental treatments. Some states, such as California, cover "investigational" treatments that meet certain criteria (that is, conventional therapy is inadequate, the provider has a record of safety and success, and the treatment is likely to succeed).[115] California's Medi-Cal also

---

[110] 42 U.S.C. § 1396a(a)(17)(D).

[111] 42 U.S.C.A. §§ 1369b(f)(2)(B), 1396a(a)(17) (West Supp. 1996).

[112] 42 C.F.R. § 440.210 (enumerating types of care states must provide to categorically eligible individuals).

[113] *Id.* § 440.220.

[114] The terms of each of these as well as the mandatory coverages are defined in 42 C.F.R. § 440.1.

[115] Cal. Welf. & Inst. Code § 14137.8.

covers medications classified by the FDA or DHS as investigational new drugs.[116] The federal government does not pay towards transplant-related procedures (including bone marrow transplants) unless the state has strict written standards in place regarding when such care is covered. It may require a legal challenge in order to get an experimental treatment covered, in which a claimant must demonstrate that the treatment reflects the community standard of care.[117]

At the very least, Medicaid should pay for off-label uses of FDA-approved drugs, if the off-label use reflects the community standard of care. In one landmark case, *Weaver v. Reagen,*[118] a class of persons with AIDS brought suit against their state's Medicaid program for limiting the availability of AZT to only those whose symptoms matched those described in the drug's FDA label. The court held that once a state undertakes to provide prescription drugs to Medicaid recipients, it may not do so in an inconsistent or arbitrary manner. In fact, if a treatment constitutes the generally accepted practice of the medical community, Medicaid must provide the drug. "The Medicaid statute and regulatory scheme create a presumption in favor of the medical judgment of the attending physician in determining the medical necessity of the treatment."[119] It is unclear how this principle will be applied as Medicaid becomes increasingly linked to managed care systems under which physicians may experience pressure to limit services.

§ 9.40   —Retroactivity

Federal law requires states to provide three months of retroactive Medicaid coverage.[120] That is, medical expenses incurred by an applicant within three months prior to the application must be covered by Medicaid upon request, if the individual would have been eligible for Medicaid at the time the expenses were incurred. Medicaid must receive the request for retroactive coverage within one year of the application. Bills too old for Medicaid coverage can always be used to satisfy the applicant's share of cost, as long as they are still due.

---

[116] *Id.* § 14137.6.

[117] *See* Irwin E. Keller, *Getting Your Insurer to Cover New HIV Treatments: A Crash Course,* AIDS Treatment News, Jan. 5, 1996 (newsl.). This article explores arguments demonstrating that a treatment is not experimental and should therefore be covered. These arguments can be used in the context of public health coverage as well. Back issues of AIDS Treatment News are available via the Internet at http:\\www.immunet.org\atn. Current issues can be accessed at http:\\www.aidsnews.org.

[118] 886 F.2d 194 (8th Cir. 1989).

[119] *Id.* at 200; 42 C.F.R. §§ 440.230(b), 440.240(b).

[120] 42 U.S.C. § 1396a(a)(34) (1994); 42 C.F.R. § 435.914(a).

§ 9.41 —Medicaid Payment of Health Insurance Premiums

Medicaid requires states to enroll Medicaid beneficiaries in a group health plan, including COBRA continuation coverage, if the individual is eligible for participation in the plan and the result would be "cost-effective."[121] The state is required to pay any premiums, deductibles, and co-payments. This works out to be a savings for the state, because the bulk of the beneficiary's health care will be paid for by a private carrier. These programs (often called HIPP, health insurance premium payment) are also advantageous for HIV-positive beneficiaries, who would be able to continue the same private care they may have been receiving prior to Medicaid eligibility.

§ 9.42 Claim Processing and Fair Hearing Rights

Any adverse decision made by Medicaid may be appealed within a reasonable period of time, not to exceed 90 days.[122] The appeal will result in a hearing before an ALJ, whose decision must, in turn, issue within 90 days of the request for the hearing.[123] If the hearing request is made prior to the adverse action, the individual has a right to "aid paid pending." In other words, if an individual receives notice that Medicaid intends to discontinue payment for a particular treatment, and the individual files for a fair hearing before payment is discontinued, Medicaid is obligated to continue paying for the treatment until a decision is made through the hearing.[124]

§ 9.43 Transfer of Assets Penalties

Medicaid penalizes individuals for transferring away nonexempt assets for less than their fair market in order to become Medicaid-eligible. The penalty consists of a period of ineligibility for Medicaid reimbursement for certain types of long-term care. The period of disqualification is equal to the uncompensated value of property transferred divided by the state Medicaid program's monthly cost for an individual's care in a nursing home.[125] So, for instance, if an individual gives away $15,000 in cash, and the state's cost for nursing home care is $3,000 per month, that individual is ineligible for Medicaid payment for long-term care for five months, beginning the month after the transfer. Multiple transfers

---

[121] 42 U.S.C. § 1396e.

[122] 42 C.F.R. § 431.221.

[123] *Id.* § 431.246.

[124] *Id.* §§ 431.205, 431.232, 431.233.

[125] 42 U.S.C.A. § 1396p(c)(1)(E) (West Supp. 1996).

create consecutive periods of ineligibility. The act of refusing to accept income or resources that one is entitled to receive may also be treated as a disqualifying transfer.[126]

Medicaid will do this calculation upon an individual's entry into long-term care. At that time, Medicaid looks back 36 months to find transfers of assets for less than fair market value and 60 months to find uncompensated transfers out of trusts.[127]

Transfers will not be penalized if they were made to a legal spouse for the spouse's sole benefit, or to a child under 21, or to a blind or disabled child of any age.[128] Also, there is no penalty if a satisfactory showing can be made that the individual intended to transfer the asset for fair market value (for instance, in exchange for personal care services),[129] or that the transfer was made exclusively for a purpose other than qualifying for Medicaid.[130] This last exception removes the penalty from all transfers of a primary residence, because the individual would not have needed to relinquish ownership of the home in order to qualify for Medicaid.

The penalty does not affect basic Medicaid coverage. It does, however, affect care received in long-term care nursing facilities, as well as nursing home level care received in any facility.[131] It also affects services provided under general home- and community-based waivers. States may also opt to have penalties apply to some services needed by noninstitutionalized individuals, including mandatory home health care. In reality, it is unclear at this point the degree to which these penalties are being applied to any sort of care other than in-patient nursing home care. Additionally, under anti-fraud provisions included in the Health Insurance Portability and Accountability Act of 1996,[132] the knowing and intentional disposal, including a transfer to a trust, that results in a period of ineligibility, may subject the transferor to criminal penalties.

§ 9.44   —Treatment of Trusts

Trusts in which an individual retains some discretion over the use of funds, or which are revocable, are considered available resources for Medicaid purposes.[133] When a portion of the funds in a trust is reachable by the individual, that amount is also considered available.

---

[126] *Id.* § 1396p(e)(1).

[127] *Id.* § 1396p(c)(1)(B).

[128] *Id.* § 1396p(c)(2)(B).

[129] *Id.* § 1396p(c)(2)(C)(i).

[130] *Id.* § 1396p(c)(2)(C)(ii).

[131] 42 U.S.C.A. § 1396p(c)(1)(C)(i).

[132] Title II, § 217, 1996 U.S.C.C.A.N. (110 Stat.) 1936, 2008–09, *amending* 42 U.S.C. § 1320a-7b(a). This provision's effective date was Jan. 1, 1997. Pub. L. No. 104-191, § 218.

[133] 42 U.S.C.A. § 1396p(d)(3).

Payments out of an irrevocable trust made directly to the Medicaid beneficiary for the beneficiary's own benefit are considered income for Medicaid purposes, even if the trust corpus is not considered available. Payments made to any other party for a purpose other than the benefit of the Medicaid beneficiary are considered transfers of assets that may trigger penalties.[134] If the trust is irrevocable and funds in it may not be used for the benefit of the individual, then the establishment of the trust itself is considered a transfer of assets that may trigger penalties.[135]

The funds in an irrevocable *special needs trust* set up for a disabled individual under age 65, funded by parents or by a court (for example, funds from a judgment or settlement), are not considered an asset as long as the trust provides that when the individual dies, any balance in the trust will be used to reimburse the state for Medicaid benefits paid on the individual's behalf.[136]

§ 9.45   —Liens and Claims

The state maintains the right to claim against a Medicaid beneficiary's property upon death if it paid for long-term care or for any care after the beneficiary was age 55.[137] Under federal law, estate recovery can even include reaching joint tenancy property.[138]

MEDICARE

§ 9.46   Eligibility

Medicare is a health insurance program sponsored by the Social Security Administration. It is available to seniors, as well as to younger adults if they are disabled and have been receiving SSDI benefits for two years. Unlike seni rs, there is no way for younger adults to purchase Medicare if they are not entitled through SSDI.

§ 9.47   Coverage

Medicare is made up of two parts: hospitalization (Part A) and medical (Part B). Entitlement to Part A is automatic after 24 months of SSDI. The SSDI beneficiary

---

[134] *Id.* § 1396p(d)(3)(A)(ii)–(iii), (B)(i).

[135] *Id.* § 1396p(d)(3)(B)(ii).

[136] *Id.* § 1396p(d)(4)(A).

[137] 42 U.S.C.A. § 1396p(b)(1)(B).

[138] *Id.* § 1396p(b)(4)(B).

cannot opt out of Part A coverage, which is free. Part B, however, is optional. If the individual decides to accept Part B, the individual must pay a small monthly premium. In 1996, for example, the premium was $41.40 per month. The premium can be automatically deducted from the SSDI benefit. If an individual is entitled to Medicaid as well, Medicaid will pay the Medicare Part B premium. If an individual receives both Medicaid and Medicare, Medicare will be the primary health insurance, and Medicaid will pay deductibles, co-payments, the Medicare Part B premium, and most expenses excluded by Medicare, such as outpatient drugs.

Medicare's coverage is much more limited than Medicaid's. Medicare pays only 80 percent of approved costs for medically necessary treatment. The beneficiary must pay the remaining 20 percent, unless the health care provider takes Medicare assignment. Medicare Part A covers the costs of inpatient treatment, including hospital care, skilled nursing facilities, home health care, and hospice care. Part B covers physician's services, durable medical equipment and supplies, psychiatric social services, chiropractic care, and ambulance service.

Neither Medicare Part A nor Part B covers outpatient pharmaceuticals. For people with HIV, this is Medicare's greatest limitation. If an individual has Medicaid as well, Medicaid will pay for drugs. Otherwise, a Medicare recipient must seek out other programs such as a state AIDS Drug Assistance Program, or private Medicare Supplemental Insurance, which is not usually available on the market to younger adults but only as "conversion" policies from certain group or individual health insurance plans.

OTHER PUBLIC HEALTH CARE PROGRAMS

§ 9.48   HIV-Specific Programs

Numerous states have some programs to assist individuals with HIV to access medical care. Those programs are usually funded through Title II of the federal Ryan White CARE Act.[139]

The most common CARE Act-funded health care programs are the AIDS Drug Assistance Programs. These programs offer some prescription drugs free of charge or on a sliding scale for people with HIV who have no other drug coverage. There are usually financial eligibility requirements for these programs, although they tend to be more generous than Medicaid eligibility.

Some states, for instance California, have health insurance premium payment (HIPP) programs, modeled on the counterpart Medicaid program but again having less stringent financial eligibility requirements. The purpose of these programs is to maximize the money that can be used in the AIDS Drug Assistance Program by keeping individuals with HIV privately insured.

---

[139] 42 U.S.C. §§ 300ff-22(a)(4), 300ff-26 (1994). The Ryan White CARE Act is also discussed in **Ch. 2.**

Titles I and II of the CARE Act fund other programs to serve the needs of HIV positive individuals. These programs include test sites, primary medical care, medical case management, psychosocial support, and advocacy. In some instances these services are offered directly by the county or the state; in other instances they are provided by community-based organizations under contract with the public entity.

REFERENCE MATERIALS

§ 9.49   Stand-Alone Disabling HIV Conditions for Adults

This section is reprinted from 20 C.F.R. part 404, subpart P, appendix 1, Listing 14.08 (1996).

BACTERIAL INFECTIONS

1. **Mycobacterial infection** (e.g., caused by M. avium-intracellulare, M. kansasii, or M. tuberculosis) at a site other than the lungs, skin, or cervical or hilar lymph nodes

2. **Pulmonary tuberculosis** resistant to treatment

3. **Nocardiosis**

4. **Salmonella bacteremia,** recurrent non-typhoid

5. **Syphillis or neurosyphillis** (e.g., meningovascular syphillis) resulting in neurologic or other sequelae

6. **Multiple or recurrent bacterial infection**(s), including pelvic inflammatory disease, requiring hospitalization or intravenous antibiotic treatment 3 or more times in 1 year

FUNGAL INFECTIONS

7. **Aspergillosis**

8. **Candidiasis,** at a site other than the skin, urinary tract, intestinal tract, or oral or vulvovaginal mucous membranes; or candidiasis involving the esophagus, trachea, bronchi, or lungs

9. **Coccidioidomycosis,** at a site other than the lungs or lymph nodes

10. **Cryptococcosis,** at a site other than the lungs (e.g., cryptococcal meningitis)

11.   **Histoplasmosis,** at a site other than the lungs or lymph nodes

12.   **Mucormycosis**

PROTOZOAN OR HELMINTHIC INFECTIONS

13.   **Cryptosporidiosis, isosporiasis, or microsporidiosis,** with diarrhea lasting for 1 month or longer

14.   **Pneumocystis carinii pneumonia or extrapulmonary pneumocystis carinii infection**

15.   **Strongyloidiasis,** extra-intestinal

16.   **Toxoplasmosis** of an organ other than the liver, spleen, or lymph nodes

VIRAL INFECTIONS

17.   **Cytomegalovirus disease,** at a site other than the liver, spleen, or lymph nodes

18.   **Herpes simplex virus** causing mucocutaneous infection (e.g., oral, genital, perianal) lasting for 1 month or longer; or infection at a site other than the skin or mucous membranes (e.g., bronchitis, pneumonitis, esophagitis, or encephalitis); or disseminated infection

19.   **Herpes zoster,** disseminated or with multidermatomal eruptions that are resistant to treatment

20.   **Progressive multifocal leukoencephalopathy**

21.   **Hepatitis,** resulting in chronic liver disease manifested by appropriate findings (e.g., persistent ascites, bleeding esophagal varices, hepatic encephalopathy)

MALIGNANT NEOPLASMS

22.   **Carcinoma of the cervix,** invasive, FIGO stage II and beyond

23.   **Kaposi's sarcoma,** with extensive oral lesions; or involvement of the gastro-intestinal tract, lungs, or other visceral organs; or involvement of the skin or mucous membranes with extensive fungating or ulcerating lesions not responding to treatment

24.   **Lymphoma** of any type (e.g., primary lymphoma of the brain, Burkitt's lymphoma, immunoblastic sarcoma, other non-Hodgkins lymphoma, Hodgkins disease)

25.   **Squamous cell carcinoma of the anus**

SKIN OR MUCOUS MEMBRANES

26. **Conditions of the skin or mucous membranes,** with extensive fungating or ulcerating lesions not responding to treatment (e.g., dermatological conditions such as eczema or psoriasis, vulvovaginal or other mucosal candida, condyloma caused by human papillomavirus, genital ulcerative disease)

HEMATOLOGIC ABNORMALITIES

27. **Anemia** (hematocrit persisting at 30 percent or less), requiring one or more blood transfusions on an average of at least once every 2 months

28. **Granulocytopenia,** with absolute neutrophil counts repeatedly below 1,000 cells/mm3 and documented recurrent systemic bacterial infections occurring at least 3 times in the last 5 months

29. **Thrombocytopenia,** with platelet counts repeatedly below 40,000/mm3; with at least one spontaneous hemorrhage, requiring transfusion in the last 5 months; or intracranial bleeding in the last 12 months

NEUROLOGICAL ABNORMALITIES

30. **HIV encephalopathy,** characterized by cognitive or motor dysfunction that limits function and progresses.

31. **Other neurological manifestations of HIV infection** (e.g., peripheral neuropathy), with significant and persistent disorganization of motor function in 2 extremities resulting in sustained disturbance of gross and dexterous movements, or gait and station

HIV WASTING SYNDROME

32. **HIV wasting syndrome,** characterized by involuntary weight loss of 10 percent or more of baseline (or other significant involuntary weight loss) and, in the absence of a concurrent illness that could explain the findings, involving: chronic diarrhea with 2 or more loose stools daily lasting for 1 month or longer; or chronic weakness and documented fever greater than 38° C (100.4° F) for the majority of 1 month or longer

DIARRHEA

33. **Diarrhea,** lasting for 1 month or longer, resistant to treatment, and requiring intravenous hydration, intravenous alimentation, or tube feeding

CARDIOMYOPATHY

34. **Cardiomyopathy** (chronic heart failure, or cor pulmonale, or other severe cardiac abnormality not responsive to treatment)

NEPHROPATHY

35. **Nephropathy,** resulting in chronic renal failure.

INFECTIONS RESISTANT TO TREATMENT OR REQUIRING HOSPITALIZATION OR INTRAVENOUS TREATMENT 3 OR MORE TIMES IN 1 YEAR

36. **Sepsis**

37. **Meningitis**

38. **Pneumonia** (non-PCP)

39. **Septic Arthritis**

40. **Endocarditis**

41. **Sinusitis,** radiographically documented

§ 9.50   Stand-Alone Disabling HIV Conditions for Children

This section is reprinted from 20 C.F.R. part 404, subpart P, appendix 1, Listing 114.08 (1996).

BACTERIAL INFECTIONS

1. **Mycobacterial infection** (e.g., caused by M. avium-intracellulare, M. kansasii, or M. tuberculosis) at a site other than the lungs, skin, or cervical or hilar lymph nodes

2. **Pulmonary tuberculosis** resistant to treatment

3. **Nocardiosis**

4. **Salmonella bacteremia,** recurrent non-typhoid

5. **Syphillis or neurosyphillis** (e.g., meningovascular syphillis) resulting in neurologic or other sequelae

6. In a child less than 13 years of age, **multiple or recurrent bacterial infection(s)** of the following types: sepsis, pneumonia, meningitis, bone or joint infection, or abscess of an internal organ or body cavity (excluding otitis media or superficial skin or mucosal abscesses) occurring 2 or more times in 2 years

7. **Multiple or recurrent bacterial infection(s)** including pelvic inflammatory disease, requiring hospitalization or intravenous antibiotic treatment 3 or more times in 1 year.

FUNGAL INFECTIONS

8. **Aspergillosis**

9. **Candidiasis,** at a site other than the skin, urinary tract, intestinal tract, or oral or vulvovaginal mucous membranes; or candidiasis involving the esophagus, trachea, bronchi, or lungs

10. **Coccidioidomycosis,** at a site other than the lungs or lymph nodes

11. **Cryptococcosis,** at a site other than the lungs (e.g., cryptococcal meningitis)

12. **Histoplasmosis,** at a site other than the lungs or lymph nodes

13. **Mucormycosis**

PROTOZOAN OR HELMINTHIC INFECTIONS

14. **Cryptosporidiosis, isosporiasis, or microsporidiosis,** with diarrhea lasting for 1 month or longer

15. **Pneumocystis carinii pneumonia or extrapulmonary pneumocystis carinii infection**

16. **Strongyloidiasis,** extra-intestinal

17. **Toxoplasmosis** of an organ other than the liver, spleen, or lymph nodes

VIRAL INFECTIONS

18. **Cytomegalovirus disease,** at a site other than the liver, spleen, or lymph nodes

19. **Herpes simplex virus** causing mucocutaneous infection (e.g., oral, genital, perianal) lasting for 1 month or longer; or infection at a site other than the skin or mucous membranes (e.g., bronchitis, pneumonitis, esophagitis, or encephalitis); or disseminated infection

20. **Herpes zoster,** disseminated or with multidermatomal eruptions that are resistant to treatment

21. **Progressive multifocal leukoencephalopathy**

22. **Hepatitis,** resulting in chronic liver disease manifested by appropriate findings (e.g., intractable ascites, esophagal varices, hepatic encephalopathy)

MALIGNANT NEOPLASMS

23. **Carcinoma of the cervix,** invasive, FIGO stage II and beyond.

24. **Kaposi's sarcoma,** with extensive oral lesions; or involvement of the gastro-intestinal tract, lungs, or other visceral organs; or involvement of the skin or mucous membranes with extensive fungating or ulcerating lesions not responding to treatment

25. **Lymphoma** of any type (e.g., primary lymphoma of the brain, Burkitt's lymphoma, immunoblastic sarcoma, other non-Hodgkins lymphoma, Hodgkins disease)

26. **Squamous cell carcinoma of the anus**

SKIN OR MUCOUS MEMBRANES

27. **Conditions of the skin or mucous membranes,** with extensive fungating or ulcerating lesions not responding to treatment (e.g., dermatological conditions such as eczema or psoriasis, vulvovaginal or other mucosal candida, condyloma caused by human papillomavirus, genital ulcerative disease)

HEMATOLOGIC ABNORMALITIES

28. **Anemia** (hematocrit persisting at 30 percent or less), requiring one or more blood transfusions on an average of at least once every 2 months

29. **Granulocytopenia,** with absolute neutrophil counts repeatedly below 1,000 cells/mm3 and documented recurrent systemic bacterial infections occurring at least 3 times in the last 5 months

30. **Thrombocytopenia,** with platelet counts of 40,000/mm3 or less despite prescribed therapy, or recurrent upon withdrawal of treatment; or platelet counts repeatedly below 40,000/mm3 with at least one spontaneous hemorrhage, requiring transfusion in the last 5 months; or intracranial bleeding in the last 12 months

NEUROLOGICAL MANIFESTATIONS OF HIV INFECTION (e.g., HIV ENCEPHALOPATHY, PERIPHERAL NEUROPATHY) RESULTING IN:

31. **Loss of previously acquired, or marked delay in achieving, developmental milestones or intellectual ability** (including the sudden acquisition of a new learning disability)

32. **Impaired brain growth** (acquired microcephaly or brain atrophy)

33. **Progressive motor dysfunction** affecting gait and station or fine and gross motor skills

GROWTH DISTURBANCE WITH:

34. **Involuntary weight loss (or failure to gain weight at an appropriate rate for age) resulting in a fall of 15 percentiles** from established growth curve (on standard growth charts) that persists for 2 months or longer

35. **Involuntary weight loss (or failure to gain weight at an appropriate rate for age) resulting in a fall to below the third percentile** from established growth curve (on standard growth charts) that persists for 2 months or longer

36. **Involuntary weight loss greater than 10 percent of baseline** that persists for 2 months or longer

37. **Growth impairment,** with a fall of greater than 15 percentiles in height which is sustained; or fall to, or persistence of, height below the third percentile

DIARRHEA

38. **Diarrhea,** lasting for 1 month or longer, resistant to treatment, and requiring intravenous hydration, intravenous alimentation, or tube feeding

CARDIOMYOPATHY

39. **Cardiomyopathy** (chronic heart failure; or other severe cardiac abnormality not responsive to treatment)

PULMONARY CONDITIONS

40. **Lymphoid interstitial pneumonia/pulmonary lymphoid hyperplasia** (LIP/PLH complex), with respiratory symptoms that significantly interfere with age-appropriate activities, and that cannot be controlled by prescribed treatment

NEPHROPATHY

41. **Nephropathy,** resulting in chronic renal failure

INFECTIONS RESISTANT TO TREATMENT OR REQUIRING HOSPITALIZATION OR INTRAVENOUS TREATMENT 3 OR MORE TIMES IN 1 YEAR

42. **Sepsis**

43. **Meningitis**

44. **Pneumonia** (non-PCP)

45. **Septic arthritis**

46. **Endocarditis**

47. **Sinusitis,** radiographically documented

§ 9.51   Other Manifestations of HIV Infection for Children

This section is reprinted from 20 C.F.R. part 404, subpart P, appendix 1, Listing 114.08 ¶ 0 (1996).

A child claimant will meet the Listings upon a showing of:

a. Any manifestation(s) of HIV infection; and any of the following functional limitation(s), based on the child's age group:

b. <u>Birth to Attainment of Age 1</u>—any of the following:

    1. **Cognitive/communicative functioning** generally acquired by children no more than one-half the child's chronological age (e.g., in infants 0-6 months, markedly diminished variation in the production or imitation of sounds and severe feeding abnormality, such as problems with sucking, swallowing, or chewing); or

    2. **Motor development** generally acquired by children no more than one-half the child's chronological age; or

    3. **Apathy, over-excitability, or fearfulness,** demonstrated by an absent or grossly excessive response to visual stimulation, auditory stimulation, or tactile stimulation; or

    4. **Failure to sustain social interaction** on an ongoing, reciprocal basis as evidenced by inability by 6 months to participate in vocal, visual, and motoric exchanges (including facial expressions); or failure by 9 months to communicate basic emotional responses, such as cuddling or exhibiting protest or anger; or failure to attend to the caregiver's voice or face or to explore an inanimate object for a period of time appropriate to the infant's age; or

    5. **Attainment of development or function** generally acquired by children no more than two-thirds of the child's chronological age in two or more areas (i.e., cognitive/communicative, motor, and social).

c. <u>Age 1 to Attainment of Age 3</u>—any of the following:

    1. **Gross or fine motor development** at a level generally acquired by children no more than one-half the child's chronological age; or

2. **Cognitive/communicative function** at a level generally acquired by children no more than one-half the child's chronological age; or

3. **Social function** at a level generally acquired by children no more than one-half the child's chronological age; or

4. **Attainment of development or function** generally acquired by children no more than two-thirds of the child's chronological age in two or more areas covered by 1, 2 or 3.

d. Age 3 to Attainment of Age 18—limitation in at least two of the following areas:

1. Marked impairment in age-appropriate **Cognitive/communicative function** (considering historical and other information from parents or other individuals who have knowledge of the child, when such information is needed and available); or

2. Marked impairment in age-appropriate **Social functioning** (considering information from parents or other individuals who have knowledge of the child, when such information is needed and available); or

3. Marked impairment in **Personal/behavioral function** as evidenced by marked restriction of age-appropriate activities of daily living (considering information from parents or other individuals who have knowledge of the child, when such information is needed and available); or persistent serious maladaptive behaviors destructive to self, others, animals, or property, requiring protective intervention; or

4. **Deficiencies of concentration, persistence, or pace** resulting in frequent failure to complete tasks in a timely manner.

§ 9.52 List of Social Security Forms

Listed here are some of the relevant SSA forms. They may be ordered in bulk; single copies are available from local SSA offices. This list does not include forms, such as daily activity questionnaires, that may be used by state agency disability evaluators. Advocates should check locally to obtain copies.

SSA-1696:	Appointment of Representative
SSA-7004:	Request for Earnings and Benefits Estimate Statement
SSA-827:	Authorization to Release Information to the Social Security Administration
SSA-4814-F5:	Medical Report on Adult with Allegation of HIV Infection
SSA-4815-F6:	Medical Report on Child with Allegation of HIV Infection

SSA-3368:	Disability Report
SSA-3369:	Vocational Report
SSA-821:	Work Activity Report - Employee
SSA-2506-BK:	Psychiatric Review Technique
SSA-561:	Request for Reconsideration
SSA-3441:	Reconsideration Disability Report
SSA-795:	Statement of Claimant or Other Person
HA-501:	Request for Hearing by ALJ
HA-4486:	Claimant's Statement When Request for Hearing is Filed and the Issue of Disability
HA-520:	Request for Review of Hearing Decision/Order

CHAPTER 10

GLOBAL ASPECTS OF AIDS

Mark E. Wojcik*

§ 10.1   Introduction

As of 1996, an estimated 30.6 million people have been infected with HIV.[1] HIV affects every region of the world. Consequently, the social and legal problems posed by AIDS, and the possible solutions to those problems, must consider the successes and failures of various responses to AIDS around the world. Public

---

* The author thanks David Austin of the Working Committee of the European Council of AIDS Service Organizations, Susan Timberlake of UNAIDS, Fernando Chang-Muy, former Legal Advisor to the United Nations High Commissioner on Refugees, Justice Michael Kirby of the High Court of Australia, Professor R.K. Nayak of the Indian Law Institute, and David W. Webber for their contributions to this chapter and to the continuing struggle to protect human rights. I also thank Deans R. Gilbert Johnston and Susan Brody of The John Marshall Law School for their continued support of research in the field of international law and AIDS.

[1] Global AIDS Policy Coalition, AIDS in the World II: Global Dimensions, Social Roots, and Responses 11 (Jonathan M. Mann & Daniel J.M. Tarantola eds., 1996) [hereinafter Mann & Tarantola].

health policy and law must learn from others and avoid ineffective or counter-productive responses.

The overwhelming scope of issues to be discussed on a global level can be understood if one considers that the social, legal, and policy issues arising in the United States have also arisen in many other countries. HIV affects issues of discrimination, criminal law and prison administration, civil liability, public health, employment and workers' benefits, family law, immigration and travel, insurance and government programs, privacy, and many other issues. Although "AIDS" is a relatively recent development, the literature, legislation, and practice on AIDS nationally and internationally is overwhelming. Many readers may feel that this chapter does not adequately address certain issues of importance on a global level. It is intended to give only an introduction to some of the international legal issues posed by the AIDS pandemic and to the potential role that law (and, more particularly, international human rights law) may play in developing effective responses to AIDS.[2]

§ 10.2   Extent of the Pandemic

By the year 2000, the global number of men, women, and children infected with HIV may reach 40 million.[3] Although the incidence of AIDS may seem to be decreasing in some industrialized nations, the World Health Organization reports an increased incidence of AIDS and HIV infection in developing countries, particularly in sub-Saharan Africa, Asia, Latin America, and the Caribbean.[4] The World Health Organization estimated that 80 percent of AIDS cases and 90 percent of new HIV infections can be localized within developing countries.[5]

The majority of new HIV infections are attributed to heterosexual transmission. Approximately 70 percent of all global HIV infections are estimated to be spread heterosexually.[6] By the end of the century, more than 80 percent of all HIV infections may be attributed to heterosexual intercourse.[7] Even among injecting drug users, heterosexual transmission is on the rise: many drug users, aware of the AIDS-related risks regarding the sharing of syringes, have altered their drug injecting practices but still seem recalcitrant to adopting consistent condom use.

---

[2] There are several useful guides for those seeking additional introductory material on international aspects of AIDS. *See, e.g.,* Global AIDS Policy Coalition, AIDS in the World (Jonathan M. Mann et al. eds., 1992). Those seeking more specific information on particular issues may wish to contact UNAIDS at 20 avenue Appia, CH-1211 Geneva 27, Switzerland. Tel: (+4122) 791.3666; fax: (+4122) 791.4187; e-mail: UNAIDS@WHO.CH; web page: www.unaids.org.

[3] *AIDS Pandemic Focus Shifts to Third World,* AIDS Pol'y & L., Feb. 20, 1992, at 7.

[4] *WHO Says Worldwide AIDS Cases Now Total More Than 1.5 Million,* AIDS Pol'y & L., May 15, 1991, at 6.

[5] *AIDS Pandemic Focus Shifts to Third World,* AIDS Pol'y & L., Feb. 20, 1992, at 7.

[6] *Third World Heterosexual Epidemic Has Many Implications,* AIDS Pol'y & L., Jan. 8, 1993, at 5.

[7] *WHO Says Worldwide AIDS Cases Now Total More Than 1.5 Million,* AIDS Pol'y & L., May 15, 1991, at 6.

One consequence of heterosexual transmission is an increasing number of children affected by the pandemic. By the end of the century in Central and East Africa alone, nearly 5.5 million children under the age of 15 will lose their mothers or both parents to AIDS.[8] By the year 2000, it is estimated that up to 10 million children under the age of 10 will have lost their mothers or both parents to AIDS.[9] The immense global impact of AIDS on individuals, families, and communities simply cannot be measured.[10] Also staggering are the increases in the number of children who are born infected with HIV. The World Health Organization estimates that as of mid-1995, over 1.5 million children had been infected with HIV, and that by the year 2000 this number could exceed 5 to 10 million infants.[11]

Frequently, infants born with HIV are held up to the light as a means of reflecting on the distinctions between "innocent" and "guilty" parties in the pandemic. Of course, such distinctions are misleading, yet their continued presence in discourse around AIDS reflects an additional burden that people with HIV and AIDS must bear: namely, they are seen as being in some way culpable of their condition. Generally, fault is attributed to the practices or behaviors in which people participate; those who are infected are perceived to be people who have "brought it on themselves." This underlying intolerance is paradoxically increasing as information on transmission routes has been included within a myriad of prevention projects. There seems to be a recurring tendency to attribute blame to those who, knowing how HIV can be avoided, have nonetheless exposed themselves to the virus.

In many regions of the world, this mentality has invested gay men and drug users in particular. Homosexuality may be viewed as an inherently immoral choice and drug addiction as a bad habit easily interrupted. AIDS activists have worked to expose the myths and denials that underlie these prejudices. If one looks at parallel messages played out in the global context, disturbing realities rise to the surface.

As the statistics show, HIV and AIDS impact on heterosexuals to a much larger degree than they do gay men.[12] However, this does not by any means further an understanding that AIDS can affect anyone. In analyzing the global data, it emerges that this infection has spread alarmingly among the dispossessed,

---

[8] *Report Encourages Charities to Extend Hand to AIDS Orphans,* AIDS Pol'y & L., June 12, 1991, at 4; *see also Africa Certain to Be Hardest Hit by AIDS Pandemic,* AIDS Pol'y & L., Jan. 9, 1992, at 8.

[9] *See, e.g., HIV/AIDS and Children,* Canadian HIV/AIDS Pol'y & L. Newsl. (Canadian HIV/AIDS Legal Network, Montreal, Quebec, Can.), Apr. 1996, at 18.

[10] *See, e.g.,* Sheldon Shaeffer, *AIDS in the World: The Impact on Infants, Children, and Youth,* Canadian HIV/AIDS Pol'y & L. Newsl. (Canadian HIV/AIDS Legal Network, Montreal, Quebec, Can.), Apr. 1996, at 18.

[11] *See, e.g., HIV/AIDS and Children,* 2 Canadian HIV/AIDS Pol'y & L. Newsl. (Canadian HIV/AIDS Legal Network, Montreal, Quebec, Can.), Apr. 1996, at 18.

[12] Women who have sex with women are perceived to be in the lowest risk category of all, although they are also at risk for HIV infection. This issue requires further study. *See* Anke A. Ehrhardt, *Sexual Behavior Among Heterosexuals, in* Mann & Tarantola at 259.

however one chooses to define them. AIDS is disproportionately a disease of those at greatest risk of discrimination: women, homosexuals, drug users, the poor, the homeless, refugees, immigrants, sex workers, people of color, the young, and generally people living in developing nations. Wherever there are difficulties in determining one's destiny, it can be argued that possible exposure to HIV is increased.

The argument that health is interconnected with the enjoyment of human rights is one that has gained increasing visibility with the advent of AIDS. This argument stems not from the incredible experience of discrimination which individuals with HIV have faced throughout the epidemic, but from a recognition that discriminatory social policies marginalize entire communities and affect access to health care, education, and other necessities.

Economic inequality has led to the inability of entire nations to achieve the health status that is currently enjoyed in industrialized countries. In many countries and cultures, inequality in gender makes it impossible for women to be the ultimate arbiters of their sexual choices. Inequality in the social recognition of diverse sexual orientations has resulted in more obstacles to stability within same-sex partnerships and promoted conditions for promiscuity. Inequality in political power has made it difficult for the young to ensure the inclusion of AIDS prevention and sexuality in school curriculum.

True prevention is, therefore, not merely a matter of providing information, but of empowering people to practice behavior change. It is only of limited use to foster an awareness of the right to recourse for individuals discriminated against because of their serostatus when a more fundamental awareness as to the reasons why certain populations are more exposed is not addressed. On a purely practical level, this discourse of empowerment is ultimately necessary inasmuch as it bring to bear on the power of people to pursue vindication for the violation of their rights. If one has routinely been discriminated against in almost all aspects of one's existence (the situation of women in some societies again comes to mind), then it becomes questionable whether one can envision the effectiveness of pursuing redress from the plank of an AIDS platform.

This interdependence between preexisting respect for human rights and the rights of those whose health has been impaired by HIV is but one aspect of a larger interconnectedness that AIDS has highlighted in more than one way. Elizabeth Reid, director of the HIV and Development Programme at the United Nations Development Programme in New York, argues that "within this ethic of interdependence, of concern and participation, there is a proper place for the language of rights and responsibilities and of justice."[13] She identifies five essential areas of global interdependence around AIDS:

1. The interdependence between men and women, with an implication that laws that permit wife inheritance, property snatching after the husband's death, infibulation, incest, female infanticide, rape in marriage and elsewhere, and dowry among others, must be changed

---

[13] Elizabeth Reid, HIV & AIDS: The Global-Interconnection 6 (1995).

2.   The interdependence between the affected and the not yet directly affected, with an implication that people with HIV represent national resources capable of empowering individuals to effect successful behavior change (and the recognition that national laws which discriminate against those with HIV further propel the pandemic)

3.   The interdependence between this generation and the next, not only in terms of avoiding infection for those to come, but also promoting among the young a culture of caring and caretaking for the multitudes of those who are or will be ill

4.   The interdependence between communities and government, with the recognition that initial responses to the issues raised by AIDS have come from affected communities and that it is government's responsibility to create an enabling environment in which such responses can be sustained

5.   The interdependence between and among nations.[14]

This last interdependence may seem the most obvious inasmuch as it once again raises issues of economic disparity and unequal access to health care. It will be imperative to address the bottom-line question of whether states and individuals have any way of obtaining redress for societal situations that promote an international epidemic.

§ 10.3   Responses to the AIDS Pandemic

AIDS presented the world with its first true *pandemic,* a global epidemic.[15] Virtually every country in the world has had first-hand experience with HIV and the myriad issues attending it.[16] Officials in the few remaining countries that may still report that they have had no cases of AIDS will admit privately that they either know of past or current cases of AIDS in their countries or that they realize the serious and imminent risks that their countries face.[17]

---

[14] *Id.* at 6–10.

[15] *See, e.g., Pandemic Predicted to Worsen as Public Interest in AIDS Drops,* AIDS Pol'y & L., Nov. 14, 1991, at 5.

[16] The global reach of HIV was recognized within a few years after the virus itself was discovered. Already in 1987, the United Nations General Assembly expressed its deep concern that AIDS "has assumed pandemic proportions affecting *all regions of the world* and represents a health threat to the attainment of health for all." G.A. Res. 42/8, 42 U.N. GAOR Supp. (No. 49) at 12, U.N. Doc. A42/49 (Oct. 26, 1987) (emphasis added), *reprinted in* Michael L. Closen et al., AIDS: Cases and Materials 922 (1989).

[17] The Pacific island nation of Palau, for example, failed to report any cases of AIDS even though at least one person died of the disease there. The rationale for saying that Palau was "AIDS free" was that the individual contracted HIV in the United States before moving to the Republic of Palau. The example is used not to isolate the nation of Palau but to point out a common problem that many nations have experienced in determining how to count the number of AIDS cases they may have.

Many readers will be familiar with the personal and collective losses engendered by the AIDS epidemic in their own countries. It is difficult to grasp the implications of the collective global experience of AIDS. Attempts to quantify the losses cannot reflect the true human struggles and tragedies reflected by each individual. AIDS highlights preexisting weaknesses in many national health care systems that struggle not only with effective responses to HIV, but also with an international resurgence of diseases such as cholera, polio, malaria, and multi-drug resistant tuberculosis.[18] The plight of many developing countries is especially acute: the exorbitant costs of adequate treatment for AIDS-related illnesses are simply not sustainable in economies in which the average annual per-capita expenditure for health amounts to little more than a couple of dollars. Thus, although it is known that a pregnant mother with HIV might benefit from taking AZT, a mother in Africa will wonder where she can find this drug and how she can afford to pay for it. The expenses of protease inhibitors are completely beyond her means as well, even if those drugs were available to her.

The collective global experience of AIDS goes beyond recognition of individual and societal loss, however. Throughout the world, local, national, and international bodies have had to consider appropriate religious, political, social, cultural, educational, medical, and legal responses to the pandemic. Although the public health issues posed by this pandemic are often identical, many countries and cultures have responded to the pandemic in vastly different ways and with dramatically different results. Each nation thus has the opportunity to share successful strategies so that others may adapt and apply successful measures and avoid mistakes already made by others. Seldom before has the world seen such a need for the free exchange of information, resources, and ideas to curb the further spread of AIDS and to treat with dignity and respect those affected by the virus.

Although some countries responded to AIDS with compassion and respect for those who were infected or who were at risk of infection, other countries responded with hostility, distrust, and irrational fear. Often, national and local debates centered on efforts to identify particular individuals responsible for spreading HIV (such as the "patient zero" theory)[19] or to identify classes of (often foreign) individuals who would be easy political targets for blame, exclusion, or isolation.[20] Consequently, an array of disempowered persons including immigrants, foreign visitors, sex workers, and prisoners became subject to various proposals for testing, identification, exclusion, and isolation. Countries debated schemes of mandatory testing and isolation of persons who tested positive for antibodies to HIV; at least 18 countries adopted laws that would allow

[18] *See, e.g.,* Allyn Taylor, *Making the World Health Organization Work: A Legal Framework for Universal Access to the Conditions for Health,* 18 Am. J.L. & Med. 301 (1992).

[19] *See, e.g.,* Randy Shilts, And The Band Played On 165 (1987); Michael L. Closen & Mark E. Wojcik, *Freedom in Eastern Europe and the Spread of HIV/AIDS,* 1 Touro J. Transnat'l L. 307, 308 (1990); *see also* David Robinson, *Criminal Sanctions and Quarantine, in* AIDS and the Law 243, 247 (2d ed. 1992).

[20] *See, e.g.,* Richard & Rosalind Chirimuuta, AIDS, Africa and Racism (London 1989); Michael Pollak, Les Homosexuels et le SIDA: Sociologie d'une Épidémie (Paris 1988).

them to isolate persons with AIDS and at least 21 countries identified particular sections of their populations for compulsory screening.[21]

Persons with HIV were isolated for short periods of time in countries including India[22] and Sweden.[23] The most extensive attempt to quarantine all persons with HIV, however, was adopted in Cuba in 1986, which tested all persons in the country and placed persons with HIV in special "sidatorios"[24] throughout the country where they were to remain for life, with some exceptions later made for supervised release, unsupervised released, and in some cases return to their homes after showing that they were "socially responsible" and would not spread AIDS.[25] Attempts to isolate persons with HIV were counterproductive in many respects. Many Cubans, for example, believed that because the government "locked up" persons with HIV, there was no need to engage in safer sex outside the sanatorium; anyone who was a danger would have already been removed from society. The same erroneous belief was found in many countries that banned persons with HIV from entering their countries for extended periods of time. It was mistakenly thought that the virus could be excluded at the border, when all realities were to the opposite.[26]

Nations have been unable to protect themselves by attempting to exclude persons with HIV from entering their countries. Discriminatory measures, including quarantine, mandatory testing, and restrictive policies dealing with travel and the freedom of movement, do not stop the spread of AIDS but rather drive it underground where it is much more difficult to combat.[27] Some countries have concluded that attempts to exclude persons with HIV are ultimately unworkable and ineffective from a public health perspective. Thailand, for example, had previously prohibited the entry of foreigners with AIDS.[28] That prohibition was

---

[21] Panos Inst., The Third Epidemic: Repercussions of the Fear of AIDS 125 (1990).

[22] In early 1989, the Indian state of Goa isolated the first HIV positive Goan, Dominic D'Souza, who was isolated under armed police guard in a former tuberculosis sanatorium. Panos Inst., The Third Epidemic: Repercussions of the Fear of AIDS 101 (1990). He was later released.

[23] A man in Sweden was isolated after he told his doctor that he would not use condoms with his girlfriend, and a prostitute had been isolated a number of times although she said she always used condoms when having sex. *Id.* at 103.

[24] "SIDA" is the Spanish word for AIDS. A "sidatorio" is a special sanatorium only for persons with HIV.

[25] *See, e.g.,* Mark E. Wojcik, *Inside Cuba's Sidatorios, in* AIDS Law and Policy 548 (Arthur S. Leonard ed., 2d ed. 1995) [hereinafter AIDS Law and Policy].

[26] *See, e.g.,* Michael L. Closen & Mark E. Wojcik, *International Health Law, International Travel Restrictions, and the Human Rights of Persons with AIDS and HIV,* 1 Touro J. Transnat'l L. 285 (1990).

[27] G.A. Res. 46/203, A/46/727 (1991), *reprinted in* AIDS Law and Policy 522 (Arthur S. Leonard ed., 2d ed. 1995).

[28] The Thai government adopted the prohibition in Ministerial Regulation No. 11 of Aug. 26, 1986. *See* Michael L. Closen & Mark E. Wojcik, *Living with HIV and Without Discrimination, in* American Bar Ass'n Section of Int'l Law & Practice, International Law & AIDS: International Response, Current Issues, and Future Directions 151, 156–57 (Lawrence Gostin & Lane Porter eds., 1992).

revoked in 1991 when the Thai Cabinet affirmed that excluding foreigners with HIV could not effectively curb the spread of the virus and that most HIV-infected foreigners in Thailand appeared to have contracted HIV from Thai citizens.[29] Other nations, however, including the United States, continue to use discriminatory measures and sometimes even invoke purely economic considerations as justifications to exclude persons on the basis of their HIV status.[30] Unfortunately, world opinion seems to have little effect on changing these exclusionary laws.[31]

§ 10.4 Denominators of Successful Programs

Two common denominators of successful AIDS prevention and treatment programs throughout the world have been: (1) the free exchange of information on public health strategies and scientific developments; and (2) respect for the human rights of persons affected by HIV and those perceived to be at greater risk of infection.[32]

First, by freely exchanging information on successful strategies and effective public health interventions, there can be effective educational programs that attempt to reduce the further spread of the virus. Unfortunately, a variety of factors may impede the process of education in many parts of the world, including other pressing problems of development, war, and lack of material resources.

---

[29] *Id.* at 157; AIDS Pol'y & L., Dec. 12, 1991, at 4.

[30] Although exclusion on the basis of HIV seropositive status is unwarranted as a public health measure, many have argued that there are economic justifications for excluding persons with HIV from the United States. These arguments assume (usually without foundation) that persons with HIV will be unable to work and will ultimately require public financial assistance for their health care. These arguments show that there is no reason to exclude short-term travelers (such as tourists, students, business travelers, or intra-company transferees) on the basis of their HIV status, but the exclusions against them continue because they, as a group, are politically powerless in most every nation. **Ch. 11** discusses U.S. immigration laws related to HIV; *see also* Ignatius Bau et al., *HIV Antibody Testing of Immigrants and International Travelers, in* AIDS: The Legal Issues 118 (AIDS Legal Council of Chicago, 1994). For a comparative analysis of similar issues, see Wesley Gryk, *AIDS and Immigration, in* AIDS: A Guide to the Law 79 (Richard Haigh & Dai Harris eds., 2d ed. 1995) (British law); John Godwin et al., Australian HIV/AIDS Legal Guide 341–58 (2d ed. 1993) (Australian law).

[31] *See, e.g., World AIDS Official 'Deeply Disappointed' About U.S. Decision on HIV Exclusion,* AIDS Pol'y & L., June 12, 1991, at 1.

[32] *See, e.g., Pandemic Predicted to Worsen as Public Interest in AIDS Drops,* AIDS Pol'y & L., Nov. 14, 1991, at 5. Dr. Jonathan Mann, former head of the World Health Organization's Global Program on AIDS, urged AIDS/HIV campaigns to be carried out with four basic principles in mind: (1) protection of individual rights, because there is a strong link between human rights and health care; (2) sexual equality, in that male dominance can be a health hazard to women; (3) wide diffusion of advances in medical science, including preventive treatments; and (4) wider public comprehension that AIDS/HIV is the first truly global pandemic.

Additionally, there are a number of social, economic, cultural, religious,[33] legal, political, and other factors that may impede effective use of knowledge imparted by public health education, including problems of access to preventive treatments, issues of denial and regression, fear of discrimination and harassment, problems of empowerment of many vulnerable population groups (including women), and the existence of laws that may impede dissemination of public health information if that information includes sexually explicit material[34] or information that might be viewed as promoting homosexuality[35] or condoning often illicit activities, such as the use of intravenous drugs and commercial sex work.

Other major factors may also impede the free exchange of information across borders, including underreporting of the extent of infection in a particular country, or international disputes between scientists claiming credit for the same work.

As to underreporting, some countries have feared that they would suffer if the true extent of HIV infection in their countries was known. Countries dependent on tourist dollars might see declining numbers of tourists when there are increasing numbers of reported cases of AIDS. This might be particularly the case for countries that profit from sexual tourism industries. Foreign investment might also be affected by research indicating negative trends regarding productivity; many countries will show declines in their GNP because of the illness or death of an AIDS-affected work force. Other nations fear the stigma associated with being blamed for initiating the epidemic. African countries have borne the brunt of such blame and, in rejecting it, have fashioned a response that sees the pandemic as an attempted African genocide promoted by Western countries. Similarly, Haiti blamed the United States for bringing AIDS to Haiti and the United States blamed Haiti for bringing AIDS to the United States. Issues of blame and

---

[33] *See, e.g., Indonesia: Islamic Scholars Call for Condom Restrictions,* HIV/AIDS Legal Link (Austl. Fed'n of AIDS Orgs. Legal Project, N.S.W., Austl.), Sept. 1995, at 28.

[34] In the United States, laws that might impede the dissemination of public health information about AIDS might include the Communications Decency Act, discussed in **Ch. 2.** *See also* Brown v. Hot, Sexy, & Safer Prods., 68 F.3d 525 (1st Cir. 1995) (dismissing claim that a high school safer-sex program should be banned because it violated moral beliefs of students and their parents), *cert. denied,* 116 S. Ct. 1044 (1996); Curtis v. School Comm., 652 N.E.2d 580 (Mass. 1995) (dismissing suit that challenged the distribution of condoms in public schools without prior parental consent), *cert. denied,* 116 S. Ct. 753 (1996).

[35] *See, e.g., Gingrich Vows to Hold Hearing to Block Use of Gay Themes in AIDS Programs,* AIDS Pol'y & L., Feb. 10, 1995, at 1. Although the content of safer sex materials used in programs in the United States might be seen as only a domestic U.S. issue, materials developed in the United States are frequently used in other countries directly or as models for similar materials. Consequently, restrictions on the content of materials can reduce their effectiveness when they are not available to populations perceived to be at higher risk of infection. *See also* Gay Lesbian Bisexual Alliance v. Sessions, 917 F. Supp. 1548 (M.D. Ala. 1996) (striking state restrictions against gay student group, noting that the restrictions could affect discussions on prevention of HIV); *Judge Voids State Law Banning Gay Student Groups From Campus,* AIDS Pol'y & L., Feb. 23, 1996, at 9.

denial have lead to a failure to report accurate statistics, and the failure to report accurate statistics, in turn, has often fostered a false sense of security, complacency, and denial. In particular, one must remark on the short-sightedness of those nations that have the economic resources necessary to maintain regular epidemiological data through anonymous or confidential screening and counselling yet choose not to promote primary or secondary prevention efforts.[36]

As to international disputes between scientists, it must be noted that disputes are an exception to the scientific norm of cooperation and free exchange of information. In a famous exception to that norm, however, scientists in the United States vied with scientists in France for credit as the discoverer of HIV-1. Dr. Robert C. Gallo, of the U.S. National Institutes of Health (NIH), claimed to be the first discoverer of virus in April 1984, when he announced that the probable cause of AIDS was HTLV-III (Human T-Cell Lymphotropic Virus Type III).[37] Dr. Luc Montagnier, of the Pasteur Institute in Paris, sued Gallo and claimed that Gallo's discovery of HTLV-III was based on a viral specimen of LAV (Lymphadenopathy-Associated Virus) that the Pasteur Institute provided to Gallo at his request. Media attention on Montagnier's lawsuit against Gallo showed a failure in international scientific cooperation, which activists and other commentators linked to monetary awards from royalties for antibody testing or to competition for a possible nomination for a Nobel Prize.[38]

---

[36] For further discussion of this issue of underreporting, see Michael L. Closen & Mark E. Wojcik, *Living With HIV and Without Discrimination, in* American Bar Ass'n Section of Int'l Law & Practice, International Law & AIDS: International Response, Current Issues, and Future Directions 151, 160–62 (Lawrence Gostin & Lane Porter eds., 1992).

[37] Margaret Heckler, then Secretary of the U.S. Department of Health and Human Services, stated at a press conference that Dr. Gallo's "discovery" of the virus was "another miracle" to be added "to the long honor roll of American medicine and science." Dennis Altman, AIDS in the Mind of America 51 (1986) (quoting *N.Y. Times* report). The controversial nature of this announcement has been the subject of numerous commentaries. *See, e.g.,* Mirko D. Grmek, History of AIDS 70 (1990); Sandra Panem, The AIDS Bureaucracy 25–26 (1988); Randy Shilts, And the Band Played On: Politics, People, and the AIDS Epidemic 450–51 (Penguin 1988).

[38] The United States Court of Claims initially dismissed Montagnier's lawsuit for lack of jurisdiction after finding that the Pasteur Institute had not complied with the claim presentation requirements of the Contract Disputes Act, 41 U.S.C. §§ 601–613 (1988). Institut Pasteur v. United States, 10 Cl. Ct. 304 (1986), *rev'd,* 814 F.2d 624 (Fed. Cir. 1987). The claims by the Pasteur Institute for breach of contract and unjust enrichment were based on allegations that Dr. Gallo's virus was actually the sample supplied to him by Dr. Montagnier. Dr. Montagnier had actually announced discovery of the virus and sought patent protection for an antibody test six months before Dr. Gallo announced his discovery. On appeal, the U.S. Court of Appeals for the Federal Circuit reversed the Court of Claims and found that the claim was not covered by the Contract Disputes Act. Institut Pasteur v. United States, 814 F.2d 624 (Fed. Cir. 1987). The court held that Dr. Montagnier had given Gallo a specimen as a "transfer of research materials among scientists engaged in a collaborative research effort" rather than as a bid for the U.S. government to procure goods or services under the Contract Disputes Act. *Id.* at 628. The Federal Circuit remanded the dispute to the Court of Claims, and the United States and the Pasteur Institute settled their dispute a short time later by an agreement that gave equal credit (and equal royalties from blood tests for antibodies to the

The dispute between the United States and France was especially unfortunate because it diverted valuable attention from research of treatments for AIDS, a fact not lost on AIDS activists and others affected by the disease. It was also a severe departure from the principle of successful intervention programs that required the free and fair exchange of information. With this precedent in mind, however, AIDS activists are quick to point out that any hopes that the discovery of an effective vaccine will put the problems of the pandemic behind us are extremely naive: should a vaccine be discovered tomorrow, it would still be years before it could be marketed. The potential wealth awaiting the successful victors in the vaccine war warrants an ethically questionable caution as contenders put into place all the procedures necessary for patenting their discovery. The expenses of new protease inhibitors have only added to the stakes.

Thus, the factors impeding free exchange of information across borders include the variety of social factors, possible underreporting, and international scientific disputes. When these factors are minimized, however, there is free exchange of information on public health strategies and scientific developments, an essential factor for a successful AIDS response.

The second common denominator of successful HIV-prevention programs throughout the world has been respect for the human rights of persons affected by HIV and those perceived to be at greater risk of infection. Nations that respect the human rights of those infected or perceived to be infected have found concrete benefits in promoting programs that do not drive the disease underground. Social policies that stigmatize carriers of the virus make it much less likely that individuals will avail themselves of counseling and screening programs; they reinforce mechanisms of denial, may cause individuals with AIDS to act out their anger through reckless behavior, and contribute to the spread of other opportunistic infections which can be more easily transmitted, such as tuberculosis. Human rights laws thus have had an important role to play in developing

---

virus) to Gallo and Montagnier as co-discoverers of HIV (human immunodeficiency virus), the new name given to LAV/HTLV-III. Two years later, a newspaper reporter in Chicago reopened the issue with an investigative report of scientific misconduct by Dr. Gallo. *See* John Crewdson, *The Great AIDS Quest,* Chi. Trib., Nov. 19, 1989, § 5, at 1. For Dr. Gallo's account of his discovery of HIV in general, and his response to the *Chicago Tribune* coverage in particular, see Robert Gallo, Virus Hunting: AIDS, Cancer, & the Human Retrovirus 324–34 (1991). Dr. Montagnier, for his part, claimed that he was the sole discoverer of the virus and that the United States unfairly negotiated the 1987 agreement. *See* Judy Sarasohn, *Battling U.S. Bureaucracy, Firm Revives AIDS Dispute,* Legal Times, June 29, 1992, at 1. The evidence revealed in the *Chicago Tribune* report prompted further government investigations of Dr. Gallo, including allegations that he misrepresented his discovery of the virus and failed to share critical research materials with other scientists. *See, e.g.,* John Crewdson, *U.S. Expands Probe of AIDS Researcher Gallo,* Chicago Trib., June 6, 1993, at 1. Charges against Gallo were later dropped when the Office of Research Integrity (ORI) claimed that it had insufficient evidence to meet an "overly restrictive" definition of scientific misconduct. Gallo and other critics of the ORI claimed that the office never had evidence of misconduct on Gallo's part. *See ORI Drops Gallo Case in Legal Dispute,* 262 Science 1202 (1993). The dispute harmed international scientific cooperation and diverted much attention from productive activities to settling disputes based on allegations of misconduct.

effective programs.[39] To this end, both the existing regime of protection for international human rights and emerging developments must be used to create and support effective public health programs. The development and use of those laws is consequently a focus of the remainder of this chapter.

§ 10.5   International Human Rights Law

In reviewing the relatively short history of responses to the AIDS pandemic, a common denominator of effective programs is respect for the human rights and dignity of persons who have HIV or who are perceived to be at higher risk of infection.[40] An understanding of effective programs, for purposes of legal analysis, consequently invokes fundamental principles of human rights under international law. Human rights principles guide those developing guidelines or protocols to assess and monitor how governments treat people with HIV.

Human rights under international law can be broadly defined as "those rights possessed by an individual that cannot be withheld by the State."[41] Human rights have also been defined as the "freedoms, immunities, and benefits which, according to widely accepted contemporary values, every human being should enjoy in the society in which he or she lives."[42] These definitions are hardly satisfactory to explain either the full range of rights covered under international and regional legal systems or the myriad fora in which claims of human rights violations might find redress.

Although these broad definitions are largely noncontroversial in abstract applications, the recognition of particular human rights under international law is often the subject of heated debate in many legal systems throughout the world. The application of human rights law to persons living with HIV (and those perceived to be at risk of infection) may be controversial for many legal systems. Controversy has arisen especially over the false dichotomy of protecting individual human rights and protecting the rights of society. Both can be protected.

In the first decade of the AIDS pandemic, most lawyers and public health advocates generally neglected international human rights law as a means to protect the

---

[39] *See, e.g., Human Rights Vital in Fighting Epidemic,* AIDS Pol'y & L., Aug. 7, 1992, at 1.

[40] *See, e.g.,* Global AIDS Policy Coalition, AIDS in the World 537–73 (Jonathan M. Mann et al. eds., 1992); Michael L. Closen & Mark E. Wojcik, *Living With HIV and Without Discrimination, in* American Bar Ass'n Section of Int'l Law & Practice, International Law and AIDS: International Responses, Current Issues, and Future Directions 151, 173 (Lawrence Gostin & Lane Porter eds., 1992). Another common denominator was effective public and community education as the only true "vaccine" against the further spread of AIDS. Education was only effective, however, when other aspects of AIDS prevention and treatment programs were based on fundamental principles of respect for human rights.

[41] William R. Slomanson, Fundamental Perspectives on International Law 490 (2d ed. 1995).

[42] Restatement (Third) of the Foreign Relations Law of the United States, § 701, cmt. a (1986).

rights of persons with HIV.[43] Perhaps this was because international human rights law has traditionally been thought to be substantively enigmatic and procedurally unavailable to individuals.

There are a number of possible ways to advance human rights under international law. Three documents frame many of the human rights principles potentially applicable to persons affected by HIV. These three documents, which are sometimes called the International Bill of Human Rights,[44] are the Universal Declaration of Human Rights,[45] the International Covenant on Civil and Political Rights (ICCPR),[46] and the International Covenant on Economic, Social, and Cultural Rights.[47]

Each of the documents in the International Bill of Human Rights contains provisions that might apply to persons living with HIV. The possible applications of these international instruments to persons living with HIV have been discussed by a number of scholars and advocates.[48] Provisions cited include affirmations such as "[e]veryone is entitled to all of the rights and freedoms set forth in this [Universal Declaration of Human Rights], without distinction of any kind, such as race, colour, sex, language, religion, political or other opinion,

---

[43] *See* Robert M. Jarvis, *Advocacy for AIDS Victims: An International Law Approach,* 20 U. Miami Inter-Am. L. Rev. 1 (1988).

[44] *See, e.g.,* Frank Newman & David Weissbrodt, Selected International Human Rights Instruments and Bibliography for Research on International Human Rights Law 22 (1996) [hereinafter Newman & Weissbrodt].

[45] G.A. Res. 217 A(III), U.N. Doc. A/810, at 71 (1948), *reprinted in* Newman & Weissbrodt at 22 *and* Mann & Tarantola at 588.

[46] G.A. Res. 2200A (XXI), 21 U.N. GAOR Supp. (No. 16) at 52, U.N. Doc. A/6316 (1966) (entered into force Mar. 23, 1976), *reprinted in* Newman & Weissbrodt at 33; *see also* James D. Wilets, *Using International Law to Vindicate the Civil Rights of Gays and Lesbians in United States Courts,* 27 Colum. Hum. Rts. L. Rev. 33 (1995) (discussing possible use of the ICCPR and other international documents). Simultaneously with the promulgation of the ICCPR, the U.N. General Assembly created an optional protocol that would permit individuals, rather than governments, to file complaints directly with the U.N. Human Rights Committee. Optional Protocol to the International Covenant on Civil and Political Rights, G.A. Res. 2200A (XXI), 21 U.N. GAOR Supp. (No. 16) at 59, U.N. Doc. A/6316 (1966) (entered into force Mar. 23, 1976), *reprinted in* Newman & Weissbrodt at 46.

[47] International Covenant on Economic, Social and Cultural Rights, G.A. Res. 2200A (XXI), 21 U.N. GAOR Supp. (No. 16) at 49, U.N. Doc. A/6316 (1966), 993 U.N.T.S. 3 (entered into force Jan. 3, 1976), *reprinted in* Newman & Weissbrodt at 26.

[48] *See, e.g.,* Robert M. Jarvis, *Advocacy for AIDS Victims: An International Law Approach,* 20 U. Miami Inter-Am. L. Rev. 1 (1988); Marcelo D. Turra, *The Defense of the Rights of Patients Infected With HIV in Brazil, in* AIDS Law and Policy 535 (Arthur S. Leonard ed., 2d ed. 1995) [hereinafter AIDS Law and Policy]; Mann & Tarantola at 463–76; *see also* Mark E. Wojcik, *Health as an International Human Right in the Contemporary Caribbean: "Healthy" Applications for the American Declaration of the Rights and Duties of Man, in* AIDS Law and Policy at 538. Additional advocacy information on specific countries may be available from the International Gay & Lesbian Hum. Rts. Comm'n, 1360 Mission Street, San Francisco, CA 94103: telephone: (415) 255-8680; World Wide Web: http://www.iglhrc.org.

national or social origin, property, birth or other status."[49] More recently, the Vienna Declaration from the World Conference of Human Rights contains two provisions on persons with disabilities; these provisions should also extend to persons affected by HIV.[50] All of these documents, and others, form a framework of international consensus that international law should respect the human rights of persons affected by HIV. The United Nations Commission on Human Rights recently reaffirmed this proposition when it stated that "discrimination on the basis of HIV or AIDS status, actual or presumed, is prohibited by existing international human rights standards, and that the terms 'or other status' in non-discrimination provisions in international human rights texts should be interpreted to cover health status, including HIV/AIDS."[51]

Although these human rights documents establish a framework to protect the rights of persons living with HIV, they are difficult to enforce. Courts in the United States, for example, may find the declarations to be persuasive only and to lack binding effect.[52] There are, however, certain procedures that are available to individuals to protest claims of discrimination on the basis of HIV or AIDS. For example, individuals living in the United States might raise a claim with the Inter-American Commission on Human Rights, an organ of the Organization of American States.[53] Among other things, the Commission can adjudicate human rights claims made under provisions of the *American Declaration of the Rights and Duties of Man*.[54] Although the provisions of the American Declaration were

---

[49] Universal Declaration of Human Rights, art. 2, G.A. Res. 217 A(III), U.N. Doc. A/810, at 71 (1948), *reprinted in* AIDS Law and Policy at 530. *AIDS Law and Policy* sets forth possible provisions that may apply to persons living with HIV. Provisions from the Universal Declaration of Human Rights include articles 1–3, 5–7, 9, 12–14, 16, 19, and 21–30.

[50] United Nations World Conference on Human Rights: Vienna Declaration and Programme of Action, adopted June 25, 1993, *reprinted in* 32 I.L.M. 1661, 1682 (1993) (¶¶ 63 and 64).

[51] *United Nations Subcommission on Prevention of Discrimination and Protection of Minorities Resolution on Discrimination in the Context of Human Immunodeficiency Virus (HIV) or Acquired Immune Deficiency Syndrome (AIDS),* Res. 1995/21, adopted Aug. 24, 1995, *reprinted in* United Nations Development Program, HIV Law, Ethics, and Human Rights 384, 386 (D.C. Jayasuriya ed., 1995); *United Nations Commission on Human Rights, Resolution on HIV/AIDS,* Res. 1995/44 (adopted Mar. 3, 1995), *reprinted in* United Nations Development Program, HIV Law, Ethics, and Human Rights 377, 380 (D.C. Jayasuriya ed., 1995).

[52] For a critical discussion of some of these cases, see James D. Wilets, *Using International Law to Vindicate the Civil Rights of Gays and Lesbians in United States Courts,* 27 Colum. Hum. Rts. L. Rev. 33 (1995); Mark E. Wojcik, *Using International Human Rights Law to Advance Queer Rights: A Case Study for the American Declaration of the Rights and Duties of Man,* 55 Ohio St. L.J. 649 (1994).

[53] Procedural regulations of the Inter-American Commission on Human Rights and a sample complaint form are reprinted in Organization of American States (O.A.S.), Basic Documents Pertaining to Human Rights in the Inter-American System 75, 157, OEA/Ser.L.V/II.71/Doc. 6 rev. 1 (1988).

[54] O.A.S. Res. XXX, adopted by the Ninth Int'l Conference of Am. States, Bogota, Colombia, Mar. 30–May 2, 1948, OEA/Ser. L./V/II.23/doc. 2 rev. 6 (1979), *reprinted in* Richard B. Lillich, International Human Rights Instruments 430.1–430.10 (2d ed. 1990).

thought to be nonbinding when the United States first underwrote them shortly after World War II, the Inter-American Court of Human Rights[55] subsequently found that the American Declaration was a source of international obligation on the United States by virtue of its membership in the Charter of the Organization of American States.[56] Consequently, those who invoke other laws or remedies to advance and protect civil liberties and civil rights "should know that if they do not prevail in a national forum—judicial, legislative, or administrative—there may be an international tribunal or other body to which they can take their case."[57] Furthermore, there has even been a call to establish an International AIDS Tribunal, although no concrete plans for such a tribunal are currently under consideration.[58]

Even when there is no procedural remedy available under international human rights law, policy decisions about persons with HIV, persons at risk of infection, and the public health generally should still be made within a human rights framework. A guiding principle is that "respect for the human rights and dignity of HIV-infected people and people with AIDS, and of members of population groups, is vital to the success of national AIDS prevention and control [programs]."[59] Thus, even if an international human rights law is not considered to be binding in a strict legal sense, it can still provide a valuable point of reference for individuals, governments, and nongovernmental organizations when creating recommendations for AIDS policies. The substantive principles of human rights can also be used as a lobbying tool for legislative and executive branches

---

[55] For further information on the substantive jurisdiction and procedures of the Court, see Scott Davidson, The Inter-American Court of Human Rights (1992).

[56] Interpretation of the American Declaration of the Rights and Duties of Man within the Framework of Article 64 of the American Convention on Human Rights, Advisory Op. OC-10/89 of July 14, 1989, Ser. A, No. 10 (Inter-Am. Ct. Hum. Rts. 1989), reprinted in 11 Hum. Rts. L.J. 118, 126 (1990); see also Charter of the Organization of American States, as amended by the Protocol of Buenas Aires in 1967 and by the Protocol of Cartegena de Indias in 1985, OAS Treaty Ser. No. 1-E, OEA/Ser.A/2 (English) Rev. 3 (1992). In light of the 1989 ruling that the American Declaration is binding on the United States and other signatories to the OAS Charter, decisions that predate that ruling or that did not consider it substantively should be reevaluated under the new standard. See, e.g., Nieves v. University of P.R., 7 F.3d 270 (1st Cir. 1993); Celestine v. Butler, 823 F.2d 74 (5th Cir.), cert. denied, 483 U.S. 1036 (1987); United States ex rel. Chunie v. Ringrose, 788 F.2d 638 (9th Cir.), cert. denied, 479 U.S. 1009 (1986); Sanchez-Espinoza v. Reagan, 568 F. Supp. 601 n.6 (D.D.C. 1983), aff'd, 770 F.2d 202 (D.C. Cir. 1985); In re Alien Children Educ. Litig., 501 F. Supp. 544, 594–96 (S.D. Tex. 1980); see also Filartiga v. Pena-Irala, 630 F.2d 876 (2d Cir. 1980).

[57] Newman & Weissbrodt at xv.

[58] Robert M. Jarvis, Advocacy for AIDS Victims: An International Law Approach, 20 U. Miami Inter.-Am. L. Rev. 1 (1988) (presenting arguments for an international AIDS tribunal).

[59] Avoidance of Discrimination in Relation to HIV-Infected People and People With AIDS, World Health Assembly Resolution WHA41.24 (1988), reprinted in AIDS Law and Policy at 527; see also Francois-Xavier Bagnoud Ctr. for Health & Hum. Rts., Harvard Sch. of Pub. Health, Toward A New Health Strategy for AIDS (1993).

of government and as a source of persuasive authority for appropriate judicial and administrative tribunals.[60]

§ 10.6   Health as a Human Right

Public health issues involving persons living with HIV might not seem to implicate issues of human rights protection under international law. After all, a virus is a virus, a disease is a disease, and human rights are human rights. Although a simple case of denial of medical treatment might be easy to identify as a denial of human rights,[61] the connection between public health and human rights is often obscure to many advocates, scholars, and jurists who look only to the field of public health or only to the field of human rights for direction and redress.

Consideration of the human rights of persons with HIV under international law might thus first consider the broader issue of health (or, alternatively, access to health care) as a human right. The World Health Organization defines *health* as "a state of complete physical, mental, and social well-being and not merely the absence of disease."[62] Furthermore, "[t]he enjoyment of the highest attainable standard of health is one of the fundamental rights of every human being without distinction of race, religion, political belief, economic or social consideration."[63] Under these definitions and others that may be found in other international human rights instruments, health is a human right that should be available to all. Universal recognition of health as a human right, however, is far from accepted doctrine.[64]

In considering health as a human right, debates about AIDS and human rights sometimes frame issues as a balance between the infected and the uninfected.

---

[60] *See* Robert Wintemute, Sexual Orientation and Human Rights (1995); James D. Wilets, *Using International Law to Vindicate the Civil Rights of Gays and Lesbians in United States Courts,* 27 Colum. Hum. Rts. L. Rev. 33 (1995); Mark E. Wojcik, *Using International Human Rights Law to Advance Queer Rights: A Case Study for the American Declaration of the Rights and Duties of Man,* 55 Ohio St. L.J. 649 (1994).

[61] *See* Abbott v. Bragdon, 912 F. Supp. 580 (D. Me. 1995) (dentist's written policy against treating patients with HIV violates ADA).

[62] Constitution of the World Health Organization, July 22, 1946, 62 Stat. 2679, 2680, 14 U.N.T.S. 185.

[63] *Id.; accord* American Declaration of the Rights and Duties of Man, art. XI, O.A.S. Res. XXX, adopted by Ninth International Conference of American States, Bogota, Colombia, Mar. 30–May 2, 1948, OEA/Ser. L./V/II.23/doc. 2 rev. 6 (1979), *reprinted in* Richard B. Lillich, International Human Rights Instruments 430.1–430.10 (2d ed. 1990) ("Every person has the right to the preservation of his health through sanitary and social measures relating to food, clothing, housing and medical care, to the extent permitted by public and community resources.").

[64] For example, Restatement (Third) of the Foreign Relations Law of the United States § 702 (1986) does not include health or access to health care as a human right. The reporter notes, however, at cmt. b that certain rights may in the future gain acceptance as human rights under international law.

Under such debates, the rights of the "general public" perceived to be at little or no risk of HIV infection can be protected only at the expense of the rights of those who are either infected or who are at a perceived higher risk of infection. This framework, however, is ultimately misleading. The debate should instead focus on the underlying requirements necessary to protect the rights of both the infected and the uninfected; protecting the human rights of one group need not be made at the expense of the other. Consequently, in considering health as a human right in the context of AIDS, public health goals can be achieved by recognizing and protecting the human rights of all persons, including persons living with HIV.

Nations have a responsibility to safeguard the health of everyone.[65] In the context of HIV prevention and treatment strategies, this duty requires nations "to protect the human rights and dignity of HIV-infected people and people with AIDS, and of members of population groups, and to avoid discriminatory action against and stigmatization of them in the provision of services, employment, and travel."[66]

§ 10.7   Human Rights Violations Against Persons with HIV

The realities of discrimination against persons living with HIV can illustrate the intersection between public health and human rights. Persons living with HIV face stigma and discrimination in several areas. They have been burned out of their homes, fired from their jobs,[67] refused medical care,[68] expelled from schools, detained in quarantine camps, deported from or refused entry to many countries, tattooed with the words "HIV POSITIVE," denied child custody and visitation, refused insurance or government benefits for health care, denied dignified funerals, and have even been charged with attempted murder when condom breakage occurred during sexual intercourse.

These and other aspects of stigma and discrimination cause many individuals with HIV to be wary of revealing their serostatus; nondisclosure is seen as a means of achieving nondiscrimination and avoiding abuse. One consequence of this concealment, however, is evidenced by the actual or perceived inability of some people with HIV to access medical care and counseling, which are crucial

---

[65] *Avoidance of Discrimination in Relation to HIV-Infected People and People With AIDS,* World Health Assembly Resolution WHA41.24 (1988), *reprinted in* AIDS Law and Policy at 527.

[66] *Id.* art. 1(2).

[67] Employment discrimination claims under U.S. law are covered in **Ch. 3.**

[68] Discrimination in access to services under U.S. law is covered in **Ch. 4;** *see also, e.g., Doctor Fined for Failing HIV Patient,* HIV/AIDS Legal Link (Austl. Fed'n of AIDS Orgs. Legal Project, N.S.W., Austl.), Sept. 1995, at 5 (reporting finding that doctor in New Zealand was guilty of conduct unbecoming a medical practitioner after he failed to examine a gay, HIV-positive patient).

in treating existing cases of HIV infection and in preventing further infection. Likewise, individuals who identify as belonging to socially stigmatized risk groups may also avoid medical care and counseling because of fears that possible violations of medical privacy may subject them to discrimination and other violations of human rights.[69] Social policies that promote images of risk categories are extremely misleading. By denying that HIV infection is a consequence of specific behavior as opposed to adopting identity affiliations, such policies encourage scapegoating and lead many individuals engaging in high risk behaviors to underestimate their exposure to the virus. It is on the basis of these presumptions that whole populations have been targeted as objects of "preventive" prejudice.

The examples listed above constitute only a superficial illustration of the discrimination faced by individuals affected by the epidemic. Many other illustrations of discrimination could be offered from countries all across the world. Additionally, other government and private actions may be found to discriminate against groups of individuals who are not infected with HIV, but who may be perceived to be at risk of infection by their associations with infected persons. Acts of discrimination can occur throughout the life of a person affected by HIV and, in some instances, may be seen even after the person has died.[70]

§ 10.8 International Instruments to Support Persons with HIV

Although there was little consensus for many years about using international human rights law to promote the rights of persons with HIV, and similarly little notice of public health benefits that would result from protecting the human rights of persons with HIV, there were many helpful declarations made to develop a human rights framework for persons with HIV. For example, the London Declaration on AIDS Prevention in January 1988 by heads of health ministries and other delegates from 148 countries emphasized the need for AIDS prevention programs "to protect human rights and human dignity."[71] The London Declaration stated that "[d]iscrimination against, and stigmatization of, HIV-infected people and people with AIDS and population groups undermine public health and must be avoided."[72]

---

[69] *See, e.g.,* Julia Cabassi, *Human Rights and Anti-Discrimination Law,* HIV/AIDS Legal Link (Austl. Fed'n of AIDS Orgs. Legal Project, N.S.W., Austl.), Mar. 1996, at 22 (discussing human rights violations in the Asia/Pacific region).

[70] *See* Mark E. Wojcik, *AIDS and Funeral Homes: Common Legal Issues Facing Funeral Directors,* 27 J. Marshall L. Rev. 411 (1994).

[71] *London Declaration on AIDS Prevention,* Jan. 28, 1988, art. 6, *reprinted in* Michael L. Closen et al., AIDS: Cases and Materials 924, 925 (1989).

[72] *Id.*

The London Declaration represented a substantive shift in international statements on AIDS. Just a few months earlier, the U.N. General Assembly adopted Resolution 42/8, which recognized the "scourge of AIDS" but called upon "all States, in addressing the AIDS problem, to take into account the legitimate concerns of other countries and the interests of inter-state relations."[73] Some nations could (and did) ignore the resolution or use it to justify human rights abuses such as travel restrictions, compulsory HIV antibody testing, and restrictions of personal liberty. These abuses not only offended the protection of human rights but also produced unsound public health policies that are ineffective, and, indeed, counterproductive. The policies created stigma that branded persons vulnerable to HIV infection. This stigma drives individuals underground, where they will not receive information about HIV and how to prevent transmission.

Not surprisingly, in 1988 the United Nations General Assembly did not acknowledge the link between public health and human rights. In that year, however, the General Assembly of the World Health Organization urged member states "to protect the human rights and dignity of HIV-infected people and people with AIDS, and of members of population groups, and to avoid discriminating action against and stigmatization of them in the provision of services, employment, and travel."[74] The U.N. General Assembly adopted this language three years later. In 1991, the U.N. General Assembly urged member nations and intergovernmental organizations "to protect the human rights and human dignity of HIV-infected people, people with AIDS and members of particular population groups, and to avoid discriminating action against and stigmatization of them in the provision of services, employment and travel."

The connection between human rights and public health, in the context of AIDS, thus appeared to be firmly established by 1991, as reflected in certain international pronouncements if not in the customary practice of how nations treated persons with HIV. Persons with HIV still faced discrimination in housing, employment, medical services, travel, and a myriad of other daily activities.

§ 10.9   Indirect Protection under International Human Rights Declarations

Although many documents included specific human rights protection for persons affected by HIV, an equal number of international documents failed to make express references to human rights in the context of AIDS. In 1992, for example,

---

[73] G.A. Res. 42/8, 42 U.N. GAOR Supp. (No. 49) at 12, U.N. Doc. A42/49, art. 4 (Oct. 26, 1987), *reprinted in* Michael L. Closen et al., AIDS: Cases and Materials 922–23 (1989).

[74] World Health Assembly Resolution on Avoidance of Discrimination in Relation to HIV-Infected People and People with AIDs, Res. WHA41.24, WHO/GPA/INF/88.2 (May 13, 1988), *reprinted in* Michael L. Closen et al., AIDS: Cases and Materials 926–27 (1989).

the Organization of African Unity (OAU) issued a Declaration on the AIDS Epidemic in Africa. The OAU did not mention the human rights of persons with HIV, but said only "that people with HIV or AIDS are to be treated with respect and compassion, in keeping with Africa's age-old tradition of tolerance."[75] As another example, the rights of persons with HIV found no express coverage in the Vienna Declaration from the U.N. World Conference on Human Rights.[76]

Although the Vienna Declaration (and other documents) may not expressly link human rights and AIDS, there is still indirect coverage in the final document to protect persons affected by HIV. This protection can be found in the provisions affecting persons with disabilities. Under U.S. law, the term *disability,* with respect to individuals, is defined as "(A) a physical or mental impairment that substantially limits one or more of the major life activities of such individuals; (B) a record of such impairment; or (C) being regarded as having such an impairment."[77] A number of courts and scholars construing this and similar statutory provisions have concluded that persons with HIV qualify as persons with disabilities, even when they are only perceived as being disabled.[78] General policies that discriminate against persons with HIV can violate the law just as specific acts of discrimination against individuals.[79] Similar rulings that HIV is protected as a disability might be found in other countries with similar antidiscrimination laws.[80] In some cases, these antidiscrimination laws might provide even greater protection. In Australia, for example, the policy of refusing to admit HIV positive recruits into the army was ruled unlawful under the Australian Disability Discrimination Act, which forbids discrimination in employment.[81] In the United States, by comparison, the Americans with Disabilities Act

---

[75] Organization of African Unity, Declaration on the AIDS Epidemic in Africa, art. 1 (1992), *reprinted in* AIDS Law and Policy at 542, 543; *but see* Centre for Applied Legal Studies of the Univ. of the Watwatersrand, The AIDS and HIV Charter of South Africa (1993), *reprinted in* AIDS Law and Policy at 545. *See also* John Godwin, *HIV/AIDS Law in the New South Africa,* HIV/AIDS Legal Link (Austl. Fed'n of AIDS Orgs. Legal Project, N.S.W., Austl.), Mar. 1996, at 10.

[76] United Nations World Conference on Human Rights, *Vienna Declaration and Programme of Action,* adopted June 25, 1993, *reprinted in* 32 I.L.M. 1661 (1993). The Vienna Declaration has been compared to "a quarry whose resources have [yet] to be tapped." Koen Davidse, *The Vienna World Conference on Human Rights: Bridge to Nowhere or Bridge Over Troubled Waters?,* 6 Touro Int'l L. Rev. 239, 257 (1995).

[77] Americans with Disabilities Act, 42 U.S.C. § 12102(2) (1994).

[78] This issue is discussed in **Ch. 3.**

[79] *See* Abbott v. Bragdon, 912 F. Supp. 580 (D. Me. 1995) (dentist's written policy against treating with HIV violates ADA); *Judge Says Dentist's Refusal to Treat Patient Was Illegal,* 11 AIDS Pol'y & L. (BNA) 11 (Jan. 26, 1996); *US: Court Finds Dentist Guilty of Discrimination,* 2 Canadian HIV/AIDS Pol'y & L. Newsl. (No. 3), at 7 (Apr. 1996).

[80] *See, e.g., Ontario Human Rights Board to Hear Discrimination Case,* AIDS Pol'y & L., Aug. 7, 1991, at 6.

[81] X v. Department of Defence, No. H94/98 (Australian Hum. Rts. & Equal Opportunity Comm'n, June 29, 1995), *reported in Sacked Army Recruit Wins HIV Discrimination Case,* HIV/AIDS Legal Link (Austl. Fed'n of AIDS Orgs. Legal Project, N.S.W., Austl.), Sept. 1995,

did not prevent the U.S. Congress from enacting a provision that would have required the Department of Defense to discharge members of the military who were HIV positive.[82]

If persons with HIV are likewise considered disabled under international human rights law, they would then find solace in paragraph 63 of the Vienna Declaration which "reaffirms that all human rights and fundamental freedoms are universal and thus unreservedly include persons with disabilities."[83] Consequently, "[a]ny direct discrimination or other negative discriminatory treatment of a disabled person is therefore a violation of his or her rights."[84]

Although persons with HIV might see advocacy for their rights as disabled persons under the Vienna Declaration, many respected scholars found nothing in the Vienna Declaration to recognize expressly "the substantial challenges that health problems pose to human rights."[85] If health law experts are skeptical about coverage for persons with HIV under the Vienna Declaration, there is some doubt as to whether nonexperts could identify such coverage without an express definition that includes persons with HIV as disabled persons. Under the

---

at 7; Michael Alexander, *Military HIV Policy under Scrutiny, id.* at 6; *Australia: Defence Force's Policy Held Discriminatory,* 2 Canadian HIV/AIDS Pol'y & L. Newsl. (Canadian HIV/AIDS Legal Network, Montreal, Quebec, Can.), Apr. 1996, at 9. The ruling was made by the Australian Human Rights and Equal Opportunities Commission, which rejected the Army's argument that the recruit would be unable to carry out duties required of a soldier because he might transmit HIV to others during combat, an accident, or by blood donation.

[82] In February 1996, President Clinton reluctantly signed legislation that would have required the U.S. military to discharge personnel who were HIV positive. *See, e.g.,* Lisa Neff, *Discharge of HIV-Positive Troops Becomes Law,* Feb. 15, 1996, at 9. He declared the provision to be unconstitutional at the time and directed the Department of Justice not to defend anticipated attacks against its constitutionality. President Clinton nonetheless signed the legislation because he favored other provisions in that bill. See **Ch. 3.** *See* Carl Brown, *A Tactical Fight Against Troops' Discharge,* Windy City Times, Feb. 15, 1996, at 12. As the President signed the legislation, he spoke out against it and urged the U.S. Congress to repeal the HIV exclusionary provision as swiftly as possible. This echoed widespread national and international press criticism of the legislation. *See, e.g., Discrimination in the Military,* 2 Canadian HIV/AIDS Pol'y & L. Newsletter (No. 3), at 9 (Apr. 1996). In April 1996, a House and Senate Conference Committee agreed to repeal the HIV exclusion law. Lou Chibbaro, Jr., *Military HIV Ban Repealed,* Washington Blade, Apr. 26, 1996, at 1; David Olson, *Discharge of HIV-Positive Troops Halted,* Windy City Times, May 2, 1996, at 1. On the same day that the Conference Committee agreed to repeal the legislation, the Congressman responsible for the original HIV exclusion legislation, Representative Bob Dornan (R-Calif.), reintroduced a bill to reinstate the ban. Sue Fox and Lou Chibbaro, Jr., *Dornan Is Down, but Not Out,* Washington Blade, Apr. 26, 1996, at 1. If the Americans with Disabilities Act applied to the U.S. military in the way that the Australian Disabilities Act applied to the Australian military, there would be no legislative debate urging the discharge of military personnel who are HIV-positive yet who are fully capable of performing their duties.

[83] United Nations World Conference on Human Rights, *Vienna Declaration and Programme of Action,* art. 63, (adopted June 25, 1993), *reprinted in* 32 I.L.M. 1661, 1682 (1993).

[84] *Id.*

[85] Lawrence O. Gostin, *Public Health and Human Rights in the AIDS Pandemic, in* Indian Law Inst., AIDS-Law and Humanity 20, 23 (New Delhi, India 1995).

principles that first placed persons with HIV under the disability laws of the United States and other countries, however, the Vienna Declaration and similar future documents should provide similar protection to persons living with HIV.

§ 10.10   Additional Specific Protection for Persons with HIV

Despite early advances in international declarations, persons with HIV were not always expressly covered by international human rights declarations. Advocacy by nongovernmental groups continued, however, and their work produced documents such as the *Rights and Humanity Declaration on Fundamental Principles of Human Rights, Ethics and Humanity Applicable in the Context of [HIV and AIDS]*, which the Permanent Mission of The Gambia to the United Nations transmitted to the U.N. Commission on Human Rights, and which the U.N. Economic and Social Council then distributed as an official document.[86] The document was drafted by the British-based nongovernmental organization Rights and Humanity. Under the *Rights and Humanity Declaration,* "[a]ll people living with illness or disability, including people with HIV and AIDS, are entitled to enjoyment of their fundamental human rights and freedoms without any unjustified restriction."[87] The Declaration also recognizes that "[r]espect for human rights and the protection of public health and well-being are interrelated and mutually dependent."[88] Consequently, the duty of nations "to protect public health requires states to introduce measures to protect people with HIV and AIDS from discrimination and social stigma."[89] These and other provisions in the *Rights and Humanity Declaration* establish firmly the affirmative connection between human rights for persons with HIV and the advancement of public health.

A companion document to the *Rights and Humanity Declaration* is the *Charter of Responsibilities to Respect Human Rights and the Principles of Ethics and Humanity in Addressing the Public Health, Social and Economic Dimensions of HIV and AIDS*. The Charter was circulated with the *Rights and Humanities Declaration* as another official document of the U.N. Economic and Social Council. The Charter is quite direct in condemning human rights violations taken in the name of public health: "An analysis of the provisions of international human rights law, the principles of ethics and humanity, and the requirements of public health indicate that most of the restrictive or coercive policies introduced as AIDS control measures both violate internationally recognized human rights norms and are ineffective as a means of controlling the spread of

---

[86] E/CN.4/1992/82 (1992).

[87] *Id.*

[88] *Id.*

[89] *Id.*

HIV infection."[90] The Charter does not identify any restrictive or coercive policies that might be effective or that protect human rights.

The Charter and the Declaration are apexes of respect for human rights and underscore the positive effect of human rights protection on public health. The Charter and Declaration, however, were documents only circulated by the U.N. Economic and Social Council at the request of the delegation from The Gambia. They were not formal resolutions of the U.N. General Assembly and are neither sources of conventional international law nor codifications of customary practice. In the future, however, these documents may been seen in a larger context that establishes an international custom to link public health policy and human rights in the specific context of HIV or other diseases.

§ 10.11   Future Trends

Two early developments in 1994 suggested a permanent shift in the thinking on the human rights protection for persons with HIV. First, in January 1994, the Executive Board of the World Health Organization voted to replace the WHO Global Programme on AIDS with a U.N. Program on AIDS (UNAIDS) that would more effectively incorporate human rights concerns into all of the program strategies. Future declarations from UNAIDS and from each of the individual agencies considering AIDS in other arenas will ground their work within a framework of human rights. By shifting responsibilities for AIDS work from the World Health Organization to a more centralized position within the United Nations structure, UN officials hoped not only to promote a more coordinated use of interagency resources but also to promote an improved understanding of the intersections between health, economics, society, and culture. Under the new UNAIDS structure, UNICEF, UNDP, UNFPA, UNESCO, and the World Bank will all be involved along with WHO in developing a joint United Nations program on HIV and AIDS. Importantly, UNAIDS will also benefit from the formal input of community-based organizations and individuals living with HIV/AIDS through its program coordinating board. The inclusion of two representatives of community-based organizations and individuals with HIV/AIDS for each continent constitutes an institutional recognition of the advocacy efforts that these groups have undertaken since the onset of the pandemic.

Second, in March 1994, the U.N. Commission on Human Rights adopted a Resolution on HIV that expressly found that HIV-related discrimination contravened the fundamental principle of nondiscrimination as reaffirmed in the Vienna Declaration adopted by the World Conference on Human Rights. This seemed to answer the question about whether the human rights of persons with HIV were included in the Vienna Declaration.[91] The Commission also expressed

---

[90] E/CN.4/1992/82, art. 30.

[91] *See* § 13.8.

its alarm "at discriminating laws and policies and the emergence of new forms of discriminatory practices which deny people with HIV infection or AIDS, their families and associates enjoyment of their fundamental rights and freedoms."[92] The Commission recognized the dual principles that antidiscrimination measures promote public health and that stigma and discrimination are counterproductive in efforts to prevent the further spread of AIDS.

A third human rights development in 1994 took place at the Paris AIDS Summit, organized in conjunction with World AIDS Day, on the first of December. The heads of government or representatives of 42 states issued a declaration that recognized that the HIV pandemic "not only causes physical and emotional suffering but it is often used as justification for grave violations of human rights." Nations declared their determination that persons with HIV can "realize the full and equal enjoyment of their fundamental rights and freedoms without distinction and under all circumstances."[93] To this end, the signatories pledged to protect the rights of persons living with or vulnerable to HIV and, in particular, to "ensure equal protection under the law for persons living with HIV/AIDS with regard to access to health care, employment, education, travel, housing and social welfare."[94]

These developments in 1994 suggest that the future trend of human rights jurisprudence and activism will incorporate concerns of individuals and communities affected by HIV.[95] Three additional developments in 1995 also confirm that the human rights of persons with HIV should be included in human rights documents and should be invoked in the continuing development of human rights law.

First, the U.N. Commission on Human Rights confirmed that discrimination based on HIV status, actual or presumed, "is prohibited by existing international human rights standards, and that the term 'or other status' in nondiscrimination provisions in international human rights texts can be interpreted to cover health status, including HIV/AIDS."[96] This simple statement opened access to several human rights declarations and, more importantly, possible enforcement mechanisms.

The second development of 1995 improved further upon the first development. The U.N. Subcommission on Prevention of Discrimination and Protection

---

[92] United Nations Commission on Human Rights, Resolution on HIV/AIDS, Res. 1994/49 (adopted Mar. 4, 1994), *reprinted in* United Nations Development Project on HIV and Development, HIV Law, Ethics, and Human Rights 372, 374 (D.C. Jayasuriya ed., 1995) [hereinafter U.N. Development Project].

[93] Paris AIDS Summit Declaration (Dec. 1, 1994), *reprinted in* U.N. Development Project at 366.

[94] *Id.*

[95] In addition to looking to future documents, various groups also recognize the importance of ensuring that governments honor commitments already made. *See, e.g.,* International Council of AIDS Services Organizations, *The Paris Summit on AIDS: One Year Later,* Canadian HIV/AIDS Pol'y & L. Newsl. (Canadian HIV/AIDS Legal Network, Montreal, Quebec, Can.), Apr. 1996, at 24.

[96] United Nations Commission on Human Rights, Resolution on HIV/AIDS, Res. 1995/44 (adopted Mar. 3, 1995), *reprinted in* U.N. Development Project at 376.

of Minorities reconfirmed that "discrimination on the basis of HIV or AIDS status, actual or presumed, is prohibited by existing international human rights standards, and that the terms 'or other status' in nondiscrimination provisions in international human rights texts should be interpreted to cover health status, including HIV/AIDS."[97] The permissive ability noted earlier by the U.N. Commission on Human Rights became an affirmative mandate to recognize and protect the human rights of persons with HIV infection, actual or presumed.

§ 10.12 A Global AIDS Law

Another development was made in 1995 by a nongovernmental organization in India, the Indian Law Institute, which attempted to create a "global law" expressly for AIDS and HIV. A conference in New Delhi, India addressed the issues of law and humanity in the context of AIDS.[98] The New Delhi Declaration resulting from the conference proposed the drafting of a model global AIDS law that would protect the human rights of all people at risk of HIV infection and that would prohibit discrimination based on HIV. The New Delhi Declaration, promulgated on December 10, 1995, recognized that "one of the most effective strategies for changing behavior and ensuring against the spread of HIV infection lies in the protection of the rights of those at risk." Such statements can be valuable in a legislative context. Lawmakers around the world face recurring debate on demands such as those to criminalize even theoretical exposure to HIV or to require foreign travelers to present HIV negative certificates when they enter a country. When a preexisting human rights framework is in place, lawmakers can make decisions guided by sound science and based on the protection and promotion of human rights and public health.

The New Delhi Declaration sets forth a role for law in the context of HIV. There are four main points. First, law must "protect human rights and empower individuals so that by their cooperation, the spread of HIV infection is contained." Second, law must "promote voluntary behavior which will protect the health of individuals, families, and children [throughout] the world." The promotion of voluntary behavior is essential because the prevention of AIDS necessarily involves the sexual sphere and there seems to be a recognition that institutional intrusion into intimacy is counterintuitive. Third, law must "prevent coercive and punitive action against persons with demonstrated or suspected HIV infection or AIDS." Fourth, law must "protect society" and "promote a sense of responsibility in the face of an epidemic which poses serious threat[s]."

The fourth point does not distinguish between individual responsibility and the responsibilities of governments to deal with AIDS. Individuals and governments

---

[97] Res. 1995/21 (adopted Aug. 24, 1995), *reprinted in* U.N. Development Project at 372, 374.

[98] For criticism of the conference, including the omission of HIV-positive speakers and Indian women from the planning stages and from many of the conference presentations, see Geoffrey Bloom et al., *The Quest for a Global AIDS Law—A Useful Exercise?*, HIV/AIDS Legal Link (Austl. Fed'n of AIDS Orgs. Legal Project, N.S.W., Austl.), Mar. 1996, at 20.

each have responsibilities to deal with AIDS without denial, without discrimination, and without the false dichotomy of rights of the infected or vulnerable versus rights of those who perceive themselves not to be at risk. There need not be such a battle of rights because the protection of individual rights has a direct correlation to the promotion of public health; the protection of one is the protection of both.

In addition to statements of broad principles, the New Delhi Declaration identifies eight specific areas that should have "priority attention in legislative action" in various countries. These areas concern:

1. Safety of blood and blood products[99]
2. Antidiscrimination, privacy, and confidentiality legislation for persons living with or suspected of having HIV
3. Access to full and accurate information on HIV and its prevention, including information "on the availability and quality of condoms and sterile injections"
4. "Protection for women in the context of marriage where their status increases their vulnerability to infection or to socio-economic impact of HIV/AIDS"
5. At least in some regions, providing sterile needles and syringes
6. Repealing criminal code provisions that contravene human rights;
7. "Forbidding discrimination in employment, education, housing, health care, social security, travel, marital and reproductive rights and other privileges of people"
8. Reforms of "laws relating to commercial sex workers to remove criminal stigma which interfere with imparting education to commercial sex workers and their clients."

Although some points are controversial, each point may be vital for successful prevention and treatment of AIDS. These points are consequently of special value to nations that may not yet treat AIDS as a human rights issue. With guidance from relevant international instruments, and with continued international advocacy for persons living with HIV, responses to the pandemic will promote public health by protecting human rights.[100] New antidiscrimination laws would not be a panacea to end discrimination, of course, even if new laws were strictly enforced. There must be a willingness to use the law and confidence in the

---

[99] Although the blood supply has been safer than it has ever been, HIV-contaminated blood still accounts for 5 percent and occasionally more of the reported HIV infections in some African countries. *Blood Supply Safer Than Ever, WHO's AIDS Policy Leader Says,* AIDS Pol'y & L., Apr. 30, 1992, at 8. Additionally, many countries do not maintain blood banks and may rely instead on direct transfusions or on donations made on an as-needed basis.

[100] *See, e.g., Human Rights Vital in Fighting Epidemic,* AIDS Pol'y & L., Aug. 7, 1992, at 1.

legal system.[101] But such laws will contribute to a climate of tolerance that will promote both public health and human rights.[102] The existence and enforcement of antidiscriminaton laws also proves a government's willingness to combat HIV while protecting human rights.[103] Experience has shown that without that willingness, the battle against HIV will be unsuccessful.

---

[101] *Cf.* Michael Tatham, *Human Rights at Risk in Thailand,* HIV/AIDS Legal Link (Austl. Fed'n of AIDS Orgs. Legal Project, N.S.W., Austl.), Mar. 1996, at 12 (describing a situation in Thailand where labor laws appear to be adequate to fight workplace discrimination yet their effectiveness is impaired by an unwillingness to use laws in a generally nonlitigious society and by lack of confidentiality in the legal system, which, in turn, produces a lack of confidence in the legal system).

[102] *Tolerant Views Said to Encourage People to Learn About HIV/AIDS,* AIDS Pol'y & L., Sept. 18, 1991, at 4.

[103] *See, e.g.,* Julia Cabassi, *Human Rights and Anti-Discrimination Law,* HIV/AIDS Legal Link (Austl. Fed'n of AIDS Orgs. Legal Project, N.S.W., Austl.), Mar. 1996, at 22 (discussing human rights violations in the Asia/Pacific region).

CHAPTER 11

IMMIGRATION LAW

Ignatius Bau

§ 11.1   Introduction

HIV is a global pandemic, present in every part of the world. National borders will not contain the spread of HIV. Unfortunately, U.S. laws and policies regarding immigrants with HIV have been dominated by partisan politics rather than sound public health policy. Despite the unanimous opposition of international and U.S. public health experts to the mandatory HIV testing and exclusion of immigrants,[1] U.S. immigration law has excluded individuals with HIV since 1987. Excluding immigrants with HIV allows U.S. government officials to appear to be doing something to prevent the spread of HIV while ignoring the real needs for HIV prevention education and for health care and services for individuals with HIV disease in the United States. At the same time, mandatory HIV testing and exclusion under U.S. immigration law hampers prevention education and early intervention efforts in immigrant communities.[2]

In the United States, the virus affects not only U.S. citizens but immigrants living legally or sometimes illegally in this country. Under U.S. immigration law, HIV status can be crucial in determining immigration status. In turn, one's immigration status determines one's eligibility for federal, state, and local government benefits such as SSI and Medicaid. Most recent immigrants are from Asia and Latin America. As the HIV epidemic continues to spread in communities of color in the United States, especially in Asian American and Latino communities, issues relating to immigration status will continue to be important for AIDS service providers and for advocates for persons with HIV disease. The current anti-immigrant sentiment sweeping the nation also threatens immigrants with disqualification from more and more essential health and social services.

---

[1] *See* WHO, Report of the Consultation on International Travel and HIV Infection, WHO/SPA/GLO/87.1 (1987), *reprinted in* 62 WHO Wkly. Epidemiological Rec. 77 (1987); Global Programme on AIDS, WHO, Statement on Screening of International Travellers for Infection With Human Immunodeficiency Virus, WHO/GPA/INF/88.3 (1988); National Comm'n on AIDS, Resolution on U.S. Visa and Immigration Policy (Dec. 1989). *See also* 56 Fed. Reg. 2484, 2485 (1991) (noting support of the American Medical Association, the American Public Health Association, the Association of State and Territorial Health Officers, the Council of State and Territorial Epidemiologists, the National Association of County Health Officials, the National Medical Association and the United States Conference of Local Health Officers for lifting HIV immigration exclusion). For commentaries, see Fernando Chang-Muy, *HIV/AIDS and International Travel: International Organizations, Regional Governments, and the United States Respond,* 23 N.Y.U.J. Int'l L. & Pol. 1047 (1991); Anthony S. DiNota, Note, *The World Health Organization's Resolution Condemning AIDS-Related Discrimination and Ongoing United States Noncompliance at the Border,* 12 N.Y.L. Sch. J. Int'l & Comp. L. 151 (1991); Nancy E. Allin, Note, *The AIDS Pandemic: International Travel and Immigration Restrictions and the World Health Organizations Response,* 28 Va. J. Int'l L. 1043 (1988). For a comparative law overview of similar immigration laws in other countries, see Sarah N. Qureshi, *Global Ostracism of HIV-Positive Aliens: International Restrictions Barring HIV-Positive Aliens,* 19 Md. J. Int'l L. & Trade 81 (1995).

[2] Many thoughtful law review articles have argued against the exclusion of immigrants with HIV. *See, e.g.,* Lia Macko, Note, *Acquiring a Better Global Vision: An Argument Against the United States' Current Exclusion of HIV-Infected Immigrants,* 9 Geo. Immigr. L.J. 545 (1995); Sarah N. Qureshi, *Global Ostracism of HIV-Positive Aliens: International Restrictions Barring HIV-Positive Aliens,* 19 Md. J. Int'l L. & Trade 81 (1995); Faith G. Pendleton, *The United States Exclusion of HIV-Positive Aliens: Realities and Illusions,* 18 Suffolk Transnat'l L. J. 269 (1995). *Cf.* Jorge L. Carro, *From Constitutional Psychopathic Inferiority to AIDS: What Is the Future for Homosexual Aliens?,* 7 Yale L. & Pol'y Rev. 201 (1989); Jason A. Pardo, Note, *Excluding Immigrants on the Basis of Health: The* Haitian Centers Council *Decision Criticized,* 11 J. Contemp. Health L. & Pol'y 523 (1995) (arguing in favor of HIV exclusion).

There are usually two critical issues raised by individuals with HIV about their immigration status. The first issue is whether their HIV status will prevent or, in a few situations, facilitate obtaining a more permanent immigration status. The second issue is whether their immigration status will prevent them from obtaining government benefits such as health and disability benefits. Although these two issues are often interrelated, it is important to discern which issues are of primary concern to an individual with HIV. In many cases, it may be easier and faster to advocate for eligibility for certain types of benefits rather than seeking or waiting for a change in immigration status.

Sections 11.2 through **11.7** provide an overview of U.S. immigration law that will enable the reader to understand how each immigration status is obtained. **Sections 11.8** through **11.13** examine the immigration issues raised by an individual's HIV status, including the exclusion based on HIV infection and the waivers of the exclusion. HIV testing and the availability of an exclusion waiver is set forth in **§ 11.14. Sections 11.15** through **11.18** review the impact of an individual's immigration status on one's eligibility for government benefits. This review includes an update on the changes made by the recently enacted welfare reform legislation.

OVERVIEW OF IMMIGRATION LAW

§ 11.2   U.S. Citizenship

There are four principal ways to obtain U.S. citizenship: birth in the United States,[3] "naturalization" or application by permanent residents to become U.S. citizens, acquisition and derivation through U.S. citizen parents,[4] and service in the U.S. military.[5] Persons born in Puerto Rico, the Panama Canal Zone, the U.S. Virgin Islands, and Guam are U.S. citizens by birth.[6] The general requirements for naturalization are residence in the United States for five years as a permanent resident, good moral character, and passage of an examination testing English language fluency and knowledge of U.S. history and civics.[7]

United States citizens have an absolute right to travel from and return to the United States. Citizens also are eligible for all federal, state, and local government benefits. It is extremely difficult to lose U.S. citizenship.[8]

---

[3] U.S. Const., amend. XIV, § 1.

[4] 8 U.S.C. §§ 1431–1432 (1994).

[5] *Id.* §§ 1439–1440.

[6] *Id.* §§ 1402–1403, 1406–1407.

[7] *Id.* §§ 1423, 1427.

[8] The United States does not recognize dual citizenship. In some cases, a citizen of another country can retain that citizenship under the laws of that country even after naturalization in the United States. Other countries also may allow U.S. citizens to retain their U.S. citizenship even after becoming citizens of that country. In such cases, the United States only recognizes the U.S. citizenship, but the other country may recognize dual citizenship.

§ 11.3   Permanent Residence

Permanent residence in the United States is the most common status for immigrants who are not yet U.S. citizens. Permanent residents are sometimes still referred to as "green card" holders although the current permanent resident card is rose-colored. Permanent residents may leave and return to the United States, but if their absence is more than temporary, they may have to reestablish their eligibility for permanent residence upon their return. The definition of *entry* to the United States is explained in § **11.7.** Prior to the enactment of the 1996 welfare reform legislation, permanent residents were eligible for almost all government benefits on the same basis as U.S. citizens. Eligibility will now vary by each state and county of residence. Welfare reform legislation and other recent legislative proposals are covered in § **11.18.**

Family Reunification.   The most common way to obtain permanent residence is through a petition by an U.S. citizen or permanent resident for the entry of another either as an immediate relative or through one of the family preference categories. There are different procedures and waiting lists for each family category. The waiting time also depends on the applicant's country of birth, a carryover of historical immigration quotas based on national origin. *Immediate relatives* include the spouses, minor unmarried children, and parents of U.S. citizens. There is no waiting time nor limit to the number of immediate relatives that can be admitted each year.

The other family categories are for adult and/or married children; for brothers and sisters, unmarried or married plus their spouses and minor children, of U.S. citizens; and for spouses and unmarried children of permanent residents. There are different waiting times for each category under a complex *family preference system.*[9] For example, there currently is no waiting time for the unmarried children of U.S. citizens. On the other hand, the waiting time for spouses and minor unmarried children of permanent residents is three and one-half years. The waiting time for brothers and sisters of U.S. citizens is at least 10 years and over 17 years for brothers and sisters from the Philippines.

Conditional Permanent Residence.   As a practical matter, one's marriage to a U.S. citizen is the fastest and most direct way to obtain permanent residence. However, the Immigration and Naturalization Service (INS) often is suspicious of these marriages, suspecting fraudulent or sham marriages.[10] There are severe criminal and civil penalties against both parties for entering into a fraudulent marriage. Moreover, since 1986, there is an additional step required for individuals seeking permanent residence through marriage. Only a two-year conditional permanent residence is granted to such spouses.[11] Prior to the two-year

---

[9] 8 U.S.C. § 1153(a) (1994).

[10] *See* Bark v. INS, 511 F.2d 1200 (9th Cir. 1975) (physical separation or marital difficulties not conclusive as to whether marriage is fraudulent).

[11] 8 U.S.C. § 1186a.

anniversary of the approval of conditional permanent residence, the couple is required to file a joint petition to remove the condition by demonstrating that the marriage remains a valid one. If the joint petition is not filed in a timely manner and approved by the INS, permanent residence is revoked and deportation proceedings are initiated against the immigrant spouse.[12] There are waivers to the requirement of the filing of the joint petition for marriages that were entered into in good faith but have now been terminated, for domestic violence and for extreme hardship.[13]

Employment-Based.   Individuals also may obtain permanent residence through the sponsorship of an U.S. employer or based on their specialized labor. The employer must demonstrate that the applicant has education, experience, and skills that are in short supply in the U.S. labor market. Most of these employment categories require the employers to complete a labor certification process that involves their state employment agency and the U.S. Department of Labor. The employer must demonstrate that there are no U.S. workers willing, qualified, and available to accept a particular job, that the employer will pay the immigrant the prevailing wage for that job, and that the employment of the immigrant will not have an adverse impact on the wages or working conditions of U.S. workers.[14]

There also is an *employment category preference system*.[15] The higher the qualifications and skills involved, the easier and faster the process. For example, there currently is no waiting for most employment categories but there is a four-year waiting time for the unskilled labor category. It also is possible to obtain permanent residence by making an investment of at least $1 million into a U.S. business and creating at least 10 U.S. jobs.[16]

Diversity Visa Lottery.   The Immigration Act of 1990[17] created a new category for obtaining permanent residence, so-called diversity visas.[18] This category was created in response to congressional concerns that too many recent immigrants were primarily from Asia and Mexico. What Congress failed to consider was that the reason for this immigration pattern was the relatively recent (1965) repeal of historical exclusions and national origin quotas against Asian and Mexican immigration, dating back to the 1882 Chinese Exclusion Act.[19] Only individuals from countries with lower levels of recent immigration are eligible

---

[12] *Id.* § 1186a(c).

[13] *Id.* § 1186a(c)(4).

[14] *Id.* § 1182(a)(5).

[15] *Id.* § 1153(b).

[16] *Id.* § 1153(b)(5). Permanent residence through this investment/job creation category also is subject to a two-year conditional period, with the investor required to demonstrate that the business continues after two years. *Id.* § 1186b.

[17] Pub. L. No. 101-649, 1990 U.S.C.C.A.N. (104 Stat.) 4978.

[18] 8 U.S.C. § 1153(c).

[19] Act of May 6, 1882, 22 Stat. 58.

for diversity visas. During the first three years of the category, Irish nationals were guaranteed 40 percent of the diversity visas each year. More recently, the diversity program has increased immigration from Africa as well as Europe. The application process for the diversity visas only requires a simple letter, with 55,000 "winners" chosen by lottery once a year. The only other requirements for eligibility are a high school education or at least two years of work experience.

Legalization under the Immigration Reform and Control Act of 1986. Over three million undocumented immigrants living in the United States were able to legalize their immigration status under three separate legalization programs enacted by the Immigration Reform and Control Act (IRCA) of 1986.[20] In order to qualify, one had to have been present and continuously residing in the United States since January 1, 1982, or have been employed in agricultural work for at least 90 days between May 1985 and May 1986, or have been admitted to the U.S. through special programs for Haitian and Cuban refugees.[21] Those who were able to qualify for legalization went through a two-step process of temporary residence prior to an adjustment of their immigration status to permanent residence.

Because the legalization programs required each individual to qualify independently, many spouses and children who either entered the United States after the eligibility date of January 1, 1982 or otherwise could not qualify for legalization independently were left separated from their legalizing family members. Congress finally recognized this oversight in 1990 by enacting a *family unity status* for such family members, which would provide a stay of deportation and employment authorization until their second family preference petitions for permanent residence through their spouses or parents were granted.[22] Congress also allocated additional visas to the second family preference category for spouses and minor unmarried children of permanent residents to meet the additional demand for visas in that category from the hundreds of thousands of new permanent residents under the legalization programs.[23]

Although most of those legalized under IRCA programs are now permanent residents or U.S. citizens, there remain several thousand unresolved legalization cases related to pending litigation about eligibility. Several hundred other cases, including some involving the waiver of the HIV exclusion, also remain unresolved at the appellate stages. HIV waivers for legalization applicants are covered in § **11.10.** However, as long as such applicants regularly renew their employment authorization each year, they are eligible to remain in the United States until their cases are finally resolved.

---

[20] Pub. L. No. 99-603, 1986 U.S.C.C.A.N. (100 Stat.) 3359.

[21] 8 U.S.C. §§ 1160, 1255a (note).

[22] Pub. L. No. 101-649, § 301, 1990 U.S.C.C.A.N. (104 Stat.) 4978, 5029.

[23] *Id.* § 112, 1990 U.S.C.C.A.N. (104 Stat.) 4978, 4987.

Registry.   The 1986 IRCA also updated provisions that allow legalization for any individual who has resided continuously in the United States, regardless of immigration status or manner of entry, since January 1, 1972.[24] The applicant must demonstrate good moral character to qualify for registry. If the applicant obtains registry, she or he becomes a permanent resident.

Adjustment from Other Statuses.   An individual also may obtain permanent residence through *adjustment* from other statuses such as refugee or asylee status.[25] Refugee and asylee status are discussed in § **11.4.**

§ 11.4   Refugees and Asylum

Refugees are individuals fleeing persecution who are admitted to the United States, usually from third countries.[26] A refugee must have been persecuted in the past or have a well-founded fear of future persecution on account of race, religion, nationality, membership in a particular social group, or political opinion.[27] Since 1980, the president and Congress jointly determine how many refugees are admitted each year, from a high of over 230,000 in 1980 to a low of 67,000 in 1986. 121,000 refugees were authorized to be admitted in fiscal year 1994.[28] In recent years, most refugees have been admitted from southeast Asia, mainly from Vietnam, and from the former Soviet Union, mainly from Russia. In contrast, very few refugees have been admitted from Africa or the Middle East, where the United Nations High Commissioner for Refugees counts the most number of refugees. Similarly, almost no refugees have been admitted from countries such as Guatemala, El Salvador, and Haiti, despite the widespread human rights abuses in those countries over the last two decades. Thus, U.S. refugee policy continues to reflect foreign policy interests.

Asylees are refugees who apply for protection from persecution while already in the United States.[29] If an individual is in deportation proceedings, he or she also may apply for *withholding* of deportation because his or her "life or freedom" may be threatened on one of the five protected grounds of race, religion, nationality, membership in a particular social group, or political opinion.[30] The

---

[24] 8 U.S.C. § 1259.

[25] *Id.* § 1159.

[26] 8 U.S.C. § 1157.

[27] *Id.* § 1101(a)(42).

[28] INS, Statistical Yearbook of the Immigration and Naturalization Service for Fiscal Year 1994, at 72 (1996).

[29] 8 U.S.C. § 1158.

[30] *Id.* § 1253(h).

standards of proof and benefits of asylum and withholding are different.[31] Asylum applicants may have entered the United States without documents illegally or may have entered as a nonimmigrant (for example, as a visitor or student).

The procedures for determining asylum applications have changed, effective January 1995. If the individual has not yet been arrested or detained by the INS, she may file an *affirmative asylum application* with the INS Asylum Office, a branch of the INS that includes specially recruited and trained asylum officers.[32] These affirmative applications must be filed within one year of physical entry into the United States.[33] These affirmative asylum applications are to be decided in a nonadversarial manner.[34] If asylum is to be granted, the asylee also is granted employment authorization and is eligible to adjust her status to permanent residence after one year.[35] If the asylum officer declines to grant asylum, however, the case is referred to the Immigration Court, and the asylum applicant will be placed in deportation proceedings.[36] The asylum applicant whose case is referred to the Immigration Court is ineligible for employment authorization, posing a dilemma: pursuing the case; working without employment authorization, which will be a negative factor in her asylum case; or subsisting without employment.

On the other hand, if an individual has not yet applied for asylum with the INS Asylum Office and is placed in either deportation or exclusion proceedings, she will have the right to apply for asylum as a "defense" to deportation or exclusion. Similarly, an asylum applicant whose case has been referred by the INS Asylum Office to the Immigration Court has the opportunity to renew the application as a defense to deportation.

The Immigration Court proceedings are adversarial and the INS is represented by a trial attorney who opposes the asylum application. The immigration judge hears all the evidence and argument and then makes a decision. However, under the 1996 amendments to the immigration law, there now will be summary asylum proceedings for individuals who either entered the United States without inspection, that is, illegally, or are stopped by the INS at the border or a port of entry with either fraudulent or incomplete immigration documents.[37]

---

[31] *See* INS v. Cardoza-Fonseca, 480 U.S. 421 (1987) (withholding requires applicant to prove that it is "more likely than not" that there would be persecution, but asylum requires only that applicant prove reasonable possibility of persecution; asylee can adjust status to permanent residence after one year but individual granted withholding remains in that status indefinitely).

[32] 8 C.F.R. §§ 208.4, 208.1(b) (1996).

[33] Illegal Immigration Reform and Immigrant Responsibility Act, Pub. L. No. 104-208, § 604, 1996 U.S.C.C.A.N. (110 Stat.) 3009 [1570], 3009 [1805], *amending* 8 U.S.C. § 1158(a)(2)(B).

[34] 8 C.F.R. § 208.9(b).

[35] 8 U.S.C. § 1159(b); 8 C.F.R. §§ 208.20, 274a.12(a)(5).

[36] 8 C.F.R. § 208.14(b)(2).

[37] Antiterrorism and Effective Death Penalty Act of 1996, Pub. L. No. 104-132, Title IV, § 422, 1996 U.S.C.C.A.N. (110 Stat.) 1214, 1270–72, and Illegal Immigration Reform and Immigrant Responsibility Act, Pub. L. No. 104-208, § 301, 1996 U.S.C.C.A.N. (110 Stat.) 3009 [1570], 3009 [1613], *amending* 8 U.S.C. §§ 1225, 1251.

Immigration courts have recognized that an asylum claim may be based on the applicant's fear of persecution on account of sexual orientation and/or HIV status.[38] The International Gay and Lesbian Human Rights Commission, which monitors asylum cases in the United States and around the world, reports that gay men from Pakistan, Brazil, Nicaragua, El Salvador, Guatemala, Romania, Venezuela, Russia, China, a lesbian from Columbia, and HIV-infected individuals from Togo and Brazil have been granted asylum by immigration courts in unreported decisions. Similarly, the INS Asylum Office has granted asylum to HIV-positive individuals from Brazil, Colombia, Chile, and El Salvador; to gay men from Mexico, Turkey, Colombia, Nicaragua, Venezuela, Singapore, Eritrea, Iran, Honduras, Lebanon, Albania, Pakistan, Brazil, Jordan, El Salvador, Peru, Russia, Romania, Yemen, Mauritania, and Hong Kong; to lesbians from Ethiopia, Iran, Guatemala, and Russia; and to a transgendered individual from Colombia.[39]

§ 11.5 Defenses to Deportation

In addition to asylum and withholding of deportation, there are several other ways to either delay or stop one's deportation. Anyone who is not a U.S. citizen, including permanent residents, can be found deportable.[40] An individual who is

---

[38] *See In re* Toboso-Alfonso, 20 I.& N. Dec. 819 (B.I.A. 1990) (gay Cuban granted asylum); *In re* Tenorio (I.J. 1993), *appeal pending* (gay Brazilian granted asylum); *In re* P., (I.J. 1995) (applicant from Togo with HIV granted asylum). *But see In re* Pitcherskaia, A72 143 932 (B.I.A. 1995) (Russian lesbian denied asylum), *petition for review filed sub nom.* Pitcherskaia v. INS, No. 95-70887 (9th Cir. Dec. 11, 1995). In 1996, the Presidential Advisory Council on AIDS released the Clinton Administration's response to its recommendations on immigration law issues relating to HIV. The administration stated in response to a recommendation about granting asylum to HIV-infected applicants that whether HIV/AIDS infection is a characteristic that may define a particular social group under asylum law depends on the practices of the government of the home country. Nothing in existing law or practice precludes recognition of persons with HIV as a particular social group, if the proof in the individual case supports such a conclusion. Presidential Advisory Council on HIV/AIDS, Progress Report: Implementation of Advisory Council Recommendations 51–52, *reprinted in* 73 Interp. Rel. 910 (1996). For commentaries on asylum issues, see Peter Margulies, *Asylum, Intersectionality, and AIDS: Women with HIV as a Persecuted Social Group,* 8 Geo. Immigr. L.J. 521 (1994); Brian J. McGoldrick, *United States Immigration Policy and Sexual Orientation: Is Asylum for Homosexuals a Possibility?,* 8 Geo. Immigr. L.J. 201 (1994); Brian F. Henes, *The Origin and Consequences of Recognizing Homosexuals as a "Particular Social Group" For Refugee Purposes,* 8 Temp. Int'l L. & Comp. L.J. 377 (1994); Suzanne B. Goldberg, *Give Me Liberty or Give Me Death: Political Asylum and the Global Persecution of Lesbians and Gay Men,* 26 Cornell Int'l L.J. 605 (1993); Stuart Grider, Recent Developments, *Sexual Orientation as Grounds for Asylum in the United States,* 35 Harv. Int'l L.J. 213 (1994).

[39] International Gay & Lesbian Human Rights Comm'n, U.S. Asylum Fact Sheet (Nov. 1996). For more information, contact the Commission at 1360 Mission Street, Suite 200, San Francisco, CA 94103.

[40] The grounds for deportation are similar to but distinct from the grounds of exclusion. *Compare* 8 U.S.C. § 1251(a) *with* 8 U.S.C. § 1182(a).

deported is prohibited from reentering the United States for five years without a special waiver from the attorney general.[41]

Suspension of Deportation. Prior to changes made by the 1996 amendments to the immigration law, an individual who had resided continuously in the United States for at least seven years, had good moral character, and could demonstrate extreme hardship resulting from deportation to himself or to an immediate family member who is a permanent resident or U.S. citizen, was eligible for suspension of deportation.[42] The prototypical case would be a situation in which the individual had a child born in the United States, who was therefore a U.S. citizen, with a serious medical condition for which appropriate care was unavailable in the home country. Several individuals have applied for suspension of deportation based on their HIV status.[43] If suspension of deportation is granted by the Immigration Judge, the applicant obtains permanent residence. Effective April 1, 1997, suspension of deportation will be replaced by *cancellation of removal.* In order to qualify for cancellation of removal, one must demonstrate at least 10 years' continuous residence, good moral character, and exceptional and extremely unusual hardship to a permanent resident or U.S. citizen spouse, parent, or child. Hardship to the applicant for cancellation of removal will no longer be relevant.[44]

Unlike asylum, however, one usually cannot apply affirmatively for suspension of deportation. It is a low priority for the INS to place anyone who meets the requirements for suspension of deportation into deportation proceedings because the INS knows that those individuals likely will obtain permanent residence. Immigrants also should be wary of attorneys, immigration counselors, and "notarios" (notary publics not licensed to practice law) who promise permanent residence to anyone who has lived in the U.S. for seven or more years. Such practices raise ethical issues such as the unauthorized practice of law by nonlawyers and false and misleading legal advertising. In fact, very few suspension applications actually are granted.

Voluntary Departure. An individual who is in deportation proceedings can admit to deportability and request permission to voluntarily depart from the United States instead of being deported.[45] The applicant must demonstrate good

---

[41] 8 U.S.C. § 1182(a)(6)(B).

[42] *Id.* § 1254.

[43] *See* Anthony Romero, *Overcoming HIV Seropositivity: Legal Authority from Extreme Hardship Cases,* Immigr. Newsl. (Nat'l Immigr. Project, Nat'l Law. Guild, Boston, MA), fall 1988, at 1, 7–14. In a February 19, 1996, memorandum, "Seroposivity for HIV and Relief from Deportation," *reprinted in* 73 Interp. Rel. 909 (1996), the INS general counsel stated that "[s]eropositivity for HIV shall be considered in requests for discretionary forms of relief from deportation."

[44] Pub. L. No. 104-208, § 304, 1996 U.S.C.C.A.N. (110 Stat.) 3009 [1570], 3009 [1633] (codified at 8 U.S.C. § 1230A).

[45] 8 U.S.C. § 1254(e).

moral character for the last five years and the financial means to leave the United States. He need not return to his home country but only to a country outside of the United States that will admit him. The advantage of voluntary departure is that the individual is not prohibited from returning legally to the United States. Most voluntary departure orders are issued in the alternative: if the individual fails to leave by the time ordered, a deportation order automatically is issued. Although the time granted for voluntary departure could be up to one year, the 1996 amendments to the immigration law have limited voluntary departure to either 60 days (from an immigration judge) or 120 days (from the INS).[46]

Deferred Action. *Deferred action* is an administrative decision by the INS to take no action to deport an individual based on humanitarian concerns.[47] The prototypical situation is when the individual is too ill to be deported. The decision is entirely discretionary and requires an admission of deportability. In some areas, individuals with AIDS have been able to obtain deferred action on their cases, in one-year increments of time, because of their AIDS diagnoses.

§ 11.6 Nonimmigrants

Nonimmigrants are individuals admitted to the United States for a temporary period of time and for a specific purpose.[48] They generally must maintain their primary residence in their home country and must intend to return to that primary residence after the purpose of their stay in the United States is completed. Nonimmigrants are categorized by the type of visa they are granted, designated with a letter. For example, B visas are granted to tourists and business visitors.

Nonimmigrant visas may be valid for single or multiple entries into the United States, which may be made during the particular period of time that the visa is valid. However, the actual period of time that a nonimmigrant is allowed to remain in the United States is controlled by the date and conditions stamped on a small white card, the INS I-94 Arrival and Departure Card, stapled to the nonimmigrant's passport upon entry to the United States. Thus, although a B visa may be valid for multiple entries during a 10-year period, the visa holder is only allowed to remain in the United States for the time stamped on the I-94, usually three or six months, unless the visa holder obtains an extension or change in immigration status.

Visitors and Tourists. Visitors and tourists account for over 20 million of the 22 million nonimmigrants admitted to the United States each year.[49] Visitors may

---

[46] Pub. L. No. 104-208, § 304, 1996 U.S.C.C.A.N. (110 Stat.) 3009 [1570], 3009 [1633] (codified at 8 U.S.C. § 1230B).

[47] INS Operations Instructions 242.1a(22).

[48] 8 U.S.C. § 1101(a)(15).

[49] INS, Statistical Yearbook of the Immigration and Naturalization Service for Fiscal Year 1994 at 108 (1996) (Table 40).

be admitted for pleasure on B-2 visas or for business on B-1 visas. Generally, visitors are admitted for three or six months, with possible extensions for a total stay of no longer than one year at a time. Under the Visa Waiver Program, individuals from most European countries and Japan are eligible to enter the United States without any visa as visitors for no longer than 90 days.[50] However, these individuals may not extend or change their immigration status beyond the 90 days.

Students.   Students are admitted to pursue a full-time course of studies on F visas, or M visas for students attending vocational schools. Students may be admitted at any educational level, for English language studies, or for specialized schools (for example, music or art schools). Students generally are admitted for the ordinary duration of their studies (for example, four years for undergraduates).

There are complex rules governing employment of foreign students. Generally, a student must demonstrate sufficient financial resources for all educational costs as a condition for admission to the United States. However, it is understood that many foreign students will seek employment, especially those enrolled in graduate studies. On-campus employment and on- or off-campus employment during summers and school vacations is permitted. In addition, after one year, a foreign student may work off-campus if his employer completes a *labor attestation* that there will be no adverse impact on U.S. workers from the temporary employment of the student. In addition, foreign students may work for a total of one year after completion of their studies if the employment is "practical training" related to their field of study.

Temporary Workers.   Temporary workers are admitted on H visas to fill temporary labor shortages or to be trained in the United States. Although some of the requirements are similar to those for an employment preference petition for permanent residence, the burden of proof to demonstrate a temporary shortage of U.S. workers is much easier to meet. In addition, there are special temporary worker programs to admit temporary agricultural workers and nurses.

Other Nonimmigrants.   There are other nonimmigrant categories for entertainers and athletes (O and P visas), religious workers (R visas), diplomats (A visas), employees of international organizations (G visas), foreign journalists (I visas) and other specialized categories of temporary visitors to the United States.[51]

§ 11.7   Exclusion in General

Both immigrants and nonimmigrants must demonstrate that none of the statutory grounds of exclusion apply to them. Waivers of some grounds of exclusion are

---

[50] 8 U.S.C. § 1187.

[51] *Id.* § 1101(a)(15).

available for some categories of nonimmigrants and immigrants. Exclusion is not relevant to certain types of applications for immigration status such as registry, suspension of deportation, asylum and withholding of deportation, and deferred action.

Grounds of Exclusion

The Immigration Act of 1990 reorganized the grounds of exclusion.[52] This discussion will focus on the health, criminal, and public charge grounds of exclusion. The 1990 Act also repealed the exclusion based on sexual orientation.[53] Accordingly, homosexuality is no longer relevant to exclusion or immigration status decisions, except as a possible basis for asylum (see **§ 11.4**). The Immigration Act of 1990 reorganized the grounds of exclusion; additional amendments and a change in name from "exclusion" to "inadmissability" were added in 1996.[54]

Health Exclusions. Since 1891, the United States has excluded individuals with "loathsome or dangerous contagious diseases."[55] In 1961, Congress delegated the authority to determine the list of excludable diseases to the Public Health Service, a branch of the Department of Health, Education and Welfare,[56] now the Department of Health and Human Services. The addition of HIV to the exclusion list has been the subject of considerable domestic and international controversy, as discussed in **§ 11.8.**

The other health exclusion is for physical or mental disorders that pose a threat to the property, safety or welfare of oneself or others,[57] and for "drug abuser[s] and addict[s]."[58] *Drug abusers* are defined to include anyone who has engaged in the nonmedical use of any controlled substance.[59] One can be excludable as a drug abuser even without any criminal arrests or convictions. There is no waiver available for the drug abuser exclusion. The 1996 amendments to the immigration law added a third health exclusion for those failing to provide evidence of a large number of immunizations.[60]

---

[52] *Id.* § 1182(a).

[53] H.R. Rep. No. 723, pt. 1, 101st Cong., 2d Sess. 52–53 (1990), *reprinted in* 1990 U.S.C.C.A.N. 6710, 6732–33.

[54] Pub. L. No. 104-208, Title III, §§ 301–388, 1996 U.S.C.C.A.N. (110 Stat.) 3009 [1570], 3009 [1613]–3009 [1747], *amending* 8 U.S.C. § 1182.

[55] Act of March 3, 1891, § 1, 26 Stat. 884, 1084. Earlier statutes authorized the National Board of Health to inspect arriving vessels and crews to prevent the introduction of infectious or contagious diseases into the United States but were not directed at excluding immigrants. 20 Stat. 484 (1879); 21 Stat. 5 (1879).

[56] Pub. L. No. 87-301, 75 Stat. 650, 654 (1961).

[57] 8 U.S.C. § 1182(a)(1)(A)(ii).

[58] *Id.* § 1182(a)(1)(A)(iii).

[59] 42 C.F.R. § 34.2(g).

[60] Pub. L. No. 104-208, § 341, 1996 U.S.C.C.A.N. (110 Stat.) 3009 [1570], 3009 [1714], (codified at 8 U.S.C. § 1182(a)(1)(A)(ii)).

Criminal Exclusions.   Individuals who have been convicted or admit to certain crimes of "moral turpitude," or two or more crimes with aggregate sentences to confinement actually imposed of five years or more, or any crime concerning controlled substances are excludable.[61] There is a separate exclusion ground for prostitution, which includes engaging in prostitution at any time within the past 10 years.[62] There are limited waivers for these criminal grounds of exclusion.[63]

Public Charge Exclusion.   Both nonimmigrants and immigrants must demonstrate that they are not likely to become a "public charge" if admitted to the United States.[64] The 1996 amendments establish specific criteria for defining public charge, including age, health, family status, assets, resources, financial status, education, and skills. Affidavits of support also are required for family preference immigrants.[65] Under the 1996 welfare reform law,[66] the affidavit of support must be signed by the relative filing the visa petition for the immigrant. In addition, the new affidavits of support will be enforceable by the immigrant for actual financial support and by federal, state, and local governments to recover the costs of any government benefits received by the immigrant, with a 10-year statute of limitations. The sponsor who signs these new affidavits of support also will be subject to fines of up to $5000 for failure to notify the INS and other government agencies of any change in address until the sponsored immigrant becomes a U.S. citizen. Finally, the income of the sponsor who signed the affidavit of support is "deemed" to be available to the immigrant until the immigrant becomes a U.S. citizen. Thus, the immigrant will be disqualified from receiving any government benefits based on income eligibility: the income of the immigrant plus the income of the sponsor completing the affidavit of support will be above the income eligibility level because those combined incomes must be at least 125 percent above the federal poverty guidelines.[67] These federal poverty guidelines are the usual income eligibility guidelines for receiving federal public benefits.

---

[61] 8 U.S.C. § 1182(a)(2).

[62] *Id.* § 1182(a)(2)(D).

[63] *Id.* § 1182(h).

[64] *Id.* § 1182(a)(4).

[65] Pub. L. No. 104-208, § 531, 1996 U.S.C.C.A.N. (110 Stat.) 3009 [1570], 3009 [1779], *amending* 8 U.S.C. § 1182(a)(4).

[66] Personal Responsibility and Work Opportunity Reconciliation Act of 1996, Pub. L. No. 104-193, Title IV, §§ 421, 423, 1996 U.S.C.C.A.N. (110 Stat.) 2105, 2270, 2271–74. The welfare reform legislation extends the deeming provisions to all federal "means-tested" programs. Prior to 1996, deeming applied only to SSI (for five years) and to AFDC and Food Stamps (three years).

[67] Pub. L. No. 104-193, Title IV, § 423, 1996 U.S.C.C.A.N. (110 Stat.) 2105, 2271–74 (codified at 8 U.S.C. § 1183A), and amended by Pub. L. No. 104-208, § 551, 1996 U.S.C.C.A.N. (110 Stat.) 3009 [1570], 3009 [1780].

Admission and Entry

The HIV status and all the other bases of exclusion only are relevant to admissions. There is a critical distinction between every literal *entry* or reentry into the United States and an *admission* under U.S. immigration law. One can enter the United States with or without authorization, with or without "inspection." On the other hand, an admission is completed only after an inspection at the border or other port of entry, or after an adjustment of immigration status interview by an INS official. Thus, individuals seeking initial admission as permanent residents at the border are subject to exclusion. Similarly, individuals already in the United States seeking admission through an adjustment of immigration status to permanent residence also are subject to exclusion. All nonimmigrants seeking admission to the United States are subject to exclusion.

There is an important exception, however, for permanent residents who leave the United States temporarily and then return. As long as the absence is "innocent, casual and brief," the returning permanent resident is not subject to exclusion.[68] The determination of whether the absence is innocent, casual, and brief depends less on the length of the absence and more on the purpose of the absence and the activities abroad. The key factor is whether the permanent resident continues to maintain her permanent residence in the United States. For example, short vacations, visits to family, or business-related travel generally are considered innocent, casual, and brief absences. On the other hand, a permanent resident who quits his job and sells his house in the United States and then returns after one week abroad may have difficulty proving that he has not abandoned his permanent residence in the United States. Similarly, a permanent resident who travels abroad for a short period of time but buys a house or starts a business abroad might have difficulty rebutting the presumption that she has abandoned her permanent residence in the United States. HIV-infected permanent residents who travel abroad should ensure that sufficient ties to the United States such as employment, housing and health care, are maintained to establish that their permanent residence remains in the United States.

EXCLUSION BASED ON HIV INFECTION

§ 11.8 History of Exclusion Based on HIV Infection

HIV infection has been a basis for exclusion under U.S. immigration law since 1987.

In April 1986, the Public Health Service (PHS) published a proposed regulation adding AIDS to the list of excludable diseases (which then included active

---

[68] Rosenberg v. Flueti, 374 U.S. 449 (1963).

tuberculosis, infectious syphilis, gonorrhea, chancroid, granuloma inguinale, lymphogranuloma venereum, and infectious leprosy).[69] The rationale for the proposed regulation was that as long as other sexually transmitted diseases remained on the list, AIDS, also classifiable as a sexually transmitted disease, needed to be added.[70] The PHS received little public comment on the proposed regulation and never acted to finalize it.

The issue exploded politically when President Ronald Reagan made his first public speech about AIDS on the eve of the Fourth International Conference on AIDS in Washington, D.C., on May 31, 1987. President Reagan called for the mandatory HIV testing of immigrants, those incarcerated in federal prisons, and applicants for state marriage licenses.[71] The federal bureaucracy then moved with unprecedented speed. Within days of the president's speech, the PHS finalized its dormant proposed regulation adding AIDS to the exclusion list[72] and simultaneously published a new proposed regulation substituting HIV infection for AIDS on the exclusion list.[73] Meanwhile, on June 2, 1987, Senator Jesse Helms attached a last-minute amendment to a supplemental appropriations bill, H.R. 1827, requiring the president to add HIV infection to the exclusion list before August 31, 1987. Among the supplemental appropriations was an additional $30 million to provide AZT to HIV-infected individuals. The Helms amendment passed the Senate by a vote of 97 to 0.[74] The bill was acceded to by the House and was signed into law by President Reagan in July.[75] The PHS in fact finalized its regulation substituting HIV infection for AIDS on the exclusion list on August 28, 1987.[76]

---

[69] 51 Fed. Reg. 15,354 (1986), *amending* 42 C.F.R. § 34.2(b).

[70] 51 Fed. Reg. 15,354 ("It is proposed that AIDS be added to the list of dangerous contagious diseases since it would be anomalous to have diseases such as chancroid and lymphogranuloma venereum on such a list and not include AIDS. AIDS is added to the list because it is a recently defined sexually transmitted disease of significant public health importance.").

[71] *See* Philip M. Boffey, *Reagan Urges Wide AIDS Testing but Does Not Call for Compulsion,* N.Y. Times, Jun. 1, 1987, at A1; Sandra G. Boodman, *Reagan Asks Expansion of AIDS Virus Testing,* Wash. Post, Jun. 1, 1987, at A1.

[72] 52 Fed. Reg. 21,532 (1987).

[73] *Id.* at 21,607. The PHS emphasized that "[t]he spread of AIDS by certain high risk sexual practices is not unlike several other diseases currently on the list of 'dangerous contagious diseases' in the regulations implementing our responsibilities under the Immigration and Nationality Act . . . . This substitution is not being made on the basis of any new scientific knowledge about the transmission of HIV infection or the natural history of AIDS.")

[74] 133 Cong. Rec. 14,290 (1987). *See* Jonathan Fuerbringer, *Senate Votes to Require Test of Aliens for AIDS Virus,* N.Y. Times, Jun. 3, 1987, at B8.

[75] Pub. L. No. 100-71, § 518, 1987 U.S.C.C.A.N. (101 Stat.) 391, 475.

[76] 52 Fed. Reg. 32,540 (1987). The exclusion became effective on December 1, 1987. There are no reliable statistics on how many HIV-infected immigrants would be excluded from the U.S. each year. The Congressional Research Service estimated the number at 200 to 300 individuals annually. J.C. Vialet, Congressional Res. Serv. Rep. for Cong., No. 93-257 EPW, HIV-Positive Aliens: Facts and Issues (1993). Others have used an estimate of 600 to 800. *See*

This regulatory change occurred during the middle of the processing of applications for legalization under the Immigration Reform and Control Act of 1986 (see § **11.3**). There was widespread confusion about the new exclusion. There was no training or orientation about HIV testing for the thousands of INS-designated "civil surgeons" who would now be administering hundreds of thousands of HIV antibody tests.[77]

Despite the problems with the implementation of the HIV immigration exclusion, there was little public attention paid to the issue until April 1989, when the INS excluded and detained a Dutch AIDS educator, Hans Paul Verhoef, who was seeking to attend a gay and lesbian health conference in the United States.[78] Although Verhoef eventually was admitted into the United States by an immigration judge over the objections of the INS, AIDS and public health organizations began to voice their opposition to the immigration exclusion. The opposition to the exclusion policy escalated into an international boycott of the Sixth International Conference on AIDS held in San Francisco in June 1990.[79] In response to the growing international pressure, the INS created a special waiver for persons with HIV seeking to attend the conference (nonimmigrant waivers are

---

Malcolm Gladwell, *U.S. Won't Lift HIV Immigration Ban; Cost of Treating Those Who Develop AIDS Called Unacceptable,* Wash. Post, Aug., 2, 1991, at A1. Another estimate, based on Department of State statistics for 1988, the first full calendar year of HIV testing, suggests that the seroprevalence rate among immigrants subject to the exclusion is about 0.13 percent, or 1.3 per 1,000. Larry O. Gostin et al., *Screening Immigrants and International Travelers For the Human Immunodeficiency Virus,* 322 New Eng. J. Med. 1743, 1744 (1990). One analysis suggests that, given the varying false positive rates among populations depending on their actual seroprevalence rate, as many as 270 false positive immigrants could be excluded each year. Rupert E.D. Whitaker & Richard K. Edwards, *A Model-Based Approach to US Policy on HIV-1 Infection and Immigration,* 6 AIDS & Pub. Pol'y J. 3 (1991) (Table 4).

[77] Ignatius Bau & Patricia Dunn, *INS HIV Antibody Testing: No Justification for Exclusion of Immigrants and Refugees,* Immigr. Newsl. (Nat'l Immigr. Project, Nat'l Law. Guild, Boston, MA), vol. 18, 1989, at 3–8, 25. INS medical examinations are covered in § **11.9**.

[78] *In re* Verhoef, A28 522 388 (I.J. 1989). *See* Paul Houston, *Jailing of Dutch Traveler who Has AIDS Stirs Protest Over U.S. Immigration Rule,* L.A. Times, Apr. 5, 1989, at A14; Victor F. Zonana, *Dutch AIDS Patient Freed, Travels to S.F.,* L.A. Times, Apr. 9, 1989, at A3; *Alien with AIDS Ordered Freed,* N.Y. Times, Apr. 8, 1989, at A9; 66 Interp. Rel. 427–28 (1989).

[79] *See* Michael Specter, *Major Groups Plan to Boycott San Francisco AIDS Meeting; U.S. Restriction on Immigration Criticized,* Wash. Post, Dec. 13, 1989, at A2; Victor F. Zonana, *Rules on AIDS Fuel Boycott of Conference,* L.A. Times, Mar. 23, 1990, at A3; Robert M. Wachter, The Fragile Coalition: Scientists, Activists and AIDS 113–49 (1991). Among the nearly 100 organizations joining the boycott were the International League of Red Cross and Red Crescent Societies, the World Hemophilia Association, the National Association of People with AIDS, the United Kingdom Nongovernmental Organization AIDS Consortium, the International Planned Parenthood Federation, Gay Men's Health Crisis, Shanti Project, and the Names Project as well as the European Parliament and the government of France. The National Commission on AIDS also weighed in, calling for the lifting of the HIV immigration exclusion. *See* Marlene Cimons, *AIDS Panel Calls for End to Stigmatizing Foreign Visitors Who Are HIV-Infected,* L.A. Times, Dec. 13, 1989, at A4; Philip J. Hilts, *U.S. Urged to End Screening on AIDS,* N.Y. Times, Dec. 13, 1989, at B14.

covered in § **11.10**). During the conference, both conference speakers and street protests condemned the immigration exclusion.[80]

Meanwhile, in early 1990, the PHS quietly had conducted its own review of the immigration exclusion and concluded that all the diseases, including HIV, should be removed except for infectious tuberculosis.[81] However, the Bush Administration never acted on this internal PHS recommendation.[82]

Later that year, the Immigration Act of 1990[83] provided the opportunity for the statutory revision of the HIV exclusion. Eventually, legislation authored by Representative Barney Frank revising all the grounds of exclusion, H.R. 1280, and by Representative J. Roy Rowland, H.R. 4506, specifically lifting the HIV exclusion, were incorporated into the final immigration bill. The new exclusion statute made clear that the authority over the health exclusion list would remain with the secretary of the Department of Health and Human Services (HHS). The new statute also revised the statutory language of the health exclusion from "dangerous contagious diseases" to "communicable diseases of public health significance" and required HHS to publish regulations with a new list of excludable diseases by June 1, 1991.[84] Congress directed the HHS secretary to establish the new list of excludable diseases based solely on "current epidemiological principles and medical standards" and to include only those diseases for which the admission of individuals with them "would constitute a public health threat to the United States."[85] The new statute also expanded the eligibility for waivers of the health-related exclusions, including the HIV exclusion.[86]

---

[80] *See* Jane Gross, *Immigration Laws Protested on Eve of AIDS Conference,* N.Y. Times, June 20, 1990, at A15; David Tuller, *Protest at Immigration Service in S.F.,* S.F. Chron., June 20, 1990, at A9; Michael Specter, *Activists Take to the Streets at AIDS Conference,* Wash. Post, June 20, 1990, at A4; Charles Petit, *AIDS Delegates Join in Immigration Protest, Armbands Show Disdain for U.S. Policy Barring People,* S.F. Chron., June 21, 1990, at A8.

[81] *See* 56 Fed. Reg. 2484, 2485 (1991) (referencing PHS review one year earlier); Philip J. Hilts, *Agency Says AIDS Should Not Bar Entry to U.S.,* N.Y. Times, Feb. 27, 1990, at A18; Jayne Garrison, *CDC Urges Removing HIV from Travel Restrictions,* S.F. Examiner, Feb. 28, 1990, at A5.

[82] One of the reasons there was no action on the PHS recommendation was confusion over whether the 1987 Helms amendment required HIV infection to remain on the exclusion list. However, in May 1990, the comptroller general issued a legal opinion that the authority over the exclusion list remained with the PHS because the Helms Amendment literally had been complied with—HIV infection has been added before August 31, 1987, and now could be removed at any time from the exclusion list—and because the Helms amendment was binding only during the one fiscal year of its underlying appropriations bill. Comp. Gen. Op. B-239598 (1990). The Bush administration also ignored this Comptroller General opinion. *See President Told He Can Lift AIDS Travel Ban,* N.Y. Times, May 23, 1990, at A9; Malcolm Gladwell, *HHS Can Lift AIDS Virus Immigration Barrier, Opinion Says,* Wash. Post, May 23, 1990, at A9; Marlene Cimons, *U.S. Restrictions on AIDS-Infected Visitors Challenged,* L.A. Times, May 23, 1990, at A14.

[83] Pub. L. No. 101-649, 1990 U.S.C.C.A.N. (104 Stat.) 4978.

[84] Pub. L. No. 101-649, § 601, *amending* 8 U.S.C. § 1182(a)(1)(A)(i). *See* Philip J. Hilts, *Landmark Accord Promises to Ease Immigration Curb,* N.Y. Times, Oct. 26, 1990, at A1.

[85] H.R. Conf. Rep. No. 955, 101st Cong., 2d Sess. 128, *reprinted in* 1990 U.S.C.C.A.N. 6784, 6793.

[86] 8 U.S.C. § 1182(g)(1). Family-based waivers are covered in § **11.10**.

Given his new statutory mandate, HHS Secretary Louis Sullivan published in January 1991 a proposed regulation removing all the diseases, including HIV infection, from the old exclusion list except for infectious tuberculosis.[87] This proposed regulation was essentially the regulation that PHS had recommended in early 1990 before the HIV exclusion became so politicized. However, opponents of the change organized an unprecedented response to the proposed regulation by sending HHS over 40,000 letters and postcards opposing the regulation. In response, HHS extended the public comment period past the statutory June 1 deadline to August 2, 1991, and temporarily adopted the former list of excludable diseases, including HIV infection, as the list under the new statute.[88] Efforts organized by immigrants, gays and lesbians, and HIV advocates then produced over 110,000 letters and postcards supporting the proposed regulation during the extended public comment period.[89] However, HHS took no further action after the extended public comment period ended, essentially nullifying the effect of the statutory revision by failing to promulgate any new regulations on the exclusion list.[90] Given the absence of any policy change, the threat of another international boycott of the Eighth International Conference on AIDS scheduled in Boston in 1992 led its sponsors to move the conference to Amsterdam.[91]

Soon after the inauguration of President Bill Clinton in 1993, his new HHS Secretary Donna Shalala announced plans to finalize her predecessor's dormant 1991 proposed regulation revising the list of exclusions, including removing HIV

---

[87] 56 Fed. Reg. 2484 (1991). *See* Philip J. Hilts, *In Shift, Health Chief Lifts Ban on Visitors with the AIDS Virus,* N.Y. Times, Jan. 4, 1991, at A1; Susan Okie, *U.S. Will Stop Excluding Immigrants, Travelers with AIDS Virus,* Wash. Post, Jan. 5, 1991, at A5.

[88] 56 Fed. Reg. 25,000 (1991). *See* Karen De Witt, *U.S., in Switch, Plans to Keep Out People Infected with AIDS Virus,* N.Y. Times, May 26, 1991, at A1; Robert Pear, *Ban on Aliens with AIDS to Continue for Now,* N.Y. Times, May 30, 1991, at A23; Marlene Cimons, *AIDS-Immigration Ban Extension Near,* L.A. Times, May 30, 1991, at A19.

[89] Memorandum to HHS Secretary on Draft Final Rule on Medical Examination of Aliens, Feb. 5, 1993, at 2–3 (on file with author).

[90] *See* Malcolm Gladwell, *U.S. Won't Lift HIV Immigration Ban,* Wash. Post, Aug. 2, 1991, at A1.

[91] *See* Dolores Kong, *Harvard Cancels AIDS Conference,* Boston Globe, Aug. 17, 1991, at 1; Marlene Cimons, *Harvard Decides Not to Hold '92 AIDS Conference in U.S.,* L.A. Times, Aug. 17, 1991, at A1; Malcolm Gladwell, *AIDS Meeting to Move Abroad Due to U.S. Immigration Rules,* Wash. Post, Aug. 17, 1991, at A2; Philip J. Hilts, *United States Policy on Infected Visitors Keeps AIDS Meeting Out of Country,* N.Y. Times, Aug. 17, 1991, at A6; Delores Kong, *Amsterdam Chosen for AIDS Conference,* Boston Globe, Sept. 11, 1991, at 4; Lawrence K. Altman, *Amsterdam Picked for AIDS Meeting,* N.Y. Times, Sept. 12, 1991, at B11. A permanent resident of the United States, Tomas Fabregas, drew international attention to the exclusion at the Amsterdam conference by challenging the Bush administration to exclude him for HIV infection upon his return to the United States. *See Man with HIV Challenges Entry Ban,* N.Y. Times, July 27, 1992, at A12; Marilyn Chase, *Resident Alien Who Has AIDS Defies U.S. Ban,* Wall St. J., July 27, 1992, at B4; Wylie Wong, *Oakland Man Dares U.S. on HIV Entry Ban,* S.F. Chron., July 26, 1992, at B8. Fabregas was not excluded and re-admitted to the United States under the *Flueti* rule but made his point that the continuing HIV immigration exclusion was unevenly applied and was ineffective as a public health measure.

from the list.[92] The congressional response was swift, amending S.1, a bill re-authorizing and reorganizing the funding for the National Institutes for Health, with a provision that added HIV infection as a statutory basis for exclusion.[93] Despite the policy arguments that Congress had recently delegated the control of the exclusion list expressly to HHS and that HHS had made its proposal to remove HIV infection from the list under both Republican and Democratic presidential administrations, congressional support for the amendment remained insurmountable.[94] Ultimately, the amendment was enacted.[95] Thus, HIV infection is now a statutory basis for exclusion, requiring an unlikely repeal by Congress.

The failure of the Clinton Administration to end the immigration exclusion based on HIV infection had a critical impact on the fate of Haitian refugees[96] who fled the repression of the 1991 military coup that ousted Haiti's first democratically elected president, Jean-Bertrand Aristide. Over 35,000 individuals fled Haiti after the coup and were interdicted by the U.S. Coast Guard and

---

[92] *See* Philip J. Hilts, *Clinton to Lift Ban on HIV-Infected Visitors,* N.Y. Times, Feb. 9, 1993, at A17; David Lauter, *Clinton to Drop Travel Ban on HIV Patients,* L.A. Times, Feb. 5, 1993, at A14.

[93] 139 Cong. Rec. S1767 (daily ed. Feb. 18, 1993). *See* Helen Dewar, *Senate, 76-23, Votes to Bar HIV-Infected Immigrants,* Wash. Post, Feb. 19, 1993, at A2; Clifford Krauss, *Senate Opposes Immigration of People with AIDS Virus,* N.Y. Times, Feb. 19, 1993, at A11; Marlene Cimons, *Senate Backs Ban on Immigrants with AIDS Virus,* L.A. Times, Feb. 19, 1993, at A1. It was ironic that the Senate attached the HIV immigration exclusion amendment to the NIH bill, which created the Office of AIDS Research and otherwise increased funding for AIDS-related research, both goals advocated by AIDS activists.

[94] The House passed the NIH legislation with a similar amendment regarding the HIV immigration exclusion on March 11. 139 Cong. Rec. 1178–79 (daily ed. Mar. 11, 1993). *See* Marlene Cimons, *House OKs Ban on Immigrants with HIV,* L.A. Times, Mar. 12, 1993, at A31; Adam Clymer, *House, Like Senate, Votes to Bar HIV Immigrants,* N.Y. Times, Mar. 12, 1993, at A11; Kenneth J. Cooper, *House Backs HIV Immigration Ban,* Wash. Post, Mar. 12, 1993, at A13.

[95] Pub. L. No. 103-43, § 2007, 1993 U.S.C.C.A.N. (107 Stat.) 122, 210, *amending* 8 U.S.C. § 1182(a)(1)(A)(i). *See* Philip J. Hilts, *Bar on HIV-Infected Immigrants Is Retained in Final Capitol Test,* N.Y. Times, May 25, 1993, at A13. For background on the legislative history of the 1993 statutory codification, see Juan P. Osuna, *The Exclusion from the United States of Aliens Infected with the AIDS Virus: Recent Developments and Prospects for the Future,* 16 Hous. J. Int'l L. 22–39 (1989). Another consequence of the failure of the Clinton Administration to lift the HIV immigration exclusion is that the other outdated disease exclusions also remain in effect, although they could be lifted at any time by HHS regulation.

[96] The fact that the HIV exclusion has ended up impacting Haitians the most raises parallels to the CDC and FDA's inappropriate classification of Haitians as a high risk group for HIV infection solely because of their national origin in the early 1980s. *See* John Wilke, *Physician Disputes Link of Haitians, AIDS Risk,* Wash. Post, Aug. 2, 1983, at A2; Christine Russell, *Haitians No Longer Listed As Known AIDS Risk,* Wash. Post, Apr. 9, 1985, at A3; Donatella Lorch, *FDA Policy to Limit Blood is Protested,* N.Y. Times, Apr. 21, 1990, at A25.

screened by the INS at the U.S. Naval Base at Guantanamo Bay, Cuba. Approximately 10,490 Haitians, or about 30 percent, were found likely to be refugees and "paroled" into the United States to pursue their asylum claims.[97] Beginning in February 1992, the INS began a second round of refugee status screening for those 215 Haitians and 52 of their family members found to be HIV-infected. Unlike the other Haitians who had been paroled into the United States, these 267 Haitians remained in detention at Guantanamo solely because of their HIV infection.[98]

Meanwhile, in May 1992, the Bush Administration began a policy of interdiction and immediate repatriation.[99] During the 1992 presidential campaign, candidate Bill Clinton pledged both to reverse the Bush Administration Haitian interdiction and immediate repatriation policy and to end the HIV immigration exclusion.[100] However, when Clinton announced even before his inauguration that he would continue the interdiction and immediate repatriation policy, the Haitian refugees detained on Guantanamo began a four-week hunger strike. Hunger strikes, primarily on college campuses, also began in the United States.[101] Clinton did attempt to lift the HIV immigration exclusion in February 1993 but could not do so in the face of congressional opposition. As part of a complex legal challenge to the U.S. policies of interdiction, screening, and repatriation, the Clinton Administration ultimately was ordered to either provide adequate medical services for the HIV infected Haitians at Guantanamo or parole them into

---

[97] *Parole status* is used to allow an individual into the United States pending determination of their immigration status. 8 U.S.C. § 1182(d)(5). *See generally,* Ruth Ellen Wasem & Larry M. Eig, Congressional Res. Serv. Rep. for Cong., No. 93-294 EPW, HIV-Positive Haitians Detained at Guantanamo (1993).

[98] Haitian Ctrs. Council, Inc. v. Sale, 823 F. Supp. 1028, 1035–36 (E.D.N.Y. 1993). The court noted their conditions of detention:

> They live in camps surrounded by razor barbed wire. They tie plastic garbage bags to the sides of the building to keep the rain out. They sleep on cots and hang sheets to create some semblance of privacy. They are guarded by the military and not permitted to leave the camp, except under military escort. The Haitian detainees have been subjected to pre-dawn military sweeps as they sleep by as many as 400 soldiers dressed in full riot gear. They are confined like prisoners and are subject to detention in the brig without a hearing for camp rule infractions.

Id. at 1037.

[99] Exec. Order No. 12,807, 3 C.F.R. § 303 (1992).

[100] *See* Bill Clinton & Al Gore, Putting People First: How We Can All Change America 41, 119 (1992); David G. Savage, *Policy Switch Easy as Stroke of Clinton Pen,* L.A. Times, Nov. 7, 1992, at A1.

[101] *See* Nadine Brozan, *Chronicle: A Fast in Support of Haitian Refugees Moves from Yale to Harvard,* N.Y. Times, Mar. 12, 1993, at B6; Matt Neufeld, *Students Plan Hunger Strikes for Haitians,* Wash. Times, Apr. 1, 1993, at B3; Sara Bowen, *Students: Haiti Policy Is Hypocritical,* USA Today, Apr. 13, 1993, at A11.

the United States.[102] The U.S. Supreme Court ultimately upheld the interdiction and immediate repatriation policy.[103]

§ 11.9 Exclusion Procedures in HIV Cases

Although one's HIV status is a basis for exclusion under U.S. immigration law, it is not a basis for deportation. Thus, although a person may be denied a change

---

[102] Haitians Ctrs. Council, Inc. v. Sale, 817 F. Supp. 336, *subsequent op.* 823 F. Supp. 1028 (E.D.N.Y. 1993). Among the findings of the district court was that the INS had demonstrated "deliberate indifference to the Haitians' medical needs in violation of their due process rights." *Id.* at 1044. The court concluded:

> Where HIV+ detainees have been held for nearly two years in prison camp conditions likely to further compromise their health, where each year other individuals carrying the HIV virus are allowed to enter the United States, and where the admission of Haitians is unlikely to affect the spread of AIDS in this country, the Government's continued imprisonment of the Screened In Plaintiffs serves no other purpose other than to punish them for being sick.

Id. at 1049. For commentary on the Haitian refugee litigation, see Kerry A. Krzynowek, Note, Haitian Centers Council, Inc. v. Sale: *Rejecting the Indefinite Detention of HIV-Infected Aliens,* 11 J. Contemp. Health L. & Pol'y 541 (1995); Creola Johnson, *Quarantining HIV-Infected Haitians: United States' Violations of International Law at Guantanamo Bay,* 37 How. L.J. 305 (1994); Jason W. Konvicka, Note, *Give Us Your Tired, Your Poor, Your Huddled Masses . . . Except When They Have HIV: An Analysis of Current United States Immigration Policy Regarding HIV-Positive Aliens in Light of Guantanamo Bay,* 27 U. Rich. L. Rev. 531 (1993); Elizabeth M. McCormick, Note, *HIV-Infected Haitian Refugees: An Argument Against Exclusion,* 7 Geo. Immigr. L.J. 149 (1993). *Cf.* Jason A. Pardo, Note, *Excluding Immigrants on the Basis of Health: The Haitian Centers Council Decision Criticized,* 11 J. Contemp. Health L. & Pol'y 523 (1995) (arguing in favor of exclusion).

[103] Sale v. Haitian Ctrs. Council, Inc., 113 S. Ct. 2549 (1993). Lead counsel Yale Law School Professor Koh and his extraordinary team of law students have written insightful reflections on their experiences of the litigation. *See* Harold Hongju Koh, *The "Haiti Paradigm" in United States Human Rights Policy,* 103 Yale L.J. 2391 (1994); *id., Reflections on Refoulement and Haitian Centers Council,* 35 Harv. Int'l L.J. 1 (1994); *id., The Haitian Refugee Litigation: A Case Study in Transnational Public Law Litigation,* 18 Md. J. Int'l L. & Trade 1 (1994); *id., The Human Face of the Haitian Interdiction Program,* 33 Va. J. Int'l L. 483 (1993); Victoria Clawson et al., Essay, *Litigating as Law Students: An Inside Look at Haitian Centers Council,* 103 Yale L.J. 2337 (1994); and Lowenstein Int'l Hum. Rts. Clinic, *Aliens and the Duty of Nonrefoulement: Haitian Centers Council v. McNary,* 6 Harv. Hum. Rts. J. 1 (1993). Professor Koh writes eloquently of the lesson of the case:

> I realized that the Haitian story reduces to a story about "we" and "they." Our government was able to depersonalize the Haitians because Americans wanted to believe that the Haitians are not us . . . . But if you have ever been a refugee, or if your forbears were refugees, then in fact, you are Haitian. If you ever lived in an internment camp or knew someone in an internment camp, then you are Haitian. If you have ever known someone shunned because they have HIV, then you are Haitian. And if you ever believed—even for one second—that the words on the Statue of Liberty are not just words, but a sacred promise, then you are Haitian.

18 Md. J. Int'l L. & Trade at 20.

of immigration status because he is HIV infected, he will not be deported solely because of that fact. Of course, he may be or may become deportable for other, unrelated reasons, such as illegal entry, staying longer than authorized, or working without employment authorization.[104] The HIV exclusion is applied by the INS at adjustment of immigration status interviews and again at the border or place of entry. The exclusion also is applied by Department of State consular officials at permanent resident interviews and during the processing of requests for nonimmigrant visas at U.S. embassies and consulates abroad.

The INS has issued guidelines for border inspections that restrict questioning by INS officials about one's HIV serostatus.[105] Specifically, the INS should not inquire about HIV status unless there are clear physical symptoms (presumably, visually detectable ones such as Karposi's sarcoma) or the individual makes an unsolicited and unambiguous declaration of his or her HIV infection. Questioning about HIV status is not to be triggered by the discovery of any literature, buttons, T-shirts, or similar items referring to HIV or AIDS. However, the discovery of AIDS-related drugs such as AZT may trigger questioning about HIV status and even referral for a medical examination. Individuals who are bringing any medications into the United States must also carry a written prescription for the medications to meet the requirements of U.S. customs laws. In order to avoid questioning about their AIDS-related medications, individuals can carry the written prescriptions separately from the medications and place the medications in unmarked containers. Unfortunately, the INS inspection guidelines are only advisory, and an individual cannot challenge his interrogation, detention, or exclusion based on any alleged violations of the guidelines.

If an individual entering the United States is suspected or discovered to be subject to the HIV exclusion at the border, the INS generally attempts to persuade the individual to return to his country of origin. The INS has the authority to detain the individual indefinitely, without any right to release on bail or bond. The individual may be transferred to a state or local jail for detention. The individual has no right to counsel at this stage and often is unable to communicate with others who may be able to provide evidence or arguments on his behalf.

However, in many cases, the INS will release individuals either on their own recognizance or on a bond and require a "deferred inspection" at the local INS office a few days later. Under a legal fiction, individuals subject to a deferred inspection still stand at the border, awaiting a determination of their right to be admitted even though they already have physically entered the country. At the deferred inspection, the individuals may have legal counsel and present evidence. The INS again attempts to persuade the individual to "withdraw the application for admission" and leave the United States. The INS also may decide

---

[104] 8 U.S.C. § 1251(a) (grounds of deportation).

[105] INS, Mem. No. CO 234-P, Admission of Individuals Who Are HIV Positive (1990), *reprinted in* 67 Interp. Rel. 569–71 (1990); INS, Mem. No. CO 234-P, Inspections Regarding Medical Exclusion Grounds (1990), *reprinted in* 67 Interp. Rel. 1100–03 (1990).

to admit the individual after all. If the individual persists in pursuing admission, the case is referred to the Immigration Court for a determination of excludability by an immigration judge. The decision of the immigration judge may be reviewed by a U.S. District Court through a writ of habeas corpus.

INS Medical Examinations

Medical examinations are required as part of the process of obtaining permanent residence. The medical examination must be conducted by an INS or Department of State designated civil surgeon, although most are general medical practitioners, not actual surgeons. A list of approved physicians is provided by each local INS office or Department of State consular office.[106] Unfortunately, there is little oversight of these physicians. The only requirement to qualify as a civil surgeon is a minimum of four years of licensed medical practice.[107] There is no formal procedure to remove any civil surgeon from the approved lists for noncompliance with either CDC or INS guidelines.

The medical examination generally consists of a medical history, a general physical examination, a chest x-ray (to detect tuberculosis), and the drawing of a blood sample to be tested for syphilis and HIV antibodies. Applicants under the age of 15 are exempt from the HIV antibody test unless there is reason to suspect HIV infection. There is no requirement that the civil surgeon obtain the immigrant's informed consent to the HIV antibody test. Although the CDC has issued guidelines encouraging pre- and post-HIV test counseling by civil surgeons, there is no monitoring and no enforcement of these guidelines.[108] The results of the medical examination are given to the immigrant in a sealed envelope to present to the INS at the adjustment of status interview. The immigrant must specifically request a copy of the examination results if she wants to know the results or have a copy of the results.

The CDC also requires that confirmatory Western Blot testing be completed in addition to repetitive ELISA tests prior to a finding of HIV seropositivity by INS civil surgeons. Again, there is neither monitoring nor enforcement of these laboratory protocols. Civil surgeons receive no training or other educational materials about HIV or HIV antibody testing by either the CDC or the INS. Fortunately, some state laws do require more extensive controls over HIV antibody testing and counseling conducted for any purpose within those states. However, these safeguards generally are not present in other countries when the INS medical examination is conducted as part of consular visa processing. Immigrants who have reason to believe that they might be at risk for HIV infection

---

[106] INS, Mem. No. HQ 234-P, Medical Examinations of Aliens Applying for Adjustment of Status in the U.S. under Section 245 of the Immigration and Nationality Act (1994), *reprinted in* 71 Interp. Rel. 727–30 (1994).

[107] 8 C.F.R. § 234.2(b).

[108] U.S. Pub. Health Serv., Technical Instructions for the Medical Examination of Aliens (1991); *see* 68 Interp. Rel. 799–800 (1991).

should obtain HIV testing at an anonymous or confidential test site prior to the INS medical examination. They can then obtain the appropriate counseling and referrals regarding their HIV status prior to continuing with their immigration status processing. They also can be assured that their test results are accurate.[109]

Nonimmigrants are generally not subject to any medical examination. However, both the INS and U.S. consular officials have the authority to require a medical examination of any noncitizen, including nonimmigrants, prior to admission.[110]

Travel Issues

In general, HIV-infected noncitizens with a legal immigration status in the United States are able to travel abroad temporarily and return to resume their immigration status in the United States.[111] However, they first should determine whether they might be subject to the HIV exclusion upon their return and, if so, whether they would be eligible for a waiver. The inspection guidelines and procedures discussed above also would be relevant.

§ 11.10   Waivers of HIV Exclusion

Certain individuals with HIV can obtain waivers of the HIV exclusion. It is vital for an HIV-infected immigrant to obtain legal advice and assistance from an immigration attorney or advocate with knowledge and experience in obtaining HIV waivers. Conversely, if an HIV-infected individual is statutorily ineligible for a waiver, he may consider withdrawing or abandoning his application with the INS or pursuing alternative immigration statuses. In some areas, special legal services projects provide legal assistance and representation to immigrants with HIV.

Eligibility for Waivers.   Eligibility for an HIV waiver depends on which immigration status is being sought. **Section 11.14** lists whether an HIV waiver is available for each immigration status. Individuals who are obtaining permanent residence through employment, the diversity lottery, and certain family preference categories such as the sibling category generally are ineligible for an HIV waiver. HIV-infected individuals who are applying for permanent residence through one of these categories should consult with an immigration attorney or advocate about alternative options.

---

[109] One of the ironies of the mandatory HIV testing of immigrants is that the opportunity to provide HIV prevention education to millions of immigrants is being missed by the failure to provide pre- and post-test counseling about HIV infection. Those who test negative on their INS medical exam are not provided any information about HIV or how they might prevent becoming infected in the future.

[110] 8 U.S.C. §§ 1201(d), 1222, 1224.

[111] There are some exceptions: obviously, refugees and asylum applicants cannot return to their home countries when they are claiming a fear of persecution in those countries.

Family-Based Waivers. HIV-infected applicants for permanent residence whose spouse or child or parent, if the applicant is unmarried, is a U.S. citizen, permanent resident, or permanent resident applicant are eligible for a waiver of the HIV exclusion.[112] The applicant must demonstrate the family relationship (already required for the family-based petition for permanent residence) and must meet the other conditions established by the INS. Waiver procedures are covered in § **11.11** through **11.13.** Thus, applicants through one of the immediate relative categories automatically are eligible for a waiver. Similarly, those applying through the second family preference for spouses and unmarried children of permanent residents and the first family preference for unmarried children of U.S. citizens also are eligible for this waiver. However, those applying through the third family preference for married children or the fourth family preference for siblings of U.S. citizens would be ineligible unless they had another qualifying family relationship.

Refugees and Asylee Adjustments. Refugee applicants are eligible for waivers of the HIV exclusion "for humanitarian purposes, to assure family unity, or when it is otherwise in the public interest."[113] Working in close cooperation with the United Nations High Commissioner for Refugees, refugee applicants from countries such as Laos, Kenya, and Zaire have been granted such waivers. Similarly, both refugees and asylees seeking adjustment of status to permanent residence are eligible for HIV waivers.[114]

Legalization Waivers. Both applicants for temporary residence and temporary residents seeking adjustment of status to permanent residence through two of the legalization programs (continuous residence since January 1, 1982, and agricultural workers programs) included in the Immigration Reform and Control Act of 1986 (see § 11.3) are eligible for waivers of the HIV exclusion "for humanitarian purposes, to assure family unity, or when it is otherwise in the public interest."[115] The INS did promulgate regulations establishing its three-prong test

---

[112] 8 U.S.C. § 1182(g)(1). These family-based waivers were not available prior to the Immigration Act of 1990. The history of the 1990 Act is provided in § **11.8.**

[113] 8 U.S.C. § 1157(c)(3).

[114] *Id.* § 1159(c). *See generally* Deborah Bartz, Comment, *The United States HIV Exclusion: Endangering Refugees' Human Rights,* 17 Hamline L. Rev. 155 (1993). The INS continues to apply its own three-prong criteria to these waivers, as discussed in §§ **11.11–11.13.** The use of the INS criteria, however, especially the third prong, may violate the statute because these two statutory waivers explicitly waive the public charge exclusion. 8 U.S.C. §§ 1157(c)(3), 1159(c).

[115] 8 U.S.C. §§ 1255a(d)(2)(B)(i), 1160(c)(2)(B)(i). Congress intended that such waivers be granted in a "liberal and generous" fashion. H.R. Rep. No. 115, 98th Cong., 1st Sess., pt. 1, 69–70 (1983); H.R. Rep. No. 28, 100th Cong., 1st Sess. 37–38 (1987).

for these waivers.[116] HIV waivers are not available for the Cuban and Haitian legalization program under the Immigration Reform and Control Act.

Nonimmigrant Waivers. Nonimmigrants also are eligible for waivers of the HIV exclusion.[117] After the public controversy over the exclusion of Hans Verhoef in the spring of 1989, the INS clarified that waivers of the HIV exclusion would be granted to visitors if they could demonstrate that the public benefit from their visit outweighed the public health risk, and it authorized 30-day waivers for individuals seeking to visit the United States for one of four reasons: to visit family, to receive pre-paid medical treatment, for business, or to attend a scientific or health-related conference.[118] In response to the adverse international publicity surrounding the HIV exclusion and the growing boycott of the Sixth International Conference on AIDS, the INS then created a special 10-day waiver for individuals attending "pre-approved" conferences and events (such as the Sixth International Conference on AIDS or the XIX International Congress of the World Federation of Hemophilia).[119] The INS and Department of State also clarified that both the request and the evidence of a grant of these special waivers would be processed under procedures that maximized confidentiality.[120]

---

[116] 8 C.F.R. § 245a.3(d)(4). *See also* INS Cable No. CO 234-P (July 6, 1987), *reprinted in* 64 Interp. Rel. 888–89 (1987); INS Cable, Mar. 2, 1988, *reprinted in* 65 Interp. Rel. 239 (1988); INS Cable No. CO 1588-C (Jul. 29, 1988), *reprinted in* 65 Interp. Rel. 850–51 (1988). *See generally* Robert S. Hilliard, *Practice Tips for Preparing HIV Waivers for Amnesty Applicants,* Immigr. Newsl. (Nat'l Immigr. Project, Nat'l Law. Guild, Boston, MA), summer 1989, at 3–6; Bettina M. Fernandez, Note, *HIV Exclusion of Immigrants Under the Immigration Reform and Control Act of 1986,* 5 La Raza L.J. 65 (1992); Court E. Columbic, *Closing the Open Door: The Impact of Human Immunodeficiency Virus Exclusion on the Legalization Program of the Immigration Reform and Control Act of 1986,* 15 Yale J. Int'l L. 162 (1990).

[117] 8 U.S.C. § 1182(d)(3). *See* Department of State Cable No. 89-State-296666 (Sept. 15, 1989), *reprinted in* 66 Interp. Rel. 1211–12 (1989).

[118] INS Cables Nos. CO 234-P & CO 212.25-P (May 25, 1989), *reprinted in* 66 Interp. Rel. 625–26 (1989). *See generally In re* Hranka, 16 I. & N. Dec. 491 (B.I.A. 1978); *In re* A., 11 I. & N. Dec. 99 (Dist. Dir. 1965).

[119] INS Cable No. CO-234P (Feb. 22, 1990), *reprinted in* 67 Interp. Rel. 262–63 (1990). *See also* Department of State Cable No. 90-State-020636 (Jan. 20, 1990), *reprinted in* 67 Interp. Rel. 190–91 (1990); Department of State Cable No. 90-State-046042 (Feb. 10, 1990), *reprinted in* 67 Interp. Rel. 320–21 (1990); Department of State Cable No. 136115 (Apr. 27, 1990), *reprinted in* 67 Interp. Rel. 535–36 (1990); INS Cable No. CO-234P, (Jun. 4, 1990), *reprinted in* 67 Interp. Rel. 666–67 (1990); Department of State Cable No. 90-State-153915 (May 12, 1990), *reprinted in* 67 Interp. Rel. 667 (1990).

[120] The INS also authorized the 10-day waiver for those attending the Gay Games IV and Stonewall 25 events in the summer of 1994. INS, Mem. No. HQ 235-C, Admission of Individuals Who Are HIV Positive or Have AIDS to Attend Gay Games IV (1994), *reprinted in* 71 Interp. Rel. 504–06 (1994).

§ 11.11   HIV Waiver Procedures

Despite the distinct statutory requirements for the various HIV waivers, the INS has applied its own criteria to adjudicate all HIV waivers.[121] Under the INS criteria, the applicant must demonstrate that:

> 1) the danger to the public health of the United States created by his or her admission is minimal; 2) the possibility of the spread of the infection created by his or her admission to the United States is minimal; and 3) there will be no cost incurred by any level of government agency of the United States without the prior consent of that agency.[122]

The INS generally treats the first two prongs together, requiring that the applicant receive counseling about HIV and make a commitment to avoid the transmission of HIV. A 1995 INS memorandum on HIV waivers states that evidence of "the applicant's awareness of the nature and severity of his or her medical condition," "the applicant's willingness to attend educational seminars and counseling sessions," and "the applicant's knowledge of the modes of transmission of the disease" would be sufficient to meet the first two prongs.[123]

The third prong of the INS criteria has proven problematic in many cases. Generally, the INS requires proof of private health insurance for the applicant. Of course, it is extremely difficult for many individuals, especially those who are HIV-infected, to purchase private health insurance. Many health insurance policies still include disqualifications based on preexisting conditions, such as HIV infection, or include limits on the amount of health care coverage available in a single year or over the insured's lifetime. Although an applicant for an HIV waiver may also demonstrate prior consent from a government agency, it is unclear how such consent is to be obtained or documented. Some waiver applicants have submitted evidence of the current receipt of benefits with the knowledge of

---

[121] Except for the regulations relating to HIV waivers for legalization applicants, 8 C.F.R. § 245a.3(d)(4), the INS has failed to promulgate any regulations establishing its three-prong test as its administrative interpretation of the various statutory waiver provisions. This failure may violate the Administrative Procedure Act, 5 U.S.C. § 553. *See* American Fed'n of Gov't Employees v. Block, 655 F.2d 1153 (D.C. Cir. 1981) (exceptions to requirement of notice and comment narrowly construed). The failure to promulgate regulations is especially critical for refugee applicants and for refugees and asylees seeking adjustment of status because the third prong appears to be in violation of the statutory waiver of the public charge exclusion. 8 U.S.C. §§ 1157(c), 1159(c).

[122] INS Cable No. CO-234-P (Jul. 6, 1987), *reprinted in* 64 Interp. Rel. 888–89 (1987); INS Cable No. CO-234-P (Mar. 2, 1988), *reprinted in* 65 Interp. Rel. 239 (1988); INS Cable Nos. CO-234-P & CO-212.25-P (May 25, 1989), *reprinted in* 66 Interp. Rel. 625–26 (1989); INS, Mem. No. HQ 212.3-P, Immigrant Waivers for Aliens Found Excludable under Section 212(a)(1)(A)(i) of the Immigration and Nationality Act (Sept. 6, 1995), *reprinted in* 72 Interp. Rel. 1347–54 (1995).

[123] INS, Mem. No. HQ 212.3-P, Immigrant Waivers for Aliens Found Excludable under Section 212(a)(1)(A)(i) of the Immigration and Nationality Act at 5 (Sept. 6, 1995), *reprinted in* 72 Interp. Rel. at 1351.

the government agency of their pending immigration status. It is unlikely that any official of any governmental agency would sign a document ensuring future health care coverage for anyone.

Although the 1995 INS memorandum clarifies some procedures and criteria for HIV waivers for immigrants, it also raises new issues that will affect the future adjudication of HIV waivers. The memorandum does not address the failure to promulgate regulations and repeats the three-prong INS criteria for HIV waivers. The memorandum also attempts to distinguish between the public charge exclusion and the third prong of the HIV waiver but ultimately combines the two issues. The memorandum first notes:

> Examiners should make it clear in their decisions that a separate finding on the ground of public charge will be made. Although both findings (eligibility for a waiver under section 212(g) of the Act and excludability under section 212(a)(4) relating to public charge) may be contained in the same decision, they should be written up as separate and distinct adjudications to show that each ground of inadmissibility was reviewed and considered on its own merits.[124]

The 1995 INS memorandum then states:

> Examiners should note that HIV infection does not automatically result in a finding that an applicant is likely to become a public charge; however, in reviewing each case, a reasonable calculation of the applicant's future ability to pay the expected costs of the illness should be made. In addition to the medical expenses, a reasonable calculation of the applicant's ability to meet basic living expenses also should be made.[125]

However, the consideration of an applicant's future ability to pay for the costs of future illnesses is a significant expansion of the public charge exclusion. The usual public charge inquiry is limited to whether the household income exceeds the poverty guidelines, or whether there is current employment. To add consideration of actual or estimated medical or living expenses goes beyond the agency's practice and is unreliably dependent on the untrained speculation of the adjudicating official.

Ultimately, the 1995 INS memorandum confuses and combines the public charge exclusion and eligibility for the HIV waiver issues in the following paragraph titled "Determining Public Charge":

> Examiners should note that publicly-funded medical treatment for HIV infection does not automatically render the applicant excludable under the public charge provision. If the applicant has received or intends to receive HIV-related treatment

---

[124] *Id.* at 5–6, *reprinted in* 72 Interp. Rel. at 1351–52.

[125] *Id.* at 3. This instruction is consistent with Department of State instructions to consider that "aliens infected with the HIV virus are more likely to be subject to the public charge provision because of the relatively high costs of treating this disease." Department of State Cable No. 92-State-093280 (Mar. 25, 1992), *reprinted in* 69 Interp. Rel. 516–17 (1992).

at a government-financed facility, the applicant must submit evidence that such treatment is available and that the appropriate government agency has consented to the treatment.[126]

Thus, despite the INS memorandum's disclaimer that it is not changing any substantive eligibility standards,[127] this last paragraph combines the public charge and HIV exclusion grounds to create a new test: an HIV-infected applicant otherwise excludable on public charge grounds because of a likelihood that he would require publicly-funded medical care can overcome both the public charge exclusion and meet the third prong of the INS criteria for an HIV waiver if he can obtain prior consent from the funding government agency. This is a significant change, because the public charge exclusion has never been overcome simply with government agency consent. Of course, how consent of the "appropriate government agency" is obtained and documented remains highly problematic. Thus, although this latest INS memorandum seems to expand the public charge exclusion by considering an applicant's ability to pay medical and living expenses, it also seems to limit the exclusion by combining it with the third prong of the INS HIV waiver criteria. Monitoring of actual INS adjudications of HIV waivers under the new memorandum will be required to resolve these eligibility issues.

§ 11.12   —Documentation to Support HIV Waivers

As a practical matter, applicants for HIV waivers will need to assemble two types of evidence in support of the waiver. First, letters from doctors, nurses, AIDS service organizations, mental health workers, or social workers that attest to the knowledge and understanding of the applicant about HIV and its transmission will be required to satisfy the first two prongs of the INS criteria. A declaration from the applicant including the applicant's commitment to avoid transmission of HIV also would be helpful. If the applicant is participating in any support groups or engaging in any HIV prevention education efforts, those activities should be emphasized as positive contributions from the applicant above and beyond his own self-awareness and care.

Second, evidence must be collected to satisfy the third prong of the INS criteria. Proof of enrollment in a private health insurance plan, with copies of the scope of benefits, is sufficient. If the applicant has a regular health care provider who already is aware of the individual's HIV status, it also may be helpful for that provider to write a letter stating that health care will be available and reimbursable through the applicant's health insurance plan without any governmental costs.

---

[126] INS, Mem. No. HQ 212.3-P (Sept. 6, 1995) at 6.
[127] *Id.* at 2.

If the applicant does not have private health insurance, affidavits of support from relatives promising to pay the health care costs of the applicant may be submitted. Those affidavits, however, will be of limited use, given the extremely high costs of health care for persons living with AIDS. Both the Department of State and the INS have estimated the average cost of care for an HIV-infected person at $85,000.[128] In addition, relatives of the applicant may be unwilling or financially unable to make a sufficient commitment of resources to satisfy the INS.

A few HIV waiver applicants successfully have submitted evidence of participation in HIV-related clinical trials that include general health care to meet the third INS prong. Although such clinical trials might involve some governmental funding, the INS has seemed to overlook the issue of prior government consent. There also is a persuasive argument that the applicant's participation in the clinical trials is in the "public interest," one of the statutory criteria for several of the HIV waivers. Finally, the applicant may attempt to obtain some documentation of "consent" by a governmental agency for future costs of health care.[129]

§ 11.13 —INS Office Procedures

There are some critical differences in the processing and adjudication of HIV waivers at INS offices in the United States and at U.S. embassies and consular offices jointly staffed by the INS and the Department of State abroad. An applicant's ability to gather evidence and documentation as well as the applicant's rights to administrative and judicial review are severely limited outside the United States. Accordingly, it is vital that applicants for HIV waivers obtain legal advice and assistance prior to traveling abroad for any overseas processing of their HIV waivers.

Applicants for permanent residence who are adjusting their immigration status to permanent residence at INS offices in the United States must bring the sealed medical examination results from their civil surgeons with them to the INS interview. The INS should discover upon opening the results of the medical examination that the applicant is subject to the HIV exclusion. The INS should

---

[128] INS, Mem. No. HQ212.3-P (Sept. 6, 1995) at 3; Department of State Cable No. 92-093280 (Mar. 25, 1992), *reprinted in* 69 Interp. Rel. 516–17 (1992). In a comparative study of long-term health costs involving Canadian immigrants, however, one study found that the costs associated with coronary heart disease over a 10-year period would be nearly $5 million more than those costs associated with HIV infection. Hanna Zowall et al., *Economic Impact of HIV Infection and Coronary Heart Disease in Immigrants to Canada,* 147 Can. Med. Ass'n J. 1163 (1992). All these cost estimates may be outdated with the new but expensive treatment alternatives with protease inhibitors.

[129] *See generally* Robert S. Hilliard, *Getting Residency when You've Got HIV: Waivers of HIV-Related Grounds of Exclusion under the 1990 Act,* Immigr. Newsl. (Nat'l Immigr. Project, Nat'l Law. Guild, Boston, Mass.), Aug. 1992, at 3–9.

then advise the applicant that he or she may seek a waiver of the HIV exclusion by filing INS form I-601. The INS also is required to notify the CDC and request that the CDC open a file on the case. The INS waits for CDC's acknowledgment, accompanied by a CDC form that the waiver applicant must complete. The INS sends the CDC form to the waiver applicant to obtain the required signatures. The CDC form is adapted from exclusion cases involving tuberculosis, requiring signatures of local public health officials acknowledging that an immigrant with an excludable contagious or communicable disease will be residing in their jurisdiction and ensuring that there will be local monitoring and followup. All this makes sense for tuberculosis, in which there is tracking of infectious cases and a specific treatment protocol that must be followed for a certain period of time. It does not make sense for an HIV-infected individual, especially one who is asymtomatic. There obviously are serious disclosure and confidentiality issues in notifying and obtaining signatures from local public health officials. The INS waits for the applicant to return the I-601, the completed CDC form, and any supporting evidence before adjudicating the waiver request.

One of the advantages of obtaining legal representation and assistance is that an attorney or advocate can bypass this cumbersome procedure. There is no assurance that all the government agencies involved will respond in a timely manner to complete each of the many steps in this process. Meanwhile, the applicant is waiting simply to submit a waiver request. The applicant already knows the result of the medical examination, so the applicant can prepare the I-601 and the supporting evidence to submit immediately at the INS interview. An attorney also can obtain a copy of the blank CDC form and obtain the required signatures prior to the INS interview. At the interview, the attorney can present all the required forms and evidence for the HIV waiver and ask that the INS official adjudicate the waiver request as quickly as possible. The attorney may have to explain to the INS official that the need to wait for a response from CDC can be bypassed. The INS still must notify CDC to open a file on the case but can otherwise proceed to adjudicate the HIV waiver.

Overseas Procedures

HIV waiver procedures at U.S. embassies and consulates overseas are generally the same as at INS offices.[130] The critical difference between adjudications of HIV waivers by INS and Department of State officials submitted by applicants outside the United States is the absence of any administrative or judicial review of such decisions.[131] In addition, the further complication of overseas communication

---

[130] Department of State Cable No. 91-State-211456 (Jun. 27, 1991), *reprinted in* 68 Interp. Rel. 969–71 (1991); Department of State Cable No. 92-227815 (Jul. 16, 1992), *reprinted in* 69 Interp. Rel. 1097–98 (1992); INS Cable No. HQ 212.25-P (June 3, 1993), *reprinted in* 70 Interp. Rel. 873 (1993).

[131] The 1995 INS memorandum ended the practice of certifying all HIV waiver decisions to the INS central office for review and final decision making. This certification process might have

between the embassy or consulate, the INS, and the CDC may result in additional delays. If the applicant is waiting to enter or return to the United States, the delay in adjudication can be for over a year. Under a 1994 change in immigration law, individuals who otherwise are ineligible to complete their adjustment of immigration status at an INS office in the United States now have the option of paying an additional INS fee of $780 to avoid overseas processing.[132] Given the risks of leaving the United States and the long delays in adjudicating HIV waivers, applicants should consider taking advantage of this change if, of course, they can afford the additional fee.[133]

§ 11.14   HIV Testing Requirements and Waiver Availability

Table 11–1 indicates whether HIV testing is required for various categories of U.S. immigrants and whether waivers are available. All immigrants who test HIV positive should obtain confirmatory testing and seek health and legal counseling.

Table 11–1

HIV Testing Requirements for Immigrants

	Immigration Status	HIV Test Required	Waiver Availability if HIV+	Comments/Remedies
1	Applicant for permanent residence ("green card") based on family relationship (spouse, unmarried child, or parent of U.S. citizen, or spouse or minor child of permanent resident).	Yes	Yes	If HIV+ get confirmatory testing, health counseling and legal representation to apply for waiver.

created venue in the United States for either administrative or judicial review, because the final decisions regarding HIV waivers would be made by INS officials in Washington, DC. Without certification, decisions by INS and Department of State consular officers abroad will be furthered insulated from administrative or judicial review.

[132] 8 U.S.C. § 1255(i).

[133] Another important change under the 1994 law is that individuals who do decide to complete their adjustment process abroad must first reside in that country, usually their country of birth, for at least ninety days prior to the adjustment interview. Applicants need to anticipate this additional delay and make arrangements for their health care while abroad.

Table 11–1
(continued)

	Immigration Status	HIV Test Required	Waiver Availability if HIV+	Comments/Remedies
2	Applicant for permanent residence ("green card") based on labor certification (employment) or if applicant is married child or a sibling of a U.S. citizen	Yes	No*	Do not apply. No confidentiality. Refer to health and legal counseling.
3	Refugee (applying from outside U.S.)	Yes	Yes	If HIV+ get confirmatory testing, health counseling and legal representation to apply for waiver.
4	Asylum applicant (within U.S.)	No	N/A	HIV+ persons should get health and legal counseling; HIV+ status may be basis of asylum.
5	Adjustment from asylum or refugee status to permanent resident	Yes	Yes	If HIV+ get confirmatory testing, health counseling and legal representation to apply for waiver
6	Applicant for temporary residence under amnesty programs (1/1/82 or Special Agricultural Worker)	Yes	Yes	If HIV+ get confirmatory testing, health counseling and legal representation to apply for waiver.
7	Amnesty applicant for permanent residence under 1/1/82 program	Yes	Yes	If HIV+ get confirmatory testing, health counseling and legal representation to apply for waiver.

	Immigration Status	HIV Test Required	Waiver Availability if HIV+	Comments/Remedies
8	Amnesty applicant for permanent residence under Special Agricultural Worker (SAW) program	No	N/A	HIV+ persons should get health and legal counseling.
9	Registry (applicants for permanent residence who arrived before 1972)	No	N/A	If HIV+ do not reveal test results (no confidentiality); get health and legal counseling.
10	Suspension of deportation (after 7 or more years of U.S. residency)	No	N/A	HIV+ persons should get health and legal counseling; HIV status may be basis for suspension.
11	Cuban/Haitian applicant for adjustment	Yes	No	Do not apply. No confidentiality. Refer to health and legal counseling.
12	Deferred Action or Extended Voluntary Departure for undocumented individual	No	N/A	If undocumented person with AIDS, get legal assistance and health counseling. HIV+ status may be basis for status.
13	Non-immigrant, e.g., visitor, student, business person	No, but INS may exclude if suspected, e.g. evidence of AZT.	Yes	Special 10-day (for pre-approved conferences) 30-day (for business, family visits or medical care) or regular non-immigrant waivers.
14	Persons accepted under lottery programs	Yes	No	Do not apply. No confidentiality. Refer for health and legal counseling.

Table 11–1

(continued)

	Immigration Status	HIV Test Required	Waiver Availability if HIV+	Comments/Remedies
15	Permanent residents applying for citizenship (naturalization)	No	N/A	HIV+ persons should get health and legal counseling.

* Waiver is not available, unless applicant has a qualifying relationship, that is, is a spouse, unmarried child, or parent of a U.S. citizen, permanent resident, or another applicant approved for permanent residence.

IMMIGRANT ELIGIBILITY FOR PUBLIC BENEFITS

§ 11.15 Immigration Status and Eligibility for Public Benefits

A major issue facing immigrants living with HIV disease is establishing eligibility for federal, state, and local public benefits, including health care and social services.[134] Prior to the 1996 welfare reform legislation,[135] permanent residents (with some exceptions for SSI, AFDC, and Food Stamps), refugees and asylees[136] were eligible for almost all federal, state, and local public benefits on the same basis as U.S. citizens. The new eligibility rules are complex and will vary in each state and county in light of federal block grants and state and local options under the welfare reform legislation.[137]

Medicaid. The most critical need for many individuals living with HIV disease is access to quality health care services. If an individual is not covered by

---

[134] For background on the eligibility of immigrants for government benefits prior to the 1996 law, see Ignatius Bau, *HIV Seropositive Immigrants and Public Benefits,* Immigr. Newsl. (Nat'l Immigr. Project, Nat'l Law. Guild, Boston, Mass.), Feb. 1993, at 3–8; Charles W. Wheeler & Robert L. Leventhal, *Aliens' Rights to Public Benefits,* 20 Clearinghouse Rev. 913 (1987); Robert Rubin, *Walking the Gray Line: The "Color of Law" Test Governing Noncitizen Eligibility for Public Benefits,* 24 San Diego L. Rev. 411 (1987). *See also* National Immigration L. Ctr., Guide to Alien Eligibility for Federal Programs (3d ed. 1994) (available from NILC, 1102 South Crenshaw Blvd., Suite 101, Los Angeles, CA 90019).

[135] Personal Responsibility and Work Opportunity Reconciliation Act of 1996, Pub. L. No. 104-193, §§ 400–451, 1996 U.S.C.C.A.N. (110 Stat.) 2105, 2260–77.

[136] Refugees and asylees remain eligible for a special program of cash and medical assistance for a limited period of time after their admission to the United States. 8 U.S.C. § 1522(e).

[137] There also have been special public benefits eligibility rules for certain categories of immigrants such as legalization applicants. *See, e.g.,* 8 U.S.C. §§ 1255a(h), 1160(f).

a private health insurance plan, eligibility for health care services can depend on immigration status. Medicaid provides federal and state government reimbursements for medical care. One must be both indigent and "categorically linked" (for example, eligible for SSI or AFDC) to qualify for Medicaid. Medicaid generally is not available to single adults. In addition, under the welfare reform legislation, any individual who is not a U.S. citizen and who is not currently receiving Medicaid as of August 1996 will be ineligible for Medicaid for the five years after entry.[138] The bill then gives each state the option of continuing the disqualification until the immigrant becomes a U.S. citizen.[139] States also will have the option of disqualifying from Medicaid those immigrants already in the United States and receiving Medicaid as of August 1996, effective no earlier than January 1, 1997.[140] If states exercise this option, immigrants infected with HIV currently receiving Medicaid may lose their health care coverage.

Since 1986, emergency Medicaid has been available to all persons regardless of immigration status.[141] *Emergency medical care* is defined as care and services necessary for the treatment of any medical condition, including emergency labor and delivery, manifesting itself by acute symptoms of sufficient severity, including severe pain, such that the absence of immediate medical attention could reasonably be expected to result in placing the patient's health in serious jeopardy, serious impairment to bodily functions, or serious dysfunction of any bodily organ or part.[142] The 1996 welfare reform legislation does not change the availability of emergency Medicaid.

Other Public Health Services. The 1996 welfare reform legislation also may impose immigration status eligibility requirements for other types of federally funded health care services, such as health services provided by community health centers, migrant health centers, and rural health centers. These facilities receive federal funding in addition to Medicaid reimbursements for their individual patients. In addition, new immigrants will be disqualified from Title XX services such as In Home Support Services, with state options to continue the disqualification until citizenship[143] is granted.

On the other hand, there are no immigration status eligibility requirements on programs funded through the Ryan White Comprehensive AIDS Response

---

[138] Personal Responsibility and Work Opportunity Reconciliation Act of 1996, Pub. L. No. 104-193, § 403(a), 1996 U.S.C.C.A.N. (110 Stat.) 2105, 2265. Prior to the 1996 welfare reform legislation, permanent residents, refugees, asylees, and those "permanently residing in the U.S. under color of law" (PRUCOL) were eligible for Medicaid. *Compare* 42 U.S.C. § 1396b(v), 42 C.F.R. § 435.408. The PRUCOL category was a difficult one to define and was interpreted differently for different public benefits.

[139] Pub. L. No. 104-193, § 402(b), 1996 U.S.C.C.A.N. (110 Stat.) 2105, 2264–65.

[140] *Id.*

[141] 42 U.S.C. § 1396b(v) (1994); 42 C.F.R. § 435.408.

[142] *Id.*

[143] Pub. L. No. 104-193, §§ 403(a), 402(b), 1996 U.S.C.C.A.N. (110 Stat.) 2105, 2265, 2264.

Emergency (CARE) Act.[144] Similarly, there are no immigration status eligibility requirements for the state AIDS Drug Assistance Programs (ADAP). Finally, there are no restrictions on participation in federally funded clinical trials.

Disability Benefits.   Individuals living with HIV disease who have worked in the past or are still working may be eligible for a variety of governmental and private disability benefits when they become too disabled to continue to work. Almost all employees have FICA contributions deducted from their wages. If that employee becomes permanently disabled and has made sufficient withholding contributions, he is eligible for Social Security disability benefits.[145] There should be no inquiry regarding immigration status.

On the other hand, persons who are both indigent and permanently disabled may apply for Supplemental Security Income (SSI), regardless of their contribution of FICA withholdings.[146] However, under the 1996 welfare reform legislation, only U.S. citizens will be eligible to receive SSI. Those poor and disabled immigrants who are now receiving SSI will lose their benefits before August 1997 unless they meet one of the very limited exceptions under the new law.[147]

Some employers provide long-term disability benefits for their disabled employees. There should not be any immigration status eligibility requirements for long-term disability benefits. Some states also provide benefits for short-term disabilities. Deductions are made from employee wages as premiums for these programs. At least one state court has ruled that an undocumented immigrant cannot be denied state disability benefits solely on the basis of immigration status.[148]

AFDC, Food Stamps, and Nutrition Programs.   Prior to 1996, parents with dependent children who were unable to work could receive benefits from the Aid to Families with Dependent Children (AFDC) program. The 1996 welfare reform legislation repeals the AFDC program and replaces it with a federal block grant to each of the states. The disqualifications from AFDC for immigrants under the new law are the same as from Medicaid: new immigrants are disqualified for the first five years and states have the option to disqualify current immigrants as well as extend the disqualification for new immigrants

---

[144] In fact, some local community planning groups mandated by the Act have prioritized immigrants, including undocumented immigrants, as a target population for services.

[145] 42 U.S.C. §§ 401–431.

[146] *Id.* § 405(c)(2)(B)(i).

[147] The only exceptions are for refugees and asylees who entered the United States after August 1991 (for the first five years after entry), veterans and those on active military duty, battered spouses and children, and those who have worked 40 qualifying Social Security quarters. Pub. L. No. 104-193, §§ 402(a)(2), 403(b), 1996 U.S.C.C.A.N. (110 Stat.) 2105, 2262–64, 2265–66. The eligibility for SSI prior to 1996 was much broader. *Compare* 42 U.S.C. § 1382c(a)(1)(B); 20 C.F.R. § 422.104.

[148] Ayala v. California Unemployment Ins. Appeals Bd., 126 Cal. Rptr. 210 (Ct. App. 1976).

beyond the five years until they acquire citizenship.[149] Similarly, the same disqualifications that apply to SSI under the 1996 law are applicable to food stamps.[150]

The 1996 legislation specifically exempts child and school nutrition programs, such as the Women, Infants and Children (WIC) program and school breakfast and lunch programs, from any immigration status restrictions for new immigrants.[151] However, it is unclear whether these benefits might be available to undocumented immigrants.

Other Public Benefits.   There may be other state and local programs available to provide public benefits or health care to those who are indigent and without any other means of support. Many states have general relief or general assistance programs that provide minimal cash benefits as a last resort. State and local governments also administer indigent health care programs. It is up to each state or local government to determine immigration status eligibility requirements for these programs. However, the 1996 federal welfare reform legislation also imposes new restrictions on these state and local programs under the rationale of the federal authority to control immigration.[152]

§ 11.16   Immigration Consequences of Receiving Public Benefits

Noncitizens also should be aware that their receipt of public benefits may affect their future immigration status because of both the exclusion and deportation statutes that relate to being a public charge. Administrative and judicial decision have limited exclusion or deportation as a public charge to circumstances in which the individual has relied on cash as opposed to medical, food, housing, or other in-kind public benefits. However, the INS can always inquire about the receipt of any public benefits and can initiate deportation proceedings against any noncitizen who has received public assistance under the deportation statute, although such proceedings are extremely rare.

More commonly, the public charge exclusion is relevant at the time an individual seeks adjustment of immigration status to permanent residence. The general rule, however, is that the INS must consider the "totality of circumstances,"

---

[149] Personal Responsibility and Work Opportunity Reconciliation Act of 1996, Pub. L. No. 104-193, §§ 403(a), 402(b), 1996 U.S.C.C.A.N. (110 Stat.) 2105, 2265, 2264. The 1996 enactment repeals the earlier AFDC eligibility based on PROCOL status. *Cf.* 42 U.S.C. § 602(a)(33) (1994); 45 C.F.R. § 233.50.

[150] Pub. L. No. 104-193, §§ 402(a), 403(a), 1996 U.S.C.C.A.N. (110 Stat.) 2105, 2262–64, 2265. *Compare* 7 U.S.C. § 2015(f); 7 C.F.R. § 273.4(d).

[151] Pub. L. No. 104-193, § 403(c)(2)(C)–(D), 1996 U.S.C.C.A.N. (110 Stat.) 2105, 2266.

[152] *Id.* §§ 411–412, 422, 1996 U.S.C.C.A.N. (110 Stat.) 2105, 2268–70, 2271.

with the receipt of public benefits being only one factor.[153] For example, if the applicant can demonstrate a change in circumstances, that could rebut the presumption that the applicant is likely to become a public charge in the future. For individuals with HIV, it would be difficult to rebut the presumption that past receipt of public benefits will continue. Moreover, if the benefits received require a determination of permanent disability or indigency, then the INS reasonably can argue that the individual is unable to demonstrate economic self-support. These individuals will have to overcome the public charge exclusion with other evidence such as a job offer or affidavits of support.

In addition, the INS may initiate deportation proceedings, even against a permanent resident, for becoming a public charge within five years of entry.[154] In practice, the INS rarely initiates deportation proceedings based solely on the public charge issue.

§ 11.17 Employment Issues

Several issues relate to an immigrant's ability to work in the United States. The Immigration Reform and Control Act of 1986 (IRCA)[155] requires all U.S. employers to verify the identity and employment authorization of all their employees hired after its date of enactment, November 6, 1986.[156] The verification requirements apply regardless of the size of the employer or the number of employees. The only exceptions to the verification requirements are for independent contractors who are not "employees" and for intermittent, domestic employment (for example, the one-time lawn mower or baby sitter is exempt but not the regular gardener or child care provider). Employers must complete an INS I-9 form for each of their employees in order to meet the IRCA verification requirements.

An employee may produce many different documents to meet the employment authorization verification requirements.[157] However, an employer may not specify which documents an employee must produce to meet the employment authorization verification requirements.[158] Civil and criminal penalties can be imposed against employers for both paperwork violations relating to the completion of the I-9's and for knowingly hiring an employee without employment authorization.[159] On the other hand, employers may not discriminate against

---

[153] *In re* Perez, 15 I. & N. Dec. 136, 137 (B.I.A. 1974); *In re* Harutunian, 14 I. & N. Dec. 583, 588–90 (Reg. Comm'r 1974); *In re* Martinez-Lopez, 10 I.& N. Dec. 409, 421 (Att'y Gen. 1964).

[154] 8 U.S.C. § 1251(a)(5).

[155] Pub. L. No. 99-603, 1986 U.S.C.C.A.N. (100 Stat.) 3359.

[156] 8 U.S.C. § 1324a.

[157] *See* INS Form I-9; INS, Handbook for Employers (INS M-274, 1987).

[158] 8 U.S.C. § 1324b(a)(6).

[159] *Id.* § 1324a(a)(1).

applicants for employment or employees based on citizenship status or national origin.[160]

Immigration Document Fraud. The Immigration Act of 1990 also created new civil penalties for the use of false or fraudulent immigration documents.[161] These penalties are independent of the grounds for exclusion and deportation. Document fraud proceedings are conducted by Department of Justice administrative law judges similarly to deportation or employer sanctions proceedings. The INS often seeks a signed admission of document fraud with a waiver of the right to an administrative hearing. A finding of the use of false or fraudulent documents is a permanent ground of exclusion.[162] Thus, an individual found to have committed document fraud is permanently prohibited from ever lawfully returning to the U.S. These provisions are critical because the use of false or fraudulent documents to complete an INS I-9 constitutes document fraud.

Social Security Numbers and Taxes. Immigrants seeking government benefits or employment face new restrictions on their use of Social Security numbers. There are now three distinct types of Social Security numbers issued: numbers without any restrictions as to their use; numbers issued to persons without employment authorization that are identified "Not for Employment Purposes"; and numbers issued to persons with temporary employment authorization that are identified "Valid Only With INS Employment Authorization." The fraudulent use of a Social Security number is punishable by both criminal and civil penalties.[163] These prosecutions, however, are generally rare. On the other hand, the use of a Social Security number that is identified "Not for Employment Purpose" for employment purposes will trigger a report from the Social Security Administration to the INS that may result in an INS enforcement action against that individual.[164]

Undocumented immigrants are caught in several dilemmas. First, it may be both document fraud and a violation of immigration status to work without employment authorization. On the other hand, the INS looks negatively on a failure to work and pay taxes when adjudicating most applications for discretionary immigration statuses. In addition, if an individual is in fact using a false number or someone else's Social Security number for employment purposes, he incurs federal and state income tax obligations. If additional income tax is owed, the individual is subject to Internal Revenue Service and state income tax agency enforcement actions. Conversely, if too much income tax has been withheld, the individual will be unable to collect a refund because the Social Security

---

[160] *Id.* § 1324b(a), 42 U.S.C. § 2000e (Title VII).

[161] 8 U.S.C. § 1324c.

[162] *Id.* § 1182(a)(6)(F).

[163] 42 U.S.C. § 408, 18 U.S.C. §§ 1001, 1546, 20 C.F.R. § 422.108.

[164] 20 C.F.R. §§ 422.104(c), 422.107(e).

number used on the tax return does not match with the name in Social Security Administration's records.

§ 11.18   Recent Legislation

In 1996, two major laws were enacted that have a major impact on both U.S. immigration standards and the eligibility of immigrants for government benefits. The enactment of both the Personal Responsibility and Work Opportunity Reconciliation Act[165] and the Illegal Immigration Reform and Immigrant Responsibility Act[166] will result in the disqualifications of almost all persons who are not U.S. citizens from many federal, state, and local benefits. This will have an immediate impact on persons living with HIV and AIDS who are not U.S. citizens and who depend on programs such as Medicaid, SSI, Title XX social services, and AFDC.

Much of the current anti-immigrant sentiment found in Congress is a federal reflection of the passage of Proposition 187 by California voters in 1994. Proposition 187 is a state initiative that requires all health providers, schools, universities, colleges, social service departments, and police departments to determine the immigration status of the patients, students, and clients with whom they have contact and to deny health, education, social service, or public safety services to any individual they suspect of being undocumented.[167] The implementation of most of Proposition 187 has been enjoined by federal and state courts in California, principally based on federal preemption over immigration issues.[168] However, provisions in the recently enacted federal welfare reform legislation now require verification of immigration status and cooperation between state government officials and the INS in reporting undocumented immigrants.[169] Moreover, the welfare reform legislation goes far beyond Proposition 187 in disqualifying both undocumented and legal immigrants from government benefits.[170]

The replacement of the AFDC program with block grants and the state options to extend the immigrant disqualifications to Medicaid, Title XX services, and

---

[165] Pub. L. No. 104-193, Title IV, §§ 400–451, 1996 U.S.C.C.A.N. (110 Stat.) 2105, 2260–77.

[166] Pub. L. No. 104-208, 1996 U.S.C.C.A.N. (110 Stat.) 3009.

[167] *Adding* Cal. Pen. Code §§ 113–114, 834b; Educ. Code §§ 48215, 66010.8; Health & Safety Code § 130; Welf. & Inst. Code § 10001.5; Gov't Code § 53069.65.

[168] League of United Latin Am. Citizens v. Wilson, 908 F. Supp. 755 (C.D. Cal. 1995) (granting partial summary judgment for plaintiffs.); Doe v. Regents of Univ. of Cal., No. 965090 (Cal. Super. Ct. Mar. 15, 1995) (prelim. inj.).

[169] Personal Responsibility and Work Opportunity Reconciliation Act of 1996, Pub. L. No. 104-193, §§ 432, 434, 1996 U.S.C.C.A.N. (110 Stat.) 2105, 2274–75.

[170] An earlier version of the legislation, H.R. 4, as passed by the Senate, disqualified even those individuals who had recently become U.S. citizens from federal public benefits. 141 Cong. Rec. S13,802 (daily ed. Sept. 19, 1995). H.R. 4 was subsequently vetoed by the president. H.R. Doc. No. 164, 104th Cong., 2d Sess., 142 Cong. Rec. H342 (daily ed. Jan. 22, 1996).

state and local government benefits also has significant policy implications for immigrants infected with HIV. Each state legislature must now take up the debate of whether immigrants should be eligible for these programs. AIDS service organizations and health care providers will have to monitor these federal, state, and local legislative developments for their impact on immigrants with HIV.

APPENDIXES

SUMMARY OF STATE STATUTES

The following appendix presents a state-by-state summary of HIV-specific statutes and regulations that address issues in the following categories: HIV reporting; standards governing HIV testing and confidentiality; quarantine; criminal transmission; insurance; and employment. References to pertinent law review literature discussing state-specific issues are also included where available.

Alabama

Reporting: Ala. Code § 22-11A-14 (Supp. 1989) (HIV status, as STD, reported)

Consent for Testing: Ala. Code § 22-11A-17 (Michie Supp. 1994) (allowing oral consent)

Mandatory Testing: Ala. Code § 22-11A-17 (Michie Supp. 1989) (all convicted prisoners upon entering and upon release from jail or prison); § 22-11A-37 (Michie Supp. 1989) (STDs)

Transmission Crimes: Ala. Code § 22-11A-21(c) (Michie Supp. 1989) (STDs) (misdemeanor)

Regulations: Rules of the State Board of Health, Division of Disease Control, § 420-4-1.03 (1987) (HIV classified as an STD)

James Paul Sizemore, *Alabama's Confidentiality Quagmire: Psychotherapists, AIDS, Mandatory Reporting and* Tarasoff, 19 L. & Psychol. Rev. 241 (1995)

Alaska

Mandatory Testing: Alaska Stat. § 18.15.310 (Michie 1994) (court-ordered HIV testing of defendants charged with sexual offenses)

* The materials in this appendix were compiled by Edwin J. Greenlee, J.D., Ph.D.

Arizona

Reporting HIV status: Ariz. Admin. Dig. R9-6-604, -701 (1990) (name reporting required)

Consent for Testing: Ariz. Rev. Stat. Ann. § 36-663 (1993) (informed consent required)

Anonymous testing: Ariz. Rev. Stat. Ann. § 36-136(H)(15) (1993)

Confidentiality: Ariz. Rev. Stat. Ann. § 36-664(A), (L) (1993)

Exceptions: Ariz. Rev. Stat. Ann. § 36-1415 (1993) (sexual offense victims), § 36-1457 (health care or emergency workers), § 36-1860 (sexual or syringe-sharing partners)

Mandatory Testing: Ariz. Rev. Stat. Ann. § 36-669 (1993) (prisoners); § 13-1415 (persons convicted of sexual offenses involving risk of transmission)

Quarantine: Ariz. Rev. Stat. Ann. § 36-136(H)(1) (1993)

Arkansas

Reporting HIV status: Ark. Code Ann. § 21-15-904 (Michie 1996) (physician reporting of HIV-positive patients to Department of Health)

Consent for Testing: Ark. Code Ann. § 21-15-905 (Michie 1996) (informed consent requirement)

Exceptions: Ark. Code Ann. § 21-15-905 (Michie 1996) (physician determines HIV testing is "medically indicated" and general consent to medical treatment has been given; health care provider exposure)

Counseling Requirement: Ark. Code Ann. § 21-15-905 (Michie 1996) ("appropriate counseling" with testing)

Mandatory Testing: Ark. Code Ann. § 16-82-101 (court-ordered testing of person arrested and charged with sexual offense), § 16-82-102 (Michie Supp. 1995) (court-ordered testing of person arrested and charged with assault/battery upon law enforcement officer, emergency medical technician)

Transmission Crimes: Ark. Code Ann. § 5-14-123 (class A felony for HIV positive individual to expose another to HIV), § 20-15-903 (Michie 1993) (class A misdemeanor if HIV positive individual fails to inform physician/dentist prior to receipt of health care services)

Education: Ark. Code Ann. § 6-18-703 (Michie 1993) (AIDS education programs for public schools emphasizing abstinence)

Michael L. Closen, *The Arkansas Criminal HIV Exposure Law: Statutory Issues, Public Policy Concerns, and Constitutional Objections,* 1993 Ark. L. Notes 47 (1993)

California

Consent for Testing: Cal. Health & Safety Code § 199.22 (a) (West 1990) (written consent required)

Partner Notification: Cal. Health & Safety Code § 199.25 (West 1990)

Confidentiality: Cal. Health & Safety Code § 199.20 (West 1990) (notification of health care or emergency workers; post-mortem notification of first responder); Cal. Civ. Code §§ 56–56.37 (West 1992 & Supp. 1995) (written consent for disclosure required)

Enforcement: Cal. Health & Safety Code § 199.7 (West 1990) (civil and criminal penalties for willful or malicious disclosure; $25 fine for negligent disclosure)

Mandatory Testing: Cal. Penal Code §§ 7511–7512.5 (West Supp. 1996) (inmates after exposure of correctional facilities employees); Cal. Welf. & Inst. Code § 1768.9 (West Supp. 1996) (juveniles under control of Youth Authority); Cal. Penal Code § 1202.1 (West Supp. 1996) (persons convicted of sexual assault, victims notified); Cal. Health & Safety Code § 199.67 (West Supp. 1996) (patient testing after exposure of health care providers; donors of semen, blood, or tissue)

Transmission Crimes: Cal. Penal Code § 647f (West Supp. 1996) (felony to continue working as prostitute after knowledge of HIV infection), § 12022.85 (West 1992) (three-year enhancement for each conviction for persons aware of their HIV infection)

Roger Doughty, Comment, *The Confidentiality of HIV-Related Information: Responding to the Resurgence of Aggressive Public Health Interventions in the AIDS Epidemic,* 82 Cal. L. Rev. 111 (1994)

Thomas S. Tanana, *Could California Reduce AIDS by Modeling Nevada Prostitution Law?,* 2 San Diego Just. J. 491 (1994)

Margaret Salmon Rivas, *California AIDS Initiative and the Food and Drug Administration: Working at Odds with Each Other,* 46 Food Drug Cosmetics L.J. 107 (1991)

Denise C. Singelton, *Nonconsensual HIV Testing in the Health Care Setting: The Case for Extending the Occupational Protections of California Proposition 96 to Health Care Workers,* 26 Loy. L.A. L. Rev. 1251 (1993)

Colorado

Reporting HIV Status: Colo. Rev. Stat. §§ 25-4-1402(1), (2), 25-4-1405(7)(b)(I) (Supp. 1996) (name reporting by physician)

Consent for Testing: Colo. Rev. Stat. § 25-4-1405(8)(a) (Supp. 1996) (exceptions for health care workers, corrections, prisoners, patient without capacity)

Confidentiality: Colo. Rev. Stat. § 25-4-1404 (Supp. 1996)

Exceptions: Colo. Rev. Stat. § 25-4-1404(1)(c) (Supp. 1996)

Penalty for Disclosure: Colo. Rev. Stat. § 25-4-1409 (Supp. 1996)

Quarantine: Colo. Rev. Stat. §§ 25-4-1406, 25-4-1407 (Supp. 1996)

Mandatory Testing: Colo. Rev. Stat. § 18-3-415 (Supp. 1996) (testing of criminal defendants after preliminary hearing establishing act of sexual penetration)

Transmission Crimes: Colo. Rev. Stat. § 18-7-201.7 (Supp. 1996) (felony for act of prostitution or to patronize a prostitute with knowledge of HIV infection)

Connecticut

Consent for Testing: Conn. Gen. Stat. Ann. § 19A-582(A) (West Supp. 1996) (written or oral informed consent documented in medical record; exceptions for significant exposure)

Confidentiality: AIDS Testing and Medical Information, Conn. Gen. Stat. Ann. §§ 19a-581 to 19a-592 (West Supp. 1996) (1989 Pub. Acts, No. 89-246), § 19a-581, amended (1993 Pub. Acts, No. 93-291) as to definition of "other person" to include volunteer emergency medical services, fire and public safety personnel, § 19a-584 (West Supp. 1996) (sexual or needle-sharing partners)

Penalties Include Civil Remedies: Conn. Gen. Stat. Ann. § 19A-590 (West Supp. 1996)

Mandatory Testing: Conn. Gen. Stat. Ann. § 19A-582 (West Supp. 1996) (prisoners—for treatment purposes or if posing a risk of transmission to others)

Delaware

Reporting HIV Status: Del. State Bd. of Health, Regs. for the Control of Contagious & Other Disease Conditions § 7.412 (no names except from Blood Bank of Delaware)

Consent for Testing: Del. Code Ann. tit. 16, § 1202(a) (Michie 1995) (allowing oral consent; informed consent unless for health care worker exposure)

Exceptions: Del. Code Ann. tit. 16, § 1202(c) (Michie 1995) (health care worker exposure), § 703 (STDs), § 708 (prenatal testing of pregnant women)

Penalties: Del. Code Ann. tit. 16, § 1204 (Michie 1995) (civil remedies)

Confidentiality: Del. Code Ann. tit. 16, §§ 711, 1203 (Michie 1995)

Exception: Del. Code Ann. tit. 16, § 1203(a)(3) (Michie 1995) (health care worker exception)

Quarantine: Del. Code Ann. tit. 16, §§ 703–705 (Michie 1995) (STDs)

District of Columbia

Confidentiality: D.C. Code Ann. § 6-117(b)(1)(B) (Michie 1995) (applicable only to reports made to D.C. government, health department; no general confidentiality provision), § 2-3305.14(a)(16) (Michie 1994) (general confidentiality provision applicable to health care professionals licensed in D.C.), § 35-1511 (Michie 1993) (lab records confidential), § 35-226(d) (Michie 1996 Supp.) (insurers)

Exceptions: D.C. Code Ann. § 6-117(b)(1)(B) (Michie 1995) (upon judicial determination that disclosure is essential to safeguard the physical health of others or if relevant to criminal prosecution)

Florida

Reporting HIV Status: Fla. Admin. Code Ann. r. 10D-3, 10D-93; Fla. Stat. Ann. § 384.25(3) (no name reporting), § 384.23 (West 1993) (HIV is STD)

Consent for Testing: Fla. Stat. Ann. § 381.004(3)(a) (West 1993) (allowing oral consent)

Counseling Requirement: Fla. Stat. Ann. § 381.004(3)(e) (West 1993) (immediate face-to-face counseling)

Confidentiality: Fla. Stat. Ann. § 381.004(3)(a) (West 1993)

Exceptions: Fla. Stat. Ann. § 381.004(3)(a) (West 1993 & Supp. 1997), § 455.2416 (sexual or syringe-sharing partners), § 960.003 (West 1993) (sexual assault complainants)

Contact Tracing: Fla. Stat. Ann. § 384.26 (West 1993)

Mandatory Testing: Fla. Stat. Ann. §§ 381.004(3)(a), 796.08(3) (prostitutes and persons injuring peace officer), 960.003 (West 1993) (persons charged with sexual offense involving transmission of body fluids)

Transmission Crimes: Fla. Stat. Ann. § 384.24 (West 1993) (STDs), § 796.08(5) (West Supp. 1996) (prostitution with knowledge of HIV status)

Robert C. Waters, *Florida's Involuntary AIDS Testing Statutes,* 19 Fla. St. U. L. Rev. 369 (1991)

Robert C. Waters, *Florida's Omnibus AIDS Act of 1988,* 16 Fla. St. U. L. Rev. 441 (1988)

Georgia

Reporting HIV Status: Ga. Code Ann. § 31-22-9.2 (Michie 1991) (Health care provider/facility required to report age/sex/race/county of residence of persons testing HIV-positive)

Exceptions: Ga. Code Ann. § 31-22-9.2 (Michie 1991) (testing after health care provider's exposure to any body fluids that create risk of HIV infection if patient refuses consent for testing)

Counseling Requirement: Ga. Code Ann. § 31-22-9.2 (Michie 1991) (pre- and post-test counseling)

Partner Notification: Ga. Code Ann. § 24-9-47 (Michie 1995) (partner notification by physician)

Confidentiality: Ga. Code Ann. § 24-9-40.1 (Michie 1995) (AIDS-related information disclosed/discovered within physician-patient relationship is confidential); Ga. Code Ann. § 24-9-47 (Michie 1995) (AIDS confidential information; written authorization for disclosure)

Exceptions: Ga. Code Ann. § 24-9-47 (Michie 1995) (court-ordered disclosure of AIDS confidential information in numerous instances)

Mandatory Testing: Ga. Code Ann. § 15-11-35.1 (Michie 1994) (court-ordered testing of child suspected of committing delinquent act constituting AIDS-transmitting crime; testing of juveniles sentenced to Dep't of Corrections/ Dep't of Children & Youth Services as per department's policies and procedures), § 17-10-15 (Michie Supp. 1996) (court-ordered testing of person arrested for sexual offense at request of victim when significant risk of exposure to HIV was involved); § 31-17A-2 and -3 (Michie 1991) (court-authorized HIV testing of individual infected or suspected of being infected with HIV who fails to consent to testing); § 42-5-52.1 (Michie 1994) (testing of persons committed to penal institution)

Transmission Crimes: Ga. Code Ann. § 16-5-60 (Michie Supp. 1995) (felony for HIV-infected individual, aware of his or her HIV status, to engage in sexual acts, share hypodermic needles, exchange sex for money, or donate blood or body fluids)

Education: Ga. Code Ann. § 20-2-143 (Michie 1996) (local boards of education to prescribe AIDS prevention program for public school students; right of parents to opt out)

Hawaii

Consent for Testing: Haw. Rev. Stat. § 325-16 (Michie 1996) (written informed consent for HIV testing)

Exceptions: Haw. Rev. Stat. § 325-16 (Michie 1996)

Counseling Requirement: Haw. Rev. Stat. § 325-16 (Michie 1996) (pre- and post-test counseling)

Confidentiality: Haw. Rev. Stat. § 325-101 (Michie 1996) (confidentiality of HIV-related information; prior written consent for release of records)

Exceptions: Haw. Rev. Stat. § 325-101 (Michie 1996)

Insurance: Haw. Rev. Stat. § 431:13-103 (Michie 1994) (unfair method of competition or deceptive act or practice to refuse to insure or continue coverage merely because individual had HIV test prior to applying for insurance)

Idaho

Reporting HIV Status: Idaho Code § 39-606 (Michie 1993) (name reporting)

Consent for Testing: Idaho Code § 39-4304 (Michie 1985) (generally)

Exception: Idaho Code § 39-4303A (Michie 1985) (health care worker significant exposure)

Confidentiality: Idaho Code § 39-610 (Michie 1993)

Exceptions: Idaho Code § 39-604 (sexual assault complainants), § 39-4303 (Michie Supp. 1996) (health or emergency workers)

Contact tracing: Idaho Code § 39-610 (Michie 1993)

Mandatory Testing: Idaho Code § 39-604(1) (Michie 1993) (all prisoners)

Transmission Crimes: Idaho Code § 39-608 (Michie 1993) (sexual contact or syringe sharing with knowledge of HIV status is felony)

Illinois

Reporting: Ill. Ann. Stat. ch. 401, § 305/9 (Smith-Hurd Supp. 1996) (AIDS/HIV positive status)

Consent for Testing: Ill. Ann. Stat. ch. 410, § 305/4-5 (Smith-Hurd 1993) (written informed consent)

Exceptions: Ill. Ann. Stat. ch. 410, § 305/7 (Smith-Hurd 1993) (including significant exposure of health care provider/fire fighter/emergency medical personnel while providing care)

Contact Tracing: Ill. Ann. Stat. ch. 410, § 325/5.5 (Smith-Hurd 1993)

Confidentiality: Ill. Ann. Stat. ch. 410, §§ 305/10, 305/11 (Smith-Hurd 1993) (AIDS Confidentiality Act)

Mandatory Testing: Ill. Ann. Stat. ch. 720, § 5/12-18 (Smith-Hurd 1993) (court-ordered testing of defendant accused of criminal sexual assault); ch. 730, § 5/3-6-2 (Smith-Hurd 1992) (testing prior to release of inmate with documented history of IV drug use); ch. 730, § 5/5-5-3 (Smith-Hurd 1992) (testing of defendant convicted under Hypodermic Syringes and Needles

Act); ch. 20, §§ 2310/55.45–.46 (Smith-Hurd 1993) (testing of blood/organ donors); ch. 20, § 505/22.3 (Smith-Hurd 1993) (testing upon request of child's adoptive parent when child in custody of Dep't of Children & Family Services is placed in adoptive care)

Transmission Crimes: Ill. Ann. Stat. ch. 720, § 5/12-16.2 (Smith-Hurd 1993) (criminal transmission when individual who knows that he/she is HIV-positive engages in intimate contact involving the exposure of another to blood/body fluid; donates/provides blood/body fluid; exchanges/transfers nonsterile intravenous drug paraphernalia; knowing consent is a defense)

Education: Ill. Ann. Stat. ch. 20, §§ 2310/55.52, /55.55–.56 (AIDS prevention education programs prepared by Dep't of Public Health); ch. 105, §§ 5/27-9.1, -9.2; 110/3 (comprehensive sex education programs for public elementary and high schools; parental opt-out provision; including AIDS education); ch. 750, § 5/204 (brochure on STDs to be provided to marriage license applicants); ch. 410, § 50/3 (Smith-Hurd 1993) (HIV testing in insurance context)

Regulations: Written Informed Consent Form, Ill. Adm. Code tit. 77, § 697, app. A, illus. A

Scott H. Isaacman, *Conflict Between Illinois Rule 1.6(b) and the AIDS Confidentiality Act,* 25 J. Marshall L. Rev. 727 (1992)

Michael L. Closen & Jeffrey S. Deutschman, *A Proposal to Repeal the Illinois HIV Transmission Statute,* 78 Ill. Bar J. 592 (1990)

Indiana

Reporting HIV Status: Ind. Code Ann. § 16-41-2-3 (Michie 1993) (physicians, hospitals, and medical laboratories shall report each case of HIV infection)

Consent for Testing: Ind. Code Ann. § 16-41-6-1 (Michie 1993) (consent of individual or representative of individual)

Exceptions: Ind. Code Ann. § 16-41-6-1 (Michie 1993) (physician has health care consent or implied consent; court order; epidemiological survey)

Mandatory Testing: Ind. Code Ann. § 35-38-1-10.5 (Michie 1994) (person convicted of a sex crime which created risk of transmission of HIV or offense related to controlled substances)

Screening of Semen Donors: Ind. Code Ann. §§ 16-41-14-1, 16-41-14-5 to 16-41-14-15, 16-41-14-18, 16-41-14-9 (Michie 1993)

Transmission Crimes: Ind. Code Ann. § 16-41-14-17 (Michie 1993) (HIV positive semen donor in artificial insemination context: Class C felony); § 35-38-1-7.1 (Michie 1993) (aggravating circumstances: person who commits offense related to use of sharp object that creates a risk of HIV transmission; knowledge that person was HIV carrier; person received risk counseling); §§ 35-42-1-7 (Michie 1994), 16-41-12-15 (Michie 1993) (felony to recklessly, knowingly, or intentionally donate, sell, or transfer blood component containing HIV); § 35-42-2-6 (Michie 1996 Supp.) (felony to knowingly or intentionally, in a rude, insolent, or angry manner, place blood or another body fluid on law enforcement or corrections officer)

Education: Ind. Code Ann. §§ 16-41-4-1, 16-41-4-2 (Michie 1993) (Department of Health and Board of Education provides literature stressing "moral aspects of abstinence"; literature not provided to school children without consent of school governing body), 20-10.1-4-10 (school corporation to include AIDS education in its curriculum), 31-7-3-3, 31-7-3-3.5 (Michie Supp. 1996) (HIV information to be provided to marriage license applicants)

Iowa

Counseling Requirement: Iowa Code § 141.22 (1989) (pre- and post-test counseling)

Partner Notification: Iowa Code § 141.6 (1989) (partner notification for persons who test HIV positive)

Confidentiality: Iowa Code § 141.10 (1989) (HIV test records strictly confidential medical information); § 141.23 (1989) (written release to disclose HIV test results); § 141.21 (1989) (statutory cause of action with breach of confidentiality)

Exceptions: Iowa Code § 141.23 (1989)

Mandatory Testing: Iowa Code § 356.48 (1994) (testing of inmate who bites another or causes exchange of body fluids); § 709B.2 (Supp. 1996) (at request of victim, court may order mandatory testing of person convicted of sexual assault or other sex crimes)

Education: Iowa Code § 141.3 (1989) (Dep't of Health to develop and implement AIDS education program for public and professionals), § 141.9 (1989) (various AIDS education programs), §§ 256.11, 279.50 (1996) (Boards of Education to implement AIDS education at all grade levels)

Employment: Iowa Code § 216.6 (1994) (no discrimination against employees or job applicants on the basis of HIV infection; no HIV testing as condition of employment)

Kansas

Reporting HIV Status: Kan. Stat. Ann. § 65-6002 (1992) (reporting to secretary of state name and address of persons suffering with/died from AIDS)

Mandatory Testing: Kan. Stat. Ann. § 22-293 (1995) (individual convicted of act involving sexual act or transmission of bodily fluids, at request of victim),

§ 65-6017 (1992) (court-ordered testing if corrections employee is in contact with blood/body fluids and offender refuses voluntary testing)

Confidentiality: Kan. Stat. Ann. § 65-6002 (1992) (HIV information confidential; written consent for disclosure)

Exceptions: Kan. Stat. Ann. § 65-6002 (1992) ("to protect public health;" medical personnel dealing with medical emergency)

Education: Kan. Stat. Ann. § 65-6006 (1992) (AIDS education material to be distributed to marriage license applicants)

Kentucky

Reporting HIV Status: Ky. Rev. Stat. Ann. § 211.180 (Michie 1995) (physician reporting of AIDS/HIV but no names or addresses)

Consent for Testing: Ky. Rev. Stat. Ann. § 214.625 (Michie 1995) (general consent for performance of medical tests/procedures, with notice that HIV test may be ordered, is sufficient)

Counseling Requirement: Ky. Rev. Stat. Ann. § 214.625 (Michie 1995) (post-test counseling)

Confidentiality: Ky. Rev. Stat. Ann. §§ 214.625, 214.420 (Michie 1995)

Exceptions: Ky. Rev. Stat. Ann. § 214.625 (Michie 1995) (numerous confidentiality exceptions)

Mandatory Testing: Ky. Rev. Stat. Ann. §§ 197.055 (Michie 1995), 71.130 (Michie Supp. 1994) (testing of inmates), § 438.250 (Michie Supp. 1994) (mandatory testing when criminal defendant/inmate bites/exposes public servant or victim of crime to blood/body fluid), § 510.320 (Michie Supp. 1994) (testing of defendant charged with sexual offense), § 510.320 (Michie Supp. 1994) (testing of person convicted of prostitution), § 635.110 (Michie Supp. 1994) (testing of juvenile adjudicated a public offender if offense is of a sexual nature)

Transmission Crimes: Ky. Rev. Stat. Ann. § 529.090 (Michie Supp. 1994) (Class D felony for individual who has tested HIV positive to engage in prostitution in a manner likely to transmit HIV)

Education: Ky. Rev. Stat. Ann. § 15.333 (Michie 1992) (AIDS education program for law enforcement officers); Ky. Rev. Stat. Ann. §§ 16.095 (Michie 1992), 72.415 (Michie 1994) (AIDS education programs for various government officials/personnel), § 164.351 (Michie 1994) (AIDS education for state college/university students), §§ 196.171 (Michie 1995), 441.115 (Michie Supp. 1994) (AIDS education for Dep't of Corrections personnel); § 197.055 (Michie 1995), (introductory/continuing AIDS education for inmates offered by Dep't of Corrections), § 214.605 (Michie 1995) (AIDS education for the general public), §§ 214.615, 311.653 (Michie 1995) (mandatory AIDS education for various health care related professionals), §§ 214.620, 311.654, 311.908 (Michie 1995) (mandatory AIDS education for licensed health care professionals)

Employment: Ky. Rev. Stat. Ann. § 207.135 (no HIV testing of individuals for hiring, promotion, or continued employment unless absence of HIV infection is bona fide occupational qualification), § 207.150 (Michie 1995) (nondiscrimination by employers on basis of HIV status)

Insurance: Ky. Rev. Stat. Ann. § 304.12-013 (HIV testing in the insurance context), § 304.14-130 (Michie Supp. 1994) (no limitation of insurance benefits because of AIDS/HIV infection)

Blood/Organ Donation: Ky. Rev. Stat. Ann. §§ 214.452, 214.458, 311.281 (Michie 1995)

Louisiana

Reporting HIV Status: La. Rev. Stat. Ann. § 33:1562 (West 1988) (misdemeanor if physician/others fail to report death of individual with HIV/AIDS or fail to notify coroner)

Consent for Testing: La. Rev. Stat. Ann. § 40:1300.13 (West 1992) (HIV-related testing only with written informed consent or oral consent with contemporaneous written documentation in medical record)

Exceptions: La. Rev. Stat. Ann. § 40:1300.13 (West 1992) (sex crime arrestees); La. Rev. Stat. Ann. § 40:1299.40 (West 1992) (testing without consent if physician, emergency medical personnel, police officers exposed to blood/body fluids); La. Code Crim. Proc. Ann. art. 499 (West 1992) (person indicted for sexual offense tested at court's discretion)

Confidentiality: La. Rev. Stat. Ann. §§ 40:1300.11–.16 (West 1992)

Exceptions: La. Rev. Stat. Ann. § 40:1300.14 (West 1992) (court-ordered disclosure of HIV-related information after showing of compelling need in criminal or civil proceeding, or in case of imminent danger to individual or public health)

Transmission Crimes: La. Rev. Stat. Ann. § 14:43.5 (West Supp. 1996) (crime of violence to intentionally expose another to HIV through sexual conduct or other means without knowing and lawful consent)

Education: La. Rev. Stat. Ann. § 17:7.2 (AIDS prevention education for grades 7 through 12), § 17:281 (West Supp. 1996) (emphasis on abstinence in sex education materials)

Maine

Reporting: Me. Rev. Stat. Ann. tit. 22, § 1011(3) (Supp. 1989) (HIV) (no names)

Consent for Testing: Me. Rev. Stat. Ann. tit. 5, §§ 19203-A(4), 19203-C (1989) (after "significant" exposure to health-care/EREs and court review; civil penalties up to $5,000)

Confidentiality: Me. Rev. Stat. Ann. tit. 5, § 19203 (1989)

Maryland

Consent for Testing: Md. Health-Gen. Code Ann. § 18-336 (Michie 1994 & Supp. 1996) (requires written informed consent for HIV test, except as provided by Article 27, § 765 of the Code; 1994 amendment changed reference from "§ 20-107" to "§ 5-605" of same title)

Partner Notification: Md. Health-Gen. Code Ann. § 18-337 (Michie 1994 & Supp. 1996) (physician may notify, if patient fails to)

Confidentiality: Md. Health-Gen. Code Ann. § 18-213.1 (notification of health care or emergency workers), § 18-213.2 (Michie 1994 & Supp. 1996) (post-mortem notification of first responder)

Mandatory Testing: Md. Health-Gen. Code Ann. § 18-338 (Michie 1994 & Supp. 1996) (inmates after exposure of correctional facilities employees), § 18-338.1 (patient testing after exposure of health care providers), § 18-334 (donors of semen, blood, or tissue)

Transmission Crimes: Md. Health-Gen. Code Ann. § 18-601.1 (Michie 1994)

Education: Md. Health-Gen. Code Ann. § 18-339 (Michie 1994) (persons convicted of certain drug and sex offenses)

Doctor-Patient Confidentiality Versus Duty to Warn in the Context of AIDS Patients and Their Partners, 47 Md. L. Rev. 675 (1988)

The AIDS Project: Creating a Public Health Policy—Rights and Obligations of Health Care Workers, 48 Md. L. Rev. 93 (1989)

Massachusetts

Consent for Testing: Mass. Ann. Laws ch. 111, § 70f (Law. Co-op. 1995) (written informed consent required)

Confidentiality: Mass. Ann. Laws ch. 111, § 70f (Law. Co-op. 1995) (written consent for disclosure of test results; notification of health care or emergency workers; post-mortem notification of first responder)

Education: Mass. Ann. Laws ch. 69, §§ 1D, 1L (Law. Co-op. Supp. 1996) (HIV/AIDS education in grades K through 12)

Employment: Mass. Ann. Laws ch. 111, § 70 F (Law. Co-op. 1995) (HIV test may not be required as condition for employment)

Michael D. Isacco, Jr., *A Massachusetts Real Estate Broker's Duty to Disclose: The Quandry Presented by AIDS-Stigmatized Property*, 27 New Eng. L. Rev. 1211 (1993)

William O. Fabbri, *Home HIV Testing and Conflicts with State HIV Testing Regulations*, 21 Am. J. L. & Med. 419 (1995)

Michigan

Reporting: Mich. Comp. Laws Ann. § 333.5114 (West Supp. 1990) (names)

Statutory Informed Consent Requirement: Mich. Comp. Laws Ann. § 333.5133(2) (West Supp. 1991)

Exceptions to Informed Consent: Mich. Comp. Laws Ann. § 333.5123 (West Supp. 1991) (prenatal testing of pregnant women, but only if woman consents), § 333.5133(12), (13) (after exposure of health care worker if patient is informed about possibility of such test upon admission to health care facility; patient unable to consent)

Confidentiality: Mich. Comp. Laws Ann. § 333.5131(1) (West Supp. 1991)

Anonymous Testing Statute: Mich. Comp. Laws Ann. § 333.5133(9) (West Supp. 1991)

Exceptions to Nondisclosure: Mich. Comp. Laws Ann. § 333.5131 (West Supp. 1991) (health care workers; sexual or needle-sharing partners; school district employees; foster care agencies), § 333.20191 (emergency workers), § 333.2843b (funeral directors)

Penalties for Wrongful Disclosure: Mich. Comp. Laws Ann. § 333.5131(8) (West Supp. 1991) (misdemeanor)

Contact Tracing: Mich. Comp. Laws Ann. § 333.5114a (West Supp. 1991)

Quarantine: Mich. Comp. Laws Ann. §§ 333.5203–.5209 (West Supp. 1991) (serious communicable diseases or infections)

Mandatory Testing: Mich. Comp. Laws Ann. § 333.5129 (West Supp. 1991) (persons convicted of prostitution, criminal sexual conduct, or intravenous use of controlled substances: victims notified if they choose), § 791.267(2) (all other prisoners tested upon arrival at reception center)

Transmission Crimes: Mich. Comp. Laws Ann. § 333.5210 (West Supp. 1991) ("sexual penetration" after knowledge of seropositivity and without informing partner is felony)

Phyllis G. Donaldson, *Management of Seropositive AIDS Inmates in the Prison Population: The Michigan Approach,* 36 Wayne L. Rev. 1589 (1990)

Minnesota

Reporting: Minn. R. 4605.7040 (1987) (names)

Statutory Informed Consent Requirement: Minn. Stat. Ann. § 144.765 (West Supp. 1991) (applicable after "significant exposure" to emergency employees)

Confidentiality: Minn. Stat. Ann. § 144.768 (West Supp. 1991) (applicable after "significant exposure" to emergency employees), § 13.38 (West 1989) (generally)

Exceptions to Nondisclosure: Minn. Stat. Ann. §§ 144.762, .767 (West Supp. 1990) (emergency workers)

Penalties for Wrongful Disclosure: Minn. Stat. Ann. § 144.769 (West Supp. 1990) (misdemeanor), §§ 13.08, .09 (West 1988 & Supp. 1990)

Contact Tracing: Minn. Stat. Ann. § 144.4172(4) (West 1989)

Quarantine: Minn. Stat. Ann. §§ 144.4173–.4186 (West 1989)

Mississippi

Reporting HIV Status: Miss. Code Ann. § 41-23-1 (1993) (reporting of AIDS deaths/AIDS cases to executive officer of State Board of Health), Miss. Code Ann. §§ 41-34-5, 41-34-7 (1993) (licensing boards may require HIV carriers to report)

Exceptions: Miss. Code Ann. § 41-41-16 (1993) (physician or hospital may conduct HIV test without specific consent if determination is made that HIV test is necessary for providing appropriate care/treatment)

Mandatory Testing: Miss. Code Ann. § 99-19-203 (1994) (mandatory HIV testing of person convicted of sex offense)

Education: Miss. Code Ann. § 41-79-5 (Supp. 1996) (school reproductive health education to include STDs with emphasis on abstinence)

Quarantine: Miss. Code Ann. § 41-23-27 (1993) (State Board of Health has power to isolate/quarantine/treat persons inflicted with infectious sexually transmitted diseases)

Missouri

Consent for Testing: Mo. Rev. Stat. §§ 191.650–.698 (West 1996)

Counseling: Mo. Rev. Stat. § 191.653 (West 1996) (pre- and post-test counseling)

Confidentiality: Mo. Rev. Stat. § 191.656 (West 1996)

Exceptions: Mo. Rev. Stat. § 191.656 (West 1996)

Mandatory Testing: Mo. Rev. Stat. § 191.226 (mandatory testing of individuals convicted of rape, sodomy, or incest), § 191.659 (mandatory testing of all inmates entering or being discharged from correctional facilities), §191.663 (mandatory testing of all persons convicted of sexual offenses), § 191.674 (West 1996) (mandatory court-ordered testing if reasonable grounds exist to believe individual is infected with HIV, refuses consent to testing, and presents serious and present health threat to others)

Transmission Crimes: Mo. Rev. Stat. § 191.677 (felony for HIV-positive individual to knowingly donate blood or organs), § 191.677 (West 1996) (felony for HIV-positive individual to deliberately risk infecting another with HIV through sexual or other contact)

Education: Mo. Rev. Stat. § 191.688 (West 1996) (HIV prevention educational programs for public primary and secondary schools)

Paula L. Andres, *Sticking It to the Fourth Amendment: The Failure of Missouri's Mandatory HIV Testing Law for Juvenile Sex Offenders,* 63 U. Mo. K.C. L. Rev. 455 (1995)

Montana

Consent for Testing: Mont. Code Ann. § 50-16-1007 (1995) (written informed consent required)

Exceptions: Mont. Code Ann. § 50-16-702 (testing without consent if emergency medical services provider is exposed to HIV risk and written informed consent from patient is unavailable), § 50-16-1007 (1995) (consent not required for HIV testing of prisoners)

Counseling Requirement: Mont. Code Ann. § 50-16-1007 (1995) (pre- and post-test counseling)

Confidentiality: Mont. Code Ann. § 50-16-1009 (1995) (confidentiality of HIV-related information)

Mandatory Testing: Mont. Code Ann. § 50-18-107 (examination and treatment of person reasonably suspected of having STD; isolation/quarantine measures available), § 46-18-25 (1995) (mandatory HIV testing of individuals convicted of sexual offenses)

Education: Mont. Code Ann. § 50-16-1002 (1995) (HIV prevention education to be directed toward individuals infected or at risk for infection)

Nebraska

Reporting HIV Status: Neb. Rev. Stat. § 71-532 (Supp. 1994) (HIV reportable in same manner as communicable diseases)

Consent for Testing: Neb. Rev. Stat. § 71-531 (Supp. 1994) (written informed consent)

Mandatory Testing: Neb. Rev. Stat. § 29-2290 (1995) (court-ordered testing at request of victim of persons convicted of sexual assault or other sex offenses), § 71-510 (1990) (mandatory testing of patient's blood when emergency medical services provider experiences significant exposure to blood/body fluid that could involve HIV transmission if patient fails to consent), § 71-514.03 (Supp. 1994) (mandatory testing of patient's blood when health care providers experiences significant exposure to blood/body fluid that could involve HIV transmission if patient fails to consent)

Employment: Neb. Rev. Stat. § 20-168 (1991) (employer prohibited from discriminating against employees/job applicants because of HIV status/perceived HIV status)

Nevada

Confidentiality: Nev. Rev. Stat. Ann. § 441A.220 (Michie 1991) (personal information about reported/suspected case of communicable disease is confidential medical information; written release required for disclosure of information)

Mandatory Testing: Nev. Rev. Stat. Ann. § 441A.320 (Michie Supp. 1993) (HIV testing of individual arrested for sexual offense), § 201.356 (Michie 1992) (HIV testing of persons arrested for prostitution/solicitation that is not in licensed house of prostitution), § 209.385 (Michie 1996) (HIV testing of offenders in custody of Correctional Department as director deems appropriate)

Transmission Crimes: Nev. Rev. Stat. Ann. § 201.205 (Michie Supp. 1993) (felony for individual who has tested HIV-positive to knowingly/willfully act in a fashion intended or likely to transmit the disease; consent is affirmative defense), § 201.358 (Michie 1992) (felony for individual who has tested HIV positive to engage in prostitution)

Education: Nev. Rev. Stat. Ann. § 389.065 (Michie 1991) (sex education to include factual information about AIDS; written consent of parent required for student to participate), § 209.385 (Michie 1996) (HIV education for inmates and Dep't of Corrections employees)

New Hampshire

Consent for Testing: N.H. Rev. Stat. Ann. § 141-F:5 (written informed consent), § 141-F:11 (1996) (crime to violate statutory requirements for informed consent for testing)

Exceptions: N.H. Rev. Stat. Ann. § 141-F:5 (1996)

Counseling Requirement: N.H. Rev. Stat. Ann. § 141-F:7 (1996) (post-test counseling)

Confidentiality: N.H. Rev. Stat. Ann. § 141-F:8 (HIV-related information to be maintained as confidential; written authorization for release of information), § 141-F:11 (1996) (crime to violate statutory restrictions meant to ensure confidentiality of HIV-related information)

Mandatory Testing: N.H. Rev. Stat. Ann. § 141-F:5 (1996) (court may order mandatory HIV testing of individuals convicted and confined to correctional facilities)

Education: N.H. Rev. Stat. Ann. § 141-F:3 (Division of Public Health Services to develop HIV prevention education and material), § 186:11 (1996) (State Board of Education to provide HIV-related educational material for public school students)

Insurance: N.H. Rev. Stat. Ann. § 417:4 (1996) (HIV testing for insurance purposes: confidentiality and informed consent requirements apply)

New Jersey

Reporting HIV Status: N.J. Stat. Ann. § 26:5C-6 (West 1996) (reporting of all diagnosed cases of AIDS/HIV infection along with identify information for the individual diagnosed).

Confidentiality: N.J. Stat. Ann. § 26:5C-7 (confidentiality of HIV-related information), § 26:5C-8 (written consent required for release of information), § 26:5C-14 (West 1996) (cause of action for illegal disclosure of information)

Exceptions: N.J. Stat. Ann. § 26:5C-8, § 26:5C-9 (West 1996) (court-ordered disclosure of HIV-related information after determination of good cause; court to weigh public interest and need with disclosure with potential injury to patient)

Mandatory Testing: N.J. Stat. Ann. § 2A:4A-43.1 (mandatory testing of juvenile adjudicated delinquent for act which, if committed by an adult, would constitute aggravated sexual assault), § 2C:43-2.2 (West Supp. 1996) (mandatory HIV testing of individual convicted of, indicted for, or formally charged with sexual assault)

Education: N.J. Stat. Ann. § 26:5C-3 (West 1996) (AIDS education program for the public developed by the Commissioner of the State Dep't of Health)

New Mexico

Consent for Testing: N.M. Stat. Ann. § 24-2B-2 (Michie 1994) (written informed consent or documentation in medical record indicating informed consent)

Exceptions: N.M. Stat. Ann. §§ 24-2B-5, 24-1-9.1 (Michie 1994) (blood or tissue donation; medical emergencies; anonymous medical research)

Counseling Requirement: N.M. Stat. Ann. § 24-B-4 (Michie 1994) (post-test counseling)

Confidentiality: N.M. Stat. Ann. § 24-2B-7 (Michie 1994) (written release for disclosure of HIV information)

Mandatory Testing: N.M. Stat. Ann. § 24-2B-5 (Michie 1994) (court-ordered testing of individuals convicted of sexual offenses or in instance of transmission of body fluids between offender and victim)

New York

Consent for Testing: N.Y. Pub. Health Law § 2781 (written consent required), § 2786 (McKinney 1993) (commissioner of health to develop forms to be used for informed consent for HIV testing and for release of HIV-related information)

Counseling: N.Y. Pub. Health Law § 2786 (McKinney 1993) (pre- and post-test counseling)

Contact Notification: N.Y. Pub. Health Law § 2782 (McKinney 1993) (physician permitted to disclose confidential HIV-related information in detailed circumstances)

Confidentiality: N.Y. Pub. Health Law § 2782 (McKinney 1993)

Exceptions: N.Y. Pub. Health Law §§ 2780 to 2790 (McKinney 1993) (court-ordered disclosure of HIV-related information upon showing of compelling need in adjudication of criminal or civil proceeding or clear and imminent danger to an individual whose life/health may be unknowingly at significant risk as result of contact)

Education: N.Y. Educ. Law § 6505-b (McKinney Supp. 1996); N.Y. Pub. Health Law § 239 (McKinney 1993) (prevention of HIV transmission for health care professionals)

Insurance: N.Y. Ins. Law § 2611 (McKinney Supp. 1996) (requirements, including informed consent, for HIV testing in the insurance context)

Wendy A. Barnhart, *Confidentiality of HIV and AIDS-Related Information in New York,* 1 Syracuse J. Legis. & Pol'y 115 (1995)

Kevin J. Curnin, *Newborn HIV Screening and New York Assembly Bill Number 6747-B: Privacy and Equal Protection of Pregnant Women,* 21 Fordham Urb. L.J. 857 (1994)

Leonardo Renna, *New York State's Proposal to Unblind HIV Testing for Newborns: A Necessary Step in Addressing a Critical Problem,* 60 Brooklyn L. Rev. 407 (1994)

North Carolina

Reporting HIV Status: N.C. Gen. Stat. § 130A-135 (Michie 1995) (physician required to report to Public Health Study Commission)

Counseling Requirement: N.C. Gen. Stat. § 130A-148 (Michie 1995)

Confidentiality: N.C. Gen. Stat. § 130A-143 (Michie 1995) (all information/ records identifying individual as having AIDS; written authorization required for release of records)

Exceptions: N.C. Gen. Stat. § 130A-143 (Michie 1995) (court order: protect public health; to court, for law enforcement purposes; preventing spread of communicable disease)

Mandatory Testing: N.C. Gen. Stat. § 15A-534.3 (court-ordered testing of criminal defendant if probable cause that individual was exposed to defendant in manner which poses significant risk of AIDS transmission), § 15A-615 (Michie Supp. 1995) (mandatory testing of defendant indicted for sexual crime with minor), § 130A-148 (Michie 1995) (mandatory AIDS testing to protect public health)

Education: N.C. Gen. Stat. § 115C-81 (Michie Supp. 1995) (comprehensive school health education program including instruction in AIDS prevention; provision for hearings and parental consent mechanism)

Employment: N.C. Gen. Stat. § 130A-148 (Michie 1995) (continued employment cannot be contingent upon HIV status; no required AIDS testing; mandatory AIDS testing in pre-employment medical examinations permitted; employer can reject job applicant solely on basis of HIV-positive status; AIDS testing as part of mandatory annual medical examinations)

North Dakota

Reporting HIV Status: N.D. Cent. Code § 23-07-01 (State Dep't of Health may require reporting of infectious and sexually transmitted diseases), § 23-07.02-2 (1991) (physicians and health care workers treating HIV-positive individuals in public or private institutions shall report individual's identity to the State Dep't of Health)

Consent for Testing: N.D. Cent. Code §§ 23-07.5-01 to .5-08 (1991) (written consent for testing)

Exceptions: N.D. Cent. Code §§ 23-07.5.01 to 08 (adoptees/foster parents; subject's health care providers; blood/tissue donation), §§ 23-07.7-01 to 02 (1991) (persons charged with alleged sexual offenses at request of victim)

Confidentiality: N.D. Cent. Code § 23-07-21 (class C felony to breach confidentiality of HIV-related information), §§ 23-07.5-01 to .5-08 (Supp. 1995) (written release for disclosure of HIV-related information)

Mandatory Testing: N.D. Cent. Code § 23-07-07.5 (1991) (mandatory HIV testing of persons convicted of a crime and imprisoned for more than 15 days; persons convicted of sexual offenses or illegal intravenous drug use)

Treatment and Confinement: N.D. Cent. Code §§ 23-07.4-01 to .4-03 (Supp. 1995) (state health officer can require persons suspected of being HIV-infected to be tested and undergo counseling and education and to cease and desist from conduct that endangers health of others; injunction and up to 90 days custody available measures)

Transmission Crimes: N.D. Cent. Code § 12.1-20-17 (Supp. 1995) (class A felony for HIV-infected individual to transmit body fluids; affirmative defenses in sexual contact setting: consent after full disclosure and use of prophylactic device), 23-07-21 (1991) (infraction for persons who know they are infected with STD to willfully expose another person to infection)

Ohio

Reporting HIV Status: Ohio Rev. Code Ann. § 3701.24 (reporting of AIDS cases and persons testing HIV positive to director of health), § 3707.06 (Anderson 1995) (physicians to report to health commissioner the name, age, sex, address of patients suffering from "disease dangerous to the public health")

Consent for Testing: Ohio Rev. Code Ann. § 3701.242 (Anderson 1995) (oral or written informed consent; details of information to be provided to patient in obtaining informed consent)

Exceptions: Ohio Rev. Code Ann. § 3701.242 (Anderson 1995) (emergency medical situation; testing of incarcerated person; patient who has given physician general consent for medical treatment)

Counseling Requirement: Ohio Rev. Code Ann. § 3701.242 (Anderson 1995) (post-test counseling)

Confidentiality: Ohio Rev. Code Ann. § 3701.243. (Anderson 1995)

Exceptions: Ohio Rev. Code Ann. § 3701.248 (emergency medical services worker/funeral director/embalmer who suffers significant exposure to risk of HIV may request information on results of tests to determine if patient/deceased had a contagious/infectious disease), § 3701.24 (release of HIV-related information: to treat test subject; pursuant to court order, search warrant, or subpoena in connection with criminal investigation/prosecution), § 3701.243 (procedure for obtaining court-ordered release of HIV-related information), § 3701.243 (Anderson 1995) (written disclosure of HIV-related information to health care provider and others who have "medical need to know")

Mandatory Testing: Ohio Rev. Code Ann. § 3701.247 (Anderson 1995) (court-ordered testing when persons rendering health care/emergency care or peace officers believe they may have been exposed to HIV infection while carrying out their duties), § 2907.27 (Anderson 1993) (HIV testing of persons accused for rape, other sexual offenses, prostitution)

Transmission Crimes: Ohio Rev. Code Ann. § 2927.13 (Anderson 1993) (third-degree felony for individuals who know they are "carriers of AIDS" to sell blood/blood products)

Insurance: Ohio Rev. Code Ann. § 3901.45 (insurers prohibited from considering applicant's sexual orientation or fact that applicant has taken HIV test), § 3901.46 (Anderson Supp. 1995) (limitations on insurer's use of HIV testing)

Oklahoma

Reporting HIV Status: Okla. Stat. tit. 63, § 1-527 (1984) (reporting by physicians, managers of hospitals, etc., of STD cases to State Commission of Health)

Confidentiality: Okla. Stat. tit. 63, § 1-502.2 (Supp. 1996) (information and records regarding venereal or communicable disease are confidential; written release required to disclose; cause of action for breach of confidentiality)

Exceptions: Okla. Stat. tit. 63, § 1-523 (correctional institution shall maintain record of all inmates infected with a venereal disease and notify correctional employees and other employees of seropositive status of AIDS/HIV positive inmates), § 1-502.2 (Supp. 1996) (release of information to health care and emergency care personnel who have had risk of exposure, as well as to health professionals, state agencies, and district courts to enforce communicable and venereal disease prevention and control rules)

Mandatory Testing: Okla. Stat. tit. 63, § 1-524 (Supp. 1996) (mandatory IV testing of all persons arrested for sexual offenses)

Transmission Crimes: Okla. Stat. tit. 21, § 1031 (felony for individuals to engage in prostitution if they know they are infected with HIV), § 1192.1 (Supp. 1996) (felony for individual with AIDS or HIV infected to engage in conduct reasonably likely to transfer body fluids into bloodstream of another)

Education: Okla. Stat. tit. 70, § 11-103.3 (1989) (education for AIDS education to be taught in public schools; parents can opt out; emphasis on abstinence)

R. Brian Leech, *Criminalizing Sexual Transmission of HIV: Oklahoma's Intentional Transmission Statute: Unconstitutional or Merely Unenforceable?*, 46 Okla. L. Rev. 687 (1993)

Oregon

Consent for Testing: Or. Rev. Stat. § 433.045 (1992) (required for HIV testing; health department specifies forms, procedures, and materials to be used in obtaining informed consent by nonphysician)

Counseling Requirement: Or. Rev. Stat. § 433.045 (1992) (explanation of testing procedure, risks, alternatives)

Mandatory Testing: Or. Rev. Stat. § 135.139 (persons arrested and charged with crime in which transmission of body fluids is involved or in which sexual act may have been involved); § 433.080 (1992) (court-ordered testing of "source persons" when defined class of workers experiences potential occupational exposure to HIV)

Education: Or. Rev. Stat. § 336.455 (1992) (public school classes on sex education to include information on HIV transmission and risk reduction strategies, with emphasis on abstinence; includes parental opt-out provision)

Pennsylvania

Consent for Testing: 35 Pa. Cons. Stat. Ann. § 7605(a) (1993) (written, informed consent required)

Counseling Required: 35 Pa. Cons. Stat. Ann. § 7605(e)(1) (1993) (pre- and post-test counseling required)

Partner Notification: 35 Pa. Cons. Stat. Ann. § 7609 (permissible physician disclosure of confidential HIV information to known contact in certain circumstances)

Confidentiality: 35 Pa. Cons. Stat. Ann. § 7607 (written consent for disclosure required), § 7611 (cause of action for violation of Confidentiality of HIV-Related Information Act)

Exceptions: 35 Pa. Cons. Stat. Ann. § 7608 (court-ordered release of confidential HIV-related information when compelling need is demonstrated)

Mandatory Testing: 35 Pa. Cons. Stat. Ann. § 7609 (testing of source patient's available blood when health care provider/first responder experiences a significant risk of exposure to HIV by being exposed to blood/body fluids while rendering health care services and patient refuses voluntary consent to testing); 18 Pa. Cons. Stat. Ann. § 521.11(a) (mandatory HIV testing of individual convicted or adjudicated delinquent of rape and various other sexual offenses)

Transmission Crimes: § 18 Pa. Cons. Stat. Ann. § 521.2 (third-degree felony for those who know they are HIV positive to engage in prostitution or to patronize a prostitute)

Molly E. Puhlman, *The AIDS Challenge Continues: Should Pennsylvania's Criminal Law Take on the Challenge?*, 30 Duq. L. Rev. 283 (1992)

Rhode Island

Consent for Testing: R.I. Gen. Laws § 23-6-11 (Michie Supp. 1995) (specification of AIDS testing and notification form), § 23-6-13 (Michie 1989) (testing requires written consent; detailed specific requirements for valid informed consent)

Exceptions: R.I. Gen. Laws §§ 23-6-14, 23-6-15 (Michie Supp. 1995) (exceptions to informed consent)

Counseling Requirement: R.I. Gen. Laws § 23-6-13 (Michie 1989) (pre- and post-test counseling)

Confidentiality: R.I. Gen. Laws § 23-6-18 (Michie Supp. 1995)

Exceptions: R.I. Gen. Laws § 23-6-17 (Michie Supp. 1995) (disclosure of HIV information without prior written consent in certain circumstances)

Mandatory Testing: R.I. Gen. Laws § 21-11-12 (Michie 1995) (misdemeanor for person suspected of having STD to refuse examination); R.I. Gen. Laws § 11-34-10 (Michie 1995) (mandatory testing of any person convicted of prostitution or lewdness), § 11-37-17 (mandatory testing of all persons convicted of sexual offenses); § 21-28-4.20 (Michie Supp. 1996) (mandatory HIV testing of any person convicted of illegal possession of hypodermic needles associated with IV drug use); § 45-56.37 (mandatory testing of all persons committed to adult correctional institutes)

Education: R.I. Gen. Laws §§ 16-22-17, 16-22-18 (Michie 1988) (AIDS prevention education, focusing on abstinence, for elementary and secondary schools)

Employment: R.I. Gen. Laws § 23-6-23 (Michie 1989) (prohibition of employment discrimination on the basis of positive AIDS test)

Insurance: R.I. Gen. Laws § 23-6-24 (Michie 1989) (special provisions for HIV testing in the insurance context, including requirement of prior written notice)

South Carolina

Reporting HIV Status: S.C. Code Ann. § 44-29-70 (Law. Co-op. Supp. 1995) (physician reporting of individuals treated for STD)

Confidentiality: S.C. Code Ann. § 44-29-135 (Law. Co-op. Supp. 1995) (confidentiality of all information concerning case of sexually transmitted disease held by Dep't of Health & Environmental Control)

Exceptions: S.C. Code Ann. § 44-29-136 (release of information for statistical purposes; consent to individual required for release of information to medical personnel), § 44-29-136 (Law. Co-op. Supp. 1995) (court-ordered release of information after determination of compelling need)

Mandatory Testing: S.C. Code Ann. § 16-3-740 (within 15 days after conviction of individual for sexual battery/conduct resulting in exposure of victim to blood/body fluid and offer; offender and victim informed of results), § 16-15-255 (testing of offender convicted of sexual offense), § 44-29-230 (Law. Co-op. Supp. 1995) (patient's blood tested after health care worker or emergency response employee is or may have been exposed to HIV while working with patient's blood or body fluids)

Transmission Crimes: S.C. Code Ann. § 44-29-145 (unlawful to knowingly expose another to HIV), § 44-29-45 (Law. Co-op. Supp. 1995) (felony for HIV-positive individual to knowingly engage in sexual activity without consent, to engage in prostitution, to sell or donate blood, or to knowingly share hypodermic needles)

Education: S.C. Code Ann. § 59-32-50 (Law. Co-op. Supp. 1995) (health education for public schools to include information on sexually transmitted diseases; includes parental opt-out provision)

South Dakota

Mandatory Testing: S.D. Codified Laws §§ 23A-35B-1 to -6 (Michie Supp. 1996) (mandatory testing of criminal defendant in case of sexual assault crimes of violence, defendant involved in motor vehicle accident when driving while intoxicated, at request of victim; testing of defendant when law enforcement officer is potentially exposed to blood or body fluids, at request of law enforcement officer)

Education: S.D. Codified Laws § 25-1-28.1 (Michie Supp. 1996) (marriage license applicants provided with educational material about HIV transmission and on locations of counseling and testing services)

Tennessee

Reporting HIV Status: Tenn. Code Ann. § 68-5-102 (1996) (physician who knows/suspects that patient/examinee is HIV positive is obligated to notify county/town health authorities)

Mandatory Testing: Tenn. Code Ann. § 39-13-521 (1991) (mandatory HIV testing of individuals arrested for rape, aggravated rape, statutory rape; test results to be reported to victim), § 39-13-521 (mandatory HIV testing of individuals convicted of prostitution)

Transmission Crimes: Tenn. Code Ann. § 39-13-109 (criminal offense for HIV-infected individual to engage in intimate contact with another, transfer body fluids, or transfer nonsterile intravenous drug paraphernalia; consent is affirmative defense), 39-13-516 (Supp. 1996) (aggravated prostitution: when HIV-positive individual engages in sexual activity as business)

Education: Tenn. Code Ann. § 49-6-1008 (1996) (AIDS prevention information aimed at K to 12 grades; emphasis on abstinence and avoidance of drug use)

Quarantine: Tenn. Code Ann. § 39-13-108 (Supp. 1996) (Dep't of Health authorized to quarantine or isolate within secure facility person when such person demonstrates willful/knowing disregard for health safety of others in context of HIV transmission and continues to pose public health and safety risk)

Texas

Reporting HIV Status: Tex. Health & Safety Code Ann. § 81.052 (West 1992) (names, addresses not required)

Consent for Testing: Tex. Health & Safety Code Ann. § 81.102 (class A misdemeanor to require individual to undergo HIV test unless permitted by statute), § 81.106 (West 1992) (general consent for performance of medical tests is sufficient)

Counseling Requirement: Tex. Health & Safety Code Ann. § 81.109 (West 1992) (post-test counseling)

Partner Notification: Tex. Health & Safety Code Ann. § 81.051 (West 1992)

Confidentiality: Tex. Health & Safety Code Ann. § 81.046 (confidentiality of information furnished to health authority or Dep't of Health), §§ 81.103, .104 (confidentiality of AIDS/HIV test results; cause of action for violation of confidentiality requirements), § 81.103 (West 1992) (criminal liability for negligent release of HIV-related information)

Mandatory Testing: Tex. Fam. Code Ann. § 54.033 (West 1996) (mandatory testing of child adjudicated delinquent), Tex. Gov't Code Ann. § 500.054 (West 1990) (HIV testing of inmates in custody of Dep't of Criminal Justice), Tex. Health & Safety Code Ann. § 81.050 (West 1992) (mandatory testing when law enforcement officer, fire fighter, emergency medical services personnel exposed to possible HIV infection), Tex. Health & Safety Code Ann. § 81.102 (West 1992) (number of instances when individual may be required to undergo HIV testing), Tex. Crim. Proc. Code Ann. art. 21.31 (West Supp. 1996) (court-ordered testing of person indicted for sexual assault)

Education: Tex. Educ. Code Ann. § 28.004 (West 1996) (AIDS education in public schools, with emphasis on abstinence; includes parental opt-out provision), Tex. Health & Safety Code Ann. §§ 163.001–.002 (West 1992) (Dep't of Health to develop AIDS education program for school age children;

emphasis on abstinence and avoidance of drug use), Tex. Educ. Code Ann. § 51.919 (West 1996) (institutions of higher education: HIV/AIDS policies and education), Tex. Gov't Code Ann. §§ 500.054, 507.023 (West 1990) (Department of Criminal Justice educational programs for employees and inmates), Tex. Health & Safety Code Ann. §§ 85.004–.011 (West 1992) (Department of Health HIV/AIDS educational programs for general public), Tex. Fam. Code Ann. §§ 1.07, 1.94 (West 1993) (county clerk who issues marriage licenses to provide applicants with printed AIDS educational material)

Employment: Tex. Health & Safety Code Ann. § 85.112 (West 1992) (workplace guidelines concerning persons with HIV infection)

Insurance: Tex. Ins. Code Ann. § 21.21-4 (West 1992) (requirements for HIV testing of applicants by insurers)

Julie Edwards, *Controlling the Epidemic: The Texas AIDS Reporting Statute,* 41 Baylor L. Rev. 399 (1989)

Utah

Reporting HIV Status: Utah Code Ann. § 26-6-3 (1995) (reporting of AIDS and HIV infection)

Partner Notification: Utah Code Ann. § 26-6-3 (1995)

Mandatory Testing: Utah Code Ann. §§ 76-10-1309, -1310 (individual convicted of prostitution/solicitation who is HIV positive and has been given written notice of HIV test results is guilty of felony in third degree), § 76-5-502 (testing of sexual offenders); § 64-13-36 (testing of all prisoners when admitted to correctional facility), § 76-5-504 (1995) (mandatory testing of minors adjudicated of having committed sexual offense), Utah Code Ann. § 78-29-102 (Supp. 1996) (court-ordered HIV testing at request of emergency medical services provider or public safety officers exposed while carrying out their duties who experience significant exposure to risk of HIV)

Education: Utah Code Ann. § 53A-13-101 (1994) (school curriculum to require instruction in prevention of communicable diseases, with emphasis on abstinence)

Vermont

Confidentiality: Vt. Stat. Ann. tit. 12, § 1705 (Supp. 1996) (confidentiality of HIV-related information)

Exceptions: Vt. Stat. Ann. tit. 12, § 1705 (Supp. 1996) (court determination of compelling need for disclosure of HIV-related information)

Education: Vt. Stat. Ann. tit. 16, § 134 (1989) (comprehensive AIDS educational programs for schools with parental opt-out for religious reasons)

Employment: Vt. Stat. Ann. tit. 3, § 961 (1995) (unfair labor practice for employer to require HIV testing of employees/applicants or to discriminate against HIV-positive employees/applicants)

Health Care: Vt. Stat. Ann. tit. 18, § 1128 (Supp. 1996) (no health care provider/facility can request/require patient/client/applicant for services to undergo HIV testing)

Virginia

Reporting HIV Status: Va. Code Ann. § 32.1-36 (Michie 1992) (physician required to report to local health department identity of individuals who test HIV positive)

Consent for Testing: Va. Code Ann. § 32.1-37.2 (Michie 1992) (informed consent need not be written; agreement to undergo routine diagnostic blood testing is deemed informed consent to HIV testing)

Exceptions: Va. Code Ann. § 32.1-45.1 (Michie 1992) (testing without consent when health care provider is directly exposed to body fluids)

Counseling Requirement: Va. Code Ann. 32.1-37.2 (Michie 1992) (post-test counseling)

Confidentiality: Va. Code Ann. 32.1-36 (Michie Supp. 1996) (HIV-related information is confidential)

Exceptions: Va. Code Ann. 32.1-36.1. (Michie Supp. 1996)

Mandatory Testing: Va. Code Ann. 18.2-346.1 (Michie 1996) (mandatory HIV testing after conviction for sexual offense)

Transmission Crimes: Va. Code Ann. 32.1-289.2 (Michie 1992) (felony for HIV-positive individual to sell or donate blood, organs)

Education: Va. Code Ann. 22.1-207.1 (K through 12 sex education), 23-9.2:3.2 (Michie 1993) (HIV prevention education for public colleges and universities)

Washington

Reporting HIV Status: Wash. Rev. Code Ann. § 70.24.050 (West 1992) (laboratories testing for HIV required to report anonymous HIV test results to Dep't of Health)

Consent for testing: Wash. Rev. Code Ann. § 70.24.330 (West 1992) (consent required for HIV testing)

Confidentiality: Wash. Rev. Code Ann. § 70.24.105 (West 1992)

Mandatory Testing: Wash. Rev. Code Ann. § 70.24.034 (health officer may order individual reasonably believed to be infected with STD to submit to medical examination, testing, counseling and treatment), § 70.24.340 (mandatory testing when law enforcement officer, fire fighter, or health care worker placed at risk of HIV because of exposure to blood, body fluids; court-ordered testing of persons convicted of sexual offense, prostitution, or drug offense), §§ 70.24.360, 70.24.370 (West 1992) (jail administration may order HIV testing of detainees)

Transmission Crimes: Wash. Rev. Code Ann. 9A.36.021 (West 1996 Supp.) (class B felony for HIV-positive individual to expose or transmit HIV to another with intent to inflict bodily harm)

Education: Wash. Rev. Code Ann. §§ 28A.230.070, 70.24.220 (West Supp. 1996) (public school education AIDS prevention programs to begin in fifth grade; parent may object in writing to exempt a student from participation)

West Virginia

Consent for Testing: West Virginia AIDS Medical Testing and Records Confidentiality Act, W. Va. Code §§ 16-3C-1 *et seq.* (1995)

Confidentiality: W. Va. Code § 16-3C-3 (1995) (notification of health care or emergency workers; post-mortem notification of first responder)

Mandatory Testing: W. Va. Code § 16-3C-2 (1995) (inmates, following exposure of correctional facilities employees; patient testing after exposure of health care providers; donors of semen, blood, or tissue)

Transmission Crimes: W. Va. Code § 18-601.1

Frank W. Volk, *HIV Positive Employees as "Handicapped" Persons under State and Federal Law: West Virginia Follows the Trend to Cast Aside Irrational Fear and Prejudice in Favor of Competent Medical Evidence and Sound Public Policy,* 93 W. Va. L. Rev. 219 (1990)

Wisconsin

Reporting: Wis. Stat. § 101.02 (1995 Supp.) (physician reporting to local health officer and Dep't of Health)

Consent for Testing: Wis. Stat. § 146.82 (Supp. 1995) (written informed consent required)

Exceptions: Wis. Stat. § 252.15 (Supp. 1995)

Counseling: Wis. Stat. § 252.14 (Supp. 1995) (counseling and referral)

Confidentiality: Wis. Stat. § 252.15 (notification of health care or emergency workers; post-mortem notification of first responder), § 252.11 (Supp. 1995) (STD records are confidential)

Exceptions: Wis. Stat. § 48.371 (Supp. 1995) (release of HIV testing records at time of placement of child in foster home)

Mandatory Testing: Wis. Stat. § 252.15 (inmates, following exposure of correctional facilities employees), § 225.15 (patient testing after exposure of health care providers; donors of semen, blood, or tissue), § 968.38 (Supp. 1995) (mandatory testing of juvenile alleged to have committed sexual assault)

Education: Wis. Stat. § 118.01 (1991) (public school education on STDs), § 118.019 (HIV/AIDS instruction in K through 12)

Employment: Wis. Stat. § 103.15 (Supp. 1995) (public employer can not require HIV testing as condition of employment)

Wyoming

Confidentiality: Wyo. Stat. § 35-4-132 (Michie 1994) (HIV-related information is confidential; written consent required for release of information)

Exceptions: Wyo. Stat. § 35-4-132 (Michie 1994) (release of HIV-related information without consent in order to protect life or health of health care professionals)

Contact Tracing: Wyo. Stat. § 35-4-133 (Michie 1994) (contact tracing by health officer when report of STD)

Mandatory Testing: Wyo. Stat. § 35-4-133 (Michie 1994) (HIV testing of patient specimen after health care worker's exposure to blood or body fluid if patient fails to consent), § 7-1-109 (Michie 1995) (testing of person accused of crime when there has been alleged exchange of body fluids), § 35-4-134 (Michie 1994) (health officer may examine individuals confined to or imprisoned in any correctional institution)

Sylvia J. Earnshaw, *An Ounce of Prevention Where There Is No Cure: AIDS and Public Health in Wyoming,* 27 Land & Water L. Rev. 471 (1992)

29 C.F.R. § 1910.1030 (Reprint)
BLOODBORNE PATHOGENS

§ 1910.1030   Bloodborne pathogens.

(a) *Scope and Application*. This section applies to all occupational exposure to blood or other potentially infectious materials as defined by paragraph (b) of this section.

(b) *Definitions*. For purposes of this section, the following shall apply:

Assistant Secretary means the Assistant Secretary of Labor for Occupational Safety and Health, or designated representative.

Blood means human blood, human blood components, and products made from human blood.

Bloodborne Pathogens means pathogenic microorganisms that are present in human blood and can cause disease in humans. These pathogens include, but are not limited to, hepatitis B virus (HBV) and human immunodeficiency virus (HIV).

Clinical Laboratory means a workplace where diagnostic or other screening procedures are performed on blood or other potentially infectious materials.

Contaminated means the presence or the reasonably anticipated presence of blood or other potentially infectious materials on an item or surface.

Contaminated Laundry means laundry which has been soiled with blood or other potentially infectious materials or may contain sharps.

Contaminated Sharps means any contaminated object that can penetrate the skin including, but not limited to, needles, scalpels, broken glass, broken capillary tubes, and exposed ends of dental wires.

Decontamination means the use of physical or chemical means to remove, inactivate, or destroy bloodborne pathogens on a surface or item to the point where they are no longer capable of transmitting infectious particles and the surface or item is rendered safe for handling, use, or disposal.

Director means the Director of the National Institute for Occupational Safety and Health, U.S. Department of Health and Human Services, or designated representative.

Engineering Controls means controls (e.g., sharps disposal containers, self-sheathing needles) that isolate or remove the bloodborne pathogens hazard from the workplace.

Exposure Incident means a specific eye, mouth, other mucous membrane, non-intact skin, or parenteral contact with blood or other potentially infectious materials that results from the performance of an employee's duties.

Handwashing Facilities means a facility providing an adequate supply of running potable water, soap and single use towels or hot air drying machines.

Licensed Healthcare Professional is a person whose legally permitted scope of practice allows him or her to independently perform the activities required by paragraph (f) Hepatitis B Vaccination and Post-exposure Evaluation and Follow-up.

HBV means hepatitis B virus.

HIV means human immunodeficiency virus.

Occupational Exposure means reasonably anticipated skin, eye, mucous membrane, or parenteral contact with blood or other potentially infectious materials that may result from the performance of an employee's duties.

Other Potentially Infectious Materials means

(1) The following human body fluids: semen, vaginal secretions, cerebrospinal fluid, synovial fluid, pleural fluid, pericardial fluid, peritoneal fluid, amniotic fluid, saliva in dental procedures, any body fluid that is visibly contaminated with blood, and all body fluids in situations where it is difficult or impossible to differentiate between body fluids;

(2) Any unfixed tissue or organ (other than intact skin) from a human (living or dead); and

(3) HIV-containing cell or tissue cultures, organ cultures, and HIV- or HBV-containing culture medium or other solutions; and blood, organs, or other tissues from experimental animals infected with HIV or HBV.

Parenteral means piercing mucous membranes or the skin barrier through such events as needlesticks, human bites, cuts, and abrasions.

Personal Protective Equipment is specialized clothing or equipment worn by an employee for protection against a hazard. General work clothes (e.g., uniforms, pants, shirts or blouses) not intended to function as protection against a hazard are not considered to be personal protective equipment.

Production Facility means a facility engaged in industrial-scale, large-volume or high concentration production of HIV or HBV.

Regulated Waste means liquid or semi-liquid blood or other potentially infectious materials; contaminated items that would release blood or other potentially infectious materials in a liquid or semi-liquid state if compressed; items that are caked with dried blood or other potentially infectious materials and are capable of releasing these materials during handling; contaminated sharps; and pathological and microbiological wastes containing blood or other potentially infectious materials.

Research Laboratory means a laboratory producing or using research-laboratory-scale amounts of HIV or HBV. Research laboratories may produce high concentrations of HIV or HBV but not in the volume found in production facilities.

Source Individual means any individual, living or dead, whose blood or other potentially infectious materials may be a source of occupational exposure to the employee. Examples include, but are not limited to, hospital and clinic patients; clients in institutions for the developmentally disabled; trauma victims; clients of drug and alcohol treatment facilities; residents of hospices and nursing homes; human remains; and individuals who donate or sell blood or blood components.

Sterilize means the use of a physical or chemical procedure to destroy all microbial life including highly resistant bacterial endospores.

Universal Precautions is an approach to infection control. According to the concept of Universal Precautions, all human blood and certain human body fluids are treated as if known to be infectious for HIV, HBV, and other bloodborne pathogens.

Work Practice Controls means controls that reduce the likelihood of exposure by altering the manner in which a task is performed (e.g., prohibiting recapping of needles by a two-handed technique).

(c) *Exposure control*—(1) *Exposure Control Plan.* (i) Each employer having an employee(s) with occupational exposure as defined by paragraph (b) of this section shall establish a written Exposure Control Plan designed to eliminate or minimize employee exposure.

(ii) The Exposure Control Plan shall contain at least the following elements:

(A) The exposure determination required by paragraph (c)(2),

(B) The schedule and method of implementation for paragraphs (d) Methods of Compliance, (e) HIV and HBV Research Laboratories and Production Facilities, (f) Hepatitis B Vaccination and Post-Exposure Evaluation and Follow-up, (g) Communication of Hazards to Employees, and (h) Recordkeeping, of this standard, and

(C) The procedure for the evaluation of circumstances surrounding exposure incidents as required by paragraph (f)(3)(i) of this standard.

(iii) Each employer shall ensure that a copy of the Exposure Control Plan is accessible to employees in accordance with 29 CFR 1910.20(e).

(iv) The Exposure Control Plan shall be reviewed and updated at least annually and whenever necessary to reflect new or modified tasks and procedures which affect occupational exposure and to reflect new or revised employee positions with occupational exposure.

(v) The Exposure Control Plan shall be made available to the Assistant Secretary and the Director upon request for examination and copying.

(2) *Exposure determination.* (i) Each employer who has an employee(s) with occupational exposure as defined by paragraph (b) of this section shall prepare an exposure determination. This exposure determination shall contain the following:

(A) A list of all job classifications in which all employees in those job classifications have occupational exposure;

(B) A list of job classifications in which some employees have occupational exposure, and

(C) A list of all tasks and procedures or groups of closely related task and procedures in which occupational exposure occurs and that are performed by employees in job classifications listed in accordance with the provisions of paragraph (c)(2)(i)(B) of this standard.

(ii) This exposure determination shall be made without regard to the use of personal protective equipment.

(d) *Methods of compliance*—(1) *General*—Universal precautions shall be observed to prevent contact with blood or other potentially infectious materials. Under circumstances in which differentiation between body fluid types is difficult or impossible, all body fluids shall be considered potentially infectious materials.

(2) *Engineering and work practice controls.* (i) Engineering and work practice controls shall be used to eliminate or minimize employee exposure. Where occupational exposure remains after institution of these controls, personal protective equipment shall also be used.

(ii) Engineering controls shall be examined and maintained or replaced on a regular schedule to ensure their effectiveness.

(iii) Employers shall provide handwashing facilities which are readily accessible to employees.

(iv) When provision of handwashing facilities is not feasible, the employer shall provide either an appropriate antiseptic hand cleanser in conjunction with clean cloth/paper towels or antiseptic towelettes. When antiseptic hand cleansers or towelettes are used, hands shall be washed with soap and running water as soon as feasible.

(v) Employers shall ensure that employees wash their hands immediately or as soon as feasible after removal of gloves or other personal protective equipment.

(vi) Employers shall ensure that employees wash hands and any other skin with soap and water, or flush mucous membranes with water immediately or as soon as feasible following contact of such body areas with blood or other potentially infectious materials.

(vii) Contaminated needles and other contaminated sharps shall not be bent, recapped, or removed except as noted in paragraphs (d)(2)(vii)(A) and (d)(2)(vii)(B) below. Shearing or breaking of contaminated needles is prohibited.

(A) Contaminated needles and other contaminated sharps shall not be bent, recapped or removed unless the employer can demonstrate that no alternative is feasible or that such action is required by a specific medical or dental procedure.

(B) Such bending, recapping or needle removal must be accomplished through the use of a mechanical device or a one-handed technique.

(viii) Immediately or as soon as possible after use, contaminated reusable sharps shall be placed in appropriate containers until properly reprocessed. These containers shall be:

(A) Puncture resistant;

(B) Labeled or color-coded in accordance with this standard;

(C) Leakproof on the sides and bottom; and

(D) In accordance with the requirements set forth in paragraph (d)(4)(ii)(E) for reusable sharps.

(ix) Eating, drinking, smoking, applying cosmetics or lip balm, and handling contact lenses are prohibited in work areas where there is a reasonable likelihood of occupational exposure.

(x) Food and drink shall not be kept in refrigerators, freezers, shelves, cabinets or on countertops or benchtops where blood or other potentially infectious materials are present.

(xi) All procedures involving blood or other potentially infectious materials shall be performed in such a manner as to minimize splashing, spraying, spattering, and generation of droplets of these substances.

(xii) Mouth pipetting/suctioning of blood or other potentially infectious materials is prohibited.

(xiii) Specimens of blood or other potentially infectious materials shall be placed in a container which prevents leakage during collection, handling, processing, storage, transport, or shipping.

(A) The container for storage, transport, or shipping shall be labeled or color-coded according to paragraph (g)(1)(i) and closed prior to being stored, transported, or shipped. When a facility utilizes Universal Precautions in the handling of all specimens, the labeling/color-coding of specimens is not necessary provided containers are recognizable as containing specimens. This exemption only applies while such specimens/containers remain within the facility. Labeling or color-coding in accordance with paragraph (g)(1)(i) is required when such specimens/containers leave the facility.

(B) If outside contamination of the primary container occurs, the primary container shall be placed within a second container which prevents leakage during handling, processing, storage, transport, or shipping and is labeled or color-coded according to the requirements of this standard.

(C) If the specimen could puncture the primary container, the primary container shall be placed within a secondary container which is puncture-resistant in addition to the above characteristics.

(xiv) Equipment which may become contaminated with blood or other potentially infectious materials shall be examined prior to servicing or shipping and shall be decontaminated as necessary, unless the employer can demonstrate that decontamination of such equipment or portions of such equipment is not feasible.

(A) A readily observable label in accordance with paragraph (g)(1)(i)(H) shall be attached to the equipment stating which portions remain contaminated.

(B) The employer shall ensure that th¹s information is conveyed to all affected employees, the servicing representative, and/or the manufacturer, as appropriate, prior to handling, servicing, or shipping so that appropriate precautions will be taken.

(3) *Personal protective equipment*—(i) Provision. When there is occupational exposure, the employer shall provide, at no cost to the employee, appropriate personal protective equipment such as, but not limited to, gloves, gowns, laboratory coats, face shields or masks and eye protection, and mouthpieces, resuscitation bags, pocket masks, or other ventilation devices. Personal protective equipment will be considered "appropriate" only if it does not permit blood or other potentially infectious materials to pass through to or reach the employee's work clothes, street clothes, undergarments, skin, eyes, mouth, or other mucous membranes under normal conditions of use and for the duration of time which the protective equipment will be used.

(ii) Use. The employer shall ensure that the employee uses appropriate personal protective equipment unless the employer shows that the employee temporarily and briefly declined to use personal protective equipment when, under rare and extraordinary circumstances, it was the employee's professional judgment that in the specific instance its use would have prevented the delivery of health care or public safety services or would have posed an increased hazard to the safety of the worker or co-worker. When the employee makes this judgement, the circumstances shall be investigated and documented in order to determine whether changes can be instituted to prevent such occurences in the future.

(iii) Accessibility. The employer shall ensure that appropriate personal protective equipment in the appro-

priate sizes is readily accessible at the worksite or is issued to employees. Hypoallergenic gloves, glove liners, powderless gloves, or other similar alternatives shall be readily accessible to those employees who are allergic to the gloves normally provided.

(iv) Cleaning, Laundering, and Disposal. The employer shall clean, launder, and dispose of personal protective equipment required by paragraphs (d) and (e) of this standard, at no cost to the employee.

(v) Repair and Replacement. The employer shall repair or replace personal protective equipment as needed to maintain its effectiveness, at no cost to the employee.

(vi) If a garment(s) is penetrated by blood or other potentially infectious materials, the garment(s) shall be removed immediately or as soon as feasible.

(vii) All personal protective equipment shall be removed prior to leaving the work area.

(viii) When personal protective equipment is removed it shall be placed in an appropriately designated area or container for storage, washing, decontamination or disposal.

(ix) Gloves. Gloves shall be worn when it can be reasonably anticipated that the employee may have hand contact with blood, other potentially infectious materials, mucous membranes, and non-intact skin; when performing vascular access procedures except as specified in paragraph (d)(3)(ix)(D); and when handling or touching contaminated items or surfaces.

(A) Disposable (single use) gloves such as surgical or examination gloves, shall be replaced as soon as practical when contaminated or as soon as feasible if they are torn, punctured, or when their ability to function as a barrier is compromised.

(B) Disposable (single use) gloves shall not be washed or decontaminated for re-use.

(C) Utility gloves may be decontaminated for re-use if the integrity of the glove is not compromised. However, they must be discarded if they are cracked, peeling, torn, punctured, or exhibit other signs of deterioration or when their ability to function as a barrier is compromised.

(D) If an employer in a volunteer blood donation center judges that routine gloving for all phlebotomies is not necessary then the employer shall:

(1) Periodically reevaluate this policy;

(2) Make gloves available to all employees who wish to use them for phlebotomy;

(3) Not discourage the use of gloves for phlebotomy; and

(4) Require that gloves be used for phlebotomy in the following circumstances:

(i) When the employee has cuts, scratches, or other breaks in his or her skin;

(ii) When the employee judges that hand contamination with blood may occur, for example, when performing phlebotomy on an uncooperative source individual; and

(iii) When the employee is receiving training in phlebotomy.

(x) Masks, Eye Protection, and Face Shields. Masks in combination with eye protection devices, such as goggles or glasses with solid side shields, or chin-length face shields, shall be worn whenever splashes, spray, spatter, or droplets of blood or other potentially infectious materials may be generated and eye, nose, or mouth contamination can be reasonably anticipated.

(xi) Gowns, Aprons, and Other Protective Body Clothing. Appropriate protective clothing such as, but not limited to, gowns, aprons, lab coats, clinic jackets, or similar outer garments shall be worn in occupational exposure situations. The type and characteristics will depend upon the task and degree of exposure anticipated.

(xii) Surgical caps or hoods and/or shoe covers or boots shall be worn in instances when gross contamination can reasonably be anticipated (e.g., autopsies, orthopaedic surgery).

(4) *Housekeeping.* (i) General. Employers shall ensure that the worksite is maintained in a clean and sanitary condition. The employer shall determine and implement an appropriate written schedule for cleaning and method of decontamination based upon the location within the facility, type of surface to be cleaned, type of soil

present, and tasks or procedures being performed in the area.

(ii) All equipment and environmental and working surfaces shall be cleaned and decontaminated after contact with blood or other potentially infectious materials.

(A) Contaminated work surfaces shall be decontaminated with an appropriate disinfectant after completion of procedures; immediately or as soon as feasible when surfaces are overtly contaminated or after any spill of blood or other potentially infectious materials; and at the end of the work shift if the surface may have become contaminated since the last cleaning.

(B) Protective coverings, such as plastic wrap, aluminum foil, or imperviously-backed absorbent paper used to cover equipment and environmental surfaces, shall be removed and replaced as soon as feasible when they become overtly contaminated or at the end of the workshift if they may have become contaminated during the shift.

(C) All bins, pails, cans, and similar receptacles intended for reuse which have a reasonable likelihood for becoming contaminated with blood or other potentially infectious materials shall be inspected and decontaminated on a regularly scheduled basis and cleaned and decontaminated immediately or as soon as feasible upon visible contamination.

(D) Broken glassware which may be contaminated shall not be picked up directly with the hands. It shall be cleaned up using mechanical means, such as a brush and dust pan, tongs, or forceps.

(E) Reusable sharps that are contaminated with blood or other potentially infectious materials shall not be stored or processed in a manner that requires employees to reach by hand into the containers where these sharps have been placed.

(iii) Regulated Waste.

(A) Contaminated Sharps Discarding and Containment. (1) Contaminated sharps shall be discarded immediately or as soon as feasible in containers that are:

(i) Closable;

(ii) Puncture resistant;

(iii) Leakproof on sides and bottom; and

(*iv*) Labeled or color-coded in accordance with paragraph (g)(1)(i) of this standard.

(*2*) During use, containers for contaminated sharps shall be:

(*i*) Easily accessible to personnel and located as close as is feasible to the immediate area where sharps are used or can be reasonably anticipated to be found (e.g., laundries);

(*ii*) Maintained upright throughout use; and

(*iii*) Replaced routinely and not be allowed to overfill.

(*3*) When moving containers of contaminated sharps from the area of use, the containers shall be:

(*i*) Closed immediately prior to removal or replacement to prevent spillage or protrusion of contents during handling, storage, transport, or shipping;

(*ii*) Placed in a secondary container if leakage is possible. The second container shall be:

(*A*) Closable;

(*B*) Constructed to contain all contents and prevent leakage during handling, storage, transport, or shipping; and

(*C*) Labeled or color-coded according to paragraph (g)(1)(i) of this standard.

(*4*) Reusable containers shall not be opened, emptied, or cleaned manually or in any other manner which would expose employees to the risk of percutaneous injury.

(B) Other Regulated Waste Containment. (*1*) Regulated waste shall be placed in containers which are:

(*i*) Closable;

(*ii*) Constructed to contain all contents and prevent leakage of fluids during handling, storage, transport or shipping;

(*iii*) Labeled or color-coded in accordance with paragraph (g)(1)(i) this standard; and

(*iv*) Closed prior to removal to prevent spillage or protrusion of contents during handling, storage, transport, or shipping.

(*2*) If outside contamination of the regulated waste container occurs, it shall be placed in a second container. The second container shall be:

(*i*) Closable;

(*ii*) Constructed to contain all contents and prevent leakage of fluids dur-

ing handling, storage, transport or shipping;

(*iii*) Labeled or color-coded in accordance with paragraph (g)(1)(i) of this standard; and

(*iv*) Closed prior to removal to prevent spillage or protrusion of contents during handling, storage, transport, or shipping.

(C) Disposal of all regulated waste shall be in accordance with applicable regulations of the United States, States and Territories, and political subdivisions of States and Territories.

(iv) Laundry.

(A) Contaminated laundry shall be handled as little as possible with a minimum of agitation. (1) Contaminated laundry shall be bagged or containerized at the location where it was used and shall not be sorted or rinsed in the location of use.

(2) Contaminated laundry shall be placed and transported in bags or containers labeled or color-coded in accordance with paragraph (g)(1)(i) of this standard. When a facility utilizes Universal Precautions in the handling of all soiled laundry, alternative labeling or color-coding is sufficient if it permits all employees to recognize the containers as requiring compliance with Universal Precautions.

(3) Whenever contaminated laundry is wet and presents a reasonable likelihood of soak-through of or leakage from the bag or container, the laundry shall be placed and transported in bags or containers which prevent soak-through and/or leakage of fluids to the exterior.

(B) The employer shall ensure that employees who have contact with contaminated laundry wear protective gloves and other appropriate personal protective equipment.

(C) When a facility ships contaminated laundry off-site to a second facility which does not utilize Universal Precautions in the handling of all laundry, the facility generating the contaminated laundry must place such laundry in bags or containers which are labeled or color-coded in accordance with paragraph (g)(1)(i).

(e) *HIV and HBV Research Laboratories and Production Facilities.* (1) This paragraph applies to research laboratories and production facilities engaged in the culture, production, concentration, experimentation, and manipulation of HIV and HBV. It does not apply to clinical or diagnostic laboratories engaged solely in the analysis of blood, tissues, or organs. These requirements apply in addition to the other requirements of the standard.

(2) Research laboratories and production facilities shall meet the following criteria:

(i) Standard microbiological practices. All regulated waste shall either be incinerated or decontaminated by a method such as autoclaving known to effectively destroy bloodborne pathogens.

(ii) Special practices.

(A) Laboratory doors shall be kept closed when work involving HIV or HBV is in progress.

(B) Contaminated materials that are to be decontaminated at a site away from the work area shall be placed in a durable, leakproof, labeled or color-coded container that is closed before being removed from the work area.

(C) Access to the work area shall be limited to authorized persons. Written policies and procedures shall be established whereby only persons who have been advised of the potential biohazard, who meet any specific entry requirements, and who comply with all entry and exit procedures shall be allowed to enter the work areas and animal rooms.

(D) When other potentially infectious materials or infected animals are present in the work area or containment module, a hazard warning sign incorporating the universal biohazard symbol shall be posted on all access doors. The hazard warning sign shall comply with paragraph (g)(1)(ii) of this standard.

(E) All activities involving other potentially infectious materials shall be conducted in biological safety cabinets or other physical-containment devices within the containment module. No work with these other potentially infectious materials shall be conducted on the open bench.

(F) Laboratory coats, gowns, smocks, uniforms, or other appropriate protective clothing shall be used in the work area and animal rooms. Protective clothing shall not be worn outside of the work area and shall be decontaminated before being laundered.

(G) Special care shall be taken to avoid skin contact with other potentially infectious materials. Gloves shall be worn when handling infected animals and when making hand contact with other potentially infectious materials is unavoidable.

(H) Before disposal all waste from work areas and from animal rooms shall either be incinerated or decontaminated by a method such as autoclaving known to effectively destroy bloodborne pathogens.

(I) Vacuum lines shall be protected with liquid disinfectant traps and high-efficiency particulate air (HEPA) filters or filters of equivalent or superior efficiency and which are checked routinely and maintained or replaced as necessary.

(J) Hypodermic needles and syringes shall be used only for parenteral injection and aspiration of fluids from laboratory animals and diaphragm bottles. Only needle-locking syringes or disposable syringe-needle units (i.e., the needle is integral to the syringe) shall be used for the injection or aspiration of other potentially infectious materials. Extreme caution shall be used when handling needles and syringes. A needle shall not be bent, sheared, replaced in the sheath or guard, or removed from the syringe following use. The needle and syringe shall be promptly placed in a puncture-resistant container and autoclaved or decontaminated before reuse or disposal.

(K) All spills shall be immediately contained and cleaned up by appropriate professional staff or others properly trained and equipped to work with potentially concentrated infectious materials.

(L) A spill or accident that results in an exposure incident shall be immediately reported to the laboratory director or other responsible person.

(M) A biosafety manual shall be prepared or adopted and periodically reviewed and updated at least annually or more often if necessary. Personnel shall be advised of potential hazards, shall be required to read instructions on practices and procedures, and shall be required to follow them.

(iii) *Containment equipment.* (A) Certified biological safety cabinets (Class I, II, or III) or other appropriate combinations of personal protection or physical containment devices, such as special protective clothing, respirators, centrifuge safety cups, sealed centrifuge rotors, and containment caging for animals, shall be used for all activities with other potentially infectious materials that pose a threat of exposure to droplets, splashes, spills, or aerosols.

(B) Biological safety cabinets shall be certified when installed, whenever they are moved and at least annually.

(3) HIV and HBV research laboratories shall meet the following criteria:

(i) Each laboratory shall contain a facility for hand washing and an eye wash facility which is readily available within the work area.

(ii) An autoclave for decontamination of regulated waste shall be available.

(4) HIV and HBV production facilities shall meet the following criteria:

(i) The work areas shall be separated from areas that are open to unrestricted traffic flow within the building. Passage through two sets of doors shall be the basic requirement for entry into the work area from access corridors or other contiguous areas. Physical separation of the high-containment work area from access corridors or other areas or activities may also be provided by a double-doored clothes-change room (showers may be included), airlock, or other access facility that requires passing through two sets of doors before entering the work area.

(ii) The surfaces of doors, walls, floors and ceilings in the work area shall be water resistant so that they can be easily cleaned. Penetrations in these surfaces shall be sealed or capable of being sealed to facilitate decontamination.

(iii) Each work area shall contain a sink for washing hands and a readily available eye wash facility. The sink shall be foot, elbow, or automatically operated and shall be located near the exit door of the work area.

(iv) Access doors to the work area or containment module shall be self-closing.

(v) An autoclave for decontamination of regulated waste shall be available within or as near as possible to the work area.

(vi) A ducted exhaust-air ventilation system shall be provided. This system shall create directional airflow that draws air into the work area through the entry area. The exhaust air shall not be recirculated to any other area of the building, shall be discharged to the outside, and shall be dispersed away from occupied areas and air intakes. The proper direction of the airflow shall be verified (i.e., into the work area).

(5) *Training Requirements.* Additional training requirements for employees in HIV and HBV research laboratories and HIV and HBV production facilities are specified in paragraph (g)(2)(ix).

(f) *Hepatitis B vaccination and post-exposure evaluation and follow-up*—(1) *General.* (i) The employer shall make available the hepatitis B vaccine and vaccination series to all employees who have occupational exposure, and post-exposure evaluation and follow-up to all employees who have had an exposure incident.

(ii) The employer shall ensure that all medical evaluations and procedures including the hepatitis B vaccine and vaccination series and post-exposure evaluation and follow-up, including prophylaxis, are:

(A) Made available at no cost to the employee;

(B) Made available to the employee at a reasonable time and place;

(C) Performed by or under the supervision of a licensed physician or by or under the supervision of another licensed healthcare professional; and

(D) Provided according to recommendations of the U.S. Public Health Service current at the time these evaluations and procedures take place, except as specified by this paragraph (f).

(iii) The employer shall ensure that all laboratory tests are conducted by an accredited laboratory at no cost to the employee.

(2) *Hepatitis B Vaccination.* (i) Hepatitis B vaccination shall be made available after the employee has received the training required in paragraph (g)(2)(vii)(I) and within 10 working days of initial assignment to all employees who have occupational exposure unless the employee has previously received the complete hepatitis B vaccination series, antibody testing has revealed that the employee is immune, or the vaccine is contraindicated for medical reasons.

(ii) The employer shall not make participation in a prescreening program a prerequisite for receiving hepatitis B vaccination.

(iii) If the employee initially declines hepatitis B vaccination but at a later date while still covered under the standard decides to accept the vaccination, the employer shall make available hepatitis B vaccination at that time.

(iv) The employer shall assure that employees who decline to accept hepatitis B vaccination offered by the employer sign the statement in appendix A.

(v) If a routine booster dose(s) of hepatitis B vaccine is recommended by the U.S. Public Health Service at a future date, such booster dose(s) shall be made available in accordance with section (f)(1)(ii).

(3) *Post-exposure Evaluation and Follow-up.* Following a report of an exposure incident, the employer shall make immediately available to the exposed employee a confidential medical evaluation and follow-up, including at least the following elements:

(i) Documentation of the route(s) of exposure, and the circumstances under which the exposure incident occurred;

(ii) Identification and documentation of the source individual, unless the employer can establish that identification is infeasible or prohibited by state or local law;

(A) The source individual's blood shall be tested as soon as feasible and after consent is obtained in order to determine HBV and HIV infectivity. If consent is not obtained, the employer shall establish that legally required consent cannot be obtained. When the source individual's consent is not required by law, the source individual's

blood, if available, shall be tested and the results documented.

(B) When the source individual is already known to be infected with HBV or HIV, testing for the source individual's known HBV or HIV status need not be repeated.

(C) Results of the source individual's testing shall be made available to the exposed employee, and the employee shall be informed of applicable laws and regulations concerning disclosure of the identity and infectious status of the source individual.

(iii) Collection and testing of blood for HBV and HIV serological status;

(A) The exposed employee's blood shall be collected as soon as feasible and tested after consent is obtained.

(B) If the employee consents to baseline blood collection, but does not give consent at that time for HIV serologic testing, the sample shall be preserved for at least 90 days. If, within 90 days of the exposure incident, the employee elects to have the baseline sample tested, such testing shall be done as soon as feasible.

(iv) Post-exposure prophylaxis, when medically indicated, as recommended by the U.S. Public Health Service;

(v) Counseling; and

(vi) Evaluation of reported illnesses.

(4) *Information Provided to the Healthcare Professional.* (i) The employer shall ensure that the healthcare professional responsible for the employee's Hepatitis B vaccination is provided a copy of this regulation.

(ii) The employer shall ensure that the healthcare professional evaluating an employee after an exposure incident is provided the following information:

(A) A copy of this regulation;

(B) A description of the exposed employee's duties as they relate to the exposure incident;

(C) Documentation of the route(s) of exposure and circumstances under which exposure occurred;

(D) Results of the source individual's blood testing, if available; and

(E) All medical records relevant to the appropriate treatment of the employee including vaccination status which are the employer's responsibility to maintain.

(5) *Healthcare Professional's Written Opinion.* The employer shall obtain and

provide the employee with a copy of the evaluating healthcare professional's written opinion within 15 days of the completion of the evaluation.

(i) The healthcare professional's written opinion for Hepatitis B vaccination shall be limited to whether Hepatitis B vaccination is indicated for an employee, and if the employee has received such vaccination.

(ii) The healthcare professional's written opinion for post-exposure evaluation and follow-up shall be limited to the following information:

(A) That the employee has been informed of the results of the evaluation; and

(B) That the employee has been told about any medical conditions resulting from exposure to blood or other potentially infectious materials which require further evaluation or treatment. (iii) All other findings or diagnoses shall remain confidential and shall not be included in the written report.

(6) *Medical recordkeeping.* Medical records required by this standard shall be maintained in accordance with paragraph (h)(1) of this section.

(g) *Communication of hazards to employees*—(1) *Labels and signs.* (i) Labels. (A) Warning labels shall be affixed to containers of regulated waste, refrigerators and freezers containing blood or other potentially infectious material; and other containers used to store, transport or ship blood or other potentially infectious materials, except as provided in paragraph (g)(1)(i)(E), (F) and (G).

(B) Labels required by this section shall include the following legend:

BIOHAZARD

(C) These labels shall be fluorescent orange or orange-red or predominantly so, with lettering and symbols in a contrasting color.

(D) Labels shall be affixed as close as feasible to the container by string, wire, adhesive, or other method that prevents their loss or unintentional removal.

(E) Red bags or red containers may be substituted for labels.

(F) Containers of blood, blood components, or blood products that are labeled as to their contents and have been released for transfusion or other clinical use are exempted from the labeling requirements of paragraph (g).

(G) Individual containers of blood or other potentially infectious materials that are placed in a labeled container during storage, transport, shipment or disposal are exempted from the labeling requirement.

(H) Labels required for contaminated equipment shall be in accordance with this paragraph and shall also state which portions of the equipment remain contaminated.

(I) Regulated waste that has been decontaminated need not be labeled or color-coded.

(ii) Signs. (A) The employer shall post signs at the entrance to work areas specified in paragraph (e), HIV and HBV Research Laboratory and Production Facilities, which shall bear the following legend:

BIOHAZARD

(Name of the Infectious Agent)
(Special requirements for entering the area)
(Name, telephone number of the laboratory director or other responsible person.)

(B) These signs shall be fluorescent orange-red or predominantly so, with lettering and symbols in a contrasting color.

(2) *Information and Training.* (i) Employers shall ensure that all employees with occupational exposure participate in a training program which must be

provided at no cost to the employee and during working hours.

(ii) Training shall be provided as follows:

(A) At the time of initial assignment to tasks where occupational exposure may take place;

(B) Within 90 days after the effective date of the standard; and

(C) At least annually thereafter.

(iii) For employees who have received training on bloodborne pathogens in the year preceding the effective date of the standard, only training with respect to the provisions of the standard which were not included need be provided.

(iv) Annual training for all employees shall be provided within one year of their previous training.

(v) Employers shall provide additional training when changes such as modification of tasks or procedures or institution of new tasks or procedures affect the employee's occupational exposure. The additional training may be limited to addressing the new exposures created.

(vi) Material appropriate in content and vocabulary to educational level, literacy, and language of employees shall be used.

(vii) The training program shall contain at a minimum the following elements:

(A) An accessible copy of the regulatory text of this standard and an explanation of its contents;

(B) A general explanation of the epidemiology and symptoms of bloodborne diseases;

(C) An explanation of the modes of transmission of bloodborne pathogens;

(D) An explanation of the employer's exposure control plan and the means by which the employee can obtain a copy of the written plan;

(E) An explanation of the appropriate methods for recognizing tasks and other activities that may involve exposure to blood and other potentially infectious materials;

(F) An explanation of the use and limitations of methods that will prevent or reduce exposure including appropriate engineering controls, work practices, and personal protective equipment;

(G) Information on the types, proper use, location, removal, handling, decontamination and disposal of personal protective equipment;

(H) An explanation of the basis for selection of personal protective equipment;

(I) Information on the hepatitis B vaccine, including information on its efficacy, safety, method of administration, the benefits of being vaccinated, and that the vaccine and vaccination will be offered free of charge;

(J) Information on the appropriate actions to take and persons to contact in an emergency involving blood or other potentially infectious materials;

(K) An explanation of the procedure to follow if an exposure incident occurs, including the method of reporting the incident and the medical follow-up that will be made available;

(L) Information on the post-exposure evaluation and follow-up that the employer is required to provide for the employee following an exposure incident;

(M) An explanation of the signs and labels and/or color coding required by paragraph (g)(1); and

(N) An opportunity for interactive questions and answers with the person conducting the training session.

(viii) The person conducting the training shall be knowledgeable in the subject matter covered by the elements contained in the training program as it relates to the workplace that the training will address.

(ix) Additional Initial Training for Employees in HIV and HBV Laboratories and Production Facilities. Employees in HIV or HBV research laboratories and HIV or HBV production facilities shall receive the following initial training in addition to the above training requirements.

(A) The employer shall assure that employees demonstrate proficiency in standard microbiological practices and techniques and in the practices and operations specific to the facility before being allowed to work with HIV or HBV.

(B) The employer shall assure that employees have prior experience in the handling of human pathogens or tissue cultures before working with HIV or HBV.

(C) The employer shall provide a training program to employees who have no prior experience in handling human pathogens. Initial work activities shall not include the handling of infectious agents. A progression of work activities shall be assigned as techniques are learned and proficiency is developed. The employer shall assure that employees participate in work activities involving infectious agents only after proficiency has been demonstrated.

(h)   *Recordkeeping*—(1)   *Medical Records.* (i) The employer shall establish and maintain an accurate record for each employee with occupational exposure, in accordance with 29 CFR 1910.20.

(ii) This record shall include:

(A) The name and social security number of the employee;

(B) A copy of the employee's hepatitis B vaccination status including the dates of all the hepatitis B vaccinations and any medical records relative to the employee's ability to receive vaccination as required by paragraph (f)(2);

(C) A copy of all results of examinations, medical testing, and follow-up procedures as required by paragraph (f)(3);

(D) The employer's copy of the healthcare professional's written opinion as required by paragraph (f)(5); and

(E) A copy of the information provided to the healthcare professional as required by paragraphs (f)(4)(ii)(B)(C) and (D).

(iii) Confidentiality. The employer shall ensure that employee medical records required by paragraph (h)(1) are:

(A) Kept confidential; and

(B) Not disclosed or reported without the employee's express written consent to any person within or outside the workplace except as required by this section or as may be required by law.

(iv) The employer shall maintain the records required by paragraph (h) for at least the duration of employment plus 30 years in accordance with 29 CFR 1910.20.

(2) *Training Records.* (i) Training records shall include the following information:

(A) The dates of the training sessions;

(B) The contents or a summary of the training sessions;

(C) The names and qualifications of persons conducting the training; and

(D) The names and job titles of all persons attending the training sessions.

(ii) Training records shall be maintained for 3 years from the date on which the training occurred.

(3) *Availability.* (i) The employer shall ensure that all records required to be maintained by this section shall be made available upon request to the Assistant Secretary and the Director for examination and copying.

(ii) Employee training records required by this paragraph shall be provided upon request for examination and copying to employees, to employee representatives, to the Director, and to the Assistant Secretary.

(iii) Employee medical records required by this paragraph shall be provided upon request for examination and copying to the subject employee, to anyone having written consent of the subject employee, to the Director, and to the Assistant Secretary in accordance with 29 CFR 1910.20.

(4) *Transfer of Records.* (i) The employer shall comply with the requirements involving transfer of records set forth in 29 CFR 1910.20(h).

(ii) If the employer ceases to do business and there is no successor employer to receive and retain the records for the prescribed period, the employer shall notify the Director, at least three months prior to their disposal and transmit them to the Director, if required by the Director to do so, within that three month period.

(i)   *Dates*—(1)   *Effective Date.* The standard shall become effective on March 6, 1992.

(2) The Exposure Control Plan required by paragraph (c) of this section shall be completed on or before May 5, 1992.

(3) Paragraph (g)(2) Information and Training and (h) Recordkeeping shall take effect on or before June 4, 1992.

(4) Paragraphs (d)(2) Engineering and Work Practice Controls, (d)(3) Personal Protective Equipment, (d)(4) Housekeeping, (e) HIV and HBV Research Laboratories and Production Facilities, (f) Hepatitis B Vaccination and Post-Exposure Evaluation and Follow-up, and (g) (1) Labels and Signs, shall take effect July 6, 1992.

RECOMMENDATIONS FOR PREVENTING TRANSMISSION OF HUMAN IMMUNODEFICIENCY VIRUS AND HEPATITIS B VIRUS TO PATIENTS DURING EXPOSURE-PRONE INVASIVE PROCEDURES

(Centers for Disease Control, 40 MMWR RR-8 (July 12, 1991))

This document has been developed by the Centers for Disease Control (CDC) to update recommendations for prevention of transmission of human immuno-deficiency virus (HIV) and hepatitis B virus (HBV) in the healthcare setting. Current data suggest that the risk for such transmission from a health-care worker (HCW) to a patient during an invasive procedure is small; a precise assessment of the risk is not yet available. This document contains recommen-dations to provide guidance for prevention of HIV and HBV transmission during those invasive procedures that are considered exposure-prone.

INTRODUCTION

Recommendations have been made by the Centers for Disease Control (CDC) for the prevention of transmission of the human immunodeficiency virus (HIV) and the hepatitis B virus (HBV) in health-care settings (1-6). These recommen-dations emphasize adherence to universal precautions that require that blood and other specified body fluids of **all** patients be handled as if they contain blood-borne pathogens (1,2).

Previous guidelines contained precautions to be used during invasive procedures (defined in Appendix) and recommendations for the management of HIV- and HBV-infected health-care workers (HCWs) (1). These guidelines did not include specific recommendations on testing HCWs for HIV or HBV infection, and they did not provide guidance on which invasive procedures may represent increased risk to the patient.

The recommendations outlined in this document are based on the following considerations:

- Infected HCWs who adhere to universal precautions and who do not perform invasive procedures pose no risk for transmitting HIV or HBV to patients.
- Infected HCWs who adhere to universal precautions and who perform certain exposure-prone procedures (see page 4) pose a small risk for transmitting HBV to patients.
- HIV is transmitted much less readily than HBV.

In the interim, until further data are available, additional precautions are prudent to prevent HIV and HBV transmission during procedures that have been linked to HCW-to-patient HBV transmission or that are considered exposure-prone.

BACKGROUND

Infection-Control Practices

Previous recommendations have specified that infection-control programs should incorporate principles of universal precautions (i.e., appropriate use of hand washing, protective barriers, and care in the use and disposal of needles and other sharp instruments) and should maintain these precautions rigorously in all health-care settings (1,2,5). Proper application of these principles will assist in minimizing the risk of transmission of HIV or HBV from patient to HCW, HCW to patient, or patient to patient.

As part of standard infection-control practice, instruments and other reusable equipment used in performing invasive procedures should be appropriately disinfected and sterilized as follows (7):

- Equipment and devices that enter the patient's vascular system or other normally sterile areas of the body should be sterilized before being used for each patient.
- Equipment and devices that touch intact mucous membranes but do not penetrate the patient's body surfaces should be sterilized when possible or undergo high-level disinfection if they cannot be sterilized before being used for each patient.
- Equipment and devices that do not touch the patient or that only touch intact skin of the patient need only be cleaned with a detergent or as indicated by the manufacturer.

Compliance with universal precautions and recommendations for disinfection and sterilization of medical devices should be scrupulously monitored in all health-care settings (*1, 7, 8*). Training of HCWs in proper infection-control technique should begin in professional and vocational schools and continue as an ongoing process. Institutions should provide all HCWs with appropriate inservice education regarding infection control and safety and should establish procedures for monitoring compliance with infection-control policies.

All HCWs who might be exposed to blood in an occupational setting should receive hepatitis B vaccine, preferably during their period of professional training and before any occupational exposures could occur (*8, 9*).

Transmission of HBV During Invasive Procedures

Since the introduction of serologic testing for HBV infection in the early 1970s, there have been published reports of 20 clusters in which a total of over 300 patients were infected with HBV in association with treatment by an HBV-infected HCW. In 12 of these clusters, the implicated HCW did not routinely wear gloves; several HCWs also had skin lesions that may have facilitated HBV transmission (*10-22*). These 12 clusters included nine linked to dentists or oral surgeons and one cluster each linked to a general practitioner, an inhalation therapist, and a cardiopulmonary-bypass-pump technician. The clusters associated with the inhalation therapist and the cardiopulmonary-bypass-pump technician— and some of the other 10 clusters—could possibly have been prevented if current recommendations on universal precautions, including glove use, had been in effect. In the remaining eight clusters, transmission occurred despite glove use by the HCWs; five clusters were linked to obstetricians or gynecologists, and three were linked to cardiovascular surgeons (*6, 22-28*). In addition, recent unpublished reports strongly suggest HBV transmission from three surgeons to patients in 1989 and 1990 during colorectal (CDC, unpublished data), abdominal, and cardiothoracic surgery (*29*).

Seven of the HCWs who were linked to published clusters in the United States were allowed to perform invasive procedures following modification of invasive techniques (e.g., double gloving and restriction of certain high-risk procedures) (*6, 11–13, 15, 16, 24*). For five HCWs, no further transmission to patients was observed. In two instances involving an obstetrician/gynecologist and an oral surgeon, HBV was transmitted to patients after techniques were modified (*6, 12*).

Review of the 20 published studies indicates that a combination of risk factors accounted for transmission of HBV from HCWs to patients. Of the HCWs whose hepatitis B e antigen (HBeAg) status was determined (17 of 20), all were HBeAg positive. The presence of HBeAg in serum is associated with higher levels of circulating virus and therefore with greater infectivity of hepatitis-B-surface-antigen (HBsAg)-positive individuals; the risk of HBV transmission to an HCW after a percutaneous exposure to HBeAg-positive blood is approximately 30% (*30-32*). In addition, each report indicated that the potential existed for contamination of surgical wounds or traumatized tissue, either from a major break in standard infection-control practices (e.g., not wearing gloves during invasive procedures) or from unintentional injury to the infected HCW during invasive procedures (e.g., needle sticks incurred while manipulating needles without being able to see them during suturing).

Most reported clusters in the United States occurred before awareness increased of the risks of transmission of blood-borne pathogens in health-care settings and before emphasis was placed on the use of universal precautions and hepatitis B vaccine among HCWs. The limited number of reports of HBV transmission from HCWs to patients in recent years may reflect the adoption of universal precautions and increased use of HBV vaccine. However, the limited number of recent reports does not preclude the occurrence of undetected or unreported small clusters or individual instances of transmission; routine use of gloves does not prevent most injuries caused by sharp instruments and does not eliminate the potential for exposure of a patient to an HCW's blood and transmission of HBV (6, 22–29).

Transmission of HIV During Invasive Procedures

The risk of HIV transmission to an HCW after percutaneous exposure to HIV-infected blood is considerably lower than the risk of HBV transmission after percutaneous exposure to HBeAg-positive blood (0.3% versus approximately 30%) (33–35). Thus, the risk of transmission of HIV from an infected HCW to a patient during an invasive procedure is likely to be proportionately lower than the risk of HBV transmission from an HBeAg-positive HCW to a patient during the same procedure. As with HBV, the relative infectivity of HIV probably varies among individuals and over time for a single individual. Unlike HBV infection, however, there is currently no readily available laboratory test for increased HIV infectivity.

Investigation of a cluster of HIV infections among patients in the practice of one dentist with acquired immunodeficiency syndrome (AIDS) strongly suggested that HIV was transmitted to five of the approximately 850 patients evaluated through June 1991 (36–38). The investigation indicates that HIV transmission occurred during dental care, although the precise mechanisms of transmission have not been determined. In two other studies, when patients cared for by a general surgeon and a surgical resident who had AIDS were tested, all patients tested, 75 and 62, respectively, were negative for HIV infection (39, 40). In a fourth study, 143 patients who had been treated by a dental student with HIV infection and were later tested were all negative for HIV infection (41). In another investigation, HIV antibody testing was offered to all patients whose surgical procedures had been performed by a general surgeon within 7 years before the surgeon's diagnosis of AIDS; the date at which the surgeon became infected with HIV is unknown (42). Of 1,340 surgical patients contacted, 616 (46%) were tested for HIV. One patient, a known intravenous drug user, was HIV positive when tested but may already have been infected at the time of surgery.

HIV test results for the 615 other surgical patients were negative (95% confidence interval for risk of transmission per operation = 0.0%-0.5%).

The limited number of participants and the differences in procedures associated with these five investigations limit the ability to generalize from them and to define precisely the risk of HIV transmission from HIV-infected HCWs to patients. A precise estimate of the risk of HIV transmission from infected HCWs to patients can be determined only after careful evaluation of a substantially larger number of patients whose exposure-prone procedures have been performed by HIV-infected HCWs.

Exposure-Prone Procedures

Despite adherence to the principles of universal precautions, certain invasive surgical and dental procedures have been implicated in the transmission of HBV from infected HCWs to patients, and should be considered exposure-prone. Reported examples include certain oral, cardiothoracic, colorectal (CDC, unpublished data), and obstetric/gynecologic procedures (6, 12, 22–29).

Certain other invasive procedures should also be considered exposure prone. In a prospective study CDC conducted in four hospitals, one or more percutaneous injuries occurred among surgical personnel during 96 (6.9%) of 1,382 operative procedures on the general surgery, gynecology, orthopedic, cardiac, and trauma services (43). Percutaneous exposure of the patient to the HCW's blood may have occurred when the sharp object causing the injury recontacted the patient's open wound in 28 (32%) of the 88 observed injuries to surgeons (range among surgical specialties = 8%-57%; range among hospitals = 24%-42%).

Characteristics of exposure-prone procedures include digital palpation of a needle tip in a body cavity or the simultaneous presence of the HCW's fingers and a needle or other sharp instrument or object in a poorly visualized or highly confined anatomic site. Performance of exposure-prone procedures presents a recognized risk of percutaneous injury to the HCW, and—if such an injury occurs—the HCW's blood is likely to contact the patient's body cavity, subcutaneous tissue, and/or mucous membranes.

Experience with HBV indicates that invasive procedures that do not have the above characteristics would be expected to pose substantially lower risk, if any, of transmission of HIV and other blood-borne pathogens from an infected HCW to patients.

RECOMMENDATIONS

Investigations of HIV and HBV transmission from HCWs to patients indicate that, when HCWs adhere to recommended infection-control procedures, the risk of transmitting HBV from an infected HCW to a patient is small, and the risk of transmitting HIV is likely to be even smaller. However, the likelihood of exposure of the patient to an HCW's blood is greater for certain procedures designated as exposure-prone. To minimize the risk of HIV or HBV transmission, the following measures are recommended:

- **All HCWs should adhere to universal precautions, including the appropriate use of hand washing, protective barriers, and care in the use and disposal of needles and other sharp instruments. HCWs who have exudative lesions or weeping dermatitis should refrain from all direct patient care and from handling patient-care equipment and devices used in performing invasive procedures until the condition resolves. HCWs should also comply with current guidelines for disinfection and sterilization of reusable devices used in invasive procedures.**

- **Currently available data provide no basis for recommendations to restrict the practice of HCWs infected with HIV or HBV who perform invasive procedures not identified as exposure-prone, provided the infected HCWs practice recommended surgical or dental technique and comply with universal precautions and current recommendations for sterilization/disinfection.**

- **Exposure-prone procedures should be identified by medical/surgical/dental organizations and institutions at which the procedures are performed.**

- **HCWs who perform exposure-prone procedures should know their HIV antibody status. HCWs who perform exposure-prone procedures and who do not have serologic evidence of immunity to HBV from vaccination or from previous infection should know their HBsAg status and, if that is positive, should also know their HBeAg status.**

- **HCWs who are infected with HIV or HBV (and are HBeAg positive) should not perform exposure-prone procedures unless they have sought counsel from an expert review panel and been advised under what circumstances, if any, they may continue to perform these procedures.* Such circumstances would include notifying prospective patients of the HCW's seropositivity before they undergo exposure-prone invasive procedures.**

---

* The review panel should include experts who represent a balanced perspective. Such experts might include all of the following: a) the HCW's personal physician(s), b) an infectious disease specialist with expertise in the epidemiology of HIV and HBV transmission, c) a health professional with expertise in the procedures performed by the HCW, and d) state or local public health official(s). If the HCW's practice is institutionally based, the expert review panel might also include a member of the infection-control committee, preferably a hospital epidemiologist. HCWs who perform exposure-prone procedures outside the hospital/institutional setting should seek advice from appropriate state and local public health officials regarding the review process. Panels must recognize the importance of confidentiality and the privacy rights of infected HCWs.

- **Mandatory testing of HCWs for HIV antibody, HBsAg, or HBeAg is not recommended. The current assessment of the risk that infected HCWs will transmit HIV or HBV to patients during exposure prone procedures does not support the diversion of resources that would be required to implement mandatory testing programs. Compliance by HCWs with recommendations can be increased through education, training, and appropriate confidentiality safeguards.**

HCWS WHOSE PRACTICES ARE MODIFIED BECAUSE OF HIV OR HBV STATUS

HCWs whose practices are modified because of their HIV or HBV infection status should, whenever possible, be provided opportunities to continue appropriate patient-care activities. Career counseling and job retraining should be encouraged to promote the continued use of the HCW's talents, knowledge, and skills. HCWs whose practices are modified because of HBV infection should be reevaluated periodically to determine whether their HBeAg status changes due to resolution of infection or as a result of treatment (*44*).

NOTIFICATION OF PATIENTS AND FOLLOW-UP STUDIES

The public health benefit of notification of patients who have had exposure-prone procedures performed by HCWs infected with HIV or positive for HBeAg should be considered on a case-by-case basis, taking into consideration an assessment of specific risks, confidentiality issues, and available resources. Carefully designed and implemented follow-up studies are necessary to determine more precisely the risk of transmission during such procedures. Decisions regarding notification and follow-up studies should be made in consultation with state and local public health officials.

ADDITIONAL NEEDS

- Clearer definition of the nature, frequency, and circumstances of blood contact between patients and HCWs during invasive procedures.
- Development and evaluation of new devices, protective barriers, and techniques that may prevent such blood contact without adversely affecting the quality of patient care.
- More information on the potential for HIV and HBV transmission through contaminated instruments.
- Improvements in sterilization and disinfection techniques for certain reusable equipment and devices.
- Identification of factors that may influence the likelihood of HIV or HBV transmission after exposure to HIV- or HBV-infected blood.

References

1. CDC. Recommendations for prevention of HIV transmission in health-care settings. MMWR 1987:36(suppl. no. 2S): I-18S.

2. CDC. Update: Universal precautions for prevention of transmission of human immunodeficiency virus, hepatitis B virus, and other bloodborne pathogens in health-care settings. MMWR 1988;37:377-82,387-8.

3. CDC. Hepatitis Surveillance Report No. 48. Atlanta: U.S. Department of Health and Human Services, Public Health Service. 1982:2-3.

4. CDC. CDC Guideline for Infection Control in Hospital Personnel, Atlanta, Georgia: Public Health Service, 1983. 24 pages. (GPO# 6AR031488305).

5. CDC. Guidelines for prevention of transmission of human immunodeficiency virus and hepatitis B virus to health-care and public-safety workers. MMWR 1989:38: (suppl. no. S-6):I-37.

6. Lettau LA, Smith JD, Williams D, et al. Transmission of hepatitis B with resultant restriction of surgical practice. JAMA 1986;255:934-7.

7. CDC. Guidelines for the prevention and control of nosocomial infections: guideline for handwashing and hospital environmental control. Atlanta, Georgia: Public Health Service, 1985. 20 pages. (GPO# 544-436/24441).

8. Department of Labor, Occupational Safety and Health Administration. Occupational exposure to bloodborne pathogens: proposed rule and notice of hearing. Federal Register 1989;54:23042-139.

9. CDC. Protection against viral hepatitis: recommendations of the immunization practices advisory committee (ACIP). MMWR 1990;39:(no. RR-2).

10. Levin ML, Maddrey WC, Wands JR, Mendeloff Al. Hepatitis B transmission by dentists. JAMA 1974; 228:1139-40.

11. Rimland D, Parkin WE, Miller GB, Schrack WD. Hepatitis B outbreak traced to an oral surgeon. N Engl J Med 1977;296:953-8.

12. Goodwin D, Fannin SL, McCracken BB. An oral-surgeon related hepatitis-B outbreak, California Morbidity 1976;14.

13. Hadler SC, Sorley DL, Acree KH, et al. An outbreak of hepatitis B in a dental practice. Ann Intern Med 1981;95:133-8.

14. Reingold AL, Kane MA, Murphy BL, Checko P, Francis DP, Maynard JE. Transmission of hepatitis B by an oral surgeon. J Infect Dis 1982;145:262-8.

15. Goodman RA, Ahtone JL, Finton RJ. Hepatitis B transmission from dental personnel to patients: unfinished business [Editorial]. Ann Intern Med 1982;96:119.

16. Ahtone J, Goodman RA. Hepatitis B and dental personnel: transmission to patients and prevention issues. J Am Dent Assoc 1983;106:219-22.

17. Shaw FE, Jr, Barren CL, Hamm R, et al. Lethal outbreak of hepatitis B in a dental practice. JAMA 1986;255:3260-4.

18. CDC. Outbreak of hepatitis B associated with an oral surgeon. New Hampshire. MMWR 87;36:132-3.

19. Grob PJ, Moeschlin P. Risk to contacts of a medical practitioner carrying HBsAg. [Letter]. N Engl J Med 1975;293:197.

20. Grob PJ, Bischof B, Naeff F. Cluster of hepatitis B transmitted by a physician. Lancet 1981;2:1218-20.

21. Snydman DR, Hindman SH, Wineland MD, Bryan JA, Maynard JE. Nosocomial viral hepatitis B. A cluster among staff with subsequent transmission to patients. Ann Intern Med 1976;85:573-7.

22. Coutinho RA, Albrecht-van Lent P, Stoutjesdijk L, et al. Hepatitis B from doctors [Letter]. Lancet 1982;1:345-6.

23. Anonymous. Acute hepatitis B associated with gynecological surgery. Lancet 1980; 1:1-6.

24. Carl M, Blakey DL, Francis DP, Maynard JE. Interruption of hepatatis B transmission by modification of a gynaecologits surgical technique. Lancet 1982;1:731-3.

25. Anonymous. Acute hepatitis B following gynecological surgery. J Hosp Infect 1987;9:34-8,

26. Welch J, Webster M, Tilzey AJ, Noah ND, Banatvala JE. Hepatitis B Infections after gynaecological surgery. Lancet 1989;1:205-7.

27. Haeram JW, Siebke JC, Ulstrup J, Geiram D, Helle I. HBsAg transmission from a cardiac surgeon incubating hepatitis resulting in chronic antigenemia in four patients. Acta Med Scand 1981;210:389–92.

28. Flower AJE, Prentice M, Morgan G, et al. Hepatitis B infection following cardio-thoracic surgery [Abstract]. 1990 International Symposium on Viral Hepatitis and Liver Diseases, Houston. 1990;94.

29. Heptonstall J. Outbreaks of hepatitis B virus infection associated with infected surgical staff in the United Kingdom. Communicable Disease Reports 1991 (in press).

30. Alter HJ, Seef LB, Kaplan PM, et al. Type B hepatitis: the infectivity of blood positive for e antigen and DNA polymerase after accidental needlestick exposure. N Engl J Med 1976;295:909-13.

31. Seeff LB, Wright EC, Zimmerman HJ, et al. Type B hepatitis after needlestick exposure: prevention with hepatitis B immunoglobulin: final report of the Veterans Administration Cooperative Study. Ann Intern Med 1978;88:285-93.

32. Grady GF, Lee VA, Prince AM, et al. Hepatitis B immune globulin for accidental exposures among medical personnel: final report of a multicenter controlled trial. J Infec Dis 1978;138:625-38.

33. Henderson DK, Fahoy BJ, Willy M, et al. Risk for occupational transmission of human immunodeficiency virus type 1 (HIV-1) associated with clinical exposures: a prospective evaluation. Ann Intern Med 1990;113:740-6.

34. Marcus R, CDC Cooperative Needlestick Study Group. Surveillance of health-care workers exposed to blood from patients infected with the human immunodeficiency virus. N Engl J Med 1988;319:1118-23.

35. Gerberding JL, Bryant-LeBlanc CE, Nelson K, et al. Risk of transmitting the human immunodeficiency virus, cytomegalovirus, and hepatitis B virus to health-care workers exposed to patients with AIDS and AIDS-related conditions. J Infect Dis 1987;156:1-8.

36. CDC. Possible transmission of human immunodeficiency virus to a patient during an invasive dental procedure. MMWR 1990;39:489-93.

37. CDC. Update: transmission of HIV infection during an invasive dental procedure - Florida. MMWR 1991;40:21-27,33.

38. CDC. Update: transmission of HIV infection during invasive dental procedures - Florida. MMWR 1991;40:377-81.

39. Porter JD, Cruikshank JG, Genrle PH, Robinson RG, Gill ON. Management of patient treated by a surgeon with HIV infection. [Letter] Lancet 1990;335:113-4.

40. Armstrong FP, Miner JC, Wolfe WH. Investigation of a health-care worker with symptomatic human immunodeficiency virus infection: an epidemiologic approach. Milit Med 1987;152:414-8.

41. Comer RW, Myers DR, Steadman CD, Carter MJ, Rissing JP, Tedesco FJ. Management considerations for an HIV positive dental student. J Dent Educ 1991;55:187-91.

42. Mishu B, Schaffner W, Horan JM, Wood LH, Hutcheson R, McNabb P. A surgeon with AIDS: lack of evidence of transmission to patients. JAMA 1990;264:467-70.

43. Tokars J, Bell D, Marcus R, et al. Percutaneous injuries during surgical procedures [Abstract]. VII International Conference on AIDS. Vol 2. Florence, Italy, June 16-21, 1991:83.

44. Perrillo RP, Schiff ER, Davis GL, et al. A randomized, controlled trial of interferon alfa-2b alone and after prednisone withdrawal for the treatment of chronic hepatitis B. N Engl J Med 1990;323:295-301.

APPENDIX

Definition of Invasive Procedure

An invasive procedure is defined as "surgical entry into tissues, cavities, or organs or repair of major traumatic injuries" associated with any of the following: "1) an operating or delivery room, emergency department, or outpatient setting, including both physicians' and dentists' offices; 2) cardiac catheterization and angiographic procedures; 3) a vaginal or cesarean delivery or other invasive obstetric procedure during which bleeding may occur; or 4) the manipulation, cutting, or removal of any oral or perioral tissues, including tooth structure, during which bleeding occurs or the potential for bleeding exists."

Reprinted from: Centers for Disease Control. Recommendation for prevention of HIV transmission in health-care settings. *MMWR* 1987;36 (suppl. no. 2S):6S-7S.

TABLE OF CASES

Case	*Book §*
Atascadero State Hosp. v. Scanlon, 473 U.S. 234 (1985)	§ 3.5
Austin v. Owens-Brockway Glass Container, Inc., 844 F. Supp. 1103 (W.D. Va. 1994)	§ 3.4
Aviles v. United States, 696 F. Supp. 217 (E.D. La. 1988)	§ 3.19
A.W. v. Northwest R-1 Sch. Dist., 813 F.2d 158 (8th Cir. 1987)	§ 5.7
Ayala v. California Unemployment Ins. Appeals Bd., 126 Cal. Rptr. 210 (Ct. App. 1976)	§ 11.15
Bamon Corp. v. City of Dayton, 923 F.2d 470 (6th Cir. 1991)	§ 2.3
Baranowski v. Torre, No. CV90-0236178, 1991 WL 240460 (Conn. Super. Ct. Nov. 8, 1991)	§ 8.9
Bark v. INS, 511 F.2d 1200 (9th Cir. 1975)	§ 11.3
Barlow v. Ground, 943 F.2d 1132 (9th Cir. 1991), *cert. denied*, 505 U.S. 1206 (1992)	§§ 3.24, 7.15, 7.17
Barlow v. Superior Court, 236 Cal. Rptr. 134 (Ct. App. 1987)	§ 7.15
Barrett v. Danbury Hosp., 654 A.2d 748 (Conn. 1995)	§§ 8.7, 8.9
Battle v. Pennsylvania, 629 F.2d 269 (3d Cir. 1980), *cert. denied*, 452 U.S. 968 (1981)	§ 5.7
Baumgardner v. HUD, 960 F.2d 572 (6th Cir. 1992)	§ 6.10
Baxter v. City of Belleville, 720 F. Supp. 720, 728-30 (S.D. Ill. 1989)	§§ 6.5, 6.6, 6.7
Beasley v. Ken Edwards Enters., Inc., No. CV-1348, AIDS Litig. Rep. (Andrews Pubs.) 6526 (N.D. Ga. June 11, 1991)	§ 6.5
Beaulieu v. Clausen, 491 N.W.2d 662 (Minn. Ct. App. 1992)	§ 4.17
Bechtel v. East Penn Sch. Dist., 1994 WL 3396 (E.D. Pa. Jan. 4, 1994)	§§ 4.6, 4.10
Beck v. Interstate Brands Corp., 953 F.2d 1275 (11th Cir. 1992)	§§ 3.28, 8.11
Behringer Estate v. Princeton Medical Ctr., 592 A.2d 1251 (N.J. Super. Ct. Law Div. (1991)	§§ 3.12, 3.31, 8.11
Bell v. Wolfish, 441 U.S. 520 (1979)	§§ 7.13, 7.14, 7.16
Benjamin R. v. Orkin Exterminating Co., 390 S.E.2d 814 (W. Va. 1990)	§§ 3.26, 3.27
Benson v. Minnesota Bd. of Medical Practice, 526 N.W.2d 634 (Minn. Ct. App. 1995)	§ 8.7
Berg v. Health & Hosp. Corp., 865 F.2d 797 (7th Cir. 1989), *aff'g*, 667 F. Supp. 639 (S.D. Ind. 1987)	§ 2.3
Bermudez Zenon v. Restaurant Compostela, Inc., 790 F. Supp. 41 (D.P.R. 1992)	§ 4.10
Betsy v. Turtle Creek Assocs., 736 F.2d 983 (4th Cir. 1984)	§ 6.10
Bevin H. v. Wright, 666 F. Supp. 71 (W.D. Pa. 1987)	§ 5.7
Billman v. Indiana Dep't of Corrections, 56 F.3d 785 (7th Cir. 1995)	§ 8.9
Blake v. May Dep't Stores Co., 882 S.W.2d 688 (Mo. Ct. App. 1994)	§ 8.10
Block v. Art Iron, Inc., 866 F. Supp. 380 (N.D. Ind. 1994)	§ 3.4
Blythe v. Radiometer Am., Inc., 866 P.2d 218 (Mont. 1993)	§ 3.33
Board of Educ. v. Cooperman, 523 A.2d 655 (N.J. Super. Ct. 1987)	§ 5.13
Board of Educ. v. Diamond, 808 F.2d 987 (3d Cir. 1986)	§ 5.5
Board of Educ. v. Rowley, 458 U.S. 176 (1982)	§§ 5.5, 5.12
Bowen v. Yuckert, 482 U.S. 137 (1987)	§ 9.11
Bowers v. Hardwick, 478 U.S. 186 (1986)	§§ 7.5, 7.8

Case	*Book §*
Equality Found., Inc. v. City of Cincinnati, 860 F. Supp. 417 (S.D. Ohio, 1994), *aff'd in part and rev'd in part,* 54 F.3d 261 (1995), *vacated,* 116 S. Ct. 2519 (1996)	§ 7.5
Estelle v. Williams, 425 U.S. 501 (1976)	§ 7.19
Ethridge v. State of Alabama, 847 F. Supp. 903 (M.D. Ala. 1993)	§ 4.6
Faison v. Parker, 823 F. Supp. 1198 (E.D. Pa. 1993)	§§ 7.19, 7.21
Farmah v. State, 789 S.W.2d 665 (Tex. Ct. App. 1990)	§ 7.19
Farmer v. Moritsugu, 742 F. Supp. 525 (W.D. Wis. 1990)	§ 3.11
Favors v. MAQ Management Corp., 753 F. Supp. 941 (N.D. Ga. 1990)	§ 6.5
Faya v. Almaraz, 620 A.2d 327 (Md. 1993)	§§ 8.4, 8.5, 8.9
Filartiga v. Pena-Irala, 630 F.2d 876 (2d Cir. 1980)	§ 10.5
Finley v. Giacobbe, 827 F. Supp. 215 (S.D.N.Y. 1993)	§§ 3.7, 3.27, 4.5
Flynn v. Doe, 553 N.Y.S.2d 288 (Sup. Ct. N.Y. County 1990)	§§ 3.4, 8.7
Fosman v. State, 664 So. 2d 1163 (Fla. Dist. Ct. App. 1995)	§§ 7.14, 7.16, 7.17
Foucha v. Louisiana, 504 U.S. 71 (1992)	§ 2.4
Frazier v. Board of Trustees, 765 F.2d 1278 (5th Cir., *modified in unrelated part,* 777 F.2d 329 (5th Cir. 1985), *cert. denied,* 476 U.S. 1142 (1986)	§ 4.16
Fry v. First Fidelity Bancorporation, 64 U.S.L.W. 1122 (E.D. Pa. Jan. 30, 1996)	§ 3.18
Funeral Servs. *ex rel.* Gregory, Inc. v. Bluefield Community Hosp., 413 S.E.2d 79 (W. Va. 1991), *overruled in part on other grounds by,* Courtney v. Courtney, 437 S.E.2d 436 (W. Va. 1993)	§§ 8.2, 8.9
FW/PBS, Inc. v. City of Dallas, 873 F.2d 1298 (5th Cir. 1988), *vacated in part on other grounds,* 493 U.S. 215 (1990)	§ 2.3
Gates v. Rowland, 39 F.3d 1439 (9th Cir. 1994)	§ 3.7
Gay Lesbian Bisexual Alliance v. Sessions, 917 F. Supp. 1548 (M.D. Ala. 1996)	§ 10.4
Gentzler v. Atlee, 660 A.2d 1378 (Pa. Super. Ct. 1995)	§ 8.5
Gerdom v. Continental Airlines, Inc., 692 F.2d 602 (9th Cir. 1982), *cert. denied,* 460 U.S. 1074 (1983)	§ 8.9
Gertz v. Robert Welch, Inc., 418 U.S. 323 (1974)	§ 8.10
Gilmer v. Interstate/Johnson Lane Corp., 500 U.S. 20 (1990)	§ 3.4
Gilson v. Knickerbocker Hosp., 116 N.Y.S.2d 745 (App. Div. 1952)	§ 8.10
Gladstone Realtors v. Village of Bellwood, 441 U.S. 91 (1979)	§ 6.10
Glanz v. Vernick, 756 F. Supp. 632 (D. Mass. 1991)	§ 3.33
Glegola v. State, 871 P.2d 950 (Nev. 1994)	§§ 7.6, 7.21
Glover v. Eastern Neb. Community Office of Retardation, 686 F. Supp. 243 (D. Neb. 1988), *aff'd,* 867 F.2d 461 (8th Cir.), *cert. denied,* 493 U.S. 932 (1989)	§§ 3.24, 3.29, 7.17
Goldman v. Weinberger, 475 U.S. 503 (1986)	§ 3.19
Gorsline v. Kansas, 1994 WL 129983 (D. Kan. Mar. 4, 1994)	§ 4.6
Government of the V.I. v. Roberts, 756 F. Supp. 898 (D.V.I. 1991)	§§ 7.13, 7.14, 7.16, 7.17

UNITED STATES CODE CITATIONS

U.S.C.	*Book §*
2 U.S.C. §§ 60m-60n (1994)	§ 3.18
5 U.S.C. § 553	§ 11.11
5 U.S.C. § 4103	§ 3.3
5 U.S.C. §§ 6381-6387 (1994)	§ 3.18
5 U.S.C. § 6381	§ 3.18
7 U.S.C. § 2015(f)	§ 11.15
8 U.S.C. § 1101(a)(15)	§ 11.6
8 U.S.C. § 1101(a)(42)	§ 11.4
8 U.S.C. § 1153(a) (1994)	§ 11.3
8 U.S.C. § 1153(b)	§ 11.3
8 U.S.C. § 1153(b)(5)	§ 11.3
8 U.S.C. § 1157	§ 11.4
8 U.S.C. § 1157(c)	§§ 11.3, 11.11
8 U.S.C. § 1157(c)(3)	§ 11.10
8 U.S.C. § 1158	§ 11.4
8 U.S.C. § 1158(a)(2)(B)	§ 11.4
8 U.S.C. § 1159	§ 11.3
8 U.S.C. § 1159(b)	§ 11.4
8 U.S.C. § 1159(c)	§§ 11.10, 11.11
8 U.S.C. § 1160	§ 11.3
8 U.S.C. § 1160(c)(2)(B)(i)	§ 11.10
8 U.S.C. § 1160(f)	§ 11.15
8 U.S.C. § 1182	§ 11.7
8 U.S.C. § 1182(a)	§§ 11.5, 11.7
8 U.S.C. § 1182(a)(1)(A)(i)	§ 11.8
8 U.S.C. § 1182(a)(1)(A)(ii)	§ 11.7
8 U.S.C. § 1182(a)(1)(A)(iii)	§ 11.7
8 U.S.C. § 1182(a)(2)	§ 11.7
8 U.S.C. § 1182(a)(2)(D)	§ 11.7
8 U.S.C. § 1182(a)(4)	§ 11.7
8 U.S.C. § 1182(a)(5)	§ 11.3
8 U.S.C. § 1182(a)(6)(B)	§ 11.5
8 U.S.C. § 1182(a)(6)(F)	§ 11.17
8 U.S.C. § 1182(d)(3)	§ 11.10
8 U.S.C. § 1182(g)(1)	§§ 11.8, 11.10
8 U.S.C. § 1182(h)	§ 11.7
8 U.S.C. § 1183A	§ 11.7

CODE OF FEDERAL REGULATIONS

INDEX

607